pro-poor land reform

SATURNINO M. BORRAS JR.

pro-poor
land reform
a critique

THE UNIVERSITY OF OTTAWA PRESS
OTTAWA

© University of Ottawa Press 2007

All rights reserved. No parts of this publication may be reproduced, stored in a retrieval system or transmitted in any form or by any means, electronic or mechanical, including photocopy, recording, or otherwise, without permission in writing from the publisher.

LIBRARY AND ARCHIVES CANADA CATALOGUING IN PUBLICATION

Borras, Saturnino M
Pro-poor land reform : a critique / Saturnino M. Borras Jr.

Includes bibliographical references and index.
ISBN 978-0-7766-0650-7

1. Land reform--Philippines. 2. Land reform. 3. Rural poor--Philippines.
4. Rural poor. 5. Land reform--Government policy--Philippines.
6. Comprehensive Agrarian Reform Program (Philippines). I. Title.

HD1333.P6B673 2007   333.3'1599   C2007-903932-4

Published by the University of Ottawa Press, 2007
542 King Edward Avenue
Ottawa, Ontario K1N 6N5
www.uopress.uottawa.ca

The University of Ottawa Press acknowledges with gratitude the support extended to its publishing list by Heritage Canada through its Book Publishing Industry Development Program, by the Canada Council for the Arts, by the Canadian Federation for the Humanities and Social Sciences through its Aid to Scholarly Publications Program, by the Social Sciences and Humanities Research Council, and by the University of Ottawa. We also gratefully acknowledge the Institute of Social Studies in The Hague whose financial support has contributed to the publication of this book.

This book is dedicated to the memory of
Eric Cabanit, secretary general of UNORKA,
assassinated in Davao in April 2006;
my dear friend and comrade Max Frivaldo,
assassinated in Irosin, Sorsogon, in January 2006; and
countless unknown land reform activists
who were killed in the course of their struggles
for land, food, freedom, and dignity
— in the Philippines and in many parts of the world.
I also dedicate this book to the memory of
some of the best leaders of agrarian reform movements
in the Philippines who passed away without seeing
the full realization of their dream of a just Philippine society:
Felicisimo "*Ka* Memong" Patayan, *Ka* Simon Sagnip,
and *Ka* Nilo Oracion.

TABLE OF CONTENTS

List of Tables ix
Foreword xi
Acknowledgments xiii

Introduction
Some Gaps in Land Reform Studies 1

Chapter 1
The Politics of Redistributive Land Reform:
Conceptual Reconsideration 21

Chapter 2
Land and Tenancy Reforms in the Philippines:
A National-Level View of Structures and Institutions,
Processes and Outcomes 81

Chapter 3
CARP's Non-redistributive Policies and Outcomes 119

Chapter 4
CARP's Redistributive Policies and Outcomes 163

Chapter 5
State–Society Interactions for Redistributive Land Reform 215

Conclusion
The Challenge of Redistributive Land Reform:
Conclusions and Implications 281

Notes	299
List of Abbreviations	323
References	329
Index	385

LIST OF TABLES

Table 1.1: Possible Outcomes of Land (Reform) Policies in
Public Lands 33
Table 1.2: Economic and Socio-political Bases of Land Reforms 47
Table 1.3: Key Features of State- and Market-Led Approaches to
Land Reform in Private Lands 58
Table 2.1: Population of the Philippines, 1961–1999 88
Table 2.2: Size Distribution of Farms, 1980 89
Table 2.3: Concentration of Agricultural Land Ownership, 1988 90
Table 2.4: Value of Total Agricultural Exports-Imports, 1971–2002 93
Table 2.5: Value of Exports of Non-traditional Crops, 1971–2002 95
Table 2.6: Comparative Yield per Hectare in Rice and Corn,
Selected Countries 96
Table 2.7: Trends in Revealed Comparative Advantage, Agriculture
and Selected Major Agricultural Exports, 1960–1998 97
Table 2.8: DAR's Land Redistribution Scope, Deductions, and
Accomplishment, 1972–2005 111
Table 2.9: Total Land Redistribution under the DAR, 1972–2005 113
Table 2.10: Total Land Redistribution under the DENR, 1987–2004 113
Table 2.11: Number of Beneficiaries of Land Reform Programs,
1972–2000 114

Table 2.12: Yearly Summary of Leasehold Accomplishment, 1986–2003 115

Table 3.1: Land Deducted from the DAR Scope, as of 31 March 2005 140

Table 3.2: DAR's Land Distribution Accomplishment, by Land Acquisition Modality, 1972–2005 148

Table 3.3: Deductions from the CARP Scope, by Region, as of 2005 151

Table 3.4.a: National Summary of Deductions Based on Legal Grounds, as of 1998 152

Table 3.4.b: Geographic (Regional) Distribution of Deductions Based on Legal Grounds, as of 1998 153

Table 3.5: Pangasinan's Land Reform Accomplishment, DAR Jurisdiction, as of 2001 155

Table 4.1: DAR Land Redistribution Output in Private Lands, 1972–2005 206

Table 4.2: DENR's Accomplishment in A&D Lands and CBFM, 1987–2001 212

Table 5.1: The KMP-Visayas Number of Participants in Mass Mobilizations, 1985–1991 223

Table 5.2: State–Society Interactions and Spatial Variations in Policy Outcomes 277

FOREWORD

Revolutions and peasant insurgencies during the 20th century often led to major land reforms, as occurred in Mexico and China. In the post-1945 Cold War climate many governments introduced land reform legislation to preempt more radical change. Some governments also viewed land reform as a precondition for industrialization and economic development. Undoubtedly land reform played a key role in the economic success of South Korea and Taiwan, a fact that is often overlooked. Overall, the record of land reforms is more mixed, as most governments failed to deliver. Far less land was redistributed than promised and those who did benefit often had to compete on disadvantageous terms in the market without any economic support from the state.

During the 1980s land reforms were no longer on the policy agenda. On the contrary, with the neoliberal agenda ushered in by the debt crisis and the World Bank–driven structural adjustment program, many governments put an end to land reform and facilitated the development of land markets. Furthermore, many developing countries liberalized and opened their economies, a process that resulted in the bankruptcy of many peasant farmers who were unable to compete with the cheap and subsidized imports from North America and the European Union. Such liberalizing measures can be described as a "counter-reform by stealth," as peasants were forced to sell their land to pay off their debts and join the army of cheap labour. A few countries even implemented counter-reform measures in which many former land reform beneficiaries were driven from the land.

The exclusionary and concentrating consequences of neoliberal policies provoked a resurgence of peasant and indigenous movements claiming their rights to a dignified livelihood as exemplified by the Zapatista rebellion in Mexico, the Landless Rural Workers Movement (MST) in Brazil, and the Movement Towards Socialism (MAS) in Bolivia. Land reform continues to be a major demand of these movements as well as of others throughout Africa, Asia, and Latin America.

Borras's book thus appears at an opportune moment. It is the most comprehensive and up-to-date study ever published on the agrarian reform in the Philippines. The Philippine case is of particular interest given the long history of land reform, which began in 1963 and is still ongoing, as the current struggles of rural workers in the countryside testify. To this day many peasant leaders are assassinated in the Philippines for daring to defend the interests of the rural poor.

This book should be read by all those interested in land reform. Borras's novel theoretical perspective and methodology extend their relevance well beyond the Philippines. His state–civil society interaction theory and conceptualization of land reform provide a completely new interpretation of the Philippines' land reform. Those who read this book will have to look at other land reform experiences with fresh eyes. Hopefully it will bolster the fulfilment of the lost promise of land reform. The struggles of millions of landless and poor peasants throughout the world demand no less.

Cristóbal Kay
Professor of Rural Development and Development Studies
Institute of Social Studies
The Hague, The Netherlands
18 October 2006

ACKNOWLEDGMENTS

The Philippine government has claimed great success in its land redistribution program. This claim is rejected and dismissed by critics who argue that nothing significant has been achieved by the state land reform. Meanwhile, various international development institutions have moved on to launch large-scale market-oriented land policies including the formalization of private property rights over land resources, alongside the so-called market-led agrarian reform model. These initiatives have been questioned widely by critics. Indeed in recent years there has been a worldwide revival of interest in the issue of land — land reform, land policies, property rights — but in significantly different ways than the previous initiatives around land reform. It is within this general global and national political context that I embarked on the research that has led to the publication of this book. The principal motivation for me was political: to get a good sense of the debates on land reform and peasant movements in the Philippines and act accordingly in order to contribute to peasant struggles for land and democracy. The subsequent research undertaking has necessarily brought me deeper into the peasant communities across the country, while at the same time it has pushed me to take a broader perspective worldwide. The same political challenge has required a rigorous academic research discipline; and fortunately the latter was provided by my doctoral studies at the Institute of Social Studies (ISS) in the Hague.

The fieldwork for this study is comprised of both formal/structured and informal/unstructured elements. The former pertains to my official affiliation with the ISS as a doctoral student, with scholarship support from the Netherlands Fellowship Programme (NFP). Under this program I conducted an intensive year of field research in the Philippines during the period 2001–

2002. The latter spans a much longer period of time, stretching far back into the early 1980s (when I was just starting my activist involvement with the peasant movement in the Philippines) and extending up to the present (during my regular field research trips to the Philippines involving a variety of other intellectual and political undertakings). It is important to note that while in the process of constructing a coherent dissertation, I started to develop the component parts of the thesis, and several of these parts have been published in academic journals. Throughout all these processes and during this entire period, as can well be imagined, I became indebted to so many institutions and individuals who, in a variety of ways, have assisted and inspired me to persist in this study. I wish to thank all of them here – but of course it is not possible to name them all. I trust that they all know how grateful I am to them. I will simply mention a few individuals and institutions:

I would like to thank the NFP for the generous support extended to me to carry out my doctoral studies and research. I also thank the Rural Development, Environment and Population Studies Group (RDEPS) at the Institute of Social Studies (ISS) for providing me with a job, an office space, and logistical support that enabled me to carry out a number of research initiatives and at the same time revise my dissertation, prepare the manuscript for this book, and go through the process of publishing this book. More particularly, I thank the "land research group" at RDEPS for its financial support to the later phase of this book project – and by implication, the land research group's funders: the Inter-Church Organization for Development and Cooperation (ICCO), Cordaid, Oxfam Novib, and the Belgian 11.11.11.

I would like to thank several academic journals and publishers for allowing me to publish my articles, or parts of them, in this book: *Development and Change, Journal of Agrarian Change, Journal of Development Studies, Journal of International Development, Review of International Political Economy, European Journal for Development Research, Critical Asian Studies,* and *Progress in Development Studies;* the Institute for Popular Democracy (IPD), the Transnational Institute (TNI), and FoodFirst Books. And I would also like to thank the Ateneo de Manila University Press, which is publishing my two volume book on agrarian reform, rural development, and social movements: There are several overlapping chapters between this current book and those two volumes, although they are significantly different.

There are several key intellectual influences on this book that I would like to acknowledge and thank, without of course attributing to them my final analysis or the errors that may remain in this work.

I am extremely grateful to Ben White and Cris Kay — my dissertation supervisors, who provided me with intellectual guidance and inspiration, allowing me space for my own exploration and innovation while providing constant reminders of the requisites of proper research. Their critical comments and helpful suggestions saved this study from embarrassing mistakes and greatly improved the quality of its arguments.

I am deeply indebted as well to Danilo Carranza, Jonathan Fox, Jennifer Franco, Ron Herring, James Putzel, and Manuel "Steve" Quiambao for their varying intellectual inputs to this study. James and Ron made their contribution by reading and commenting on several other related papers, in addition to their official task as members of the examination committee of my dissertation. I am also grateful to Rosanne Rutten, Bridget O'Laughlin, Otto van den Muijzenberg, and Erhard Berner — all of whom were involved in the process of my thesis writing and defence, providing much needed intellectual assistance and raising critical and challenging questions.

I am also grateful to my other teachers and colleagues at ISS, some of whom I have already mentioned above: Haroon Akram Lodhi, David Dunham, Cris Kay, Wicky Meynen, Eric Ross, Ashwani Saith, Antonella Sorrentino, Max Spoor, Ben White, and Marc Wuyts. They have provided me with an inspiring and stimulating intellectual community and have been extremely supportive to my research projects during my stay at ISS. I also thank many former fellow doctoral students as well as the Filipino community at the ISS with whom I shared great intellectual and personal experiences.

As mentioned earlier, several parts of this book have been published in a number of journals and as chapters in books. In the process of these publications, I became indebted to several people for giving their comments and suggestions on how to improve my draft papers. Of course many of these people were anonymous, especially the reviewers; I thank them anyway. But several people were known to me — and I thank them here: Walden Bello, Henry Bernstein, Paula Bownas, Terry Byres, Dominique Caouette, the late Ranjit Dwivedi, Tom Fenton, Tim Forsyth, John Gershman, Krishna Ghimire, Paolo Groppo, John Harriss, Frank Hirtz, Peter Houtzager, Ben Kerkvliet, Hans Meliczek, Sarah O'Byrne, Joel Rocamora, Sergio Sauer, and David Wurfel.

Three parallel intellectual initiatives were going on at the time when I was revising the manuscript for this book. The first one was the Land Reform, Poverty Reduction and Public Action joint research by the ISS and UNDP. It brought together more than a dozen scholars to study and compare lessons from ten developing and transition countries. The debates, discussions, and exchanges of information and ideas were so rich and insightful and have benefited this book in so many ways. I am grateful to all my fellow workshop participants in this project, especially Terry McKinley. The other initiative was the Citizen Engagement in National Policy Change. Sponsored by the Institute of Development Studies (IDS) in Sussex, the project brought together eight scholars to study different experiences of state–civil society interactions in eight countries. Many of the ideas from the series of brainstorming sessions in this research were very useful in sharpening the arguments of this book. I would like to thank my fellow workshop participants in this project, especially John Gaventa, Gary Hawes, and Mark Robinson. Finally, this book benefited so much from my deep involvement in the preparation for and in the actual conduct of the International Conference on Land, Poverty, Social Justice and Development at the ISS in The Hague in January 2006, which brought together more than three hundred scholars, peasant leaders, civil society activists, and development policy experts from all over the world. The exchanges of information and heated debates in this conference have enhanced my knowledge about other experiences outside the Philippines as well as new theoretical thinking related to land policies.

Moreover, I would also like to thank the two anonymous reviewers for the University of Ottawa Press (UOP) for their critical but very useful comments and suggestions to the final draft of the book manuscript. I also thank Eric Nelson and Marie Clausén at UOP for their support and assistance with this project, as well as Trish O'Reilly for her excellent copy-editing work.

Political discussions with activists and development practitioners in the Philippines and internationally have equally been helpful in this study. It might require several pages to list all the organizations and people who have, one way or another, helped in this process, so I will list here just a few special ones: Armin Paasch and Sofia Monsalve at the FoodFirst Information and Action Network (FIAN); Evert de Boer at the Filipijnen Groep Nederland (FGN), and Malu Padilla of Bayanihan in Utrecht; fellow development practitioners at ICCO; friends and comrades at the Transnational Institute (TNI) and XminY both in Amsterdam and at 11.11.11 in Brussels.

To friends and comrades at the PEACE Foundation, UNORKA, PARRDS, Padayon, MFDC, and AFRIM — it is too risky to name names, because I'm sure I will miss several: I am deeply indebted to all of them for their friendship and solidarity, patience and support all these years. In countless ways they have helped facilitate my fieldwork and my access to key social movement information and have provided constant inspiration.

I also thank all those who agreed to be interviewed for this study — and as can be seen from the list of interviewees in the references, there are many of them. I was tempted many times to name a few of them here, but I could not decide whom to select: the top officials who gave me rare insiders' views or the rank and file DAR officials who provided me critical front-line information; a famous peasant leader or an ordinary land claim–maker? It is not easy to choose. In the end, I decided not to name names.

Finally, I thank my long-time intellectual collaborator, critic, fellow activist and best friend Jennifer Franco for all her great input to this research and for her patience, understanding, and self-sacrifice during the long years of my doctoral studies.

Salamatunon tabi sa iyo intero!

SOME GAPS IN LAND REFORM STUDIES

I.1 INTRODUCTION

The resurgence of land-based peasant and indigenous peoples' movements in many parts of the world since the 1990s on the one hand and the aggressive neoliberal push for land market reforms on the other have put the issue of redistributive land reform back onto the official agendas of international development institutions, national governments, and academics. However the key themes being discussed are significantly different from the conventional land reform scholarship: willing buyer–willing seller transactions instead of expropriation, private and decentralized land sales and land rental transactions instead of public policies on land redistribution and restitution by central governments, cutting back on public spending instead of more budget allocation for agrarian reform, among others. The current debate has put land reform theory and practice in the critical spotlight.[1]

Written within this global context, this book offers a critique and contribution from the Philippine experience, where a significant land redistribution outcome has recently been officially reported and claimed by government but has been questioned by critics. Between the optimistic official claims and the pessimistic critiques, we attempt to determine what has actually happened in the Philippine land reform process and what insights can be drawn from this national experience that are relevant to the current global land reform studies and debates.

I.2 THE PROBLEM

Five types of agrarian cases from the Philippines are presented below. The cases were lumped together with thousands of others in the nationally aggregated reports of the Philippine Comprehensive Agrarian Reform Program (CARP). Alongside hundreds of thousands of specific cases reported nationwide as "land redistribution accomplishments," the cases cited below were lost as individual stories, as they became depersonalized quantitative data — the type of data used by scholars, policymakers, and political activists to analyze land reform programs. The analytic lens of conventional land reform literature has difficulty fully accounting for and explaining the nature and implications of these cases. This largely sets the stage for the problematic addressed in this study.

Case One: *A piece of public land has long been under the effective control of a landlord despite the absence of a formal land title. According to government documents, the land is public forest, and so without agricultural tenants. In reality, it is productive farmland planted to coconut and worked by peasants under a share tenancy arrangement. Learning about the state land reform program, the peasants petitioned the government for the redistribution of the landholding despite harassment from the landlord. Largely due to sustained peasant mobilization, the government acted on the petition and redistributed the land to the peasants. Subsequently, the transaction was reported as land redistribution accomplishment under the public forest land component of the land reform program.*

Case Two: *A parcel of private land is owned by a landlord. It has been planted with mangoes and worked by several farmworkers. This landholding is under the scope of the land reform law. The landlord complied with the law by redistributing the farm via the voluntary land transfer scheme. In fact the landlord "redistributed" the land to his family members and to "paper beneficiaries" through this voluntary scheme. On paper, the beneficiaries paid the landlord for the land, but in reality no payment was made. There is no need for it because the landlord remains the land's real owner, the estate remains a single operational farm unit, and farm surplus extraction and disposition remain under the landlord's absolute control. In fact, nothing has changed, except the formal documents claiming that the farm has been subjected to redistributive land reform and is now owned by worker beneficiaries. This case has been reported as an accomplishment of the land reform program under its private land category.*

Based on the conventional wisdom in the land reform literature, Case One, having been reported as accomplishment in public lands, is not considered a redistributive land reform, and its significance is dismissed. Case Two, having been reported as accomplishment in private lands, is considered a redistributive land reform, and its importance is underscored. These readings are obviously wrong. In fact, the first case is a real redistributive case, while the second is an "apparent-but-not-real" redistributive land reform. Case One has real impact on the actually existing agrarian structure, while Case Two has none.

Case Three: *This case involves dozens of tenants tilling the rice farm of a politically powerful landlord. One day, the landlord asked them to sign a paper claiming that the land had been "sold" to the tenants at a specified price and on cash basis in compliance with the land reform program (that allows for direct payment as a legal land redistribution mechanism). The so-called sale is fake, and the landlord made this clear to the tenants. The landlord also warned that all those who refused to sign the document would have to leave the home lots allotted to tenants within the hacienda and would no longer be taken on as tenants or as hired farm labourers. All of the tenants signed the documents. Thus, on paper they are the owners of the land, but in reality they are not; they are "coerced on-paper beneficiaries" of the land reform program. This case has been reported as land redistribution accomplishment in the private land category of the land reform program.*

Case Four: *Two years after receiving a parcel of land under the land reform program, a beneficiary was forced to sell her land after her child fell ill in order to raise money for the medical expenses. The buyer was the son of the former landlord who suffered expropriation under the land reform program. However, the land reform law prohibits the sale of awarded lands within ten years of the award. Thus, in all legal documents, the owner of the land is still the peasant beneficiary, but in reality she has nothing to do with the land in any way. The sale was not coerced; it was mutually agreed between her and the buyer.*

Case Five: *A landlord donated his orchard to his workers. There was no payment required, but there was a condition: the worker beneficiaries had to put the land into a joint venture agreement with the (former) landlord for sixty years, wherein the land reform beneficiaries/new owners could continue to be farmworkers and were promised dividends if and when the joint corporation made a profit. An almost absolute right was given to the joint corporation whose majority stocks were controlled by the landlord due to what was claimed to be capital intensive investments made by the latter compared to the (deliberately depressed) assessed value of the land, which was provided as equity by the land reform beneficiaries. Thus, on paper the worker-beneficiaries own the land, but in reality the landlord maintains effective control. The change occurred only on paper. The case was reported as land redistribution accomplishment of the land reform program under its private land category.*

Cases Three to Five demonstrate varying forms of the phenomenon of "apparent-but-not-real" ownership of land. As these cases show, such a condition can either be forcibly imposed upon peasants by a powerful landlord, it can be mutually agreed between a landlord and poor peasants through the (illegal) sale of land, or it can be a result of some "trick" through promises of better economic arrangements around a particular land use.

These five cases are both real and familiar in the contemporary Philippine land reform process. In addition to the cases presented, there are many more situations in the actually existing agrarian structure in the Philippines — and very likely elsewhere — that, like the five cases, are not fully captured or explained by the dominant land reform theoretical perspectives. When such phenomena are detected, scholars and policymakers tend to dismiss them as policy implementation anomalies or as administrative problems and operational aberrations.

This study is undertaken on the assumption that such cases are actually quite commonplace and that therefore the causes and consequences of these phenomena should be investigated; in the end, this may require a re-examination of the theory and practice of land reform. This study aims to provide better understanding of the "anomalies" that surfaced in the cases cited above. It also aims to examine the implications of such cases for the broader theory and practice of redistributive land reform. For these purposes, the study investigates land reform in the Philippines.

Historically, most land reform scholars have believed that only through state-led public policies can significant movement be achieved toward resolution of the problem of skewed land-ownership distribution in agrarian societies in favour of poor peasants (in this study, the term "peasants" is taken in a loose definition to mean landless and near-landless tenants and farmers, farmworkers, and other rural wage labourers and rural semi-proletariat).[2] Considering land as having a multidimensional character, that is, it interlinks political, economic, social, and cultural functions,[3] this approach relies on the interventionist central state to exercise its redistributive and regulatory powers, as well as on strong, independent peasant movements to mount political pressure to implement the reform.[4] This approach is expropriationary to varying degrees. Its revolutionary variant is confiscatory — not compensating landlords and redistributing lands to beneficiaries for free. The less revolutionary expropriationary type of land reform compensates landlords at below the market price and redistributes land either for free or under subsidized repayment schemes.[5] Likewise, within this tradition post–land transfer development is state-led, via agricultural extension services, production and trade subsidies, and infrastructure provision, while beneficiaries are organized either into collectives or associations of individual farmers. In this approach, the role of the market is not altogether dismissed, but it is highly regulated, ostensibly to protect the emerging small family farms and farm collectives from the perceived harshness of unregulated market forces.

To varying extents and in different versions, state-led agrarian reforms have been widely enacted and somewhat less widely implemented in many countries for the greater part of the past century until the late 1970s. Past initiatives have shown that achieving a substantial degree of success in redistributive land reform is possible but not automatic, difficult but not altogether impossible. In any case, the outcomes have almost always been partial (Borras, 2006a).[6] For various reasons, including the debt crises of the 1980s, land reform was dropped from many policy agendas from the late 1970s onward.[7]

Despite the series of land reforms carried out in earlier decades, lack of effective control over and ownership of land by the rural poor remains a major problem today.[8] Sporadic but dramatic land-based political conflicts since the 1990s are among the more obvious symptoms of the persistence of the land problem. But while militant political actions by some peasant movements, such as those in Brazil, Chiapas (in Mexico), and Zimbabwe, have helped put land reform back onto the theoretical and policy agendas,[9] it is, arguably, the push from the pro-market academic and policy circles[10] that has provided the crucial impetus for the resurrection of the issue. It is not surprising therefore that current scholarship as well as policy and political debates on land reform revolve largely around the terms and issues set by the pro-market literature.

The dominance of neoliberal ideas in mainstream development policy thinking has put the issue of land into a new perspective. The limitations of the earlier neoliberal policies, especially the income-centred and growth-oriented views on poverty and development, became more apparent in the late 1980s. The persistence of poverty and growing inequality have in fact brought this mainstream development framework into question. Revisions of the dominant paradigm were then introduced. In this context, the issue of rural poor people's access to productive assets, especially land, was brought (back) in. The notion of "insecurity" in rural livelihoods as well as that of investments in the countryside have become an important foundation of the revised framework, anchored on the assumption that it is the insecure access to productive resources that has led to unstable livelihoods and lack of investments.[11] The task for the mainstream development framework has become quite clear: to develop formal private (and usually individualized) landed property rights. For public lands, this entails the development of more efficient cadastral records and surveying programs, with the end view of establishing clearer property rights, either through individualized titles or via "community" land rights with individualized land use rights within them.[12] These policies concern most of the remaining lands that are not fully privatized or whose registration and titles are not formalized (yet), including state-owned and collectively organized landholdings that were the outcomes of previous land reform programs, such as the many cases in Africa, Latin America, Asia, and the transition countries.[13] For private lands, the principal bias is to take away all legal prohibitions on freer land sales and rental transactions in the market, with emphasis on developing land rentals. Under certain conditions, lands sales will be encouraged but strictly on a voluntary basis, which has become widely known as "market-led agrarian reform" (World Bank, 2003; Deininger, 1999; Deininger and Binswanger, 1999). Hence, land policies have become quite important in the current mainstream international development institutions, and in turn, among national government agencies and civil society organizations. Specifically, in Latin America, but with global implications, Carter and Salgado (2001; see also World Bank, 2003) sum it up:

> Despite the renewed prominence of [issues related to access to land], the traditional policy instrument of state-mandated redistributive land reform is decidedly off the agenda in most Latin American countries. Contemporary land policy is primarily comprised of two instruments: (1) land titling, including the assignment of individual, marketable land titles to the beneficiaries of earlier redistributive reforms; and (2) negotiated or market-assisted land reform. (246–247)

The emergence of the pro-market approach as a proposition challenging the state-led approach has provoked debate in academic, policy, and political circles. The contemporary debate has shaped, and been reshaped by, two dominant currents in land reform scholarship. The first is the "limits-centred" approach. Today, many scholars of state-led agrarian reform believe that the recent socioeconomic and political changes at the international, national, and local levels have called into question the feasibility of carrying out an ideal type state-led agrarian reform. This thinking rests on two assumptions: (i) that there is a "weakening" of the regulatory and redistributive powers of the central state and (ii) that market reforms impose greater constraints on peasant movements. Others emphasize the political near-impossibility of redistributive land reform today, arguing that some segments of the landowning class have been provided with even more incentives to resist reform amidst the new possibilities for agricultural exports that have been opened up by neoliberal reforms. Policymakers' renewed interest in economic efficiency partly via the reduction of transaction costs through cutbacks in public spending has also imposed limits on redistributive land reforms, which have tended to be financially expensive.[14] Finally, the waning of peasant-based communist insurgencies in most developing countries and the end of the Cold War have taken away two crucial factors that motivated many governments to implement land reform in the past.[15]

The second current is the "opportunities-centred" approach. The same recent political and economic changes considered by many scholars as obstacles to land reform are, interestingly, viewed by others as opportunities for land reform. Some academics blame past failures to solve the problem of lack of access to land and underdevelopment in agriculture to what they label as the coercive "statist," "highly centralized," and "supply-driven" approaches in classic agrarian reform. Pro-market scholars and policymakers celebrate recent initiatives worldwide toward a less interventionary role for the central state in the economy and public administration. The marginalization of inward-oriented development policy and its substitution by an outward, export-oriented paradigm constitutes a key opportunity for land reform, according to these scholars.[16] The World Bank (n.d.) celebrates these changes:

> As structural adjustment programs in many parts of the world have reduced subsidies to large farms, privatized government collective farms, and created better financial instruments for the wealthy than land, a potentially transferable supply of land has come onto the market. The latent demand for that land by the poor often cannot be realized because they lack the capital. Market assisted land reform helps activate the market and create the environment in which land can be transferred from large to small farms. (1)

The persistence of these dichotomous views in the land reform literature poses an analytic challenge. Arguably, a fundamental misconception underlying the contemporary views of the prospects of land reform is the confusion about, and conflation of, what is redistributive reform and what is not. An incomplete, and at times muddled, understanding about the meaning of redistributive reform has permitted the entry of non-redistributive types of "land reform" into the land reform literature. The inclusion of some concepts and exclusion of others in the literature has blurred, not clarified, important ideas crucial to understanding redistributive land reform. But even if the concepts used are clarified, confusion can still persist if scholars are vague about the nature of the empirical data they are working on. Here an insight from Herring (1983) is relevant:

> Much of the literature on land reform in [South Asia] dismisses the reforms as mere charades manipulated by ruling elites to pacify the peasantry, coopt leftist critics, and satisfy modernist elite sectors while effecting little structural change in rural areas. Such a view, while certainly accurate in part ... requires considerable modification. The case studies [in this book] clearly indicate change induced by land reforms, though not always in directions indicated by reform rhetoric. This structural change is of two kinds — apparent and real. Though it seems contradictory to write of "apparent" structural change, the usage is meaningful. Land reforms produce important alterations in the *observable* structure of agrarian systems — land records are altered, census data collected, reports are made — all presenting a picture of the rural world that is more congruent with the needs of landed elites, administrators, and ruling politicians than with reality on the ground. Landowners have strong incentives to show that they own very little land and that there are no tenants on it; reform administrators are pressured to show progress in implementation .... The apparent change is important because it is this data-built facade which goes into planning documents, policy debates, reports of international agencies, and all too many scholarly treatments. The distortions become social facts, the primary sources for understanding the rural world for nonrural groups who are, after all, the primary movers of rural policy. (269, italics original)

In putting forward the issue of discrepancies between what is officially recorded and claimed on the one side, and what actually exists, on the other, Herring raises a crucial issue with implications for the current debate on redistributive land reform. A deeper examination reveals that there are numerous types of real and apparent redistributive land reforms, far more even than the types shown by Herring in the case of South Asia. This is partly shown in the five cases presented in this chapter's introduction.

The theoretical problem facing contemporary land reform scholarship therefore is fundamental in nature. It is impossible for scholars and policymakers to resolve among themselves the critical issue of redistributive land reform if there is no clarity and unity among them about its basic concepts. While historically there seems to be an understanding about the core land reform concept, closer inspection reveals that this unity is more assumed than demonstrated. Rather than reproduce uncritically the conventional assumption, this research opts to problematize — in a manner explained in the first section of this introduction — the concept of redistributive land reform before examining the current questions with regard to opportunities for and limits to redistributive land reform.

I.3   RESEARCH QUESTIONS AND ARGUMENTS

The study poses three central research questions: (i) When do land policies and policy outcomes constitute redistributive land reform? (ii) How and to what extent do pre-existing structural and institutional settings shape and condition the nature of land reform policies and the types of land reform policy outcomes? (iii) How and to what extent do political actions and strategies of pro-reform state and societal actors influence the nature, pace, extent, and direction of land reform policy implementation processes and outcomes?

By answering the first question, this book aims to contribute toward a clearer understanding of the basic building block of land reform studies today, that is, the notion of "redistributive reform." This critical reflection is not simply a question of semantics; it is a fundamental issue that must be clarified theoretically, empirically, and methodologically. Consequently, a clearer view about this basic point aims to facilitate a more systematic discussion about the limits to, opportunities for, and state–society interactions around redistributive land reform. It aims to better frame the discussion on the importance of political actions and the strategies of state and societal actors with regard to redistributive reform.

The main arguments are as follows: First, redistributive land reform policies and their outcomes are, in reality, of two types: "real" and "apparent-but-not-real." Most land reform studies fail to distinguish these two types systematically, leading to, at best, partial, or, worse, flawed understanding of redistributive land reforms. The lack of clarity as to what is and what is not a redistributive land reform is rooted mainly in the use of frameworks fixated on the official and static private-public land property rights dichotomy. This has led to the problematic dominant views in land reform theory and practice because it: (i) excluded actually existing land-based production and distribution relationships that occur in lands that are officially classified as "public"; (ii) inconsistently included — or excluded — real redistributive reform achieved via share tenancy or leasehold reform; and (iii) inadvertently included land transfers involving private lands that do not actually constitute real redistributive reform.

To better understand what is redistributive land reform and what is not, the definition of redistributive reform is problematized, emphasizing two key issues: (i) the actual and effective control over the land resource — meaning, the power to control the nature, pace, extent, and direction of surplus production and extraction from the land and the disposition of such surplus and (ii) the transfer of power to control land resources, which has to occur, but such transfer must flow from landed elite to the landless and land-poor peasants — meaning, the direction of change must categorically traverse social classes but favour the landless and near-landless poor and not remain within a social class, or within elite classes, or, worse, be from the landless and land-poor to the landowning classes. Thus, redistributive reform is achieved only when there is actual net transfer of (power for) effective control over the land resource. This can happen when peasants are able to secure, exercise, and maintain effective control over the nature, pace, extent, and direction of surplus production and extraction from the land and disposition of such surplus, regardless of whether it is in private or public lands, or whether it involves a formal change in the right to alienate (full ownership) or not (e.g., leasehold or stewardship).

Second, the current global agrarian restructuring and changes in international political economy have transformed the structure of, limits to, and opportunities for redistributive reforms like land reform. This has, in turn, inspired the emergence of studies that emphasize either the limits or the opportunities. While the limits-centred and opportunities-centred approaches both have explanatory power, both have weaknesses also. The problem with the limits-centred approach is its over-emphasis on the obstacles to redistributive land reform; this overlooks actual and potential opportunities. In fact, there is a tendency among some scholars to over-emphasize the limits to redistributive land reform in the neoliberal era. They generally give so much attention to pre-existing structural and institutional constraints and obstacles that they overlook latent, and even actual, opportunities. Most critical land reform scholars tend to focus their analyses on only those social and political institutions and relationships that reinforce anti-reform power. They tend to take structural and institutional limits as something fixed and static and, so, insurmountable. Therefore, they have difficulty explaining redistributive land reforms when they do occur in unexpected circumstances. Such structural and institutional factors favouring anti-reform forces are certainly operative in the real world. But there are also institutions and relationships that, while they do not automatically undermine anti-reform power, can be mobilized to counteract manoeuvres by anti-reform forces. Meanwhile, the problem with the opportunities-centred perspective is its over-emphasis on the favourable factors for land reform today; this approach fails to understand and acknowledge the actual and potential limits to reforms. The tendency among other scholars to highlight individual human agency and policy and institutional reforms assumes that, given proper institutional incentives and disincentives, individuals will behave in a rational manner (i.e., to maximize their individual, usually assumed to be economic, interests). Founded on the premise that recent pro-market policy and institutional reforms encourage and promote the maximization of individual interests in a rational way, these scholars highlight the opportunities recently opened up for land reform. This approach tends to overlook the crucial role of pre-existing macro-socioeconomic structures and socio-political institutions that either hinder "rational" behaviour or promote "irrational" actions from a range of actors.

More fundamentally, the two camps' partial understanding of redistributive land reforms has resulted in the conflation of and confusion over several concepts in land reform. This has resulted in even more confusion in the discussion about limits to and possibilities for redistributive land reform. One camp may be discussing limits to land reform, the other camp may be discussing opportunities for a non-redistributive land reform, and so on. Therefore, problematizing the fundamental concept of redistributive land reform and placing the discussion about the limits to and possibilities for land reform within this core concept can contribute toward a better understanding of land reform in theory and practice. Building on the strength of both approaches, but addressing their weaknesses, this study argues that pre-existing structural and institutional settings are important determinants of the nature of limits to and opportunities for land reform, and therefore, of its outcomes, but they are never the sole determinants. The nature and extent of influence that pre-existing structures and institutions bear upon land reform processes and outcomes are, in turn, largely determined by the extent to which the structures and institutions shape and condition the pre-existing distribution of power of the various actors that ally or compete with each other to control land resources. Such structures and institutions provide the *context* within which actors amass, maintain, or lose some degree of power in the recursive, dynamic multi-actor contestations over control of land. But this is not a one-way relationship, because the same structures and institutions are, at the same time, the *objects* of these contestations.

Finally, the political actions and strategies of state and societal actors do matter. The alliance between state reformists and autonomous reformist societal groups can, under certain conditions, surmount obstacles, overcome limits, and harness opportunities to allow a redistributive land reform to occur. This alliance is achieved at various levels of the polity, but in a highly varied and uneven manner, geographically, across crops and farm types, across land reform policy components, and over time. The character and extent of this coalition, in turn, largely account for the highly uneven and varied outcomes of land reform policies through time.

I.4 THE RELEVANCE OF THE PHILIPPINE LAND REFORM EXPERIENCE

The Philippine land reform experience provides an excellent case study to examine the problematic of this research. The Philippines still has an important agricultural sector relative to the country's economy as a whole. During the past decade, the share of the agriculture sector in the Philippine GDP shrank from around one-third in the 1960s–1970s to around one-fifth by 2004. During the same period, the industrial sector registered a marginal increase, eventually stagnating at around one-third. Most of the economy's development was accounted for by the phenomenal expansion of the services sector, which grew from about 30 percent to around 50 percent of GDP during the same period. The agriculture sector has remained a key sector, with a current share of one-fifth of GDP and two-fifths of employment. But as Balisacan and Hill (2003: 25) have explained, when "a broader definition that encompasses agricultural processing and related activities is adopted, the indirect share [of agriculture] rises to about 40 percent and 67 percent, respectively." However, the performance of the Philippine agriculture sector between 1980 and 2000 was dismal, at an average of 1.4 percent annual growth rate (David, 2003: 177; Borras, 2007).

The agrarian structure of the Philippines is marked by widespread landlessness and near-landlessness and inequality, with the Gini coefficient for land-ownership distribution 0.64 in 1988, the year CARP implementation began (Putzel, 1992: 30). The persistence of land monopolies has perpetuated massive poverty in the countryside. The 2005 Philippine poverty analysis and report released by the Asian Development Bank (ADB) showed that "the poverty incidence of families fell by 10.5% over the period 1985–2000" (or from 44.2% to 33.7%), but that "this was negated by very high population growth rates of 2.36% per year." By 2004, 75 percent of the country's poor were rural poor. According to the ADB report, "Of the 26.5 million poor people in the country in 2000 ... 7.1 million were urban and 19.4 million live in rural areas. In other words, nearly 75% of the poor are rural poor" (ADB, 2005: 64). And the poverty incidence among farming households during the period 1985–2000 has remained almost unchanged. It was 56.7 percent and 55.8 percent, in 1985 and 2000, respectively (ibid: 98).

Historically, hundreds of peasant revolts have erupted in different parts of the archipelago, most of which were rooted in problems of land and tenancy relations. Yet persistent peasant mobilizations over time have effected only intermittent concessions from the country's landowning classes and the central government in the combined forms of limited land and tenancy reform and resettlement — as well as persistent efforts at co-optation and repression. None of the political administrations during the past century has ever seriously addressed the underlying cause of the peasant revolts, that is, landlessness. When Marcos was overthrown in 1986, land reform remained most peasants' main concern. It was during the regime transition in 1986–1988 that the contemporary, most comprehensive land reform program — CARP — was passed into law (in 1988).

The Philippine CARP is among the few state-led land reforms being implemented in the world today. The recent officially reported accomplishment for land redistribution under CARP is far greater than that of other such reforms, such as those in South Africa (since 1994), Brazil (from the mid-1980s), and Zimbabwe (since 1980). Many other national land reform policies remain in place (in theory) but are usually relatively dormant (in practice), as for example, the Basic Agrarian Law of 1960 in Indonesia (see, e.g., Wiradi, 2005; Bachriadi and Fauzi, 2006). By 2006, CARP was officially reported to have redistributed nearly 6 million hectares of land to 3 million peasant households over a period of more than thirty years (1972–2006; the 1972 Marcos land reform in rice and corn lands was subsumed by CARP in 1988). If true, these figures account for nearly half of the country's farmlands and two-fifths of peasant households. In addition, 1.5 million hectares were officially reported to have been placed under compulsory leasehold reform benefiting one million tenant-farmer households over the same period. To what extent this data is true is the subject of the rest of this book. Moreover, the Philippines has long experience in land and tenancy reforms, beginning at the start of the past century. In addition, this experience has unfolded across different macropolitical and economic development regimes over time. Furthermore, significant "positive" (or redistributive) and "negative" (or non-redistributive) outcomes are both found in CARP's land redistribution outcomes. Finally, together with the expropriationary approaches within CARP, market-based land transfer schemes have also been carried out and, recently, the World

Bank has started to pilot-test its "land reform" model in the country. Taken together, these provide rich empirical materials for our analysis.

I.5 SOME METHODOLOGICAL ISSUES

This research looks into "institutions," broadly defined here as "formal and informal rules and procedures and organizations that structure conduct" of a range of actors (Thelen and Steinmo, 1992: 2), as important variables, both dependent and independent, in understanding the theoretical problems presented briefly above. Analyzing institutions does not deny the importance of socioeconomic structures; rather, as Thelen and Steinmo (ibid.: 2–3) explain, crucial in the conception of "historical institutionalism" is "that institutions constrain and refract politics but they are never the sole 'cause' of outcomes" (see also Fox, 1993: 21–39). Moreover, this research gives due importance to human agency (of actors) and macro-socioeconomic structures. Here, the term "agency" means that people are not passive victims of socio-political processes; people have the capacity to act, which, in turn, affects the social relationships within which they are embedded (Layder, 1994: 4; see also the works of James Scott, especially 1990, 1985, 1976; and of Benedict Kerkvliet, especially 1990; and Scott and Kerkvliet, 1986). Some scholars loosely refer to this approach as a combined structural-institutional-actor-oriented approach, or simply, structural-actor-oriented approach (e.g., Long, 1988; see Layder, 1994: Ch. 1). Having said this, however, it is important to emphasize the critical role played by the political-economic structural factors on the nature of, character of, and limits to the power of actors and on the opportunities that can be opened up by institutions. Actors and institutions shape and are shaped by the structures, the social and production relations, within which they are embedded (see, e.g., Byres, 1995; Bernstein, 2006; Harriss, 1982, 2002; but see also, e.g., McMichael, 2006a, 2006b; Fox, 1993: Ch. 2).

Furthermore, this research employs a combination of research strategies: the case study and cross-sectional/longitudinal methods. It also has elements of both quantitative and qualitative methods (see related discussions in Hammersley, 1992: 159–173; Ragin, 1992: 53; Mukherjee and Wuyts, 1998: 237).

The units of analysis in this study are both the political processes and their outcomes, both of which are marked by incessant struggles between different actors within the state and in society, who constantly compete to gain effective control over land resources. In these units of analysis, some categories of actors are often used, and it is useful to introduce them here. "State" and "societal actors" are treated not as actors independent of each other, but as actors closely interlinked via power relations. State and societal actors are thus analyzed as actors embedded within existing social and political-economic structures and institutions of a given setting and so necessarily connected with each other (Migdal, 2001). Here, societal actors are defined as "groups of people who identify common interests and share ideas about how to pursue their goals," while state actors are defined as "groups of officials whose actions push or pull in the same political direction" (Fox, 1993: 10–12). They can thus be located within a state agency or societal classes, and/or can cross such organizational and group divides to link with others based on common agendas and interests. In this study, state and societal actors include peasants and peasant organizations, land reform beneficiary groups, nongovernmental organizations (NGOs), political movements, landlords and their organizations, agribusiness groups, real estate firms, banks, local government units, courts, police, anti-reform state actors, international inter-governmental organizations, and international financial institutions. State reformists are defined in broad terms: state actors who are tolerant, even supportive, of social pressures from below in order to implement the redistributive land reform policy (ibid.). Likewise, the levels of analysis are inherently interlinked. A combined macro-micro approach is thus used as these two levels are closely intertwined (Layder, 1994: 3–6). That means that political process and outcomes related to the struggles to gain effective control over land resources are analyzed at different levels, namely, national, regional, provincial, municipal, village, farm and plantation, and international. The interplay between the political processes at these different levels is an important area of analysis.

Data and data collection

Historically, in the Philippines and elsewhere, one difficulty in systematically examining agrarian structure and land reform is the fact that most of the official statistics are, for various reasons, "polluted" or partial accounts of the more complex reality (see, e.g., the introduction of Barraclough, 1973: xiv–xix, with reference to Latin America). Hence, data in the current research have been chosen and researched carefully.

Secondary data used in this study include published and unpublished materials: books, journal articles, conference papers, government documents, newspaper accounts, and videos. Primary data include interviews with key informants; internal documents of peasant organizations, NGOs, and other political organizations; and the author's personal perceptions and recollections of relevant events. Each data type has distinct strengths and weaknesses.

The current research attempts to harness their strengths and isolate their weaknesses (see, e.g., related discussion in Mukherjee and Wuyts, 1998: 13–14). Thus, this study uses official data as well as non-official quantitative and qualitative data, information from within and outside the state, and data aggregated at the national and sub-national levels.

Key informants are broadly categorized into four types. The first is state actors, including top government officials from the national centre down to the regional, provincial, and municipal village levels. These are mainly from the executive branch of government, primarily from the Department of Agrarian Reform (DAR) bureaucracy. The second category of informant is rural social movement actors. These comprise NGOs and peasant organizations from national networks, federations, and alliances through regional-provincial organizations down to the local level (i.e., municipal-, village-, and farm- or plantation-based associations and individuals). They also include other non-rural social political movements and experts from academe. Private sector actors is the third category of informant. These are mainly landlords, agribusiness people, and experts from the private sector. The final category is that of individual peasants, including land reform beneficiaries, aspiring land reform beneficiaries, former applicants who were rejected, and members of a beneficiary household. These informants were selected based on their knowledge about particular cases and in order to verify the views expressed by leaders of organizations and NGO activists. These key informants were chosen based on the author's previous knowledge of people's and organizations' roles in the processes that this study investigates; although some were included in the list after initial interviews with other informants led to the necessity to gather information from other sources.

Data were solicited from the key informants through one-on-one semi-structured interviews and focus group discussions (FGDs). The former is semi-structured so that while preconceived questions based on the initial formulation of the problematic of the research are put forward, the interviews remain flexible and it is possible to pursue an unanticipated line of discussion during the interview with the end view of gaining as much relevant information as possible.

The choice of which government documents would be used for this research was difficult. Large government departments (ministries) have different offices within them, and each separately generates and manages data and documents regarding broadly similar information from the field. On some occasions, different offices within one department generate different, at times conflicting, sets of data. The Philippine DAR is notorious in this regard.

Making the best choices between alternative data requires familiarity with the entire process of the land reform implementation and the internal dynamics of the bureaucracy. Hence, a researcher is confronted with a dilemma: In order to understand the land reform process and outcomes one has to use the best quality data; but in order to identify the best quality data, one has to understand the land reform processes and outcomes. To break out of this chicken-and-egg dilemma requires some degree of prior understanding of the land reform processes and outcomes on the one hand and the types and nature of data on the other. It is a recursive exercise carried out keenly and carefully over time. Nevertheless, it is important to note that perhaps one of the most important reformist achievements of the Garilao administration at the DAR (1992–1998) was the modernization, including national computerization, and professionalization of data generation and management. This has helped ensure relatively better longitudinal quality data.[17]

Whenever it is important to explain the choice of data used in this research or whenever flaws in the data are suspected, notes are made.

Another source of primary information for this research is the author's own perception and recollection of key events, processes, and actions that he witnessed personally over a period of more than two decades (since 1982). The author's direct involvement in land reform struggles provides a rare opportunity to gain access to information about the actions and thinking of various relevant actors. At the same time, it poses the danger that the partisan nature of these political engagements may affect the objective perception of reality. To lessen the probability of subjective and selective perceptions and remembering (and forgetting), facts were double-checked and validated via the other data collection methods mentioned earlier.

Finally, the case studies in this research focus on the experiences of the "national-democratic" (ND) movement and a subsequent splinter group from it. Specifically, this means focusing attention on the PEACE (Philippine Ecumenical Action for Community Empowerment) Foundation network of NGOs and the "ND" and "ex-ND" peasant organizations: KMP, DKMP, and UNORKA (introduced and examined in chapter 5). The study analyzes the ideological frameworks and political strategies of these organizations toward redistributive land reform in order to partly answer the question raised earlier about the role played by political actions and strategies of pro-reform actors in determining the nature of land reform processes and outcomes. There are three reasons for focusing on these organizations. First, the ND and ex-ND rural social movement groups, in various periods of their struggle for land reform, were the most important in terms of organizational and political influence.

Second, analyzing social movement groups that share a *common political history* offers better comparative insights than comparisons of politically disparate groups. Finally, the author had a twenty-year uninterrupted, close political work engagement with these groups that provides a rare opportunity to access valuable data and insights.

I.6 OVERVIEW OF CHAPTERS

There are five chapters in this study and a conclusion. Chapter 1, The Politics of Redistributive Land Reform: Conceptual Reconsideration, discusses three distinct but interlinked theoretical themes in order to lay the analytic groundwork for this study: redistributive land reform, the limits to and opportunities for land reform in the contemporary era, and state–society interactions for redistributive land reform. These three themes form the first three sections of the chapter. It is inconceivable that we discuss any of these themes completely separately from the others if the issue of land reform is to be fully understood. For instance, it is impossible to fully explain the limits to and opportunities for land reform without an understanding of the meaning of redistributive land reform. Likewise, the limits to and opportunities for land reform cannot be explained without a full examination of the actors and the political processes that make or unmake such limits and opportunities.

Chapter 2, Land and Tenancy Reforms in the Philippines: A National-Level View of Structures and Institutions, Processes and Outcomes, provides an overview of the structures and institutions, policy processes and outcomes relating to land and tenancy reforms in the Philippines at the national level. This chapter locates the land reform imperatives and initiatives within the broader socioeconomic and political history of the country. It explains the key features of CARP and examines its initial nationally aggregated outcomes. Chapter 2 begins with a discussion of the structural and institutional context for the land reforms in the country's history. It then focuses on the nation's agrarian structure and rural politics, followed by an analysis of the key features of CARP. The chapter concludes by providing an initial view of the nationally aggregated CARP outcomes.

Chapter 3, CARP's Non-redistributive Policies and Outcomes, examines evidence showing that some of the officially reported and popularly accepted accomplishment data in land redistribution are in fact devoid of the essential elements of redistributive reform. It also looks into the extent to which such outcomes have been carried out nationally. The chapter has two goals: On the one hand, it seeks to demonstrate empirically when and how outcomes do not actually constitute redistributive reform. On the other hand, it aspires to assess the possible extent to which these types of outcomes have been implemented nationwide. The chapter analyzes policy issues and outcomes. It establishes the empirical bases for systematic classification of some policies and outcomes as non-redistributive. Case studies are presented and analyzed. It also shows the possible extent and geographic distribution of outcomes.

The weight of evidence presented in chapter 3 calls into question official government claims about CARP's massive land redistribution and tenancy reform accomplishment. Yet this does not necessarily mean that the pessimistic camp that had earlier predicted and currently claims insignificant achievement of CARP is fully vindicated. Chapter 4, CARP's Redistributive Policies and Outcomes, examines evidence showing that parts of the officially reported redistribution accomplishment are in fact gains in redistributive reform, whether or not popularly accepted as such. It also looks into the extent to which such outcomes have been carried out nationally. This chapter demonstrates empirically when and how such outcomes do constitute real redistributive reform and how these reforms were achieved and maintained. It also assesses the extent to which these types of outcomes were carried out nationwide.

The kinds of CARP land redistribution outcomes, their extent and geographic distribution, are largely reflective of the nature and extent of the pro-reform state–society coalitions pushing for redistributive land reform. Chapter 5, State–Society Interactions for Redistributive Land Reform, analyzes the state–society interactions for redistributive land reform. Its primary aim is to better understand the role played by state and societal actors in shaping and reshaping the CARP process, resulting in the kinds of outcomes examined in the preceding chapters. This chapter has four sections: Section 1 analyzes the peasant movements and their allies (collectively and loosely referred to here as "rural social movement organizations") and their struggles for land. Their agendas, repertoire of collective actions, degree of organizational and political influence, and geographic spread over time are examined. Section 2 traces the general contours of the emergence of pro–land reform state actors within the DAR over time. Section 3 examines the evolution of the pro-reform state–society alliance for land reform and the role it played in CARP implementation. Section 4 analyzes how the pro- and anti-reform state–society coalitions clash with each other over the issue of redistributive land reform and with what outcomes.

The conclusion, The Challenge of Redistributive Land Reform: Conclusions and Implications, returns the discussion to the key research questions raised in the introduction, but this time with the power of empirical evidence from the Philippines as discussed in chapters 2 through 5. The study concludes by suggesting possible implications of the research for the theories, policies, and politics of redistributive land reform in the Philippines and elsewhere.

CHAPTER ONE

THE POLITICS OF REDISTRIBUTIVE LAND REFORM: CONCEPTUAL RECONSIDERATION

1.1 RETHINKING LAND REFORM

According to Jonathan Fox, redistributive reforms are public policies that change the relative shares between groups in society (Fox, 1993). He elaborates:

> Distributive reforms are qualitative changes in the way states allocate public resources to large social groups .... Redistributive reforms are a special case of distributive policies: they change the relative shares between groups. This distinction is important for two principal reasons. First, many apparently redistributive reforms are not, and to call them so implicitly begins with what should be the ultimate outcome of analysis: determining what a social reform actually does, and why. Second, redistribution implies zero-sum action, whereas social programs often are carried out precisely because they avoid clearly taking from one group to give to another. In a context of economic growth, moreover, antipoverty spending may well rise in absolute terms without changing its relative share of the government budget. The label "redistribution" builds in an assumption about where the resources come from, whereas the notion of distribution limits the focus to who gets what. (10)

Applied to property rights reform, redistributive land reform means the net transfer of wealth and power from the landed to landless and land-poor classes. Griffin, Khan and Ickowitz (2002: 279–280) have explained land reform as being about redistributing "land ownership from large private landowners to small peasant farmers and landless agricultural workers," emphasizing that it is "concerned with a redistribution of wealth." Moreover, Anna Tsing (2002: 97) has explained that property rights are social relationships; that "property is a social relationship between nonowners and owners, in which nonowners are expected to respect the rights of owners to their claimed objects." It is these social relationships that are ought to be the subject of land reform.

This study understands that, to be truly redistributive, a land reform must effect on a pre-existing agrarian structure a change in ownership of and/or control over land resources wherein such a change flows strictly from the landed to the landless and land-poor classes or from rich landlords to poor peasants and rural workers. Here "ownership and/or control over land resources" means the *effective control* over the nature, pace, extent, and direction of surplus production and distribution. In other words, according to Tuma (1965: 251), land redistribution aims to create "purposive change" that can result in the improvement of the situation of the landless and land-poor peasants and rural workers. Such purposive change or "reform" is inherently relational: it must result in a net increase in poor peasants' and rural workers' power to control land resources with a corresponding decrease in the share of power of those who used to have such power over the same land resources and production processes. In fact, land redistribution is essentially power redistribution. This can occur through the transfer of the entire bundle of property rights, including the "right to alienate," but it can also be realized without involving full, formal ownership of the land, for example, through leasehold reform and stewardship (see Putzel, 1992: 3; Herring, 1983: 13; Byres, 2004b: 27–32). Thus, what is essentially meant here by "reform" is not simply "change" in production and distribution relationships in a given agrarian structure. The latter ("change") can happen in multiple directions and both within and between social classes, as it may include elite-to-elite or even poor-to-elite transfer of effective control over land resources. The former ("reform") limits the direction of change to that which transfers power between social classes, specifically, from landed to landless and land-poor classes, or from rich to poor. The redistributed lands can be held either collectively or individually, the organization of production can take the form of family farm or corporate-type plantation, while the newly formed family farm can be a stand-alone livelihood or just a part of a multiple household livelihood strategies (see, e.g. Hart, 1995; Bernstein, 2002; Razavi, 2003; Borras and Franco, 2005).

Redistributive reform, in terms of its nature and extent, is essentially a *matter of degree*. The redistributive *nature* of a land reform transaction in a given landholding, and the change that it causes in the relative shares between the landlord on the one side and the peasants on the other side, is seldom either one hundred percent redistributive or one hundred percent non-redistributive; it is usually somewhere in between. The *extent* to which redistributive land reform is implemented in a given society is also a matter of degree, with redistributive outcomes seldom being all or nothing. Traditionally, two interrelated elements have defined the redistributive character of a land reform policy, namely, the compensation to landlords and the payment made by peasants. On the one hand, compensation to the landlord can be between zero and somewhere below the "market price" of the land; the difference between the "market price" and the actual compensation partly defines the degree of redistribution.[1] On the other hand, the payment made by peasants and rural workers for the land can be between zero and somewhere below the acquisition cost, with the difference between the two also partly defining the degree of redistribution.

Taking redistributive land reform as inherently a matter of degree provides us with an analytic tool to understand and compare land reforms between and within countries. Using this perspective, analysis can move beyond the crude "success" or "failure" comparative divide, which is also overly quantitatively oriented, and bring qualitative aspects into the analysis to allow more nuanced comparisons, especially on the social and political-economic aspects of land reform. For example, a land reform that confiscates lands without compensation to landlords and distributes such lands to peasants and workers for free constitutes redistributive reform. Similarly, a land reform that expropriates lands with compensation to landlords at below market price and distributes such lands to peasants and workers at reduced or subsidized cost is also redistributive. However, the degree of redistributive reform is higher in the former than in the latter. Such is the case comparing land reforms, by both nature and extent, in China and Taiwan immediately after World War II (see Griffin, Khan and Ickowitz, 2002; Apthorpe, 1979). Similarly, in extent, Mexico's land reform outcomes are more redistributive than Brazil's. This perspective also allows for a better sub-national analysis of land reform: the surge of redistribution of irrigated private lands in northern Mexico in the 1960s is, arguably, by nature more redistributive than the redistributions of many marginal public lands in the central part of the country in the 1920s (see Sanderson, 1984). The land reform outcome during the Allende administration was, in nature and extent, more redistributive than that during the Frei administration in Chile (see Thome, 1971, 1989: 196; Kay and Silva, 1992; Loveman, 1976: 238; Bellisario, 2007a, 2007b, 2006). True, it is difficult to devise a tool for actually measuring the degree of redistribution in this context, and this makes statistical generalizations on land reform outcomes even more difficult. But this must not stop us from stating that land redistribution is a matter of degree.

Following this framework, this study argues that a land transfer scheme does not constitute redistributive land reform where the landlord is paid one hundred percent spot-cash for one hundred percent (or higher) of the "market value" of the land and where the buyer shoulders one hundred percent of the land cost, including the sales transaction costs. Such is a simple capitalist real-estate transaction which, of itself, is highly unlikely to favour the landless rural poor (see also Flores, 1970: 149; Levin and Weiner, 1997: 258). "Exchange" of goods and money in the market between sellers and buyers is not the same as, nor does it necessarily constitute, "pro-poor" redistribution of wealth and power.

The two minimum requirements for redistributive land reform, namely, compensation to landlords at below market price and payment by peasants and workers at below actual acquisition cost must, in turn, be linked to the principle that land is not a simple economic factor of production. Rather, land has a multidimensional function and character, that is, it has political, economic, social, and cultural dimensions. In fact the "value" of land cannot be reduced to strictly monetary terms, and so the "market price" of a parcel of land is actually a contested notion involving political-economic and socio-cultural factors that, themselves, depend on who is attaching the value to the land. The notion of land having a multidimensional character (i) provides the basis for bringing in issues imbued with value judgment such as "social justice," "social function of the land," "purposive change," and "empowerment," which cannot be understood in purely monetary terms and (ii) inherently requires the intervention of the state to achieve the desired multiple goals of land reform policy. Thus, landlord compensation–related mechanisms ranging from land confiscation without compensation to expropriation with compensation at below market prices (usually inflation adjustment is not factored in) are also largely determined, and should also be determined, by non-economic factors such as socio-historical circumstances and the politics of pre-existing land monopoly and reform. The same consideration applies in determining the level of peasants' and workers' payment. Hence, the multidimensional character of land renders the monetary-based valuation method an important but incomplete way to assess the land's actual and full value.

Finally, while conceptual clarification about redistributive land reform is crucial to understand the nature and implications of a land reform policy, confusion among scholars and policymakers can arise regarding the empirical data they are working with. Specifically, changes in who supposedly controls land might be registered in formal, official records, while such changes do not occur in reality, as explained by Herring (1983: 269).

The conceptual clarification that land reform is about redistribution of wealth and power necessarily implies and requires that analysis of land reform investigate actually existing conditions rather than rely wholly and uncritically on what the official data claim or convey. This is because dynamic land-based production and distribution relationships that are essentially power relations — the very subject of reform — cannot be fully and properly captured by static official statistics alone. The literature on natural resource management, especially in light of popular calls for decentralization and "self-governance" of management (e.g., Ostrom, 2001; Bromley, 1991; Agarwal, 2005; Meinzen-Dick and Knox, 1999; Ribot and Larson, 2005) and law and development (e.g., von Benda-Beckmann, 2001, 1993; Manji, 2006; Nyamu-Musembi, 2006; but see also Peters 2004; Roquas, 2002; McAuslan, 2000; Houtzager and Franco, 2003) offers useful tools to better understand the problematic in this study. Ostrom (2001: 129) correctly criticized the conventional theory on "idealized models of private property and government property." She explained that from such a traditional perspective, "the concept of private property is conceptualized narrowly with a primary focus on the right to alienate through sale or inheritance as *the* defining attribute of private property" (emphasis original). Ostrom explained the different types of claims made over different types of rights over various resources. These rights include the right of access, withdrawal, management, exclusion, and alienation. Only a full owner has the complete set of the enumerated rights, while other types of claimants have varying rights or combinations thereof, but not alienation (Ostrom, 2001: 135; see also Toulmin and Quan, 2000). Ostrom's schema is a powerful critique of the conventional wisdom founded on the simplistic conception of property rights that refers mainly to the right to alienate.

In general, this study employs Ostrom's schema. However, it puts forth additional insights from the specific context of the research, as there are some limitations in the Ostrom schema's ability to capture some realities, such as those in the agrarian cases related in the introduction of this chapter. For example, there are cases where a person is the full owner of a parcel of land but has no power to fully and effectively exercise ownership rights (the entire range, from the right of access to the right to alienate). This is because the degree of power of an elite to exercise effective control over the same land is much higher than that of the formal (nominal) owner; in this case, the elite's power may cover almost the entire range of rights, except the formal right to alienate. However, for the elite, the right to alienate is superfluous because the formal-nominal owner's right to alienate has been effectively clipped through legal and illegal, violent and non-violent means. Indeed, the elite has no need or want to dispose of the owner's control over the land, at least not in the medium term, and so the right to alienate has no significant value. To the landed elite what is important is the effective control over the land, that is, all the rights except the right to alienate, which also means effective control over non-economic benefits, such as the captive seasonal electoral votes of the people on the land. In fact, Herring (2002: 288) concludes that "real property rights are inevitably local; right means what the claimant can make it mean, with or without the state's help." Such largely class-based relationships have been imposed and enforced by the landowning classes through violence or threat of violence, usually outside formal state institutions or through mutually agreed (real) sales transactions in settings where such sales are not allowed by state law. Thus, it is crucial to include in the analysis the power to effectively control land resources regardless of what the formal bundles of property rights demonstrate.[2]

From the discussion thus far, it is useful to identify further gaps in the literature. This is done in three broad categories: public lands, private lands, and share tenancy reform through leasehold contracts.

1.2 PROBLEMS WITH THE DOMINANT VIEWS

Public lands

According to the conventional definition, redistributive land reform is a public policy that transfers property rights over large *private* landholdings to small farmers and landless farmworkers (see, e.g., Griffin, Khan and Ickowitz, 2002: 279–280). The universally accepted definition, implicitly and explicitly, excludes non-private lands (i.e., "public," "state," or "communal" lands). The underlying assumption in the dominant land reform literature is that lands that are officially classified as "public/state" properties, especially those used to open up resettlement areas, are lands that are generally not cultivated and inhabited and are without pre-existing private control. In such conditions, it is logical to conclude that land policies that concern these lands do not recast any land-based production and distribution relationships. The literature on land reform is strong on this point, and rightly so. Yet, it becomes problematic when the use of the same lens is stretched as far as to examine "public" lands that are in fact under varying degrees of cultivation, imbued with private interests, and marked by production and distribution relationships between the landed and the landless and land-poor, between the elite and non-elite — interests and relationships that are often not captured by official census. The failure to recognize the potentially and actually contested nature of much of "public lands" risks removing them from the reach of redistributive reform, and so risks the continuation of many of the economic, social, and political problems associated with an agrarian structure that is dominated by the landed classes as well.

Most scholars understand land reform to apply only to land officially classified as private. Private lands are those where the entire bundle of property rights, from the right to use to the right to alienate, is under the formal ownership and control of a private entity that commands respect from nonowners and is legally sanctioned by the state (see, e.g., Tsing, 2002: 97). Here, "public" land is taken in its broadest sense, to mean lands where full private property rights have not been applied and sanctioned by the state. The "public land" category takes a variety of forms from one setting to another, but for the purposes of this book, it loosely includes state-owned (forest), indigenous, or communal lands and lands operated under customary arrangements. In some cases, the social relations in these types of lands are also referred to as "informal tenure" (World Bank, 2003: xxv; see also Delville, 2000; Cousins and Claassens, 2006).

When a land reform policy is directed to and implemented in "public lands," it is called a "public settlement program" or "colonization." Because few bother to interrogate the official story about such areas and compare with ground level reality, many scholars, activists, and policymakers alike simply assume that such a policy does not alter pre-existing distributions of wealth and power in society, hence does not constitute and promote redistributive reform, and therefore is politically non-contentious. On the basis of the official classification data alone, rather than empirical investigation, even some of the most important land reform scholars have made explicit their rejection of the idea that public lands can play a significantly positive role in the pursuit of land reform objectives. Hence, Feder (1970) once called the policy of land reform in public lands "counter-reform." Thiesenhusen (1971: 210) explained, "[L]and reform usually connotes a drastic change in ownership patterns in the established private sector. On the other hand directed colonization patterns on state lands or on a small number of formerly private farms frequently have little to do with making overall resource or income distribution more egalitarian: only a few settlers benefit." Tai (1974: 234) explained that "public land settlement (or colonization) is an attractive idea. To settle people on new land and to develop it for agricultural use does not involve any basic alteration of the property rights of existing landowners; hence a public-land settlement program will generate no opposition from the landed class." Lipton (1974: 272, original emphasis) argued that "the two Great evasions of land policy [are] settlement schemes and reform of tenure conditions. Both are often included in a too-weak definition …. Such programmes fail to achieve their stated goals because they do not attack the rural power structure, which is rooted in an extremely unequal distribution of owned land." Finally, de Janvry, Sadoulet and Wolford (2001: 279) have said that "countries with open frontiers have engaged in settlement programs, but we do not include this form of access to land as part of land reform."

Specifically in the context of the Philippines, Riedinger, Yang and Brook (2001) exclude redistribution of public lands from land reform accomplishment for the same reasons, as cited by other scholars elsewhere and historically. They declared,

> This figure ... reflects the area distributed by the Department of Agrarian Reform (2,562,089 hectares) in the period 1972–1997 net of lands distributed as settlements (662,727 hectares), as *Kilusang Kabuhayan at Kaunlaran* (606,347 hectares), and the rice and corn lands redistributed under Operation Land Transfer prior to 1986 (258,638 hectares) .... The former two elements of the distribution program are netted out because they do not involve *re*-distribution of *private* agricultural lands. The latter category of lands is excluded because they were redistributed prior to CARP. (376, footnote 2, emphasis original)

The dominant view on public land has far-reaching, problematic implications for land reform theory and practice, and this is especially important because of the significance of public lands to the livelihoods of a vast number of rural poor in the world today. A significant number of the rural poor are located in lands marked by what Sato (2000) calls "ambiguous" lands or property rights, as in the cases of several countries in southern Africa, Latin America, and Asia (Christodoulou, 1990: 20; Van Acker 2005; Cousins and Claassens, 2006; Nyamu-Musembi, 2006; Peters 2004). For example, 70 percent of Indonesia's land is officially categorized as "state forest land" despite "unofficial" private appropriation and use of these lands; in reality, many of these lands are productive farmlands (Peluso, 1992; Tsing, 2002; Li, 1996). In sub-Saharan Africa, "the vast majority of the land area is operated under customary tenure arrangements that, until very recently, were not even recognized by the state and therefore remained outside the realm of law" (World Bank, 2003: xviii; but see Manji, 2006; Toulmin and Quan, 2000). In Bolivia, despite the sweeping land reform that was implemented decades ago and recent attempts at "regularization" of landed property rights through land titling, the majority of lands have remained mottled by ambiguous property rights (i.e., contested "public" lands), fuelling escalating class- and ethnic-based conflict linked to competing land claims and socio-cultural and political animosities (Kay and Urioste, 2007).

Despite growing evidence to the contrary, the conventional land reform literature continues to imply that the public lands being "colonized" for resettlement projects, as a substitute for or as part of land reform programs, are mainly uninhabited, unproductive, and uncultivated forest and free from private elite control or interest. Employing a deductive method of reasoning, it is logical that the concept of *re*distribution would not apply here. But this conclusion is correct only if the assumption about the actually existing land-based production and distribution relationships holds true, which may not always, or even often, be the case. In fact, as has been suggested, the social realities obtaining in much of the land formally categorized as public are much more complex than the conventional land reform literature admits and thus require a different analytic approach. The "reality" that is captured in the official statistics, however flawed, is the "reality" that is most often accepted by or integrated into the dominant discourse. As Herring (1983: 269) has explained, flawed nationally aggregated data are too often uncritically reproduced and used by scholars, policymakers, and activists, and in the process, the number of problematic state policies are multiplied. The over-reliance on nationally aggregated official data does not result in studies that fully and accurately reflect the complexity and dynamism of property relations in agrarian societies, but rather produces "findings" that remain blind to them. To be sure, the social relationships that animate local agrarian societies are not static but endlessly negotiated and renegotiated between actors over time (see, e.g., Tsing, 2002: 95; Li, 1996; Fortmann, 1995; Juul and Lund, 2002; Mathieu, Zongo and Paré, 2002). One landlord may have control over the land at one point, only to be replaced by another later; or the terms of a sharing arrangement between landlord and tenants may change over time. Neither is the agronomic condition of land permanent: it could have been forest in the past, then deforested, then planted to various crops or converted into pasture, or reforested. All of these changes can occur while official categories and documents remain unchanged, opening up gaps in the historical record and eventually leading to state interventions that simply do not make sense and can in fact do much harm. Herring (2002: 286) goes so far as to contend that "states claim more than they know, and the mass publics know it."

Looking from the "bottom up," in terms of demographic and agro-economic conditions, there are two broad types of public lands, namely, uninhabited and idle land on the one side and populated and cultivated land on the other side. The former (uninhabited and idle land) is what most land reform scholars refer to simply as "public land." In this case and context, their argument that land policies here do not constitute *re*distributive reform (or could even be a "counter-reform") may be accepted as valid and unproblematic. For the other type (populated and cultivated), the conventional assumptions in the land reform literature emerge as so problematic as to require rethinking. Many of these lands have pre-existing inhabitants and productive activities. Despite official classification as public, these lands have been the object of complex overlapping and conflicting private land claims that have subsequently emerged and that are not easy to untangle or resolve. The implementation of state resettlement programs, for example, has impacted on the pre-existing communities in these lands. As James Scott (1998: 191) has explained, "The concentration of population in planned settlements may not create what state planners had in mind, but it has almost always disrupted or destroyed prior communities whose cohesion derived mostly from non-state sources."

This understanding of variable "public" land types more accurately reflects ground-level realities, including the reality of agriculturally productive landholdings that are controlled by private entities in many parts of the agrarian world but that have escaped the lens of land reform scholars. Even decades back, in Latin America and Asia, many so-called public lands had already witnessed varying degrees of settlement and cultivation and the creeping grip of private interests, though not always through formal institutional property rights instruments such as private land titles or formal stewardship rights. In Asia, the significant share of public lands that were highly productive even before redistribution in the Taiwanese and South Korean land reforms attests to this. The land reform beneficiaries were even made to pay for the plots carved out of blocks of public land in Taiwan (King, 1977: 211). In Latin America, the evidence shows similar conditions. As Felstehausen (1971: 168–169; see also Hobsbawm, 1974) revealed,

> An estimated 3 million hectares of well-drained, level savannahs are potentially suitable for agriculture, but many of these lands are already claimed and used by private ranchers. Technical observers report that since "land has long been available for the taking, ranches are expansive. Ranch size varies from 500 to 50,000 hectares or more" .... This statement suggests the problem associated with figures used to show the theoretical availability of land in Colombia. Much of the land listed as available is already in farms and ranches but is not included in statistical reports because it is not titled or recorded. Such lands are often held under informal possession and use arrangements. Occupation rights, in turn, are bought, sold and exchanged outside the recorded land transfer system. (125–126)

This observation appears not to have been picked up by either Felstehausen's contemporaries or succeeding scholars despite its important implications for land reform studies. Meanwhile, a process similar to that observed by Felstehausen in Colombia in the 1960s — that is, a kind of informal privatization of public land over time and outside the purview of state authorities — also transpired in some Asian countries such as Indonesia (see, e.g., White, 1997: 124–125; Peluso, 1992) and the Philippines (see Wurfel, 1958 cited in Tai, 1974: 261).

The growing literatures on community-based natural resource management, legal pluralism and related fields of research, and more recently environmental studies have been generating powerful new analytic tools that help deepen our understanding of the complex nature of landed property rights in public (forest) lands.[3] Yet, so far the findings about existing complex resource uses and the management and control of these so-called public lands have not been systematically integrated into the land reform literature. The recent surge of interest in public lands, mainly in an effort to transform them into commercial commodities via formal, private land titling procedures (see, e.g., de Soto, 2000; World Bank, 2003 — but see Manji, 2006; Nyamu-Musembi, 2006), partly contradicts the earlier (flawed) assumptions about these lands. More specifically, using cases from Thailand, Sato (2000) showed some important aspects of what these "forests" might look like on the ground. He explained,

> [A] more effective analysis begins with the study of a specific people residing in a specific location, who are likely to be caught between various interests and power relations representing forces beyond the locale. The analysis of "ambiguous lands" and the people who inhabit them is particularly revealing for understanding environmental deterioration in Thailand. "Ambiguous lands" are those which are legally owned by the state but are used and cultivated by local people. They do not fit neatly into the private property regime based on fictions of exclusive rights and alienability, and consist of residual lands of state simplification processes on land tenure. (156)

Thus, as in Colombia, many of Thailand's so-called forest lands, which official government documents claim are "public" lands, are in reality under the effective control of private entities, elite or otherwise.

The historical empirical evidence uncovered by different scholars coming from diverse social science disciplines, as described above, shows us that there is a great diversity of socioeconomic and political conditions existing in so-called public lands. But in terms of the land-based production and distribution relations that exist in these lands, it is possible and useful to construct a typology, and three broad types are in fact observable. Type 1 involves land where landed elite (we include here landlords, as well as companies engaged in logging, mining, livestock, and agribusiness) have effective control over lands officially classified as public, and have imposed varying land-based production and distribution relations with peasants and rural workers. Examples of these include numerous corporate-controlled plantations in Indonesia. Type 2 concerns land where private individuals who are neither poor nor as rich or "big" as other landed and corporate elite have effective control over land officially categorized as public as well as over the terms of farm production and distribution arrangements with peasants and workers. Type 3 involves land where poor peasants have actual control over parcels of so-called public lands that they directly till. The reality of course is far more diverse and dynamic than the typology presented here, but the latter is useful in terms of providing concrete picture of the reality hidden underneath the architecture of state law.

In short, as these examples show, existing land-based production and distribution relations in many public (forest) lands are diverse, complex, and dynamic, and thus by implication, when carried out on certain land types, a land (reform) policy can result in multi-directional outcomes, as shown in table 1.1.

Private lands

Many studies on land reform were cautious and relatively critical of official land redistribution accomplishment data offered by governments. Scholars often express doubts about the veracity of official data, leading to contentious debates about statistics. Analyses tended to focus on the possibility of deliberate padding of official land redistribution data. This is of course important. But what is lacking in the dominant critical thinking is a questioning that delves into the very essence of what is, and is not, a redistributive policy outcome.

Again, evidence from the Philippines elucidates this problem. While, on one hand, Riedinger, Yang and Brook (2001) explicitly dismiss redistribution on public lands as non-redistributive, on the other hand, they tend to be uncritical toward official reports of private land redistribution, essentially accepting "land transfers" on private lands via the voluntary offer-to-sell (VOS) and voluntary land transfer (VLT) schemes as redistributive:

> CARP had redistributed over 1.03 million hectares of private agricultural land by 1997. Half of this area was fully redistributed through programs of "Voluntary Offer-To-Sell" (265,744 hectares) and "Voluntary Land Transfer"

Table 1.1
Possible outcomes of land (reform) policies in public lands

Existing Condition	Property Rights *Prior* to Land (Reform) Policy Implementation		Property Rights *After* Land (Reform) Policy Implementation	
	Formal	*Effective*	*Formal*	*Effective*
Outcome 1: Landed elite (e.g. landlord/logging/ livestock/ agribusiness/ mining company) control over land, imposing tenurial relations w/ peasants	State/Public	Private landed elite	Private landed elite	Private landed elite
Outcome 2: Non-poor (but also not major landed elite) control over land, imposing tenurial relations with peasants	State/Public	Private Non-poor	Private non-poor	Private non-poor
Outcome 3: Poor peasants control over, and working on, land	State/Public	Private poor peasants	Private landed elite or non-poor	Private landed elite or non-poor
Outcome 4: Poor peasants control over and working on land	State/Public	Private poor peasants	Private poor peasants	Private poor peasants
Outcome 5: Landed elite (e.g. landlord/ agribusiness/logging/ livestock company) + other non-poor control over land, imposing tenurial relations with peasants	State/Public	Landed elite (e.g. landlord/ logging/ agribusiness/ livestock company) + other non-poor control over land, imposing tenurial relations w/ peasants	Private poor peasants	Private poor peasants

Source: Borras (2006b)

(276,307 hectares), suggesting that CARP — which is based on compulsory acquisition — provided a powerful incentive for landowners to enter into voluntary "market" transactions to transfer their lands to the agrarian reform agency or to erstwhile tenants and farm laborers. (373)

This analysis — commonly shared by NGOs and peasant movement activists in the Philippines and elsewhere — is problematic for a number of reasons. First, by taking an uncritical stance toward the officially reported accomplishment data on private lands, they essentially recognize all the reported output in this category as redistributive. This is problematic because there are officially reported land redistributions (carried out within a conventional state-driven land reform policy) that are simply "on-paper" land transfers where in reality reforms never took place. Examples of these are intra-family land transfers to evade expropriation, "manipulated" land transfer processes, and overpriced land transfer transactions that have a net effect of securing the effective control over land resources in the hands of the landlord or corporate elite or even achieve a net transfer of wealth from the poor to the rich. It is true that expropriationary land reforms can, under certain conditions, force — and have in some cases actually forced — some landlords to sell their lands under the government land reform program and to bargain for better compensation schemes. But this happens (as will be shown in the empirical chapters of this study) through VOS and not via VLT. This happened historically in many countries of Latin America (de Janvry, 1981; de Janvry and Sadoulet, 1989), such as in Mexico right after the revolution (Tannenbaum, 1929: 333) and in Chile during the Frei era (Thome, 1997), and it happened in Zimbabwe in 1980–1983 (Bratton, 1990). However, not all of these transactions were redistributive.

Another problematic implication of this dominant view is the relative weakness in the critical examination of neoliberal land reform that is founded on the voluntary, "willing seller, willing buyer" land sales principle. While most critics have raised valid and important issues regarding the problems in this kind of "land reform," they have generally focused on operational and administrative questions, instead of substantive issues. Specifically, critics have questioned market-led agrarian reform on the grounds that it is inherently financially expensive and for the reason that it is likely to distribute lands only on a limited scale (see, e.g., Riedinger, Yang and Brook 2001; El-Ghonemy, 2001; Griffin, Khan and Ickowitz, 2002). But this argument, wittingly or unwittingly, also implies acceptance, not rejection, of the neoliberal market-led agrarian reform as a valid concept of land reform. This study disagrees because one hundred percent commercial land sales transactions often in essence do not constitute real redistributive reform. An alternative critique of the market-led agrarian reform formula should be based on substantive issues, while highlighting operational and administrative questions as well.

In short, there are land redistributions that have been made "apparent" in official records that do not actually exist in reality. The analytic problems lies not on mere administrative issue concerning "proper accounting" but on the very framework that guides and influences any reform outcome accounting.

Share tenancy and leasehold reform

Share tenancy has existed since ancient times and this arrangement has been widespread. Different forms of share tenancy arrangements have appeared, disappeared, and reappeared in various places and times (Byres, 1983: 7–40, 2004b). But the literature on share tenancy and leasehold reforms (in this study, we refer both to share tenancy and leasehold reforms in their various possible forms) is largely contradictory and inconsistent: many scholars and activists contend that share tenancy/leasehold reform does not significantly challenge and alter pre-existing exploitative agrarian structures. However, they go on elaborately about the difficulty of implementing such reforms due to strong landlord resistance. On the one hand, Tai (1974: 218–219) explained that "the measures to improve tenancy do not as vitally affect the interest of the landlord class as does land redistribution, thus arousing not as much vigorous opposition. The central issue in the land reform remains the question of land ownership, not land use." And Jacoby (1971: 253–254) argued that "reforms of landlord-tenant relationships are less dramatic than changes in the land redistribution pattern …. Land redistribution is a surgical operation, whereas tenancy reform is an internal cure." On the other hand, Tai (ibid.: 219) admitted that "a tenancy reform law is easier to enact than to enforce," citing various political and administrative reasons, including landlords' evasive tactics. And Jacoby (ibid.) conceded that tenancy reform is "far more difficult to accomplish," citing two problems that, according to him, need to be resolved: "first, how to encourage the tenant cultivator to insist on his [sic] legal rights and secondly how to prevent the landlord from either bringing into contempt the new regulations or contriving arrangements that in reality evade the spirit of the reform." There is an inherent tension in this typical explanation about share tenancy or leasehold reform because while it claims that leasehold reform is, strictly speaking, non-redistributive, it underscores the difficulty in implementing such a policy due to reasons which boil down to landlord opposition. This tension betrays the land reform literature's built-in bias toward formal private property rights, with over-emphasis on the right to alienate, as the framework for defining what redistributive reform is or is not (see Lipton, 1974; Griffin, Khan and Ickowitz, 2002 — but see Byres, 2004b: 27–32).

Recently, broadly pro-market scholars have pushed for share tenancy reforms as a distinct, "stand-alone" policy and with a largely modified definition, rather than in its conventional form as a complementary scheme. Deininger (1999: 666) argued that only in settings where rental arrangements were not feasible should land reform through land sales be considered. The recent flurry of studies on share tenancy reform is thus identified more with the pro-market camp. The issue of tenancy reform is taken within the context of developing the so-called (liberalized) land rental market as the crucial way to provide the rural poor with access to land (see Banerjee, 1999; Banerjee, Gertler and Ghatak, 2002; Sadoulet, Murgai and de Janvry, 2001). Alain de Janvry and colleagues (2001a; see also Sadoulet, Murgai and de Janvry, 2001) explained,

> Land rental markets tend to be friendlier to the rural poor than land sales markets in allowing them access to land …. Fixed rent tenancy gives full incentive to the tenant, but high risk and liquidity constraints reduce demand for the contract while the risk of asset mismanagement … reduces its supply, limiting access to land under this form of tenancy for the rural poor. … Share tenancy can be the entry point in accessing land, leading toward land ownership through an "agricultural ladder." Sharecropping allows capitalization of rent accrued to the tenant's non-tradable assets which are given value by access to land. It also allows the accumulation of managerial experience. (15, 16)

The share tenancy reform that the pro-market scholars have recently advocated does not necessarily constitute and promote redistributive reform. It is more of a "formalization" of the system rather than "reform-then-formalization." It is founded solely on the principle of the most efficient economic use of land as a scarce resource, and it is concerned about the transfer of farm management and production organization decisions from the landowner to any willing-and-efficient tenant — the latter can be anyone, the bottom line being that they must be potentially a more efficient manager or producer on the land. Thus, in this thinking, elite-to-elite, or even poor-to-elite, transfer of control over land resources is included and is even most likely to be the dominant type because it is the elite, or at least the non-poor, who have the capital (or access to its sources) necessary to become an efficient producer. In this conception of share tenancy reform, intra-family transfers within the landowning households are included.

But despite the numerous critical studies on share tenancy reform, some gaps have persisted and so warrant further clarification. Share tenancy reform can occur in a variety of ways. It can take policy frameworks ranging from a mere formalization and registration of sharecropping arrangement without actual reform in the existing land-based production and distribution relations (for the purpose of attaining tenure security) to a more radical version that involves real reform in these relationships (to attain both tenure security and actual redistribution of wealth and power). In this study, share tenancy reform or leasehold means the latter. Leasehold reform can also take place in a variety of contexts, from being an alternative or substitute policy to redistributive land reform to being a complementary/parallel one. Most land reform studies have been framed as critiques of the former, and so they have focused on comparing the pros and cons of having share tenancy reform *instead of* land redistribution, as well as on the strengths and weaknesses of each of the two taken as *separate* policies. But leasehold reform can also be, and has been, conceived of and carried out as a policy that is *complementary* or *parallel* to land redistribution. This perspective has received relatively less attention in the literature, and is especially underscored in this study (see, also Lahiff, 2003: 41).

In short, the lack of clarity as to what is, and is not, a redistributive land reform is rooted in the use of a framework that is biased towards official private property rights. This has led to problematic *a priori* rejection of land redistribution in public lands, *a priori* acceptance of officially reported "redistribution" of private lands, and the inconsistent inclusion — or exclusion — of share tenancy/leasehold reform in the dominant land reform theory and practice. This in turn has led to, at best, partial or, worse, flawed analysis of redistributive land reform, both for country case studies and crossnational comparisons (Borras, 2006a, 2006b). This will be explained further in the succeeding discussion.

Reliance on official census data to explain land redistribution

Most land reform analyses centre around the use of relatively handy official census data that are moulded within formal property rights categories, between public lands and private lands, between those who are tenants and those who are not, and so on. The already problematic reliance on nationally aggregated official data is aggravated by the pre-existing dominant discourse related to underlying assumptions about the nature and character of public lands, especially forest lands. The "reality" that is captured in and projected from the official statistics is the "reality" that has been assumed and popularly believed in the dominant discourse. This happened, for example, in the forest policy discourse in West Africa critically examined and exposed by Fairhead and Leach (2000). Flawed nationally aggregated data are reproduced and used by scholars, policymakers, and activists in the process, multiplying the number of problematic state policies (see also Herring, 1983: 269).

As explained earlier, the over-reliance on nationally aggregated official data amidst a flawed but dominant discourse does not lead to studies that fully and accurately reflect the complex property relations in most agrarian societies, where many property rights claims are in the grey area between the strictly public and strictly private domains. Social and production relations within agrarian structures are complex and dynamic. Many of these relationships operate in "informal" institutions, for example, when actually existing tenants are non-existent in official documents or when actually privately-controlled lands are public lands in official documents. These relationships are not static; they are endlessly negotiated and renegotiated between actors.

The issue of "effective control" as the central factor defining redistributive land reform

While many conventional studies acknowledge the critical issue of power relations in the context of land reform, the analyses remain incomplete and tend to miss cases in the "grey" areas explained here. Using the concept of "effective control" over land resources – regardless of what the official documents and popular discourse would have us believe – as our analytic lens, rather than the conventional "formal property rights" lens, reveals different images of the ground-level realities in many agrarian settings. For example, many land reform beneficiaries remain the officially registered owners of their land despite the fact that they have already sold the land or rented it out for a very long period. However, because most land reform laws prohibit sales and rental of awarded lands, such transactions go unreported and unrecorded. These are the so-called informal land market transactions that have become the subject of much interest in academic and policy research in recent years (see, e.g., Carter and Salgado, 2001; Sadoulet, Murgai and de Janvry, 2001; Banerjee, 1999; Gordillo, 1997; Gordillo and Boening, 1999; Baumeister, 2000). On the other side, the people, usually landed elite, who took over the effective control over, or even full ownership of, these (black market) traded (land reformed) lands are not officially registered in their new status as owners. From another perspective, this is demonstrated by the example of Zimbabwe, where it is widely believed that perhaps 600 of the 4,400 commercial farmers by the late 1980s were already black Africans, mainly top officials and influential figures within the Mugabe government. But partly because government officials were legally limited to owning less than fifty acres of land, these new, real owners were never registered as owners (Bratton, 1990: 282–283). Rikki Broegaard's (2005) notion of "perceived tenure security" in the context of land title holders in Nicaragua is equally enlightening along the lines of argument advanced in this study.

In a related issue, it is widely known in the Philippines, as elsewhere, historically, that several multinational agribusiness corporations have effectively controlled vast tracts of public land through long-term, effectively lifetime, lease agreements with governments (see, e.g., Hawes, 1987; David et al., 1983; Tadem, Reyes and Magno, 1984; Putzel, 1992; de la Rosa, 2005, for the southern Philippines). These multinational corporations are not, however, the owners of the lands.

By implication then, the conventional thinking in this regard suggests that redistribution of these government-owned lands would be insignificant and non-redistributive. Some examples are the lands previously controlled by Dole in the southern Philippines (see, e.g., Borras and Franco, 2005) and the experience in Mexico in the 1920s wherein numerous public lands illegally appropriated by private entities, including American companies, were taken back and redistributed among poor peasants (Tannenbaum, 1929: 315–334; see also Striffler, 2002, for the Ecuadorian experience, and Griffin, Khan and Ickowitz, 2002, for the Taiwanese experience).

Thus, looking into the question of actual and effective control over land resources offers great advantages in terms of a deeper and more complete understanding of the political-economic dynamics in the agrarian structure, and so of reform initiatives. This study identifies with the "theory of access" developed by Jesse Ribot and Nancy Peluso (2003), where it has been persuasively argued that the concept of "bundle of powers" rather than "bundle of property rights" is more useful in understanding current struggles over (land) resources. They explain,

> The term "access" is frequently used by property and nature resource analysts without adequate definition .... We define access as "the *ability* to derive benefits from things," broadening from property's classical definition as "the *right* to benefit from things." Access, following this definition, is more akin to "a bundle of powers" than to property's notion of a "bundle of rights." This

formulation includes a wider range of social relationships that constrain or enable benefits from resource use than property relations alone. (153)

In addition, and finally, the discussions above also follow Bina Agarwal's work on land rights. In her critically acclaimed classic work on gender and land rights, Agarwal (1994: 19–20) has also explained broadly similar notion of rights and power over landed property. She said that in relation to this question, four distinctions are relevant: (i) "to distinguish between the legal recognition of a claim and its social recognition, and between recognition and enforcement"; (ii) to distinguish "between the ownership of land and its effective control. (Control itself can have multiple meanings, such as the ability to decide how the land is used, how its produce is disposed of, whether it can be leased out, mortgaged, bequeathed, sold, and so on.)"; (iii) "to distinguish between ownership and use rights vested in individuals and those vested in a group"; and (iv) to "distinguish between rights conferred via inheritance and those conferred by State transfers of land …."[4]

The notion of "bundle of powers" explained by Ribot and Peluso and the discussion offered by Agarwal are closely related to recent argument for the notion of "a political economy of rights" put forward by Peter Newell and Joanna Wheeler (2006) in the broader but related context of citizenship rights and access to resources. They said,

> Contests over rights of access to resources and to the benefits that derive from their exploitation define many contemporary and historical struggles in development. They affect the interests of the powerful and the poor simultaneously, often bringing them into conflict with one another …. What emerges, then, is a *political economy of rights* in which questions of access to and distribution and production of resources are paramount. A focus on resources changes the way we think about the relationship between rights and accountability. The challenge is not to over-emphasize the material dimensions of this relationship and to acknowledge instead that economic rights are in many ways indivisible from social, political and cultural rights. Realizing the former is in many ways contingent on having access to the latter rights. (9, emphasis original)

A firm understanding of the actual dynamics of access to and control over resources drawing from various social science disciplines will greatly benefit the land reform scholarship. Using these frameworks and insights, we now turn to the issues of opportunities for and limits to redistributive land reform in the contemporary era of neoliberal globalization.

1.3 THE LIMITS-CENTRED AND OPPORTUNITIES-CENTRED APPROACHES

Current interest in land reform has given birth to a steady growth of academic and policy-oriented works on the subject. Some are new publications essentially about old evidence and old insights. Others ignore past serious works and put forward completely new, almost ahistorical, interpretations of land questions and the way to resolve them. A few have embarked on truly fresher examination of past and present evidence. This highly diverse thinking about land reform today has led to diverse literature. Nevertheless, it can be analytically segregated and clustered into two broad competing camps: the "limits-centred" approach and the "opportunities-centred" approach. More or less, the former traces its provenance from the classic state-led land reform tradition, while the latter invents, packages, and presents itself as a brand new alternative, the market-led approach.

State-led land reforms: Imperatives and initiatives

Different imperatives have pushed nation-states to adopt multiple varieties of land reform initiatives in differing circumstances since ancient times (see, e.g., Tuma, 1965; see also Jorgensen, 2006, for some eastern European cases), but becoming more common during the 20th century (see, e.g., King, 1977). Most, if not all, of what was considered "land reform" in the past has been state sponsored. The permanent twin agendas of the state, namely, to achieve and maintain the necessary minimum degree of political legitimacy on the one hand, and to maintain conditions for capital accumulation on the other (see Fox, 1993: Ch. 2), have in varying degrees and forms provided the imperatives and contexts for past land redistribution initiatives.

These two broad state agendas have taken numerous forms. In one, the fear of those in state power of some cataclysmic social upheaval by the mass of hungry and desperate landless and land-poor peasants that might lead to more radical societal changes has almost always led to broadly pre-emptive types of reforms, such as the Stolypin reform in Russia in the early 20th century (Huizer, 2001: 167–169), that in South Vietnam before the 1975 communist victory, and that in El Salvador in 1980 (Paige, 1975, 1996; Diskin, 1989). Many of the reforms within this context were also broadly conceived as part of a counter-revolutionary containment strategy against communism, chiefly sponsored by the United States and its allies. The land reform initiative in Latin America undertaken under the auspices of the US-sponsored Alliance for Progress is a classic example. Wolf Ladejinsky pioneered the land reform model adopted in these situations immediately after World War II (see Walinsky, 1977; Ross, 1998: Ch. 5). Roy Prosterman more or less continued this tradition onward (see Prosterman, 1976; Prosterman and Riedinger, 1987; but also White, 1989: 16–17, on Prosterman; Putzel, 1992).

A closely related perspective is the fact that land reform has been an important policy instrument in geopolitics. The special cases of post–World War II land reforms in Japan, South Korea, and Taiwan that were conceived, imposed, and enforced by the United States were the concrete cases in which land reform was used to strengthen the politico-military position of the United States against the possible resurgence of fascism in Japan and the advance of communist groups from China and North Korea. This became the precedent of and model for the subsequent use of land reform as a policy weapon against communism (see Ross, 1998: Ch. 5).

Land reform has also been an important policy instrument in political consolidation efforts during (different types of) regime transitions. One type is the regime transition after a non-socialist revolution, such as the land reforms immediately after the French Revolution (Tuma, 1965; Moore, 1967; Jones, 1991), right after the 1910 Mexican Revolution (Tannenbaum, 1929; Sanderson, 1984), and after the early 1950s revolution in Guatemala (Handy, 1994). Another type is regime transition after a socialist revolution, such as the land reforms in China (Shillinglaw, 1974; Saith, 1985; Bramall, 2004), Cuba (Deere, 2000), Nicaragua (Collins, Lappé and Allen, 1982; Fitzgerald, 1985), and Mozambique (O'Laughlin, 1995, 1996). Yet another type is the transition ending a colonial regime, such as in many countries in Africa (Moyo, 2000; Gasper, 1990; Bratton, 1990; Worby, 2001; Palmer, 2000a; Berry, 2002) and in post-apartheid South Africa (Levin and Weiner, 1997; Cousins, 1997; Bernstein, 1998; Adams and Howell, 2001; Lahiff and Scoones, 2000; Ntsebeza, 2006; Ntsebeza and Hall, 2006; Walker, 2003). Consolidation of an electoral victory of radical groups paving the way for a new regime type is another example, such as the case during the Allende presidency in Chile in the early 1970s (Kay and Silva, 1992; Kay, 1992a, 1992b; Loveman, 1976; Thiesenhusen, 1971), the 1957 communist electoral victory in Kerala (Herring, 1983, 1990), and the 1977 communist victory in West Bengal (Lieten, 1996; Baruah, 1990; Harriss, 1993). Finally, the assumption to power by an authoritarian, militarist regime has tended to be followed by initiatives for land reform, partly to debase the ousted traditional elite, such as what happened in Peru in the late 1960s and early 1970s (Kay, 1983; Mosley, 1985), in Egypt in the early 1950s (Migdal, 1988: Ch. 3), and in the Philippines in 1972 (Kerkvliet, 1979; Wurfel, 1983).

Permeating the various imperatives and contexts, land reform was widely adopted (at least formally) and implemented generally as an instrument for changing existing relationships within agrarian structures in societies, either as a prerequisite for capitalist development or for socialist construction (see, e.g., Bernstein, 2002, 2003, 2004; Saith, 1985; O'Laughlin, 1996), for national development campaigns either in the rural or urban bias path (Lipton, 1974; Byres, 1974; Byres, 2004a, 2004b; Karshenas, 2004; Griffin, Khan and Ickowitz, 2002; Kay, 2002b), or for straightforward poverty reduction campaigns (see, e.g., Quan, 2000). In no national case can a single imperative and intention fully account for and explain a land reform policy. Always a mixture of socio-political and economic intentions, a convergence of factors and actors, as well as a confluence of events pushed for a particular national land reform initiative.

The diversity of imperatives and contexts within which land reforms have been conceived has given birth to equally diverse land reform policies. It is almost impossible to capture such diversity in writing, but they can be grouped into three ideal types, namely, revolutionary, conservative, and liberal. Partly following the typology by James Putzel (1992 — see also the one by Sobhan, 1993), this study defines a revolutionary land reform as one that confiscates estates from landlords without compensation and redistributes them to landless and land-poor peasants for free; it targets large private landholdings. A conservative land reform is one that de-emphasizes expropriation of private lands and instead focuses on tenancy reforms, resettlement programs on (unoccupied) public lands, and, at times, formally includes a small portion of private land with full compensation to amenable landlords. In this last case, the beneficiaries are usually made to pay the full cost of the land. Finally, a liberal land reform is somewhere between the first two, combining expropriationary elements with conservative components. Most actually existing land reforms fall within this third broad category, e.g., the contemporary policies in Brazil (Sauer, 2003: 48-49; Deere and Medeiros, 2007) and the Philippines (Borras, 2001). These land reforms are redistributive to varying degrees — either closer to the conservative model or nearer the revolutionary ideal. Most of these policies compensate landlords at essentially below market prices (either by putting below market price tags on the land or by paying the landlords over a long period so that the real value of the money is eroded, especially when computed against annual inflation, or a combination of both) and redistribute lands to peasants usually at subsidized prices. Broadly liberal land reforms have effected a significant degree of land redistribution, such as in the cases of Japan, Taiwan, South Korea, and Chile. Thus, land reform outcomes with high degrees of success are not the monopoly of revolutionary land reforms, socialist or otherwise, like those in China and Mexico.

A universe of multiple forms of land reform policies has been implemented under different specific conditions and contexts by different types of state and societal actors and their alliances. These have resulted in equally diverse outcomes between and within nation-states described above. Many studies have attempted to underscore the diversity of outcomes between nation-states to achieve fuller understanding of land reform. Ironically, however, these have tended to simplify the diversity by coming up with simplistic categories of "success" and "failure." Following this perspective, successful cases are understood as those able to redistribute more land to more landless and land-poor peasants, and the opposite are the failed cases. Yet, interestingly, whenever partial categories appear in the literature, the connotation is almost always nearer to the "failed" type, rather than having a distinct category: partial. This tendency is common both among the pro–state-led land reform scholars and their pro-market critics (see, e.g., Deininger and Binswanger 1999; El-Ghonemy, 2001). This is unfortunate because almost all land reform initiatives, except perhaps for a few socialist-revolutionary types, have delivered varying degrees of outcomes, but always partial; they are neither completely successful nor a total failure, and they must be understood as such. Thus, in fact redistributive land reform is a matter of degree both in the nature and extent of its outcomes. As Thiesenhusen (1989: 35) admitted, "Usually land reforms do not accomplish all they set out to do. Often, accomplishment on one score is mixed with less satisfactory results on another; sometimes, to the chagrin and embarrassment of all, results are nearly the opposite of what was intended" (see also Byres, 1974: 224).

There is an inherent tension within the land reform literature with regard to measurement of success or failure. In their eagerness to come up with exact or precise measurements of success or failure of land reform outcomes, most studies apply techniques that require relatively easily accessible data, both quantitative, such as nationally aggregated formal and official reports, and qualitative, such as vague concepts like "strong political will" of the state or "strong independent peasant organizations." Yet as already explained, while different types of data are important for analysis, these are incomplete and not totally reliable when one is to examine land reform based on its redistributive nature. Even more difficult to evaluate is the success or failure of the impact of land reforms on the overall socio-political and economic conditions of each country. As Kay (1998) explained, it may require a longer period after land redistribution has been completed, and even then, it becomes complicated because other relevant factors are also at work. Kay's assessment of the strategic impact of earlier land redistribution on current agribusiness in Chile is illuminating (see Kay 2002a: 488–489 and 2002b; Bellisario, 2007b; see also Byres, 1974: 224 in the context of India; Borras, 2007, for Southeast Asia; and Meliczek, 1999). To Kay's assertion, it can be added that rigorous analysis of the impact of land redistribution on the overall national development of a country must be premised on a firm grasp of the real and apparent-but-not-real outcomes of land redistribution.[5]

Moreover, Borras and Franco (2006) have explained, "The social, political and cultural aspects of successful land redistribution are difficult to measure and assess. Some studies posit a straightforward breaking of the nexus between peasants and landlord and transformation of the former into relatively 'freeer' agents, with a greater degree of autonomy in social and political decision-making and action vis-à-vis both state and non-state actors" (1). They continue to explain that meanwhile, "others show that while clientelistic tenant-landlord ties may be cut through land reform, other unequal relationships can emerge to take their place, such as between government officials and merchants on the one side and newly created small family farmers on the other. Or, in the case of commercial plantations, farmworkers' key relationship may shift from being with a domestic landlord to a transnational company, where the underlying issue of control of the land resource and its products is not resolved in their favour" (ibid.: 1). But Borras and Franco conclude that "in the contemporary Philippines, the overall picture may be mixed, but one thing is clear: fuelled by the break-up of landlord-peasant ties through partial land reform implementation, the social-political power of the landed elite has experienced an unprecedented degree of erosion, albeit in localised patches scattered across the country" (ibid.: 1).

The point is that it is possible that while one may be looking for the strategic impact of land redistribution on development or democratization, what is actually being analyzed is an apparent-but-not-real type of land redistribution. A faulty frame can lead to erroneous conclusions. On the one hand, one may conclude that land reform is working because the "land reformed estates" are economically productive and competitive, when in fact the estates being analyzed remain under the control of the landowning elite despite the land reform claims in official records. On the other hand, one may conclude that land reform is not working because the farms are not economically productive and competitive, when in fact the landholdings being analyzed have not undergone real redistributive reform despite the claims in official records. More generally, some may conclude that land reform is not a workable concept because of the experience in this or that country, when in reality, redistributive land reforms were never carried out to any significant extent in those countries despite claims to the contrary in official records. These are, for example, the cases of recent market-led agrarian reform programs as officially claimed by their proponents (e.g., Deininger and Binswanger, 1999; Buainain et al., 1999). These were exposed by various critical analyses, for example, those by van Donge, Eiseb and Mosimane (2007) in the case of Namibia, Andrews (2006) for South Africa, or Gauster (2006) for Guatemala. Finally, in measuring the success of land redistribution, we may be looking for robust small family farms created by the land reform process but missing the fact that it is possible that for many land reform beneficiaries the awarded landholdings form only one part of their asset complex and serve only one part of their combination of livelihood strategies — a reality that has earlier been underscored by Gillian Hart (1995: 46; see also Rigg, 2006; Razavi, 2003). Insights drawn from wrong empirical bases thus lead to problematic conclusions.

By the time the world entered the eighth decade of the past century, land reform had lost most of its ground in policy and academic terrain, internationally and nationally, although as Herring (2003) explained, it did not really exit the political arena and agenda. Thus, land reform was written off from international and national policy agendas and only a few cases were carried out (see Zoomers and van der Haar, 2000; Carter and Salgado, 2001; Ghimire, 2001c, 2001a; Ghimire and Moore, 2001; Akram-Lodhi, Borras and Kay, 2007; Rosset, Patel and Courville, 2006). Around the mid-1990s, however, a confluence of events occurred to bring land reform back onto the policy agendas. Various sporadic but dramatic land-based political conflicts, such as that in Brazil (Petras, 1997, 1998; Petras and Veltmeyer, 2001; Veltmeyer, 2005a, 2005b; Deere, 2003; Wright and Wolford, 2003; Robles 2001; Branford and Rocha, 2002; Meszaros, 2000a, 2000b), Zimbabwe (Worby, 2001; Moyo, 2000; Palmer, 2000b; Waeterloos and Rutherford 2004), and Chiapas in Mexico (Harvey, 1998; Bobrow-Strain, 2004) contributed to this policy revival (see also Pons-Vignon and Lecomte, 2004). Also responsible was the realization by pro-market scholars that neoliberal policy reforms had difficulty taking off in most developing countries, which are saddled with the problem of highly skewed land ownership in which most of the rural poor cannot actively participate in the market, or when land markets were distorted by state regulation.[6] This latter has been perhaps even more influential for the land reform policy resurrection (World Bank, 2003; Deininger and Binswanger, 1999; de Soto, 2000; but see Stiglitz, 2002: 80–81; Manji, 2006). Combined, these two factors

Table 1.2
Economic and socio-political bases of, and imperatives for, land reforms

Pre-1980s period	1990s onward
Economic	
Existing large landed estates are economically inefficient and must be restructured through land reform	Continuing relevance/currency
Creation of privatized and individualized landed property rights in order to boost investments in the rural economy	Continuing — and has seen greater expansion in coverage
	Issues related to inefficiency (and accountability) in (former) socialist state farms and cooperatives, e.g., Eastern Europe, central Asia, Vietnam, China
	Issues related to efficiency in farm collectives brought about by past land reforms, e.g., Mexico and Peru
Socio-political	
De-colonization	While to a large extent it is not a burning issue with the same intensity as decades ago, decolonization process–related issues have persisted in many countries, such as Zimbabwe
Cold War	Not any more
Central state's "management" of rural unrest usually instigated by liberation movements	Diminished substantially as liberation movements waned. But rural unrest persisted in different forms, usually not in the context of armed groups wanting to seize state power but to push for radical reforms, e.g., Chiapas, Brazil
As a strategy to legitimize and/or consolidate one elite faction's hold on state power against that of another, e.g., Left electoral victories, military *coups d'état*	Continuing, e.g., Zimbabwe, tenancy reform by the Left Front in West Bengal
As an integral component of the central state's aspiration of "modernization," i.e., standardized cadastral maps, etc. for taxation purposes, etc.	Continuing, and has seen unprecedented degree of technological sophistication (e.g., satellite/digital mapping, computerized data-banking)
	i) Post-conflict democratic construction and consolidation, e.g., post-apartheid South Africa, post–civil war El Salvador (de Bremond, 2006; Pearce, 1998; Foley, 1997), Colombia (Ross, 2003, 2007)

ii) Advancement of knowledge about the distinct rights of indigenous peoples (e.g., Yashar, 1999; Hirtz, 2003; Korovkin, 2000; Assies, van der Haar and Hoekma, 1998)

iii) Advancement of knowledge about gender and rights issues, see, e.g., Razavi (2003); Agarwal (1994), Kabeer (1999); Deere (1985), and Deere and León (2001), Resurreccion (2006); Walker (2003); Whitehead and Tsikata (2003)

iv) Greater concern about the environment (see, e.g., Herring, 2002; Holt-Gimenez, 2006)

v) Persistence and resurgence of violence including that related to drugs and ethnic issues (see, e.g., Pons-Vignon and Lecomte, 2004; Peluso, 2007; Borras and Ross, 2007; Bush, 2002; Cramer, 2003)

vi) Emerging "[human] rights-based approaches" to development (see, e.g., Molyneux and Razavi (2002) Patel, Balakrishna and Narayan, 2007; Franco, 2006; Monsalve, 2003)

vii) The phenomenal rise of NGOs as important actors in development questions at the local, national, and international levels

viii) "rule of law" reforms (see, e.g., Franco, forthcoming; Houtzager and Franco, 2003; Manji, 2006; Nyamu-Musembi, 2006; McAuslan, 2000; Meszaros, 2000a, 2000b)

Note: Table adapted from Borras, Kay and Akram-Lodhi (2007)

have pushed the slow but steady resurgence of land reform back onto the policy and political agendas nationally and internationally since the late 1990s. However, the terms and parameters of this policy debate have been set more by the pro-market scholars (see World Bank, 2003; de Janvry et al., 2001b).

The global agrarian restructuring (see, e.g., Bernstein, 2006; McMichael, 2006a; Patel, 2006; Friedmann, 2005; Kay, 2004; Rigg, 2006; Edelman, 1999) and its impact on redistributive land reforms (Fortin, 2005; Hall, 2004; Bush, 2002) has been interpreted differently by different land reform scholars. Those who were part of the peak years of state-led land reforms tend to concede that the classic approaches to state-led land reform must be revised because such an approach is (supposedly) difficult to carry out in the current changed and changing global and national conditions (see, e.g., Dorner, 2001, 1992).

Therefore, it is not surprising that among scholars from the state-led tradition who continue to believe and argue that state-led land reform is necessary and urgent (e.g., Barraclough, 2001) are many who are to varying degrees pessimistic about its prospects in recent writings (see, e.g., Dorner, 2001; El-Ghonemy, 2001). Moreover, many scholars have tended to become eclectic, endorsing some principles from both the classic state-led approaches and some from the new market-led proposition (e.g., Dorner, 1992; Ciamarra, 2003; Lipton, 1993; Carter, 2000; Carter and Salgado, 2001; de Janvry and Sadoulet, 1989; Gordillo, 1997; Gordillo and Boening, 1999; Banerjee, 1999; de Janvry et al., 2001a, 2001b). For instance, Dorner (1992: 92) concluded, "There is likely to be a major role for various land-market interventions that may provide increased access to land and productive opportunities for at least some of the rural poor, and yield some prospect for evolutionary change in such markets in the future." A few scholars have (re)argued for redistributive land reform from the basic standpoint of the classic state-led approach and have actually tried to analyze the changes in the contemporary setting that could be favourable to land redistribution today. An outstanding work in this context is Herring (2003), which boldly argues that the proposition of the demise of redistributive land reform is premature and without basis and that the various social policy issues and the (new) social movements that have emerged around these concerns could serve as an impetus for the revival of land reform on development policy agendas (see also Putzel, 2000).

Contemporary pro-market thinking on land reform

The perceived limits to redistributive land reform have been highlighted by the emergence of a competing model. The pro-market land policies have challenged the conventional wisdom that land reform must be imposed and enforced by the state from above. In contrast, the neoliberal policy model identifies the forces of the free market as the principal mechanism for (re)allocation of land resources. These mechanisms are necessarily privatized and decentralized. Such a model has been constructed partly believing that the newly changed and changing global and national socioeconomic and political settings provide unprecedented opportunities for "land reform." Our discussion on this theme is divided into two parts, namely, (i) a pro-market critique of the state-led agrarian reform and (ii) an exposition of the pro-market policy.

Pro-market critique of the state-led agrarian reform

For the mainstream economists, the key problem of past land policies was the fact that the state was given the power to intervene in the (re)allocation of land resources, leading to the distortion of the land markets that in turn resulted in the "insecurity" of property rights and investments in the rural economy (Deininger and Binswanger, 1999). They pointed out the problems with public lands where there are no clear private property rights, as well as with the state and collectivized farms that are outcomes of past land reforms. Thus, the mainstream advocacy is to develop clear, formal private property rights in the remaining public lands in most developing countries and transition economies (see de Soto, 2000; but see also the different but arguably very similar arguments by the World Bank, 2003; see Nyamu-Musembi, 2006; Manji, 2006; Whitehead and Tsikata, 2003; Van Acker 2005; and Cousins and Claassens, 2006 for critical insights in the context of Africa).

Meanwhile, as to private lands, the pro-market critique holds that the main cause of the "failure" of state-led land reforms is their land acquisition method: expropriationary and coercive. It is argued that compensation to landlords via cash-bonds payment for the expropriated land at a below market price level is a thin veil for confiscation that provokes and promotes landlord opposition to reform. The critique is particularly hostile to the state-led approach's concept of a "land size ceiling," which allows landlords to own only a limited amount of land. Deininger and Binswanger (1999: 263) argued, "Ceiling laws have been expensive to enforce, have imposed costs on landowners who took measures to avoid them, and have generated corruption, tenure insecurity, and red tape." The same scholars go on to explain that the usual mode of payment to landlords at below market prices and through staggered, partly government bonds allows time to erode the real value of the landowners' money, and so, provokes landlords' resistance to reform (Binswanger and Deininger, 1996: 71). Landlords have subverted the policy, evading coverage by subdividing their farms or retaining the best parts of the land. Legal battles launched by landlords have slowed, if not prevented, much land reform implementation (see also de Janvry and Sadoulet, 1989).

Moreover, according to this critique, the "supply-driven" approach in state-led land reform with regard to selection of beneficiaries and land is responsible for taking in "unfit beneficiaries" and "unfit lands" to become part of the reform, leading to greater inefficiency in land use and a "dole-out" mentality among beneficiaries that, in turn, has led to the "failure" of land reforms in the past. According to pro-market scholars, a state-led land reform usually starts either by first identifying lands for expropriation and then looking for possible peasant beneficiaries, or by first identifying potential peasant beneficiaries then looking for lands to be expropriated. This leads to economic inefficiency (i) when productive farms are expropriated and subdivided into smaller, less productive units or when environmentally fragile, usually public lands are distributed by the state, and (ii) when peasant households "unfit" to become beneficiaries (i.e., those with no potential to become economically efficient and competitive producers) are given lands to farm (World Bank, n.d.: 2; Deininger and Binswanger, 1999).

Furthermore, according to the pro-market critique, state-led land reforms have been "statist" and "centralized" and so have been inherently slow and corruption-ridden in implementation. The pro-market critique argues that the state-led approach relies heavily on the central state and its huge bureaucracy for implementation through top-down methods that fail to capture the diversity between and within local communities and are unable to respond to the actual needs in the local villages at quick pace (Gordillo, 1997: 12). Binswanger (1996a) explained,

> Public sector bureaucracies develop their own set of interests that is in conflict with the rapid redistribution of land ... expropriation at below market prices requires that the state purchase the land rather than the beneficiaries. While not inevitable, this is likely to lead to the emergence of a land reform agency whose personnel will eventually engage in rent-seeking behaviour of its own. (141-142)

Meanwhile, according to the critique, another consequence of the state-led approach is the distortion of the land market. According to Deininger and Binswanger (1999: 262-263), most developing countries are plagued with distorted land markets caused primarily by prohibitions on land sales and rentals by land reform beneficiaries and landlords already marked for expropriation. This is thought to have prevented more efficient producers from acquiring or accumulating lands, blocked the entry of potential external investors, and prevented inefficient and bankrupt beneficiaries from getting out of production. These prohibitions have led to informal land market transactions that, in turn, breed corruption within state agencies and drive land prices upward to further distort land markets (see Carter and Salgado, 2001; Banerjee, 1999; Gordillo, 1997: 12-19; de Janvry, Sadoulet and Murgai, 1999). Furthermore, the pro-market critique laments that state-led agrarian reforms have been implemented usually without prior or accompanying progressive land taxation and a systematic land titling program, the absence of which contributes to land price increases beyond their proper levels, encourages landlords to practice "land banking" or speculation, and leads to complex competing claims over land that, again, result in land market distortions (Bryant, 1996). The latter measures, such as land taxation, are partly hoping to carry out what Hirschman (1967) has observed in the early 1960s in Colombia as "reform by stealth" — gaining reformist inroads while avoiding premature backlash from the landlords.

The pro-market critique further complains that state-led land reforms adopt the sequence of "farm plans and development *after* land redistribution," causing the "failure" of agrarian reforms in particular and of the agricultural sector in general. The pro-market critique laments most state-led land reforms as, at best, land redistribution–centred, because in most cases, the state has failed to deliver support services to beneficiaries. Extension services have tended to be inefficient, with, on most occasions, support services extended mainly via production and trade subsidies that are universal in nature. Therefore, in reality, the politically influential sector of large farmers and landlords have benefited more than small farmers. In addition, Deininger and Binswanger (1999: 266–267) concluded, "Centralized government bureaucracies — charged with providing technical assistance and other support services to beneficiaries — proved to be corrupt, expensive, and ineffective in responding to beneficiary demands." Therefore, post-redistribution land development has been uncertain and less than dynamic, without widespread efficiency gains, and has "resulted in widespread default [in repayments] and nonrecoverable loans" by beneficiaries (ibid.). The critique holds that the state-led approach drives away credit sources because expropriation pushes landlords (a traditional source of capital) away from farming, while formal credit institutions do not honour land award certificates due to land sales and rental prohibitions. For the same reasons, potential external investors are discouraged from entering into the agricultural sector (Gordillo, 1997: 13).

Finally, according to the pro-market critique, the state-led approach is too costly because it is too expensive for the state to buy the land from landlords. Landlords are paid regardless of whether the beneficiaries pay for the land. This is the concept of sovereign guarantee that has been applied in government-sponsored credit programs that have failed in general. Moreover, production- and trade-related universal subsidies are costly and wasteful, while the huge land reform bureaucracy itself eats up much of the program budget (Binswanger and Deininger, 1997).

In short, Deininger and Binswanger (1999: 267) captured the essence of the pro-market critique of the state-led agrarian reforms when they concluded, "Most land reforms have relied on expropriation and have been more successful in creating bureaucratic behemoths and in colonizing frontiers than in redistributing land from large to small farmers."

The pro-market critique is the most unsympathetic, but arguably the most systematic, critique of state-led approaches to agrarian reform — from a pro-market perspective. The alternative pro-market land policy model was constructed from this critique. Deininger (1999: 651) explained the market-led agrarian reform (MLAR) model as a "mechanism to provide an efficiency- and equity-enhancing redistribution of assets." According to Deininger and Binswanger (1999: 249), "This approach can help overcome long-standing problems of asset distribution and social exclusion."

The pro-market land policy model
The neoliberal land policies on public/communal lands and state and collective farms (in both socialist and capitalist settings) have been carried out through different land policy instruments, resulting in variegated and uneven outcomes between and within countries over time — but not always in favour of the poor. By public/state lands, we mean the remaining public and communal lands in most developing countries today, as well as state and collective farms both in (ex-)socialist and capitalist settings. The main pro-market critique is that due to conventional land policies many of the public/state lands have remained economically under-utilized. The key pro-market philosophy and goal is the promotion of privatized and individualized property rights in these lands. In instances where customary and communal tenure is supported, individualized rights within such "community-controlled" areas are prescribed (see World Bank, 2003; but see also Cousins and Claassens, 2006). For mainstream perspectives, see Deininger (1995, 2002), Deininger and Binswanger (1999) and the World Bank (2003). For critical examination, especially in the context of transition countries, see Spoor (forthcoming, 2003, 1997), Spoor and Visser (2004), Ho and Spoor (2006), Akram-Lodhi (2004, 2005), Sikor (2006). See Kerkvliet (2005, 2006) for a particularly nuanced analysis of the case of Vietnam regarding the dynamic interplay between the state, community and family in facilitating access to land to the peasantry after the period of state collectivization.-

For private lands, a combination of liberalized land sales and rental policies has been advocated. The key features of the MLAR model can be explained in three parts: (i) gaining access to land, (ii) post–land purchase farm development, and (iii) financing mechanisms. But before going into the features of the pro-market proposition, it is important to point out that, according to MLAR proponents, land transfer schemes must be taken only as a second option for improving access to land by the landless. The preferred policy is to implement some adjustment in share tenancy regulations and/or to promote a full liberalization of the land rental market aimed mainly to achieve the most efficient use of land (Deininger, 1999: 666; Banerjee, 1999; Sadoulet, Murgai, de Janvry, 2001; Carter and Salgado, 2001; Carter and Mesbah, 1993). Only under certain conditions should land transfer be implemented in addition to, or instead of, share tenancy reform. Deininger (1999: 666) explained, "Negotiated land reform [i.e., MLAR] is a complement rather than a substitute for other forms of gaining access to land, especially land rental." Sadoulet, Murgai and de Janvry (1998) explain further:

> Tenancy contracts serve as instruments for the landless to gain access to land and for landowners to adjust their ownership units into operational units of a size closer to their optimum. In providing an entry point into farming, tenancy for the landless holds promise for eventual land ownership and vertical mobility in the "agricultural ladder" .... We conclude with policy recommendations to preserve and promote access to land for the rural poor via land rental markets. (1)

The first part of the MLAR model is gaining access to land. According to MLAR proponents, the cooperation of the landlords is the most important factor for any successful implementation of land reform. This is MLAR's guiding principle. Hence, it is a voluntary program: Only the land of landlords who voluntarily sell is touched; landlords who do not want to sell are not compelled to do so. Deininger and Binswanger (1999: 267) clarified that "this approach ... aims to replace the confrontational atmosphere that has characterized land reforms." The willing sellers, in turn, are paid one hundred percent spot cash for one hundred percent of the value of their lands. Deininger (1999: 663) claimed that this would provide "a strong incentive for landowners ... to sell land." But Gordillo and Boening (1999: 10) cautioned, "[MLAR] is targeted in regions with enough excess supply of land relative to the program of land purchases in order to avoid triggering an increase in land prices." Deininger (1999 : 659) supported this warning, explaining that the ideal ratio is 3:1 of land supply to demand.

The MLAR model adopts a "demand-driven" approach in land and beneficiary targeting. Only poor families who explicitly demand land and only the lands being demanded by potential buyers are negotiated for the reform program (qualified beneficiaries are provided funds to enable them to buy lands, as will be discussed later). But Buainain et al. (1999: 29–30) explained that to ensure success "only individuals with human capital, previous savings, and adequate knowledge of how to make use of the opportunities would make the decision to participate in the Program ... [MLAR will select] local people, who [have] closer relations with landowners, better access to networks of social relations and information" on the local land market. The creation and development of efficient and competitive individual family farms is the main objective of the MLAR project. In order to find the "fittest" beneficiaries, and to strengthen the bargaining power of the buyers during the land purchase negotiations, beneficiaries are required to form an organization. The formation of a beneficiary organization is also necessary to achieve economies of scale in the input and output markets. These organizations carry out a "peer monitoring" process in order to bring down the program's transaction costs (Deininger and Binswanger, 1999). This excludes less promising applicants because they would not be allowed by their peers to join the organization negotiating the land purchase and credit access.

Moreover, the model adopts a decentralized method of implementation for speedy transactions and for transparency and accountability. "It privatizes and thereby decentralizes the essential process [of land reform]," according to Binswanger (1996b: 155). Agrarian reform scholars van Zyl, Kirsten and Binswanger (1996: 9) explained, "The role of government should be to establish a comprehensive legal, institutional and policy framework which will ensure a level playing field for all players." It is partly in this context that MLAR needs local governments, for land purchase mediation and tax collection. Local governments are thought to be nearer to the people and so should be more responsive to actual needs of the local communities. Moreover, Deininger and Binswanger (1999: 267–268) explained, "the [MLAR] promises to overcome some of the informational imperfections that have plagued the implementation of land reform by government bureaucracies" via localized market information systems set up by local government units.

In addition, the MLAR model is faster because, as Binswanger (1996b: 155) observed, "It avoids years of delays associated with disputes about compensation levels." Moreover, land prices are expected to be lower because of the one hundred percent cash payment made to landlords, which would factor out transaction costs incurred under the state-led approach's cash-bond, staggered mode of payment.

Meanwhile, "in a clear departure from the traditional approach, the new model would stimulate, rather than undermine, land markets" (Deininger and Binswanger, 1999: 267). Prohibitions on land sales and rentals are abolished to allow for a more fluid land market (ibid.: 269; see Banerjee, 1999; Carter and Salgado, 2001). "[C]losing the gap between agricultural land values and market values of the land makes land more affordable and enhances repayment ability because buyers of land will now find it easier to repay a loan from the productive capacity of the land itself" (van Schalkwyk and van Zyl, 1996: 333). This is done partly through subsidy withdrawal (from large farmers), progressive land taxation, systematic land titling, land sales and rental liberalization, and better market information systems. The MLAR model has a better chance of success if there is an efficient land titling system. According to Bryant (1996: 1543), a "'willing-buyers, willing-sellers' formal land market requires that the sellers can certify that boundaries have been demarcated and that the land in question is legally owned by the seller." Buyers are not as willing to buy land where those characteristics are absent. Meanwhile, de Janvry, Sadoulet and Wolford (2001: 293–294) observed, "The introduction of land markets would allow better farmers to replace older or less skilled farmers, inducing a slow process of social differentiation. This process would gradually transfer the land toward the most competitive farm sizes and the better farmers" (but see Baranyi, Deere, Morales, 2004: 32–35).

The second part of the MLAR model is *post–land purchase farm and beneficiary development*. MLAR takes on the program implementation sequence of farm plans *before* land purchase and so, the argument goes, farm development is assured because no land will be purchased without viable farm plans that emphasize diversified, commercial farming. Moreover, because beneficiaries are given cash grants to develop their farms, development will be quick (Deininger, 1999: 666). A portion of this grant must be spent on privatized-decentralized extension services that are strictly demand driven. Beneficiaries can hire consultants (e.g., NGOs and cooperatives) to assist them with project plans, an approach that Deininger (1999) sees as efficient, since accountability between beneficiaries and service providers should be direct and the process transparent. Moreover, widespread credit and investments are expected to come in quickly because the lands are acquired via outright purchase and so titles are honoured as collateral for bank loans (Deininger and Binswanger, 1999: 265).

Program financing is the third part of the MLAR model. MLAR adopts a flexible loan-grant financing scheme. Each beneficiary is given a fixed sum of money, which they are free to use in accordance with this rule: the portion of the sum that is used to buy the land is considered a loan and must be repaid by the beneficiary (one hundred percent of the amount at market interest rates). Whatever amount is left after the land purchase is given to the beneficiary as a grant to be used for post–land transfer development projects and is not to be repaid by the beneficiary. This flexible approach safeguards against possible fund manipulation and instils the value of co-sharing of risks to avoid a "dole-out mentality" among beneficiaries (Deininger, 1999). It also veers away from universal subsidies, arguing that "[grants] are superior to subsidies because they are immediate, transparent, can be targeted and their distortive effects are small" (van Zyl and Binswanger, 1996: 419). This mechanism is also thought to be a key factor that would reduce the cost of land, because peasants will try to get the best bargain for their money (Deininger, 1999). Finally, the MLAR model is much cheaper than state-led land reforms, primarily because it does away with huge, expensive government bureaucracies, land prices are lower, and beneficiaries shoulder one hundred percent of the land cost. The model requires national governments to bankroll the initial phase of the program, but in the long term, it counts on private banks to provide the primary financing of the project. Multilateral and bilateral aid agencies are also expected to invest in the program (van den Brink, de Klerk and Binswanger 1996: 451), especially on the "grant side" for post–land transfer development.

In short, in pursuit of its goals, the MLAR model has developed strategies that are exactly the opposite of those in the state-led approach; for example, from statist-centralized to privatized-decentralized, from supply-driven to demand-driven, from compulsory to voluntary. Table 1.3 summarizes these contrasts.

Meanwhile, the MLAR model has, to varying extents, been implemented in Brazil through the *Projeto Cédula da Terra* (PCT) from 1998 to 2001 (Navarro, 1998; Sauer, 2003; Pereira, forthcoming), which was renewed and expanded during the Lula administration (Deere and Medeiros, 2007), in Colombia through the *Agrarian Law 160 of 1994* from 1995 to 2003 (Mondragon, 2003), and in South Africa since 1995 (Lahiff, 2001), among other places. A small pilot project was also carried out in the Philippines, although a much bigger MLAR-like voluntary land transfer (VLT) scheme has been implemented more significantly (Borras, 2005; de Asis, forthcoming). Proponents of MLAR have claimed impressive success in these countries (Deininger, 1999; Buainain et al., 1999; World Bank, 2003). However, such claims are now seriously questioned by many scholars (e.g., Rosset, Patel and Courville, 2006; Barros, Sauer and Schwartzman, 2003; Borras, 2003a, 2003c), while others have urged caution in rushing to conclusions (see, e.g., Carter and Salgado, 2001). Most civil society organizations oppose these land policies and have launched coordinated local, national, and international campaigns to stop them. Such an initiative is currently being coordinated internationally by *La Via Campesina*, the FoodFirst Information and Action Network or FIAN, and the Land Research and Action Network or LRAN (see, e.g., FIAN-Via Campesina, 2003; Borras, 2004; Paasch, 2003; Monsalve, 2003; Rosset, Patel and Courville 2006; McMichael, 2006a, 2006b).

Table 1.3
Key features of state- and market-led approaches to land reform in private lands (based on the pro-market explanations)

Issues	State-led	Market-led
Getting access to land		
Acquisition method	Coercive; cash-bonds payments at below market price, therefore is opposed by landlords leading to policy "failures"	Voluntary; 100% cash payment based on 100% market value of land, and so will not be opposed by landlords thereby increasing chances of policy success
Beneficiaries	Supply-driven; beneficiaries state-selected therefore "unfit" beneficiaries have usually been included	Demand-driven; self-selected, therefore only "fit" beneficiaries will be included in the program
Implementation method	Statist-centralized; transparency and accountability = low degree	Privatized-decentralized; transparency and accountability = high degree
Pace and nature	Protracted; politically and legally contentious	Quick; politically and legally noncontentious
Land prices	Higher	Lower
Land markets	Land reform: cause of/ aggravates land market distortions; progressive land tax and land titling program not required = all resulting in the inefficient allocation and use of land resources	Land reform: cause and effect of land market stimulation; progressive land tax and titling program required, and so will result in the efficient allocation and use of land
Post–land transfer farm and beneficiary development		
Program sequence; Pace of dev't Extension service	Farm developments plans *after* land redistribution: Protracted, uncertain and anemic post–land transfer Dev't; extension service statist-centralized = inefficient	Farm development plans *before* land redistribution Quick, certain, and dynamic Post–land transfer dev't. extension service privatized- decentralized = efficient

Credit and investments	Low credit supply and low investments, resulting in economic stagnation and poverty	Increased credit and investments, and will result in economic growth and therefore poverty eradication
Exit options	None	Ample
Financing		
Mechanism	State "universal" subsidies; sovereign guarantee; beneficiaries pay subsidized land price; "dole-out" mentality among beneficiaries = resulting in the waste of public funds and persistence of inefficient land users/producers	Flexible loan-grant mechanism; co-sharing of risks; beneficiaries shoulder full cost of land; farm dev't cost given via grant, and so will result in greater economic/fiscal efficiency
Cost of reform	HIGH	LOW

Source: Borras (2003a)

Closer examination of documents, however, reveals contradictory claims about the initial outcomes of MLAR policy implementation. On the one hand and more generally, they claim that early implementation in these countries has been successful and impressive (Deininger and Binswanger, 1999: 268; Deininger, 1999; World Bank, 2003, n.d.). On the other hand, preliminary accounts cast doubt on such optimistic claims. These differentiated views fall into three main groups: (i) direct references by MLAR proponents to varying degrees of problems and failures, although they are quick to point out that such problems are operational and administrative in nature (see, e.g., Deininger, 1999; Buainain et al., 1999; but see also Gershman, 1999); (ii) critical views and reminders from scholars who are generally supportive of the MLAR model and experiment (see, e.g., Carter and Salgado, 2001; Banerjee, 1999; de Janvry et al., 2001b; Lipton, 1993); (iii) a few critical works arguing that the problems in MLAR implementation in Brazil, Colombia, and South Africa are fundamental in nature (see, e.g., Barros, Sauer and Schwartzman, 2003; Levin and Weiner, 1997, 1996; Rosset, Patel and Courville, 2006; Borras, 2003a, 2003c, 2002a; Lahiff, 2003, 2006; Murray, 1996; Lebert, 2001; Mondragon, 2003; Paasch, 2003; Groppo et al., 1998; Deere and Medeiros, 2007; Bobrow-Strain 2004; Pereria, forthcoming). These findings are more or less corroborated by emerging studies from other countries (e.g., Ray Bush, 2002, brands this neoliberal land reform as "counter-revolution" in the Egyptian context; see also van Donge, Eiseb and Mosimane, 2007, for Namibia; Bhandari, 2006, for Nepal, and so on). Moreover, refer to tables 1.4 and 1.5 in Borras and McKinley (2006) to get a comparative overview of state-led and market-led land redistribution accomplishments from different countries over time. Finally, refer to the forthcoming special issue of the Third World Quarterly journal (December 2007) edited by Borras, Kay and Lahiff for a collection of critical thematic and country case studies on MLAR

1.4 BEYOND THE LIMITS-CENTRED AND OPPORTUNITIES-CENTRED PERSPECTIVES

As discussed earlier, historically, most land reform policies have in fact been less than ideal. As such, elements of both limits and opportunities have usually been simultaneously operative in land reforms, past and present. Even in situations where opportunities for land reform seemed to have been absent, closer examination has revealed that it is not so — that opportunities actually do exist in varying forms and extents. For example, arguably, the mere passage of a land redistribution law constitutes a political opportunity for peasants and pro-land reform advocates; even the maintenance of such a law in a dormant state (as many land reform laws have been in the contemporary era) can be considered an opportunity. Herring (2003: 64) explained that even dead land reforms are not dead, as they "often form nodes around which politics may precipitate." The Indonesian experience in the Basic Agrarian Law of 1960 is an example of this (Bachriadi and Fauzi, 2006; Tsing, 2002; Wiradi, 2005). Meanwhile, the mere fact that most, if not all, land reform initiatives historically have delivered varying degrees of partial outcomes reveals what seems to be their built-in limits (and opportunities).

The limits-centred and the opportunities-centred approaches both have explanatory power. The limits to redistributive reform outlined by one set of scholars cannot be dismissed; many of them are real. Neither are the opportunities mentioned by other scholars altogether unbelievable; opportunities cannot be summarily dismissed, as explained earlier. However, while building on the strength of these two perspectives, it is necessary to point out their weaknesses.

There are at least three problematic issues related to the limits-centred approach to agrarian reform studies today. First, most of the evidence used by scholars in arguing the structural and institutional limits to redistributive reforms in the neoliberal era is the same evidence that could, arguably, be counted as opportunities, as is being done by pro-market scholars. For example, the withdrawal of direct subsidies from agriculture would hurt, and is hurting, not only the would-be small farmers to be created via land reform (as well as actually existing small farms) but also some of the large farms, plunging many of the latter into bankruptcy. Thus, the meaning, that is, whether limits or opportunities, of these recent developments is contested.[7] For example, and interestingly, while Dorner (2001) listed technological advancement in the neoliberal era as a minus-factor for redistributive land reform, Herring (2003) included it as a plus-factor (see also relevant discussion in Brass, 2003a). Second, it is unclear whether all the cited limits are inherent to neoliberalism. For instance, the assumption that neoliberalism has caused the waning of militant forms of collective actions by peasant movements and provoked divisions among the peasantry (see, e.g., Dorner, 2001) need evidence on causal relationships. Such an argument may have difficulty confronting the question of whether neoliberalism is in fact supposed to provoke more militant actions from the marginalized sectors of the rural world, as in Brazil and Mexico.[8] Or, was it not that cleavages — class-based or not — among peasant movements were widespread even in the pre-neoliberal past? (See, e.g., Landsberger, 1974; Landsberger and Hewitt, 1970; Alavi, 1973; Huizer, 1975, 1972; Shanin, 1987; Brass, 2003b). Finally, and related to the two issues raised above, the limits-centred school tends to assume rather than demonstrate how and to what extent these limiting factors are actually operative in the real world. For example, claims about globalization as having a "weakening" effect on nation-states and peasant movements are not backed up with convincing evidence demonstrating why and how actually this is operative in the real world. Moreover, a fuller understanding of the limits of redistributive land reform requires an understanding of the opportunities and of the dialectical relationship between them.

Furthermore, the recent thinking about state-led agrarian reform is generally based on retrospective studies of agrarian reforms implemented before the onslaught of neoliberal reforms. These retrospective studies are important in setting straight the historical accounts of land reform as relevant building blocks for current theorizing. However, except perhaps for Brazil, South Africa and Zimbabwe the experiences of land reform *during* the neoliberal period, particularly for understanding how and the extent to which neoliberalism actually impacted the power (i.e., autonomy and capacity) of central states and peasant organizations to push for redistributive land reform, are left relatively under-studied despite the numerous studies on land policies' in general. This relative dearth in studies is explained by two interrelated developments on the agrarian reform front. On the one hand, very few national land reform policies were implemented during the 1980s and 1990s, and fewer still were policies that delivered significant outcomes. On the other, and influenced by the former, there was a significant drop of research interest in agrarian reform in academic circles in the 1990s.

Meanwhile, there are also a number of problems with the "opportunities-centred" approach. First, some of the basic pro-market criticisms of the state-led land reform that, in turn, form part of the premises for the pro-market model are quite problematic (see Borras, e.g., 2003c). For example: the criticism pertaining to the top-down, "supply-driven" approaches in land reform that claims that lands were not really demanded by peasants is problematic, especially when many land reforms have actually been actively "demanded" by poor peasants; the criticism that the use of coercive approaches is said to be a cause of land reform failures is problematic because most land reforms with higher degrees of success were those that employed highly coercive measures; the assumption that the inward-looking orientation of agricultural policies during the Import-Substitution Industrialization (ISI) were among the causes of the failure of agrarian reforms is problematic because in fact the records of both inward-looking and outward-looking development strategies were mixed (see, e.g., Spoor, 2002; Kay, 2002b; Gwynne and Kay, 2004; Bryceson, Kay and Mooij, 2000; Saith, 1990).

Second, the opportunities-centred arguments are founded on assumptions about the workings of the forces of the "free" market: vibrant land markets, free trade, perfect market information and perfect competition, a level playing field, and the like. On most occasions and in most developing countries, contrary to textbook predictions, these conditions are not present. Thus, many of the so-called "opportunities" are mere theoretical assumptions; they are (projected) ideal-type constructs rather than realities. One example is the complete deregulation of agriculture; in fact, agricultural sectors in developing countries continue to receive state subsidies or (re)regulation in various, sometimes new, forms (e.g., Fox 1994c, 1995, for the Mexican experience). Arguably, if the MLAR model is strictly followed, it could not be implemented in any country today because its own requirements do not actually exist anywhere (such as the three-to-one land supply-demand ratio, progressive land tax, "rational" landlords, and so on).

Third, at best, many of the so-called opportunities are in fact "potential" opportunities, which do not automatically lead to operational mechanisms capable of effecting actual redistributive land reforms. Some examples are noteworthy: In the 1990s, the surge in the number of bankrupt cattle ranchers in Colombia did not result in an influx of land traded on the market (see Forero, 1999); and despite the 60 percent drop in the price of agricultural land in

Brazil between 1990 and 1997 due to various neoliberal policies, no significant quantity of farmland was voluntarily brought to the market at the low price levels (see Buainain, da Silveira, and Teófilo, 1998: 6).[9] These experiences were shared by financially troubled white commercial farmers in neoliberal South Africa, despite earlier optimistic predictions made by pro-market scholars that a great volume of farmland transactions would emerge under the liberalized agriculture system (see van Zyl, Kirsten, and Binswanger, 1996; Deininger and May, 2000). Along these same lines, the early flurry of white commercial farmers selling land to the Zimbabwean government under its land reform program was concentrated in abandoned and run-down farms and limited to marginal zones of Manicaland on the country's eastern border; the flow of commercial farms into the land market had dried up by 1983 (Bratton, 1990: 280–281; see also Matondi and Moyo, 2003; but see Gasper, 1990).

Thus, a preliminary reading of the Philippine land reform process shows that the limits and opportunities for redistributive land reforms are not static. They are dynamically altered across geographic spaces, between policy realms, by and for various groups and individuals, and over time. These changes are influenced by macro-socioeconomic structural conditions, prior distribution of power in society and within the state, by constellations of state and societal actors and their alliances, actions, and strategies, as well as by the institutions that structure the way that these actors try to shape, and are reshaped by the limits and opportunities for redistributive land reforms. It is through these dynamic political processes that the neoliberal reforms and the subsequent development processes and outcomes the former has spurred have altered the structural-institutional terrain for redistributive land reform, oscillating between the two opposing poles of obstacles and possibilities.

1.5 STATE-CENTRED AND SOCIETY-CENTRED APPROACHES TO STATE–SOCIETY RELATIONS

Parsons (1956: 9) explained that "in a very deep sense, land tenure problems are power problems, problems of disparity in economic, social, and political power." This is a perspective expressed earlier (in what has now become quite a famous quote) by John K. Galbraith (1951, cited in Tai, 1974: 18; see also Paige, 1996): "In fact, a land reform is a revolutionary step; it passes power, property and status from one group in the community to another. If the government is dominated or strongly influenced by the landholding group … no one should expect effective land legislation as an act of grace." Thus, the central state is necessarily called in to carry out reform because, as Tai (1974: 13–14) argued, "a basic and broad alteration of the tenure structure cannot be brought about under private auspices." Yet, in doing so, the state has to interact with a range of societal actors with varying, often competing and conflicting, interests. Thus, a rigorous analysis of land reform requires the full understanding of state–society relations dynamics. Moreover, state land reform laws largely (although not always solely, see von Benda-Beckmann, 2001; Hirtz, 1998) define the rules and parameters of state–society interactions in the push toward or pull away from redistributive reform. As Kristine Juul and Christian Lund (2002: 3) explained in the context of Africa, "State institutions compete over unclear jurisdictional boundaries, constituting political 'turfs' and obfuscating the notion of state authority .... The result is that laws ... play important roles in processes of property negotiation; however, they are neither universally respected, nor entirely neglected" (but see also Peters, 2004: 269–314; Nyamu-Musembi, 2006; Razavi, 2003; Whitehead and Tsikata, 2003). However, by themselves, state agrarian laws do not make policy outcomes, but the way such rules are defined heavily influences the nature, pace, extent, and direction of outcomes in reforms (Houtzager and Franco, 2003). In this context, state–society interactions can work and rework such institutional rules and parameters toward, or away from, redistributive land reforms (Franco, forthcoming, 2005). This is illustrated, for example, in the statement of a Chinese official during the 1947–1950 land reform in China: "Laws and decrees ... in land reform should be treated as weapons in the struggle against landlords .... Many things cannot be decided in a text .... Texts can be interpreted in every way, and should be interpreted to the advantage of the poor and hired" (cited in Shillinglaw, 1974: 152). And to think that it was a revolutionary land reform that was being carried out in this context.

Yet, like the land reform literature, the state–society relations literature is also marked by dichotomous views: between those who emphasize the role of "policy elites" (in the Grindle-ian sense) in implementing land reform and those who view the outcomes of land reform policy as predetermined by structural factors (in the 1981 de Janvry-ian sense). Following Fox (1993: Ch. 2), these views are referred to here as the state-centred and society-centred approaches respectively (e.g., compare Alain de Janvry, 1981, with Merilee Grindle, 1986, as classic examples of the two competing perspectives in the context of agrarian reform and rural development).

The state-centred approach

The units of analysis in the state-centred approach are the state policy elites (policymakers and managers, see Grindle and Thomas, 1989; Thomas and

Grindle, 1990; Grindle, 1986) and the agencies and organizations responsible for carrying out public policies. Exponents of this approach, many of whom come from the Weberian theoretical tradition, see the state as an institution of governance autonomous from society. Taking the state as an independent actor and independent variable, state-centred scholars often assume that the state is autonomous in making policy choices and in transforming them into authoritative actions, even when these run counter to the interests of the dominant classes or groups in society (Grindle and Thomas, 1989; Nordlinger, 1987; see Warriner, 1969: 436). Many scholars and policy practitioners of this approach place a premium on the administrative design of the policy, believing that such a policy, if carried out by an efficient state organization, has little reason to fail.

State-centred approaches often view social actors such as peasant organizations and NGOs as necessary complements to the state's reformist efforts, recognizing the practical administrative and fiscal limitations of the state. This realization has led many policy elites to try to form government-sponsored peasant organizations or to reach out to existing community organizations in order to reshape them within their own parameters by assigning them specific supporting roles in policy implementation. Concerned with efficient policy implementation, policy elites tend to assume that there is a need to avoid conflict; they therefore do not generally challenge entrenched elites and do not usually encourage criticism from societal actors.

Finally, founded on the premise of state autonomy, state-centred approaches posit that state intervention can overcome structural and institutional obstacles mounted by landlords by mustering sufficient "political will" to effect reform (see Tai, 1974: 267), by efficient administrative and technical organization, and by ensuring sufficient funding to finance redistributive land reform (see Thomas and Grindle, 1990; Grindle, 1986). When they do explain temporal and spatial variations, adherents of this approach tend to place a premium on the role of policy elites in the given time and space. In short, the essence of the state-centred approach is captured by Tai's (1974) conclusion:

> Political commitment to reform — i.e., the willingness and readiness of the political elite to mobilize all available resources to carry out a reform program — is of critical importance, *outweighing all other factors*. With strong political commitment, a country is likely to achieve extensive implementation of its program even though some of the other factors are unfavourable. (267, emphasis added)

The society-centred approach

Taking social classes and interest group formations in society as their units of analysis, advocates of a society-centred approach identify social mobilization from below as the key to successful land reform implementation. These scholars, mostly from the Marxist tradition, emphasize the inherent structural and institutional obstacles to reform and the "captivity" of the state to the interests of the dominant social classes; the state then is assumed to have no autonomy (some examples are de Janvry, 1981; Lehmann, 1974b; Paige, 1975). Some stress the influence that social forces exert directly on the state, while others highlight the external constraints they impose. This approach assumes either that the state is monolithic or that any internal differences within the state are direct reflections of societal interests. The activities of the state and policy elites are understood to be dependent variables. Thus, the policy choices and the behaviour of policy elites can be predicted on the basis of an analysis of class and group formations in society or in the international arena (see, e.g., El-Ghonemy, 1990).

Proponents of this framework tend to argue that pro-reform forces must pressure the state into implementing land reform. Thus, effective peasant organizations, NGOs, and political movements must necessarily be "independent" from the state. Moreover, social mobilization from below sets the parameters, extent, and location of reforms; state actors only react to such pressures. The relationship between pro-reform societal actors and the state is necessarily conflict ridden, and oppositional pressure politics is the most effective way to press for reforms. Focusing the analysis on social classes and class alignments based on prior distribution of power in society, this approach argues that to overcome the structural and institutional obstacles to land reform, substantial, even if partial, structural and institutional changes must first occur within the state and in society. When they do explain temporal and spatial variations, adherents of this approach tend to place a premium on the influence of pre-existing structures and institutions or on the role of militant peasant movements in the given time and space (see, e.g., Sanderson, 1984: 71–72). In short, the society-centred approach is captured by Lehmann's (1974a) conclusion:

> [There is an] illusion of bureaucratic or technocratic omnipotence which tends to overtake advocates of one policy or another – an illusion rampant in the entire field of development studies …. The bureaucracy … is not an "autonomous" force …. Bureaucracy, like "the government," is a dependent variable. (18)

Comparing the two approaches

Both approaches have strong explanatory power, but both have limitations. The state-centred approach over-emphasizes the autonomy of the state and the capacity of policy elites to overcome structural obstacles to and institutional constraints in carrying out redistributive reforms. This approach finds it difficult to explain why good public policies on redistributive reform, implemented by capable administrative organizations that are sufficiently funded, can still fail. The society-centred approach, on the other hand, over-emphasizes the significance of structural-institutional factors, societal groups, and international institutions, neglecting the role of the state and policy elites in conceptualizing and implementing redistributive reforms. This approach cannot easily explain why, in some cases, state actors undertake autonomous actions that run counter to the interests of the dominant classes in society.

By adopting such one-dimensional views of state–society relations, both approaches have difficulty explaining why, in many cases, societal actors attempt to influence and transform state actors, but in the process are themselves transformed, and vice versa (Fox, 1993: Ch. 2). On peasant mobilization specifically, society-centred approaches often struggle with the issue of why the actions of strong, independent peasant movements have led in many cases not to sustained and widespread land redistribution but to violent retribution by the state and landlords. At the same time, state-centred approaches cannot fully explain why co-opted peasant organizations, often organized by policy elites as part of the state's extended administrative machinery, usually fail to perform even the supporting roles assigned to them.

The evidence from the Philippine CARP implementation throws doubt upon the ability of either the state-centred or the society-centred approach to fully explain policy processes and outcomes. For instance, society-centred initiatives for land reform, specifically through peasant land occupations in the 1980s, did not lead to sustained land redistribution but to violent landlord retribution and state repression. Meanwhile, the state-centred push under the Aquino administration (1986–1992), with the use of state co-opted peasant associations, did not improve CARP implementation. Implementation started to gain momentum and modest success only during the Ramos administration (1992–1998). At this time, as I have argued elsewhere, the pro-reform alliance between state reformists and autonomous social movements was principally responsible for the progressive change in the course of the CARP process (Borras, 2001, 1999).

Finally, the highly varied and uneven processes and outcomes of land reform implementation at the sub-national level, across geographic spaces, land

and farm types, policy components, and over time, cannot be easily and fully explained by either the state-centred or the society-centred approach. A quick look at major land reforms, especially those in large countries, suggests that the outcomes of land redistribution tend to be highly varied and uneven not only temporally but also spatially. But the land reform literature has not offered any significant attention to and explanation for this sub-national unevenness and variations. One of the few exceptions to the convention is the body of work of the American geographer Wendy Wolford in her examination and explanation of the land reform process in Brazil, especially the land occupation settlements by MST. Wolford's (see, e.g., 2005, 2004) explanation is focused on the production and reproduction variation between geographic spaces that largely influence whether and how small family farmers and farmworkers join the MST. Refer to equally relevant discussions by James Petras (1998), Wolford (2003a), and Heredia et al. (2006) about the regional variation of land occupation activities of MST; see also Redclift (1978), in the case of Ecuador. Wolford's insights are extremely useful to the understanding of the Philippine experience. My own treatment in this book however is slightly different, taking state–society interaction as an important independent variable that accounts for the sub-national variation and unevenness in land redistribution pattern in the Philippines; see especially chapters 5 and 6.

In this light, an alternative "interactive" approach to the study of state–society relations developed by Fox (1993) is better equipped to help to construct a theoretical framework with which to find answers to the key questions put forward in this study.

1.6 TOWARDS AN "INTERACTIVE APPROACH" IN THE STUDY OF STATE–SOCIETY INTERACTIONS FOR REDISTRIBUTIVE LAND REFORM

The highlight of Fox's (1993; see also 1996, 2005) interactive approach is captured in the following extended quote:

> The challenge is to develop an explanation of state action that can effectively balance both state and societal factors. The most promising approaches focus on the interaction between state and society, the institutions that mediate such interaction, and the factors that account for how those institutions are in turn transformed .... An interactive approach ... requires recasting conventional notions of state power, carefully distinguishing between the autonomy and the capacity of state actors. The challenge is to develop an approach that can

account for how shifts in the balance of power within the state recursively interact with shifts in the correlation of forces in society .... This approach suggests that prospects for distributive reform *depend less on the insulation and coherence of a strong state than on internal divisions that favour reformists*. Pro-reform policy currents must pursue strategies that strengthen them and their allies while weakening their opponents. Some reforms are initiated from above while others are responses to pressures from below — but in both cases it often takes pressure from below to carry them out .... *The successful implementation of distributive policies depends on the nature of the political interaction between the pro-reform forces in state and society*. If their actions are mutually reinforcing, then the reform effort internalizes social conflict within the state. This reciprocal interaction between state and social actors can lead to unexpected political outcomes. (39–40, emphasis added)

Following Fox, an important assumption in this research is that political actions and strategies of a range of state and societal actors do matter in determining the nature, pace, extent, and direction of redistributive land reform policies and outcomes. These political actions and strategies are shaped and reshaped by macro-socioeconomic structures and political institutions, and vice versa. This study assumes that "institutions" are important variables — both dependent and independent — in understanding land reform processes and outcomes. Institutions are both the context *and* object of contestations within the state, within society, and between the state and society.

As Fox explained, an interactive approach requires a recasting of the dichotomous views of the state as either autonomous from or an instrument of social classes, a dichotomy largely influenced by the contending perspectives of Marx and Weber. Neither of the two can, on its own, fully explain the land reform implementation process in the Philippines. As Bright and Harding (1984) argued,

> States are neither static givens lording over society nor subservient by-products of other social forces .... [States] are institutions of governance, as in Weber, and they are central agents of social order and reproduction, as in Marx, but such characterizations pale before the fantastic diversity and fluidity of form, function and malfunction that current studies of states and political processes reveal. (4)

The "state" is thus defined here as that which "comprises the *ensemble* of political, social, economic, and coercive institutions that exercise 'public' authority in a given territory" (Fox, 1993: 11–12, emphasis original). However, there is consensus that in societies with an important agrarian sector, the central state has almost always been heavily influenced by the landowning classes (see, e.g., Moore, 1967; Putzel, 1992). Still following Fox (1993: Ch. 2), an explanation of the actions of the state requires a clarification of the two dimensions of state power, namely autonomy and capacity. Autonomy refers here to the independent goal-formation of the state, while state capacity is defined as the ability of state leaders to use the agencies of the state to get people in society to do what they want them to do (Migdal, 1988: xi). Distinguishing autonomy from capacity clarifies the understanding of state actions and helps to move the analysis beyond the widely used dichotomy between state "strength" and "weakness," which implicitly treats the state as a single actor and inherently conflates autonomy and capacity (Fox, 1993: 10–30). For instance, a state may have the autonomy to pursue redistributive land reform but no capacity to implement it; conversely, it may have the capacity to implement the reform but not the autonomy to pursue it. Either way, land reform will not be carried out.

The state has its own distinct agendas as an institution. These agendas are constantly pursued through the state-building process. But the state-building process always tends to be partial and uneven in space and time (see, e.g., Scott, 1998: 183–191; Abinales, 2000) and this has profound impact on the actual implementation of redistributive land reform policies. In his examination of Mexican state-building over time and across geographic spaces in order to explain the contemporary Chiapas political condition, Harvey (1998: 227) concluded that "history reveals not only the contested nature of state formation, but also the impossibility of any social order ever fully constituting itself." The waves of regime transitions during the 1980s and 1990s have exposed the unevenness of previous and contemporary state-building processes, partly through the persistence of "local authoritarian enclaves" despite relatively successful national transitions (Fox, 1994a, 1994b, 1994c, 1990; O'Donnell, 1993; Franco, 2001a, 2004). Furthermore, the recent surge in the study of decentralization has likewise exposed the highly uneven process of state-building across geographic spaces and over time (see, e.g., Boone, 1998; Blair, 2000; Slater, 1989, 1990; Griffin, 1980) as well as the possible conflict and violence that the decentralization process can provoke, especially in the context of resource control, as explained by Nancy Peluso (2007).

Moreover, policies are not static. During the conflict-ridden process of implementation, policies are transformed by politics, and vice versa, as policies are put into the crucible of state–society relations, where changes in the balance of power within the state dynamically interact with the shifting alignments of forces in society. State and societal actors are each transformed through conflict (Fox, 1993: Ch. 2; Herring, 1983: 217–218; Evans, 1997, 1995; Migdal, 2001: 263–264; Migdal, Kohli and Shue 1994; Houtzager and Moore 2003; Tendler 1997; Wang 1999, 1997). John Gaventa (2002) explained, in the same light, that state–society negotiations around a reformist policy that matters to poor people are not smooth and conflict free. He said,

> Negotiation often means entering spaces for participation and expression of citizen voice. Our discussion of policy spaces, however, reminds us that they are rarely neutral. The fact that public spaces for participation exist, whether in rule of law or social practice, does not mean that they will always be used equally by various actors for realising rights of citizens. Rather, such space is itself socially and politically located, with dynamics of participation varying across different levels and arenas of citizen engagement, and across different types of policy spaces. (10)

Still on the conflictive state–society interaction, Patrick Heller (2000), drawing lessons from India, argues that what he calls as "redistributive conflict" could in fact lead to redistributive gains for working classes and could strengthen the latter. Heller (2000: 519) explains that "repeated cycles of mobilization have created organizations and networks that cut across traditional social cleavages, thus broadening the associational scope and quality of public life." He elaborates further, "Class-based mobilization has created forms of conflict that lend themselves to compromise and encompassing solutions. Unlike many other forms of claim making, pursuing redistributive demands in a capitalist economy … reveals the interdependence of class interests."

Meanwhile, Fox's interactive approach to state–society relations and its application to the study of land reform dynamics is captured in Franco's (2005; see also Franco, forthcoming) analysis of the political-legal institutional terrain, within which key actors in the Philippine land reform process ally with, or struggle against, each other in order to influence the interpretation and enforcement of agrarian laws:

> What kind of law is authoritative in a given space and time is contingent upon the "interactions between actors in society and the state over the setting, interpreting, and complying with authoritative rules" …. Recognizing the plurality of actors in rural areas in the Philippines, we begin to see why progressive legal rules governing agrarian relations are neither self-enforcing

nor self-interpreting. Rural social change in the form of redistribution of wealth and power in land, mandated by state law, is just one possible outcome of a three-way battle between the state, regional authoritarian land-based elites, and autonomous peasant movements for control of the political-legal process around agrarian law making and its outcomes. In examining how these actors operate and interact in this battle, we can also begin to understand how rural poor people's legal land rights might still be claimed. (3)

This brief conceptual clarification should guide our further discussion about the "interactive approach" in search for answers to the key questions posed by this study. Four related themes are important in the study of state–society relations in the context of redistributive land reform: (i) autonomous rural social mobilizations "from below," (ii) pro-reform initiatives "from above," (iii) positive interaction between pro-reform forces within the state and in society, and (iv) ability to overcome landlords' resistance to redistributive land reform. These are examined below.

Autonomous rural social mobilizations "from below"

Peasants are not passive societal actors. The literature on peasant mobilization reveals the extent of peasants' participation in grand historical wars that have transformed societies, such as the German peasant war of 1525 (Bak, 1975; see also Engels, 1956; and Marx, 1968; Moore, 1967; Skocpol, 1979; Hobsbawm, 1965; Kurtz, 2000) and numerous revolutions or "peasant wars" during the 20th century (Wolf, 1969; Paige, 1975; Rutten, 2000a, 2000b). On the other hand, the literature on "everyday forms of peasant resistance" shows the daily texture of peasant politics (Scott, 1985, 1976, 1990; Scott and Kerkvliet, 1986; Kerkvliet, 1977, 1990, 1993, 2005, 2006).[10] These works have greatly contributed to understanding of the political behaviour of peasants. However, the dichotomy in the literature between all-out peasant revolution and "everyday politics," like pilfering and foot-dragging, tends to overlook a large chunk of rural political dynamics and activities ranging from land occupation to organization-building to negotiations with the state (Fox, 1992; Brockett, 1991: 260; Lund, 1998; Houtzager, 2000, 2001; Petras, 1997, 1998; Petras and Veltmeyer, 2001; Veltmeyer, 1997; Brass, 1994, 2000, 2003a, 2003b). Although there have been several studies of these middle-range activities, a significant number have been in the context of understanding the revolutionary character of peasants, or how these activities lead to full-scale revolution (see, e.g., Huizer, 1972, 1975, 2001; Paige, 1975; see also Lichbach, 1994; Skocpol, 1988; McClintock, 1984; Walt, 1992; Hawes, 1990; Migdal, 1974). In most cases, however, these mid-range peasant actions do not lead to full-scale revolutions. Exploring the mid-range peasant politics, Shapan Adnan (2007: 222), in the context of Bangladesh, explains, "It is perhaps more useful to use an approach that can accommodate flexibility and substitution in the strategies adopted, rather than giving overwhelming emphasis to only one kind of normative strategy or primary 'weapon' of the weak (or the powerful). This consideration also highlights the need for further exploration and analysis of the middle ground between everyday and exceptional forms of resistance."

Peasant collective action requires a number of minimum factors. First, there should be a perception of shared interests or identities among peasants. This is "a collective process of interpretation, attribution and social construction that mediates opportunity and action" (McAdam, McCarthy and Zald, 1996: 2; see also Tilly, 1988: xv). Collective identity is inherently dynamic, as "it is constructed and negotiated through a repeated process of 'activation' of social relationships connecting the actors" (Melucci, 1985: 793, 1992). This collective perception may cut "horizontally" based on social class divisions, or "vertically" by transcending social class divisions to include other social identities such as community, gender, ethnicity, ideology, or even a shared elite patron (see Alavi, 1973; see also Brass, 1994, 2000, 2003b; Harvey, 1998; Deere, 2003; Platteau, 1995; Rutten, 2000a, 2000b; Petras and Veltmeyer, 2003). Second, peasants do not usually immediately engage in overt actions, as the "everyday forms of resistance" literature demonstrates. Most peasant collective actions are preceded by a general feeling that there is a good chance of goals being realized (see Fox, 1993, 1992; Kerkvliet, 1990: 191–194, 1993, 2005). A further prerequisite to collective action is the opening up of political opportunity. Tarrow (1994: 54) defined political opportunities as "the consistent (but not necessarily formal, permanent, or national) signals to social or political actors which either encourage or discourage them to use their internal resources to form a social movement" (see also Brockett, 1991: 254; Tarrow, 1998, 1996).

Most literature on peasant movements shows that when peasants mobilize, the initial activity is usually confined to the boundaries of their community, partly because of limited political and logistical resources (see Kerkvliet, 1977, 1990). This level of collective action is rarely sufficient for goals to be achieved, however, chiefly because (in the case of land reform) landlords resist reforms at a level far beyond the municipality. But it is at this local level that the basic building blocks for sturdier regional and national peasant movements are laid (or not). If the local organizations are weak, it is inconceivable for them to build together a strong regional or national coalition (see Fox, 1992). It is at the local level where centres of power of the peasant movement organizations are created in order to form stronger regional or national coalitions.

When confronted by an initial failure to realize their goals, many peasants recoil, but some persist. The opening up of political opportunities can encourage them to sustain and expand their mobilization beyond the municipality. Political opportunities for peasants may come in the form of allies who provide the political and logistical support that is necessary but frequently inaccessible and unaffordable to them, such as transportation costs to and from provincial and national government offices, accommodation expenses in urban centres, where they may have to stay for several days doing lobby work, propaganda materials to amplify their demands in public, contact with the media and other influential groups, and further understanding of the technical aspects of the law, as well as legal advice and aid (see, e.g., Franco, 2005; Fox, 1992; Ghimire, 2001b). Allies can also help peasant groups to identify the proper state actors and "access routes" to state power for the maximum impact of their mobilization (Fox, 1993).

The concept of peasant allies is widely studied, and peasants' wariness toward outsiders and outsiders' disdain of peasants' political behaviour is often highlighted in the literature. But as Fox (1993: 38–42) pointed out, it is not the need to have allies that peasants tend to be wary of but rather the terms of such a relationship. Allies support peasants' demands and actions because of the former's own motivations, ranging from ideological to political to institutional agendas. Often, these agendas encourage allies (e.g., NGOs, political parties and movements) to try to reshape and stretch the parameters and targets of peasant collective action below or beyond what the peasants might have originally intended. The peasants may still subscribe to this set-up, as long as their major, usually immediate, concerns are addressed in such a relationship. But when these allies neglect the peasants' compelling concerns, the latter gradually demobilize or abandon the alliance and seek out other allies (see, e.g., Rutten, 2000b: 423–468; Boudreau, 2001; Franco and Borras, 2005).

Such allies have their own motivations for supporting the peasants' demands and actions, ranging from ideological to political and institutional agendas. Some may support the peasant organizations' interest in autonomy (see, e.g., Franco, 2001b), while others may not (see, e.g., Putzel, 1995; Rutten, 1996). The *caudillo* phenomenon, referring to a "type of leader [may or may not be a peasant] who exercises undisputed control within popular movements" (Harvey, 1998: 8), is an example of the latter; and it has been quite prevalent among peasant organizations historically (see, e.g., Salamini, 1971: 142; Huizer,

1975, 1972; Landsberger, 1974; Landsberger and Hewitt, 1970). It is however important to think of the interaction between peasant movements and their allies such as political parties as highly dynamic and constantly (re)negotiated over time, and it is not always the case that the peasant movements lose their autonomy; they can also, as explained by Judith Adler Hellman (1992: 59–60) transform their allies. Even where a pro-reform alliance is vibrant, however, the combined force may still lag behind the resistance of landlords as this escalates and expands, provoked by social mobilization from below into counter-mobilization (see Meyer and Staggenborg, 1996). When this occurs, peasant action is insufficient to effect reforms, and state actors are increasingly drawn into the conflict.

Pro-reform initiatives "from above"

The state itself is a socially and politically contested terrain, and as such is a highly heterogeneous institution comprised of various actors. Thus, this study uses "state actors" to refer to the groups of officials whose actions push or pull in the same political direction (Fox, 1993: 28–33). This analytic category is different from Grindle's concept of "policy elites" (see Grindle, 1986; Grindle and Thomas, 1989; Thomas and Grindle, 1990). According to Fox (1993: 28–33), many state organizations are "composed of a range of actors with different interests, who struggle to control the agency, to determine its goals, and to decide how to pursue them." A combination of complex "material, institutional and ideological goals motivates state actors." In most cases too, "state actors with any power share a common interest in perpetuating state rule because it is a necessary precondition for advancing whatever their particular agendas might be." These interests are partly evident in political party affiliations and the nature of appointments.

No single explanation can fully account for the actions of state actors, but as Fox (1993: 30–31) showed, the concept of the twin foundations of state rule — accumulation and legitimation ("the continuation of private capital accumulation and the preservation of some historically conditioned minimum of political legitimacy," respectively) — offers useful insights in terms of the broader context in which state actors can exercise autonomy. For example, on the one hand, some state actors oppose land reform on productive estates because they put a premium on the contribution of these farms to national capital accumulation. Other state actors may invoke issues of social justice or democratization. These two foundations represent two permanent but often contradictory tasks which must be performed by all state actors. These tasks partly explain why reformists are recruited into the state (generally, in the executive branch, see Fox, 1995). Moreover, popular struggles traverse the state from top to bottom so that different agencies and actors feel social pressures differently. In this process, state institutions are pried open, revealing previously latent adversaries or allies (see Tarrow, 1998).

Social forces may thus take different access routes in pursuing their interests within the state. Some state actors are inclined to pursue the state's private capital accumulation interests, while others may value the task of strengthening political legitimacy even more. Still others "may simply be concerned with career advancement or material gain. But this does not mean that state actors are completely free to respond as they wish — they face structural-institutional constraints and limitations" (Fox, 1993: 29–32). A state actor's bargaining power within the state "is closely related to the influence of social forces that are pushing in the same direction, whether or not they consider themselves allies." Such state allies, having resources and power, can strengthen and increase the impact of social mobilization "from below" (ibid.). Specifically, these state allies pose a countervailing force against the state allies of the landlords. They provide additional political and logistical support to the peasants and security against possible violence of other state and non-state actors against the peasants. This was observed by Kay (1992b: 130) in Latin American cases where "governments encourage peasant organizations to increase their power base and, in some cases, may lessen peasant repression and redirect the repressive apparatus of the state to check resistance by landlords" (see also Kay, 2001, 1992a).

Positive interaction between pro-reform forces within the state and in society

The process of formulating and implementing policy entails an interaction between state actors and societal actors, despite the latter's usual claim that they are independent groups. How and to what extent the state centralizes and brokers political interests and conflicts in and around the land reform issue is partly explained in Hart (1989; see also Tilly, 1984):

> Bringing the state into the analysis is not simply a matter of viewing agrarian processes as "an epiphenomenon of state power" .... Nor is it a question of the "inefficiency" of state intervention .... Rather, it entails understanding how power struggles at different levels of society are connected with one another and related to access to and control over resources and people. (48)

Still following Fox (1993), two concepts must be clarified here: independence and autonomy. Independence is largely seen as an absolute either/or question; groups are either co-opted by or are independent from the state. To be independent means that the internal dynamics of societal organizations are (and can be) insulated from any form of state interference or influence. Meanwhile, autonomy is a matter of degree and refers here to "the amount of state intervention in the societal actor's internal decision-making" (ibid.). But as Harvey (1998: 26) explained, "Associational autonomy is something to be won rather than assumed," but once won it is not guaranteed to stay permanently (see also Hellman, 1992; Edelman, 1999; Franco, 1998a, 1999c, 2004). The degree of autonomy of a particular peasant organization vis-à-vis the state is endlessly and dynamically altered over time in the course of land reform implementation. It can increase or decrease within the political and policy dynamics that shape and reshape the process and outcomes of land reform (Fox, 1992: 24). The experience of peasant organizations in Veracruz, Mexico, during the period 1920–1938 is an example (see Salamini, 1971).

In the history of peasant movements, independent organizations can go as far as putting issues onto the state's agenda (see Foley, 1991), but they are largely unable to directly influence policy outcomes without close interaction with state actors. Co-opted organizations do not make an important impact, since they are basically administrative adjuncts of the state and can rarely go beyond what the state defines as their parameters of action (Foley and Yambert, 1989: 63). Autonomous organizations have more potential. While they are able to penetrate the state from top to bottom and to influence it from within, they can also pull out from such interaction when disengagement is necessary and preserve themselves when the windows of opportunity close, still retaining some degree of strength from previous interactions with the state, which can be utilized for the next reformist opening (see Fox, 1992, 1996; Fox and Gershman, 2000).

Even in revolutionary land reforms where the state is thought to be absolutely powerful, a pro-reform state–society alliance is necessary. This was, for instance, the case in China, or at least some parts of it, in the 1947–1950 period. A communist government official aptly explained that "the implementation of land reform would be far harder than assumed by the 'optimists,' and that only a policy of organizing and mobilizing the peasantry into an 'anti-feudal united front' for 'resolute and appropriate struggle against reactionary landlords' would secure the obedience of the landlord class to the law" (Shillinglaw, 1974: 134).

There may be occasions when state reformists and pro-reform social groups exist without fully and positively interacting with each other. In such situations, political opportunities are not fully harnessed. In other cases, they do interact but instead of supporting each other, they undermine each other: Pro-reform forces are then generally weakened and prospects for land reform implementation are remote (see, e.g., Franco, 2004). The most promising situation is when the two streams of pro-reform forces interact positively in pursuit of the common goal of implementing land reform, despite differences in agendas and motivations between them. This strategy was necessary in China in the late 1940s and early 1950s (Shillinglaw, 1974), in Kerala (India) after 1957 (Herring, 1990), in Chile (Kay and Silva, 1992), and in Taiwan (Tai, 1974), for example.

Such positive interaction does not necessarily entail explicit coalitions between state and societal actors. Parallel initiatives of state and societal actors (who may even consider themselves adversaries) toward a common aim also form "objective alliances." These types of parallel pro-reform actions might have even been the more common experiences in many countries historically.

In short, in a pro-reform state–society alliance, one actor might pressure the other to give in, but they share a broader interest in each other's gaining strength. The different motivations underlying the actions of the state and those of societal actors are responsible for the inherent potential for conflict in the relationship between state and societal actors (see Fox, 1993: 21–32). Maintaining a high degree of autonomy while coalescing with state reformists is a difficult task, but one which peasant organizations must perform at all times (see also Foweraker, 1990: 8–9). Moreover, the dynamic state–society interactions also have direct influence on the constant changes in the forms of collective actions preferred and actually taken by rural social movements as well as on the degree of conflict in such interactions. Marc Edelman (1999: 188) in the Costa Rican context explains, "Both state officials and movement leaders may stand to gain by the substitution of prolonged negotiations for militant actions and threats of disturbances."

Ability to overcome landlords' resistance to land reform

Achieving a symbiotic interaction between pro-reform state and societal actors does not automatically lead to land reform implementation. The pro-reform forces have to surmount various anti-reform obstacles. In the context of evading land reform, landlords usually recruit allies within the state, from top to bottom. It is quite rare to see successful landlord evasion of expropriation without an alliance with anti-reform state actors. However, it must be noted that landlords also recruit "allies" from among the peasantry by cajoling, tricking, buying, or coercing them into the landlords' camp (see, e.g., Kerkvliet, 1995, 1990, 1977; Scott and Kerkvliet, 1986; Scott, 1990). This fits well with the classic "divide and conquer" tactic. Thus, in fact, the conflict can very well take the form of peasants versus peasants when in reality it is a peasants-versus-landlord battle as shown in the sugarcane and banana plantation sectors in the Philippines (see, e.g., Franco, 1999b, 2004; Franco and Acosta, 1999). This situation can work very effectively in favour of a landlord who wants to carry out an apparent-but-not-real land redistribution scheme.

To understand how poor peasants and their allies can defeat the landlords' anti-reform manoeuvres, it is important to stress what Herring (1983: 218) said about the landowning classes: "The political power of the landed is often, and rightly, given emphasis in the explanation of ineffectual land reform. But ruling elites have for a long time been more plural than the landlord-dominated caricature allows. Moreover land reforms of more or less serious intent continue to be promulgated despite objections from landed strata."

This reminder can, in turn, facilitate a better understanding of Tarrow's concept of political opportunity structure, which explains the number of ways in which the anti-reform coalition can be weakened. Tarrow (1998) identified four important political opportunities: access to power, shifting alignments, availability of influential elites, and cleavages within and among elites. The availability of all or some of these opportunities can create possibilities that even weak and disorganized actors can take advantage of; conversely, the strong may also grow weak. Regime transitions, even periodic administration turnover through competitive elections, offer changes in the political opportunity structure, as described by Tarrow, that can be potentially favourable to the landless poor, especially when the ruling classes are fragmented into competing factions. Moreover, as explained by Vince Boudreau (2001: 176) in his study of Philippine social movements, "Recruitment, cooperation, conflict, and demobilization are all closely associated with the different influences produced upon heterogeneous movement constituencies by shifting external opportunities and constraints." Thus, the pro–land reform forces can overcome anti-reform obstacles when their ranks remain solid and persistent, while the landlords may fail to muster sufficient state allies, may be abandoned by state allies, or may face a split from other elites. Furthermore, their co-opted peasant groups may fail to deliver, or may simply be overpowered by the composite force of pro-reform actors. This political opportunity perspective, as explained by Tarrow, offers better understanding of the rich variation and enormous unevenness in land redistribution outcomes at the sub-national level over time.

CHAPTER TWO

LAND AND TENANCY REFORMS IN THE PHILIPPINES: A NATIONAL-LEVEL VIEW OF STRUCTURES AND INSTITUTIONS, PROCESSES AND OUTCOMES

[L]andlessness and poverty continue to dominate the rural landscape in the Philippines, and calls for redistributive reform continue to be heard throughout the archipelago. (James Putzel, 1992: 376)

2.1 INTRODUCTION

This chapter offers an overview of the relevant socioeconomic structures and socio-political institutions, policy processes, and outcomes of land and tenancy reforms in the Philippines. It aims to locate the land reform imperatives and initiatives within the country's socioeconomic and political history. The chapter explains the main features of CARP and its nationally aggregated outcomes. It presents both the context and subject of this study.

2.2 STRUCTURAL AND INSTITUTIONAL CONTEXT

The Philippine agricultural sector remains important both in terms of financial value of the sector as a percentage of the national economy and with regard to the number of people dependent on it. The agricultural and rural transformation during the past century occurred in a highly uneven manner, geographically and over time. Such transformation has occurred against the backdrop of a highly skewed landownership distribution and widespread rural poverty (Borras, 2007).

The Marcos authoritarian regime (1965–1986) collapsed under the weight of popular mobilizations that culminated in a combined military and civilian uprising in early 1986.[1] Marcos' promise of land reform and agricultural-economic development did not fully materialize despite years of sponsorship from international financial institutions and the launching of the Green Revolution (see, e.g., Boyce, 1993; Bello et al, 1982; Feder, 1983). Landlessness, economic underdevelopment, and political repression dominated the national landscape during this period (Wurfel, 1988; Geremia, 1986; Thompson, 1996). The regime transition under the administration of Corazón Aquino (1986-1992) succeeded in restoring a number of important political institutions such as competitive national elections (Franco, 2001a; see also Quimpo, 2005). However, this period failed to deliver most of the promises and aspirations of the 1986 people's uprising. Political turmoil persisted and economic problems continued (see, e.g., Bello and Gershman, 1992).

A significant degree of political stability and economic invigoration was achieved by Aquino's successor. The administration of Fidel Ramos (1992-1998), who was among Marcos' top military officers, did not veer away from the export-oriented agricultural and economic development paradigm; neoliberal policy reforms started to gain ground during this period. Like its predecessors, the administration continued to squeeze agriculture of "surplus" factors of production for industrial development while maintaining and consolidating productive farms that generated export earnings. But while agriculture continued to be important in financing the industrial project of the elite, two other key sources emerged over time: foreign direct investment and remittances from Filipinos working abroad (but see Bello, 2001; Bello et al., 2004: 11; Sta. Ana, 1998). Inflows of significant foreign direct investment started toward the mid-1990s; the dollar remittances of overseas Filipinos, at present estimated at around 10 percent of the total population, or from 7 to 8 million migrants, continue to be a crucial pillar upon which the economy rests, with their remittances cornering up to 15 percent of the annual GDP.[2] Altogether this change in socioeconomic make up during the past decades has transformed the Philippine countryside, making the sources of income of a rural household increasingly more plural and diversified, as partly shown in the 1993 study by Rosanne Rutten (see also Rigg, 2006; Lim, 1998).

Like the Ramos presidency, the short-lived administration of Joseph Estrada (1998-January 2001) pinned its hope for development on the three main pillars of the national economy (i.e., exports, foreign direct investment, and remittances from overseas Filipino workers). The Macapagal-Arroyo administration (from January 2001 to the present) remains within this broad development framework but has promised to deepen and expand the neoliberal reforms even further.[3] But a combination of massive corruption, popular belief that the president cheated in the 2004 presidential election, and neoliberal reforms has resulted in a political crisis beginning in mid-2005 that might affect the national economy.

The agrarian structure

Philippine agriculture is diverse in terms of products and production systems but can be broadly differentiated into two types. The traditional sector — rice, corn, coconut, and sugar cane — continues to predominate in terms of nationally aggregated monetary value and land use: not less than 90 percent of total farmland. Characterized by high-volume, low-value crops, this sector is dominated by "traditional" landlords whose provenance dates back to colonial times. In contrast, the non-traditional sector produces low-volume, high-value crops and products such as banana, mango, pineapple, and aquatic products, and has seen expansion, albeit less than expected, in recent years. Marked by production and exchange relations different from the traditional sector, such as contract growing schemes and wage relations, this sector is where non-traditional landed elites, including urban-based entrepreneurs and multinational corporations, have gained the most ground. Modern technology and equipment, as well as a capitalist management system, also characterize these modern farm enclaves. Rene Ofreneo (1980) provides an excellent critical analysis of the early phase of the development of this sector.

Thus, the development of capitalism in Philippine agriculture has been highly uneven over time and across sectors and geographic spaces.[4] It has impacted upon, and contributed toward, the emergence of a complex agrarian structure in the country. The development of capitalism, specifically in agriculture, can be traced back to changes in international trade in the mid-19th century, when the Philippines, then under Spanish colonialism, emerged into the global economy.[5] The country's main engagement in global trade during the 19th century was its exports of abaca hemp, coconut, sugar cane, and minerals.[6] The current agrarian structure can be traced from this period when landownership started to become concentrated in the hands of Spanish *conquistadores*, the *mestizos*, their local Filipino collaborators, and the Roman Catholic Church. The haciendas proliferated. More and more local people lost their formal claims of ownership, control, or rights over these lands (Constantino, 1975). Share tenancy expanded geographically and by crop to include sugar cane plantations (Aguilar, 1994).

Spanish colonialism ended in 1898 under the weight of the Philippine Revolution of 1896, which various authors have seen as the culmination of hundreds of pockets of peasant-based revolts during more than three hundred years of Spanish colonialism (Constantino, 1975; Sturtevant, 1976; Agoncillo, 1965; Ileto, 1979). Most of these revolts were land and tenancy related. But the Filipinos failed to secure their independence, since the United States came in to snatch the revolutionary victory having bought the Philippines for US$ 20 million from the Spaniards. In its politico-military consolidation effort, the United States co-opted the landowning classes. The Filipinos revolted against the US invasion and against the betrayal by the local elite of the goals of the revolution (broader access to land, for instance). The revolt was violently crushed (Constantino, 1975).

The American military campaign was complemented by other "reforms," among which were several land-related laws. For example, confronted by the controversial issue of the landholdings grabbed by the Spanish Catholic friars, the Americans (who also needed the Catholic Church in the politico-military consolidation) decided to buy these estates from the church at a commercial price and resell them in the market. As a result, individual and corporate elites, both local and American, were able to re-amass these lands (Corpuz, 1997; see also Connolly, 1992). Another law passed during the early years of the past century pertained to the implementation of the Torrens land titling system, which had a far-reaching impact on property rights (a concept that was introduced during the Spanish era) and agrarian structure. Ostensibly, this program was an effort to help systematize private property ownership, which was crucial for the planned agricultural and economic development campaign. The policy ushered in an era in Philippine history where the western concept of property rights broadly categorized between private and public became the dominant formal institution, pushing to the periphery, and an "informal" status, the pre-existing indigenous concept of "rights" over resources such as land. The same law led, on the one hand, to wholesale land-grabbing by those who knew about the law and had access to courts and, on the other, to the displacement of many poor peasants and indigenous communities who did not know about it and had no access to the new cadastral registration system. Sugar cane, abaca, and coconut farm enclaves mushroomed across the country as the United States encouraged production of and trade in these products.[7] American-owned sugar, coconut oil, and timber mills had been established, at times in partnership with the Philippine landowning classes.[8] During this period, tenancy incidence multiplied, and the number of landless peasants increased steadily (Constantino, 1975; Corpuz, 1997).

Resettlement programs to open new land frontiers got started as early as the first quarter of the past century. Over the years these were pushed by the convergence of a number of imperatives: the requirements of the state-building process, capital accumulation needs of both private and state interests, and the need to diffuse politico-military tension in Luzon (Abinales, 2000; Putzel, 1992). Settlement programs and the conquest of new land frontiers came in various forms: state-organized settlements, state-facilitated entry of multinational companies to pave the way for timber exploitation and initial opening of plantations, enterprising middle classes and bureaucrats who took advantage of the program to amass land, land-grabbing domestic elite, and desperate landless poor who resorted to voluntary settlements on what they thought were public lands (see Abinales, 2000; David et al., 1983; Tadem, Reyes and Magno,1984; Gutierrez and Borras, 2004). The formal, state-organized settlement programs involving poor people in general failed to achieve their goals of developing small family farms, citing prohibitive cost as the main reason (Velmonte, 1956; Lichauco, 1956).[9]

However, these various forms of entry into the land frontier had a profound impact on the pre-existing agrarian structure in these frontiers. For example, (i) vast territories of the indigenous communities were invaded; (ii) vast tracts of public land ended up in the hands of the elite with or without formal private titles, many of these public lands were awarded to elite through timberland concessions or pasture lease agreements, though decades later, the lands were converted into productive croplands; and (iii) a variety of social and production relations emerged on these landholdings. Altogether, the series of settlements in their different forms altered the agrarian structure, creating webs of complex social relations that would prove quite difficult to untangle and resolve in the decades to come (Leonen 1993).[10] State laws were passed from the remote capital of the country over time, many of which have started to contradict each other. This is akin to the "stacked law" Esther Roquas (2002) talks about in the context of Central America.

Yet, the goal of pacifying peasant unrest in many parts of Luzon failed. Armed peasant-based rebellions partly rooted in land- and tenancy-based grievances persisted in the period from the 1930s to the 1950s. During the Japanese occupation, peasant guerrillas invaded the estates of landlords who fled to the cities or abroad. However, the peasants were violently driven away by the returning landlords allied with the state after the war (Kerkvliet, 1977). Thus, land- and tenancy-related peasant unrest persisted after the war, but at this time in a far more widespread and organized manner, having a relatively sophisticated armed struggle component, the *Huk* (ibid.). The reaction of the post-war Philippine state was broadly the same: a settlement program combined with promises of limited tenancy reform and state repression. Again, despite US Central Intelligence Agency sponsorship of the early 1950s counter-insurgency tenancy reform and settlement program, the state failed to solve the growing land-based political and economic problems. The early 1960s witnessed the first significant state policy on land redistribution (there was a less significant similar policy in the 1930s under the Rural Progress Administration). A land reform law was passed that called for redistribution of tenanted rice and corn lands above a certain land size ceiling, which was very high and so exempted the overwhelming majority of farms in the country.[11] This same law declared share tenancy illegal (German, 1995). But the law did not see any significant degree of implementation.

In 1972, Ferdinand Marcos started his land reform, which also called for the redistribution of tenanted rice and corn lands (see Putzel, 1992: 127–156). This initiative had many intentions: to recruit popular support for the Marcos martial law regime, to debase the then-fledgling peasant-based communist guerrilla movement, and to crush some of Marcos' land-based elite political opponents (see Kerkvliet, 1979; Putzel, 1992). In the Marcos land reform (Presidential Decree No. 27), land was to be bought at below market price (computed based on productivity-related features: see Putzel, 1992; Riedinger, 1995) and re-sold to the beneficiaries at a subsidized price and on an amortizing basis; landlords were given the right to retain land but at a much lower ceiling than in the Macapagal law. Moreover, leasehold conversion was a component of this land reform program, wherein sharing arrangements on rice and corn lands under the retention rights of landlords were converted to leasehold contracts where tenants were to pay fixed lease rents pegged at not more than 25 percent of the average harvest. At the same time, a number of resettlement programs on public lands were carried out.

After more than a decade of implementation, the land redistribution outcome of Marcos' program was far below the level of its original intentions and promises. As documented by James Putzel (1992: 138–139), from 1972 to 1986 under the Operation Land Transfer (OLT) program, the government claimed to have released certificates of land transfer (CLTs) to 444,277 peasant beneficiaries covering 766,630 hectares of land. Moreover, the government reported that during the same period, 690,207 leasehold contracts were awarded to 645,808 tenants through the Operation Leasehold (OLH) program. Finally, the Marcos administration opened up new settlements covering 180,000 hectares of public lands and benefiting 12,000 peasant households.

If true, these figures of land and tenancy reform accomplishment are relatively significant, though far from being able to resolve the land monopoly in the country, because the program's limited coverage to tenanted rice and corn farms spared landlords in other agricultural sub-sectors. There are, however, several problems with the data presented above. For example, it is unclear how many beneficiaries actually got their CLTs and were able to take possession of the awarded lands. It is also unclear from the data how many of the peasant beneficiaries were able to fully pay for the lands and thus secure the actual land titles (see, e.g., Hirtz, 1998).

But while there may be problems with the data on land reform accomplishment during the period 1972–1986, it is impossible to deny that the Marcos land reform, regardless of its original intentions, contributed to the reform efforts in the country. It led to actual, albeit limited, land and tenancy reform and to the general weakening of the political power of landlords of rice and corn farms (Wurfel, 1983, 1988; Riedinger, 1995; Boyce, 1993; Wolters, 1984; van den Muijzenberg, 1991). Furthermore, the Marcos regime can be partly credited for the establishment of the land reform administrative machinery that would be useful in the CARP era. It was during this period that the Ministry/Department of Agrarian Reform (DAR) was established, together with local agrarian courts nationwide. These institutional innovations would have profound impact on state–society interactions around land reform far beyond the Marcos regime.

The limited land reform program was carried out against the background of several attempts by the regime to facilitate the development of capitalism in certain agricultural sub-sectors, mainly through a combination of the introduction and promotion of the Green Revolution package of technology (the Philippines hosts the International Rice Research Institute, which has been at the forefront of this modernization campaign) and plantation-based agro-export agricultural modernization. It was also during this time that several crony-controlled special agricultural groupings or monopolies were established, such as those in the coconut and sugar cane sectors.[12]

Meanwhile, rural dissent, which erupted into full-blown peasant-based communist-directed revolution from the 1970s onward, was met with violent militarization of the countryside (Hawes, 1990). The unresolved landlessness therefore persisted into the post-authoritarian era. Share tenancy relations were marked by onerous terms, such as *tersyuhan* — one-third/two-thirds crop sharing in favour of the landlord wherein the tenant-peasants usually shoulder most of the production costs.

On the eve of the promulgation of the 1988 CARP law, or in 1985, at an average of six members per household, there were more or less 5.2 million rural households in the Philippines, accounting for 57 percent of the national population; 4.4 million of these were agricultural households (table 2.1). There is no definitive way of coming up with exact figures about the population

Table 2.1
Population of the Philippines, 1961–1999

	1961	1970	1980	1985
Population				
National	28,380,000	37,540,000	48,317,000	54,668,000
Rural	19,708,000	25,160,000	30,207,000	31,134,000
% national	70	67	63	57
Agricultural	17,843,000	21,667,000	25,177,000	26,655,000
% national	63	58	52	49

	1990	1995	1999
Population			
National	60,687,000	68,354,000	74,184,000
Rural	31,075,000	31,414,000	31,335,000
% national	51	46	42
Agricultural	27,687,000	28,969,000	29,645,000
% national	46	42	40

Source: Calculated from data on the website of the United Nations Food and Agriculture Organization, Statistics Division, at: www.faostat.org. Percentages are rounded.

of landless peasants, as explained by Putzel (1992: 24–26).[13] This study uses the estimate commonly employed among peasant organizations and by the DAR; that is, in 1988 roughly 70 percent of the total agricultural population were landless or near-landless households.[14] The landless and near-landless agricultural population is, in turn, categorized as tenants (fixed-cash rent or variations of sharecropping), owner-cultivators below subsistence, cultivators of land without secure property rights, seasonal and plantation (more or less permanent) farmworkers, and part-time subsistence fisherfolk. Again, there are no systematic means to know exactly how many households belong to each category, although it is widely assumed that the seasonal farmworkers (rural semi-proletariat) are the most numerous. It is most probable that many peasant households did not make it into the official census because they reside in isolated upland areas inaccessible to government census takers. It is also likely that landlords deliberately kept tenancy data out of the census due to illegal arrangements, for example, tenants on supposedly public lands. Landlords also fear that divulging data about tenancy relations could lead to their land being subjected to state reforms. This problem with regard to the actual data on share tenancy is closely linked to the lack of any systematic databank on land use and land titles. The absence of clear and systematic land titling and administration in the country has in fact significantly contributed to the problematic process of land reform (see Putzel, 1992, 2002). The current government initiative to address the problem of land titling and administration has been through the World Bank–initiated and AusAid-funded Land Administration and Management Program (LAMP), the long-term impact of which remains to be seen, although initial outcomes appear not to be favouring the landless poor.

Meanwhile, the agricultural population increased to 5 million households in 1999, pointing to a rising number of potential beneficiaries/claim-makers for land reform from 1988 onward (see table 2.1), amidst a marginal increase in the area of farmland and irrigated land between 1985 and 1999 and against the backdrop of a total of more or less 10 million hectares of farm land, based on the 1980 census (see, e.g., Putzel, 1992: 19, 40, n. 106).

Available data is suggestive of a highly skewed landownership distribution before the 1988 land reform was implemented. Table 2.2 shows the following: (i) small farms, or those 2.99 hectares and less, account for some two-thirds of the total number of farms but for less than one-third of total hectares of agricultural land; (ii) farms 5 hectares or more, which are the potentially

Table 2.2
Size distribution of farms, 1980

Farm size (ha)	No. of farms	% of farms	Area (ha)	% of area
Under 0.5	288,962	8.5	68,900	0.7
0.50–0.99	485,829	14.2	300,200	3.1
1.00–1.99	964,220	28.2	1,189,900	12.2
2.00–2.99	613,824	18.0	1,332,300	13.7
3.00–4.99	588,151	17.2	2,066,700	21.2
5.00–7.00	283,585	8.3	1,612,100	16.6
7.01–9.99	76,421	2.2	630,900	6.5
10.00–24.99	103,723	3.0	1,406,300	14.5
25.00 and above	14,608	0.4	1,117,800	11.5
Total	3,420,323		9,725,100	

Source: Putzel (1992: 28).

expropriable farms (those above the land size ceiling of 5 hectares), account for almost 14 percent of the total number of farms but less than half of the total hectares of agricultural land. Other estimates place the total farmland area at 10.3 million hectares. Table 2.3 shows the result of the land registration program in 1988 (*"Listasaka"*).

Based on this initial data, Putzel (1992: 29) calculated the Gini coefficient in landownership in 1988 to be 0.647, showing a high degree of inequality. But official censuses do not, cannot, show the actual extent of land monopoly in quantitative terms due to (i) landlords' subdivision of their landholdings into smaller units to evade the land size ceiling; (ii) unregistered farm holdings, especially those that are on public lands, or lands under other classifications that are not directly expropriable, such as those classified as "forest" or "timberland" but which in fact are croplands under tenancy arrangements; (iii) other public lands formally leased to private companies, foreign or domestic; (iv) other farms of various classifications that are not formally included in land redistribution, such as military reservations or church lands but where

Table 2.3
Concentration of agricultural land ownership, 1988

Farm size (ha.)	Number of owners	% of owners	Area (ha.)	% of area	% of rural families	% of agricultural families
<3.0	1,021,446	65.7	1,257,074	16.4	16.7	26.1
3.1–7.0	319,595	20.6	1,471,149	19.2	5.2	8.2
7.1–12.0	123,507	7.9	1,126,197	14.7	2.0	3.2
12.1–15.0	27,243	1.8	363,173	4.7	0.4	0.7
15.1–24.0	37,797	2.4	710,844	9.3	0.6	1.0
24.1–50.0	16,781	1.1	545,475	7.1	0.3	0.4
50.1–100.0	4,990	0.3	337,843	4.4	0.1	0.1
>100.0	3,235	0.2	1,854,888	24.2	0.1	0.1
Total	*1,554,594*	*100*	*7,666,643*	*100*	*25*	*39*

Note: Agricultural families = 3,919,241; rural families = 6,132,339. Percentages are rounded.

Source: Putzel (1992: 29) based on partial "Listasaka I: Final Report on Landholders Registration by Regions as of July 18, 1988."

in fact tenancy and labour relations exist informally; (v) unregistered tenancy arrangements for reasons explained earlier; and (vi) the "owners-on-paper" category, which is likely to have ballooned in recent years because of the large numbers of land reform beneficiaries who have already sold their awarded lands or rights over them but who hide such transactions from the government, and so from the census, because of the legal prohibition on land sales and rentals. There are other grey areas on landlessness, landholdings, and farm size distribution that aggregated statistics failed to capture. Yet, these farms are part of the agrarian structure. From these landholdings, farm surpluses are created, extracted, and disposed under varying landlord-peasant relationships.

There are two broad types of small- and medium-sized landholdings. The first type are those that are registered as small- and medium-sized holdings but are in fact part of larger estates controlled by a single landlord; up to this time, there are no systematic cadastral records that can show exactly how much land landlords own or control. The second type is the landholdings that really are small- and medium-sized. While it is nearly impossible to pin down how many belong to this category, it is safe to say that they are significant in number (see Putzel, 1992, for more elaborate discussion on this issue).

The agricultural sector within the national economy

As mentioned in the Introduction, during the past decades, the share of the agriculture sector in the Philippine GDP shrank from around one-third in the 1960s to 1970s to around one-fifth by 2006. During the same period, the industry sector registered a marginal increase, eventually stagnating at around one-third. Most of the economy's development was accounted for by the phenomenal expansion of the services sector, which grew from about 30 percent to around 50 percent of GDP during the same period. The agriculture sector has remained a key sector, with a current share of one-fifth of GDP and two-fifths of employment. But as Balisacan and Hill (2003: 25) have explained, when "a broader definition that encompasses agricultural processing and related activities is adopted, the indirect share [of agriculture] rises to about 40 percent and 67 percent, respectively." However, the performance of the Philippine agriculture sector between 1980 and 2000 was dismal, at an average of 1.4 percent annual growth rate (David, 2003: 177; Borras, 2007).

The poverty incidence has been high. The 2005 Philippine poverty analysis and report released by the Asian Development Bank (ADB) showed that "the poverty incidence of families fell by 10.5% over the period 1985–2000" (or from 44.2 percent to 33.7 percent), but that "this was negated by very high population growth rates of 2.36% per year."[15] Poverty in the Philippines is a rural phenomenon. According to the ADB report, "Of the 26.5 million poor people in the country in 2000 ... 7.1 million were urban and 19.4 million live in rural areas. In other words, nearly 75% of the poor are rural poor" (ADB, 2005: 64). And the poverty incidence among farming households during the period 1985-2000 has remained almost unchanged. It was 56.7 percent and 55.8 percent, in 1985 and 2000, respectively (ibid: 98). The Gini coefficient for income distribution was a high 0.46 in 2004 (CPRC, 2005: 102, 116),[16] but poverty is highly uneven across geographic spaces in the country (Monsod and Monsod, 1999).

Persistent rural poverty can be partly accounted for by the state of agriculture relative to other sectors of the economy during the past few decades. The gross value added (GVA) of agriculture was a low 1.0 in 1980-1990 and 1.8 in 1990-2000 in the Philippines. Meanwhile, the real value added per worker during the period 1970-2000 also showed the dismal performance of the agriculture sector: It was quite low and had increased much more slowly than the industry sector's at PhP 15,800 in 1970 and PhP 17,100 in 2000 — in contrast to the industry sector's PhP 62,300 and PhP 72,000, respectively (Balisacan and Hill, 2003: 13). Hence, despite the modest growth in agriculture during the 1990s, it did not translate into real value added gains for the agricultural households. Thus Philippine agriculture failed to achieve the promise of Green Revolution that was inaugurated in the Philippines in the early 1970s.

Agriculture has not reflected the bullish character of economic development during the past decade. In fact, the sector may be in for more problems in the future if current trends continue. Some insights from table 2.4 are noteworthy. Contrary to the goals of and earlier claims by agricultural trade reformers (i.e., to boost the agricultural sector's global competitiveness), the initial results seem to be the opposite: Since 1991, the country has been transformed from a net agricultural exporting country to a net agricultural importing country, in contrast to the performance of its Southeast Asian neighbours.

A disaggregated glance at the Philippine agriculture sector can give us a clearer picture of some of the factors that have caused the anomalous negative performance of the country relative to its regional counterparts. First, driven by its, arguably, short-sighted rice policy, the government has been flooding the domestic market with rice imported from its Asian neighbors and the United States in order to ensure sufficient supply of cheap rice for its urban-based consumers, especially urban-based workers (for political and economic reasons). Second, enticed by the cheap ("dumping") prices of maize

Table 2.4 Value of total agricultural exports-imports (in US$), 1971–2002

	1971–1974	1975–1978	1979–1982	1983–1986	1987–1990	1991–1994	1995–1998	1999–2002
Philippines								
Exports	3,456,288	5,533,916	7,121,570	5,340,551	4,854,905	5,440,135	7,152,650	5,851,500
Imports	1,095,292	1,655,647	2,686,723	2,505,581	4,144,210	5,697,601	10,500,096	10,293,519
Balance	2,360,996	3,878,269	4,434,847	2,834,970	710,695	(257,466)	(3,347,446)	(4,442,019)
Indonesia								
Exports	2,716,864	5,742,853	8,523,340	9,522,321	11,857,847	14,985,995	22,492,113	20,652,338
Imports	1,770,643	3,983,167	5,983,276	3,377,856	5,656,582	9,945,234	18,629,462	17,042,862
Balance	946,221	1,759,686	2,540,064	6,144,465	6,201,265	5,040,761	3,862,651	3,609,476
Malaysia								
Exports	4,707,318	8,917,966	14,168,735	15,337,010	18,398,840	20,958,595	31,110,514	25,833,424
Imports	1,942,225	3,210,261	3,123,882	5,885,799	7,576,555	10,910,318	16,160,069	15,853,830
Balance	2,765,093	5,707,705	11,044,853	9,451,211	10,822,285	10,048,277	14,950,445	9,979,594
Thailand								
Exports	3,854,712	8,046,682	14,180,809	13,994,994	20,392,518	25,663,875	33,642,782	30,021,387
Imports	594,790	1,201,118	2,181,170	2,348,731	4,678,507	8,498,990	10,855,770	10,907,895
Balance	3,259,922	6,845,564	11,999,639	11,646,263	15,714,011	17,164,885	22,787,012	19,113,492
Vietnam								
Exports	118,280	316,481	458,585	951,845	2,042,037	3,545,078	7,674,665	8,894,943
Imports	1,594,976	1,655,620	1,322,411	728,579	1,013,781	1,388,910	3,954,573	5,313,921
Balance	(1,476,696)	(1,339,139)	(863,826)	223,266	1,028,256	2,156,168	3,720,092	3,581,022

Source: Calculated from data on the website of the United Nations Food and Agriculture Organization, Statistics Division, at: www.faostat.org; see Borras (2007).

in the world market, the Philippines opened up its domestic maize markets for massive importation largely due to the successful lobby of politically and economically powerful and well-connected livestock-based capital. The radical reduction of farms devoted to corn affected an estimated half a million subsistence farmers in the Philippines in the 1990s (Watkins, 1996). Third, in addition to the country losing substantial ground in its basic grains sectors (rice and corn), it has also lost ground in traditional export crops, particularly coconut and sugar cane. In the coconut sector, the Philippines' share of the world market began to diminish; while in the sugar cane sector, the country has even started to import (see also de la Rosa, 1994; Boyce, 1992).

Meanwhile, the so-called export-winners, the non-traditional export crops, have also, in general, failed to deliver their promise of export gains. Table 2.5 shows either a negligible gain, such as in asparagus and papaya, or a boom-bust cycle, such as in cocoa, coffee, and ramie. The only relatively stable export crops that have substantial aggregate value are banana and pineapple. While the Philippines has remained unrivalled in the banana sector, this is not the case with the pineapple sector, where Thailand is a major competitor. While mango has indeed demonstrated great promise, the total value of this sector remains relatively small. Oil palm and rubber have been doomed from the start by stiff competition from Malaysia and Indonesia. The Philippines is also a poor third in ranking in the export of shrimps and prawns, with Indonesia and Thailand being the most dominant, although the former remains a major tuna exporter as well (ASEAN, 2004). The Philippines has also been significantly left out in the export of processed, canned/bottled food products within and outside the region — a sector that is clearly dominated now by Thailand. Finally, the country's livestock sector, especially the cattle sector, has also suffered significant setbacks amidst cheap imports during the past decade or so (Borras, 2007).

A closer look at some of the basic data on agriculture partly explains the loss of Philippine competitiveness. For the basic grains, the Philippine average yield per hectare is one of the lowest in East and Southeast Asia (see table 2.6). For rice, while Thailand has the lowest yield per hectare in rice production, it is still a leader in both quantity and quality, making it the world's top rice exporter. The Philippines, with a very low yield per hectare, has failed to secure the necessary quantity (and so it has to import) and quality (and so it fails to export). Meanwhile, Vietnam has an impressive record of increasing its average yield per hectare, putting it second to Thailand in the global export of rice, while the United States, a regular source of cheap "California" rice for

Table 2.5 Value of exports of non-traditional crops (in US$ 1,000), 1971–2002

	1971–1974	1975–1978	1979–1982	1983–1986	1987–1990	1991–1994	1995–1998	1999–2002
Asparagus	0	0	0	0	463	17,563	43,181	40,068
Banana*	112,173	305,310	481,001	470,695	562,724	769,838	893,605	1,138,612
Cocoa**	—	—	7,455	5,886	6,863	412	2,223	157
Coffee§	2,754	105,494	177,214	311,139	130,547	15,482	11,271	1,099
Mango§§	3,395	11,479	27,879	55,100	62,181	117,260	175,951	141,055
Papaya	—	—	2	7	738	3,168	1,326	14,974
Pineapple†	111,084	231,932	418,962	456,316	522,410	567,887	515,418	474,264
Ramie	2,856	6,660	19,110	50,496	74,818	5,426	727	51

Notes: * includes area planted to non-export variety — export variety covers around 50,000 hectares; ** beans; § green and roast; §§ fruit and juice; †fruit, concentrate and canned.

Source: Calculated from data on the website of the United Nations Food and Agriculture Organization, Statistics Division, at: www.faostat.org.

the Philippines has an average yield three times than that of the Philippines'. The situation is even worse for the Philippines in terms of corn productivity, at below two tons per hectare, as compared to its regional counterparts (see table 2.6).

It is clear that the Philippines has failed to gain any significant ground in agricultural exports, while at the same time losing its foothold in the basic grains (rice and corn) sectors and other traditional export farm sectors.

The dismal performance of Philippine agriculture, which is directly traced to low labour and land productivity levels (David, 2003), which in turn is partly linked to the low level of development of rural infrastructure, such as road networks and irrigation (see, e.g., Ramos, 2000; Oorthuizen, 2003), has been a significant part of the country's overall loss in comparative advantage, as demonstrated in table 2.7 (borrowed from Cristina David, 2003). Even the comparative advantage in bananas and pineapple, two of the relatively stable export crops, has been eroded over time.

The land reform literature assumes that the problematic condition, if not the outright bankruptcy, of a given agricultural sector will lead to a greater

Table 2.6
Comparative yield per hectare in rice and corn in selected countries

	1961	1970	1980	1985	1990	1995	1999
Rice, yield/hectare (in MT)							
Philippines	1.22	1.74	2.21	2.58	2.97	2.80	2.86
Thailand	1.65	2.02	1.88	2.06	1.95	2.41	2.32
Vietnam	1.89	2.15	2.07	2.78	3.18	3.68	4.10
Indonesia	1.76	2.37	3.29	3.94	4.30	4.34	4.26
China	2.07	3.41	4.14	5.24	5.71	6.02	6.32
United States	3.82	5.17	4.94	6.07	6.19	6.30	6.62
Corn (Maize), yield/hectare (in MT)							
Philippines	0.62	0.82	0.96	1.11	1.27	1.52	1.71
Thailand	2.00	2.58	2.22	2.57	2.40	3.28	3.56
Indonesia	0.92	0.96	1.45	1.77	2.13	2.25	2.64
China	1.18	2.08	3.07	3.61	4.52	4.91	4.88
United States	3.91	4.54	5.71	7.40	7.43	7.12	8.39

Source: Calculated from data on the website of the United Nations Food and Agriculture Organization, Statistics Division, at: www.faostat.org.

Table 2.7
Trends in revealed comparative advantage, agriculture and selected major agricultural exports, 1960–1998*

Year	Agriculture**	Coconut	Sugar***	Bananas	Pineapple (canned)	(fresh)
1960	3.0	—	—	—	—	—
1965	2.7	131.8	15.3	—	—	—
1970	2.6	145.0	21.4	—	—	—
1975	3.8	211.2	22.0	29.3	—	—
1980	2.9	224.1	12.1	30.4	82.2	48.9
1985	2.4	212.3	7.6	31.2	91.6	59.7
1990	1.6	212.4	3.8	23.4	70.2	54.6
1995	1.1	153.5	2.0	14.1	41.5	23.6
1998	0.8	105.3	1.4	8.8	33.2	11.5

Notes:
* Estimated as the ratio of the share of a commodity group in a country's exports to that commodity group's share of world exports. Except for 1960 and 1998, years represent a three-year average centred on the year shown.
** Includes fisheries.
*** Sugar has historically been exported to the United States at a premium price.[17] Hence a value greater than unity does not reveal comparative advantage in this case. However, the sharp declining trend may still be interpreted as a rapid deterioration in comparative advantage.

Source: David (2003: 182).

supply of land in the market at cheaper prices and will therefore facilitate non-confrontational land reform (see, e.g., Deininger 1999). If we follow this assumption, then the current problematic state of Philippine agriculture can indeed partly explain the relative success of land redistribution during the past two decades. It cannot however fully explain the Philippine land reform processes and outcomes. For example, among the agricultural sectors most adversely affected by neoliberal reforms were the livestock and sugar cane sectors. However, landlords in these sectors turned out to be among the most recalcitrant and determinedly opposed to land reform despite the fact that their farms are generally unable to compete in the changed neoliberal setting. This can easily be seen through the pockets of high-intensity land reform opposition, for example, in the provinces of Negros Occidental, Camarines

Sur, and Masbate (see, e.g., Peña, 1996; Carranza and Mato, 2006). Landlords in these sectors and provinces were, to a large extent, able to successfully resist land reform through their alliances with local government officials, key national state actors in the executive and legislative branches, and members of the judiciary. A good example is the 2006 decision of the Supreme Court to decisively exempt livestock areas from agrarian reform. According to Danilo Carranza and Pepito Mato (2006: 8), this decision will exempt 200,000 hectares of privately owned lands, and 300,000 hectares of public lands leased to private entities from the land reform process, and deny 250,000 peasant households their land rights. The persistent landlord resistance from within these problematic agricultural sectors illustrates quite clearly that land has not only economic value but also a more multidimensional character; it connotes political power, as discussed in chapter 1. It is to this political dimension that we now turn.

2.3 RURAL POLITICS

The character of the agrarian structure has had a profound impact on the structure of power relations and political institutions in the rural polity.[18] Rural politics is dominated by local political bosses (*caciques*), most of them landed, who lord over the countryside through a complex combination of network, patronage, and the use and threat of coercion (Kerkvliet, 1977, 1990; Anderson, 1988, Sidel, 1999; McCoy, 1993a; Franco, 2001a; Hutchcroft, 2000).[19]

As discussed earlier, national and local elite classes, landed or otherwise, from the start of the past century until 1988, confronted the persistent peasant unrest rooted in land and tenancy relations with a combination of minor and largely unimplemented tenancy reforms and minor attempts at land redistribution, as well as continuing settlement programs. Co-optation of previously autonomous rural people's organizations, or the creation of less autonomous peasant associations, has been an integral component of the state's strategy in managing rural protest. Yet, the threat and actual use of repression through the state police and military apparatus was always employed whenever such limited reforms failed to contain peasant upheavals. The landed classes' violence against the peasants has been generally condoned by the state. Yet, due to various imperatives, land and tenancy reform issues have always featured prominently on the state agenda. In summarized presentation, these imperatives can be seen in various ways.

First, each national administration's permanent agenda to maintain a minimum level of political legitimacy has brought the state face to face with its rural constituency. While it was possible to ignore the persistent calls for reforms from the rural poor, periodic popular upheavals forced the central state to act on such grievances (Kerkvliet, 1977). Second, the rural constituency has remained an important source of votes for any faction of the elite who wanted to take state power. Thus, issues related to reforming the agrarian structure, or even some parts of it, have remained an important electoral issue, then and now (Franco, 2001a, 1998b). Third, intra-elite conflicts and realignments occur quite regularly, between different factions of the landowning classes and/or between landed and non-landed elites. Land and tenancy problems have become important weapons for some factions of the ruling elites in their attempts to politically and electorally dislodge their opponents, either nationally or locally (Kerkvliet, 1979; Franco, 2001a, 2004). Fourth, land and tenancy reforms have been explicitly addressed in the pursuit of capital accumulation for private and state interests. Fifth, this rural capital accumulation process has to proceed in a relatively stable political environment. Thus, political stability becomes an important requisite that the central state needs to guarantee, especially when local capitalist activities are tied in with foreign investors. Sixth, and closely related to the fifth, land and tenancy reforms have become components of the various counter-insurgency measures taken up by the central state in different periods of time (Wurfel, 1988; Putzel, 1992; Rutten, 2000b). Limited reforms have been carried out, particularly in areas of serious insurgency threat; these were complementary measures to the mainly military approaches to combating rebellions (Kerkvliet, 1979). Seventh, and related to the previous points, tackling the land and tenancy problems serves the interest of the central state in its state-building process (Abinales, 2000). Finally, land and tenancy reforms have been advanced by some state actors who believe that democratic and economic dividends can be derived from such an approach (Borras, 1999, 2001). In short, land and tenancy reforms have been pursued within the inseparable obligations of the state to maintain political legitimacy and pursue capital accumulation both for private and for state interests.

The above implies that the state is a differentiated entity. In a similar manner, the ruling elites are plural and highly heterogeneous, politically and economically; the landowning classes are likewise differentiated, economically and politically. This study suffices to classify the landowning classes into two broad categories: "traditional" and "non-traditional," as reflected in the two broad types of agricultural sectors explained earlier. The former is the most opposed (in a high-profile manner) to any form of land and tenancy reform, mainly because its principal source of economic power is land rent and because land gains it political power in a variety of ways, such as tenants as captive voters. The latter type is broadly comprised of modernizing landlord-entrepreneurs whose economic power derives not mainly from land rent but also from agricultural processing, manufacturing, and trading; some members of this group may even be engaged in non-agricultural sectors (see, e.g., Angeles, 1999; Rivera, 1994; de la Rosa, 2005). Hence, in general, they no longer employ share tenancy arrangements, preferring wage or trade-based arrangements. While they are basically opposed to redistributive land reform, they may employ more "creative" ways, such as joint venture agreements, to undermine the land reform policy, compared to the simplistic outright rejection stance of traditional landlords toward such reformist policy.

Naturally, these two elite camps are both influential in the central state and local governments; they clash with or diverge from each other from time to time on land and agriculture-related policy questions. In recent decades, the rise in economic significance of the non-traditional export crops sector in the national economy has entailed a surge in the political influence of landlord-entrepreneurs, challenging the historical political influence of traditional landlords. This is best illustrated on the one hand by the fact that during negotiations on CARP policymaking, the concession that the rice and corn landlords received was a modest adjustment of the compensation package for their land (Riedinger, 1995: 203; see also Banzon-Bautista, 1984). Meanwhile, Temario Rivera explains in 1994 (31) that "reflecting the power of the landlord class in export agriculture, the major land reform laws enacted by various administrations from 1930 to 1972 targeted only the lands in the rice and corn areas and exempted the export plantation crops like sugar, coconut, pineapples, and bananas." On the other hand, and in the context of the favoured export sectors as just explained by Rivera, owners of big commercial farms were able to secure a land redistribution deferment for ten years, from 1988 to 1998 (Borras and Franco, 2005; de la Rosa, 2005). Hence, historically, and in general, the central state's elites have been reluctant to antagonize the landowning classes with expropriationary land reform, but especially those engaged in agricultural exports. And while the influence of the landed classes within the central state has been entrenched historically, the local governments and congressional districts have been their traditional bailiwick.

This is the political background of past cycles of violent peasant-based upheavals (see also Sturtevant, 1976; Constantino, 1975; Constantino and Constantino, 1978). But while landlessness, poverty, and exploitation have marked the condition of the rural poor since the colonial era, peasant revolts and overt peasant collective actions have occurred in an uneven manner, marked by periodic ebb and flow. This can be seen in a number of ways. First, as most studies on peasant behaviour in the Philippines and elsewhere have concluded, it is not landlessness and poverty per se that instigate peasants to mobilize and eventually revolt against landlords and governments. Rather, the spark to revolt is caused by the deep feeling and realization at given points in time that injustice committed against them has reached an intolerable level, as in the numerous uprisings during the Spanish era, in the 1930s, the 1950s, and the 1970s (see Scott's "moral economy," 1976; see also 1985, 1990; Kerkvliet, 1977; Ileto, 1979).

Second, the emergence and availability of allies has been a crucial factor determining whether the rural poor engage in covert collective actions or even revolt. Allies can come in the form of charismatic persons who become leaders; on most occasions these leaders are from the peasant class but have urban and/or higher educational exposure, or they might come from the middle class and have sympathy with the rural poor.[20] Sympathetic political parties are another usual ally for the peasants, such as the communist parties in the 1930s and the 1970s and 1980s (Rutten, 2000a). Progressive elements within churches can, at times and under certain conditions, be crucial allies to peasants; an example is the widespread church-based conscientization and organizing work among the rural poor in the 1960s and 1970s, which led to the radicalization of many Federation of Free Farmers (FFF) activists and the subsequent formation of consistently more militant organizations, such as the KMP in the mid-1980s (Franco, 1994; Patayan, 1998). Moreover, since the 1980s, the emergence and proliferation of various types of progressive NGOs — local community-based groups, national policy think-tanks, and international donors — have provided the rural poor with a pool of allies (see Clarke, 1998; Silliman and Noble, 1998; Hilhorst, 2003). The works of the PEACE Foundation and the Philippine Peasant Institute (PPI), for example, contributed enormously in the earlier stages of formation and consolidation work of national-democratic (ND) rural people's organizations, such as the KMP (Franco, 2001b, 1994). Finally, broader alliances, either sectoral or multisectoral, have been important allies for peasants, especially those organized in local and singular associations. Such alliances have provided the vertical and horizontal linkages necessary to extend the political reach of peasants' collective actions (Huizer, 1972). Some examples of these coalitions are the alliances between peasant associations and trade unions in the 1930s (Tatang, 1988), as well as the ideologically broad national coalitions like the Congress for a People's Agrarian Reform (CPAR) in the late 1980s and early 1990s (Putzel, 1995, 1998), and the Partnership for Agrarian Reform and Rural Development Services (PARRDS) (Franco, 1999a). It is, however, important to note that unlike in many other countries where electoral political parties played an important role as allies (or not) of landless peasants for land reform (e.g., in Chile and in Kerala in India), this did not occur in the Philippines. This is partly because of the way members of the House of Representatives are elected, which is by congressional districts and by the individual candidates and not by party. And because the local districts are known bailiwicks of the landowning classes, the national congress has always been landlord dominated (see Gutierrez, 1994; Gutierrez, Torrente and Narca,1992). It is partly for this reason that party-based electoral politics in the country has remained weak and has not become a significant actor in the redistributive land reform politics (see Franco, 2001a; see also Montinola, 1999).

Third, grievances around and demands for land and tenancy reforms have been generally centralized within the state. State laws have increasingly become the defining parameter within which grievances are voiced and collective actions launched. Hence, the Philippine state has become an important context within which such grievances are partly defined and where contestations are engaged in between different social classes and interest groups, as well as the object of such contestations, as these groups compete against, or coalesce with, each other to influence or control the state and its public policies. Therefore, decisions made by peasants and their allies on the type of actions to engage in (overt or covert, armed or unarmed) and the set of demands put forward (tenancy and labour reforms or land redistribution) have been calculated partly against their perception of the balance of forces within and outside the state. This is seen in the calibration of peasant demands before the state from the colonial era to the present — always trying to capitalize on state official promises and then push the official boundaries farther than what state actors originally intended.

Fourth, the state is a principal source of political opportunities for peasants and their allies against which collective actions are planned and launched. Philippine state laws, dormant or otherwise, have been crucial contexts and objects of peasant mobilizations: They influence the level, scale, and nature of peasant demands; in turn, such demands have influenced subsequent state policymaking and choices. Hence, the Philippine state's pronouncements on land and tenancy reforms, even when state actors did not really mean to implement them, historically became rallying points for claim-making mobilizations by peasants. During the past century in the Philippines, there appears to have been a "ratchet effect" in the cycles of reforms or reform promises: from the most limited (and essentially flawed) friar land reform, to homestead and resettlement, to tenancy reforms in selected land types, to land redistribution of some land categories, to land redistribution of and tenancy reforms in all types of farmland. Peasant demands have tended to be calculated based on the actual political opportunity structure, including the way that Philippine state laws pertaining to land and tenancy reforms as well as to public/community forested lands have been (re)formulated at different periods (see Putzel, 1992; Franco, 2005).[21] Thus, in this context, perhaps the most important unintended outcome of Marcos' largely unimplemented land reform was that it set the benchmark in the popular discourse on land reform: This is now taken to mean expropriationary land redistribution. Succeeding peasant mobilizations would be anchored in this period and the level of reform discourse it promoted; there was no turning back in terms of the nature and scale of demands from the peasants and their allies. Hence, while indeed the history of land and tenancy reforms in the Philippines has been quite long and protracted, as well as marked by dozens of state laws, it has to be understood in the context of upward calibration in terms of reform content and extent.

Fifth, the escalation of peasant mobilization for reforms on the one hand and state actors' initiatives for land and tenancy reforms on the other usually occurred during an important national political transition and/or administration turnover: the Commonwealth era in the mid-1930s onward to the post–World War II transition (Kerkvliet, 1977), the Macapagal assumption of power onward to the 1972 shift to authoritarian rule (Kerkvliet, 1979), the 1986 regime transition (Putzel, 1992; Riedinger, 1995; Kasuya, 1995; Kerkvliet, 1993), and periodic administration turnovers since then (Franco, 2004). The efforts of competing elites to court peasant votes and/or to shore up eroded political legitimacy might have been keenly perceived and taken advantage of by poor peasants and their allies in order to put forward, or even increase, their demands for reform. In cases of ideologically and politically sophisticated peasant allies, such as communist and socialist parties, the potential for further ruling classes' fragmentation during such transitions was even greater, with these classes pried wider apart by divisive and anti-elite popular demands such as land and tenancy reforms. These demand-making initiatives were usually complemented by both spontaneous and organized mobilizations of the rural poor, such as the land occupations during the regime transitions in the 1940s (see, e.g., Kerkvliet, 1977) and in 1986–1990 (Kerkvliet, 1993).

Sixth, peasants' decisions to pursue covert actions in order to advance their demands and interests have been premised on their collective perception that there was a good chance that their goals could be better realized in this way (Kerkvliet, 1993). This also partly explains why on most occasions peasant demands have tended to match what the state already offered, at least formally and legally, like tenancy reforms during the first three quarters of the past century, or the contemporary demand to implement CARP (see Franco, 2005).

Finally, having explained the various ways in which peasants launched their collective actions to overtly engage the state on issues of rural reforms, it is important to note that on most occasions, Filipino peasants actually have not engaged in overt mass actions. Instead they have employed "everyday forms of resistance," from pilferage to misdeclaration of crop harvests, from foot-dragging to arson (see Scott, 1976, 1985, 1990; Scott and Kerkvliet, 1986; Kerkvliet, 1990). Decisions to engage in open collective mass action are usually calculated against the weight of their gains through everyday forms of resistance or claim-making. This is demonstrated in Kerkvliet's (1993) explanation of the 1980s peasant land occupations and in Franco's (2005) analysis of the peasant struggle for land and democracy in Bondoc peninsula, Quezon.

As mentioned earlier, the elite response to peasant unrest has traditionally been a combination of repression, co-optation, resettlement, and limited land and tenancy reforms. There have been several dozen such periods in the past, with the peasants having been able to gain only intermittent concessions from the state. None of the past tenancy and land reform programs significantly addressed the underlying causes of peasant unrest, which is widespread lack of control over land by the rural poor. So peasant unrest has remained an important part of Philippine rural politics throughout the past century. The most important post-war peasant-based revolution is the insurgency led by the Communist Party of the Philippines (CPP) together with its armed wing, the New People's Army (NPA) (see Weekley, 2001; Caouette, 2004; Pimentel, 1991; Rutten, 1996, 2000a).

Furthermore, the transition from an authoritarian to a "national clientilist electoral regime" in 1986 did not lead to complete democratization of the countryside, since even today entrenched political elites continue to dominate the rural polity (Franco, 2001a; see also Lara and Morales, 1990; Kerkvliet, 1995; Putzel, 1999). Their power connects with the centre. As Alfred McCoy (1993a: 20) explains, "We could identify both national [political] entrepreneurs without a provincial base and local warlords with only tenuous ties to the capital. Most political families, however, fused local power with national access." McCoy (ibid.) continues to explain that indeed, many found that they could not compete effectively in Manila for rents unless they could deliver, by whatever means, a substantial bloc of votes to national politicians. Even the most violent of provincial warlords tried to win lucrative rents, either through allies in Manila or by exercise of their de facto local autonomy.

Moreover, in his study of the Philippine state and regime transition in the mid-1980s, Gary Hawes (1987: 162) found out that "the change in regimes has had little impact at the level of the state. The pattern of class domination, while no longer so harshly repressive, remains relatively unchanged." He further concluded that "there is little prospect for change in landownership. The Philippines remains dependent on agriculture for the bulk of its export earnings …." However, elite classes' control of the economy and politics has never been totally stable and secure, and it has been persistently challenged historically, from within and outside the state. The Canadian political scientist David Wurfel (1988: 21) explained that

> the interaction of intra-elite competition and organized mass pressures go a long way to explain the patterns of Filipino politics for more than fifty years. This interaction was shaped by three long-term trends. First, the economic interests of the politico-economic elite were becoming more diversified by the rise of Filipino commerce and manufacturing, and with diversity came the potential for deeper and more persistent intra-elite conflict, especially after exchange controls were imposed in 1948. Second, mass mobilization grew steadily as a result of education, media exposure, urbanization, and the reorganization of hierarchies of patron-client relations, which did much to structure the pattern of both intra-elite competition and elite-mass relations, the salience of such hierarchies was eroded by the first two trends mentioned.

From this historical perspective, recent years can reveal that there has been only a very partial erosion of "rural local authoritarian enclaves," in a political process that can be traced back partly to the factors explained by Wurfel, partly to the series of highly constrained elections held during and immediately after the period of authoritarian rule, as well as to sustained social mobilizations from below demanding some forms redistributive reforms, mainly land reform. As argued and demonstrated by Franco (2001a), Sidel (1999) and McCoy (1993b), many localities in the countryside, despite the regime transition in the mid-1980s, remain in martial law–type authoritarian settings. Many of Marcos' local elite allies survived the political changes and remain local political bosses — the latter being defined in John Sidel (1999: 141) as "power brokers with monopolistic personal control over coercive and economic resources in their territorial jurisdictions or bailiwicks." Meanwhile, many of the elites disenfranchised during the Marcos dictatorship were able to regain their political-economic "fiefdoms" as well.[22] Nevertheless, the transition era brought new political opportunities for democratization, which have led to a heated policy debate on agrarian reform.

After initially dragging its feet on the issue, the Aquino administration was forced to act after thirteen peasants were gunned down by government troops at the foot of Mendiola Bridge near Malacañang Palace during a huge peasant demonstration for agrarian reform sponsored by KMP and its allies. The president asked the Congress to pass a land reform law based on the general guidelines the president had promulgated. Thus, the main battlefront was the Congress, which was landlord-dominated. The policy issue of land reform was bitterly fought between the majority of congress members, who themselves were landlords or closely linked to landowning families on one side, and a few articulate members of congress allied with then vibrant rural social movements clamouring for a more progressive, even revolutionary, land reform, on the other side. But the anti-reform lobby proved to be too strong, having allies within the executive branch including President Aquino herself, who comes from one of the largest landed families in the country. The final version of the law (i.e., CARP) that was passed therefore reflected the actual balance of power between pro-reform and anti-reform forces within and outside the Philippine state: It was not revolutionary, but neither was it a blatantly conservative piece of legislation (Lara, 1986; see also Hayami, Quisumbing and Adriano, 1990; Riedinger, 1995).[23]

Almost all peasant organizations and their NGO and social movement allies across the political spectrum rejected CARP. It was too far from the popular demand for a progressive, if not revolutionary, type of land reform (Lara, 1986; Lara and Morales, 1990; Rodriguez, 1987). The passage of a less-than-desired version of land reform led to the consolidation of various national peasant organizations in the country under the umbrella of CPAR, the first-ever ideologically and politically broad national coalition of peasant associations in the country's history. CPAR was at the forefront of the advocacy to reject CARP and call for new legislation on land reform; at the same time it called for widespread peasant-initiated land reform through land occupation (Putzel, 1995, 1998; Franco, 1999a; Magadia, 2003). The rejection stance of peasant organizations vis-à-vis CARP was the main feature of state–society relations in land reform implementation throughout the Aquino administration, which lasted until mid-1992 (Lara and Morales, 1990).

2.4 KEY FEATURES OF CARP

CARP is a public policy that falls into neither the ideal type of voluntary-non-redistributive nor expropriationary-redistributive reform. While having some degree of expropriationary power, it incorporates elements that are voluntary and non-redistributive. The CARP law mandates that all farmlands, private and public, regardless of tenurial and productivity conditions be subject to agrarian reform (with a relatively few exceptions such as military reservations and religious and educational sites). There are three broad types of reform: redistribution of private and public lands, lease (including leasehold on lands legally retained by landlords and stewardship contracts for some public lands), and, on a small scale and limited to the first few years of CARP implementation, a stock distribution option for some large corporate farms.

The far-reaching formal coverage of the CARP law makes it more progressive than most other post-1980 land reform laws elsewhere. Such laws elsewhere, as in Brazil (Hall, 1990), Kerala, India (Herring, 1990), and Zimbabwe (Bratton, 1990), do not cover productive, commercial farmlands. Thus, based on the original 1988 scope, CARP intended to reform tenure relations on 10.3 million hectares of the country's farmland via land redistribution (and to a limited extent, stock distribution); the estimated number of beneficiaries could reach some 4 million landless and land-poor peasant households, comprising close to 80 percent of the agricultural population. Additionally, some 2 million hectares of farms smaller than 5 hectares (retained farms by landlords) were made subject to leasehold reform that would benefit an estimated 1 million poor tenant households. Though landlords would have the right to retain 5 hectares, they could also hold 3 hectares for each legitimate heir on the condition that any such heir should be fifteen years of age by June 1988 and be willing to directly work or manage the farm. Private lands and some government-owned lands were to be redistributed by the DAR, while redistribution of public alienable and disposable (A&D) lands and forest lands under the Community-Based Forest Management (CBFM) program were to be implemented by the Department of Environment and Natural Resources (DENR).[24] It should be noted that the average farm size in the country is 2 hectares, while the land reform award ceiling is fixed at 3 hectares.

CARP is being implemented within the structural and institutional constraints of the Philippine political setting — indeed within the very setting that it aims to change. During implementation, CARP has thus been brought to the crucible of state–society relations, where various dynamic factors influence policy processes and outcomes. The implementation process has been a tale of struggle between pro-reform and anti-reform forces within the state and society, pushing CARP in the direction of either the voluntary-non-redistributive or expropriationary-redistributive policy currents.

The pro- and anti-reform conflict internalized within CARP is reflected partly in the various CARP land acquisition modes for private lands. First is the OLT program, which was the mechanism used for tenanted rice and corn lands under the Marcos-era land reform program and later was integrated within CARP. Second, devised to reduce landlord resistance to reform, the VOS increases the cash portion of landlord compensation by 5 percent with a corresponding 5 percent decrease in the bonds portion. Third is the VLT mode, which aspires to win landlord cooperation with the program. The VLT provides for the direct transfer of land to peasants under terms mutually agreed between peasants and landlords with the government's role confined to information provision and contract enforcement. A landlord who is interested in complying with the CARP law via VLT is expected to discuss and agree with the potential beneficiaries the transaction terms: land price, mode of payment, and set of beneficiaries. Upon full agreement, the parties submit their VLT proposal to the DAR, which approves or rejects the plan. If the proposal is rejected, the CARP process restarts and may or may not take the VLT route. If the proposal is accepted, the transaction is deemed a successful CARP land redistribution process and is officially reported as such. The difference between VOS and VLT is that in the former the landlord sells land to the state while in the latter the landlord sells directly to the peasants. It is a significant difference that has strategic implications for these schemes' potential for redistributive reform (or absence of it). Both VOS and VLT operate in the context of expropriation; that is, if landlords refuse VOS or VLT, their estates could nonetheless be acquired by the state. Finally, CARP's last acquisition mode is compulsory acquisition (CA) through which land is expropriated with or without the landlord's cooperation. OLT is akin to CA.

Moreover, landholdings under the control of government financial institutions (GFIs) are subject to redistribution; public lands earlier segregated and earmarked for the Marcos livelihood program, KKK (*Kilusang Kabuhayan at Kaunlaran*), are included in the coverage. The remainder of the friar lands (landed estates) is likewise included, and public lands set aside for settlement programs, before and after the CARP law, are also up for redistribution. Finally, other public lands under different legal classifications can be distributed via DENR's A&D lands and CBFM programs. Some related acquisition and distribution policies and mechanisms are important to note. For one, the stock distribution option (SDO) is a distinct mode designed for corporate farms. CARP exempts such lands from redistribution if the owner opts for corporate stock sharing with peasant beneficiaries through the option. Moreover, the acquisition of more or less 50,000 hectares of large, productive commercial farms, for example, banana plantations, was deferred in 1988 for a ten-year period, ostensibly to allow plantation owners to recoup their investments and to prepare farmworkers for eventual takeover (de León and Escobido, 2004; Borras and Franco, 2005). During this deferment period, the plantation owners were compelled by law to implement production and profit-sharing schemes. Under certain conditions, peasant beneficiaries are allowed to lease out (leaseback) awarded lands to an investor. Acquired landholdings can be transferred to individuals or cooperatives, although the bias is toward the former (Hayami, Quisumbing and Adriano, 1990).

Meanwhile, the modes of payment to landlords and by peasants follow the more common approaches to agrarian reform. Landlord compensation is based on "just compensation" and computed based on various factors such as land productivity and tax declaration; it is supposed to be computed at slightly below the market price of the land. Land distribution is a transaction between government and peasant recipients, who pay for land parcels at rates determined by "affordability." The gap between just compensation and affordable price is subsidized by government. The beneficiaries are issued a Certificate of Land Ownership Award (CLOA). Stewardship contracts good for twenty-five years, renewable for another twenty-five years, are issued to CBFM beneficiaries. Public A&D land beneficiaries can secure similar instruments, or free patents, or even CLOAs depending on the actual condition of the land. Awarded landholdings cannot be sold or rented out by the beneficiary for ten years after the award.

CARP was provided a fund of PhP 50 billion in 1988 and was mandated to finish the land acquisition and distribution components within ten years' time, or by 1998. All proceeds of the government's effort to recover the so-called ill-gotten wealth of Marcos and his cronies were supposed to be automatically transferred to the CARP fund, in addition to its regular fund allocation from the General Appropriations Act (GAA).[25] By the end of 1997, it was clear that the program would not be fully completed. After a series of complex political events, a new law was passed extending the implementation period for another ten years, or until 2008, with a new budget cap of PhP 50 billion (Borras, 1999: 80–84).

CARP contains a number of exclusions, among them military reservations, penal colonies, educational and research fields, timberlands, and some church areas. Undeveloped hills with a slope of 18 degrees or more are also excluded. In the mid-1990s, further exemptions were introduced, namely agricultural sectors that are "less dependent on land," for example, poultry, livestock, salt beds, and fishponds. Yet, these exemptions are not automatic. The owners of these lands must be able to demonstrate at all times that the lands are indeed used for the purposes cited. For cattle ranches, a ratio of one head of cattle for every hectare of land must be upheld, otherwise the land will be expropriated and redistributed. These farms are also compelled by law to implement labour-related reforms, including compulsory production and profit sharing.

The CARP scope (DAR and DENR jurisdictions) has undergone a series of revisions. Between 1988 and 1996, the scope was reduced from 10.3 to 8.1 million hectares (see Borras, 2003b). This is part of what the DAR under Garilao called "data cleanup." Table 2.8 presents the DAR scope before and after the series of revisions made between 1988 and 2005. Major revisions were also made in the DENR scope, with some of its original scope transferred to DAR jurisdiction and some dropped altogether. There has been no full and satisfactory explanation for such a huge deduction in scope except for the government claim that it was due to legal and administrative reasons.

More than twenty state agencies, large and small, are directly involved in land redistribution processes for different purposes. Within the DAR bureaucracy, various bureaus are involved at different levels in land reform implementation. These bureaus are of three broad types: quasi-judicial, policy, and executive. The quasi-judicial body is the DAR Adjudication Board (DARAB), which functions as the main adjudicator of legal cases related to agrarian disputes. This organization has representatives at the regional and provincial levels, the Regional Agrarian Reform Adjudicators (RARADs) and the Provincial Agrarian Reform Adjudicators (PARADs) respectively. Among other legal cases, DARAB handles disputes about just compensation, although a landlord can opt to apply to a Special Agrarian Court (SAC) for such appeals. The SAC is a special arm directly linked with the regular courts; a SAC judge is a regular court judge. DAR decisions on agrarian disputes can be appealed before the Office of the President (OP), which, in turn, can be appealed before the Supreme Court. But the CARP law states that the land acquisition and distribution process can proceed despite pending appeals by landlords. The process of land value assessment, compensation to landlords, and amortization payments by peasants is handled by the government-owned Land Bank of the Philippines (LBP).[26] Meanwhile, the highest oversight, policy-related body for CARP is the PARC, a multi-agency and multisectoral body

Table 2.8
DAR's land redistribution scope(s), deductions, and accomplishment, 1972–2005

Land type (in hectares)	Original scope	Deductions			Working scope	"Balance"
		Quantity	% of original scope	% of total deduction		
OLT	705,725	65,567	9.3	2.76	640,158	59,839
PAL>50	1,081,433	367,861	34.02	15.48	713,572	218,371
VOS	308,893	34,341	11.12	1.45	274,551	46,630
CA	652,488	323,080	49.52	13.6	329,408	141,601
VLT	120,052	10,440	8.7	0.44	109,612	30,140
PAL24–50	488,101	273,558	56.05	11.52	214,542	91,404
VOS	85,744	9,920	11.57	0.42	75,823	21,894
CA	340,506	251,958	74.0	10.62	88,549	62,357
VLT	61,850	11,680	18.9	0.5	50,170	7,153
PAL5–24	2,241,100	1,383,712	61.74	58.25	857,388	234,289
VOS	272,325	21,664	7.95	0.91	250,661	53,293
CA	1,511,777	1,303,863	86.25	54.9	207,914	131,696
VLT	456,998	58,185	12.73	2.45	398,813	49,300
PAL<5	98,715	29,149	29.53	1.23	69,566	7,375
VOS	25,013	623	2.5	0.02	24,389	5,347
VLT	73,702	28,526	38.7	1.2	45,176	2,028
GFI	284,099	81,404	28.65	3.43	202,695	33,137
KKK	934,971	160,104	17.12	6.74	774,866	24,696
LE	71,807	605	0.84	0.02	71,201	543
SETT	770,495	13,651	1.77	0.57	756,844	16,299
TOTAL	6,676,444	2,375,612	35.58	100.00	4,300,832	685,954

Notes: OLT = Operation Land Transfer (from the 1972 Marcos land reform on tenanted rice and corn land); PAL = private agricultural land; PAL>50 = private agricultural land 50 hectares and above; PAL24–50 = private agricultural land 24 to 50 hectares in size; VOS = voluntary offer-to-sell; VLT = voluntary land transfer; GFI = government financial institution; KKK = *Kilusang Kabuhayan at Kaunlaran* — a development program started by Marcos that segregated some government-owned land for redistribution; LE = landed estate — this mainly concerns the outstanding balance in the century-old (Spanish) friar lands; SETT = settlement program that involves government-owned land. See also memorandum from the Presidential Agrarian Reform Council (PARC) Secretariat addressed to the PARC Executive Committee regarding DENR's newly revised scope on public A&D lands dated 27 January 1997 (PARC, 1997; PARC-EC, 1997).

Source: DAR-MIS (2005).

formally headed by the president of the republic. PARC is anchored at the DAR and comprised of all CARP implementing agencies, with representation of the landlord group and the peasant sector. It functions as a consultative council at the national level. At the provincial level, PARC takes the form of the Provincial Agrarian Reform Consultative Committee (PARCCOM), and at the village level, the *Barangay* Agrarian Reform Committee (BARC). In 1994, the PARC's Audit Management and Investigation Committee (AMIC) was created to conduct annual comprehensive internal program audits. The bulk of implementation tasks, however, rests with the main executive body of the DAR, headed by the DAR Secretary, with powers filtering down through the regional directors, Provincial Agrarian Reform Officers (PAROs), and Municipal Agrarian Reform Officers (MAROs) to the lowest ranked employee, the Agrarian Reform Program Technician (ARPT). There are 15,000 DAR employees nationwide.

Critics of CARP, academics and activists, predicted that no significant redistribution of land would be achieved through CARP because of its various flaws. Among the key criticisms are the following: (i) the 5-hectare retention limit is too high and will exempt a substantial portion of agricultural lands; (ii) the additional 3-hectare award for every qualified heir of the landlord will exempt more lands from redistribution; (iii) the adoption of the principle of just compensation means essentially full market price and will thus make the program unaffordable for both the government and the beneficiaries; (iv) the inclusion of SDO as an option for landlords will effectively exclude large corporate farms from reform; (v) the leaseback option will facilitate awarded lands being reverted back to landlords; (vi) the deferment of the land acquisition and distribution process on big commercial farms will give plantation owners a way to evade land reform in the end. Such criticisms are not merely theoretical but are firmly grounded in a concrete analysis of the historical political and economic conditions of the country.[27]

2.5 INITIAL OUTCOMES

The actual land redistribution accomplishment of CARP by 2006 is unexpected from two perspectives: on the one hand, it is far below the earlier optimistic projections by government; on the other hand, it significantly surpasses the earlier pessimistic predictions of CARP critics. Thus, CARP's land redistribution accomplishment is somewhere between these two poles.[28] As Putzel (2002: 219) admits, "The programme has certainly touched a far greater proportion of the country's land and rural population than its early critics predicted." While the nationally aggregated data (tables 2.9 and 2.10) tends to be nearer the claims of the government, closer examination reveals that this is unlikely to be the case. Succeeding chapters provide a more complete explanation.

Table 2.9
Total land redistribution by land type under the Department of Agrarian Reform (DAR),* 1972–2005

Land area (in hectares)	
Private lands	*2,036,201*
OLT	576,556
CA	289,250
VOS	494,133
VLT	514,277
GFI	161,985
Government-owned lands:	*1,530,790*
KKK	737,512
LE	70,658
Settlement	722,620
Total	*3,566,991*

Table 2.10
Total land redistribution by land type under the Department of Environment and Natural Resources (DENR), 1987–2004**

Land area (in hectares)	
Public/state lands	*2,337,647*
A&D	1,295,559
CBFM	1,042,088

Notes:
* DAR data = 1972 to 31 March 2005
** DENR data = beginning 1987 to 31 December 2004
OLT = Operation Land Transfer; CA = compulsory acquisition; VOS = voluntary offer-to-sell; VLT = voluntary land transfer; GFI = government financial institution; KKK = *Kilusang Kabuhayan at Kaunlaran*; LE = landed estate; A&D = alienable and disposable land; CBFM = Community-Based Forest Management.

Sources: DAR-MIS (2005); DENR (2004).

A number of observations can be drawn from the tabulated data. First, nearly three-fourths of CARP's total working scope has apparently been redistributed to peasant beneficiaries (see tables 2.9 and 2.10). The number of beneficiary households is some 3 million. The total redistributed land accounts for a little more than 50 percent of the total farmland, while the number of household beneficiaries accounts for two-fifths of the total rural population (see table 2.11). The leasehold accomplishment is also likely to be incomplete, but it is substantial at 1.5 million hectares, which has the potential to benefit one million tenant households (see table 2.12). This set of data is comparable to significant land reform initiatives elsewhere historically. Second, the bulk of the accomplishment is in public lands (DAR and DENR), accounting for two-thirds of the total CARP output. (The GFI category essentially involves private lands.) Third, the bulk of the DAR's balance is mainly in private lands outside of OLT (rice and corn land) coverage. Fourth, the DENR data is unclear on whether and how many hectares of ancestral domain claims were included, because circumstantial evidence shows that some ancestral domain claims are also reported in the earlier CBFM accomplishment reports.

In short, the land redistribution outcome is mainly in public lands and on OLT rice and corn farms, which is partly an indication of the government's inconsistency in confronting private landlords. Thus, this study shares the common criticisms of Philippine land redistribution, but it goes beyond them. If we follow the argument of some land reform scholars and most Philippine activists that there is no real redistributive reform in public lands, then what CARP has achieved in real terms according to this assumption is not more than 1.7 million hectares of private lands.[29] This could benefit not more than a million peasant households. Most land reform observers and analysts

Table 2.11
Number of beneficiaries of land reform programs, 1972–2000

Program	Number of beneficiary households
Land transfer under DAR	1,697,566
Land transfer under DENR	1,273,845
Leasehold operations	1,098,948
Stock distribution option (SDO)	8,975
Total	4,079,334

Source: Reyes (2002: 15).

Table 2.12 Yearly summary of leasehold accomplishment, area in hectares, by region and by year, 1986–2003

	Phil	1	2	CAR	3	4	5	6	7	8	9	10	11	12	13
up to 1986	572,999	80,736	55,312	4,209	112,636	68,284	30,090	73,759	18,980	33,691	12,343	24,885	36,975	21,099	0
1987	5,250	92	2,206	93	1,884	0	0	0	554	0	422	0	0	(1)	0
1988	17,330	95	2,400	1,647	944	0	0	0	0	0	11,583	0	661	0	0
1989	17,643	0	0	1,871	0	614	0	0	12,797	138	23	0	2,201	0	0
1990	75,267	5,388	1,808	213	6,713	1,211	23	2,358	1321	3,534	8,221	12,662	30,918	897	0
1991	258,900	13,753	1,921	396	6,289	26,810	410	3,991	11,396	30,945	50,731	77,878	34,380	0	0
1992	203,646	11,473	18,015	340	4,272	17,035	1,631	5,681	20,087	35,597	28,929	34,847	22,728	3,011	0
1993	123,269	11,141	3,517	93	4,222	9,740	2,570	8,171	8,750	22,858	17,703	16,022	15,530	2,952	0
1994	89,521	11,585	3,666	74	1,626	8,218	1,402	6,310	4,819	20,325	3,321	10,651	14,922	2,602	0
1995	33,976	2,963	1,988	25	849	3,061	1,194	1,579	1,769	9,191	1,663	403	7,311	1,980	0
1996	27,527	1,183	1,453	0	1,086	1,505	886	1,828	1,118	9,170	523	3,766	4,990	19	0
1997	14,762	191	489	9	433	1,415	2,060	579	317	2,532	375	2,978	2,691	396	297
1998	13,450	111	1,338	12	396	486	790	1,431	530	3,485	166	1,451	2,657	398	199
1999	15,202	108	1,031	24	341	1,976	670	1,172	820	2,727	290	1,196	2,716	1,681	450
2000	14,297	224	853	11	315	758	853	1,148	1,289	3,008	648	823	1,743	2,290	334
2001	15,190	5	620	0	312	1,776	2,492	900	729	5,200	360	945	622	1,185	294
2002	18,349	204	887	7	525	2,524	1,553	1,172	1,266	4,533	297	2,975	674	1,851	402
2003	29,983	223	1,117	0	493	4,298	4,002	1,397	1,269	6,242	1,445	2,660	709	6,962	577
Total	1,483,039	139,043	95,997	9,017	142,006	141,113	42,579	108,007	84,546	17,7201	136,941	187,562	180,423	37,324	1,280

Notes: Excluding the Autonomous Region of Muslim Mindanao (ARMM). Phil = the Philippines, national total; Region 1 = Ilocos; Region 2 = Cagayan Valley; CAR = Cordillera Autonomous Region; Region 3 = Central Luzon; Region 4 = Southern Tagalog; Region 5 = Bicol; Region 6 = Western Visayas; Region 7 = Central Visayas; Region 8 = Eastern Visayas; Region 9 = Southwestern Mindanao; Region 10 = Northern Mindanao; Region 11 = Southern Mindanao; Region 12 = Central Mindanao; Region 13 = Northeastern Mindanao.

Source: DAR-PS (2003).

in the Philippines and elsewhere (political activists, media practitioners, and academics) tend to follow this line of reasoning, using the nationally aggregated data to cross-examine the land reform process and outcomes, draw conclusions, and chart policy or political or research actions based on the private-public lands divide. This type of data and analysis is relevant; it is also powerful. It can explain several observable processes and events, as demonstrated in this chapter. In fact, using broadly the same methodology, the World Bank has joined the pessimistic chorus against CARP, but with a different agenda: It wants to put a stop to the state-led CARP in order to replace it with its market-led agrarian reform (World Bank, 1996, 1997a, 1997b; Deininger et al., 2000). Nevertheless, these nationally aggregated data reveal less than they conceal. They are informative in part, but in part deceiving and misleading. On the one hand, some land redistribution outcomes reported under the private land category involve no real redistribution and reform. On the other hand, some land redistribution outcomes reported under the public land category involve real redistribution and reform. Limiting analysis to the aggregated data (usually quantitative) at the national level and within the private-public land dichotomy can lead to, at best, a partially correct analysis and, at worst, a grossly erroneous reading of the reality, as will be demonstrated in succeeding chapters.

2.6 CONCLUDING REMARKS

This chapter presented an overview of the socioeconomic structures and sociopolitical institutions of the Philippines, focusing on the agrarian structure, which is both the context and the object of the empirical inquiry of this study. It showed that popular demand for land and tenancy reforms has been significant in the political and policy discourse of the country during the past century, and that the Philippine state responded to this demand with a combination of limited tenancy and land reforms, and settlements combined with co-optation, and repression. The demands and actual gains for redistributive reforms, however, have been ratcheted up over time, leading to today's comprehensive land redistribution program (CARP). By 2006, CARP officially claimed to have redistributed nearly 6 million hectares of land to more than 3 million peasant households. If this is true, it accounts for nearly half of the country's total agricultural lands and two-fifths of the total rural households, respectively. This nationally aggregated land redistribution outcome falls below the optimistic projections and claims of its ardent supporters, but it also reaches significantly beyond the pessimistic predictions and claims of CARP critics.

But this data is contested, and the criticisms are not without solid basis, despite their being unsystematic. In the next chapter it will be revealed that the probable actual land redistribution outcome is likely to be far less than the official claims. Meanwhile, chapter 2 has shown that population growth rates continue to be quite high, and the land frontier has been exhausted — at the same time as global agrarian restructuring has had quite a negative impact on the Philippine agricultural sector. This is likely to lessen even further any possible positive impact of the partial but significant accomplishment of land reform. A fuller understanding of this officially reported CARP outcome requires careful inquiry into the disaggregated parts of the official data, in order to reveal actual processes and outcomes at the more local level, including those not captured by government data. Guided by the theoretical discussions in the introduction and chapter 1, and following the central aim of this study, the following chapters proceed with further empirical investigation.

CHAPTER THREE

CARP'S NON-REDISTRIBUTIVE POLICIES AND OUTCOMES

> When doctrines command widespread agreement, the time has usually come for a re-examination; when men [sic] who otherwise disagree on fundamental political values agree on an issue of importance, they are probably using crucial terms in widely differing senses; when radical rhetoric becomes fashionable, it may well acquire non-radical implications .... So it is with land reform today .... [P]eople think they are talking about the same thing, when in fact they define crucial terms in radically different ways. More perverse still, there are those who use terms precisely on account of their ambiguity. (David Lehmann, 1974a: 13, 14)

3.1 INTRODUCTION

This chapter aims to demonstrate when and how land reform outcomes do not constitute redistributive reform. Policies and outcomes would be considered non-redistributive when there was no real transfer of wealth and power from the landed to the landless and near-landless classes — that is, there was no real pro-poor reform in the actually existing social and production relations. This chapter also aspires to assess the extent of these types of outcomes nationwide. Section 3.2 provides the empirical bases for the classification of some policies and outcomes as non-redistributive with reference to specific cases. Section 3.3 examines the possible extent and geographic distribution of non-redistributive outcomes.

3.2 NON-REDISTRIBUTIVE POLICIES AND OUTCOMES

There are various ways non-redistributive policies and policy outcomes can be seen in a land reform policy, and there are at least eleven ways in which these types of outcomes have manifested in the CARP process: (i) voluntary land transfer (VLT), (ii) stock distribution option (SDO), (iii) overpriced land transfers, (iv) "uninstalled" beneficiaries, (v) land reform reversals, (vi) deliberate padding of reports, (vii) non-redistributive practices in settlement areas and on other public lands, (viii) cheating in pre-expropriation mandatory production and profit sharing, (ix) shrinking the CARP scope, (x) clear-cut failed attempts at land redistribution, and (xi) fictitious titles sold to the DAR. These are examined here, along with the World Bank's MLAR initiative.

Voluntary land transfer (VLT)

The concept of the market-oriented VLT scheme as a policy option in the context of land reform policy discourse is not new in Philippine history. When the American colonial government took over at the beginning of the past century, instead of confiscating the lands amassed by the Catholic Church during the Spanish era and redistributing them to poor peasants, it decided to employ a market-based approach. In 1903, the colonial government purchased at market price 158,676 hectares of the "friar lands" for the amount of US$ 6,043,217. It paid the church cash from loans secured from commercial banks in the United States at commercial interest rates and resold the lands at full acquisition cost, including the cost of loan interest. Only the rich, including American corporations, were able to buy the lands (Corpuz, 1997: 266–270). These "friar lands" remained an issue during the several peasant revolts in the 1930s (Constantino, 1975: 303–305, 375; Connolly, 1992; McAndrew, 1994). Despite the friar lands fiasco, and reacting to persistent peasant unrest, succeeding Filipino administrations attempted to combine limited tenancy reforms with a land sales transactions–oriented approach. According to Benedict Kerkvliet (1977: 198–199), "The Roxas administration (1946–1948) also began to purchase a few landed estates ... that were to be resold to tenants." This was nothing new, however. President Quezon's administration (1935–1940) began similar purchases in the late 1930s. Kerkvliet (ibid.) explains, "The purchases never could have solved agrarian problems in Central Luzon. The acreage involved was infinitesimal. Furthermore, high prices for the land prohibited most tenants from paying for the land later. Beyond that, improprieties and corruption plagued the government agencies responsible for the administration of these lands." In 1988, the VLT scheme was enshrined within the CARP law. Since then, it has been implemented to an unprecedented extent. In early 2002, the Macapagal-Arroyo administration announced that it had adopted VLT as the main strategy for land redistribution.

Closer examination of the VLT transactions reveals their non-redistributive nature. This is done by analyzing empirical evidence from the annual CARP internal program audit and other cases. First, however, it is important to introduce the CARP internal audit system. One of the reforms carried out by DAR Secretary Ernesto Garilao (1992–1998) was the creation in early 1994 of the AMIC under the inter-agency PARC. This was partly the Garilao DAR's response to public clamour for greater transparency and accountability in CARP implementation. The AMIC is composed of representatives of the DAR Internal Audit Service, the PARC Secretariat, and peasant and landowner sectors represented in the PARC. Among the main tasks of the AMIC is to validate official land redistribution reports by confirming beneficiaries; inspection, verification, and approval of surveys; validation of the land valuation process; and verification of landowner compensation, title registration, and distribution of land award certificates. AMIC works via sampling, examining two provinces in every region and three municipalities from each of the two pre-selected provinces:

> [T]he first two provinces in the region in terms of [land acquisition and distribution] accomplishments will be selected for the audit. In case the first two provinces have already been covered by the previous CARP audit activities, get the next two ranking provinces; and ... in choosing the three municipalities to be audited within the selected province, the three municipalities will be randomly selected from the top 50% of the municipalities in terms of [land acquisition and distribution] accomplishments within the province. (PARC-AMIC, 2001: 3)

Moreover, in each audited municipality about 10 percent of land acquisition and distribution is closely examined. The AMIC's systematic and thorough audits since 1994 cover all provinces in the country.[1] Qualitatively and quantitatively, they are thus a reliable source of rich empirical data about the internal workings of CARP implementation; its large sample population provides evidence of the possible extent of problems in VLT. This study draws on case studies from these reports to provide a better idea about the nature of VLT. To deepen our understanding of VLT transactions, this study also examines additional case studies researched first-hand by the author. It identifies four main ways in which VLT has produced non-redistributive outcomes in land reform: (i) straightforward land reform evasion; (ii) petty but widespread rent-seeking; (iii) the lease-to-own scheme; and (iv) VLT-based integrated schemes.

Straightforward land reform evasion
Straightforward evasions of expropriation via VLT are seen in three broad patterns: First, a quite common evasion tactic is to declare children, relatives, and other dummies as beneficiaries. The CARP law allows children and other relatives to become "preferred" beneficiaries only if they were at least fifteen years of age as of 1988 and were actually tilling or willing to till the land. In normal administrative procedures, such transactions are listed as retention rights claims of landlords and so are excluded from the land acquisition and distribution accomplishment reports (being in the "non-reform sector"). However, by reporting such transfers as VLT transactions, these cases can be categorized as land reform accomplishment (in the "reform sector"). Evidence shows not only that many of the VLT "transfers" sampled from the AMIC audit reports were made in favour of family members but also that these family members were often not legally qualified to become beneficiaries because they were minors and/or not working on the farm. For example, "In the sample municipalities of Masbate and Sorsogon, most of the awardees under the VLT scheme were members of the family and relatives of the landowners. Hence the partitioning of the landowner's properties among ... heirs was merely facilitated and costs for documentation, transfer taxes, surveys, and titling all charged to CARP funds." In another case in Iligan, Lanao del Norte, of the twenty-six farmer beneficiaries interviewed during the audit, some were not actually tilling the lands awarded to them, "one being a manager of a drugstore, two having migrated to the USA prior to distribution of the said land, nine being full-time students and still minors and one being manager of a printing press" (PARC-AMIC, 1997: 10).[2]

The second type of evasion is the practice of declaring as beneficiaries people who are completely unaware of the transaction. While likely not as widespread as the first, this second type is indicative of the creativity and daring of some landlords in connivance with corrupt local government officials in their attempts to circumvent a potentially redistributive land reform policy. The CARP law imposes a ten-year land rental/sales prohibition. After this period the anticipation is that the land will be formally "resold" to the "former" owner or family members thereof, thus completing a cycle of land transfer on paper without any change in actual control of property rights and agrarian relations. An AMIC-documented case hints at this practice: "In Tandag, Surigao del Sur, CLOAs ... were awarded to three farmer-beneficiaries ... who were not aware of the award, ignorant of the owner and location of the landholding, and not willing to till the land."

The third type is where peasants are coerced to agree to become "paper beneficiaries." In this type, the landlord is declared to have complied with the land reform law, while the old tenancy sharing arrangement between landlord and tenants/farmworkers continues, despite the formalities of land transfer in official documents. Again, the landlord anticipates an on-paper resale after the ten-year rental/sales prohibition. This evasion type is perhaps the most difficult to document since when it occurs, it involves a politically and economically powerful, usually despotic landlord. This is the case of a large landholding in Central Luzon, but the on-paper beneficiaries refused to talk openly about it for fear of reprisal from their landlord-patron.[3]

Petty but widespread rent-seeking
The VLT scheme is also used as a money-making enterprise by some local DAR officials. Though similar to the cases cited above, the difference in this second method of rendering transactions non-redistributive is that it happens more at the initiative of local DAR officials than the landlords. This seems to occur in two main ways: First, it is a well-known "secret" within the internal circles of the agencies associated with land reform that some government officials coach the landlords on how to evade land reform via VLT. This is done on the condition that a set of beneficiaries that the government official provides, in addition to the landlord's preferred and paper beneficiaries, are included in the final set of beneficiaries. For example,

> Four (4) children aged 9, 11, 13, and 15 years of Pangasinan's incumbent [provincial agrarian reform officer (PARO)] were made beneficiaries .... DARMO-Matalam [North Cotabato] awarded CLOAs to four absentee tillers .... Same is true to the landholding of Brigida Cubita whose properties were awarded to her 12 children who are mostly non-occupants of the said landholdings. The rest of her landholdings were further subdivided to the children of her brothers Domingo Cubita and Victor Cubita, who was a former PARO of North Cotabato province .... In Pigcawayan, North Cotabato, [the municipal office's] 1993 record showed that there were 64 CLOAs actually received by the farmer-beneficiaries involving 80 hectares mostly under the VLT scheme. Five (5) sample beneficiaries were confirmed, but two ... were professional government employees.[4]

Second, DAR officials report ordinary land sales that occur in the village or *municipio* as land redistribution accomplishment under the VLT scheme. In so doing, local DAR officials effectively give the parties to the land sales attractive incentives to commit fraud: free survey and title generation and exemption from transfer taxes. For example, "In Esperanza, Agusan del Sur, a sale transaction of an agricultural land in *Barangay* Dacutan owned by Carmen Sire and sold to Antonio Polizon ... covering an area of 5 hectares was processed as VLT."[5] Moreover, a former provincial DAR official confided,

> I even discovered that through VLT the buyer in an ordinary land sale deal is declared a beneficiary and the land sale process a CARP transaction. I knew personally a VLT transaction in Camarines Sur where the buyer who did not know that the seller made the land sale transaction within VLT came to my office to have his CLOA cancelled because he said he is not a land reform beneficiary but a legitimate land buyer .... Most VLT reports are for accomplishment padding by municipal DAR officials; you would know because these are landholdings that are not even part of the CARP working scope, then suddenly they are reported as accomplishment.[6]

It must be noted that the CARP land redistribution scheme should include only farms with a land size of 5 hectares or more. However, in the VLT land redistribution accomplishment report, a category has been included for a "5 hectares and less" farm size.

"Lease to own" schemes
A lease-to-own type of evasion appears to have become popular among landlords, multinational corporations, and DAR officials in some parts of Mindanao since 2000.[7] These are the regions where global fruit giants such as Dole are rapidly expanding their production of fruits such as banana and pineapple. This production expansion is of a relatively newer kind, as it is no longer based on plantation production, where huge tracts of contiguous lands are directly controlled and managed by a multinational company or large domestic landed elite. Rather, the current expansion is founded on smaller farms, and production and exchange relations revolve around various types of either contract farming or lease arrangements (see de la Rosa, 2005; Vellema, 2002; Borras and Franco, 2005).

Such a lease-type arrangement works as follows: The landlord and the beneficiary enter into a VLT arrangement; the landlord is thus deemed to have complied with the land reform law. A key aspect of the arrangement is that the set of beneficiaries must be totally acceptable to and approved by the landlord, otherwise the latter will not voluntarily transfer the land. Naturally, the priority beneficiaries — those most acceptable to the landlord — are the landlord's children and relatives and other dummies. But on many occasions, legitimate tenants and farmworkers become beneficiaries as well. The terms of reference of the contract are then submitted to the local DAR which, it appears, automatically approves such contracts and quickly reports the transaction as land redistribution accomplishment. Then the landlord and the beneficiaries, together with the local DAR officials, submit the same landholding to a multinational company — Dole in the case of North Cotabato province — for a special lease arrangement. Dole's standard terms for such an arrangement are (i) lease rental for the land is set at PhP 12,000 per hectare per year (US$ 200 at the 2004 foreign exchange rate); (ii) the contract is for ten years, renewable for another ten years at the sole option of Dole; (iii) during the first seven years all of the monthly rentals are paid by Dole to the landlord; (iv) after seven years of regular payment by Dole to the landlord, the beneficiary shall be deemed to have fully paid for the land, and so the land shall be fully the beneficiary's property; (v) starting the eighth year the beneficiary shall begin to receive the yearly rental of PhP 12,000 per hectare until the end of the contract in the tenth (or 20th) year; (vi) meanwhile, starting in the first year until the end of the contract, the beneficiary shall be employed as a worker on the Dole-operated farm at minimum wage, which was PhP 160 per day in early 2002; (vii) Dole bankrolls the entire VLT process, paying a "finder's fee" of PhP 1,000 per hectare to whoever can bring in a landlord with a set of beneficiaries for the scheme (reportedly, many local DAR and local government officials have ended up being paid handsomely with finder's fees). Dole also awards a "signing bonus" to contracted peasants and pays for notarization and production of documents. Dole retains all documents, however, including the CLOAs.

VLT-based integrated schemes
There are also VLT-based integrated arrangements. Four such cases are examined here: (i) the Danding Cojuangco joint venture, (ii) the Dole-DARBCI leaseback, (iii) the Floirendo leaseback, and (iv) the Marsman profit-sharing scheme. Combined, these cases directly affect some 20,000 farmworkers. Although no official data are available on the extent to which VLT-based integrated schemes have been implemented nationwide, perhaps more important is the profound impact of cases such as these on the politics of land reform more generally: These cases involve big landowning families and multinational companies in the country, and their actions are likely to influence the course of land reform implementation throughout the nation.

The estate involved in the *Danding Cojuangco joint venture scheme* is the more than 4,000-hectare orchard worked by more than 1,000 farmworkers in the province of Negros Occidental (central-western Philippines). This world-class, modern orchard, formerly a sugar cane plantation, is owned by one of the most powerful landlord-businessmen in the country, Eduardo "Danding" Cojuangco, Jr. A crony of former president Ferdinand Marcos, Danding was accused of amassing tens of thousands of hectares of land under questionable circumstances. But Danding is a resilient politician. He survived the 1986–1988 regime transition and became influential in the subsequent administrations of Joseph Estrada and Gloria Macapagal-Arroyo (Parreño, 2003).

Some time in the mid-1990s, Danding started to negotiate with the DAR (Ramos administration, 1992–1998) regarding how CARP could be implemented at the orchard. His proposal was to employ VLT to enable his farmworkers to buy the land directly on the condition that it would automatically be placed under a joint venture agreement between his company and the worker-beneficiaries' cooperative. Payment for the land was to come from the dividends that beneficiaries were expected to earn. The terms of the joint venture proposal were as follows: (i) the government would not spend money on land acquisition, since it would be a direct deal between Danding and his workers via VLT; (ii) Danding would retain ownership of the newly installed modern plantation infrastructure, such as irrigation pipes and farm machinery; (iii) Danding would invest in the installation of processing plants and a modern management system; (iv) the land price would be set at PhP 350,000 per hectare; (v) the workers would be employed in the joint venture company; (vi) ownership of the land would be collective in the name of the farmworker-beneficiaries' cooperative; (vii) joint venture shares were to be allotted 30 percent–70 percent in favour of Danding; (viii) the joint venture agreement would be in effect for twenty-five years renewable for another twenty-five years at the sole option of Danding; (ix) the beneficiaries' cooperative would put its CLOA into the joint venture company as equity. The negotiation of this special land reform deal was not concluded at the time, however, because the term of office of the Ramos administration ended (in mid-1998), although the CLOA was generated during that period.[8]

A new round of negotiation started when the Estrada administration assumed office in mid-1998. Danding's offer remained basically the same as under the previous administration, with two exceptions: First, Danding had purged from "his" list of beneficiaries several dozen workers who had been critical of the scheme. Effectively, Danding was the one deciding who would be included in and excluded from the beneficiary list. Moreover, this was done in the context of Danding's systematic harassment of autonomous organizing initiatives among the farmworkers, the latter having failed to gain substantial ground.⁹ Second, though Danding originally negotiated a purchase price of PhP 350,000 per hectare for his land, during President Estrada's visit to the orchard in late 1998 he made the surprise announcement that he instead would give his land to the workers for free, but still on the condition that the land would be put into the joint venture. This prompted Estrada to declare Danding the "godfather of land reform," a pronouncement that was met by popular protest from agrarian reform activists.¹⁰

Reacting to various public criticisms, the DAR came up with a counter proposal with the following features: First, the equity that the worker-beneficiaries were to put into the joint venture was to be "land use" and not the land title (or CLOA) so as to protect the workers' claim over the land in event of bankruptcy of the joint venture. Second, the government, represented by the DAR, was to be allowed to join the joint venture with a 30 percent share reserved for the beneficiaries, a 65 percent share for Danding, and a 5 percent share for the government, supposedly to deny Danding an automatic two-thirds majority vote in the company and to enable the government to provide protection to the beneficiaries. Finally, the duration of the joint venture was to be shortened to ten years, renewable upon mutual agreement of all parties involved. Unsurprisingly, Danding rejected the DAR's proposal, leading to a long impasse in the case (up to the time of writing in mid-2006).¹¹

The *Dole-DARBCI leaseback case* involves more than 9,000 hectares of government-owned land in South Cotabato (in southern Mindanao) planted to pineapple.¹² While it is not a VLT transaction, it provides lessons with regard to leaseback arrangements, which, in recent years, have become an integral component of most VLT transactions. In this case, the government leased the land to global fruit giant Dole decades before CARP. In 1988, the land was redistributed to the more than 7,000 farmworkers who were employed by Dole on the vast plantation. Each farmworker-beneficiary received a little more than a hectare. A cooperative of the farmworkers was formed for the purpose of the land redistribution: the Dole Agrarian Reform Beneficiaries Cooperative Incorporated (DARBCI). It owns the reformed plantation through a "collective CLOA"; that is, no individual beneficiary was awarded a particular plot, nor could beneficiaries quit the CLOA and the cooperative without losing their beneficiary rights. Pre-arranged in the deal was that the plantation would be automatically placed under leaseback scheme with Dole — a deal described by veteran activist Billy de la Rosa as a "pre-nuptial" arrangement between the landlord/company and farmworkers (see de la Rosa, 2005); thus at the same time as the announcement that the plantation was redistributed to farmworkers, a leaseback arrangement was formally commenced. The lease contract was to run for ten years, during which Dole could use the land under the pre-CARP plantation operational setup. In exchange, Dole would pay each beneficiary PhP 3,200 per hectare per year.

During the ten-year lease contract (1988–1998), Dole retrenched some 3,300 farmworkers, which is nearly half the total number of beneficiaries, while hiring new workers who were not land reform beneficiaries, ostensibly as part of the company's efficiency drive. Most of those retrenched were left without any other source of income except for the meagre lease rent.[13] Meanwhile, conflicts within the leadership of DARBCI emerged and started to intensify around cooperative policy directions and fund management, although in the main the cooperative remained intact during the ten-year period. Toward the end of 1998, when the lease agreement was to expire, the divisions within DARBCI became more serious. The negotiation of a new lease contract with Dole became the main fault line that resulted in a major rift within the cooperative.

In 1998, Dole offered to renew the lease agreement with the following terms: lease for twenty-five years, renewable for another twenty-five years at the sole option of Dole, and PhP 5,000 per hectare per year lease rent. One group of (actively) employed farmworker-beneficiaries supported the proposal, while another group rejected it on the grounds that the lease rent was too low. During this period, the prevailing market rate for land leases on banana and pineapple plantations was six times higher than Dole's offer. Thus, the second group put forward a proposal for the renewal of the leaseback arrangement with Dole but at PhP 30,000-per-hectare-per-year lease rent. Dole rejected it. A legal battle over which group was the rightful representative of the cooperative ensued. (As of this writing, the legal question between the two farmworker-beneficiary groups remained pending at the Supreme Court.) Meanwhile, Dole entered into a de facto arrangement with the first group at a lease rental agreement of PhP 7,500 per hectare per year for twenty-five years and has since continued its operations, capitalizing on the support of a significant portion of the, for the most part, disorganized retrenched farmworker-beneficiaries, who were given a substantial cash advance on the projected lease rentals. There is, however, an emerging movement from a small section of the retrenched farmworker-beneficiaries for individual parcelization of the plantation and for multiple exit options for all. But this movement remains weak, and their demands have so far been ignored by the government. The mainstream anti-Dole group has adopted a purely legalistic strategy.

The agrarian reform–related intra-beneficiary conflict in this case is the largest in CARP's history both in terms of the amount of land involved and the number of beneficiaries affected. It is noteworthy that both groups have so far failed to address the fundamental issue confronting the retrenched farmworker-beneficiaries. No longer being able to work on the land has separated these farmworkers from their stake in the land and in the cooperative. The more than 3,300 farmworker-beneficiaries who were retrenched have no significant stake or interest in any type of renewed leaseback with Dole, because Dole will not rehire them. For most, the main interest is either to get their individual parcels of lands and cultivate them directly or to enter into an individual contract farming arrangement with any interested fruit company, foreign or domestic — regarding a more stable farm employment opportunity as key to their livelihoods (Borras and Franco, 2005). They are even under threat of being delisted from the beneficiary roll since they are "non-working" or "absentee" beneficiaries, and under the CARP law, such beneficiaries should be expelled and replaced by active farmworkers, a move being initiated now by the pro-Dole group of farmworkers. Moreover, many of the retrenched farmworker-beneficiaries — who are unorganized and to a large degree geographically scattered — have found the immediate cash offered by the pro-Dole group irresistible.

The *Floirendo leaseback scheme* involves the Floirendo family, one of the Philippines' most influential political-economic elites since the 1960s.[14] Like Danding, the family survived the 1986–1988 regime transition and subsequent national administration changes. One of the largest of the domestic banana sector–based elites, the family has links to multinational companies like Chiquita and controls thousands of hectares of land, both privately owned and leased from the government.[15] For their privately owned plantations, they originally tried to frustrate land reform by setting a sky-high asking price for their lands: PhP 750,000 per hectare in 1997. However, in 1998 the government-owned LBP assessed the value at only PhP 275,000 per hectare.[16] Meanwhile, in 2001, a local court declared the value of a banana plantation like that owned by the Floirendos to be PhP 1.6 million per hectare.

Thus, many were surprised when the Floirendos sold their plantation in 2002 for PhP 92,000 per hectare. But the sale was made through VLT integrated in a leaseback contract with six main features: (i) the land was to be bought directly by the farmworkers from the Floirendo family; (ii) the farmworker-beneficiaries would lease the land back to the Floirendo family for thirty years, renewable for another thirty years at the sole option of the Floirendos; (iii) payment for the land was to be amortized within thirty years and be automatically deducted from the lease rental due to the worker-beneficiaries; (iv) the lease rental was set at PhP 5,000 per hectare per year;

(v) the beneficiaries would remain employed as workers on the plantation; and (vi) the Floirendo family would have the sole right to buy back the land if any of the beneficiaries were to give up their land or were later disqualified as beneficiary.

The terms of such integrated contracts reveal landlords' attempts to transform the VLT leaseback scheme into a powerful anti-reform formula. The Floirendo family's decision to radically lower their asking price for the land was tied to the leaseback arrangement: the lower the land price, the lower the lease rent would be.[17] The sixty-year lease contract is virtually a lifetime; before the sixtieth year, most beneficiaries would have died without ever owning the land they were supposed to have gotten from land reform. The Floirendo family offered cash advances for the rentals to the would-be beneficiaries and exerted vigorous efforts to "delist" from the beneficiary roll any farmworkers belonging to autonomous organizations that were demanding expropriation of the plantations. Splits in the farmworkers' ranks erupted as the Floirendos moved to consummate contracts — with support from the VLT-inspired DAR leadership.[18] The main leader of the anti-leaseback workers' group, Eric Cabanit, was assassinated by masked men in Panabo, Daval del Norte, in April 2006. The case remains unresolved as of this writing.

The *Marsman profit-sharing scheme* involves Roberto Sebastian, former secretary of the Department of Agriculture (1992–1995) and president and chief executive officer of Marsman banana company. Sebastian came up with a modified arrangement for the Marsman plantation, a farm that is near that of the Floirendos' and on which Marsman originally put a price tag of PhP 1.2 million per hectare in 1997.[19] The land would be donated, not sold, to farmworker-beneficiaries (in a transaction classified as VLT), but on four conditions: (i) the farmworker-beneficiaries would allow Marsman to use the land free of charge for thirty years, renewable for another thirty years at the sole option of Marsman; (ii) the worker-beneficiaries would be hired as farm labourers; (iii) unlike the straightforward leaseback of the Floirendo family, the Marsman formula was to provide annual production and profit shares to the beneficiaries which it claimed was superior to the lease rental arrangement because profits and profit shares could rise unlike a fixed land rent; and (iv) Marsman would have the sole right to buy back the land if any beneficiaries gave up their land or were disqualified as beneficiary (Marsman, 2002).

The government moved to approve this proposed contract. President Gloria Macapagal-Arroyo herself ordered its approval. During the PARC meeting where Marsman was asked to present its proposal, President Arroyo confidently declared, "The formula for land reform is acquisition and redistribution. [In this Marsman formula] we are saving acquisition.

We are going straight to distribution. Praise God!" To which DAR Secretary Hernani Braganza replied, "In the long term, Madame President, this could serve as a model to the whole industry. The productivity is not lost. The value of the land is not lost." Finance Department Secretary Camacho concluded, "Madame President, we like your formula very much. With your formula, we are in full support. We think that it is excellent." Roberto Sebastian was elated. The Marsman farmworkers directly affected by the proposal were not even invited to take part in this meeting that would decide their fate (PARC, 2002b, 2002c).

The stock distribution option

Either to lessen landlord opposition to CARP by providing middle-ground arrangements that are not expropriationary or to deliberately facilitate the ultimate evasion by landlords of land expropriation, the stock distribution option (SDO) was provided. Simply put, under SDO arrangements, landholdings of landlords who run their farm as corporate entities are exempted from land redistribution if the landlords opt instead to distribute corporate stocks equivalent to the value of the land in the total assets of the corporation. The workers, who then become co-owners, continue to get their main earnings from their daily work in the corporation, but they get extra income from corporate dividends if the corporation realizes a net profit. Legally, the corporation has to apply for the SDO and it is the PARC that has the authority to approve or reject such an application. Once approved, a contract under the SDO is not permanent; it is subject to regular monitoring by the DAR. Any violations of the contract, such as cheating in income reports, are grounds for PARC to revoke the SDO contract, expropriate the landholdings, and redistribute them to peasants. The cut-off period for SDO application was set as 1990.[20]

The potential for redistributive reform under this arrangement is realized only if the land asset occupies a majority portion of the total corporate assets. Thus, the peasant beneficiaries would become the controlling majority in the corporation. But if the value of the land is depressed while the value of the non-land assets, which are not included in the land reform, is jacked up, then the doors for real redistributive reform are shut, and the agrarian structure of the estate remains unchanged.

The best known example of SDO is the 6,400-hectare sugar cane hacienda owned by former President Corazon Cojuangco-Aquino and her family (Cojuangco) in Central Luzon. Anticipating the possibility of a CARP provision for SDO, the Cojuangco family created a number of spin-off corporations related to sugar cane production, transportation, milling, and marketing. The entity created to settle with the more or less 4,000 farmworkers on the issue of land reform was the Hacienda Luisita, Inc. (HLI). Only 4,900 hectares of land were declared as land assets of HLI. The rest, the more expensive portions of land located near roads and residential/commercial areas, were segregated and declared property of other Cojuangco corporations outside HLI. The Cojuangcos depressed the cost of the land, pegging it at one-third of the total value of HLI, so the land reform beneficiaries own only one-third of the corporation. The Cojuangco family thus retained control of the corporation by ensuring that the assessed value of non-land assets was at least two-thirds of HLI's value (Putzel, 1992: 332–335). Putzel found that by mere "accounting manipulation," HLI was able to overvalue its non-land assets. In this case a rather marginalized autonomous initiative to organize farmworkers of the hacienda failed to surmount the anti-reform manoeuvres of the landlords (Carranza, 2005, 1994).

Between 1989 and 2002, there was no evidence to show that the socioeconomic condition of the farmworker-beneficiaries had improved. In fact, there were reports that hundreds of hectares of lands included in the SDO had already been taken back by the Cojuangcos and converted to commercial, residential, and recreational (golf course) purposes without corresponding compensation to the beneficiaries, in clear violation of the SDO contract. Persistent calls from NGOs to investigate these reports fell on deaf ears. There were also reports that sugar cane production at HLI was radically scaled down, throwing hundreds of farmworkers out of jobs. The reality is that hundreds of farmworkers have a weekly pay slip worth only a few pesos, while the promise of big dividends from the corporation's profits never materialized (Carranza, 1994, 2005).[21]

Farmworkers have been restive, but apparently the DAR refused to confront the Cojuangcos: It never ordered serious investigation of whether the terms of the SDO had been violated. However, at the height of the anti-Estrada campaign in the latter part of 2000, the Morales DAR did order an investigation of possible violations of the Cojuangcos on the SDO contract. This move was clearly politically motivated, because Corazon Cojuangco-Aquino and her family were outspokenly anti-Estrada. DAR Secretary Morales joined forces with Tarlac Provincial Governor Apeng Yap (a political opponent of the Cojuangcos) in fanning the flames among the disgruntled HLI farmworkers. Several hundred HLI farmworker-beneficiaries signed a petition against the Cojuangcos. Thus, finding equally powerful elite allies, hundreds of farmworkers took the risk of collective action, holding rallies and daring to speak of their predicament under the SDO. This state of affairs, however, was short lived. The media (and even the pro-land reform NGOs and activists) interpreted such actions as politically motivated and instigated by the Estrada administration. Before the movement could gain further momentum, Estrada was ousted as president, as was Morales as DAR secretary (see Franco, 2004).[22] The succeeding Macapagal-Arroyo administration refused to investigate the possible violations in the Hacienda Luisita SDO, until the bloody incident in late 2004 when seven of the workers who went to join a strike in protest against labour-related issues were killed by the police and military forces who were called in by the Cojuangcos to break the strikers' barricade. Then once again the media spotlight was focused on the case, but, unfortunately, the attention was again short lived. The discussion in the media, and even amongst policymakers and analysts, focused on the labour issues and not on the underlying key problem — the voluntary, market-driven stock distribution option (Carranza, 2005; Borras, Carranza and Reyes, 2007). However, in mid-2005, the Cojuangcos joined the opposition against the Macapagal-Arroyo administration on issues of corruption and possible cheating in the 2004 presidential election. In retaliation, the administration ordered the revocation of the SDO contract for HLI and the redistribution of the land. It remains to be seen whether the estate will indeed be redistributed to farmworkers, and whether the newly formed autonomous farmworkers' group (FARM, affiliated with UNORKA — see Chapter 5) will survive the political challenges ahead (see Carranza, 2005).

Overpriced land acquisition

Redistributive reform is absent when the land the government purchases for redistribution is overpriced. However, establishing a standard national benchmark that enables one to conclude whether a land acquisition transaction is overpriced or not is highly contentious, especially when land is viewed as having a multidimensional, and not just monetary, character. In this study, "overpriced" land acquisitions are considered to be those holdings whose price is set at levels significantly higher than the price set by the LBP. This is not the most ideal way of determining overpricing (and could, in fact, underestimate the extent of overpricing, since LBP valuation can also be elevated), but because it provides a standard of measurement that is — at least to some degree — consistent, it can provide critical insights relevant to this study's purposes. The level of government subsidy for the beneficiaries' amortized payment for the land is also a significant factor in assessing this issue.

One notable example of overpricing is that of the Hijo Plantation, Inc. (HPI).[23] The LBP assessed the value of this banana plantation, which was earlier placed under VOS, at PhP 296,665 per hectare, for a total value of PhP 411.9 million for the 1,388-hectare plantation. The landlord appealed the ruling in a civil court (the Special Agrarian Court of Tagum City), which decided to raise the plantation's price to PhP 1,665,781 per hectare, with a resulting total value of PhP 2.85 billion — or nearly six times the LBP assessment. The LBP filed an appeal against the SAC decision. In another case in Nueva Ecija, similar jacking up of the land price was done by the DAR's provincial adjudicator (PARAD). When the LBP refused to pay the landlord pending appeal, the PARAD issued a "contempt of court" order against the LBP that led to the arrest and detention of LBP President Margarito Teves. This created a national controversy that caused embarrassment to the government. Later, the DAR investigation committee found that the PARAD had abused its authority.[24]

"Uninstalled" land reform beneficiaries

When a land transfer is reported in government records but the beneficiaries are in fact unable to take possession of the awarded lands due to ongoing landlord resistance, redistributive reform has not occurred on the given landholding. In a DAR land redistribution report, the 231-hectare Benedicto sugar cane plantation in La Carlota City, Negros Occidental, was included; CLOAs were issued in October of that year to seventy-seven beneficiaries, each one having been awarded 3 hectares (the top amount allowed by the regulations). But this amounted to an apparent-but-not-real redistributive outcome, because the said awarded lands were never occupied by the seventy-seven beneficiaries due to the violent opposition of the landlord. Benedicto was among the closest cronies of Ferdinand Marcos and owned the estate through a company called Malibu Agro Corporation. This is just one of the many estates owned by the Benedictos and subject to an earlier negotiated settlement with the post-Marcos governments.

The seventy-seven beneficiaries, who formed an organization called Nagasi Agrarian Reform Beneficiaries Multi-Purpose Cooperative, Inc. (NARBMCI), enjoyed being the new owners of the land for only a few months beginning in October 1999, after which the landlord petitioned that the CLOA be revoked and that the DAR commence a new process on the grounds that (i) the landlord had a pending land valuation protest, (ii) some of the workers whom the company claimed to be "bona fide" were excluded, (iii) some of the seventy-seven beneficiaries were not "bona fide" workers, and (iv) the landowner had a claim on the standing crop. The landlord was able to get favourable decisions from the sub-national DAR offices; and the peasants who tried to harvest the standing crop were driven off the estate by armed security guards hired by the company.

DAR Secretary Morales, however, ruled in favour of the peasants in October 2000. But by then the landlord had filed an appeal before the Office of the President (OP), with the current president still being Estrada with Ronaldo Zamora as executive secretary. A month before Estrada was driven out of the office, Secretary Zamora reversed the decision of DAR Secretary Morales and ruled in favour of the landlord. This decision emboldened the landlord to escalate harassment of the peasants, barricading the estate and beefing up the armed security. Intermittent shootings by the security guards at the peasants ensued. The peasants mobilized their allied peasant organizations and NGOs at the national and international levels. But the anti-reform powers seemed formidable. However, with the peasants' renewed lobby before the then new (Macapagal-Arroyo) administration and with a new executive secretary at the OP, the Zamora order was reversed in April 2001, ruling in favour of the 77 peasants.[25] Yet the DAR was unable to implement the new order because of the armed resistance of the landlord. The landlord filed an appeal which was pending for several years. In 2004, the beneficiaries were finally able to occupy the awarded land — but whether temporarily or permanently is still an open question (see Feranil, 2005).[26]

Land reform reversals

The non-redistributive nature of "land reform reversal" through cancellation of an award is obvious and straightforward. An award is made that is redistributive; it enters the official records as such; later, and for various reasons, the award is cancelled and the official records may or may not be altered accordingly (see, e.g., Lo, 2004). The Hacienda Looc case in Batangas is a classic example. The case involved some 8,650 hectares located near the coastal town of Nasugbu. These lands were previously awarded to peasants under the land reform program. Toward the mid-1990s, real estate companies came in enticed by the tourist potential of the hacienda and lobbied the government to acquire the property. In 1996, the Garilao DAR cancelled the CLOAs. By mid-1998, and by virtue of another national DAR decision, the property effectively came under the control of the real estate company, Fil-Estate, a financial giant in the sector, politically well-connected and rumoured to be close to President Ramos. Subsequent efforts to assert the prior and superior right of the peasants over the land proved futile amidst an extremely powerful united front of anti–land reform individuals and entities who did not hesitate to use violence against the peasants.[27] The divisions that later emerged among the ranks of the peasant beneficiaries and their external allies did not help the cause of the peasants either.

If a case like this enters the records as land redistribution accomplishment, and despite a later reversal, remains included as accomplishment in the official records, then it is a clear case of an apparent-but-not-real outcome. If it is subtracted from the official records accordingly, then it is a straightforward case of a failed attempt in land redistribution. In either case, there is no redistributive reform. In the case of Hacienda Looc, the officially recorded land reform achievement was subtracted from the Batangas land redistribution accomplishment.

Deliberate padding of accomplishment reports

Perhaps the most commonly discussed type of apparent-but-not-real land reform accomplishment is the padding of achievement reports. This takes a variety of forms, many of which were discussed earlier. Two examples are offered here. Between January and December 2001 under the Braganza DAR, Region 2 reported an accomplishment of 4,031 hectares for 2001 under the KKK land category; however, as of the previous September (September 2000), the remaining available balance under this category for that region was only 119 hectares.[28] Similarly, Region 8 reported an accomplishment of 10,178 hectares for the same period for the KKK land category; yet as of September 2000, there was no more available land in this category from that region — in fact it had already registered a more than one hundred percent accomplishment rate. Region 12 posted an output of 9,974 hectares under the settlement category; yet in September 2000, there was an available balance of only 2,071 hectares for that category in that region. Still in Region 12 but on the DENR CARP program, the PARC-AMIC (2001: 13) audit team discovered a similar case where the DENR provincial head "padded their accomplishments by a combined total of 42 percent." While deeper investigation is necessary, this information strongly suggests something anomalous.

The other example is a grey area in leasehold output reports. By the end of 2003, about 1.5 million hectares were reported as put under a leasehold arrangement benefiting some one million tenant households. Some 573,000 hectares of this had been reformed during the Marcos era. But under the CARP law, leasehold can be used in two ways: as a permanent tenurial instrument for lands under the retention rights of the landlords or as a transitory scheme toward eventual expropriation. The official report on leasehold is an aggregate of supposedly permanent leasehold. However, several cases of leasehold reform implemented as transitory schemes were included in the reports from 1990 to 1993, and during a portion of 1994, effectively bloating the output totals in leasehold.[29] This study estimates that the figures could have been bloated possibly by as much as 650,000 hectares.[30] It would require Herculean effort to reconstruct the data for these years in order to segregate what are permanent and what are transitory types of leasehold. Whether leasehold reports were deliberately padded as window-dressing for DAR's accomplishment in leasehold is difficult to determine. To complicate the matter, it is even more difficult to determine whether the reported compliance on the more permanent type of leasehold is real. The essential point here is that there clearly are apparent-but-not-real leasehold outputs created through padding in reports.

Problems in settlement areas and public lands

Another widely cited example of an apparent-but-not-real redistributive land reform is the redistribution of previously unoccupied and uncultivated public lands marked by a complete absence of any prior or existing landlord control or interest. Many colonization projects in the Philippines and elsewhere in the past have a significant component of this. The current CARP implementation also includes such cases, but, arguably, not as much as most people tend to assume because, as pointed out earlier, most public lands in the Philippines today are imbued with private interests and under varying degrees of cultivation and elite control. One specific case of a huge tract of this type of public land was reported in Samar. The case involves several thousand hectares of marginal lands awarded to a variety of landless rural poor in the vicinity who subsequently refused to occupy the land due to lack of settlement and farming infrastructure: no roads, no drinking water facilities, very remote location, no irrigation, and no parcellary survey to determine which land was to go to whom. It was a case of "voluntary non-installation." In this case, of course, there was no redistributive reform.[31]

Perhaps more serious is how land redistribution has been carried out in settlement areas. Settlement areas are usually huge blocks (thousands of hectares) of contiguous public lands that are to be redistributed under land reform. In Central Mindanao (Region 12) many such lands have been cultivated and settled despite the absence of formal property documents. Share tenancy arrangements exist in these settlements. Hundreds of thousands of hectares of land under the settlement category have entered the official CARP accomplishment reports. However, recent field investigation in Central Mindanao settlements reveals the high probability of widespread apparent-but-not-real redistributive outcomes (see Borras, 2002a). The DAR has been implementing CARP in the settlement areas with careless haste — most likely because these vast chunks of land could boost the periodic national accomplishment reports. In so doing, the DAR simply recognizes and formalizes the actually existing cultivation and settlement claims of various households in these settlement blocks, regardless of whether beneficiaries are landless peasants, tenant-farmers, non-peasant households, or even landlords. Some (usually petty) landlords in fact have been able to formalize their own claims within these settlement blocks by putting up several claims in the name of family members and other dummies. The case of the settlement in Tulunan, North Cotabato, is strongly suggestive of such a practice.[32]

Moreover, some of these lands overlap with ancestral domains, bringing the issues of land reform under the CARP law and ancestral domain claims under the IPRA law into conflict with each other. The example of Columbio settlement in Sultan Kudarat (Region 12) shows that while a large portion of the settlement is clearly an ancestral domain claimed by a *Lumad* group (also claimed by Muslims), the DAR insisted it be covered through a CLOA under CARP and not a CADC (Certificate of Ancestral Domain Claim) — for the obvious reason that DAR needed the vast tract of land for accomplishment report purposes. Non-indigenous beneficiaries were likewise included to a substantial degree. The implication of covering such lands under CARP (with a CLOA) is far-reaching and irreversible: the ancestral domain is effectively privatized and parcelized. The process generates serious tensions with regard to indigenous peoples' rights and welfare. In this case, redistribution of these ancestral domains under the mainstream land reform program is, arguably, "anti-reform" and non-redistributive in a profound sense.[33]

Finally, non-redistributive outcomes have most likely resulted from CARP implementation processes in the DENR-controlled portion of CARP (public A&D lands and the CBFM program), in particular because of the absence of any pro-reform state–society interaction over this CARP component. Evidence provided in the PARC-AMIC annual internal audits show that the beneficiary selection and inclusion processes and outcomes have suffered the same fate as that of DAR's VLT. Moreover, dubious reclassification of public lands, including questionable timetables of A&D reclassifications and land type reclassifications (timberlands, pasturelands, 18-degree slope lands, forest lands, and so on) to benefit the elite, are among the documented problems under DENR's A&D and CBFM programs (see also Carranza, 2006).[34]

Pre-expropriation compulsory production and profit sharing

Land acquisition and redistribution on big commercial plantations (those with a yearly gross income of more than PhP 5 million) was deferred for ten years, from 1988 to 1998. The most important sub-sector affected in terms of financial value was banana agribusiness. During the deferment period (1988–1998), the plantation companies were required by the CARP law to implement a production and profit sharing (PPS) scheme: 3 percent of annual gross sales plus 5 percent of annual net income were supposed to be distributed each year to farmworkers on the plantations in question. Plantation companies availed themselves of the CARP's deferment provision to protect some 50,000 hectares of modern plantations from land redistribution for that decade. The PPS scheme, arguably, does have some degree of redistributory value, especially in view of the significant sums of money involved. Yet, not surprisingly, plantation owners have manipulated the scheme. To evade the redistributive PPS, between 1988 and 1998, plantation owners retrenched an estimated 20,000 farmworkers in the banana sector (a sector that previously had a labour force of 50,000), an effort suggestive of a company manoeuvre to rid plantations of land and PPS claim-makers. There are also strong indications that many of the retrenched farmworkers were those who were involved with autonomous unions (and later, peasant organizations) (de la Rosa, 2005). Most banana companies complied with the mandatory PPS (though most rubber plantations did not) but abruptly lowered their annual production and profit reports beginning in 1989. The PPS dividends given to farmworkers were a small fraction, usually one-tenth, of what ought to have been given, according to various estimates. For example, a worker in Floirendo's Tagum Agricultural Development Corporation (TADECO) got a daily PPS dividend of PhP 7 in 1995, an amount that, at the time, could buy only 500 grams of the lowest quality rice (DAR-XI, 1998). The aggregate total of PPS shares that should have been paid out but were not was estimated at some PhP 5 billion in the banana sector alone — equal to the value of all the expropriated banana plantations, based on prices computed by the LBP.[35] The United Floirendo Employees Agrarian Reform Beneficiaries, Inc. (UFEARBAI, a network member of UNORKA) filed a case before the DARAB petitioning for a recomputation of the 1988–1998 PPS. The case, however, has continued to "sleep" up to the time of this writing (Borras and Franco, 2005).

Shrinking CARP scope

Yet another issue that seems to have escaped the critical lens of most CARP critics is the problem of the continually shrinking CARP land redistribution scope (see table 3.1). The absence of any systematic analysis of this issue in most CARP critiques is noticeable; among the few exceptions is Putzel (2002).

Table 3.1
Land deducted from the DAR scope as of 31 March 2005, in hectares

Land type	Scope	Deducted	Working scope
OLT	705,725	65,567	640,158
PAL>50	1,081,433	367,861	713,572
VOS	308,893	34,341	274,551
CA	652,488	323,080	329,408
VLT	120,052	10,440	109,612
PAL 24–50	488,101	273,558	214,542
VOS	85,744	9,920	75,823
CA	340,506	251,958	88,549
VLT	61,850	11,680	50,170
PAL 5–24	2,241,100	1,383,712	857,388
VOS	272,325	21,664	250,661
CA	1,511,777	1,303,863	207,914
VLT	456,998	58,185	398,813
PAL<5	98,715	29,149	69,566
VOS	25,013	623	24,389
VLT	73,702	28,526	45,176
GFI	284,0992	81,404	202,695
GOL/KKK	934,971	160,104	774,866
LE	71,807	605	71,201
SETT	770,495	13,561	756,844
Grand total	6,676,444	2,375,612	4,300,832

Notes: OLT = Operation Land Transfer (from the 1972 Marcos land reform on tenanted rice and corn land); PAL = private agricultural land; PAL>50 = private agricultural land 50 hectares and above; PAL24–50 = private agricultural land 24 to 50 hectares in size; VOS = voluntary offer-to-sell; VLT = voluntary land transfer; GFI = government financial institution; KKK = *Kilusang Kabuhayan at Kaunlaran* — a development program started by Marcos that segregated some government-owned land for redistribution; LE = landed estate, which mainly concerns the outstanding balance in the century-old (Spanish) friar lands; SETT = settlement program that involves government-owned land.

Source: DAR-MIS (2005), table 4, 31 March 2005. Percentages are rounded.

The sheer volume of land taken out of CARP's formal scope makes this issue the largest non-redistributive policy component and "outcome" of CARP. The original 1988 CARP scope was 10.3 million hectares of land, all the agricultural lands in the country at that time; this was then reduced to 8.1 million hectares through a decision by the PARC in early 1996. Since then this lower figure has become the official reference point. The official brief explanation is that the data on the scope had to be "cleaned-up" because the 1988 land registration was "not systematic" and landlords had misdeclared/under-declared their land assets. Neither the DAR nor the PARC made further public explanation. The NGOs and peasant movements undertook only marginal and superficial questioning of this assertion, nothing serious and sustained enough to earn a reaction or attention from the government.[36] The data set used in this study is from the Field Operations Office of the central DAR (the so-called Table 4 produced by FOSSO/MIS). While there are other slightly different sets of data from other DAR bureaus, the FOSSO/MIS data set is the one used in daily DAR operations.

Having made such clarification, the official explanation about the deduction becomes problematic. This is seen by analyzing the facts from four perspectives: the distribution pattern of the deducted lands based on legal grounds, the distribution of the deducted lands by land acquisition types, the patterns in processes through which land deductions were made, and the geographic distribution of land deductions. These issues are examined further below.

Clear-cut failed attempts to redistribute lands

Failed attempts to redistribute lands means an ultimate absence of redistributive reform for the affected estates and peasant households. Unfortunately, the DAR monitors and tabulates only cases and data regarding land redistribution *accomplishment*; it is not data-banking the *failed* attempts, including the portions of estates that underwent partial redistribution as part of some "negotiated" settlement on the issue of land reform. The latter has emerged recently as one of the routes taken by some DAR officials when landlords mount opposition to expropriation. There are a variety of reasons for the failure to redistribute lands, and they are discussed throughout this study. The well-publicized case of Mapalad in Bukidnon is a classic example of a failed attempt (Villarin, 1999; Gatmaytan, 2000; Quitoriano, 2000). And the partial coverage of the Floirendo banana plantations is an example of a "negotiated" partial coverage, as are the DAR decisions in the Puyat estates in Bulacan and the Benedicto landholdings in Negros Occidental.

Fictitious titles sold to DAR
Another straightforward case of an apparent-but-not-real outcome is the selling of fictitious land titles to the land reform program. This is a simple case of fraud: fake titles of either existing or non-existing landholdings are sold by a fake landlord to the DAR. The DAR pays for the fake title through the VOS program and reports the sale as land redistribution accomplishment.

The World Bank's market-led agrarian reform
The literature, both by the World Bank and its critics, makes frequent reference to the fact that MLAR has been implemented full scale in the Philippines since 1998 (see, e.g., Deininger and Binswanger, 1999; El-Ghonemy, 2001). This is not the case, as some scholars have deduced (e.g., Franco, 1999d, 1999e; Reyes, 1999) and as shown below, and it is important to clarify the matter.

Since the early 1970s, the World Bank has played an important role in shaping the policy directions for rural development in the Philippines. Together with some key organizations in US foreign policy circles, such as the US Agency for International Development (USAID), the World Bank has generally maintained a policy position against redistributive land reform in the country, though this position has, at times, been challenged from within. Historically, the World Bank has worked for an agricultural and rural development approach in the country that is based more on economic growth than on equity (see Putzel, 1992; Bello, Kinley and Elinson, 1982). Thus, while the World Bank eventually supported CARP, its assistance was limited to infrastructure construction (e.g., roads and bridges) in communities where lands had been redistributed, rather than extending to the land redistribution itself (see Fox and Gershman, 2000).

The World Bank and USAID worked together to pilot test the concept of voluntary, market-led land transfer schemes in Latin America in the 1970s and 1980s (Dorner, 1992: 86–91). Similar advocacy by the two agencies was evident in the Philippines during the CARP policymaking process (Putzel, 1992). But while USAID was more vocal in advocating voluntary land transfer schemes during the CARP policymaking process (ibid.: 293–295), it was the World Bank that later systematically lobbied the Philippine government to veer away from expropriation and to adopt voluntary-non-expropriationary modes of "land reform."

The first attempt by the World Bank to recruit government officials to embrace MLAR was in 1996, when it insinuated in its country policy papers that the Philippine government must halt CARP's land distribution implementation, especially in the 5–24-hectare farm size category, because it was said to be "distorting" the land market and was financially expensive

(World Bank, 1996, 1997a, 1997b). Under Garilao, the DAR rejected the World Bank proposal, and subsequent noisy public protest from agrarian reform activist circles drove the World Bank officials away from CARP. They came back three years later, however, with renewed vigour and persistence, and made some modest policy inroads (Franco, 1999e). In early 1999, the World Bank officials tried to convince the then new DAR leadership to at least support a small pilot MLAR project in the context of exploring other "complementary approaches" in implementing land reform. For different reasons, including the hope of receiving new loans from the World Bank amidst a creeping shortage of public funds, the DAR leadership expressed interest in exploring the possibilities of MLAR.[37] In late 2000, and after a long, complex negotiation process, it was agreed that a much smaller project — a feasibility study — would be carried out.[38]

The MLAR feasibility study largely involved desk-bound macro-policy studies and it produced papers favourable to the pro-market policy model. For example, Esguerra (2001) predicted MLAR's economic viability, though he warned about the less controllable institutional, organizational, and financial factors that could prevent a demand-driven process, among others. Edillion (2001) presented elaborate comparative data between different land acquisition schemes in different crops, and likewise predicted MLAR's financial viability; though like Esguerra, she cautioned about the unpredictability of factors in the field. Mamon (2001) endorsed the continuation of the feasibility-cum-pilot project but underscored the crucial role of autonomous social preparation in the communities involved. Finally, an operational manual (DAR-ARCDP, 2001) was produced, outlining the ways and means through which MLAR could be implemented in the country.

The feasibility project also involved two community-based test cases from which reports were produced. The contents of these documents, however, are routine, pre-project evaluations of standard operating procedures: profiles of prospective buyers and sellers, characteristics of the lands for sale, and so on. Going through the documents and interviewing some of those directly involved in the feasibility study at the community level, however, yielded additional data and insights.

The first project site, in *Barangay* Sibula, Lopez Jaena, Misamis Occidental, involved a tenanted 178-hectare stretch of (provincial) government-owned land (48 hectares of which lie idle, while 130 hectares were planted to coconut and subsistence crops). There were 178 potential buyer-beneficiaries. The buyers were chosen through the usual DAR/CARP process, that is, mainly by the DAR but with the participation of all potential beneficiaries and an assisting NGO. The government — the seller in this case — originally set the land price at PhP 31,000 per hectare, but that price was rejected by the local beneficiaries and other parties in the arrangement. The government's final offer was PhP 16,000 per hectare, payable in ten years (UPSARDFI, 2001: 94–95). Under this proposed agreement, the buyers would shoulder the full cost of the land (MUCEP, 2001).

The other project site, in *Barangay* Hagonghong, Buenavista, Bondoc Peninsula Quezon, involved a tenanted 48-hectare stretch of private marginal farmland planted to coconut and subsistence crops. The land had been for sale since 1989 and was being sold to the DAR when discussions about the MLAR feasibility project began. The landlord originally set the land price at PhP 35,000 per hectare, payable through a 25 percent downpayment, with the balance paid in instalments over ten years. Nineteen potential beneficiary households were chosen through the normal DAR/CARP process (again, mainly by the DAR but with active participation of the potential beneficiaries and an assisting NGO). The relatively organized potential beneficiary households rejected the landlord's asking price and bargained for a much lower price. The final price was set at PhP 6,000 per hectare. The buyers were to shoulder the full cost of the land, to be paid in cash through a loan from the LBP at commercial interest rates (UPSARDFI, 2001: 94).[39]

From the first case, the key lesson seems to be that even a government entity can be tempted to overprice land slated for sale to peasants under the direct sale process. The second case is also interesting, especially the way the land price was bargained down. Yet we should not take this case as representative, because the balance of power was overwhelmingly in favour of the peasants due to the direct assistance of national-provincial-local government and nongovernment actors in pressuring the landlord to abide by the prevailing land price levels in this isolated village. Such concerted intervention from highly autonomous and militant groups is unlikely to be replicated on a wide scale.

Despite, or because of, the limited insights that could be derived from the feasibility study, the World Bank decided to continue and expand it into a small pilot program. The pilot program, called the Community-Managed Agrarian Reform and Poverty Reduction Program (CMARPRP), started in mid-2003. It aimed to facilitate the sale of 1,000 hectares to 1,000 rural poor households in ten provinces across the country. Its basic operational method does not differ much from the feasibility study, that is, it is technically and legally anchored in the use of the VLT scheme. The MLAR pilot program has been integrated in the ongoing World Bank–funded Agrarian Reform Community Development Program, a support program for agrarian reform beneficiaries heavily oriented toward infrastructure building. The pilot program is supposed to be completed within two years. The short period of implementation was used by the program managers to justify dropping the supposedly required component of civil society (NGO) involvement in the project, as their inclusion would most likely result in extended project implementation processes. While this may be true, another most likely reason is the fact that almost all NGOs and peasant organizations in the Philippines are opposed to the World Bank's MLAR concept and are opposed to any form of pilot-testing of this system (see, e.g., UNORKA, 2000a, 2000b; Reyes, 1999). Initial data from the field are suggestive of a number of anomalous transactions within the scheme, including the problematic use of VLT and overpricing in land valuation. But again, its coverage in terms of number of peasant households and quantity of land is minuscule as compared to the scale of the state-driven CARP.

Preliminary evidence suggests that this project suffered the same fate as the other market-friendly transfer schemes — that is, it is stripped of any real pro-poor process and outcome, at least in the four (out of ten) project sites visited for this study.[40]

First, in a project site in Zambales province, many of the beneficiaries of CMARPRP were the "beneficiaries" of fraudulent VLT transactions completed more than ten years before CMARPRP came into being. This means that those who committed fraud in the VLT transactions in the 1990s in the community were not only not penalized but even rewarded with new grants/projects more than ten years after through the CMARPRP. The local government was responsible for the key decisions in this project, including the site and the beneficiaries.

Second, in another site (Mindoro Occidental), a long and complicated story can be summarized as follows: The lands involved were part of an ancestral domain of an indigenous community (Mangyan). When the large territory was awarded to the Mangyan community through a CADC, some portions of the territory came under the control and ownership of non-Mangyan lowlanders, in what the Mangyans charge was a fraudulent process of land acquisition. The so-called private landlords voluntarily sold the (Mangyan) land to the identified potential beneficiaries living in the community: the Mangyan indigenous community. Officials of both the local agrarian reform agency and the local government told the Mangyans that if they refused to buy the land, they would be forcibly and legally ejected from the land and their community. Under enormous pressure, the Mangyans "bought" the land under the CMARPRP project. Hence, their territory was stolen from them, and then they were forced to buy it back.

Third, in another site (Quezon Province), two opposing landlords were claiming rights over a piece of public land, contesting the distinct claim by poor peasants working the same land for decades already. No claimants have any title to the land. The CMARPRP project staff, supported by local government officials, eventually recognized the land claim by one of the landlords. This claim was questioned by the peasants. But the decision favoring the landlord stood. Then, the peasants were asked to 'willingly buy' the land, under the threat of expulsion from the land. They resisted, but eventually they were forced to accept the CMARPRP offer to buy that land that they previously claimed to be theirs.

Fourth, in a site in Samal Island (Davao Province), the land sold to the CMARPRP project was part of the territory of an indigenous people. A non-indigenous person was able to somehow "buy" a piece of land in this territory which was already covered by a CADC. He then re-sold "his" land through the CMARPRP project. The buyers were the same local people who had previously lost part of their territory through such a questionable "open market" process. The cost of the land was higher than the prevailing market price. The Samal government put up a significant cash partial payment for the landlord's land (the peasants would then repay the local government), enticed by the promise of infrastructure projects for the community to be funded by the CMARPRP project.

In sum, partial evidence shows that CMARPRP is far from having the essence of redistributive land reform: it institutionalizes, instead of correcting, historical injustice committed against the rural poor, especially indigenous peoples; it rewards, instead of penalizing, people who acquire (public) lands through fraud.[41]

In short, in various forms and through various methods, non-redistributive outcomes of CARP did, and do, occur. Yet most of these transactions entered the official records as accomplishment in redistributive land reform.

3.3 EXTENT AND GEOGRAPHIC DISTRIBUTION OF NON-REDISTRIBUTIVE POLICIES AND OUTCOMES

It is extremely difficult to determine the exact extent of non-redistributive outcomes of a land reform program. But it is not impossible to make a general estimation based on available data and information. Moreover, a disaggregated view at the sub-national, regional level reveals insights about the uneven and varied outcomes between geographic spaces that, in turn, hint at the causal relationships between policies, actors, and outcomes.

Table 3.2 shows the extent of VLT transactions nationwide over time, but like other aggregated official quantitative data it fails to reveal the full extent of the dynamic power relations that determine land redistribution on a given estate. The exact extent of non-redistributive VLT-based land transfers is difficult, if not impossible, to determine for two principal reasons: First, as discussed earlier, land redistribution is power redistribution. A case-by-case assessment is therefore necessary to determine whether and to what extent a redistribution did occur on a particular landholding contested by various competing actors. This is true for all land redistribution modalities within CARP, including VLT. Second, as demonstrated in the cases cited above, when VLT is used by landlords to comply with the land reform law it is usually accompanied by transaction processes that too are controlled by landlords, which makes it impossible to determine the exact quantity of fraudulent VLTs.

However, reliable informants provide alternative estimates of the extent of non-redistributive VLT. Three former DAR undersecretaries for field operations and support services, the top officials who oversee CARP implementation nationwide, were unanimous in their negative view of VLT. Ding Navarro said, "I don't know the exact percentage but the majority [of VLT-based land transfers], maybe as much as 70 percent were resorted to by the landowners ... to evade coverage."[42] According to Gerry Bulatao, VLT is often a transaction between relatives (*"malimit na transaksyon ng magkakamag-anak"*).[43] Hector Soliman proposed setting aside all official VLT land transfer accomplishments and having them reviewed.[44] Soliman's position is supported by the former head of DAR's Internal Audit Service, Ding San Andres, who is also the head of the AMIC and has been lobbying top DAR leadership to require a review of all VLT cases.[45] In most of the VLT cases discussed above, the transactions were registered as land sales based on 100 percent spot-cash, prompting Lorenz Reyes, a senior member of the national DAR Adjudication Board, to comment, "You will have serious doubts because these VLT schemes are mostly on a cash basis. How can a poor tenant afford to pay one hundred percent spot-cash for the land? It is most likely that these are just stage-managed, especially where the landowners are politically strong enough to control their tenants."[46]

Table 3.2 conceals more than it reveals about the reality of VLT. Nonetheless, preliminary examination of the tabulated data shows a broad pattern of non-redistributive VLT, which has likely been carried out more systematically than previously assumed. Two critical points can be raised here: On one hand, VLT, while not a dominant mode within CARP, is not insignificant in terms of scale of outcomes. By mid-2005, VLT was directly responsible for the reported "accomplishment" of 525,847 hectares of land, involving some 150,000 peasant households (DAR-MIS, 2005). It accounts for around 14 percent of the national DAR achievement in both private and public lands, while making up one-fourth of the total DAR output in private lands. On the other hand, evidence

Table 3.2 DAR's land distribution accomplishment (in hectares), by region/island group, by land acquisition modality, 1972–May 2005

Island/group/region	Total output	% Accomplishment	OLT	GFI	VOS	CA	VLT	SETT	LE	KKK
Total for the Philippines, including ARMM	3,591,055	81	554,220	156,909	512,620	243,422	525,847	699,648	80,497	817,859
CAR	81,670	105	1,257	1,115	715	144	17,784	—	—	60,655
Region 1	1422,490	87	29,835	1,790	8,646	1,237	63,803	1,969	298	14,912
Region 2	311,489	104	76,884	8,993	38,994	11,775	34,556	43,527	4,579	92,181
Region 3	376,536	93	195,100	5,222	24,062	23,708	30,154	14,725	56,808	26,757
Region 4-A (CALABARZON)	138,453	68	15,399	719	22,510	35,863	19,057	25,575	5,435	13,895
Region 4-B (MIMAROPA)	141,039	83	15,653	1,165	9,617	15,019	33,533	14,176	4,972	46,904
Region 5	237,061	52	47,302	17,041	51,224	36,862	37,216	12,001	3,016	32,399
Region 6	323,756	58	37,934	60,617	97,341	26,767	27,360	19,640	74	54,023
Region 7	117,418	70	17,685	3,880	27,028	19,198	3,021	6,623	—	39,983
Region 8	342,364	89	19,049	8,060	21,949	20,801	13,531	90,870	615	167,489
Region 9	182,500	115	10,663	7,556	15,717	12,668	59,636	20,998	2,983	52,279
Region 10	255,686	95	16,705	2,548	16,499	9,478	57,202	95,726	—	57,528
Region 11	196,975	97	8,613	6,781	60,335	19,317	34,750	33,691	—	33,488
Region 12	403,381	94	33,455	11,213	74,855	3,718	34,867	228,085	212	16,976
Region 13	187,513	94	6,481	3,333	24,621	4,720	24,145	19,259	1,474	103,480
ARMM	172,691	57	22,205	16,876	18,507	2,147	35,232	72,783	31	4,910

Notes: OLT = Operation Land Transfer; GFI = government financial institution; VOS = voluntary offer-to-sell; CA = compulsory acquisition; VLT = voluntary land transfer; SETT = settlements; LE = landed estates; KKK = *Kilusang Kabuhayan at Kaunlaran*; ARMM = Autonomous Region of Muslim Mindanao; CAR = Cordillera Autonomous Region; CALABARZON = Cavite, Laguna, Batangas, Rizal, Quezon; MIMAROPA = Mindoro, Marinduque, Romblon, Palawan.

Source: DAR-MIS (2005).

shows a highly uneven and varied distribution of VLT transactions at the regional level regardless of pre-existing structural settings.

A closer examination of table 3.2 shows VLT cases to be highly concentrated in a relatively few regions, with six of the seventeen regions and island groups (regions 1, 9, 10, 11, 21, and ARMM) accounting for a little over half of the total VLT output in hectares. These six regions, except for ARMM, are also among the top achievers in terms of officially reported land redistribution, suggesting that VLT could have played an important role in their land transfer output. In the case of ARMM, VLT-based "land transfers" made up about two-fifths of the total land distribution outcome in private agricultural land in that region. The regions (and provinces) that posted generous percentages of VLT cases in relation to their total redistribution output are mixed in terms of structural and institutional settings: generally low agricultural development in Region 1 (Ilocos, the top VLT producer) and Regions 9, 10, and ARMM; and massive urban sprawl in Regions 11 and 4 (Southern Tagalog). In contrast, provinces with insignificant VLT transactions as a percentage of reported total redistribution accomplishment figures include provinces notorious for their strong anti-reform landlords, such as Negros Occidental and Masbate (see Borras, 2005).

By implication, and on one hand, the geographic distribution of VLT transactions does not support claims that it was systematically and uniformly carried out as a key strategy from the national level down to the lowest levels of the DAR bureaucracy. On the other hand, this geographic distribution also does not support the predeterministic (structuralist) view that certain settings with structural and institutional factors resistant to redistributive land reform have systematically carried out VLT as a major way to evade redistribution. The data suggest partly that the presence or absence of certain types of political dynamics between and among various state and societal actors tends to have influenced the degree to which VLT was carried out in particular geographic locations. This is discussed further in chapter 4.

Extent and geographic distribution of CARP scope deduction

By early 2005, a total of 2.37 million hectares of land had been scooped out of the DAR's redistribution scope (DAR-MIS, 2005). This is equivalent to roughly two-fifths of the original DAR scope. But the actual extent of lands not reflected in the current official CARP scope may be higher than the official records claim. As Putzel (1992) explained,

> In 1988, as part of its preparations for agrarian reform, the government launched *"Listasaka,"* a land registration programme …. It is likely that the

Listasaka itself underestimates the extent of inequality in landownership, since owners probably did not report the full extent of their holdings, and there was no way of identifying owners who registered lands in more than one province or who were part of a larger landowning family. (28–29)

However, the process of reducing CARP's scope did not stop in 1988. In fact, after 1988, more landholdings that were already marked for redistribution through CARP were struck out of the official scope.

Extent and geographic distribution of the deductions
A careful look at table 3.3 reveals that the total national reduction is highly concentrated in a few regions: nearly 8 out of every 10 hectares deducted nationally came from only six of the seventeen regions and island groups (i.e., regions 13, 10, 11, 2, 4-A, and 5). In fact, three regions alone (10, 11, and 13/Caraga) account for a million hectares of land deducted from the scope, representing two-fifths of the total DAR reduction nationally. In four regions (4-A, 9, 10, and 11) the original scope was reduced by half or more. Region 12 registered a nearly zero reduction and is the top region in overall land redistribution performance by quantity; at a glance this region is "anomalous" in a positive way, but a deeper contextual investigation shows otherwise: there is nothing more to deduct because the private agricultural land category marked for compulsory acquisition in that region's original scope was already too negligible to merit further deduction (9 out of 10 hectares of land deducted nationally come from the private agricultural land category marked for compulsory acquisition; see the section below on extent and deduction by land type and legal grounds). The data for ARMM is similar to that of Region 12's.

These regions have varied structural and institutional settings. For example, Regions 13 and 12 are geographically remote from important urban and financial centres and are marked by the dominance of food-based and subsistence farming. Region 11 is dominated by the same type of farming systems; but it is at the same time the country's main site for modern plantations for banana and pineapple and has seen rapid urbanization. Region 4-A is marked by massive urban sprawl, which has emerged in the past two decades. In short, the distribution pattern of scope deduction is highly uneven, suggesting the likelihood of anti-reform manipulation in the reduction process.

Legal grounds for deductions
Among the usual, almost automatic replies from DAR officials when asked about CARP scope reduction is "You cannot redistribute rivers, roads and

Table 3.3
Deductions from the CARP scope, in hectares, by region, as of 31 March 2005

Island group/Region	Original scope	Deductions	Working scope
Total for the Philippines, including ARMM	6,676,444	2,375,612	3,591,055
CAR	149,846	68,891	4,300,832
Region 1	212,085	73,838	138,247
Region 2	527,822	177,800	350,022
Region 3	460,855	47,520	413,335
Region 4-A (CALABARZON)	480,584	318,048	162,536
Region 4-B (MIMAROPA)	184,518	22,201	162,317
Region 5	510,334	163,020	347,314
Region 6	553,914	92,869	461,045
Region 7	212,870	69,091	143,779
Region 8	555,197	156,804	398,393
Region 9	251,783	66,431	185,353
Region 10	491,259	229,967	261,292
Region 11	635,206	.428,139	207,067
Region 12	604,699	147,899	456,800
Region 13	504,614	304,698	199,916
ARMM	340,858	8,397	332,461

Source: DAR-MIS (2005).

watersheds," and "the landlords have their retention rights guaranteed under the law," or "these were not defined in the 1988 land registration, and so, after data clean-up that could be done only during the process of actual land acquisition, these landholdings had to be taken out of the scope." These explanations sound reasonable, until one examines the disaggregated data on reductions in tables 3.4a and 3.4b.

Several questions are raised by the data in these two tables. Perhaps the most critical point to notice is that the mysterious category of "others" accounts for nearly half the total deduction, at 42 percent. The category "others" also tops the reasons cited for the deductions in the five regions that made the biggest cuts to their original scope. Meaning, in the top five regions, nearly a million hectares of land that could involve nearly half a million peasant households were dropped from the original scope without any clear legal grounds or explanation — except for the vague category of "others." The combined total of hectares taken out of the top five regions based on the amorphous reason "others" accounted for 8 out of every 10 hectares deducted from the national scope. Another question is raised when we look at the most commonly cited legal grounds for deductions within the DAR bureaucracy (reason no. 7, order of retention and exemption) and notice that only four regions (2, 8, 10, and 11) accounted for nearly all (84 percent) of the national deduction made based on these grounds.

Deductions based on "problematic lands"

The DAR has also devised a mechanism for further classifying lands according to the degree of difficulty in land reform implementation. In particular, it has labelled some landholdings as "problematic." Problematic lands are those whose official land title registration could not be found, landholdings with

Table 3.4a
National summary of deductions based on legal grounds, as of the end of 1998

	Legal grounds	National deductions	
		in ha.	% share
1	18 degree slope and undeveloped	167,883	6.6
2	watershed/timberlands/rivers	351,486	13.8
3	used for infrastructure	120,082	4.7
4	eroded/silted	34,866	1.4
5	areas zoned/classified as non-agricultural prior to 1988	21,455	0.8
6	legally and illegally converted lands	14,867	0.6
7	with order of retention and exemption	318,496	12.5
8	EO 447/448 non-"CARPable" portion	148,021	5.8
9	alienable and disposable (A&D) after 1984	253,125	9.9
10	fishponds/CFD/for leasehold	43,556	1.7
11	"others"	1,077,898	42.2
Total		*2,551,735*	*100*

CARP's Non-redistributive Policies and Outcomes | 153

Table 3.4b Geographic (regional) distribution of deductions based on legal grounds, in hectares, as of the end of 1998*

Region	Legal grounds										
	1	2	3	4	5	6	7	8	9	10	11
CAR	9,475	22,362	228	1,317	216	36	10,666	25,923	2,708	0	25,205
1	25,233	18,303	527	1,809	1,154	623	4,546	1,046	962	0	21,478
2	15,503	10,648	112,876	2,114	3,515	1,400	42,760	10,432	1,663	0	0
3	4,794	43	147	0	0	64	1,887	0	0	15,763	16,621
4	44,110	26,393	912	547	4,694	5,407	15,536	1,201	31,363	4,140	223,712
5	13,948	21,274	740	1,306	0	516	4,818	8,226	1,564	2,663	89,394
6	14,668	3,791	944	17	1,294	1,050	5,757	2,015	0	4,417	40,377
7	3,209	14,892	448	1	2,378	394	3,293	0	561	198	40,509
8	1,756	7,963	74	5	64	414	48,799	8,837	30,128	0	28,354
9	27	2,034	222	313	131	131	1,237	72	1,940	14,653	23,678
10	11,552	27,259	419	814	2,219	609	71,842	6,936	113,102	0	16,701
11	7,393	92,095	1,519	26,540	5,779	3,340	105,008	51,858	69,136	0	329,236
12	0	0	0	0	0	0	0	0	0	0	0
Caraga**	16,215	104,429	1,025	82	10	883	2,347	31,476	0	1,722	222,633

* Numbered columns correspond to the formal legal grounds for deductions; the same numbers are used here as are shown in column 1 of Table 3.4a,
** Caraga = Region 13

Notes: This table does not give figures for ARMM, since many official national census data do not include ARMM — although some do (e.g., tables 3.2 and 3.3). Region 12 did not submit a report. However, this is unlikely to matter, since by the end of 2001, that region had only 1,607 hectares in total deductions. This detailed data on the formal justifications for deductions made from the CARP scope have not been made available publicly; the information remains accessible only through an internal document within the DAR.
Source: DAR-MIS (1998a; see also Borras, 2003b).

legally contested ownership, farms with existing boundary disputes, or simply farms whose owners vigorously resist land reform. Once labelled as "problematic," the land acquisition and distribution process for this particular landholding usually comes to a halt. It is widely believed that after some time many of these lands are dropped from the scope altogether. By early 2005, there were 211,350 hectares that were labelled problematic, involving probably around 75,000 potential peasant beneficiary households (DAR-MIS, 2005: 1); this accounts for around two-fifths of the official land distribution, which was placed at 685,954 hectares for that period.

Deductions by land type and legal grounds
Focusing on the private agricultural land (PAL) category and legal grounds for deduction, the following observations may be made (refer to table 3.1). Nearly nine out of every ten hectares deducted from the DAR scope as of 1998 were accounted for by the PAL category, the overwhelming majority of which came from lands marked for compulsory acquisition. These PAL deductions were concentrated in a small number of regions: three regions (4, 5, and 11) accounted for exactly half of the total deductions made in the land size category of 50 hectares and above; three regions (4, 11, and 13) accounted for half of the lands deducted from the PAL in the category 24–40 hectares; the same three regions accounted for 56 percent of the total deduction in the PAL 5–24 hectare category. Nearly half of all landholdings deducted from PAL were in the "others" legal grounds category. Legal grounds nos. 1, 2, and 9 (18-degree slope, timberlands, and A&D lands after 1984) also posted significant totals; these figures may be suggestive of elite encroachment on supposedly public lands that are usually in upland locations.

The scope deduction has therefore been significant in terms of quantity and furthermore has been concentrated in the private agricultural land category; it is thus quite unfortunate that few land reform analyses have inquired into this question more deeply (see Borras, 2003b). Moreover, the data on sub-national outcomes of the DAR scope reduction process have been extremely varied and uneven and cannot be fully explained by simplified national-level, generalized views. The particular case of the province of Pangasinan is quite interesting, because that province produced several personalities connected to land and rural reform policies: Conrado Estrella (Marcos' top official for land reform from the 1960s onward), President Fidel Ramos, Jose de Venecia (speaker of the House of Representatives), Roberto Sebastian and Leonardo Montemayor (secretaries of the Department of Agriculture), and Hernani Braganza (DAR

Table 3.5 Pangasinan's land reform accomplishment, DAR jurisdiction, in hectares, as of 2001

Type	Scope	Deductibles	Working scope	Accomplished as of Dec. 2001 (net)	Accomplished in 2001	Balance	Problematic	Workable scope
OLT	31,423	1,627	29,796	29,350	120	334	331	3
PAL >50	*15,038*	*10,993*	*4,044*	*3,701*	*55*	*343*	*237*	*106*
VOS	223	6	217	217	0	0	0	0
CA	12,347	10,987	1,360	1,017	3	343	237	106
VLT	2,467	0	2,467	2,467	52	0	0	0
PAL 24–50	*11,073*	*8,182*	*2,891*	*2,835*	*62*	*56*	*56*	*0*
VOS	1,026	659	367	337	0	29	29	0
CA	7,657	7,523	134	108	0	26	26	0
VLT	2,390	0	2,390	2,390	62	0	0	0
PAL 5–24	*39,276*	*21,197*	*18,079*	*17,932*	*66*	*131*	*65*	*65*
VOS	1,174	311	863	814	17	49	0	49
CA	21,035	20,865	170	99	0	71	65	6
VLT	17,067	21	17,046	17,020	49	10	0	10
PAL <5	*3,811*	*0*	*3,811*	*3,808*	*0*	*3*	*3*	*0*
VOS	45	0	45	45	0	0	0	0
VLT	3,766	0	3,766	3,763	0	3	3	0
GOL								
GFI	3,058	1,422	1,636	1,566	3	70	36	34
KKK	8,717	739	7,978	7,960	67	0	0	0
LE	3,266	0	3,266	3,266	0	0	0	0
SETT	4,496	393	4,103	4,103	0	0	0	0
TOTAL	120,158	44,554	75,604	74,521	373	936	729	208

Source: DAR-MIS (2001a).

Secretary). Despite — or because of — this, the scope deduction in that province was so extreme in terms of reductions of the private lands marked for compulsory acquisition that very few private landholdings were left for redistribution (see table 3.5).

Extent and geographic distribution of "uninstalled" beneficiaries

By the end of 1997, according to official reports, there were almost 11,000 beneficiaries who could not actually occupy their awarded lands due to landlord opposition, which was often violent. Though some of these disputes might have finally been settled by 2002, new cases have undoubtedly emerged. Overall, such incidence is likely to have increased after 1997, as the government started to concentrate redistribution initiatives on the highly contentious private lands (unfortunately, this study was not successful in securing updated data). The phenomenon of uninstalled beneficiaries is unevenly spread across the country. In fact, six out of the fourteen regions (regions 5, 6, 7, 8, 10, and 13) accounted for 88 percent of the total hectares affected by this problem. Moreover, half of the total hectares affected were in only four provinces (Garilao, 1998). Negros Occidental is host to perhaps the most numerous instances of such cases. It is possible that the actual extent of this problem may be higher and that not all local DAR officials report such cases. However, field investigations revealed no strong indications of a huge discrepancy between the official data and reality on the ground.

Extent and geographic distribution of land reform reversals

The problem of land reform reversals, where previously issued CLOAs and emancipation patents (EPs, in the case of rice and corn lands under PD 27) have been recalled and cancelled by the DAR is a serious one, because it demonstrates the capacity of anti-reform forces to reverse previous redistributive reforms. By mid-1998, 18,000 hectares that had previously been awarded to peasants had been recalled and cancelled. It is most likely that the quantity in hectares and number of beneficiaries affected by this problem have increased since then. Unfortunately, efforts to secure updated data on land reform reversals were unsuccessful. But the phenomenon of these reversals is sporadic. For example, only three regions (2, 4, and 5) accounted for 9 out of every 10 hectares cancelled nationwide. Meanwhile, some of the land reform beneficiaries affected were re-awarded land elsewhere and some of the official records adjusted accordingly (see DAR-MIS, 1998b). But again, it is likely that the actual extent of this phenomenon is higher than has been officially reported.

Extent and geographic distribution of land use conversions

Land use conversion is an emotionally and politically charged issue in the context of CARP implementation. It is widely believed that landlords connive with government officials to approve land use conversions (usually to non-agricultural uses) as a way to evade land reform or in order to avail themselves of the higher value of land in the non-agricultural market — or for both reasons.

There are illegal and legal land use conversions. The illegal conversions are difficult to ascertain due to the absence of formal records, but when driving along the highways of the urbanizing areas in a number of urban enclaves in the country it is easy to see that these conversions are taking place: In many areas, the former ricelands on either side of the highway now have commercial, industrial, and residential developments built on them. Local government units (empowered by the 1992 Local Government Code to make land use zoning ordinances in their localities) are known for their propensity to ignore the DAR rules and regulations on land use conversions, and they do not normally report land use conversions. Certainly illegal land use conversions have affected far more hectares of land than the legal conversions. As for the legal land use conversions, this study could secure only data from between July 1992 and September 1997. Fortunately, this period is likely to capture the bulk of land use conversions in the country, as this period was marked by a real estate boom which started to taper off in 1998.

Official data show that the approval rate for land use conversions filed (LUCFs) during the period 1992-1998 was 85 percent. This rate was maintained during the Morales DAR (from mid-1998 to 2000). The geographic distribution of legal land use conversions is highly skewed: five regions (3, 4, 6, 10, and 11) accounted for nearly 9 out of every 10 hectares affected by approved conversions. These are regions where urban sprawl has grown massive over the past two decades. The same regions accounted for two-thirds of the total number of approved LUCFs, with regions 4 and 11 topping the list of regions with the highest approval rates (in terms of number of LUCFs) (see Garilao, 1998).

Extent and geographic distribution of leaseback

Leaseback is the term used when the land reform beneficiaries who were awarded the land enter into a lease contract with another entity, usually the former owner of the land. This CARP provision was ostensibly meant to maintain the operation of major agribusiness multinationals in the country. By early 1994, there had been few leaseback contracts: There were only eight major leaseback contracts, which involved some 32,000 hectares and 19,500 beneficiaries. These include the two best known leaseback arrangements: the Del Monte contract in Bukidnon, involving 8,000 hectares and 9,000 beneficiaries, and the Dole contract in South Cotabato, involving 8,900 hectares and 7,500 beneficiaries. Both plantations are devoted to pineapple, both had ten years for their first contract (beginning in 1988–1989), and both had very low lease rental rates (PhP 3,000 per hectare per year). As the deferment period of other commercial farms began expiring in the late 1990s, additional leaseback arrangements started to trickle in (some of which were mentioned earlier in this chapter). Yet, most of these arrangements are located on selected farms in the plantation enclaves of Mindanao. Leaseback was not a nationwide phenomenon in the 1990s, however the post-2000 flurry of VLT transactions on commercial plantations and VOS schemes in sugar cane haciendas in Negros Occidental is likely to usher in an era marked by widespread leaseback arrangements.

Extent and geographic distribution of SDO

Contrary to earlier pessimistic predictions, SDO was not implemented on a wide scale: From 1988 to early 1992, eighty-nine SDO applications were made affecting nearly 34,000 hectares and reportedly involving close to 24,000 tenants and farmworkers. Of these, fourteen applications were approved by the PARC, covering more than 6,000 hectares and affecting almost 7,000 peasant households; another fourteen applications were rejected, affecting nearly 6,000 hectares and involving more than 4,000 peasant households. By the end of 2000, there were still a number of pending applications at the PARC: 20 applications involving more than 4,000 hectares and nearly 3,000 peasant households (PARC-EC, 2002).

Yet the geographic and sectoral distribution of SDO applications has been highly skewed: It has been carried out mainly in sugar cane plantation enclaves, and two giant corporations have a combined percentage share of two-thirds of existing SDO arrangements in total hectares and three-fourths of total beneficiaries (Hacienda Luisita Inc. and the Arsenio A. Acuña Corporation). One possible explanation for the unexpectedly low extent of SDO implementation is that the arrangement might have really been intended only for former president Aquino's Hacienda Luisita. Another possibility is that landlords were turned off by the cumbersome processes of application, monitoring, and evaluation, as well as political uncertainty (since it is a conditional arrangement) as compared to other more straightforward evasive schemes. One thing that must be said about the anti-reform use of the SDO provision is that several applications were allowed to remain pending for many years, especially in Negros island, effectively maintaining the status quo on these farms — meaning effectively no redistributive reform (Carranza, 2005). On the eve of his departure from office, and pressed by the peasant group UNORKA, Secretary Morales publicly announced that he would declare all pending SDO applications to be placed under immediate expropriation. This was at the same time that he announced that he was ordering an investigation of the Hacienda Luisita SDO case. The Macapagal-Arroyo administration did not take up the general SDO case, however, nor the Luisita issue — until the bloody incident in November 2004 where seven workers were killed on the picket line. But the government has still refused to reopen the case of Hacienda Luisita in terms of land reform, demonstrating the degree of influence the family of former President Aquino has within the central state — at least until 2005, when the Cojuangcos and the Aquinos joined the political opposition against the Macapagal-Arroyo presidency, calling for the resignation of the president on charges of corruption and electoral fraud.

Extent and geographic distribution of overpriced land valuation

As explained earlier, it is not easy to establish a nationwide benchmark for determining overpricing, although obviously wide differences in valuation between LBP and judicial and quasi-judicial bodies provide one indicator. What is certain is that average prices for land acquired under CARP have increased steadily, although the average land price for rice and corn lands under OLT remains much lower than the non-OLT private lands. Based on LBP records, the average price for landholdings outside the OLT's rice and corn lands was more or less PhP 18,000 per hectare in the period 1988–1992, jumping to PhP 53,000 in the period 1998–2001 (LBP, 2001). The higher average prices for banana plantations (PhP 300,000 per hectare) and some sugar cane farms (PhP 90,000) could have pulled up the national average, since coconut lands tend to be priced much lower. Meanwhile, OLT rice and corn lands have generally been priced at a still lower level: an average of nearly PhP 7,000 between 1988 and 2001. This is startlingly low, since a hectare of irrigated riceland can easily sell for PhP 100,000. The lower national average price for OLT rice and corn lands might be explained by the likelihood that most of the rice and corn lands sold under the land reform program were the upland, marginal, and isolated farms, which would have been sold quite cheaply. It is very likely that most irrigated rice lands along the highways and near municipal centres were successfully excluded by their owners from the land reform process. Under PD 27, the per hectare prices of rice and corn lands were based solely on their levels of productivity. This resulted in a very low national average land value before the start of CARP in 1988. The bases for pricing were revised under CARP, and new factors, such as proximity to roads, potential value for other uses other than rice, and so on, were introduced in response to lobbying by the rice landlords. The latter were only successful to a limited extent, however, because while they were able to achieve modest increases in the prices of their land, they were not able to have ricelands excluded from the land reform process or even delay the land reform process in this sector — as was achieved, for example, by the commercial plantation owners (see Riedinger, 1995).

Nationally, it is quite difficult to assess the actual prices to be paid, or being paid, by the beneficiaries, mainly because most beneficiaries have not yet made their amortization payments, principally due to administrative and technical problems within the LBP and the DAR, and also because many beneficiaries have already defaulted, deliberately or otherwise, on their payments for the awarded land. Moreover, when LBP President Margarito Teves was arrested and detained in 2002 on charges of contempt of court, filed by the PARAD of Nueva Ecija for the LBP's refusal to pay the abnormally high price of land in that province, the LBP admitted the existence of about a dozen more similar cases of overpricing (LBP, 2001). The LBP refuses to pay for these landholdings. While it is difficult to prove that overpricing is sporadic rather than systematic, it is equally difficult to scientifically back up activists' usual sweeping claims of wholesale and systematic overpricing and valuation rigging. The case of the Autonomous Region of Muslim Mindanao (ARMM) is, however, different. Overpriced VOS transactions (quite apart from the fictitious land sales discussed below) are widely reported to be systematic in that region (see Gutierrez and Borras, 2004).

Extent and geographic distribution of record padding

It is difficult to pin down the exact extent of deliberate padding of records. One reason for this difficulty is the fact that it is unlikely to be a national state policy to deliberately rig the accomplishment records, at least not during the Garilao and Morales administrations (1992–2000). Hence, as stated earlier, this phenomenon is sporadic and happens more likely at the initiative of some middle- to lower-level DAR employees. However, and again, the case of the ARMM is different: It is widely believed that deliberate padding of accomplishment reports is systematic in that region. It is so clear that there are problems in that region that the central DAR does not even include the ARMM's figures in its national report.

Easier to locate than record padding are the cases of double entries in the leasehold accomplishment report. The extent of this problem is significant, possibly bloating the output reports by as much as 650,000 hectares and 500,000 beneficiary households. The years 1991 to 1994 are the "bloated years" due to the inclusion of "transitional leasehold" in the report, with regions 8, 9, 10, and 11 posting unbelievably high accomplishment reports for that period (see data in chapter 2).

Record padding is also strongly suggested by the appearance of more than one hundred percent land distribution accomplishment rates in some regions (see, e.g., table 3.2, this chapter, and table 4.1, chapter 4). In his discussions with DAR officials and peasant groups in the field, the author discovered that some local officials continue to report land distribution accomplishment even after completing distribution of all the officially registered official scope of the program, thus resulting in more than one hundred percent accomplishment rate.

Fictitious titles sold to DAR

The extent of sales of fictitious titles is also difficult to pin down. Annual internal audits of AMIC-PARC have not reported any cases as such. This practice may be peculiar to ARMM, where, as discussed above, fake titles sold to the DAR through VOS amounted to around PhP 2 billion between 1996 and 1999. When these titles were double-checked for authenticity at the Central Bank in Manila, it was found that eight out of every ten land titles paid for by the ARMM-DAR were actually fake. These practices reportedly spilled over to some extent to the nearby provinces of Sultan Kudarat, North Cotabato, and Lanao del Norte. VOS implementation in the ARMM was stopped by the Morales DAR in 1999.[47]

Failed attempts to redistribute land

There is no known government databank that systematically gathers data about failed attempts to redistribute land. Unfortunately, even civil society organizations tend to databank only those landholdings that have ongoing land tenure reform engagement. This study is thus unable to estimate the extent and geographic distribution of this particular non-reform CARP outcome.

3.4 CONCLUSION

There are several land transfer schemes enshrined within the official state land reform law as well as introduced through the initiative of the World Bank that were included in the land redistribution accomplishment of CARP. It has been demonstrated in this chapter, however, that it is wrong to count them as redistributive land reform gain. We must consider these non-redistributive policies and outcomes because there was no real transfer of wealth and power from the landed to the landless and near-landless classes — meaning, there was no real pro-poor reform in the actually existing social and production relationships. The evidence gathered in this chapter is sufficient to justify the belief that the extent of redistributive land reform accomplishment in the country is far below the official claims. There are a number of land transfer schemes that do not constitute real redistributive reform.

Moreover, the findings in this chapter support Putzel's recent observation about MLAR and MLAR-like market-friendly land transfer schemes in the Philippines. He said,

> The [World] Bank's model provided a convenient justification for the movement toward voluntary land transfers. Because it ignores the institutional and political dimensions of the market, it can offer little hope for accelerating redistributive reform in the country; instead, it seems to be gaining influence precisely as a means to wind down further redistributive reform efforts. (2002: 224–225).

CHAPTER FOUR
CARP'S REDISTRIBUTIVE POLICIES AND OUTCOMES

> Inertial dynamics ... means ... that any social system forms routines and institutions that tend to reproduce existing distributions of power and privilege, placing limits on the extent of redistribution possible under normal conditions .... [T]he most basic structures of society are supported by a formidable array of ideological and institutional props that resist fundamental change. In agrarian societies, institutions surrounding land control are the most fundamental of these structures .... The real puzzle of land reforms is therefore not that so many fail, but that some succeed in overturning systems that have operated for generations, buttressed by cultural expression, multidimensional dominance of individuals at the bottom of society, and embedded administrative and legal routines ultimately guaranteed by the coercive power of the state. How is the inertia of reproduction of the basic outlines of such structures broken? (Ronald Herring, 1990: 50–51)

4.1 INTRODUCTION

Evidence presented in the preceding chapter calls into question the official claim about CARP's massive land redistribution and tenancy reform accomplishment. Yet, this does not mean that critics who earlier predicted and currently claim insignificant achievements of CARP are fully vindicated. This chapter analyzes the evidence showing that portions of the officially reported land redistribution achievement are in fact gains in redistributive reform, regardless of whether they are popularly accepted as such. It also looks into the extent to which such outcomes have been achieved nationally. Section 4.2, the longer portion, analyzes disaggregated themes around policy issues and outcomes. It establishes the empirical bases for the systematic classification of some policies and outcomes as truly redistributive reform with reference to specific cases. Section 4.3 goes on to explore the likely extent and geographic spread of land redistribution outcomes.

4.2 THEMATIC VIEW OF REDISTRIBUTIVE POLICIES AND OUTCOMES

As noted in the introduction and chapter 1, the dominant thinking in the land reform literature is private property biased (with over-emphasis on the transfer of the right to alienate), positing that redistributive land reform occurs only through the expropriation of private lands. In the Philippines, this takes the form of a general assumption that the compulsory acquisition (CA) mode in land acquisition and distribution is the only CARP component that constitutes real redistributive reform. Therefore, in the quest to determine the extent to which CARP has produced redistributive outcomes, scholars and activists alike tend to simply divide the nationally aggregated data into private and public lands, and to take only the private lands as those that constitute redistributive reform (e.g., Riedinger, Yang and Brook, 2001). A few scholars go further to consider as redistributive reform only those private lands redistributed via compulsory acquisition (see, e.g., Bello, with de Guzman, 2001: 192–199; Reyes, 2000).

This study agrees with the critics but only partially. It is argued and demonstrated here that there are multiple institutional ways through which redistribution of land-based wealth and power are potentially and actually achieved. In fact, pro-poor redistributive reforms within CARP can, under certain conditions, occur in six broad ways: (i) compulsory acquisition (CA), (ii) operation land transfer (OLT) in rice and corn lands, (iii) "coerced volunteerism" through voluntary offer-to-sell (VOS), (iv) redistribution of landholdings owned or controlled by government financial institutions (GFIs), (v) redistribution of public lands, either under the DAR jurisdiction (KKK and settlement lands or landed estates) or under the jurisdiction of the DENR (A&D and CBFM), and (vi) share tenancy reform via the leasehold program. A further understanding of redistributive reform within CARP can be achieved by clarifying the commonly misunderstood policy question of "inclusion-exclusion" processes among landholdings and land reform beneficiaries. This is the final theme addressed in this section of the chapter.

Compulsory acquisition (CA)

Fundamentally and formally, CARP is compulsory in nature. It declares that all agricultural lands are subject to reform: land redistribution, conversion from share tenancy to leasehold arrangements, and other forms of mandatory production and profit sharing schemes. While exemptions are allowed, these are not automatic exclusions: Landlords have to apply for them and undergo formal approval processes. Neither are exemptions permanent: Landlords have to comply with certain conditions at all times to have the lands maintained outside the expropriation parameter. For these reasons, while such exclusions and exemptions have provided favourable mechanisms for landlords to evade land reform, this has not been an absolute and permanent anti-reform victory. This kind of institutional terrain is quite difficult for pro-reform forces to navigate, but it has, arguably, provided space for further political contestations. This situation in the Philippines can better be appreciated in comparison with experiences elsewhere, such as in Brazil, where there is a constitutional prohibition that excludes productive land from redistribution programs; in Zimbabwe, where the 1980 Lancaster House agreement imposed limitations on the Zimbabwean land reform coverage to exclude white commercial farms; or in the Kerala land reform, where some commercial, for-export producing farms were officially excluded.

The two straightforward expropriationary policies enshrined within CARP, both of which can lead to actually breaking the nexus between landlords and peasants, are the CA mode of expropriating privately owned landholdings and the OLT scheme for private rice and corn lands (OLT is discussed in its own section below). These are the most direct methods of expropriation, and they can be effectively carried out despite landlords' opposition to reform or disagreement over the terms under which their landholding is being expropriated. Control over the land is transferred from the landed elite to the landless and land-poor peasants. CARP states that the compulsory acquisition mode will be used on lands where landlords fail to take other options made available to them, such as VOS or VLT. Thus, CA and its potential and actual value within the CARP process must be assessed not only on the basis of the actual hectares of land and number of beneficiaries listed as CA accomplishment but also for its role in motivating landlords to voluntarily employ the "softer" modes available within CARP, particularly VOS (see Riedinger, Yang and Brook, 2001).

In many instances, the state carries out compulsory acquisition with the active support of autonomous peasant associations and NGOs. Almost always, it is the preferred mode of autonomous peasant organizations and NGOs in the specific landholdings where they have intervened. In CARP's experience, the compulsory acquisition process can be completed within a year. On many occasions, landlords contest the land valuation or coverage, although the CA-acquired lands can, in principle, be redistributed to peasants despite pending landlord protest.

The land reform literature tends to assume or imply that expropriation can occur successfully only under certain structural and institutional settings. It is logical to believe that in sectors where landlords have been politically and economically weakened (generally, those that are no longer significant in terms of foreign exchange earnings, e.g., rice and corn lands — see Riedinger, 1995) can be subjected to land redistribution with relative ease. This is in contrast to the rising sector of modernizing non-traditional export crops usually engaged in agribusiness, such as the Cavendish banana sector. A few others are somewhere in between, that is, their foreign exchange earning capacity is declining, but the enterprises are run by politically entrenched landlords who are able to extract a variety of "subsidies" (or "rent") from the state — for instance, the sugar cane sector. In the two latter sectors, land redistribution efforts are more challenging than in the first sector.[1]

Yet, although it has been employed to a relatively limited extent compared to other land acquisition methods, the CARP's compulsory acquisition mode has witnessed some degree of successful implementation in different structural and institutional settings — regardless of whether the land was extremely productive, export-oriented, large or small. But there are also cases where despite the persistence of state reformists, landholders were able to avoid expropriation. We will examine a number of cases of successful CA-based redistributive land reform.

De los Reyes estate, Laguna[2]

The landholding in this case involves a landlord who has special ties with the national ruling elites: Geronimo de los Reyes is the father of Margarita "Tingting" Cojuangco, who is the wife of Jose "Peping" Cojuangco, who is, in turn, the co-owner of Hacienda Luisita Inc. and brother of former President Aquino. Peping Cojuangco is active in national politics, being an influential member of congress, and is ardently opposed to redistributive land reform. The landlord (Cojuangco's father-in-law, Geronimo de los Reyes) was also influential in local politics (especially during the administration of a former town mayor, who was later convicted of rape and murder and is currently languishing in the national penitentiary). The disputed estate is a 246-hectare hacienda planted mainly to coconut and some subsistence crops like *gabi* (yam). It is located in *Barangay* Imok, Calauan, Laguna, a two- to three-hour drive south of Manila (Region 4, Southern Tagalog). An estimated 400 families live within the *barangay*, most of them located in and around the hacienda. In varying degrees and capacities, they are associated with farm work at the hacienda. The prevailing sharing arrangement between the landlord and the tenants has been the common *tersyuhan*, or 70-30 in favour of the landlord, with the tenants shouldering the bulk of production expenses.

When talk about CARP reached the hacienda in the late 1980s, the landlord began to insist before the peasants and the local DAR that there were only fifteen tenants on his hacienda; the rest, he said, were seasonal farmworkers. It was clear that the landlord was aiming for limited CARP coverage of his estate, if it had to be covered at all, despite the fact that, in principle, CARP covers all land regardless of tenurial relations. Fearing that they would be excluded if they did not assert their claims, most of the peasants who had been said to be seasonal farmworkers overtly challenged that claim before the local DAR personnel. The landlord began his own manoeuvres among the ranks of the peasants, employing the classic divide-and-conquer strategy of consolidating the ranks of his favoured tenants against the other claimants. He also used threats of violence. At this point, the tension at the hacienda was palpable.

Some time in 1990, local Imok residents and claimants to the estate got in contact with the community organizers of a provincial NGO, the Laguna Development Center (LDC). The LDC specializes in assisting landless peasants in their claims for land and is a network member of the PEACE Foundation. The LDC was in fact actively (re)searching land conflicts with "national political significance" combined with concrete local struggles as part of its policy advocacy.[3] Hence, the de los Reyes estate became a land struggle the LDC actively pursued.

Their lack of success with local efforts encouraged the peasant claimants to forge a friendly relationship with the activist community organizers from the LDC. At this point, the peasants feared that the landlord was planning a more systematic effort to decisively disenfranchise them from the land reform process; there were signs that they were going to be evicted from the hacienda. A series of consultations among the peasant claimants, assisted by the LDC, resulted in their forming an organization, the *Tinig ng Magsasaka sa Imok* (TMI, "Voice of Peasants in Imok"). This association was independent of the landlord and his co-opted peasant organization. TMI involved about 100 of the more or less 400 households in the *barangay*.

After a series of consultations with their NGO ally, the TMI formally pushed for the compulsory acquisition of the landholding. The landlord was able to block this move without much effort. The president of the country at that time was Corazon Aquino, and the landlord's family was extremely influential. This was also the time when the DAR was essentially in the hands of conservative forces. The DAR argued that the landholding fell within the "50 hectare and above" land size category and so could not yet be acquired compulsorily because of the calibrated acquisition scheduling within CARP that put this land size category in the later stage. This was true at that time. However, it was also well known within the DAR bureaucracy that this rule was just a guideline and not mandatory. In fact, the main reason for not covering the de los Reyes estate was more political.

Partly due to frustration that their petition was not being seriously considered by the DAR, and partly at the instigation of their ally, which wanted to make a national political case out of the de los Reyes estate, the TMI-affiliated peasants launched a land occupation of the hacienda. They forcibly invaded the farm. They harvested coconuts. They refused to give the landlord any share from the harvest. The landlord quickly retaliated and the peasants were faced with criminal charges (*estafa* [qualified theft] and theft) filed by the landlord before the municipal court. In what turned out to be a sustained tug-of-war between the landlord and the peasants, a series of criminal charges was filed against a number of peasants. The TMI and LDC then thought it was time to bring the battle to the national political stage. The peasants pitched camp at the DAR national office and launched pickets and other forms of mobilization. The media picked up the case because of the landlord's relationship with President Aquino. At this point, the PEACE Foundation became actively involved in the collective action, providing logistical assistance and media work. Through this NGO network, the TMI also became a member the national peasant movement KMP. Pressured by the peasants' activism, the DAR decided to place the estate under compulsory acquisition, but only a portion of it: 146 of its 246 hectares. For various reasons, the landlord was allowed to retain 100 hectares; this was a compromise decision by the DAR. And while the peasants did not fully agree, the landlord continued to resist outright the implementation of even the partial expropriation: The CA occurred only on paper. And so militant actions persisted at the national level.

Back in the village, the landlord retaliated by escalating harassment of peasants. He now prohibited any planting and harvesting within the hacienda. Guards helped secure the estate. Thus, even doing repairs on peasants' huts located within the hacienda could lead to criminal charges. The municipal judge and mayor backed up the landlord. Evangeline Mendoza, a daughter of one of the older peasants and herself a young peasant, recounts,

Talagang mahirap ang buhay namin noon ... hindi kami makagalaw ng kahit anong tanim namin sa loob. Bawal. Pag nasira ang bahay namin di namin pwedeng palitan o ayusin nang maigi, bawal ... may kaso agad sa munisipyo ... Napakalakas ng may-ari sa munisipyo. Yung judge, ni wala ngang ebidensyang pini-present yung may-ari, lalabasan agad kami ng warrant of arrest. Ganun kabilis nung panahon ni mayor Sanchez. [Our life was really hard at that time ... we could not touch any of our crops. When our houses needed repairs, we could not repair them, it was prohibited ... we automatically had a legal case. The landlord was so close to the town officials. The judge would almost automatically sign a warrant of arrest despite lack of evidence. That is how it was during the time of Mayor Sanchez.][4]

However, at the height of the intense struggle against the landlord, in 1993, a serious split within TMI occurred. This was a direct effect of the split within the national-democratic movement (discussed in the next chapter): One group remained affiliated with the KMP while the other faction opted to dissociate itself from the KMP and formed the DKMP (*Demokratikong Kilusang Magbubukid ng Pilipinas*, the Democratic Peasant Movement of the Philippines).[5] This was only a temporary setback in the campaign for land redistribution at the hacienda. Not long after the split, the local DKMP group began to regain momentum and persisted in the struggle to subject the landholding to CARP. But during the second half of the 1990s, the political environment for the peasants changed: A more reformist leadership rose at the DAR, Aquino was no longer president, and the local mayor was ousted from municipal politics. These events led to the partial erosion of the landlord's political clout. The reformist local DKMP group persisted in the struggle, keeping the pressure on national DAR officials.

Finally, in 2000, the DAR was able to decisively settle the dispute, successfully carrying out the surveying of the estate. There were 116 beneficiaries: 25 tenants each got three hectares, while the rest of the seasonal farmworkers got half a hectare each (which is relatively significant especially given that they had their own home lots on the land). The land was valued at PhP 18,000 per hectare. Thus, in 2001, victory was secured, albeit a partial one in terms of land area. Evangeline had become a beneficiary with a half hectare of coconut land. She and her husband now intensively farm the parcel with various intercrops such as *lanzones* and *gabi*.[6] The small parcel of land is certainly not enough, but there is an observable sense of pride and dignity in Evangeline's having a piece of land she now calls her own — secured after a hard struggle. The peasants no longer pay the onerous and oppressive 70 percent share to de los Reyes. Evangeline, more popularly known as "*Ka Vangie*," later became a well-known leader in the new national peasant movement, UNORKA.

Mitra Farm, Albay[7]
The landholding in this dispute involves the Ligao Farm Systems, Inc., called "Mitra Farm" within the DAR and among peasants, because it was owned by Ramon Mitra, who had served as speaker of the House of Representatives during the Aquino administration. The 385-hectare farm, devoted mainly to coconut and cattle, is located in Ligao, Albay (Region 5, Bicol). In 1992, a 264-hectare portion of the landholding was subject to compulsory acquisition, while the rest was excluded, ostensibly due to its being devoted to livestock. But the landlord resisted expropriation of any part of the estate. Thus, it took many years before a "mother" (i.e., collective) CLOA was generated covering the 152 beneficiaries as a group. However, even after the CLOA was generated and awarded to the beneficiaries, the land remained under the landlord's effective control. The survey of the landholding could not be carried out, because armed guards prevented the DAR officials from entering the property. Meanwhile, the beneficiaries were not allowed on the farm. A long impasse followed. And although during this time DAR records showed that the landholding had already been redistributed via CA, in reality, the peasants were not in control of the land.

Since 2000, the peasants have been in contact with community organizers of the PEACE Foundation, which started a land redistribution campaign in the province. Slowly, the militant spirit among the peasants was re-ignited and they began a series of dialogues with and pickets at the DAR offices at the provincial, regional, and national levels. Regrettably, no positive results were achieved from these actions. The peasants and their allies knew that the late Ramon Mitra had lobbied the DAR for the exclusion of his farm from land reform. Earlier, the DAR central office had in fact issued another order declaring that only 154 hectares were to be covered by the compulsory acquisition order and urged the peasants to accept this decision and, if necessary, to start a separate negotiation for the remaining portion of the estate. The peasants did not agree. They wanted all the land contained in the original CLOA: 264 hectares, no less. They launched a series of collective actions at the regional level, including the padlocking of the DAR regional office in Legaspi City, to dramatize their protest against the unfavourable decision on their case. However, little progress was made in the land claim.

On 12 March 2002, the peasants, now organized under PACOFA (Paulog Coconut Farmers' Association, which has affiliated with UNORKA), launched an invasion of the property. They numbered some 120 people, composed both of beneficiaries and of other landless peasants who were not in the CLOA list of beneficiaries. They erected a makeshift camp and started to cultivate the land. The landlord retaliated by filing six criminal charges of theft against eighty-nine peasants, twenty-four of whom were arrested and jailed. Since the peasants had to hide from the police to evade arrest and detention, there was a temporary setback to the campaign. A few months later, however, the peasants regained their political momentum. A series of dialogues, negotiations, and petitions were carried out at the national offices of the DAR. The PACOFA peasant leaders, together with their national allies (UNORKA and PEACE) also held dialogue-negotiations with the national police and the Department of Interior and Local Government to complain about the landlord's use of the local police to harass the peasants and confiscate their coconut harvests. The peasants also held dialogues with the Department of Justice and the Supreme Court Administrator to address the "criminalization" of land reform–related cases, which, they believe, is unjust. The national DAR affirmed its decision to expropriate the 264 hectares. The landlord appealed the case to the Office of the President (OP). The peasants and their allies launched a lobby of the OP, assisted by elite allies who had access to the presidential office. The OP affirmed the DAR's decision.

Emboldened by the series of legal victories, the peasants re-invaded the estate. By November 2002, the peasants were able to retake and maintain firm control of about 150 hectares of land; they have been able to harvest coconuts and plant other crops. This time they have enjoyed the full support of the DAR. Meanwhile, the landlord has pursued his criminal case against the peasants in court, while a petition for exclusion of some portion of the land has also been filed before the Court of Appeals. Clearly, however, at least for the time being, the peasants have been able to take effective control over the land.

DAPCO, Davao del Norte[8]
In this case study, farmworkers were pitted against a multinational corporation (MNC). The estate in dispute, located in Panabo, Davao del Norte (Region 11, Southern Mindanao), involved 1,024 hectares planted to banana and controlled by Stanfilco, the plantation division of global giant Dole. In 1965 the actual landowners, under the name of their joint corporation, Davao Abaca Plantation Corporation (DAPCO), leased the estate to the Standard Philippine Fruit Company or Stanfilco. Dole-Stanfilco used to run their plantations directly, but began experimenting with a contract farming scheme.[9] The contract farming mode of operation tends to be more profitable and less risky

to MNCs, because under this arrangement foreign companies are no longer confronted with perennial irritants like the minimum wage law, autonomous unions, lease rental issues (when the land is privately owned and landlords demand high lease rental rates), and other risks (natural or otherwise). Contract farming squeezes optimal profits from small producers, especially when there is a near monopoly over the marketing and processing of products by one MNC or a few big ones, as is the situation in the Philippines (see, e.g., Watts, 1994; White, 1997; Vellema, 2002). Equally important, these companies are attracted to the contract farming scheme for political reasons, since with this arrangement they are no longer adversely affected by land reform. This case can be better viewed with these considerations in mind.

Right after CARP was promulgated, the landlords of this estate seized the opportunity for coverage deferment of ten years. In 1991 the regional DAR office in Davao gave them a deferment permit for the 870 hectares they had leased to Stanfilco, the contract for which was set to expire in 1995. The remaining 134 hectares, devoted mainly to rice production under the name Mindanao Rice Company (Minrico), were placed under CARP, although the expropriation process did not begin until later. The post-1992 period, however, brought a confluence of factors that, working against the landlords, facilitated redistribution of the previously excluded 870 hectares to the farmworkers as well. On the one hand, after the policy debate on the land reform program in 1987–1988, the MNCs realized that better profits could be made on a "reformed plantation" where contract farming would supersede the direct operation system or land lease contracts with private landlords.[10] At this time, Stanfilco was paying the landlords US$ 700 per hectare per year lease rent (DAPCO, 1985). On the other hand, the new DAR leadership had by then begun looking for an opportunity to publicly demonstrate its resolve to implement land reform on MNC-controlled plantations in Mindanao. As a consequence of their altered mindset, both Stanfilco and the DAR directly encouraged the mobilization of the estate's unionized farmworkers in favour of land redistribution. The interests of Stanfilco and DAR converged: For Stanfilco, the goal was to secure a favourable contract with the beneficiary cooperative that was better than the deal with the landlord; for the DAR, it was to use a "successful" land redistribution case in a major plantation to shore up its sagging public image prior to Garilao's take over of the central leadership.

Thus in 1993 the existing association SEARBAI (Stanfilco Employees' Agrarian Reform Beneficiaries Association, Inc.) moved to legally challenge the deferment permit that had been granted for the 870 hectares. Backed by

Stanfilco and the DAR national leadership, the DAR regional office decided in favour of the farmworkers' petition, revoking the deferment order for the 870 hectares and subjecting the estate to expropriation upon expiration of the lease contract with Dole.[11] The landlords appealed the case twice before the DAR national office but were rejected both times. In January 1995, in a highly publicized ceremony graced by the DAR secretary himself, a "mother" (collective) CLOA for both the 134-hectare Minrico area and the 870-hectare Stanfilco plantation was issued. On the same occasion, a new contract between Stanfilco and the "new landowners," represented by SEARBAI, was publicly presented and hailed by the DAR secretary as the "model" for other plantations. But the subsequent turn of events revealed the model's onerous nature.

SEARBAI, the farmworkers' association, had been formed in 1991. This gave legal status to the workers, who had sought such status in response to a series of retrenchment campaigns implemented by Stanfilco since the late 1980s. The retrenchments aimed to purge the plantation of claim-makers within the CARP framework, and particularly to get rid of militant union leaders and members. The formation of SEARBAI was also part of a widespread campaign launched by various labour unions in anticipation of land reform implementation on plantations. The campaign, however, was rather hastily organized and various trade union issues were largely left off of the agenda (e.g., the plight of seasonal and retrenched farmworkers, production and profit shares, separation pay). These omissions would ultimately prove disastrous to the struggle of farmworkers for land reform.

Before the formation of SEARBAI, many of the workers had been members of a farmworkers' union, NAMASTAN (*Nagkakaisang Manggagawa ng Stanfilco* or United Workers of Stanfilco). The original incorporators and master list of SEARBAI members were all NAMASTAN members. Prior to 1993, the chairperson of NAMASTAN and 48 other workers were laid off by Stanfilco after leading a strike against the company based on contested union issues and demands. From then on, Stanfilco stood firm in excluding the retrenched workers from land reform benefits. But the third wave of leadership in NAMASTAN, which assumed leadership of SEARBAI shortly before 1993 (despite the absence of a formal election or assembly), showed a willingness to cooperate with Stanfilco. This was motivated by the fact that the lease contract of the MNC with the landlords was about to expire, meaning an opportunity was at hand to review the case of the estate for land reform.

By the end of 1994, a memorandum of understanding (MOU) governing the new relationship between the company and SEARBAI had been drawn up. At this point, the declared membership of the cooperative was 482. Eager to begin contract growing arrangements, Stanfilco even helped SEARBAI expedite the expropriation by lending it a huge amount of money for the land survey and other expenses. The MOU, which was endorsed by the PARO, committed the farmworkers-turned-landowners to a twenty-five-year contract with Stanfilco. But several SEARBAI members who had not been part of the negotiations were surprised by the MOU and outraged by its contents. They questioned the contract on the basis of process and substance. They contended, first, that it had not resulted from a process of consultation with all SEARBAI members and, second, that it was disadvantageous to the workers since their incomes would be substantially reduced.

Under the new contract, Stanfilco would pay PhP 22.50 (US$ 0.60 at 1994 foreign exchange rates) per 13-kilogram box of bananas, a very low price by the standards of the banana business. Many of the farmworkers also questioned the MOU's provision for separation pay, which Stanfilco had used as leverage to clinch the onerous contract. The company had made it appear that giving separation pay was an act of generosity from their side, even though Philippine labour laws required them to do so. (When an employee-employer relationship is severed, under certain conditions, the employer is obliged by law to pay separation pay, which is computed based on the worker's length of service. In the context of the banana plantation, this meant a substantial amount of money.) Stanfilco explicitly stated that it would not give separation pay if the farmworkers did not agree to the MOU. Moreover, the same MOU excluded thirty-seven farmworkers plus some other employees. Many of those excluded were the leaders of the earlier strike against Stanfilco who were subsequently laid off on the eve of the expropriation process.

The problems concerning the terms of the MOU revealed the relatively uncritical stance the DAR national leadership had taken toward Stanfilco's earlier moves and its rather narrow concern only with formal transfer of land from private landlords to farmworker-beneficiaries without probing deeper into the question of effective control over the awarded lands. The workers' criticisms were later accepted by many regional DAR officials, who began to be vocal about them when more dissidents from the workers' ranks began to emerge.

The disagreement over the terms of the MOU eventually caused a split in SEARBAI: one group (SEARBAI-1) defended the MOU and another (SEARBAI-2) rejected it. The anti-MOU SEARBAI-2 filed a case with the DAR Adjudication Board (DARAB), calling for nullification of the MOU due to its onerous terms, the issue of inclusion/exclusion of several farmworkers, and SEARBAI-1's questionable mandate to represent the farmworkers. From mid-

1995 to the end of 1996, three successive cooperative elections were held by "SEARBAI members" through the initiatives of SEARBAI-2. In all elections, SEARBAI-2 candidates won the presidency. The first two elections, however, were legally contested by SEARBAI-1 and eventually declared null and void by the SEC on technical grounds.

SEARBAI-2's apparent influence over the majority of farmworkers, as highlighted by the election results, prompted Stanfilco to negotiate with the second group. After some improvements were made in the wage conversion terms of the MOU, a new covenant was forged between the company and SEARBAI-2. But the second group still failed to address contentious issues that had motivated many workers to reject the first MOU: exclusion of a number of farmworkers and other wage and non-wage benefits. Meanwhile, SEARBAI-1, put on the defensive, petitioned the DAR to split the estate between the members of the two cooperatives, signalling its acquiescence to the new covenant forged between SEARBAI-2 and Stanfilco. In October 1996, the PARAD granted the petition, giving formal recognition to the two cooperatives. This new arrangement, however, also implied the exclusion of farmworkers outside of the cooperatives, a pre-emptive move by the two cooperatives, since it was widely believed that those excluded were precisely the ones Stanfilco had vowed to "punish" for their militant unionism in the past.

Feeling betrayed again, most of the twice-excluded farmworkers, joined by others from the two SEARBAI cooperatives who were dissatisfied with the terms of the second MOU, began to strategize on a possible course of action. They sought the assistance of a group of community organizers affiliated with the Mindanao Farmworkers Development Foundation (MFDF), a network of the PEACE Foundation. Among the farmworkers within this group, a common sentiment emerged in favour of "individual titling" as a way to escape any onerous contract that Stanfilco might try to impose under a collectively owned farm. Several sympathetic regional and national NGOs and political organizations were called in to assist, including media groups, which started to train their lens on the Stanfilco case. Also at this point, international solidarity groups extended political support by reporting the issues in their newsletters, raising "action alert" calls, and sending petitions to the government.[12] This international solidarity was sustained throughout the conflict.

The emerging coalition of forces was later joined by an unexpected actor: one of the expropriated landlords (the late Antonio Javellana), who also felt betrayed. This landlord had wanted full market rate compensation for the estate after his appeal for land reform deferment was rejected. (DAPCO land was valued at only PhP 65,000/hectare, while an adjacent similar estate was valued at PhP 125,000/hectare; by 2000, the average estimate of the LBP of the value of a hectare of prime banana farm was some PhP 275,000/hectare; the Floirendos originally asked for PhP 750,000/hectare price for their land.) DAPCO has a pending appeal before the court for a higher valuation. Yet this appeal has been frustrated by both the company and the DAR. For the DAR, which might have viewed Stanfilco as strategically a more important player than the landlord, a lower price for the estate was desirable and justifiable. For its part, Stanfilco preferred a lower value for the land because it would translate into a lower production cost for bananas and therefore lower farm gate prices. Motivated by the desire to get even with both the company and the DAR, the landlord politically and logistically supported the actions of the third group of farmworkers. He started to divulge to the farmworkers' groups and their allies the "ins and outs" of the banana business, especially its oligopolistic practices. Public criticism by many DAR officials of the contents of the MOU also served as indirect encouragement to the twice-excluded but now doubly determined farmworkers.

Emboldened by the convergence of external allies, the disenfranchised farmworkers launched a series of land occupations. Three waves of land invasion began in mid-January 1997, placing more than 200 hectares under their control. The first invasion was accomplished by thirty-seven farmworkers who occupied 40 hectares; the numbers of succeeding land-invaders swelled and the areas expanded. The actions, which lasted for two months, brought the company's operations to a halt. As if to demonstrate a more just and feasible alternative, the group harvested bananas and sold them to buyers at a much higher price — PhP 60 per box compared to the PhP 22.50 in the original MOU.

Meanwhile, Stanfilco, together with SEARBAIs 1 and 2, was able to secure a temporary restraining order from the court to stop the land invasion initiatives of farmworkers, who by then were calling themselves ALDA (Active Leadership for the Development of AgriWorkers). The restraint order was enforced by the military, police, and paramilitary groups who remained in the area as the land invasions continued. This combined force was later responsible for breaking through the barricades erected by the farmworkers. Twelve farmworker leaders were arrested and imprisoned for several days on robbery charges filed by Stanfilco and the two SEARBAIs. But ALDA members held their ground.

From its first day the land invasion was covered by the regional and national press. The media attention lasted several months and had a significant impact on the players. Media reports of the conflict put Stanfilco on the defensive, at the same time embarrassing the DAR national leadership. Political support from allies heightened and widened as a result. The media's timely and high-profile projection of the controversy helped to avert violence when the military came into the picture. During the standoff, the DAR initiated a mediation session between all the farmworkers' groups and Stanfilco to thrash out the question of inclusion/exclusion of farmworkers as CARP beneficiaries. A well known national trade union leader who had previous connections with the farmworkers' organizations was asked to lead the mediation process. This was preceded by top-level negotiations between allied NGOs (PEACE and PARRDS) and pro-reform forces within the DAR on how to resolve the conflict. For three days and two nights, while the meeting was going on, ALDA members pitched camp in front of the mediation centre to keep up the pressure on the different parties. The result was a consensus decision to recognize all three groups as legitimate farmworker beneficiaries of land redistribution. ALDA, with its 124 members, was allotted 134 hectares, while the largest farmworkers' group, SEARBAI-2, got the biggest chunk of land. The ALDA members returned to work as usual in early April. Although the terms of the second MOU were not tackled during the mediation session, the groups did agree to address the matter in a different venue in the future. That meant that, for the time being, ALDA was bound by the old MOU and had to sell its bananas only to Dole under the onerous terms. In addition, it was made clear that ALDA's advocacy position was to press for individual titling to give the farmworkers-turned-landowners room to manoeuvre in case no fair contract could be forged with Stanfilco. Individual titling would also serve as a built-in check on possible corruption in a cooperative mode of land ownership. Thus, the peasants would have the option of individual farming in the future. The partial resolution of the conflict gave farmworkers the breathing space they needed to intensify their post–land reform struggle.

After a year, however, a major mobilization erupted. In August 1997, ALDA padlocked the gate of the DAR office in Davao after the farmworkers became frustrated by the DAR's slow action on their demands to be freed from the MOU binding them to the onerous terms of the Stanfilco contract. ALDA was furious because other buyers were willing to pay US$ 2.80 per box compared to Dole's US$ 0.60. The two SEARBAIs joined ALDA in its petition for higher banana prices. Further negotiations with DAR and Dole-Stanfilco were to no avail. The three groups decided to go on a farm strike: They refused to pick bananas for several weeks. Both Stanfilco and the beneficiaries were losing money, but the beneficiaries sustained their action. The DAR was forced to release a "disengagement order" for Stanfilco and the beneficiaries with regard the old contract. Politically and legally on the defensive, Stanfilco offered to buy the bananas at US$ 2.60 per box. The two SEARBAIs quickly agreed and resumed normal operations.

ALDA, however, refused to take the offer, demanding $2.80 per box and a "re-opening clause" in the contract — a safety valve in case there was a need to review the contract later — since the contract with Stanfilco was for twenty-five years. ALDA remained confident because another buyer was offering a contract with better terms. The DAR did not act on the ALDA petition, however. In February 1998, ALDA members pitched camp in front of the DAR regional office in Davao. This action lasted for weeks with no positive action coming from the DAR. Frustrated and desperate, with their families going hungry, they hauled truckloads of bananas from their farm and dumped them at the main gate of the DAR office, blocking the entire compound with a huge mound of bananas. This *tambak saging* (banana dumping) was played up in the national and regional media, the city mayor intervened, and the DAR was furious. The action ended after three days, with the DAR giving in to ALDA's demands. In the first week of May 1998, almost five years after the process of land redistribution was started, the ALDA beneficiaries had their most decisive victory: the freedom, through a DARAB decision, to sell their bananas to whomever they wanted — breaking free of Stanfilco's control.

In late 1999, the DAR granted ALDA's demand for individual titles to the land — a significant breakthrough in the plantation belt of Mindanao. Subsequent struggles for land redistribution of Mindanao plantations, even those earlier redistributed through collective CLOAs, started to look at and follow the experience of ALDA. The group chose to shift production strategy: from Cavendish bananas for export, to a local variety (*lakatan*) for the domestic market; from collective farming in a collective CLOA, to individually owned and farmed plots but using a cooperative processing and marketing operation. The new strategy has been promising financially and operationally despite difficulties. Subsequent organizational divisions occurred in all of the different groups, but these divisions were based more on farm operational differences. Finally, in 2001, yet another group of former Stanfilco farmworkers who had not joined any of the three groups launched sustained invasions of the untilled portions of the former plantation. As of this writing, their case was being deliberated within the DAR.

The Salomon Estate, Nueva Ecija[13]
In *Sitio* Poultry, *Barangay* Magsalisi, Jaen, Nueva Ecija (Region 3, Central Luzon), about a four-hour drive north of Manila, thirty-eight tenant-peasant

households have been cultivating the 49-hectare Salomon estate. Planted to mango trees and vegetables, the farm was part of a bigger estate, Hacienda Gonzales, where most of the Salomon tenants used to work. In 1972 the farm was bought by the wealthy and politically powerful Pablo Salomon, who established the standard 70-30 tenancy arrangement, in favour of the landlord and with the tenants shouldering the bulk of farm expenses. A former mayor of the nearby town of San Leonardo, the landlord had built and maintained a network of elite allies at the provincial level. His reliance on more "carrots" and fewer "sticks" marked the patron-client relationship with the tenants who worked his farm. By the late 1980s, the mango industry began experiencing a dramatic market boom domestically and internationally, prompting the government to declare this sector an "export winner" and grant a ten-year deferment of the redistribution of untenanted lands planted to mango under CARP. These became the twin incentives for Salomon to oppose the land reform program.

In 1988, anticipating possible expropriation of his farm under CARP because it was a tenanted mango farm, the landlord manoeuvred to evade reform. Using the existing patronage relationship, he "borrowed" from the tenants the right to cultivate the land for one year, ostensibly to pay off his heavy personal debts. Feeling morally obligated, the tenants readily complied with this special, temporary arrangement, even though it jeopardized their own subsistence. To complicate the matter, the landlord induced the tenants to sign a document about this special arrangement, a weapon he would later use against them in court. In addition, the peasants, whose forebears had been tenants on the same land, had no receipts of the land rentals that had been paid to Salomon since 1972.

Unbeknownst to the tenants, the landlord had in 1989 applied for a ten-year deferment of CARP coverage of his estate, claiming it was an untenanted orchard. When the one-year special arrangement ended, he refused to give the peasants back their tenancy rights, despite appeals by peasants to resume the old tenancy relationship. Feeling betrayed and deprived of their main source of livelihood, the peasants resolved to fight for resumption of the previous arrangement. Despite the existence of the signed agreement and their lack of receipts to bolster their claim to the land, the tenants decided to bring their case to the BARC and the MARO. Instead of responding immediately to their inquiry, the local DAR officials passed the petition to higher DAR offices. The peasants later learned from local DAR officials that the landlord had pressured them to decide in his favour.

After a cautious calculation of the overall situation, the BARC-MARO handed down a decision that went way beyond the peasants' demand for tenancy resumption: It ruled that the land ought to be redistributed to the peasants. The peasants, with the memory of how the landlord had stripped them of their source of livelihood still fresh, unanimously agreed to elevate their demand to land redistribution. Confronted by a tactical defeat, the landlord apparently laid down a fallback position. While his petition for deferment was pending, he applied for the retention rights of his children, involving a total of 18 hectares, and at the same time took his case to the provincial level, where he seemed to have greater influence. This evasive move was revealed later when the PARAD, reversing the earlier decision of the BARC-MARO, ruled in favour of the landlord's petition for a ten-year deferment. With this decision, the window of opportunity for the peasants to gain ownership and control of the land seemed to close. Indeed, from 1989 to 1991 the *Sitio* Poultry families mobilized amongst themselves in their municipality without making any significant progress toward getting back the land.

Then in early 1992, they made contact with an NGO, which led to an important breakthrough for them in their ongoing struggle for the land. The NGO, the Nueva Ecija People's Assistance for Development (NEPAD), a network member of the PEACE Foundation, was actively involved in land reform initiatives in the province. The NEPAD was working with the *Malayang Kaisahan ng mga Samahang Magbubukid sa Nueva Ecija* (MAKISAKA, Movement of Free Peasant Associations), which was a member of the national federation BUTIL (*Bukluran ng mga Tagapaglikha ng Butil* or Federation of Grain Producers). Hearing of the peasants' dilemma through MAKISAKA, the NEPAD activists contacted them and offered assistance in the form of organized support and legal advice. The peasants, who were in dire need of allies, welcomed the NEPAD's offer. Together, the peasants and the NEPAD activists reviewed the Salomon estate case, consulting lawyers about the legal parameters of the dispute.

Reinvigorated now by the entry of their allies, the peasants took the case beyond the municipal level, since the local DAR, though sympathetic to them, had earlier been overruled by the PARAD. Together with the NEPAD activists, the peasants put pressure on the provincial DAR office, demanding the recall of the earlier PARAD decision to defer land redistribution on the Salomon estate. But despite a series of mobilizations — demonstrations, pickets and dialogue-confrontations — the provincial DAR stood firm on its decision favouring the landlord. The peasants then took their case to the DAR national office, a move facilitated by the NEPAD, which coordinated with its national network NGO based in Manila to provide legal, political, logistical, and media support. These NGOs shouldered a substantial portion of the peasants' transportation costs, provided them with food and accommodation in Manila for several days, helped to produce public information materials, and sought further legal assistance. A series of collective actions were conducted at the national level: pickets, a dialogue-confrontation, mobilizing media groups to report their plight, and pitching camp in front of the national DAR office. Yet despite the effort, nothing seemed to move in the peasants' favour. The DAR at this point was still controlled by the conservatives. Despite the mobilizations, therefore, the case seemed to have "slept" at the DAR national office. When the new DAR leadership under Garilao took over in July 1992, however, the *Sitio* Poultry peasants and their allies saw some signs of hope. But the new DAR leadership could not yet attend to many local cases. In fact, it would take Garilao's DAR more than a year just to complete the internal "clean-up" it launched when he came to power.

In August 1992 the tenants decided to assert their claim over the land by forcibly occupying it and commencing crop cultivation. They were encouraged by the new leadership in the DAR and their new political-organizational network. Their invasion of the land was a major, albeit calculated, gamble, since CARP contains a clause against "premature entry" of peasants onto contested lands. But these considerations did not deter *Sitio* Poultry peasants from invading the land, perhaps partly because of conflicting legal advice from lawyers who pointed out the ambiguity of the law on premature entry. Meanwhile, the peasants' NGO allies mobilized media from Manila to cover their action in order to publicize the problem nationally.

The landlord was furious. Surprised and angered by the action of those who used to be his timid clients, he sent three armed men to harass them on 3 August 1992, the first day of the land invasion. Unfazed, the peasants continued their barricade and farm work. But at midnight that same day, while they were evaluating the day's activity, known goons of the landlord fired at them with automatic rifles. Two local paramilitary personnel (Citizens Armed Force Geographic Units, CAFGU) who were members of the peasant organization and involved in the land invasion fired back. Gunshots were exchanged for several minutes, killing four peasants and two of the landlord's goons and wounding several others.

The violent incident captured the headlines of the country's major newspapers — especially because one of the wounded was a field reporter from a national newspaper covering the land invasion. The violence put strong pressure on the new DAR leadership to act expeditiously on the land dispute, while placing the landlord in a defensive position that saw many of his provincial political patrons distancing themselves from him. The peasants, even more determined now, continued to occupy the land. In addition, the group formally affiliated itself with the provincial peasant organization MAKISAKA, which in turn later became affiliated with DKMP. Thus from late 1993 onward the national organization used its political muscle to exert added pressure on the DAR to resolve the dispute positively and quickly. The process of mobilizations at the national level, facilitated by their allies, also gave the *Sitio* Poultry peasants the opportunity to meet other peasants from different parts of the country who were likewise involved in land reform struggles. Such encounters played an important role in providing a broader (i.e., national) perspective to their local initiatives. But the landlord continued to employ various legal tactics to block the implementation of land reform on his estate, while the new DAR leadership remained caught in the complicated process of reorganization and reorientation.

As a result, it took 17 months of persistent pressure from the peasants and their allies for the DAR to disentangle itself from the landlord's legal machinations. In January 1994, the DAR revoked the earlier deferment clearance and issued a "mother" CLOA, but only for 23 hectares. Eight hectares were awarded to the landlord's son as his retention rights. The 18 hectares planted to some 500 mango trees were not awarded to the peasants, pending an appeal by the landlord in court. But unlike in the past, the DAR national office at this stage rejected all of the landlord's petitions, forcing him in 1995 to appeal his case to the OP for deferment. The DAR prodded the peasants to file a counter-claim at the same office. Eventually in 1996 the remaining 18 hectares were awarded to the peasants.

The *Sitio* Poultry peasants' victory had a spillover effect in the adjacent towns. The defeat of a landlord, the active role demonstrated by the new DAR leadership, the valuable assistance extended by the NGO allies, and the positive role the media played in the land dispute were all captured by the keen, observant eyes of other peasants in the province. By mid-1997, within the network of NEPAD[14] and its partner peasant organizations, more than 12,000 hectares, both private and public, were redistributed to peasant beneficiaries.

Roxas Hacienda, Batangas[15]
The land dispute in this case involves a sugar cane plantation of some 2,000 hectares in Nasugbu, Batangas (Region 4), a two- to three-hour drive south of Manila. The hacienda, located along the national highway, is owned by a powerful landowning family in Batangas that also controls sugar mills. The landlord's political connections transcend the provincial boundaries to reach the national political centre.

For a long time, the *kasamá* (share tenancy) system prevailed at the hacienda under 50-50 sharing terms, with the tenants shouldering all production costs. There was resentment among the tenants, however, with regard to the terms of tenancy. Negotiations with the landlord led to a tenurial change some years before the CARP era. The sharing system was transformed into leasehold: The peasants paid fixed rental to the landlord equivalent to 25 percent of the average net produce, and the peasants shouldered all production costs. Side by side with the tenants were many farmworkers. Thus, in all about 1,000 peasants were working the land.

In 1991 talk of possible expropriation of the hacienda under CARP reached the peasants. The local DAR started to visit the peasants to talk with them about the possible expropriation of the estate, and community organizers from an NGO (the PEACE Foundation) approached them on the same issue. The possibility of full ownership of the land pushed the tenants to agree to the proposals to acquire the land through CARP. The DAR and the NGO activists started to work with the peasants — but only the tenants, because the farmworkers formed their own network with militant trade union, the National Federation of Sugar Workers, or NFSW. A series of collective actions were launched, from the local DAR all the way up to the central office. In an interview with the author, one beneficiary proudly recalled that they pitched camp in front of the central DAR office and were almost literally blown away by a strong typhoon. But they, together with their allies, persisted in pressuring the national DAR to give in to their demand that the estate be expropriated.[16]

In October 1993, the Garilao DAR issued a compulsory acquisition order expropriating the hacienda. The tenant group formed the cooperative *Katipunan ng mga Magbubukid sa Hacienda Roxas, Inc.* (KAMAHARI, Council of Peasants in Hacienda Roxas), although this arrangement was legally formalized only in 1995. KAMAHARI, with its nearly 500 members, was awarded about 1,400 hectares of land, although this was mostly in the form of several collective CLOAs for a number of smaller expropriated land parcels. The tenants recognized that there were farmworkers even within their own ranks who were family members of beneficiaries and thus also had rights to land, and ultimately their demand for land was also met. In the end, some beneficiaries got a hectare, others three hectares, and still others one and a half hectares. The separate group of trade union-organized farmworkers also got about 500 hectares. A little over 100 hectares was retained by the landlord. The hacienda was valued at some PhP 70,000 per hectare.

However, from the start, the landlord objected to the expropriation, arguing that some portions of the land were in fact exempt from CARP because of an earlier (Marco-era) zoning order that declared those parts of the hacienda tourism areas. Also the landlord claimed there were technical problems in the expropriation process because the Notice of Coverage served by the DAR was given not to the owner but to the hacienda administrator, who is not authorized to receive such a document. The landlord pursued his case to the Supreme Court. Meanwhile, the DAR proceeded with the expropriation and redistribution.

While it has not been an easy transition for the peasants, their progress in farming their own land has been promising. External assistance from NGOs, both Philippine-based and from abroad, has been relatively generous and has proved crucial during the difficult process of making a plantation under new terms and keeping the reformed plantation as financially viable as possible. A large national NGO, Philippine Business for Social Progress (PBSP), was asked by the Garilao DAR to assist the KAMAHARI peasants. The PBSP's assistance began in the late 1990s and continues up to the time of this writing. This assistance covers socioeconomic programs and, recently, legal defence.

The landlord won a partial tactical victory when the Supreme Court recently ruled that some technical errors might have been committed in the expropriation process, and so ordered the resurvey of the plantation. It was a vague ruling, but enough for the peasants and their allies to feel an immediate threat: They had reason to fear that their farm could be reverted back to the landlord. In "backdoor" negotiations to settle the case, the landlord indicated that he was not keen on taking back all of the land. But he was interested in getting back the most commercially valuable portions, those along the national highway. The peasants did not agree, however, and the negotiations collapsed. As of the time of writing, the peasants were fighting back legally, emboldened by the assistance of their ally, the PBSP, which has recruited an activist lawyer to defend their land. Yet, the battle is not over, and the peasants and their allies remain worried.

Operation Land Transfer (OLT) in rice and corn lands

There are ambivalences and contradictions in the attitude of many activists on the issue of rice and corn lands within CARP. Many tend to dismiss the importance of CARP-era achievements in the rice and corn sector through OLT, generally insinuating that it is an "old" reform project and so cannot be claimed by CARP, or that rice and corn are no longer important in the national economy and thus land redistribution can be easily implemented. Yet, these same critics are at the forefront of protests against land use conversions and land reform reversals, which have usually occurred on ricelands. The local case analyzed below calls the dominant assumptions about OLT into question; it shows that there are few essential differences between the compulsory acquisition and OLT modes.

The conflict in this case involved some 6,000 hectares of irrigated ricelands in Candaba and San Luis in Pampanga, Central Luzon.[17] This area, popularly known as the Candaba swamp, produces an annual rice and vegetable crop during the dry season. During the rainy months the whole area is submerged by runoff from the Pampanga River. The overflow from the river brings freshwater fish onto the flooded farms, giving the area its unique dual character as a farmland and fishery ground. The unique natural endowment of the swamp makes its fishery potentials financially attractive to landlords. These farms were left untouched by the Marcos land reform.

The area has a history of violent peasant protest. The Candaba swamp was a hotbed of uprisings in the past, notably in the 1930s and during the *Huk* rebellion of the 1940s and 50s. Candaba was one of the cradles of the *Hukbong Mapagpalaya ng Bayan* (HMB, People's Liberation Army) of the (old) *Partido Komunista ng Pilipinas* (PKP).[18] The area is also known as *Huklandia*, and the peasants there are conscious of their history of organized and militant armed struggle. Even after the demise of the HMB-PKP, the peasants continued to struggle, and have succeeded in lowering land rents since the 1960s. According to villagers, some sixty of their comrades have been killed over the past few decades in these struggles. But all this persistent peasant protest still did not succeed in changing the land property relations in these communities — until an opportunity from above emerged in the shape of CARP.

In the late 1980s, CARP created an atmosphere of "guarded optimism" among the peasants. After several years of implementation, however, there was still no sign of CARP reaching the Candaba–San Luis farms. In 1991, unknown to the peasants, the landlords had tried to secure deferment permits for their estates from the DAR regional office on the grounds that the farms were essentially fishponds and not rice farms. The peasants discovered the landlords' scheme only later, when they began to mobilize by seeking an audience with local DAR officials. Discovering that the local DAR was said to be ready to grant the landlords' requests, and aware of their landlords' political clout, the peasants used their historical and individual connections with political organizations to contact the provincial centre of the PEACE Foundation, which was engaged in similar land disputes in adjacent towns. After carefully studying the parameters of their struggle with regard to the provisions of the law, the peasants, together with their new NGO ally, started to mobilize representatives to the local and regional DAR offices. They made little progress, however, since the local DAR personnel were apparently influenced by the powerful landlords and would not respond to their counterclaim.

The change in the national DAR leadership in mid-1992 renewed the peasants' hopes. During the delay in the process of resolving their case caused by the transition in the DAR bureaucracy, the peasants and their allies were able to consolidate, joining a number of villages into a relatively coherent force. Seasonal farmworkers also became active participants in these mobilizations. In April 1994, they formed an ad hoc organization of tenants and farmworkers called *Malayang Magsasaka ng Candaba at San Luis* (MMCSL, Free Farmers of Candaba and San Luis). The peasants carried out a series of picket-dialogues and street demonstrations directed at local and national DAR bureaucracies. Their NGO ally provided a substantial portion of their logistical needs, from transportation to food and accommodation in Manila. They also brought in the media to cover the issue and facilitated a direct interface between the peasants and the proper authorities within the DAR bureaucracy. These mobilizations brought to the fore the key features of this specific land dispute, which, in turn, caused a split among the local DAR officials between those who supported the deferment permit and others who wanted to push for immediate expropriation. But the same process led to a consensus within the new DAR leadership, which may have seen in the case an opportunity to demonstrate its commitment to reform. The DAR national leadership seemed to realize that, for the same amount of effort needed to deal with a 10-hectare landholding, they could acquire and redistribute 6,000 hectares. The positive response from the national DAR boosted the morale of the pro-reform alliance that had formed around the Candaba–San Luis community, encouraging the mass entry into the organization of thousands more tenants and farmworkers who had previously stayed away for fear of reprisals from their landlords. This broadening participation in the struggle, which at this point numbered some 3,000 peasants, inspired the members to escalate their collective actions. They began setting up camps in front of the provincial and national DAR offices, a move that brought them coverage in the national media, putting the landlords on the defensive politically.

Finally, in August 1994 the DAR rejected the landlords' petition for deferment and ordered the expropriation of 3,000 hectares. The landlords made a last attempt to block the reform, but when they realized the decisiveness of the pro-reform moves, they backed off and shifted their strategy to demanding very high compensation. Victory was secured, since under CARP provisions, land redistribution can proceed despite the protests of the landlords over the issue of compensation. Subsequently, even the landlords' demand for high compensation was rejected by the LBP. However, at this point the victory was only partial, because the DAR was willing to redistribute only 3,000 hectares, benefiting around 1,000 peasants (out of some 3,000 potential beneficiaries). Suspecting that either the landlords had been able to manipulate the process or that the local DAR offices had simply been inefficient, the peasants and their allies resumed their mobilizations to press for the entire 6,000 hectares to be redistributed and for more peasants to be included as beneficiaries. Finally, in January 1995, the DAR announced the expropriation of some 5,000 hectares, pending LBP procedures related to the landlords' compensation protest. Victory was clinched. But the land struggle in Candaba–San Luis is not yet over. At the time of this writing the conflict continued over the remaining 1,000 hectares, which was still not covered by expropriation and redistribution.

"Coerced volunteerism" via VOS

Many observers of the CARP process continue to conflate VOS with VLT, and vice versa (e.g., Riedinger, Yang and Brook, 2001; see also Bello, with de Guzman, 2001). As the discussion on VLT in the previous chapter shows, the two schemes are not the same, nor are they related despite the word "voluntary" being common to both. In fact, on many occasions, VOS is closer to the CA mode (i.e., it can be expropriationary and lead to redistributive reform). But again, even this phenomenon must be understood in a context in which the compulsory acquisition mode hangs over the landlords. In relative terms, the VOS scheme is "softer" than a CA: The cash portion in the compensation to the landlord is 5 percent more than when land is expropriated under the CA mode. But there is also a corresponding decrease of 5 percent in the bonds portion, so that there is no actual price difference. Moreover, DAR officials tolerate the landlords' putting forward "special requests" under VOS, the most usual ones being additional hectares under effective retention, choice lands under retention, and additional beneficiaries recommended by the landlord. This does not necessarily significantly dilute the essentially redistributive character of VOS. Many of the VOS-based land transfers in fact involve land where the previous owners at first opposed expropriation. As the pro-reform forces tilt the balance of power in the peasants' favour, and the landlords realize the futility of their opposition, the latter tended to strike a last-minute compromise with the DAR to shift the expropriation process from the CA mode to VOS. The VOS scheme, under such circumstances, is essentially "coerced volunteerism." The case of Superior Agro is a good example of this.

The estate involved in this case is the Superior Agro corporation located in San Francisco, Quezon (Bondoc Peninsula; Region 4).[19] It is a 540-hectare coconut farm with some cattle on it, worked by more than 200 peasants (tenants and seasonal farmworkers). It used to be owned by two families, Ang and Yao, both based in Manila. The Ang family used to be the direct managers of the farm and employed the classic "carrot and stick" approach in dealing with the peasants, but with more "carrots" than "sticks" on most occasions. For this reason, the Ang family enjoyed the popular support of the peasants, or at least, a portion of them. The dominant sharing arrangement was 60-40 in favour of the landlords. In the early 1990s, the unified landlords got a favourable decision from the DAR on their petition to exclude the entire property from expropriation on the pretext that it was a livestock farm that complied with the exclusion rules stipulated in the CARP law. Most of the peasants did not object to the exclusion petition of the landlords and the DAR decision, at least not overtly. In fact, some of them even supported the move by the landlords.

However, in 1994, the Ang and Yao families reportedly had a serious quarrel that led the Ang family to sell its entire share in the corporation to the Yao family. When the Yao family took over the direct management of the farm, it dealt with the peasants differently, more with "sticks" than with "carrots." The reason for the constant harassment was that the peasants were perceived as being loyal to the Ang family. At this point some NGO community organizers came to the farm to discuss the possibility of subjecting the landholding to CARP expropriation. The NGO was a partner of the Bondoc Development Program (BDP), a German government-funded (GTZ-operated) development project in the peninsula that included a component on land reform.[20]

The deep feeling of having been betrayed by the landlord and the entrance on the scene of an ally emboldened the peasants to challenge the landlord. In 1995, 68 peasants petitioned for the expropriation of the property. The DAR was forced to review its earlier decision on the case. It soon decided to place 82 of the 540 hectares under compulsory acquisition. The landlord resisted and filed a legal appeal, reaching the Court of Appeals. But while the case was progressing through the courts, the landlord began to seriously harass the peasant-petitioners. In 1995–1997, fifty of the sixty-eight petitioners were forcibly ejected from the farm. This harsh move led to an impasse within the peasant group, which was aggravated by the departure of their NGO ally, which for various reasons had severed its contract with the BDP. At this point, demoralization among the peasants was deep and widespread.

In 1998, the BDP found another partner NGO (the PEACE Foundation) to take up where the previous NGO had left off in giving assistance to the peasants. Joint peasant-NGO planning sessions to assess and possibly reinvigorate the campaign for expropriation were held. A three-pronged strategy was finalized: (i) reinvigoration of the petition for expropriation of the entire property, (ii) re-instatement of the ejected peasants onto the farm, and (iii) (temporary) leasehold contract enforcement invoking the law that bans share tenancy arrangements. The peasants' morale was improved by this new sense of direction. They even formed their own organization: SMBSAI (*Samahan ng mga Magsasakang Benepisyaryo ng Superior Agro Inc.*, the Association of Peasant Beneficiaries in Superior Agro, Inc.), whose well-known leader is an articulate, militant peasant woman popularly named *Ate* Becca.

In April/May 1999, the demand "from below" for leasehold contracts took the form of unilateral harvesting, copra-making, and marketing collectively done by the peasants. They refused to give the landlord the usual share. The landlord retaliated by filing numerous criminal cases against the peasants (*estafa* and theft), cordoned the property with barbed wire and hired armed security guards. The peasants and their allies escalated their campaign all the way to the national DAR. They joined other peasant groups from the Bondoc Peninsula in collective petitions for land redistribution. The SMBSAI become a founding member of the Bondoc peninsula–wide peasant coalition called *Kilusang Magbubukid ng Bondoc Peninsula* (KMBP, Peasant Movement of Bondoc Peninsula), which would later become a founding member of the national coalition, UNORKA. The Superior Agro peasant-petitioners joined the numerous peasant mobilizations in Manila, pitching camp in front of the DAR and confronting national government officials. They were also able to mobilize sympathetic national media. A television feature film was made about the peasant struggle and aired nationally.[21] The landlord was beginning to feel the strength of the pro-reform forces — and the DAR was feeling the escalating tension.

In 1999, the Morales DAR ordered the reinstatement of the ejected peasants. It was a tactical victory for the peasants with strategic value. They could once again penetrate the farm and carry out a rent boycott. The landlord refused to obey the DAR order and managed to have three peasant leaders thrown into the municipal jail on charges of theft and *estafa*. But the peasants persisted in their rent boycott. Encouraged by the positive DAR decision, more peasants joined in the campaign. Politically on the defensive, organizationally unable to prevent widespread and simultaneous unilateral peasant claim-making initiatives such as rent boycotts, and legally uncertain, the landlord found his resolve to fight expropriation effectively broken. In 2002, he applied for VOS. At the time of this writing, the DAR was finalizing the details of the VOS, but with the current degree of power of the peasant organization and its allies, it appears likely that the terms will be redistributive.

Government financial institution–owned lands

The category of government financial institution (GFI)–owned lands within CARP pertains to estates owned by institutions such as the LBP or the Philippine National Bank, either as regular assets or through foreclosure. But it also includes landholdings of Marcos cronies taken over by the Presidential Commission on Good Government (PCGG). Some observers treat these lands as government-owned because, of course, by the time the formal land transfer is made, it is the government entity (the GFI) that is engaged by the DAR. Yet, under certain conditions, redistribution of these types of land to poor peasants can be real and significant: There is, in effect, a net transfer of effective control and ownership from a private elite entity to landless and land-poor peasants. A short story about a long drawn out battle over a GFI landholding demonstrates this.

The land dispute in this story involves the 279 hectares of coconut land owned by the Coconut Industry Investment Fund (CIIF).[22] The CIIF is a government-controlled corporation formed during the Marcos regime. It is connected with the controversial "coconut levy fund," a fund made up of monies from the levy imposed by the government on every kilo of copra that peasants sold. The amount of the fund was enormous in the early 1980s, running to billions of pesos. However, it is widely believed that through complex legal manoeuvres, some Marcos cronies, led by Danding Cojuangco, were able to gain control of the fund for their private interests. The legal case over who the real owners of the fund are was still being fought up to the time of this writing.

The CIIF is part of the extensive assets acquired through the levy fund.[23] Some 120 peasants worked the CIIF land, which is located on the boundaries of the towns of Mulanay and San Narciso in Bondoc Peninsula, Quezon. Since the CIIF took over the land, there had been no clear, formal tenancy arrangement between the peasants and the corporation, although in general the peasants were not giving the CIIF any share of the harvest. Even so, they did not have full control and ownership of the land. In the early to mid-1980s, the communist NPA, which had begun to have influence over the villages that include the CIIF communities, began to agitate for the peasants to demand the redistribution of the land for free to the peasant occupants. The underground movement was well aware of the possible national political value of the CIIF because of its association with Marcos crony Danding Cojuangco. The peasants also felt that the land belonged to them because the previous owner's title was legally dubious. With the support of the NPA, the peasant agitation for the expropriation of the CIIF land went on unsuccessfully for years. One of the reasons for the failure of their attempts was obvious: There was as yet no land reform law that covered landholdings outside rice and corn lands. The peasant campaign was stopped short during the 1986–1988 national regime transition, principally because the area where the CIIF was located became a major target in the escalating militarization of the countryside that was part of the Aquino administration's effort to launch a "total war" against the insurgent communists. The principal peasant leader in the campaign for the expropriation of the CIIF was killed by the military during this period.

The discussion about expropriation of the CIIF was resumed in the early 1990s, when the DAR officials approached the peasants about the process through which the landholding could be acquired and redistributed. The DAR officials suggested that the value of the land should be PhP 5,000 per hectare. The peasants refused. They wanted the land expropriated and redistributed for free. After this, there was a long impasse, until 1996, when the peasants contacted the PEACE Foundation, which had started to assist peasant communities on the peninsula in their land reform struggles. The chairperson of the PEACE Foundation was former Quezon member of congress Oscar Santos. He was also a former cabinet member in the Ramos administration and had once been a member of the board of the CIIF. A series of negotiations with the CIIF and the peasants in Manila were facilitated by the peasants' NGO ally. The contentious issue was whether or not the peasants should pay for the land. The peasants were firm in their demand: They thought the land was titled by the previous landlord through less than legal means; they did not intend to pay for the land. The peasants' persistence and the PEACE Foundation's connections within the CIIF leadership finally led to the resolution of the dispute. In August 1997, the CIIF land was redistributed to the peasants, at no cost.

Redistributive reform on public lands

As explained in chapter 1, generally, the literature does not consider distribution of public lands as redistributive land reform. Under certain conditions, however, distribution of non-private lands can amount to a redistributive reform, as a number of cases show:

NDC land, South Cotabato

One example is the case of the 9,000-hectare pineapple plantation in South Cotabato that was presented as a case study in the preceding chapter. But for the purpose of this section, we will quickly sketch the case again:

The Philippine government prohibits foreign companies from owning more than 1,024 hectares of land. This land size ceiling has posed an obstacle to foreign agribusiness companies. Yet it has been successfully circumvented on different occasions, such as in the case of the resale of "friar lands" during the first quarter of the past century.[24] However, the most systematic manoeuvre was made through the formation of the government-owned National Development Corporation (NDC) in 1919.[25] As a corporate entity, the NDC could enter into long-term lease agreements with other corporate entities, domestic or foreign. Huge tracts of land were set apart for the NDC. Later, major transnational companies like Del Monte and Dole would strike long-term agreements with the NDC for large areas of land, far beyond the legal land size ceiling of 1,024 hectares. One of these NDC lands was the 9,000 hectares located in South Cotabato. It was leased to Dole in the 1960s and by 1988, the number of farmworkers on this sprawling pineapple plantation had swelled to some 7,500.

This was the first huge plantation to be redistributed to farmworkers under CARP. It was redistributed to about 7,500 workers. The NDC, having a semi-private purpose and character, demanded payment for the land. The price was set at PhP 17,000 per hectare. The redistribution of the plantation was consummated in 1988. At the time, the redistribution was real. This land redistribution was entered into the DAR official report as accomplishment under the government-owned land category. However, as explained in the preceding chapter, the post–land transfer leaseback arrangement (1988–1998), and the succeeding, contested contract (1998 to present) essentially robbed the farmworkers of the redistributive reform gains they had made. Dole remains in full control of the land, and the set-up is even more financially advantageous to Dole than the arrangement in the NDC era. As demonstrated in the DARBCI discussion in the preceding chapter, the "one-plantation, one-collective-title, one-cooperative" policy bias of the government fits in well with Dole's agenda of power and control and the somewhat elitist tendency among the cooperative leaders (who were usually the "labour aristocrats" under the former plantation set-up). It was the government's policy that was largely responsible for locking 7,500 farmworkers into the onerous contract with Dole, along with the elitist machinations of the cooperative leaders. And it was this policy that, to a significant extent, prevented individual beneficiaries from exercising their own rights and power over their awarded parcels of land.

The Aquino Estate, Quezon
Perhaps the least understood components of CARP are the ones under the jurisdiction of the DENR: the alienable and disposable (A&D) lands and the

Community-Based Forest Management (CBFM) programs. The redistribution of A&D lands is essentially an act of privatizing land ownership; on many occasions CLOAs are given to the beneficiaries. The CBFM program, on the other hand, does not constitute full formal ownership of the awarded lands; generally a stewardship type of arrangement is institutionalized partly through the issuance of a certificate of stewardship contract (CSC) under the old ISFP (together with other forestry-related programs, this was subsumed by CBFM in the mid-1990s — see also, Broad, 1994; Carranza, 2006) and a CBFM contract under the current arrangement. The contract is for a virtual lifetime: twenty-five years, renewable for another twenty-five years. In the past, ISFP awards were given to individuals; since 1999, however, the CBFM agreement is provided to a group of beneficiaries. Under the latter arrangement, while the contract is on a group basis, the actual plot assignment and farm work is done on an individual basis. These two types of land category within CARP have been confronted by a number of policy questions that pose major dilemmas, one of which is the issue of timberlands: Timberlands are formally excluded from CARP's land redistribution program, but neither can they be privately titled. Moreover, many so-called timberlands in the country are in fact no longer devoted to timber exploitation but have been converted to croplands. Some have already been privately titled (although this is illegal), while others remain untitled but under the control of local elites. Tenancy relations on this type of landholding tend to be entrenched. The case discussed below is a complex dispute involving such public lands.

The landholding in this dispute is a 201-hectare farm with rolling hills, tilled by seventy-six tenants and planted to coconut and citrus trees, located in Mulanay, Bondoc Peninsula, Quezon, an isolated town a fourteen-hour bus ride from Manila (the length of the trip is mainly due to bad roads in the area).[26] It is "owned" by the politically and economically influential Aquino family, which is related to other equally powerful families in the *municipio* and has been allied with the political elite of the peninsula. The town of Mulanay, like the rest of Bondoc, is a settler area: it was one of the land frontiers opened for settlement in the 1930s to 1960s, although elites from other areas of the country were the ones able to secure contracts with government to make use of these vast tracts of land as timberlands or pastures. Slowly, some of these elites were able to secure private titles to these lands through fraudulent means, often in connivance with corrupt judges. Others opted not to secure private titles but nevertheless exercise effective control over the land (Carranza, 2006; Franco, 2005; Borras, 2006b). Meanwhile, since the 1970s, the general pattern of land use has been transformed from timberlands to crop cultivation, mainly coconut, and with the influx of settler-peasants coming from various parts of southern Luzon and the Visayas, share tenancy emerged and persisted.

The Aquino estate has this typical historical profile, although the Aquino family was able to secure a private title to this "timberland." Since the 1960s, the Aquino family has imposed tenancy arrangements, with sharing percentages ranging from 70-30 to 80-20 in favour of the landlord, while the peasants shoulder the bulk of production expenses. The Aquino family administered the coconut farm and controlled the tenants through the overseer (*katiwala*). Peasants' lives under this arrangement were hard.

In the early 1980s, the underground communist NPA movement began to organize the peasants in and around the village where the estate is located. During that time, at least seven of the Aquino estate tenants joined the guerrillas in various capacities. In the open, the same tenants became leaders of the militant peasant association organized in the municipality and controlled by the NPA. The NPA's indoctrination on "genuine agrarian reform through agrarian revolution" became the most important campaign issue for organizing the landless peasants (see Putzel, 1995; Kerkvliet, 1993; Rutten, 2000a). In fact the NPA became quite popular in the countryside in the 1970s and 1980s, partly because of its campaign for *tersyung baliktad* (the inverted sharing arrangement). This means that instead of the 70-30 sharing arrangement in favour the landlord, the sharing scheme would be inverted to 30-70 in favour of the peasants. The Aquino estate tenants were hopeful that the NPA campaign would be implemented on their farm, as promised by the guerrillas.

In the mid-1980s, the NPA told the tenants that a meeting with the landlord had been arranged, and that the tenants must themselves put forward the demand for a *tersyung baliktad*. The guerrillas would be present at the meeting to intimidate the landlord into agreeing to the peasants' proposal. The meeting occurred, but the NPA did not show up. The peasants were unable to even open their mouths to say what they wanted. The landlord verbally abused them, and the peasants were made to apologize for taking up the landlord's time. The peasants later suspected that the NPA had failed to show because it was able to strike a deal with the landlord on a "revolutionary tax."[27] This incident changed the peasants' attitude toward the NPA. It was a major setback for the peasants' effort to alleviate their difficult living conditions. Meanwhile, during the period 1986–1989, the village was subjected to militarization as part of the government's "total war" policy against the communist insurgents. Two tenant-farmers from the village were killed due to the indiscriminate bombings by the military.

By the early 1990s, the NPA's presence was waning in the village. Yet the peasants still toiled under the onerous share tenancy arrangement. Around this time, the DAR information campaign about CARP reached the village. The peasants became interested. But it was only toward the mid-1990s that they started to organize themselves around the issue of reforming the tenancy arrangement based on the CARP law that declares share tenancy illegal and requires a shift to leasehold. The peasants got excited; to them, CARP's leasehold was just like the NPA's *tersyung baliktad*, or even better, since their share would be slightly higher and such a contract would be legally secure, unlike the NPA-brokered arrangement. Hence, the tenants preferred leasehold reform to land redistribution.

In 1995, they formed an association, SAMALA (*Samahan ng Malayang Magsasaka sa Lupaing Aquino*, Association of Free Peasants of the Aquino Estate). They then petitioned for leasehold reform. In the meeting at the municipal DAR office, the landlord came and shouted at and berated the tenants in public, insulting them as stupid, ignorant peasants who did not even know how to compute a leasehold arrangement of 25 percent and 75 percent. This outburst only served to solidify the peasant ranks and effectively cement the cooperation between them and the local DAR officials. Jointly, they elevated their demand to compulsory acquisition. By now, the peasants were agitated.

Part of the expropriation process involves securing from the DENR the classification of the landholding to be acquired for land reform. When the certification from the DENR came through in 1995, they were faced with the biggest surprise in their lives: The DENR declared that the landholding in question was in fact "timberland" based on a 1953 government classification; it thus could not possibly be titled legally to any private entity. The peasants had mixed feelings: They were elated by the fact that the Aquinos did not own the land, but dismayed that their own hopes to own the land themselves would not be realized because timberlands are not within the CARP scope for redistribution. The issue came to a temporary halt at this point and the peasant organization gave in to inertia for a short time.

Momentum was regained in the following year when the BDP — directly funded and operated by GTZ and its partner NGO, the PEACE Foundation — reached the village and began to assist the peasants with their case. Because of their desperate situation, the peasants quickly embraced the offer of the assisting NGO. In addition, the *barangay* and municipal councils had recently elected new sets of officials who were sympathetic to the peasants, and they passed resolutions supporting the peasants' claim to the land. The emergence of this broader alliance proved strategic in their struggle.

Emboldened by the discovery of the illegal nature of the Aquino's claim over the land and by the emergence of a broad front of allies, the peasants decided to declare a boycott on land rent. The landlord, in return, filed criminal charges (*estafa* and theft) before the municipal court. Several waves of arrests and detention of the tenants and peasant leaders occurred between September 1995 and October 1998. During this period, the landlord filed a total of 108 *estafa* charges against the peasants. The peasants were jailed for a few days, then were able to bail themselves out, drawing mainly on the common fund they had collected when they decided to launch the rent boycott (they had set aside 25 percent of their harvest as a "battle fund").

The NPA came back around this period. However, instead of supporting the boycott campaign of the peasants, the guerrillas tried to persuade the peasants to stop the boycott, promising that the NPA would mediate with the landlord to reform the share tenancy arrangement from the onerous 70-30 to the government's more generous leasehold arrangement of 25-75. This approach ran counter to the momentum of the peasants' campaign, however, and the peasants rejected these offers.

Together with their allies, the peasants brought the case all the way to the top-level officials of the DENR and the Office of the Solicitor General (OSG) in Manila. Their demand was now stepped up to the cancellation of the private title of the landlord, on the grounds that it was illegal in the first place. They had a tactical purpose: The declaration of the private title as illegal would effectively quash all the criminal charges filed against the peasants. It was not, however, an easy campaign: The peasants participated in marches, demonstrations, and pickets, pitching camp for several days and on many occasions at the DENR national headquarters and visiting the OSG in Manila six times. Realizing the need to forge a broader coalition with other peasant groups in order to strengthen their demands from the state, SAMALA peasants co-founded the Bondoc-wide peasant alliance, KMBP (already mentioned above in the context of the battle over the Superior Agro corporation estate). The KMBP would later coalesce with a national peasant movement, UNORKA. Through these movement networks, the political reach of the local struggle of SAMALA peasants was extended to the very centre of state power. After persistent collective actions by the peasants, in 1998 a strategic victory was achieved: The OSG filed for the cancellation of the title of the Aquino family.

The DENR was slow in processing the case. But finally, in November 2001, the DENR awarded the estate to the peasants under the CBFM program. It was a standard CBFM contract for twenty-five years, renewable for another twenty-five years, and the peasants were not to pay for the land. The case was entered in the official records as accomplishment in the CBFM program (i.e., public land category). This was a decisive victory for the peasants. The tenants who, since the land rent boycott in 1995, had begun to engage in intensive intercropping on the land, were able to start harvesting farm products without having to pay any land rent. They planned to maintain their demand for the re-classification of their land from timberland to cropland so as to secure full ownership title over the landholding. Meanwhile, the victory in the Aquino case was watched carefully by other peasants in Bondoc Peninsula who were in a similar situation. Not surprisingly, several group claims by Bondoc peasants in situations similar to SAMALA's have already been filed before the DAR and DENR offices (see Franco, 2005).

Leasehold

The CARP law declares share tenancy illegal and mandates that leasehold be implemented on all lands within the landlords' retention right (see German, 1995). Leasehold, under CARP, means a formal, secure long-term lease contract between landlord and tenants, with the latter paying the landlord 25 percent of the average net harvest from the farm either in cash or in kind. Under CARP, leasehold is also used as a transitory scheme to break the nexus between landlord and peasants; later, expropriation can be carried out.

Leasehold has the potential to double the tenant's income (and cut the landlord's share significantly) merely by adjusting the sharing arrangement. It is thus redistributive, especially in settings like the Philippines, where dominant share tenancy arrangements have been highly oppressive, for example, 80-20, 50-50, and *tersyuhan* (70-30) — always in favour of the landlord. In fact, the essential redistributive element within leasehold reform has provoked much opposition from landlords in the Philippines and elsewhere, despite the absence of ownership change, revealing the importance of the issue of power to control land resources. It is not always easy to convert tenancy arrangements into leasehold contracts — and enforce the conversion; the case of the Zoleta property in San Francisco, Quezon, demonstrates this.[28]

The estate involved is the Zoleta property owned by the eighteen heirs of the family. The 126-hectare farm is devoted to coconut and is worked by twenty-six tenant farmers. For a long time, the tenants were under a 60-40 sharing arrangement (in favour of the landlord) with the tenants shouldering all the production costs, which are mostly labour related. The tenants were convinced that a leasehold contract would be better than either a perpetual 60-40 sharing scheme or a full land redistribution. They contacted the PEACE Foundation, which was working in the municipality (see the Superior Agro case for a similar background). The peasants, thanks to the NGO's legal literacy program, fully understood that in fact share tenancy was already illegal and that leasehold must be enforced on their farm.

They petitioned for leasehold. In February 1999, the PARAD supported and confirmed the application of the twenty-six tenants, and the leasehold contract was formalized. The peasants started to pay 25 percent of the net harvest to the landlord. The amount per beneficiary varied according to the size of the awarded land and the number of coconut trees. However, the landlords petitioned for the review of the terms of the leasehold contract, arguing that the secondary crops (corn, vegetables, and citrus trees) must be included in the leasehold contract and not only coconuts. The landlords also argued that they were not provided due process during the preliminary process for leasehold conversion. Later that year, the PARAD ordered a return to the "status quo ante"; meaning that the terms of the relationship be reverted back to the 60-40 sharing arrangement while the PARAD was studying the landlords' petitions. The peasants refused to abide by the PARAD's order, arguing that share tenancy is illegal as declared by the CARP law, and, as such, the PARAD's order to revert back to the 60-40 share tenancy was illegal. The peasants continued to "forcibly pay" (via escrow at a bank) the landlord during the subsequent harvest — but based on the leasehold contract.

The landlords retaliated by filing criminal charges against the peasants (the usual *estafa* and theft) before the Municipal Trial Court in early 2000. The peasants were only able to evade being jailed through of the assistance of their allies, the NGO and some sympathetic municipal officials who provided bail. But because of their fear of being dragged to jail again, the peasants agreed to revert back to the old 60-40 share tenancy. However, while doing this, the peasant group and its ally NGO escalated their campaign all the way to the regional and national DAR offices, putting on heavy pressure on the PARAD to decide in their favour. In early 2002, the PARAD eventually issued an order in favour of the peasants. The leasehold contract was upheld and re-enforced; redistributive reform was achieved.

Contested boundaries: The inclusion of some landholdings and peasant beneficiaries and the exclusion of others

Among the important bases of many analysts' assessments of the redistributive nature of a land reform policy is the character and extent of inclusion of some farms and potential beneficiaries and exclusion of others (the "inclusion-exclusion" question) as legally and formally stipulated in the law. Thus, for example, among the criticisms of CARP is the law's allowing the exclusion of some farms and the lower priority it gives to some (usually seasonal) farmworkers (see, e.g., IBON, 1988). While these criticisms are generally valid, they tend to be static, and so they miss the dynamic nature of the contested boundaries of inclusion-exclusion issues in landholdings and with regard to peasant claim-makers. A brief examination of these issues can contribute to a better understanding of CARP's redistributive outcomes.

Farmland "inclusion-exclusion" issues
The CARP law provides for a number of exemptions and exclusions (discussed in chapter 2). These exemptions and exclusions, however, are not automatic; the landowners must apply for them. Hence, they are conditional. Once they are granted, the landlords must maintain certain legal conditions. Thus they are not permanent. Therefore, political dynamics can, under certain conditions, lead to the realization of redistributive reform on such lands. An example of this is the timberland case cited earlier; others worth mentioning are summarized here:

One example is that of Fort Magsaysay, Nueva Ecija.[29] The sprawling 22,000-hectare Fort Magsaysay military reservation in Laur, Nueva Ecija, Central Luzon, is exempted from CARP despite the fact that most of the reservation has been cultivated to varying extents. Private interests are fairly entrenched in this reservation, as evidenced by the fact that legal claims of private ownership have been lodged in courts. After a series of mobilizations by local peasants and their NGO allies, especially in the context of relocating thousands of peasants displaced by the eruption of Mt. Pinatubo in the early 1990s from different communities in Central Luzon, about 5,000 hectares of the military reservation were acquired by the DAR and redistributed to thousands of peasant families.

A second example is that of the cattle ranches. A cattle ranch is exempted from land redistribution only on the condition that it maintains a one hectare of land to one head of cattle ratio at all times. The excess lands are subject to expropriation and redistributed to peasants. While such a rule has posed problems for peasant claim-makers, it has been equally difficult for the landlords. Most landlords are unable to maintain the required ratio; they then employ various schemes in order to continue circumventing the law. The most popular manoeuvre is to borrow cattle from nearby ranches during the periodic DAR inspections, in order to appear to meet the required ratio; the DAR is working on ways to counter this scheme. Neither are peasants passive actors. They also mount counter-manoeuvres. There are cases in Luzon, for example, where peasants have killed cattle: *"Bawat bakang napapatay mamin, e katumbas ng isang ektaryang mapupunta amin; kaya mas maraming kaming mapatay na baka, mas maraming lupang mapupunta sa amin.*" [Every head of cattle that we kill is equivalent to a hectare of land that can go to us; thus, the more cattle we kill, the more lands there will be for us], related a peasant leader.[30] Many cattle ranchers have become very defensive indeed — especially given that since the late 1990s the cattle industry has been in bad shape, due, in part, to the massive cheap imports resulting from neoliberal trade reforms (see Carranza and Mato, 2006, for most recent critical analysis).

Some farmlands controlled by educational institutions, including state educational institutions, have been redistributed despite exclusion provisions in CARP. An example is the more than 4,000-hectare rubber and coconut plantation in Basilan (southwestern Mindanao).[31] The University of the Philippines (UP) owned this property, which was put under a lease contract with a multinational corporation that, in turn, transformed the vast tract of rolling hills into a rubber and coconut plantation. Under pressure from the farmworkers, the university turned the lands over to the DAR for redistribution. Since then, the more than 1,000 farmworker-beneficiaries have been trying to operate the former plantation on their own, while facing serious challenges in their effort to make it productive and financially viable.

CARP also grants fishponds exemption from land redistribution, but only on the condition of their continued operation as fishponds and with the implementation of a mandatory production and profit sharing scheme among the workers. If the fishpond fails to operate continuously for three years, and if the land use is changed, then the land would become subject to expropriation. Again, such conditional provisions have made it difficult for farmworkers to push for the expropriation of fishpond farms. But the same legal requirements impose a burden on fishpond owners, especially since the 1990s slump in fresh-fish production and exports. As a result, many fishponds failed to sustain operations and became vulnerable to expropriation. Such is the case of the controversial Aquafil estate in San Jose, Mindoro Occidental.[32] The close to 1,000-hectare Aquafil estate was the subject of one of the most public land-occupation initiatives launched by the KMP in the mid-1980s, led by local peasant leader Simon Sagnip. After a brief, successful invasion of the estate, the peasants were violently driven away by the company's armed security guards, aided by the police and the military. It took more than a decade before the leader of the peasants staged a comeback and reoccupied the land. Simon Sagnip, this time with DKMP (and later with UNORKA), led another invasion in mid-1998. The peasants were again harassed, arrested, and thrown into jail. But through persistent militant actions, combined with legal tactics and lobbying at all levels of the DAR bureaucracy, and with the assistance of their allies, the peasants were able to force the DAR to expropriate the property and redistribute it to various peasant claimant groups. The legal ground that justified the expropriation was the estate's failure to operate fully and continuously as a fishpond.

The continuing "battle" to expropriate a penal colony owned by the government illustrates another aspect of the contested boundaries of official exclusions. This is the case of the Davao Penal Colony (DAPECOL) in Davao del Norte.[33] This penal colony was created in the early 1930s and was allocated about 33,000 hectares of prime lands. The same site became the main area for the development of Cavendish banana production when the abaca sector dipped in the 1950s due to competition from synthetic alternatives. Since the 1940s, however, DAPECOL has been privatized piece by piece in what might be fraudulent sales at ridiculously low prices. In the late 1960s, Cavendish banana production got into full swing. And by the early 1970s, there were only 5,200 hectares left to DAPECOL.

The family of Don Antonio Floirendo, one of the most important cronies of Marcos, was among those who were able to "buy" lands from DAPECOL and in nearby areas. Today, the Floirendos have some 3,500 hectares of privately owned banana plantation. On top of these, the Floirendos effectively control the remaining 5,200 hectares of DAPECOL through a long-term contract that started in 1969. Through his connection with Marcos, Antonio Floirendo was able to secure the long-term lease contract with the Department of Justice (DOJ), the agency that controls the penal colony.

The plantation started to operate fully under a purchase contract with the global giant Chiquita. Prisoners in the penal colony worked on the banana plantation for meagre wages, but only until the late 1970s. Japanese buyers (the biggest market for the Philippine bananas) reportedly protested against the use of prison labour to produce the bananas sold to them. Since then, prisoners have provided only marginal amounts of labour in banana production. Sixteen years after Marcos was overthrown, the Floirendos remain politically powerful. They survived the regime transition in 1986, and all the administration changes since then; they have controlled the district representation in Congress and the governorship of the province. As of this writing, Floirendo was paying the government a meagre PhP 1,000 per hectare per year lease rent, despite the fact that the prevailing market rate for land rental for banana plantations in adjacent areas was already around PhP 30,000 per hectare per year.

A series of collective actions by farmworkers and the ejected original settlers, in Davao and Manila, have failed to yield a favourable government response in this case. DAR secretaries Garilao and Morales repeatedly requested the DOJ to turn over the land to the DAR for redistribution, but were met with a negative response. It is widely believed that the lease deal between the Floirendos and the DOJ is graft-ridden.

The DAPECOL is government-owned penal colony land. Yet its case demonstrates how difficult it is to have such lands redistributed. The private elite interest is thoroughly entrenched. Arguably, and legally, these lands should have been redistributed under CARP, because the law exempts only penal colonies that are directly tilled by prisoners. Besides, the lease contract here is tantamount to a contract disadvantageous to the government, which is illegal. If, hypothetically, DAPECOL were to be redistributed, it would certainly constitute redistributive reform.

Peasant claimant "inclusion-exclusion" issues
The contentious issue of beneficiary inclusion-exclusion has plagued most land reforms throughout the world and historically. Among the usual losers in land redistribution are the seasonal farmworkers, who also happen, on many occasions, to be women and children.[34] This problem also occurs within the CARP process. For example, during the early period of CARP implementation, the female spouses of beneficiaries did not usually have a distinct right to get land from land reform, despite their individual status as farmworkers on the same plantation. In the case of a rubber-coffee plantation in southwestern Mindanao, some 1,000 hectares were redistributed to nearly 500 beneficiaries — all of them men — completely excluding all female farmworkers.[35] Worse, when the all-men beneficiary cooperative took over the operation of the plantation, they also took over the plantation work traditionally controlled by women, completing the exclusion of women from the land reform process. The peasant women got fed up, got organized, and protested against such treatment. The case, which became a national controversy in the mid-1990s, was instrumental for the revision of the CARP rules on women beneficiaries. Since then, CARP formally respects the distinct right of women to have their own land regardless of whether their spouse has already been declared a beneficiary. While it is not an automatic guarantee, the revised policy has altered the terrain on which peasant women can launch their claim-making initiatives in land reform.

Furthermore, a number of banana farmworkers in the Davao-Cotabato regions, men and women, who were earlier retrenched from employment, would have been denied land reform benefits had it not been for a policy reform. Between 1988 and 1998 (the deferment period for land reform on banana plantations), about 20,000 farmworkers were retrenched in an apparent effort by plantation owners to purge their companies of land and production/profit share claim-makers (de la Rosa, 2005). Where local elites realized the imminent eventuality of land reform, they tried to forge different forms of joint venture agreements with the would-be beneficiaries. This led companies to consolidate their hold on less autonomous farmworkers' organizations. In order to increase their chances of forging post–land transfer joint venture agreements, the companies targeted for retrenchment mainly those workers who identified with the militant trade union tradition or who had formed autonomous organizations. Then, the companies lobbied for the exclusion of retrenched farmworkers from land reform. Reluctant to antagonize banana plantation owners, and facing the problem of insufficient funds to purchase the expensive banana lands, the DAR has been encouraging farmworkers and plantation owners to employ the VLT scheme.

Thus since 1998, in the banana sector there has been a confluence of events that is double-edged: It may further consolidate the economic and political power of transnational corporations and local elites in the banana sector at the expense of the farmworkers, or it may open a path for radical change. Both scenarios, however, depend on various factors and actors. For a more redistributive path to emerge, the development of highly autonomous and capable farmworkers' organizations allied with reformists within the state is likely to be crucial. While there are reasons to be alarmed at the market forces and state trying to advance their interests at the expense of poor farmworkers, there are also reasons to hope that progressive change may occur. The case of DAR Administrative Order (AO) No. 9 series of 1998 is a good example (Borras and Franco, 2005).[36]

In May 1998, a month before the Ramos administration's term of office ended, the DAR issued an administrative order to guide the implementation of CARP on commercial plantations, especially in the banana sector, the deferment of land reform coverage of which would expire the following month, June 1998. While DAR AO No. 6 series of 1998 ordered the expropriation of all deferred commercial plantations, this guideline, had it been implemented, would also have excluded from land reform all retrenched farmworkers.[37] Thousands of retrenched farmworkers were furious about the guideline and campaigned for its recall. To these farmworkers, AO 6 would permanently institutionalize the historical injustice committed against them.

Enrico worked on a Floirendo banana plantation in Davao del Norte from 1974 until he was retrenched in 1994. He served the company for twenty years. Since he was not actively employed at the time of the land reform implementation, from 1998 onward, he would not, under AO 6, become a land reform beneficiary. Meanwhile, in late 1996, Pablo was employed by the Floirendo banana plantation where Enrico used to work. Since Pablo was actively employed from 1998 onward when land reform would have been implemented, he would have, under AO 6, become a land reform beneficiary despite having worked in the company for only a little more than a year. There would have been no conflict among potential beneficiaries had there been enough land for every potential beneficiary. However, there were at least two potential beneficiaries for every hectare of banana land and the ideal beneficiary-land ratio in the banana sector is 1:1; hence, the critical issue of prioritizing beneficiaries.

Thousands of farmworkers, who would later organize themselves under the umbrella coalition of UFEARBAI (which is a founding member of UNORKA) campaigned hard for the inclusion of retrenched farmworkers by pushing for the adoption of the "principle of length of service" as the basis for prioritizing beneficiaries. This means prioritizing "those who worked the longest on the farm regardless of their employment status at the time of the actual land reform process," as opposed to the ahistorical "those who are actually working" (AO 6) principle. Plantation owners, however, had been working behind the scenes, lobbying to prioritize as beneficiaries only those actively employed at the time of the actual land reform coverage and those at the management and supervisory levels of the company. It is not surprising that the most contentious division occurred between different groups of farmworkers, a conflict-ridden split instigated by transnational and local elites and indirectly intensified by the DAR's ineptitude on the issue.

The following month, Horacio Morales Jr. took office as DAR secretary. After several months of collective action by farmworkers, both locally and nationally, the Morales DAR gave in. In December 1998, the DAR issued AO No. 9 series of 1998, declaring that the key guiding principle in prioritizing beneficiaries would be the principle of "those who worked the longest on the farm regardless of their employment status at the time of the actual land reform process." It was a big victory for thousands of retrenched farmworkers. However, while it constituted an important "reform of the agrarian reform," the implementation of AO 9 has not been automatic, because final decisions will partly depend on the resolution of pending labour cases and because some local DAR officials appear to be continually influenced by the banana elite in circumventing the law. Yet, AO 9 altered the institutional terrain on which retrenched farmworkers can assert their rights and launch their collective actions for redistributive reform.

4.3 POSSIBLE EXTENT OF REDISTRIBUTIVE OUTCOMES

Analyses based on nationally aggregated quantitative data can be powerful because they provide insights about overall trends and the extent of policy implementation, as well as policy trajectories. They are however inherently limited because they tend to miss the great variations of outcomes based on policy components and geographic distribution. Combined national/sub-national, aggregated/disaggregated perspectives offer better and more complete explanations of policy outcomes. Following the themes discussed in section 4.2, this section provides a better sense of the extent of CARP's redistributive outcomes and examines their geographic distribution.

Extent and geographic distribution of accomplishment in private lands
Table 4.1 shows the land redistribution output in the private land category disaggregated based on land acquisition modes: CA, OLT, GFI, VOS, and VLT. By the end of 2005, the aggregated output of these modalities was 1.99 million hectares of private lands, redistributed to nearly one million previously landless and land-poor peasant households.[38] This nationally aggregated data represents less than 16 percent of the total private and public agricultural lands and 16 percent of the total agricultural households in the country by end 2005. In fact, the proportion is even slightly less after subtracting some anomalous VOS cases (if they could actually be quantified scientifically) and all the VLT cases. If this dataset is the one used for constructing a cross-national comparative perspective, then the CARP outcome is way below the levels of significant land reforms elsewhere (but then most land reform data elsewhere are also undifferentiated; thus, the same quality problem might affect them as well). As I explained elsewhere (Borras, 2006a), some scholars also compare CARP's low output in private lands with other successful land reforms elsewhere, usually Taiwan, Japan, and South Korea, but they fail to recognize that they use quantitative data in those countries that also includes redistribution output in public lands.

Such a simple extrapolation of quantitative data is problematic and contradiction-ridden. A brief explanation is needed. As explained in chapter 1, most scholars consider private lands as the only category that qualifies for redistributive land reform. Following such logic, one must take the total redistribution outcome in private lands and assess it against the total quantity of the country's private lands to get a logical comparative percentage share of the redistributed land. Unfortunately, most studies seem to be inconsistent: They usually take the total redistribution outcome in private lands and assess

Table 4.1 DAR land redistribution output in private lands by land type and by region, in hectares (1972–2005)

Island group/ Region output accomplishment	Total	%	OLT	GFI	VOS	CA	VLT	SETT	LE	KKK
Total for the Philippines, including ARMM	3,591,055	81	554,220	156,909	512,620	243,422	525,847	699,648	80,497	817,859
CAR	81,670	105	1,257	1,115	715	144	17,784	—	—	60,655
Region 1	1,422,490	87	29,835	1,790	8,646	1,237	63,803	1,969	298	14,912
Region 2	311,489	104	76,884	8,993	38,994	11,775	34,556	43,527	4,579	92,181
Region 3	376,536	93	195,100	5,222	24,062	23,708	30,154	14,725	56,808	26,757
Region 4-A (CALABARZON)	138,453	68	15,399	719	22,510	35,863	19,057	25,575	5,435	13,895
Region 4-B (MIMAROPA)	141,039	83	15,653	1,165	9,617	15,019	33,533	14,176	4,972	46,904
Region 5	237,061	52	47,302	17,041	51,224	36,862	37,216	12,001	3,016	32,399
Region 6	323,756	58	37,934	60,617	97,341	26,767	27,360	19,640	74	54,023
Region 7	117,418	70	17,685	3,880	27,028	19,198	3,021	6,623	—	39,983
Region 8	342,364	89	19,049	8,060	21,949	20,801	13,531	90,870	615	167,489
Region 9	182,500	115	10,663	7,556	15,717	12,668	59,636	20,998	2,983	52,279
Region 10	255,686	95	16,705	2,548	16,499	9,478	57,202	95,726	—	57,528
Region 11	196,975	97	8,613	6,781	60,335	19,317	34,750	33,691	—	33,488
Region 12	403,381	94	33,455	11,213	74,855	3,718	34,867	228,085	212	16,976
Region 13	187,513	94	6,481	3,333	24,621	4,720	24,145	19,259	1,474	103,480
ARMM	172,691	57	22,205	16,876	18,507	2,147	35,232	72,783	31	4,910

Notes: OLT = Operation Land Transfer; GFI = government financial institution; VOS = voluntary offer-to-sell; CA = compulsory acquisition; VLT = voluntary land transfer; SETT = settlements; LE = landed estates; KKK = *Kilusang Kabuhayan at Kaunlaran*; ARMM = Autonomous Region of Muslim Mindanao; CALABARZON = Cavite, Laguna, Batangas, Rizal, Quezon; MIMAROPA = Mindoro, Marinduque, Romblon, Palawan.

Source: DAR-MIS (2005).

it against the combined total quantity of private *and* public lands, which are usually lumped together and labelled "total agricultural lands." While the comparative perspective that it presents is relevant, a problematic flow of logic detracts from the comparative analysis and produces a rather distorted comparison.

Since this study is interested in finding out when and how land reform policy outcomes actually constitute redistributive reform (or otherwise), the units and levels of analysis are further disaggregated based on land acquisition and geographic distribution of outcomes. The national-level and aggregated perspectives put forward above will remain within sight.

In trying to assess the possible extent and geographic distribution of outcomes in the private land category, a number of observations can be drawn from the combined data on private lands (the OLT, GFI, VOS, CA, and VLT columns) in table 4.1. The total volume of private lands in redistribution output is highly concentrated in a few regions: four regions (3, 11, 5, and 4) account for nearly half of the total output in private land. By percentage shares, the output is likewise highly uneven, with five regions (1, 3, 11, 7, and 5) having a two-thirds or greater share of private lands in total DAR output; conversely, in four regions (13, 12, CAR, and 8), private land output accounts for one-third or less of the total private-public redistribution output. At the provincial level, in almost half of the provinces in the country (thirty-four out of seventy-eight — not shown in the table) the private land share of redistribution output vis-à-vis total DAR private-public redistribution accomplishment is two-thirds or more; conversely, only nineteen provinces have a one-third or more percentage share of private land output in total DAR accomplishment.

These disaggregated data contradict the national-level generalizations about redistribution in private lands and therefore the explanations as to what causes such outcomes — that is, that a low percentage share of private lands in total DAR output is said to be evidence of the successful anti-reform campaign of landlords. While the nationally aggregated data tend to support this argument, the disaggregated data demand a better explanation. If we follow the logic of the dominant explanations, we would argue that in the thirty-four provinces where the percentage share of private lands is high, the landlords were unsuccessful in blocking the land reform process; landlords were successful in blocking land reform in nineteen provinces. This argument is not convincing however. Therefore, explaining the causes of high or low percentage shares of private lands in the total DAR private-public land accomplishment requires that we go beyond the level and unit of analysis of the dominant explanations. Finally — and interestingly — the socioeconomic structures and institutional makeup of regions that have high private land outcomes are varied: from a modern plantation belt (Region 11) to a region of urban sprawl (Region 4) to a region of anaemic economic development (Region 5); the same is true of those with low percentage shares of private land outcomes.

Extent and geographic distribution of private lands except VLT

Chapter 3 demonstrated that VLT cases are likely to be devoid of a redistributive dimension, so if we want a true picture of the situation, they must be counted out of the accomplishment report. Taking VLT out of the private land redistribution report reduces the total accomplishment in the private land category by 25 percent. The actual quantity of private lands redistributed as of May 2005 was 1.467 million hectares under OLT + GFI + VOS + CA modes of acquisition — the generally "safer" modes in terms of ensuring the redistributive content of land transfers (excluding VLT, which, as we have said, is a less accurate reflection of the redistributive reality). This reduced quantity shifts the percentage share of private lands in DAR's total accomplishment from 55 to 41 percent.

Following this assumption, five regions (1, 9, 10, 12, and CAR) would have to reduce their accomplishment data in private lands by two-fifths or more. In these regions, VLT was clearly the dominant "land acquisition" mode used to produce official policy outcomes. This is a reminder of the dangers of uncritically accepting VLT cases as gains in redistributive reform. VLT output is highly uneven geographically: At the national level VLT might be only a small part of the whole; in some regions however, it is the dominant mode. Finally, it is interesting to note that the regions that have high percentages of VLT are not homogenous; they are quite varied in terms of their structural and institutional settings. I have explained this issue in more depth elsewhere (see Borras, 2005).

Extent and geographic distribution of VOS

The VOS land acquisition mode accounted for nearly one-quarter of the total DAR output in private lands, and for 12 percent of the total output in private and public lands. The VOS in ARMM is certainly non-redistributive, as explained in the preceding chapter. But again, VOS outcomes are varied subnationally, and its geographic distribution is highly skewed. Three regions (11, 6, and 5) account for half of the total VOS transactions nationwide. The province of Negros Occidental had the biggest VOS output, with 63,837 hectares, accounting for 12 percent of all VOS output nationwide. The large numbers of bankrupt sugar cane plantations and fishpond-prawn farms that were forced to submit to the land reform program voluntarily could partly explain the high VOS percentage in this province; the evasive scheme of VOS-then-leaseback is another possible explanation (by mid-2006 sugar prices were rising again, although it is not clear whether this constitutes an actual increasing trend or just one of the usual periodic fluctuations — see, e.g., Billig, 2003). But there are provinces where the VOS percentage shares are fantastically out of proportion, such as in Davao Oriental and Sultan Kudarat where, respectively, 62 percent and 55 percent of the overall output in private lands was accomplished via the VOS mode. This raises suspicion about the quality of the "land transfers" in these areas. Finally, as for VLT, the provinces with high VOS output have a varied socioeconomic and institutional make-up, ranging from a coconut-producing province (Davao Oriental) to a sugar cane enclave (Negros Occidental).

Extent and geographic distribution of OLT

There is less controversy around the rice and corn (OLT) land, because the bulk of the achievements in redistribution are indeed concentrated in the rice-producing regions and provinces. These accounted for nearly one-third of the total DAR redistribution in private lands as of 2005. This also explains the relatively higher outputs in private lands of regions 3 and 2, two of the country's most important "rice bowls," with the latter also being the most important corn-producing region. The same land category pulled up the private land outputs of regions 5 and 1, and "saved" Region 12 from a total "disaster" in its performance in private lands. This partly explains the low CA output in regions 3 and 2, but it does not explain the low CA output in Region 1.

Extent and geographic distribution of CA

The CA mode represents a low percentage share — just 12.3 percent — of the total distribution outcome in private lands. Here, a number of observations can be made about this mode: First, the general conclusion that the CA mode is only marginally used is true — from a national perspective. However, this does not apply in all locations and at all times; this can be seen from two opposite perspectives: On the one hand, it is an understatement for regions (and provinces) where the CA mode was almost completely ignored, so that their percentage shares of CA vis-à-vis total output in private lands are almost zero. Examples of this are Region 12 with 0.15 percent, CAR with 0.5 percent, and Region 1 with 1.4 percent. On the other hand, it fails to capture the fact that the CA mode's share in some regions is *not* marginal. Regions 4 and 7, for example, both have CA shares above the national average, at 27 percent and 23 percent, respectively.

Second, the geographic distribution of the land redistribution output of CA is highly uneven, very much concentrated in a few regions: The four regions with the highest CA output in hectares (regions 4, 5, 11, and 6) together account for 56 percent of the total CA output. And conversely, the bottom four regions (12, 1, 13, and CAR) have only a 3 percent share (see table 4.1). The aggregate land areas of the two clusters of regions are comparable in size. Immediately, one notices that in the first cluster, where the CA mode is used relatively often, are (except for Region 5) regions considered to be "difficult" because the structural and institutional setup appear unfavourable to land redistribution (i.e., booming export agriculture, massive urban sprawl, heavy state subsidy of sugar cane). Conversely, the second cluster is made up of regions that are not into production of non-traditional agricultural export commodities (nor is there massive urban sprawl) and whose agriculture is dominated by subsistence farming (where you would, therefore, expect a high percentage of CA transactions). Yet the CA performance in these regions was not significant.

Third, the variations are more pronounced at the provincial level. For one, of the 78 provinces (table 4.1 does not show a breakdown by province), only 15 have CA output of more than 5,000 hectares, and the latter's combined CA output accounts for 61 percent of the total CA. These top-15 provinces are mixed in terms of structural and institutional settings: There are the relatively "softer" provinces such as Cagayan, but also "difficult" provinces like Davao del Norte (which is a modern export-oriented plantation enclave) and Quezon II (a "local authoritarian enclave"). Furthermore, almost half of the provinces have a CA output of less than 1,000 hectares each, and their combined CA output is only 3 percent of the country's total CA output. Of these provinces, amazingly, eleven have zero CA output. These eleven provinces include both small areas, like Batanes, and large ones, like Lanao del Sur. The provinces with the least CA output comprise a mixture in terms of structural and institutional settings, from a large province like Sultan Kudarat to a small island like Catanduanes, from a plantation-based province like South Cotabato to a traditional upland subsistence farming area like Kalinga.

Finally, the conclusion, based on nationally aggregated data, that the CA mode has been employed marginally within the CARP process is valid only insofar as the national picture is concerned. Some provinces have relatively high CA percentages — even more so when seen from a comparative view in the context of province-to-province diversity and not only in province-to-national or province-to-regional diversity. For example, the frequency of CA may be quite different between two provinces from two different regions, as in the cases of North Cotabato (very low at 0.1 percent) and Quezon I (high at 46 percent), or within two provinces between a region, as in the cases of Mindoro Oriental (at 14 percent) compared to Quezon I.

Extent and geographic distribution of DAR's government-owned land

As explained earlier, critics argue, in generalized terms, that CARP's output is largely from public lands and that the redistribution of public land does not constitute redistributive reform. The latter assumption was criticized in the preceding chapter. However, critics are partly correct in drawing attention to the DAR's focus on government-owned lands. A closer examination of the reported land redistribution output in the government-owned land category under DAR jurisdiction (table 4.1, columns: SETT, LE, and KKK) reveals some insights: The government-owned lands under the DAR jurisdiction were nearly completely redistributed as early as 2002, confirming the popular assumption that past DAR administrations prioritized this land type in their redistribution campaigns. As of 2005, 44.4 percent of DAR's total accomplishment came from the government-owned land type, and KKK and settlement lands accounted for the bulk of this category, at almost 95 percent.

The geographic distribution of government-owned land output is skewed, concentrated in five regions (13, 2, 12, 8, and 6). Four regions have two-thirds or more percentage shares of government-owned lands in their total DAR output;[39] region 12 has more than two-fifths of the total settlement land output. Moreover, seven provinces represent 36 percent of the country's total output in government-owned land. The pattern of geographic distribution of government-owned lands follows the distribution of the various land frontiers that earlier in history had been declared as part of the government's official (re)settlement program, while some of these were later classified as KKK lands.

Extent and geographic distribution of DENR's A&D and CBFM programs

This section casts light on the DENR accomplishment data. Table 4.2 is DENR's accomplishment report broken down by region. There are discrepancies with the data presented in chapter 2. The data in chapter 2 is from the PARC Secretariat; the data here is from the DENR CARP Secretariat and is used here due to its regional breakdown.

Table 4.2
DENR's accomplishment in A&D lands and CBFM by region, in hectares (1987–2001)

Region	A&D		CBFM	
	Quantity (ha)	% accomplished	Quantity (ha)	% accomplished
Philippines	1,141,538	55	1,042,632	81
CAR	39,745	44	36,184	89
1	95,595	50	24,323	35
2	93,961	64	97,868	75
3	66,808	33	31,855	37
4	156,535	58	109,753	89
5	69,368	47	54,609	92
6	70,614	48	67,850	86
7	66,263	49	41,589	41
8	89,337	56	81,332	96
9	59,543	56	113,647	62
10	91,909	62	108,240	100
11	92,496	73	139,293	105
12	128,511	84	89,538	139
13	13,472	55	46,549	314
ARMM	7,381	27	—	—

Notes: (1) The regional breakdown of the working scope was not made available to this study. (2) Figures for ARMM and Region 13 were reported by the national DENR only from 1997. It is unclear how much land, if any, was distributed under the program in these two regions earlier. Percentages were rounded.

Source: DENR (n.d.a, n.d.c).

A few observations can be made. Based on table 4.2, DENR output is nearly 2.2 million hectares of land (compared with 2.5 million claimed in chapter 2), almost equally divided between the two DENR programs under CARP. In relative terms, the DENR was slow in redistributing A&D lands and faster in (ISFP/) CBFM, at 55 and 81 percent, respectively. One of the reasons given for the slow processing of A&D lands is technical, administrative, and funding problems with regard to the reclassification and survey of A&D lands. The CBFM is the favoured program, but its outcomes are highly uneven subnationally. Four regions (10, 11, 12, and 13) have one hundred percent or more accomplishment rates; and as mentioned elsewhere, the data above does not clarify whether and to what extent ancestral domain claims are included in the DENR CARP accomplishment reports. Overall, these data suggest that there is no clear baseline figure for the working scope of DENR, especially in the CBFM program.

Extent and geographic distribution of leasehold reform

In the Philippines, there are no precise records of how many farms and how much land and tenants are to be covered by the mandatory conversion to leasehold. A rough estimate would place a minimum of 3 million hectares and a minimum of 1.5 million peasant households as potentially affected by this law.[40] By the end of 2003, 1.5 million hectares of land were reported to have been converted to leasehold contracts (see chapter 2).

However, as noted in chapter 2, about 650,000 hectares of this must be taken out because they are "transitory leasehold" (in transition to various land acquisition processes like CA). Another critical issue here is the difficulty of ascertaining which leasehold contracts are real and actually working. Some landowners of small- to medium-sized farms could have recruited family members as their contracting party in the leasehold arrangement (whether fake or legitimate). Other leasehold contracts could have been reverted back to the old share tenancy. The contract enforcement capacity of the state is extremely low in this type of reform, which is widespread and scattered and involves numerous individuals and individual contracts.

4.4 CONCLUDING REMARKS

This chapter analyzed evidence showing that portions of the officially reported land reform accomplishment in fact constitute gains in redistributive reform, regardless of whether they are popularly accepted as such. Under certain conditions, these CARP outcomes occurred through different land acquisition and distribution modalities in different land property rights categories; for example, both in private and public lands and under both the DAR and the DENR programs. Specifically, redistributive reforms were achieved through land transfers via the compulsory acquisition (CA) and operation land transfer (OLT) modes, through "coerced volunteerism" via the voluntary offer-to-sell (VOS) scheme, through redistribution of landholdings owned by government financial institutions, and in public lands through the various programs under the DAR and the DENR (i.e., KKK, settlement, A&D, and CBFM programs).

This type of outcome also occurred through the leasehold reform program. Moreover, outcomes that constitute redistributive reform were achieved in landholding types that were formally classified as, and popularly assumed to be, excluded from the reform process, including fishponds, military reservations, and educational facilities.

The redistributive reform attained so far through the CARP process has been significant in scale, and while it is unlikely to approach the optimistic projections and current claims by some of its official supporters, it certainly has surpassed the earlier pessimistic predictions made by critics. Finally, the redistributive outcomes of CARP have been uneven and varied between the different policy components and land acquisition modalities of the land reform policy, between different regions, and over time. The nature and extent of CARP's redistributive outcomes in land redistribution are largely influenced by the nature and extent of the pro-reform state–society coalition that has been pushing for this kind of reform. This will be discussed in the next chapter.

CHAPTER FIVE

STATE–SOCIETY INTERACTIONS FOR REDISTRIBUTIVE LAND REFORM

> The successful implementation of distributive policies depends on the nature of the political interaction between the pro-reform forces in state and society. If their actions are mutually reinforcing, then the reform effort internalizes social conflict within the state. This reciprocal interaction between state and social actors can lead to unexpected political outcomes (Jonathan Fox, 1993: 40).

5.1 INTRODUCTION

The kinds of CARP land redistribution outcomes, their extent, and their geographic distribution are largely reflective of the nature, extent, and geographic spread of the pro-reform state–society coalitions pushing for redistributive land reform. This chapter analyzes state–society interactions for redistributive land reform. Its aim is to better understand the role played by state and societal actors in shaping and reshaping the CARP process, resulting in the kinds of outcomes explained in the preceding chapters. The case studies in chapter 4 showed how state and non-state actors surmounted obstacles, overcame limits, and harnessed opportunities, resulting in redistributive land reform. The case studies in chapter 3 showed how these actors failed in their attempts to carry out land redistribution. The nationally aggregated data on land redistribution in chapter 2 showed that partial but substantial redistribution outcomes have been achieved, although critical treatment of the official data is necessary.

This chapter is devoted to a more systematic analysis of the various pro-reform state and non-state actors, focusing on their political strategies and forms of collective action and on how dynamic state–society political interactions resulted in uneven outcomes in redistributive land reform, spatially and temporally. Moreover, this chapter focuses its analysis at the national level to provide a broader perspective on the earlier discussion of state–society interactions in the local case studies.

This chapter has six sections. Following section 5.1, the introduction, section 5.2 analyzes the peasant movements and their allies (collectively and loosely referred to here as "rural social movement organizations") and their struggle for land. Continuity and change in their agendas, repertoire of collective actions, degree of organizational and political influence, political strategies, network of allies, and geographic spread over time are examined in an attempt to explain what causes these changes and what impact these changes have on the implementation of redistributive land reform policy. How reformist autonomous peasant groups emerged that explore the reform opportunities offered within the CARP legal framework is also examined. Section 5.3 traces the general contour of the emergence of pro–land reform state actors within the DAR during a specific period. Building on the assumption that pro-reform state actors do matter in policy implementation, this section examines the causes of their emergence and their impact on implementation processes and outcomes of redistributive land reform. These first two sections thus show the distinct roles that rural social movements "from below" and pro-reform state actors "from above" each play in the push for redistributive land reform, including the strengths and weaknesses of each set of actors. Section 5.4 examines the evolution of pro-reform state–society alliances and interactions for land reform and the role they have played in CARP implementation. It explains how and why such alliances and interactions emerged over time and with what impact on land reform implementation. Section 5.5 analyzes clashes between pro- and anti-reform state–society coalitions over the issue of redistributive land reform, and the outcomes of these conflicts. This section demonstrates the strengths and limitations of the pro-reform state–society coalition in pushing for redistributive land reform, which partly accounts for the policy's highly uneven and varied implementation processes and outcomes. Section 5.6 analyzes the sub-national spatial variations in land reform outcomes and demonstrates that it is the state–society interaction that largely determines patterns of variations. Section 5.7 offers a short conclusion.

5.2 AUTONOMOUS RURAL SOCIAL MOVEMENTS "FROM BELOW"

As explained in the theoretical section of this study, the most promising type of peasant movements in the context of pushing for redistributive land reform are those that have a high degree of both *autonomy* and *capacity*, the twin foundations of peasant organizational power. This section maps and examines the different types of peasant associations that have emerged in the Philippines since the early 1970s. Important national peasant movements and organizations are also presented and examined, with emphasis on their aims and agendas, repertoire of collective actions, and political strategies. Significant attention will be given to the types of allies these peasant groups have and their degree of autonomy from those allies. Moreover, this section analyzes continuity and change in the different peasant groups' land reform agendas and their political strategies in pursuit of these agendas. Specifically, it explains why most of the peasant groups that originally rejected CARP and stayed away from its early implementation would, some years later, change their attitude and eventually interact with the state to push for the implementation of the same land reform program they had earlier rejected.

Cycles of peasant collective actions for various types of rural reforms, small-scale and large-scale, armed and unarmed, have been a remarkable characteristic of the Philippine history from the Spanish colonial era to today.[1] Almost always, allies have played important roles in these peasant actions. During the first three quarters of the past century, peasant allies were usually political movements or parties (usually communist or socialist parties),[2] influential middle-class professionals, and some progressive church leaders (as in the case of the Federation of Free Farmers, or FFF).[3] These allies have been largely responsible for forging horizontal linkages among local peasant groups, stretching the political reach of peasant collective actions, and systematizing, even modifying, peasant demands addressed to the state. As state-building took more coherent form, peasant demands began to be centralized before the state, and peasant actions tended to veer away from direct confrontation with landlords."[4]

The mass political agitation in the 1960s, part of and influenced by the global and national political upheavals of that decade, included the call for land reform. Urban-based left wing political activists were able to penetrate the mainstream, conservative FFF and recruited peasant leaders and supporters into radical politics. Militant forms of collective action were launched. One of the victories with strategic importance during this period of mobilizations was the creation of the DAR. In 1972, however, martial law was imposed. The conservative leadership of the FFF quickly moved to support Marcos. There was no room left for legal, above-ground political opposition, thereby forcing the radical activists to go underground and join the communist-led clandestine movement.⁵ Most of these peasant leaders and political activists would later resurface above ground through varying and more sophisticated organizational forms.⁶

The beginning of the last quarter of the past century witnessed major development of the rural social movement front: rural reform-oriented NGOs were being set up primarily by the Catholic and Protestant churches (see Franco, 1994, 2001b).⁷ This development would strategically alter the political-organizational terrain for, and character of, rural social movements in the country. Meanwhile, other traditional allies of the peasantry remained entrenched, whether in conservative or radical political communities. Many of them had allied with the dictatorship and provided the latter with the needed semblance of peasant support, while others had joined the progressive social movements. The communist-led ND movement would become the most influential among the rural social movement organizations from the 1960s through the 1980s, ideologically, organizationally, and politically. It would largely be credited for the sustained demand and political agitation for land reform.

From the early 1970s until the late 1980s, the country's rural polity was marked by the rapid growth of the communist insurgency led by the Maoist CPP and its armed wing, the NPA. This CPP-led movement became known as the National-Democratic movement, or "Nat-Dem" or "ND," because of its program of a two-stage revolution (i.e., first to achieve "national democracy" by overthrowing imperialism, feudalism, and bureaucrat-capitalism; then moving on to the second stage, the socialist revolution). The principal form of struggle was armed, patterned after the Maoist dictum of "wave by wave, surround the cities from the countryside" within the politico-military strategy of a "protracted people's war." The ND movement subordinated all other forms of struggle (e.g., legal and electoral) to the principal armed form. It identified the "proletariat" as the "leading force" and the peasantry as the "main force" (Guerrero, 1970, but see Putzel, 1995; Caouette, 2004). The subsequent ideological, political, and organizational makeup of the legal ND peasant movements and organizations was influenced by this orientation.⁸ Two aspects of this orientation have to be reiterated. First, it held that "genuine agrarian reform" could be achieved only after the victory of the revolution. Yet second, while the revolution was being waged, partial and selective implementation of revolutionary agrarian reform could be carried out. Included in the "minimum" program was the NPA's *tersyung baliktad* campaign, the terms of which are similar to CARP's leasehold. *Tersyo* literally means "a third," referring to the usual share of the peasants in 67-33 (or more commonly 70-30) share tenancy arrangements. Inverting (*baliktad*) in favour of the peasants was a powerful rallying campaign that involved tens of thousands of peasants across the country in the 1970s and 1980s.

This orientation partly accounted for the phenomenal growth of the ND movement in the 1970s and 1980s under the authoritarian regime (Franco, 1994; Rutten, 1996). But that same ideological and political framing became the source of the movement's weakening after the late 1980s, amidst significant political-economic changes in the global, national, and local setting. The intensification of internal conflicts within the CPP leadership — which occurred amidst the movement's political isolation during and after the people's uprising in February 1986 that overthrew the Marcos government — led many of the movement's key leaders to question the basic "protracted people's war" strategy of the revolution. This debate led to in-fighting; and the in-fighting led to the movement's split in 1993.

The KMP was formally launched in July 1985 and immediately became the main open, legal national peasant movement opposed to the authoritarian regime. The KMP's biggest contribution during the remaining months of the Marcos regime was to publicly expose the failure of the land reform program, the deteriorating economic condition of the peasants, and the widespread violations of human rights in the countryside.[9] The KMP remained the most vocal and active peasant organization even during the early years of the Aquino administration. It was able to play a significant role in the subsequent policy debate about agrarian reform. It also led a march of some 20,000 peasants to Malacañang Palace on 22 January 1987 to press for land reform, in which the protesters were fired upon by the police and military forces, killing thirteen and wounding dozens more. This bloody incident forced the Aquino administration to address the demand for land reform.[10]

During the subsequent legislative debate about land reform, however, the KMP was no longer the only organization publicly projected and popularly recognized. Other progressive peasant organizations developed, such as the highly differentiated social-democratic group, during the political opening in 1986. This social-democratic bloc pushed for the formation of a broad national coalition of peasant organizations: The Congress for a People's Agrarian Reform (CPAR) launched in mid-1987. The KMP and other ND rural people's organizations joined the coalition. They did so with reservations, principally rooted in their ideological differences with the politically moderate social democrats. The CPAR was at the forefront of the peasants' lobby for a more progressive land reform policy, often receiving more publicity than the KMP. The KMP never believed that a meaningful land reform policy could be enacted by a national legislative body overwhelmingly dominated by big landlords. And its scepticism was not without basis. Thus the stress of the KMP was to "expose and oppose" the anti-land reform character of the Aquino regime and at the same time put forward a radical version of land reform as an alternative. The KMP intensified its national campaign for widespread peasant occupation of idle and abandoned land and Marcos crony-owned land, more in order to project the land reform issue politically than to actually secure ownership and control of land to address the peasants' pressing needs.

When CARP was made law in June 1988, it was rejected by almost all peasant organizations across the political spectrum. This rejection was based on the key issues of reform coverage and landlord compensation, which the peasant groups thought were too far from their radical proposals. The CPAR formulated its alternative policy proposal of land reform called the People's Agrarian Reform Code, or PARCode, and vowed to amend CARP through a nationwide signature campaign, invoking the "people's initiative" clause enshrined in the Constitution.[11] However, this campaign did not succeed (see Putzel, 1998).

The KMP rejected CARP, criticizing the policy as "pro-landlord" and "anti-peasant" (KMP, 2000, 1993). Effectively ignoring the CPAR signature campaign, the KMP intensified its land occupation campaign, with the goal of polarizing the political situation and thus putting the ND radical form of struggle, which was then beginning to lose vigour, back on the agenda as the most viable option for meaningful societal transformation. In some cases, the KMP conducted its land occupations with the participation of the NPA. In other cases, the areas that were projected as KMP-occupied lands were the same communities that had in fact earlier been subjected to the ND "agrarian revolution" program. In still other cases, peasants occupied land and later sought assistance from the KMP (see Putzel, 1995; Kerkvliet, 1993; KMP, 1992a). Overall, and by the late 1980s, the KMP claimed to have occupied 75,000 hectares of land, benefiting 50,000 peasant households. However, most of these land occupations were not sustained.

In an assessment made by the KMP in early 1992, the organization's secretary general, who was from Negros Island in the Visayas where the KMP reported to have occupied 45,000 hectares, admitted two crucial points about land occupation:[12] First, most of the invaded lands were later recovered by the landlords with the aid of private armies and the military. Second, but related, those lands that were maintained under the control of the organization had not been made productive. Specifically, he pointed out that not more than 10 percent of the total occupied lands had been made productive (KMP, 1992a).

Within the KMP, several reasons for such failure were identified. First, most of the areas were heavily militarized and so the peasants could not resume their normal farming activities. Second, almost no government or private institution wanted to give credit to the peasants occupying the lands. Third, the pool of cadres, peasants or otherwise, assigned in their communities were trained as political activists and not as development activists who could help these communities organize profitable farming enterprises. This was especially difficult because, and this is the fourth reason, most of the occupied lands were marginal. Fifth, and perhaps reflecting all these factors, when the communities started to be militarized, the peasants seldom made exhaustive efforts to stay, perhaps because they felt there was not much at stake in the land: neither legal title nor productive activities (KMP, 1992a).[13]

In short, the KMP's land occupation campaign during the second half of the 1980s contributed to keeping the issue of land reform on the national agenda, but it failed as an alternative land reform program that could be implemented outside of the state. And internally for the ND movement, the campaign failed to create the political polarization that would be necessary to put the revolutionary movement back on track.

Meanwhile, the revolutionary land reform program being carried out selectively in some areas where the NPA was strong suffered a fate similar to the KMP's land occupations. The communist insurgents' campaigns for land rent reduction, the abolition of usury, and selective land confiscation made initial and partial gains for the peasants, as some lands were redistributed to landless peasants while land rents and loan interests were reduced in areas where the NPA was strong.[14] But as soon as the general politico-military condition began to be unfavourable to the communist rebels in the late 1980s, most of these partial gains were rolled back, as landlords violently took back their land or resumed the onerous sharing arrangements. The campaign to eradicate usury proved to be contentious even within the revolutionary movement, because in many cases where this campaign was launched, local moneylenders simply withdrew from their activities, draining the community of the much-needed cash to finance rural village production. In the end, many peasants, even in the guerrilla zones, contracted loans from these moneylenders anyway but concealed them from the guerrillas (see Putzel, 1995). Even the *tersyung baliktad* campaign was not sustained (see Franco, 2001b).[15]

The same ideological, political, and organizational factors that accounted for the KMP's strength during its early years, especially under an authoritarian regime, led to its weakening toward the 1990s. The ND movement's analysis of Philippine society as static, semi-feudal, and semi-colonial locked the KMP into a situation of inflexibility amidst a profoundly and rapidly changing context. The "statist" and thus "maximalist" (i.e., "all or nothing") attitude of the ND movement with regard to the question of state power imprisoned the ND rural movements in a situation where these were unable to take full advantage of political opportunities opened on the agrarian front.

At the height of the KMP's popularity in 1985–1992, its political influence was, to varying degrees, significantly felt in most regions of the country. However, between and within these regions, its influence was highly varied and uneven. Organizationally, the KMP's mass base was amorphous, relying mainly on the mass of supporters and sympathizers of the ND movement in general; it was unclear even to the KMP leaders who their members were and who actually "called the shots," so to speak, as to when and how to carry out political mobilizations. After 1985, the KMP claimed to have a membership of 800,000 individual peasants. Internally, however, KMP leaders knew this was a deliberately bloated claim for propaganda purposes. The question of who the movement's supporters, followers, and members were was a perennial issue of internal debate with the KMP, at least between 1985 and 1993. In a major internal assessment by the KMP's National Council in early 1992, an "honest accounting" was made of membership and mobilization performance. A few citations from these records are revealing. In Central Luzon, the KMP's chapter AMGL (*Alyansa ng Magsasaka sa Gitnang Luson*, Alliance of Central Luzon Farmers) had publicly claimed 35,000 members; its leader admitted that by 1991 AMGL had only 3,706 members and could barely mobilize 3,000 peasants in any protest action (KMP, 1992a: 20). In Southern Tagalog, the regional chapter KASAMA-TK (*Katipunan ng mga Samahang Magbubukid sa Timog Katagalugan*, Council of Peasant Organizations in Southern Tagalog) had publicly claimed 100,000 members; its leader, however, admitted that by 1991 it had in fact only 1,962 members (KMP, 1992a: 24).

Publicly, when confronted with the contentious issue of exact membership numbers, the KMP would argue that it was a "movement" rather than a formal organization and so it was difficult to do head-counting of members. Internally, it explained that the most crucial indicator of the number of "members" was the number of peasants that the KMP could mobilize. The KMP called this its "mobilizeable base." Even using this argument, however, it appears that the KMP's base had shrunk by the late 1980s. An interesting case in this regard is that of the KMP-Visayas, where there was a sharp decline in the number of people mobilized from 1985 onward. Table 5.1 shows the number of people mobilized by the KMP in the different provinces in the Visayas during the two most important protest months (i.e., October, which marked Marcos' "fake

Table 5.1
The KMP-Visayas number of participants in mass mobilizations (1985–1991)

Date of KMP mobilization	Number of peasant participants
October 1985	42,500
October 1986	53,200
October 1987	29,000
October 1988	3,000
June 1989	4,000
June 1990	3,000
June 1991	6,000

Note: Until 1988, the KMP launched major mobilizations in October to protest against the "fake" land reform program of Marcos, which was started in October 1972. Beginning in 1989, June became the KMP's protest month against the "new fake land reform" (i.e., CARP).

Source: KMP (1992a: 15).

land reform," and June, which marked the "fake CARP"). The data shows that the peak years of the KMP-Visayas were 1985–1987. Beginning in 1988, a sharp decline occurred in the number of participants in mobilizations. During the 1990s and beyond, the size of the KMP's actions would not come near those seen in 1985–1987. The same trend of sharp reductions in the size and frequency of mass mobilizations of the KMP occurred in the rest of the country during the same period (KMP, 1992a). It even got worse for KMP in the 1990s. The fall of the Marcos dictatorship in early 1986 and the massive military assault against the ND base areas in the countryside beginning in 1987 were among the most important reasons for the declining peasant participation in the KMP mobilizations. But other reasons were equally important, and these will be discussed later.

Nevertheless, and more significantly, the KMP was able to project itself publicly and politically as the most important militant peasant movement in the country during the 1980s and beyond. It had, arguably, a near hegemony in the policy and political debates about land reform in the country.[16] The broad ND movement mobilized its supporters within the mainstream media to project the KMP as "the" largest and "only" genuine peasant movement in the Philippines — the rest were portrayed as either insignificant or "fake." The

KMP invested resources and deployed cadres to carry out media-related and political networking activities, nationally and internationally. This worked for some time in the 1980s and 1990s, nationally and even internationally.

Meanwhile, between 1987 and 1989, the Aquino administration launched its "total war" policy against the communist insurgents. Most of the victims of the military's indiscriminate bombings and arrests were peasants and peasant leaders broadly associated with the ND rural social movement. At the local level, the KMP-affiliated organizations almost completely disappeared, trying to evade harassment from the Aquino's military. Participation in the KMP's mobilizations dwindled dramatically, but it was not only due to fear of military reprisal. Most KMP leaders also reported that ordinary peasants persistently complained about purely political "agit-prop" (agitation-propaganda) campaigns without any concrete, especially immediate, socioeconomic objectives and gains: *"Pudpod na ang tsinelas namin sa kama-martsa, pag-uwi namin sa bahay, wala pa ring mai-saing"* [Our slippers were already worn out amidst so many marches that we attended, but when we come back to our homes, we still had nothing to cook]. This became a popularly articulated sentiment among the ND-influenced peasant communities, and slowly it trickled into the sympathetic consciousness of the corps of cadres within the KMP and its NGO allies.

By the late 1980s, when it was clear that the mass base of the ND movement had been seriously affected by the government's counterinsurgency operations, the general call within the movement was to recover the lost mass base. In response, the NPS (the group tasked with spearheading the "open peasant mass movement") of the CPP Central Committee revised much of the orthodoxy in the strategy and tactics of the CPP. Relative to other CPP organs, the NPS came up with one of the earlier critiques of the CPP analyses and strategy with regard to the rural mass movement's role in the revolution. Among other key issues, the NPS called for reinvigorated organizing work in the more populous lowland areas (the CPP's stress had been upland, mainly for guerrilla base-building) through "inclusive," "fast-track," and "issue-based" organizing methods aimed at achieving palpable gains for the peasants.[17] The organizing method was "inclusive" in that it included strata of the peasantry that had marketable farm surpluses (poor and middle-income peasants and not just the landless rural (semi)proletariat). This is partly in recognition of the preponderance of legitimate small and medium-sized farm holdings in the country, especially in the rice, corn, and coconut sectors (recall the data presented in chapter 2). The imperative for cross-class and multisectoral alliances — for example peasant-worker alliances, rural-urban alliances —

became even more important amidst the onslaught of neoliberal agricultural policies of deregulation, privatization, and import liberalization. The approach was "fast-track" as opposed to the guerrilla zone preparatory-work method of slow accumulation of core cadres through "step-by-step," "solid" organizing work. This also meant veering away from the concept of an "amorphous" mass of supporters (as exemplified by the traditional movement framing of membership — that is, "all those who would not divulge our presence to the military and despotic landlords are our members") and toward specifically defined movement followers and organizational membership.

The new method was issue-based as opposed to the movement's previous approach of broad and quite vague "motherhood" (general policy) issues like *"buwagin ang pyudalismo!"* (dismantle feudalism!). The approach aimed for immediate, palpable socioeconomic gains while still maintaining strategic perspective. The implications of the adjustment were three: First, clandestine or illegal organizers could not play a key role within this type of movement; open and legal organizers were the most appropriate. Second, legal peasant organizations and their leaderships had to have a greater role in the broader rural social movement. Third, these organizations had to directly engage the state in their struggles if they were after tangible gains on issues such as land, irrigation, price subsidies, and infrastructure.[18]

From late 1989 until 1993, the new approach proved effective in recovering lost mass base areas, organizing new communities, and securing concrete socioeconomic gains for the peasants. By 1992, different non-KMP, ND-influenced peasant organizations were formed along crop sector lines, such as the rice and corn peasants' national coalition and the BUTIL, which engaged in massive rice and corn dumping (*tambak-palay* or *tambak-butil*) in front of the government National Food Authority (NFA) offices to press for higher prices for *palay* (unhusked rice) and to protest against the NFA's privatization and import liberalization policies. Another organization was the KAMMPIL (*Kalipunan ng Maliliit na Magniniyog sa Pilipinas*, Federation of Small Coconut Farmers and Farmworkers' Organizations), which started to engage the government on the issue of recovering the billions of pesos from the coconut levy fund collected during the Marcos era, which was widely believed to have somehow ended up under the private control of Marcos cronies like Danding Cojuangco. Separate renewed organizing work among plantation workers in Mindanao in the context of the land reform struggle was also spearheaded by the NPS. At this point, tactical struggles for land using the positive provisions of CARP could be carried out only sporadically, since the DAR bureaucracy did not want to work with progressive peasant organizations.

Meanwhile, many national and local NGOs under varying degrees of influence of the NPS worked according to this adjusted concept of political and organizational tasks. At the height of the CPP influence, many of the well-known NGOs supporting the peasant movement had been brought firmly into the fold of the ND movement. In fact, many of the decisions on the direction and conduct of the peasant movement had been carried out through these NGOs, which were heavily influenced by party intellectuals. But these same NGO-based party intellectuals, who were directly exposed to open, legal peasant struggles, were the first ones to be critical of the "instrumentalist" attitude of the ND toward peasant organizations and NGOs (i.e., using these organizations for the strengthening and solidifying of the ND's power and influence rather than genuinely seeking to help achieve the peasants' goals). It was not surprising that they were the most active cadres in the internal reorientation drive within the ND movement. At the forefront was the PEACE Foundation.

The PEACE Foundation was founded in 1977 by several progressive bishops from the Protestant and Catholic churches. It became one of the biggest and most important NGOs influenced by the ND movement. Many of the PEACE community organizers in the 1970s and 1980s were directly responsible for carrying out organizing work in the rural areas. The organizing method then, however, was framed within the "guerrilla zone preparation" (internally referred to as "GZPrep") purpose. The PEACE Foundation network was crucial in the subsequent formation of major ND rural organizations such as the KMP. The reform-oriented NPS cadres were quite entrenched within the PEACE network from the 1970s to 1992.[19] Thus, the revisionist and reformist tendencies of the NPS were experimented with first through this NGO's vast national network. Nevertheless, other ND-oriented NGOs were more or less convinced of the need to carry out some reorientation of the NPS strategy. In fact, the KMP itself, or at least its national leaders, became convinced by the unconventional approaches being experimented with by the NPS. The reorientation in strategy led by the NPS between 1988 and 1992 gained most ground in the regions of Central Luzon, Southern Tagalog, Central Philippines, and the plantation belt of Davao-Cotabato in Mindanao, although within these regions the degree of their organizational and political influence was highly varied and uneven.[20] Due to the strategic political value of regions 3 and 4 (Central Luzon and Southern Tagalog, respectively) to national political-propaganda campaigns, being regions that are geographically adjacent to the national capital, the NPS reorientation campaign gave priority to these two regions.

The CPP, however, was unconvinced by the "revisionist" and "reformist" orientation of the "new" strategy of the NPS. In a 1989 political bureau decision, the CPP leadership rejected the NPS strategy (then labelled the "September Thesis") and ordered the cadres in the legal peasant mass movement to go back to the original framework of peasant organizing work, that is, "GZPrep" (Franco, 2001b).[21] The CPP Central Committee even rejected the land occupation campaign because it was "making the armed struggle serve the mass movement" (Weekley, 2001: 203, 215).[22]

By early 1992, the KMP geared up to institutionalize the new orientation. It produced a blueprint on how to carry out the new strategy in organizing work and political mobilization that included engaging the state on the land issue via CARP. In early 1992, the KMP (1992b: 2) admitted thus:

> Central among the weaknesses identified was KMP's inability to readily adjust to the post-EDSA [1986] situation during which KMP focused on mere political advocacy of fundamental social alternatives instead of shifting its stress on struggle for reforms and economic concessions. This shift was needed then to sustain KMP's grounding on the larger mass of peasants whose level of politicization have not been raised beyond pure anti-Marcos slogans. They became the most vulnerable victims of anti-communist propaganda. However, they are also the same mass of peasants who suffer the worst economic hardships but whose immediate interest for reforms and economic concessions were not promptly addressed by KMP.

Furthermore,

> The ambiguity in the Aquino government's Comprehensive Agrarian Reform Law or CARL has accorded chances for big landowners to evade land reform. But while so, it has also given KMP's chapters tactical opportunities to use the law in defending their right for the land. They have learned to combine the legal and metalegal forms of struggle to strengthen and legitimize their position *vis-à-vis* the big landowning class (KMP, 1992b: 26).

However, by the end of 1992, a serious split had occurred within the CPP that had far-reaching effects in all ND organizations, both open/legal and clandestine/illegal, so that the initial momentum of the KMP reorientation had to be substantially realized later and outside the ND organizational framework. In 1993, all the organizations of the ND movement and the legal organizations under their influence, such as the KMP, split over differences on ideological and political strategies. There were three major splinter groups, at least initially: One group reaffirmed the basic principles of the Marxist-Leninist-Maoist line under the leadership of Armando Liwanag (pseudonym).[23] Another major bloc was led by (the late) Popoy Lagman, who was able to win over the majority of the CPP support base in Metro Manila. Subsequently, this group adopted a "workerist-Leninist" ideological framework. The last major group came to be known as the "third bloc," also known at that time as the "democratic bloc." This was a highly heterogeneous group composed of various smaller groups that had opted to undergo a process of rethinking and renewal without fixing any ideological or political line immediately after the split. This group would later split into smaller groups, though both the first and second blocs would also be plagued by internal divisions. It is to be noted that among these splinter groups, only one would later pursue a "non-party, social movement" orientation — that is, Padayon (the Visayan word for "continue"), which counts as its principal support base much of the former CPP-NPS's peasant mass base and many of its former cadres (Padayon later joined other political blocs for the establishment of the party-list group Akbayan). Yet, still many other former ND cadres opted to completely detach from both the party- and social movement–oriented groups, and concentrated their work within the (narrow) parameters of specific projects of their NGOs. Further realignments occurred during the next ten years, but none of the groups would be able to regain the level of organizational and political influence enjoyed by the unified ND movement in the mid-1980s, although the Maoist CPP and its allied organizations would be able to consolidate their forces toward the end of the 1990s onward (see Caouette, 2004).[24] In mid-2005, all the former ND groups, plus a number of other non-ND radical socialist groups such as BISIG (*Bukluran sa Ikauunlad ng Sosyalismo sa Isip at Gawa* or Unity for the Advancement of Socialism in Theory and Practice) and Pandayan, forged a historic coalition with possible strategic orientation. The coalition is called *Laban ng Masa* or "Struggle of the Masses." Whether this alliance can be sustained remains to be seen.

Meanwhile, going back to the early 1990s ND peasant movement, some key national leaders opted to dissociate themselves from the KMP and the tarnished name of the organization, and instead formed the *Demokratikong Kilusang Magbubukid ng Pilipinas* (DKMP, Democratic Peasant Movement of the Philippines).[25] On the one hand, the KMP retained control of a sizeable portion of the original, but largely constricted (i.e., with a reduced number of supporters), mass base of the organization, mostly in upland interior areas. On the other hand, the DKMP, while taking a modest share of the original support base with it, was composed more of local peasant groups that emerged during the reorientation period after the late 1980s. The DKMP vowed to pursue the militant tradition of the KMP but to further develop the aborted ideological, political and organizational reorientation.[26] Liberated from the ND dogmatism, the DKMP loosely identified itself with the "third bloc," as well as with the PEACE Foundation, which had been able to break free from the CPP influence, although not without major organizational setbacks.

The first major resolution by the PEACE-DKMP alliance was to engage the government on the issue of land reform, using CARP as a starting point. This opening of the DKMP was partly internally driven (the desire to continue the reorientation to reposition itself politically) and partly externally driven, as political opportunities opened up. At this point, the new DAR leadership was demonstrating its reformist tendencies, and some of the earlier identified "positive provisions" within the CARP law were showing some concrete promise of delivering actual land reform gains to peasants. Organizationally and politically, the DKMP's influence during its first few years was significantly felt in areas where PEACE had made earlier inroads in organizing work, notably in Central Luzon, Southern Tagalog, Central Philippines, and the Davao-Cotabato plantation belt in Mindanao. But again, progress was highly varied and uneven upon a closer examination from the regional to the municipal level.

Meanwhile, the dynamic changes in the political opportunity structure for rural mobilizations and land claim–making, as well as the far-reaching realignment of forces within the political left and civil society groups, have also partly influenced and have been influenced by the changes in the priorities in funding commitment by northern development agencies. In the 1970s to 1980s, the national-democratic civil society groups had enjoyed the generous support of European and North American funding agencies. However, toward the late 1980s, the moderate social democrats began to erode the ND share of foreign funding, when the former started to get substantial funds from Catholic agencies such as the German Misereor, the Dutch Cebemo (which later would be reorganized as Cordaid), and the Ford Foundation. Other significant European funding agencies such as the German Bread for the World and the Dutch Inter-Church Organization for Development and Cooperation (ICCO) continued their support for the ND rural-oriented groups; however, the 1992–1993 split in the ND movement spelled the end of most of the funding support to these organizations. Thus, in terms of foreign funding support, the 1990s witnessed generous funding to the moderate social democrats, while the NDs and the ex-NDs became marginalized. The PEACE Foundation for example had no significant external funding beginning in 1993. But toward the late

1990s, the social democrats eventually lost most of this foreign funding, partly due to their inability to deliver their promised output. For example, these groups had marginal output in terms of successful land redistribution in their land reform campaigns — compared to some ex-NDs that persevered in their work despite marginal funding and in the end were able to demonstrate far more land reform successes. By the late 1990s, there was no significant external funding for land reform campaigns for any rural social movement organizations. It was not until 2001 that the Dutch ICCO started to entertain funding land reform campaigns again, starting with the PEACE Foundation. This support would later broaden and expand.

In short, the ND split and the subsequent erosion of ND hegemony in rural social movements coincided with other political changes on the rural front that, taken together, had a profound and far-reaching impact on the political dynamics within rural social movements and between them and the state. The CARP process would be an important context *and* object of these state–society political dynamics. These political actors and the CARP institutional processes and outcomes would shape and reshape each other over time.

The post-1992 period was marked by the proliferation of autonomous rural social movement organizations — partly due to the widespread realignments of different left and centre-left political organizations. The degree of influence of these peasant organizations would partly cause the highly uneven and varied, but relatively positive, outcomes in CARP implementation from 1992 onward. It is thus important to analyze these kinds of movements in detail.

After Ramos' election in mid-1992, CPAR was disbanded, mainly because about half of the member organizations had opted to support Ramos' presidential bid, even though he campaigned for a 50-hectare retention limit for land (Franco, 1999a).[27] (The law states that a landlord can retain only 5 hectares of land. This legal limit has several "loopholes" through which a landlord can effectively increase his/her retained area; see Putzel, 1992. Increasing the retention limit to 50 hectares, however, would automatically exclude majority of the farmlands in the country from land reform.) The demise of CPAR and the ND split in turn created an opportunity for realignments within the broad left and centre-left peasant movements and the NGO community. A coalition of NGOs and peasant organizations was formed, the Partnership for Agrarian Reform and Rural Development Services (PARRDS), which brought together several former ND organizations (e.g., DKMP and the PEACE Foundation), including the "popular democrats"[28] and the independent socialist group BISIG,[29] plus other autonomous groups. In addition, various associations across the political spectrum began to cooperate around advocacy for some policy issues despite the absence of formal organizational coalitions.

Moreover, during this period other non-ND progressive peasant organizations became stronger and more widespread — the PAKISAMA (*Pambansang Kilusan ng mga Samahang Magsasaka*, National Movement of Farmers' Associations), for instance, which identified with the broad social-democratic political group. The PAKISAMA teamed up with a huge and then well-funded national network of rural-oriented NGOs: PhilDHRRA (Philippine Partnership for the Development of Human Resources in Rural Areas).[30] The break-up of CPAR also freed this network from its obligation to toe the CPAR campaign line of complete and perpetual opposition to CARP. Immediately after the breakup of CPAR, the network started to engage the new DAR leadership headed by Ernesto Garilao, himself being identified with the broad social-democratic community, on the land reform issue (see Liamzon, 1996).

Generously funded by European Catholic development agencies and by the Ford Foundation, the social-democratic rural social movement organizations had their most widespread presence nationwide and conducted their most consistent and sustained political campaign for land reform in the mid-1990s. During that period, they formed a national coalition called Agrarian Reform Now!, or AR Now!. This group was well funded and run by a committed, talented, and articulate corps of urban-based activists. This network became organizationally and politically influential in Southern Luzon, parts of Central Mindanao, and parts of southern and northern Philippines, but the degree of its organizational and political influence at the provincial level in these regions was, again, varied and uneven. The sustained national and international campaign for the local Mapalad agrarian case (Bukidnon) had been a crucial rallying point for the coalition (see Quitoriano, 2000). By 2000, however, the network started to experience funding problems, when the Ford Foundation, Cordaid, and Misereor radically reduced support — or in some cases totally stopped support. This sudden reduction in funding would significantly affect its capacity to continue organizing work among peasants for land reform and to sustain national-level advocacy. In early 2003, personality differences between the PAKISAMA national leaders created further paralysis and setbacks for the network.[31] A member organization of AR Now!, Task Force Mapalad (TFM), would continue much of the network's work, but on a limited scale and mainly in the province of Negros Occidental.[32] TFM, formerly funded by the Canadian CIDA and later by the Dutch ICCO, is an unusual organization (by Philippine standards): It is a hybrid NGO–peasant organization entity — having mass support from among poor peasants but with leadership roles taken by city-based professionals. By 2006, enjoying generous funding support from ICCO, among others, TFM was seeking to expand its work in areas outside Negros Occidental.

By 2000, further reconfigurations occurred in the peasant movements and the ranks of their allies directly engaged in the land reform struggle; these were partly internally driven (by ideological and institutional turf conflicts and even personality differences) and partly externally influenced (by realignments of state actors to different sections of the broad rural social movements).

By this time, the DKMP had been seriously weakened due to numerous internal defections of its member organizations, in part caused by personality differences. Moreover, DKMP's leader, Jaime Tadeo, was appointed by former president Joseph Estrada to the board of directors of the Land Bank of the Philippines (LBP). This appointment prevented Tadeo from being a vocal critic of the government's agrarian policies. But the majority of cadres who bolted from the ND movement in 1992-1993 had long planned to develop a different breed of rural social movement, at least in the context of the Philippines during that time. Unlike most other groups and individuals who left the Maoist movement, the groups associated with the peasant sector did not opt to establish communist parties. They were deeply interested in a non-party social movement framework, of which the key concepts of "autonomy," "internal democracy," "leadership-membership accountability," "poly-centric leadership," among others, are critical building blocks.[33]

Their serious aspirations to establish this type of movement, added to the realization that DKMP's organizational structure, political orientation and entrenched leadership did not match what they wanted to do, prompted these groups and newly emerging local peasant leaders to pursue their social movement renewal outside DKMP. By the second half of the 1990s, most DKMP member organizations had slowly drifted away from their national federation. They would later gravitate towards each other in a loose political community. And this initiative would lead to the official formation of UNORKA.

The formal birth of UNORKA in 2000, and its teaming up with the PEACE Foundation network, provided a boost in the national land reform campaign. This was further boosted when the Dutch agency ICCO decided to once again support land reform campaigns and offered support to PEACE and to UNORKA. UNORKA fast became a robust new type of peasant movement. It is a highly polycentric rural social movement, or political network, with its local member groups themselves being centres of power. Moreover, it is very much land reform focused. By 2001, UNORKA had become directly engaged in the struggle for land redistribution of some 200,000 hectares and in 500 legal disputes involving at least 90,000 landless rural poor households (or around half million people), an unprecedented scale in the peasant movement history in the context of the CARP framework. By 2003, organizationally and politically, the influence of UNORKA-PEACE had been significantly felt in virtually the whole of Luzon, central Philippines, and the plantation belt of Davao-Cotabato, although it was uneven and varied between and within these regions. But this network was able to position itself in areas where major land reform "battles" were being fought, such as Bondoc Peninsula, Central Luzon, in Bicol provinces (including Masbate and Camarines Sur), Negros Island, and in the plantation belt of the Davao-Cotabato provinces. By 2001, according to interviews with various peasant organizations, NGOs, and DAR officials, and based on NGO and DAR records, it appears that the UNORKA-PEACE network had the widest extent of organizational and political influence in terms of quantity of land, number of agrarian disputes, and number of peasant households directly engaged in the land reform struggle within the reformist framework of CARP.[34]

Other peasant groups, although with relatively less influence in the context of land struggles, emerged during this period. One of these groups is the PKSK (*Pambansang Kilusan ng mga Samahan sa Kanayunan*, National Federation of Organizations in the Countryside).[35] The PKSK traces its provenance to its association with the independent socialist group BISIG and its NGO allies.[36] The KAISAHAN (*Kaisahan Tungo sa Kaunlaran ng Kanayunan at Repormang Pansakahan* or Unity towards the Development of the Countryside and Agrarian Reform), an NGO specializing in legal assistance to peasants also supported the formation of PKSK. Organizationally and politically, PKSK's significant presence has been felt in regions 3, 4, and 8 and on some plantations in Southwestern Mindanao. Again, like all other peasant organizations and NGOs, the degree of its organizational and political influence is highly uneven and varied between and within these regions. Moreover, the PKSK tends to focus its work on local governance-related policy advocacy aimed at strengthening the electoral political party that the PKSK is closely identified with, the Citizens' Action Party or Akbayan.

Another group to emerge during this period is the *Pambansang Katipunan ng Makabayang Magbubukid* (PKMM, National Federation of Nationalist Peasants), which is a relatively vibrant national peasant movement associated with the *Kilusan para sa Pambansang Demokrasya* (KPD, Movement for National Democracy). They are national in scope, although their support is strongest in Central Luzon, Negros, and some parts of northern Mindanao.

Another group to come into being during this period was the KASAMA-KA, or Federation of People's Organizations in the Countryside (*Kalipunan ng mga Samahaang Magsasaka sa Kanayunan*). This group is a mixture of peasant groups engaged in watershed management, sustainable agriculture, cooperative-building, and land reform struggle.[37] Its orientation can be traced to its relationship with a national network of NGOs, PhilNET-RDI (Philippine Network of Rural Development Institutes), which is a spinoff NGO from the socioeconomic section of the PPI, another major ex-ND NGO. In terms of land reform–related initiatives, this network has significant presence in regions 6, 7, 8, 9, and 11. Again, like all other networks, the degree of political and organizational influence of KASAMA-KA/PhilNET-RDI in terms of the land redistribution campaign is highly uneven between and within these regions.

Meanwhile, the coconut sector–based KAMMPIL has been able to maintain some of its mass base; it has varying degrees of influence in Southern Luzon, central Philippines, and southern and northern Mindanao.[38] The BUKLOD (*Bukluran ng Malayang Magbubukid*, a breakaway group from the FFF) has been able to maintain a presence in a few areas in regions 4 and 5, but undertaking less important land reform struggles and amidst some internal organizational problems. The FFF, which has remained under the firm control of the Montemayor family, is a more or less constant advocate for land reform, with a high profile leadership (the Montemayors) and has been able to maintain enclaves of loyal followers in a few areas of the country.[39] Finally, the AMA, which has been closely identified with the (old) *Partido Komunista ng Pilipinas* (PKP), has been able to maintain some of its original mass base in regions 2 and 3, though on a much constricted scale, amidst series of internal divisions.

In addition, relatively smaller peasant groups within the reformist framework of CARP have emerged from the evolving ex-ND political communities. One of these is the "Makabayan," which is identified with one of the groups originally associated with the "third bloc" that later merged with the vibrant trade-union based political movement Sanlakas. Another is PKMP which is a peasant organization connected to some ex-CPP cadres who first joined the Maoist bloc in the 1993 split, but who were later expelled; they subsequently helped form the KPD. These cadres later organized some service NGOs, and together with PKMP have been focusing their work on international issues such as neoliberal agricultural trade.

The PPI itself has continued to assist scattered local peasant groups in their claim-making campaigns within the CARP framework, particularly in some areas in Central Luzon, Southern Tagalog, and Central Mindanao; some groups it has worked with include surviving portions of the DKMP,[40] as well as what remains of the FFF. The PPI made several unsuccessful attempts to build broad coalitions of rural-oriented organizations, including the Kilos-Saka, which is a coalition that focuses on agricultural trade-related policy issues. For legal reasons linked to the 1992–1993 ND split, the PPI would assume a new, different corporate name and identity by 2005: Centro Saka, Inc. (CSI).

Moreover, the Philippine Development Institute (PDI), an NGO that was originally founded to do relief and rehabilitation work for communities adversely affected by the eruption of Mt. Pinatubo in the early 1990s, expanded its work to include land reform in Central Luzon, and has assisted in establishing a region-wide organization called *Nagkakaisang Magsasaka sa Gitnang Luson* (NMGL, United Farmers in Central Luzon). And the Kasangyahan Foundation, Inc. (KFI) continues to work with some land reformed rubber plantations in Southwestern Mindanao.

Finally, there are other NGOs that, while not engaging in direct organizing work and political mobilizations with peasants, have played important roles in the land reform struggle. KAISAHAN and Saligan are two groups that provide legal assistance to peasants struggling for land within the reformist framework of CARP.[41] Meanwhile, three major NGOs continue to carry out systematic research related to land reform: the PPI (later as CSI), Management and Organizational Development for Empowerment (MODE), and AFRIM. To varying extents, different peasant organizations work with these NGOs.

Most of these NGOs are funded by the Dutch agency ICCO. In 2005, these ICCO-supported groups formed a loose coalition called "Kilos AR" tasked to coordinate common national campaigns. Unfortunately, however, by 2006, there were no other significant development funding agencies (apart from ICCO) that provided support to the various organizations working on agrarian reform in the Philippines. This leaves the social movement and civil society efforts in particular and the land reform campaign in general in a very uncertain and precarious condition: If ICCO were to decide to pull their funding from land reform campaigns, the adverse effect on pro-poor redistributive reform efforts in the country would be far reaching. The creeping trend within ICCO by 2006 towards more "development-oriented projects" as opposed to the inherently political redistributive reform campaigns is starting to sound the alarm bells with many rural activists. Although there is no doubt these organizations are well rooted and so would continue to exist somehow even if external funding pulled out, their capacity as national reform campaigners would undoubtedly be adversely affected.

It is important to note that since the Garilao DAR, the old state co-opted peasant organizations that were used by the past conservative DAR leadership have been almost completely isolated and relegated to the periphery of the land reform process.

These various peasant groups relate with each other in a variety of fraternal ways, formal and informal. Formally, the most politically important peasant groups that are engaging the state on the land reform agenda (UNORKA, PAKISAMA, and PKSK) are organizationally united within an electoral political party (i.e., the Citizens Action Party or Akbayan). Formed by a variety of left wing political groups not identified with either the Maoist or Leninist groups, Akbayan has garnered seats in Congress and numerous local government positions. One of its strategic political and policy agendas is land reform, and among its most important political and electoral sources of support are members and sympathizers of the three major peasant associations cited above. Hence, despite historically and ideologically charged animosities between these three peasant groups, they have still been able to discuss and pursue common agendas and actions facilitated within the institutional framework of Akbayan. More broadly, the three peasant groups mentioned above, plus other peasant organizations, have debated and converged on common political and policy issues and launched common collective actions between 1988 and 2002 through various state–society interface mechanisms, such as "Project 40 Now" from 1995 to 1998 and the "Task Force Fast-Track" in 2000.

However, due to various historical, ideological, political (and even personality) differences between these different peasant groups and their allies, relationships between them have continued to be tension filled, and cleavages have persisted. Tensions over territory (both political and geographic) and competition for ever-shrinking funds from abroad continue to fuel animosities between the various groups and their NGO allies. Since 2003, there have been several efforts to organize broader coalitions of peasant organizations and NGOs but without much success. Arguably, the only two prospects for a stable ideologically and politically broad peasant coalition are the *Laban ng Masa* (LnM, Struggle of the Masses), which has political movements as its base, and Kilos-AR, which has NGOs as its main base. Under attack from the Maoists (the latter started to assassinate some of the leaders of other leftist groups) on the one hand, and in the midst of the crisis of national governance in 2005, with President Arroyo accused of massive corruption and electoral fraud, on the other, all non-Maoist left wing political organizations and other autonomous NGOs and social movements gathered together and forged a historic unity: *Laban ng Masa*. Chaired by left wing activists and an academic, former University of the Philippines president Francisco Nemenzo, *Laban ng Masa* has been trying to develop a kind of progressive alternative that would exist somewhere between the Arroyo administration and the Maoist communist party. Whether or not and to what extent *Laban ng Masa* will become a viable and important political actor will be seen soon. A recent important cross-sectoral coalition has been spearheaded by PARRDS and UNORKA together with Kilos-AR in their particular work with the politically influential Catholic Bishops Conference of the Philippines (CBCP). Responding to various agrarian reform-related pressing issues, partly sparked by the assassination of UNORKA leader Eric Cabanit in April 2006, and the unabated killings of peasant activists nationwide, the CBCP decided to (re)convene its National Rural Congress (NRC) in January 2008 (the first NRC was convened by the CBCP in 1967) largely in order to activate the support of the Church to the peasant struggle for land, food and dignity.

As a result of the emergence of these various formations of autonomous peasant organizations, NGOs, and political movements, combined with the widespread erosion of the CPP's influence both within the progressive movement's circle and in the national polity more generally, an era marked by militant but pragmatic rural social movements has ensued. This has had a positive impact on CARP implementation.

There are, however, common weaknesses among these peasant organizations and their allies, in addition to their continued relative fragmentation: For one, their political strategies are overly focused on the expropriation of big private landholdings within the scope of CARP. Overemphasis on this land type has, on most occasions, been at the expense of other crucial issues such as the redistribution of public lands and tenancy reforms through leasehold. The explicit or implicit acceptance among most autonomous rural social movements of the mistaken notion that redistributive reform does not occur in public lands and leasehold largely accounts for the lack of attention given to these issues. The lack of systematic attention to the "missing" landholdings within the CARP scope is also common to organizations. These peasant associations engage the state only on policy issues that are included on the official policy scope, such as the landholdings included in the official land redistribution targets. This explains the absence of any significant, coherent, and sustained protest from the peasant groups and NGOs against the exclusion of huge quantities of land from the official redistribution scope. In addition, these peasant groups and NGOs generally give attention only to the specific landholdings on which they can directly intervene, which are, in general, those areas included in their foreign-funded projects; they tend to lose sight of their strategic role in the more comprehensive (political) challenge to resolve the land question in society as a whole.

Furthermore, between and within these organizations and networks, political strategies on how to carry out effective campaigns for land reform differ quite remarkably. An extreme case is the KMP, which continues to uphold its "expose and oppose" "genuine land reform will be implemented after the seizure of state power by the worker-peasant alliance" framework. Thus, it does not support CARP, and instead works to undermine it. As such, its strategy is to focus on media work and political networking, nationally and internationally, capitalizing on carefully selected negative land reform cases that have big political value to convince the national and international public that CARP is "pro-landlord" and "anti-peasant." This explains its intermittent national/international campaigns such as that involving the Hacienda Looc in Batangas. However, a few local peasant groups associated with the KMP have actually worked within CARP for redistributive reform gains.[42]

The other extreme is more of a "tendency" than a systematic strategy (and there are really no specific peasant groups and NGOs that fit it more generally and permanently): traditional and conservative organizations relying on a few charismatic, well-connected leaders and NGO staff to follow up cases in various DAR and government offices, not using militant forms of actions and avoiding confrontation with state officials. These make use of what is pejoratively called a "paper-chasing strategy," amounting to the mere follow-up of the whereabouts of a case and its documents. They fully support some DAR officials' mistaken notion of "conflict-free partnership" achieved through peaceful dialogues and friendly negotiations. The organizing work at the ground level in this kind of strategy is unsystematic and sporadic. Some peasant organizations and their NGO allies mentioned earlier have demonstrated this tendency from time to time.

In the end, what matters is not only the quantity of peasant organizations but also their "quality." "Quality" here means a high degree of the twin foundations of peasant organizational power discussed in Chapter 1 — autonomy and capacity — relative to the task of pushing for land redistribution. Not all of the organizations mentioned above, not all of the NGOs working with the peasants, possess, in consistent fashion in the context of the struggle for land, these twin foundations. This is partly demonstrated in the degree of political and organizational influence they have.

Overall, and in longer historical view despite the encouraging emergence of militant but pragmatic peasant organizations and NGOs, the ranks of those that engage in consistent and coherent work on land reform remain thin and weak relative to the Herculean challenge of redistributive land reform.

5.3 REFORMIST INITIATIVES BY PRO-REFORM STATE ACTORS "FROM ABOVE"

As explained in the theoretical chapter of this study, state actors do not only implement public policies in response to societal pressures. On many occasions, pro-reform state actors, motivated by a variety of factors, such as concern for political legitimacy and democratization, autonomously push for progressive policy, institutional reforms, and reformist policies such as redistributive land reform, even when these run counter to elite interests. This section demonstrates and explains how, why, and to what extent pro-reform state actors within the Philippine agrarian reform bureaucracy emerged over time. It also looks at the impact of the emergence of these state reformists on the implementation processes and outcomes of redistributive land reform. The section underscores the strengths and weaknesses of state actors in the context of redistributive land reform policy implementation.

The DAR has a huge bureaucracy: 15,000 personnel nationwide. The staff has been recruited into the bureaucracy at different times, many dating as early as the Marcos era. The top DAR leadership (secretary, undersecretaries, assistant secretaries) are "political appointees," their terms of office are co-terminous with the appointing power (i.e., the president of the republic). Middle level officials (bureau chiefs, regional and provincial directors, and national-regional-provincial adjudicators) are also presidential appointees, but their terms of office are not co-terminous with the appointing power; they can secure permanent positions according to the rules of the Civil Service Commission. Below the director and PARO levels are numerous rank-and-file employees. Like other government employees, the DAR employees and officials are not well paid.[43]

As said earlier, the various employees and officials enter the DAR bureaucracy through a variety of appointment and recruitment channels, and like other government agencies, "political patrons" play a role in many such appointments and recruitment. For example, a member of Congress, before a vote for the DAR's annual budget, could ask the DAR to hire this or that person for this or that position.[44] Local and national politicians and other influential elite are widely believed to have been able to facilitate the employment of many DAR officials and employees. Moreover, many of these elites are able to block efforts of the DAR leadership to discharge or transfer DAR employees or officials.[45]

Over time and to varying degrees, the DAR bureaucracy has been subject to the power influences of anti- and pro-reform state and societal actors. However, the political and geographic locations of lower level employees and officials put them in a situation that makes them most vulnerable to anti-reform influences and manipulation. Most of these employees live and work in local communities that are the bastions of power of the landlords and their allies. They face the daily risk of landlord reprisal and constant harassment. This is aggravated by the fact that if a landlord accuses them of any administrative or criminal wrongdoing (e.g., "abuse of authority" or "trespassing on private property") when carrying out their official duties, they are left alone to defend themselves. Legally the DAR cannot provide them with lawyers or money to hire lawyers. Employees retiring from service are unable to receive retirement benefits as long as such cases are pending against them. The anti-reform forces have in fact exploited this legal technicality to pressure lower level officials not to proceed with expropriation. Some PAROs and MAROs have dozens of administrative and criminal charges filed against them by landlords.[46] Thus, many local DAR officials, who are supposed to be frontline CARP implementers, have become effectively immobilized. In comparison, and more generally, regional and national level DAR officials do not suffer as much the daily pressure and harassment by the landlords.

This brief background on the institutional set up of the DAR bureaucracy provides insights into the internal dynamics within the bureaucracy and how it engages other state and societal actors. Against this background, we can derive a better understanding of the various types of DAR employees and officials: "fence-sitters," rent-seekers, those who are outright anti–land reform, and those who are actively pro–land reform. These various categories are found not only in the national-level bureaucracy but also within the intermediate (regional and provincial) and local (municipal) levels. But such categories are dynamically altered in every location and level of the bureaucracy over time through the recursive interactions between state and societal actors, both pro-reform and anti-reform.

It is important to note that the local-level bureaucracies, just like the local peasant groups, need allies at the top of the DAR bureaucracy. If they do not perceive support from allies at the top, they usually remain fence-sitters or are even recruited to anti-reformism. Thus, the leadership at the national DAR tends to be mirrored at the lower levels of the bureaucracy. The influence of national reformists plus the direct engagement by autonomous rural social movement actors is crucial to the eventual behaviour of the numerous lower echelon, front line DAR employees.

Moreover, the DAR is embedded within the broader state apparatus and bureaucracy that directly and indirectly facilitates or blocks the former's efforts to implement land reform. For example, the DAR must contend with Congress in terms of yearly decisions on its budget allocations to the various CARP components. Yet historically, Congress has been the bastion of landowning classes and their allies. The most serious anti-reform attacks against CARP have thus come from this institution. The DAR also contends with a judiciary that, like Congress, is known to be heavily influenced by the elite, including the landed elite. It is therefore not uncommon to see landlords use the judiciary (from the local courts up to the Supreme Court) to block the implementation of land reform.

Finally, the DAR deals directly with a complex web of state agencies, large and small, in the everyday implementation of land reform. As explained elsewhere in this study, more than twenty agencies are directly involved in the various aspects of CARP implementation. Many of these agencies have demonstrated little sympathy for the cause of land reform and the interests of the landless and land-poor peasants and small farmers. For example, the Department of Agriculture (DA, and many of its attached bureaus) has almost always been led by anti–land reform secretaries who have advocated agribusiness-led agriculture, except perhaps for the short-lived stint as DA secretary by FFF's Leonardo Montemayor under the Macapagal-Arroyo presidency. Another agency, the DENR, which has a big role in CARP implementation, has been interested more in mining and commercial forestry than in the plight of landless and land-poor peasants and land reform. Other strategic and influential departments, especially Finance and Trade and Industry, have, time and time again, demonstrated their lack of sympathy for agrarian reform. This lack of widespread support for agrarian reform within the Philippine bureaucracy not only makes land reform implementation difficult; it obstructs the reform process periodically.

Nevertheless, it has to be underscored that despite the entrenched anti–land reform leaderships of these agencies, smaller pro–land reform enclaves have emerged within some of these agencies since the early 1990s. For example, within the DENR some progressive tendencies were demonstrated at the top and middle levels of leadership in the 1990s. There have also been some reformist enclaves within the Philippine Coconut Authority (PCA), an agency that used to be attached to the DA. Formed in the mid-1990s, the National Anti-Poverty Commission (NAPC), an inter-agency group tasked with addressing the poverty problem in the country has worked closely with DAR leaderships. While the NAPC has not delivered its promise of dramatic poverty reduction (see, e.g., Reid, 2005), it has nevertheless contributed to shielding agrarian reform from systematic anti-reform attacks from within the state bureaucracy, at least in the 1990s.

Before Ernesto Garilao and his team took office at the DAR and launched reformist initiatives within the bureaucracy in mid-1992, the DAR had been largely in the hands of the combined power blocs of politically conservative as well as technical-bureaucratic officials, neither of which were effective in carrying out redistributive land reform.

The Marcos regime installed Conrado Estrella at the helm of PD 27 (rice and corn land reform) implementation. His perspective on peasant organizations was as necessary administrative adjuncts to the state bureaucracy. He treated peasants as "clientele" and his DAR personnel as "change agents" (see Estrella, 1978). Thus, state co-opted peasant organizations were formed and maintained. The result, however, in terms of effective land redistribution, was not as optimistically predicted or claimed.[47]

The first four years of CARP implementation under the Aquino administration were marked by public scandals involving the rigging of the 1988 land registration campaign, anomalous real estate deals, widespread land reform evasion by landlords, effective evasion of land reform by Hacienda Luisita (the then president's sugar cane plantation), several changes in the DAR leadership, and the non-participation of major autonomous peasant organizations, as well as a steady stream of landlord-sponsored legislative initiatives intended to further dilute CARP. Within this overall unfavourable political climate for land reform, program implementation was slow and limited.

Many real estate speculators exploited the program's provisions on voluntarily offered land (VOS). In direct collusion with corrupt DAR officials, they sold marginal lands to the government at sky-high prices. The discovery of such widespread fraud during the late 1980s caused a public scandal, leading to the fall of several top DAR officials, including the department's first secretary under the CARP era, Philip Juico (1987–1989). Personally close to President Aquino, Juico was unwilling to provoke either the landlords or the military, and so he refused to subject any private landholdings to compulsory acquisition. He focused instead on distributing public lands and rice and corn lands, the landlords of which were relatively less politically influential. He was also responsible for the early facilitation of leaseback contracts with a number of multinationals in Mindanao. These contract terms would prove onerous, including the "one-plantation, one-collective-title, one-cooperative" policy for the large plantations that would later prove disastrous to the interests of poor farm workers. He facilitated the early efforts for the effective exclusion of Hacienda Luisita from actual land redistribution as well. While tolerating a handful of liberal reform advocates within the DAR bureaucracy, the politically conservative Juico headed a department known to be plagued by widespread rent-seeking and inefficiency and dominated by supporters of conservative reform; each reinforced the other.[48]

Mirian Defensor-Santiago (June to December 1989), a former judge and chief of the immigration commission, was handpicked by President Aquino to replace Juico. Like her predecessor, Santiago had no experience with land reform. By that time, however, she had gained a reputation as an effective and committed "graft-buster" and was considered the most popular national official in the Aquino administration. The administration badly needed a person like Santiago to restore the public's trust and confidence in CARP. But Santiago appeared to have a different idea about priorities. Under her administration, one of the DAR's achievements was to clinch a formal agreement with the Department of National Defense for the latter to help the DAR take back lands "illegally occupied by peasants" or distributed by the communist NPA.[49] She would later claim that the DAR's top level bureaucracy had been infiltrated by communists, referring to the liberal reform advocates (which included Gerry Bulatao, who would later become an undersecretary for operations) who had become critical of her. While it appeared that Santiago was the type of DAR secretary that the landlords might have wanted (her husband was from a landowning family), her well-known ambition in national politics got her into trouble with political leaders in Congress who were already worried about her media popularity. The imperatives of party politics within Congress prevailed. Santiago was not confirmed as secretary (the appointment of a cabinet member must be confirmed by a bicameral committee composed of representatives of both houses of the Congress).[50]

When President Aquino appointed Florencio Abad (December 1989 to April 1990), a left wing social-democrat and member of the House of Representatives, as the new DAR secretary, many observers interpreted the move as an effort to win back the confidence of the progressive section of the peasantry and to restore public and media confidence in CARP. A liberal reform advocate, Abad had authored a progressive land reform bill in 1987 that called for a zero retention right for landlords.[51] His bill was defeated, and he later voted against the final law that was approved (i.e., CARP). Vowing to stretch the limits of the law to favour the peasants, Abad accepted the challenge of implementing a law that he had voted against, banking on collaboration with autonomous peasant organizations to help him succeed. He also vowed to continue and expand the pro-reform state–society alliance strategy being pursued by a minority group of reformers led by Gerry Bulatao. But he was immediately confronted with a difficult case in which the Department of Trade and Industry (DTI), headed by an influential elite (particularly Jose Concepcion, who was close to President Aquino and the top leadership of the Catholic Church), wanted to convert a 230-hectare government-owned stretch of farmland in Cavite into an industrial complex. The peasants opposed the land use conversion; Abad sided with the peasants. However, the pro–land use conversion forces within and outside the state overpowered this pro-reform alliance. In retaliation for his position in the Cavite case, Abad was summarily refused confirmation as DAR secretary by Congress despite unanimous support by peasant organizations across the political spectrum. President Aquino did not defend Abad before Congress. He resigned in April 1990.

The last DAR secretary during the Aquino administration was Benjamin Leong (mid-1990 to June 1992), a senior undersecretary and representative of the conservative reform bloc in the department. Described as "neither pro-peasant nor anti-landlord," he got quick confirmation of his appointment.[52] In the meantime, many of the liberal reformists within the DAR had already resigned after the Abad controversy, leaving the bureaucracy in the hands of conservative officials and ensuring the department's uncontested focus on the less contentious components of CARP through the use of less contentious land acquisition and distribution modalities. The department cemented relationships with peasant groups that had been traditionally co-opted by the state.[53]

The quick turnover in the national DAR leadership during this period negatively impacted the local DAR bureaucracy, where the frontline CARP implementers were positioned. The five turnovers in rapid succession contributed to demoralization and demobilization among local officials and ordinary employees. During the transition periods, CARP implementation at the local level usually came to a stop. Ordinary employees were uninspired to work. In many cases too, anticipating a new national leadership, local officials withheld their accomplishment reports, awaiting the new DAR leadership to which they would submit achievement reports to impress the incoming administration. Finally, during these periods of internal bureaucratic problems, local DAR officials who were traditionally fence-sitters (the most numerous type nationwide) tended to remain fence-sitters, and some were even recruited to outright anti-reformism, taking part in illegal land use conversions and overpriced VOS transactions, as typified by the Garchitorena land scam in Bicol.[54]

In short, from 1988 to 1992, the reform implementation landscape was dominated by several issues which demonstrated or contributed to the further weakening of the program: the successful evasion of President Aquino's Hacienda Luisita of effective land redistribution; onerous terms in the early leaseback arrangements with multinational corporations in Mindanao; corruption scandals within the bureaucracy; and the arrest of KMP's chairperson, Jaime Tadeo, in an *estafa* case filed by Marcos in 1981 in an apparent attempt to silence Tadeo, who was then the leader of AMGL in

Central Luzon. Tadeo was jailed for three years and three months. (President Ramos granted Tadeo parole in August 1993 partly due to the sustained lobbying by DAR Secretary Ernesto Garilao as part of the government's effort to politically stabilize the agrarian reform front.) These events helped dampen the interest in the program among the foreign donors that the government had earlier hoped would take the lead in financing it. Ironically, the problem during this period was not that the funds were less than expected but rather the inability of the DAR to spend the funds, limited as they were.[55] Seriously hobbled by these unfavourable developments, the program would need the fresh, activist leadership of Ernesto Garilao under the Ramos administration to bolster its remaining capabilities.

The 1992 electoral victory of Fidel Ramos, a former Phillipine Constabulary general during the Marcos dictatorship and defence minister in the Aquino administration, elicited grim predictions about the fate of the already much weakened CARP. Initial predictions about the imminent demise of CARP were framed within the broader projection that Ramos would be a "military general-president," and that a return to an authoritarian regime was forthcoming. Indeed one of the plans in Ramos's campaign platform had been to increase the retention limit under CARP from 5 to 50 hectares in an apparent attempt to court the support of the landowning class. Soon after being sworn to office, the new president started to recruit military officers into his administration. But it did not take long for the grim predictions to be proven partly incorrect, at least on the agrarian reform front.

When Ramos took office in June 1992, the land reform agenda within the state was somehow transformed. The elections had greatly divided the elite, while the candidacy of Fidel Ramos failed to rally a majority of voters, and the new president thus entered office with a very weak electoral mandate. As a result, he sought to broaden his political base, and it was in this context that some reform-minded civil society activists were recruited into important positions in the state bureaucracy, including the DAR. Meanwhile, it is also relevant to note that Fidel Ramos and his wife did not come from any big landowning families in the country. This could also partly explain what Gerry Bulatao, who was a top DAR official during the Aquino administration and part of the Ramos period, said in comparing the attitude towards land reform between the Aquino and Ramos administrations: "There were more pressure from the family of Cory Aquino than from the family of Fidel Ramos" for us to make anti–land reform decisions or favour presidential friends in our decisions. "And," Bulatao continued, "if there was pressure [from President Ramos], it was done in a subtle way. It was so subtle that you cannot even

... you're not even sure, that it was there .... I think there is not much debate to say that Ramos was never an anti-land reform president, as compared to Aquino."[56]

Fidel Ramos appointed Ernesto Garilao as the new DAR secretary. Garilao had previously been the head of the politically conservative PBSP, one of the country's largest mainstream NGOs, which was funded by the country's top corporations and foreign donors. He was loosely identified with the broad social-democratic political community. Garilao himself believed that he had been selected by Ramos to become the DAR secretary among other possible appointees because he was "not politically controversial — considering that at that time agrarian reform was very controversial."[57] He had not really been directly involved with land reform before 1992 despite his NGO background, and he had been loosely identified with the political community of the conservative reformists. But in his first few days in office, he made the crucial move to convince Ramos to drop his campaign promise of a 50-hectare retention limit, which he succeeded in doing without much opposition. Ramos, according to Garilao, explained that the talk about a possible shift to a 50-hectare retention limit had been mere "election propaganda." Garilao said that when he asked Ramos whether the latter has landholdings in any farm size categories that the DAR should be extra sensitive about, the president replied no and subsequently gave him the go ahead to proceed and cover all farm landholdings based on what the law stated.[58]

To do this, Garilao brought several respected NGO activists into the DAR and gave them key positions — for example, Hector Soliman (undersecretary for legal affairs), Clifford Burkeley (head executive assistant and later assistant secretary for legal affairs), Joe Grageda (bureau director and later a provincial and regional top official) and Jose Olano (undersecretary for operations), to name a few — as well as Gerry Bulatao (undersecretary for operations) later in Garilao's term of office.[59] After making sure that President Ramos and his family did not have any landed interest, Garilao proceed to frame his plan: "The vision was there, and it was very simple — more lands to be distributed at a shorter time, faster rate of resolving agrarian disputes. So I approached some friends from the NGO community, and I told them that since it's them who know how to make these things work they should join me in running the department. And most of them did."[60] He also consolidated the ranks of the liberal reformers within the bureaucracy and gave more important positions to some of them. He then proceeded to launch a "clean-up" operation within the bureaucracy. His other major step was to seek informal consultations with members of the broad community of autonomous NGOs and peasant organizations, to the surprise of many of them. Garilao explained, "When

President Ramos appointed me secretary ... I brought in a number of NGO development practitioners to become agrarian reform state implementers. We adhered to the principle that for the redistributive program to succeed, it must have the support of the public in general, and of major constituency in particular, the landless farmers. Since that was not present in 1992, we had to develop strong constituency support."[61] He later instituted both formal and informal consultative groups involving various peasant groups and NGOs. Taken together, these moves suggested that he would be more concerned with ensuring political legitimacy — rather than private capital accumulation — of the Philippine state.

Garilao's sense of belonging to the politically progressive, even left wing social democrats from the Ateneo de Manila University, many of whom were staunch land reform advocates, like Abad, would largely explain his consistent pro-reform stance. Further, Garilao's reformist stance after 1992 can be largely explained by the influence of the radical reformers who were able to position themselves within the DAR bureaucracy. Moreover, Garilao's political calculation that it was highly likely that the sympathy and support of the broad peasant movements and their allies for his reformist actions would in turn strengthen his leverage within the broader state bureaucracy also partly proved correct.[62]

Recognizing CARP's flaws and ongoing landlord opposition to it, Garilao largely followed the main approach and focus of his predecessors: redistributing relatively less politically contentious lands through the relatively less contentious land acquisition and distribution modalities. The main difference he made could be seen in the relatively swift implementation of these components. He more than doubled the combined achievements of the twenty years of the Marcos and Aquino administrations (1972–1992) within the much shorter span of six years.

The position of the DAR between 1992 and 1998 thus differed from that in the first four years of CARP implementation in several ways. Garilao appears to have had a dynamic "two-way" relationship with the executive branch of government, especially with the Office of the President. He was able to "stabilize" the agrarian reform front, and in doing so, earned the government's confidence, or tolerance, as partly demonstrated by his appointment as head of the anti-poverty program. This appointment put the role of the DAR, and Garilao himself, in a broader anti-poverty framework, further strengthening the pro–(land) reform policy current within the government. Garilao demonstrated ability and willingness at times to challenge anti–(land) reform policy currents in other agencies and groups of state actors. Initially paired with a DA secretary who was anti-land reform (Roberto Sebastian, President of banana export company Marsman), Garilao showed most of the time that he could withstand conflicting interagency priorities and push their outcomes in his favour, though at times when the private capital accumulation imperatives for the government were too great, he set the political legitimacy task aside. The Garilao DAR lost a considerable number of "battles," like the Mapalad and Hacienda Looc cases — most of which had something to do with land use conversions from farmlands to non-agricultural uses involving elites who were well-connected at the national level in the context of the real estate boom of that period. Moreover, through Garilao's efforts, liberal reform advocates became deeply and widely entrenched within the DAR. One way Garilao used to convert officials and employees to a reformist orientation was to expose them to militant, autonomous peasant groups and NGOs. The Garilao DAR also gave priority to systematic data-banking and improving the quality of DAR data: computerizing the data-banking system, appointing professionals to do the job, and setting up checks and balances for data input, output, and processing.

The reformist tendency at the national DAR had an effect on the local bureaucracies. For one, the appointment of progressive, radical reformers in regional and provincial DAR positions brought the reformist leadership closer to the rank-and-file field officials and employees. The signal from the national leadership of its seriousness about reform was picked up by field personnel, leading numerous fence-sitters to jump onto the nationwide bandwagon of reformism. This signal also directly helped neutralize, if not isolate, openly anti-reform DAR officials and employees. Overall, the reformist signals at the top contributed to the consolidation and expansion of pro-reform field personnel. Autonomous peasant groups and NGOs started to interact with these local DAR reformers, arguably leading to the earlier-mentioned reformist "ratchet effect."

Through such reformist initiatives, the Garilao DAR had almost completed the implementation of redistribution of "softer" landholdings. This strategy was a conscious one on the part of Garilao, because he did not want to antagonize the landowning classes, at least not prematurely, so as not to invite any untimely backlash while trying to gain more ground with reform.[63] In a lot of ways this approach reminds us of Hirschman's notion of "reform by stealth" in the context of Colombian land reform in the early 1960s (see Hirschman, 1967). But the two post-Marcos administrations of Aquino and Ramos also left pending the full and decisive expropriation and redistribution of the vast landholdings of Marcos' cronies, particularly the lands of Danding Cojuangco, the Benedictos, and the Floirendos, despite the CARP mandate to quickly expropriate and redistribute these landholdings to peasants (see, e.g., data in Garilao, 1998; Morales, 1999).[64]

Unlike Fidel Ramos, whose electoral mandate was extremely narrow, Joseph Estrada (July 1998 to January 2001) was elected with a phenomenally high electoral mandate. Partly for this reason, unlike the Ramos administration, which consistently sought broad political alliances and consensus among various political groups and sectors, the Estrada presidency banked on its popular mandate and may not have felt obligated to reach out to other sectors and groups that did not support him in the electoral contest. However, some influential sectors and groups (like the top leadership of the Catholic Church, as well as factions of the elite and the media) opposed Estrada from the very start. He did not have the typical profile of an elite occupying the top government post in the country. A former movie actor, Estrada was a university dropout with *carabao* ("bad") English, a well-known womanizer, and a gambler. While he was not part of the landed elite (coming from an urban family), like his predecessors (and successor), he had close allies in the ranks of the landowning classes. During his stint as senator from 1987 to 1992, he is best remembered for voting to oust the US military bases in the country and for sponsoring two famous rural reform–oriented bills: expansion of irrigation infrastructures and protection and further breeding of the Philippine water buffaloes (*carabaos*), two laws that were never fully funded.

President Estrada appointed Horacio Morales Jr. as DAR secretary. Morales was a well-known figure among NGOs. He was the former chairperson of the underground revolutionary National Democratic Front (NDF) in the 1970s until his arrest and detention in the early 1980s. Released from jail during the 1986 regime transition, he then joined and headed the PRRM, a politically conservative NGO founded in the 1950s, and transformed it into an autonomous, progressive organization.[65] He also co-founded the Movement for Popular Democracy (MPD, or simply, "PopDem"), which soon became a spinoff of the ND movement.

In fact Morales at first did not want the DAR position. What he wanted was the DA secretary post. However, President Estrada apparently already promised the DA post to his running mate Edgardo Angara who lost the vice-presidential race. Angara would assume an appointed cabinet position only a year after the election. Besides, President Estrada thought that somebody who knew the left politics and social movement dynamics should head the politically contentious DAR bureaucracy and implement the land reform program. For such a job, Morales was the clear choice. Morales eventually agreed.[66]

In general, Morales took his cue from Ernesto Garilao on how to work as DAR secretary, but with some revisions and modifications, both deliberate and otherwise. Like Garilao, Morales recruited progressive NGO and academic activists to occupy top positions within the DAR, most of whom had long and deep knowledge of agrarian and rural reform and extensive exposure to militant peasant movements (e.g., Pancho Lara, Toinette Raquiza, Carlito Añonuevo, and Conrado Navarro, to name a few). Like Garilao, Morales recruited within the ranks of his immediate political community: ex-NDs and "PopDems," and, like the Garilao DAR, the Morales DAR first consolidated its own alliances with its political community. Like the Garilao DAR, the Morales DAR adopted as a strategy the pro-reform alliance with a broad spectrum of autonomous rural social movements. Morales decided basically to continue the reforms started by Garilao (see Morales, 1999).

Changes within and outside the DAR, however, would result in differences between the Garilao and Morales administrations in terms of implementation processes and actual redistribution outcomes. First, a substantial portion of the autonomous rural social movement groups refused to critically engage the Estrada-Morales administration on the issue of agrarian reform. The subsequent problems in the relationship between some of these rural social movement groups and the Morales DAR were subject to varying, often competing, interpretations. But whatever the differences between Morales and these rural social movements, their impacts would be quite substantially negative on the process and outcome of land reform, since the pro-reform forces were divided, and so, relatively weakened.[67] Second, the Morales DAR suffered amidst the negative political developments at the presidential level that affected CARP (e.g., President Estrada calling Danding Cojuangco "godfather of land reform" and directly lobbying for some of the land use conversion applications of his friends).[68] By 2000, the political turmoil leading to the ouster of Estrada (on charges of corruption — see Reyes, 2001) had, in one way or another, derailed the course of land reform. Third, these unfavourable political developments in state–society relations aggravated the already difficult and problematic state of the land reform front. Recall that unlike the Garilao DAR, the Morales DAR was confronted with the most politically contentious private landholdings.[69] Fourth, Morales failed to resist the demands of President Estrada that he take on as undersecretary for the Policy Planning and Legal Affairs Office (PPLAO) Danilo Lara, who was a former vice governor of Cavite, and close associate Juanito Remulla, both of whom were well-known anti–land reform officials in Cavite engaged in massive land use conversions for speculative real estate deals.[70] Finally, in contrast to Garilao's, the Morales management style was not "hands-on." This had some adverse impacts on his work within the bureaucracy.

The continuity and change of reformist leadership at the DAR national office during the Morales period also had an effect on the local bureaucracy. There was, to some extent, a demoralization and relative demobilization among the DAR field personnel during the period of increasing likelihood of Estrada (and so Morales) being ousted from power. Many local DAR personnel stopped reporting local accomplishments, trying to "save" them for the anticipated new leadership in the event of the ouster of Estrada. Again, land redistribution during 2000 and 2001 suffered due to transition politics.[71]

As a result of these interlinked negative currents, the Morales DAR had a yearly average redistribution output that was half that of the Garilao DAR, although the percentage shares of highly contentious lands and highly contentious land acquisition and distribution modalities were far higher than his predecessor's.[72] The Estrada presidency, and so the Morales DAR, lasted for only thirty months; it was ousted through a popular mobilization by largely urban-based middle and upper classes, supported by the church and the media, and backed by the military with charges of corruption.[73]

Vice President Gloria Macapagal-Arroyo, daughter of Diosdado Macapagal, who had formerly served as president (1961–1965), took over the presidential seat in January 2001. Macapagal-Arroyo is best known for her neoliberal economics; she sponsored the neoliberal agricultural policy reforms while she was senator, and after assuming the presidency, she vowed to deepen and widen such reforms. Her husband, Miguel Arroyo, hailed from a big landowning family in Negros Occidental. But as Ernesto Garilao correctly observed, the Arroyo Cabinet had the greatest number of pro–land reform personalities (e.g., Dinky Soliman, Ging Deles, Leonardo Montemayor, Karina Constantino-David, and Rigoberto Tiglao, to name a few) compared to previous CARP-era national administrations. These were the same land reform activists who had been extremely vocal critics of the land reform process under the Estrada-Morales tandem. Thus, hopes for a reinvigorated CARP were on the horizon, especially because land reform was one of the issues used against Estrada.

President Macapagal-Arroyo appointed a young member of congress as DAR secretary: Hernani Braganza, nephew of former president Ramos and a former ND activist during his university years (initially paired with the FFF's Leonardo Montemayor at the DA, who was later replaced by banana magnate and anti–land reform elite Luis Lorenzo Jr.[74]). Braganza did not have a background in the peasant struggle and agrarian reform issues. He very quickly broke up most of the pro-reform traditions and infrastructures instilled and installed by Garilao — which had, arguably, been maintained by Morales, at least to some extent. Braganza recruited lawyers with no prior knowledge of land reform or history of interactions with rural social movements to occupy the top DAR positions, due to his uninformed belief that land reform was purely the adjudication of land cases.[75] He refused any intense and sustained interactions with autonomous rural social movement organizations. Instead, he imposed the idea that "partnership" between DAR and rural social movements must be "conflict-free" and its form limited to peaceful dialogues and "paper chasing." He called in the elite police SWAT team to disperse demonstrating peasants in front of the DAR offices. Finally, he was out of his office most of the time.[76]

During the Macapagal-Arroyo presidency, the significant erosion of reformist traditions and institutions within the DAR bureaucracy and its interface mechanisms with peasant groups and NGOs negatively impacted the local DAR bureaucracies. The most important impact would be the absence of any systematic interactive mechanism between the DAR, either at the national or local level, and peasant groups and NGOs. Moreover, internally, the arrogant leadership displayed by Braganza antagonized the rank-and-file employees of the DAR. This would later lead to the mainstream DAR employees' union filing charges of corruption against Braganza (PAGC, 2002). While this would prove to be strategically important to the cause of land reform, especially because it would indeed lead to the ouster of Braganza, its immediate impact was widespread demoralization and demobilization of DAR officials and employees.

In many respects, Braganza was especially in the context of the politically contentious land reform process. Soon most of the autonomous peasant organizations and NGOs called for his ouster (UNORKA, 2001b, 2002; PARRDS, 2002). The DAR employees' association (DAREA) itself formally filed graft and corruption charges against Braganza, and they too called for his ouster. The combined collective actions of UNORKA, PARRDS, and DAREA forced president Macapagal-Arroyo to take Braganza out of the DAR. After more than a year in office, and after causing serious harm to the reformist momentum in the land reform process, he was "ousted" — but given a graceful exit: He was reassigned as press secretary. President Arroyo was unwilling to antagonize the Ramos camp. In the end, Braganza's average land redistribution accomplishment was less than that of the Morales DAR, in terms of both quantity and quality (PARC, 2002a). Unfortunately, during Braganza's period at the DAR, when the peasants were having great problems with him and calling for his ouster, the supposedly pro-land reform cabinet members who were extremely critical of the Estrada-Morales land reform performance were completely silent.

In February 2003, President Arroyo appointed a new DAR secretary: Roberto Pagdanganan, former governor of Bulacan (the northern province adjacent to Metro Manila). He had run and lost the past senatorial race under the president's party. His appointment was made by Arroyo, despite the sustained lobby of peasant groups and NGOs for some names who were highly acceptable to them as DAR secretary (e.g., Gerry Bulatao and Wigberto Tañada). Most, if not all, peasant groups and NGOs called for Pagdanganan's ouster, accusing him of orchestrating the widespread land use conversion and land reform evasions in Bulacan during his time as governor. While he did not make any dramatic changes to the DAR left him by his predecessor, Pagdanganan did restore to some extent the progressive tradition of interacting with autonomous rural social movements, at least during his first few months in office — the most probable motivation for this approach on his part likely being his senatorial ambition. However, months later and closer to the May 2004 national elections, Pagdanganan began to release decisions favouring big landlords in agrarian cases. Moreover, it was at this time that the government was able to decisively recover more than US$ 600 million from the Marcos loot, and by law the money was to be used to finance CARP. The various rural social movement organizations were demanding that at least 70 percent of the money be used to expropriate new private landholdings and only 30 percent dedicated to support services and development projects. The Pagdanganan DAR and president, Macapagal-Arroyo, had a different view: They wanted it 70 percent in favour of development projects. The social movement organizations suspected that this was a scheme in order to use the money for the forthcoming elections and thus protested strongly against it. Confronted by the anti-peasant decisions by Pagdanganan on several agrarian disputes and the fear that the administration was going to misuse the recovered Marcos wealth, peasant organizations, especially those directly affected by the negative decisions, were incensed. Led by UNORKA, a series of mobilizations were organized at the DAR central office. Pagdanganan, like Braganza, called in the SWAT team to violently disperse the protesting peasants. The UNORKA protest, however, escalated; it spread to DAR regional and provincial offices. Worried about the negative impact of this conflict on her election bid, President Macapagal-Arroyo removed Pagdanganan from office (but, like Braganza, he was simply transferred to another department). He was temporarily replaced by DAR insider Cheli Ponce, who was then succeeded by two more secretaries within short intervals, before Secretary Nasser Pangandaman was appointed to the post in mid-2005. Reformism within the executive branch had almost completely disappeared since President Macapagal-Arroyo took power (see Rimban, 2005). Macapagal-Arroyo's administration also ushered in an era of violence against political activists in general, and many of the victims of such violence were agrarian activists — creating a situation marked by what Franco describes as "lawlessness, murder and impunity"; one of the victims of this violence was UNORKA national Secretary-General Eric Cabanit who was assassinated in April 2006 (Franco, 2007; Franco and Borras, 2007).

In many ways, President Macapagal-Arroyo was like her predecessor, Joseph Estrada, when it came to land reform: Both were overconfident that they knew the program, while their actions and their statements betrayed their ignorance about the subject, if not their outright anti-reform bias. Estrada may have declared Danding Cojuangco to be the "godfather of land reform," but it was Macapagal-Arroyo who perpetuated the special land reform deal with Danding Cojuangco. She also made uninformed policy statements, such as,

> [Leasehold] is the way to do land reform without having to look for all that money for land acquisition …. In [Estrada's] time they never put any money in the budget for acquisition. I tried to improve by putting money. But the way our budget works, if you put something over nothing [previous year] that's not much. But in this way we can go very strong in leasehold, at least in the coconut area.[77]

For one, in taking leasehold as a substitute for land redistribution she would be violating the CARP law. Neither did she seem to know that Estrada's land redistribution output was greater than her administration's — and that Estrada's budget for land redistribution was higher than the annual budget of the Ramos and Macapagal-Arroyo administrations.[78]

5.4 PRO-REFORM STATE–SOCIETY ALLIANCES AND INTERACTIONS

While autonomous rural social movements from below and pro-reform state actors from above can each contribute toward the success of redistributive land reform, their combined forces offer more promise. This was elaborated in the theoretical chapter of this study. The aim here is to demonstrate how, why, and to what extent the pro-reform state–society alliance for redistributive land reform has emerged and with what impact on CARP implementation.[79] This provides an improved perspective on the case studies discussed in chapter 3 and chapter 4 and on the national overview of CARP outcomes presented in chapter 2.

The organized and politically coherent pro-reform alliance between state actors within the DAR and autonomous rural social movement groups started to gain more ground only after 1992. Before then, the mainstream DAR leaderships opted to work only with state co-opted peasant organizations and societal groups (although a minority group of DAR reformists led by Gerry Bulatao was already pursuing a pro-reform state–society alliance — but without much political and policy impact). Their politically conservative and technocratic approach treated peasant associations as important actors only insofar as they were administrative adjuncts to the state. The state defined the parameters of the agenda, the forms of action, and the nature of such "partnership." It was an unequal relationship. Ordinary peasants who were engaged in agrarian disputes were forced to follow up their cases at the DAR offices by themselves, or they availed themselves of the services of individual "brokers," who had some connections within the bureaucracy or used the channels provided by traditional, state co-opted peasant organizations, whose leaders, in turn, appealed to DAR offices using personal connections. This dominant conservative approach — the "paper chasing" method alluded to earlier — progressed at the mercy of DAR officials' whims. The character of pre-1992 state–society interactions just described largely explains the low level of land redistribution accomplishment during that period. This approach was relegated to the periphery only after 1992, through a convergence of factors and actors. The emergence of a relatively coherent pro-reform state–society alliance for land reform largely accounts for the significant level of land redistribution accomplishment in the 1990s, as shown in chapter 2 and in chapter 4.

The interactions between autonomous rural social movement organizations and state reformists for land reform occurred in a variety of ways and used a number of different approaches, resulting in a variety of outcomes. This is illustrated by the three main types of pro-reform state–society interface: collective action with specific demands, reformist initiatives "from below," and reformist initiatives "from above."

Collective action with specific demands

The most common form of pro-reform state–society interface has been the collective actions launched by peasant organizations and their urban-based allies addressed to the state. These collective actions have taken a variety of forms: from friendly to confrontational dialogues and pickets, from small to large street demonstrations, pitching camp in front of DAR offices to maintain political pressure on DAR officials, and small but dramatic actions designed to catch media attention, such as bringing live turtles to the DAR offices to protest the tortoise-like pace of the actions of DAR officials on land disputes. The padlocking of the gates of DAR offices to symbolize the ineptitude of the offices in resolving their cases was yet another form of collective action. These forms of action have been well calculated by peasant groups and their allies to apply maximum pressure on the DAR to act on their cases and to gain attention for their issue through the media, both nationally and internationally. In a pro-reform, symbiotic state–society relationship, such actions are meant to weaken the anti-reform state actors and to pressure them to give in to the demands of the autonomous rural social movement groups. However, they are so targeted as not to politically weaken the state reformists vis-à-vis the anti-reform forces within and outside the state. (Where there are no state reformists, the rural social movements' actions are calculated to oust anti-reform officials, as in the cases of Hernani Braganza and Roberto Pagdanganan.) In short, these interactions are better seen as inherently conflict ridden and as recursive political bargaining processes between pro-reform state and societal actors.

Moreover, and on most occasions, the forms and conduct of these collective actions were designed so that they would be picked up by the media. For example, depending on the specific aim of the action, a day-long mobilization of 5,000 peasants in front of a regional DAR office may have less impact on the media than five peasants staging a hunger strike in front of DAR headquarters in Manila. In real life, the forms of action and their duration were calculated largely based on the available logistics of the peasants and their allies in the context of the aims of the mobilization. Transporting peasants to Manila is quite expensive. In the 1990s, hiring a *"jeepney"* that could accommodate twenty people from the provinces of Central Luzon and Southern Tagalog would have cost some PhP 2,500 (US$ 50) round-trip. Thus, to organize a 2,000-strong peasant mobilization in Manila from Central Luzon and Southern Tagalog would cost at least PhP 250,000 (US$ 5,000) for a single day, not including food and other expenses. A budget of a million pesos would be insufficient to mobilize 10,000 peasants to Manila for one day. And only a minuscule amount of this could be raised from among the peasants. So it can be seen that these kinds of mobilizations drain NGO finances quite rapidly. This issue has also become a permanent source of conflict between NGOs and funding agencies — that is, the question of diverting funds from their original and official purposes. Hence, over time, the evolution of forms of collective action and approaches to organizing work has been greatly influenced by logistical considerations. This can be seen from a historical perspective:

During the Marcos dictatorship, the main agenda among ND peasant mobilizations was to expose and oppose the bankruptcy of agrarian and agricultural policies and protest against the massive human rights violations in the countryside. This type of agenda and the forms of collective action that came with it were well within the left wing tradition of political agitation-propaganda ("agit-prop") mobilizations aimed at politically isolating the ruling classes and the elite faction that held state power. The demands therefore were framed within "motherhood" slogans like "genuine land reform!," "dismantle feudalism!," or "down with the US-Marcos dictatorship!" Most of these mobilizations were carried out in urban centres, such as Manila, Cebu, or Davao, for maximum media attention. These mobilizations were highly centralized in terms of coordination, agenda, and sites of actions. To reduce the costs of peasant mobilizations, the urban-based organizers usually recruited poor urban communities — students and workers from Manila (or other cities) — to join the peasant demonstrations in order to enlarge the size without too much additional expense. These mobilizations were funded not by the peasants or their local associations, but by their allies: either the national peasant federations they belonged to (such as the KMP), their NGO allies (such as the PEACE Foundation), or political movements (such as the ND movement). NGOs abroad supplied most of their funds, some of which were intended for these types of peasant actions, but most of which were not. Funds were in fact intended, or at least officially requested for and reported as, development projects, but they were re-channelled to these agit-prop actions. During the Marcos era, the NDs had political and organizational hegemony over rural social movements and important mass mobilizations. The KMP and its allies could raise millions of pesos and mobilize 10,000 peasants combined with contingents of the urban poor, workers, and students. The NDs enjoyed massive external funding from abroad during the Marcos era. Most foreign donors explicitly and implicitly tolerated the use of their funds for mass mobilizations in the context of the intense political campaign to oust the Marcos dictatorship.

When Marcos was ousted, mass mobilizations continued, but in a slightly different form. The period 1986–1989 witnessed the prioritization of agendas that were specifically and concretely related to peasant issues, especially during the debates over the framing of the Constitution (the KMP's Tadeo was a member of the forty-eight-person Constitutional Commission) and in the subsequent policymaking process for CARP (1987–1988). Moreover, the ND peasant movement introduced the combination of selective "land invasion/occupation" of landholdings that were politically controversial and used these politically controversial cases to challenge, embarrass, and politically isolate the government over the weaknesses of its land reform program. Such mobilizations were absolutely necessary and relatively effective. In fact, this type of mobilization was adopted by other non-ND social movement groups, such as the social-democrats. The CPAR mobilizations in 1987–1989 were similar in nature. The adoption of a constitutional provision on land reform and the passage of the CARP law to some degree reflected the extent and intensity of peasant mass mobilizations during this period.

In the latter 1980s, however, internal and external factors started to work against the continued practice of agit-prop mobilizations. Internally, the rural bases of the ND movement, including those in Central Luzon and Southern Tagalog (the traditional sources of peasant political mobilizations in Manila), were adversely affected by the "total war" policy launched by the Aquino administration against the communist insurgents. Most of the victims of the Aquino war were civilian peasants who were members of or sympathetic to the KMP and other ND organizations. It became increasingly difficult to launch big peasant-based mobilizations. Externally, and for various reasons, including the collapse of the Marcos dictatorship, many foreign donor organizations were no longer tolerant of spending large amounts of money on agit-prop campaigns. They became critical of the purely political projects of the ND organizations. Soon, they began to diversify their partners to include non-ND groups, a move that meant a corresponding decrease in the ND share of funding assistance, and a relative increase in the political capacity of non-ND rural social movement organizations and networks.

It was during this period that the NPS-CPP was tasked with devising ways to recover lost mass base and reinvigorate political mass mobilizations by the peasantry. By using some new approaches, and despite the internal and external constraints, politically and logistically, the ND peasant mass mobilizations again gathered momentum, but with a different character and form. However, few of these mobilizations focused on the land reform issue, since the DAR leaderships during this period were unwilling to engage with the autonomous organized peasantry and the NGO community. The nature and character of peasant-based mass mobilizations was altered to a significant degree after the ND splits in 1993, which coincided with the rise of the state reformists within the DAR. The subsequent reformist mobilizations continued to uphold the militant and confrontational stance of the ND political tradition, but the agenda, scale, target, and form were substantially revised.

After 1993, peasant-based collective actions for land reform launched by the ex-NDs (e.g., DKMP, then UNORKA, were marked by a number of changes: The main objective of the mobilizations was redefined from the conventional ND framework of purely agit-prop, "expose and oppose," to "maximization" of opportunities available within CARP toward the successful redistribution of as many landholdings as possible to landless and land-poor peasants. Concretely, the shift was from "taking up land disputes to demonstrate that CARP cannot redistribute land" to "taking up land disputes to actually achieve redistributive reform." This also meant simultaneous actions at the national level (or in urban/media centres) and at the local, estate-level, unlike the purely urban-located, media-directed orientation of the agit-prop campaigns. (This naturally influenced the later swing toward the polycentric type of a peasant movement among reformist rural social movement groups.) But these reformist agendas were largely confined to within the specific landholdings in which the mobilizing peasant organizations and their allies had actual organizing work or members. The main targets of these mobilizations were the various DAR offices, from local (municipal) all the way up to the national DAR headquarters.

The scale of peasant mobilizations in urban centres was greatly reduced compared to the 1980s in terms of the number of "warm bodies." During the 1990s, it was rare to witness a peasant mobilization in Manila that exceeded 1,000 peasant participants. There are a number of reasons for this change. For one, the high cost of mobilization became unaffordable to most political movements and NGOs, whose external funding was generally reduced toward the end of the 1990s. In addition, the rules for fund use and management became stricter against re-channelling to uses other than those specified in the contracts (and project contracts seldom had a budget for political mobilizations). In some cases, this actually resulted in a positive development: Mobilizations were increasingly funded by the peasants themselves. But peasants were willing and able to finance part of their collective actions' logistical requirements only if the agenda centred on, or included, their particular land claims. Many of the land disputes were from geographically remote places from where the transportation cost to Manila or other regional urban centres was extremely expensive. For example, to transport a jeep-load of twenty peasant land claimants from Bondoc Peninsula, Quezon, cost more than PhP 10,000 (US$ 200) not including food expenses. This meant bringing in only the key leaders of peasant organizations that had specific land claims.[80] Finally, partly due to the changes in the nature of peasant claim-making, some of the autonomous peasant organizations that emerged after the late 1990s naturally developed the polycentric political and organizational character mentioned above: local groups were responsible for the actions demanded at the local level, such as forcible occupation of an estate and mobilizations before the local and intermediate (municipal-provincial-regional) DAR offices. But the need to increase the power and extend the reach of political actions to the national (and even international) level, required horizontal and vertical linkages with other autonomous peasant groups and their allies. These types of peasant associations and mobilizations signified a qualitative departure from peasant organizations like the KMP, which remained fixated on an urban-located, nationally and internationally oriented, media-directed political agit-prop orientation requiring tightly centralized structures of organization, leadership, and coordination. Perhaps the UNORKA experience is the best example of the polycentric type of movement emerging in the Philippines.

The reduced capacity of peasant organizations and their allies to finance large-scale peasant-based mobilizations in urban centres, especially Manila, forced activists to develop what are called "small but dramatic" peasant actions, primarily to catch media attention. Examples of these are the aforementioned PAKISAMA and AR Now!'s bringing live turtles to the DAR central office to demonstrate how slowly the DAR was acting on their land cases,[81] the Task Force Mapalad's chaining and padlocking themselves to bulletin board posts within the DAR headquarters, ALDA-UFEARBAI's paralysing the DAR regional office in Davao by dumping truckloads of bananas to block the main gates, and UNORKA's forcible occupation of the office of the DAR secretary for three days and three nights. Peasants pitching camp in front of DAR offices for weeks, even months, was another technique in the repertoire of collective actions at the national level. Peasant organizations, or rather, their NGO allies, thus increasingly invested in media work to increase the impact of their collective actions. However, the media is a private entity wherein elite influence is well entrenched; it is therefore at best a vacillating ally of the peasants in their struggle for land reform. (This is, for example, the situation confronting UFEARBAI in Davao.) Its corps of reporters is not immune to ideological biases that spill over to the slant they take in their newspaper reports.

This evolving repertoire of peasant collective actions beyond their localities differently impacted the various DAR officials, employees, and leaderships. The most tolerant of all DAR leaderships to these kinds of actions was the Garilao administration, although it was, internally, deeply angered by some of the actions, specifically the *tambak saging* (banana dumping) by farm workers in Davao and the padlocking of DAR offices. In striking contrast to the Garilao DAR were the Braganza and Pagdanganan DARs, which brought in heavily armed SWAT teams to disperse peasant actions.

But more generally, the DAR was able to reorient itself to the evolving patterns of peasant-based collective actions. Even before a peasant delegation arrived, research and preparation was already being done at the national and regional DAR, studying the particular cases pursued by the peasant delegation, bringing the key local DAR officials to the central and regional offices for briefings, coordinating with other government agencies when necessary, and, at times, preparing formal decisions on cases even before the peasant action occurred. In many cases, "backdoor" clarification between DAR officials and NGO supporters of the peasants was carried out on the issues. In the actual interface between peasants and DAR officials, the former usually took a confrontational stance: banging tables and shouting at the officials. For the peasants, these were rare opportunities to speak aloud and air their pent-up frustration and feelings of social exclusion, oppression, and suffering. To some DAR officials, though, these actions seemed unnecessary and disrespectful. When DAR officials said they would decide on a case within three days, the peasants would ask them to put it in writing and affix their signatures to their promises. Then the peasants would inform the DAR officials that they would await the decision in a makeshift camp in front of the office. This put pressure on the DAR officials to deliver and brought the peasants nearer to their objective of obtaining favourable decisions. Flooded with such encounters, the Garilao DAR in fact organized a separate office called "Special Concerns Staff" (SCS) that handled the administrative requirements of this type of interface. The DAR also devised a system to track down cases put forward by autonomous peasant groups and NGOs. It coined the term "flash-point case" to pertain to specific land cases that had the potential for violence to erupt between the competing actors; all concerned offices within the DAR bureaucracy, from local to national, were ordered to prioritize resolution of such cases.

This type of collective action ("specific case" mobilizations) by peasant organizations and their allies had very concrete advantages. For one, it forced interaction with DAR officials, who preferred avoiding such face-to-face meetings, and so brought concrete legal cases to the attention of officials who had the power, or at least the obligation, to resolve them. Mobilizations around particular cases provided systematic tracking of the course that the case had taken and sustained the pressure on DAR officials to find a resolution. Peasants and peasant leaders who were directly affected by a particular case were usually represented in these mobilizations, if they did not take the actual lead role. For example, it was impressive to see that UNORKA maintained a complete tracking, in computerized and written forms, of the progress (or not) of each case of the 519 land disputes its member organizations had filed before the government for resolution, affecting some 200,000 hectares and involving 90,000 peasant households, or about a half million people. Each case had its own systematically monitored history. The case tracking system included the name and location of the landholding, land area, crops, tenancy relations, profiles of claimants involved, type of land acquisition and distribution, counter-actions of the landlord, types of human rights violations, the actual status of the case, what needed to be done politically, legally, and organizationally, the set of demands addressed to the DAR, and the status of the latest confrontation with the DAR (UNORKA, 2001a). Hence, the interface between peasant groups and state officials revolved around concrete and specific but land case-oriented issues. The constant tracking of and political pressure applied with regard to these specific land cases pushed redistributive land reform, as demonstrated in chapter 4, nearer to reality. The proliferation of such actions largely accounted for the relative rise in the quantity of successfully resolved land cases, albeit limited in scale as shown in chapters 2, 3, and 4. This includes the case of the sugar cane sector-dominated Negros Occidental province and the subsequent mobilizations by UNORKA and the Task Force Mapalad (TFM) group.

However, from a broader and longer perspective, there are weaknesses in this kind of peasant collective action, which partly explains the character and extent of CARP's land redistribution outcomes over time. The biggest weakness is perhaps that such actions tend to focus only on the particular cases in which the said peasant organizations and their allies have direct involvement (organizing, mobilizing, and providing legal assistance). While it is perfectly understandable that local peasant groups directly affected by specific disputes focus on the resolution of their own cases, there is a great danger that national peasant organizations will lose sight of the strategic and broad perspective: the issue of land redistribution affecting the landless and land-poor peasants more generally.

This is worrisome because the ranks of autonomous peasant organizations can actually and organizationally represent only a fraction of the entire landless and land-poor peasants in the country. This also holds true for NGOs that tend to work solely on the agrarian disputes in their direct area of operations. If these organizations fail to address peasant issues outside the circle of their partner peasant groups — for example, through advocating concrete reforms in policies and implementation mechanisms, they may end up victorious in some cases, but against a larger society-wide backdrop of unresolved land questions. Unfortunately, the ranks of NGOs engaged in systematic and rigorous policy advocacy on land reform have been thin and weak, geographically uneven, and sometimes politically inconsistent and incoherent. Moreover, the specific, estate-by-estate approach has necessarily restricted (perhaps most evidently in the Davao plantation belt and the Negros Occidental sugar cane sector), on many occasions, the pro-reform societal forces within the limited confines of the agenda set by the state. For example, save for intermittent and superficial questions raised about the "missing" land redistribution scope in CARP, no peasant organization or NGO has actually systematically pursued the issue of "missing landholdings," the scale of which is enormous, as demonstrated in chapter 3. Furthermore, most of the efforts of the autonomous peasant organizations and their allies in the struggle for land reform have focused on private landholdings, effectively endorsing the mistaken notion that there is no real redistributive land reform on public lands, either lands under the DAR or under the DENR. Thus, it is rare to find organized, systematic, and sustained claim-making initiatives by rural social movements in and around these types of land, except perhaps the initiatives by the PEACE network of NGOs and peasant organizations.

In addition, while it is encouraging to see the autonomous rural social movement organizations sustain their attention on the DAR bureaucracy, from a broader perspective these actions have actually been overly DAR-centred. Recall that at least twenty different state agencies, large and small, are directly or indirectly involved in land reform. These are related to land titles (the Registry of Deeds, ROD), approval of land use conversion (the DA, local government units, the National Housing Regulatory Board, and the National Irrigation Authority), land valuation or amortization payments (the LBP), surveying (the DENR), legal appeals (the Office of the President, the Supreme Court, and the DAR Adjudication Board), and so on. Nonetheless, peasant actions have tended to be DAR centred: Legal cases at the Supreme Court provoke demonstrations at the DAR; delays in surveys provoke protests at the DAR; delays in land valuation processes and subsequent delays in land redistribution provoke rallies at the DAR; and so on. While the DAR is the lead agency in CARP implementation and so it is justifiable for DAR to receive the brunt of peasant collective action, such an approach, on most occasions, may not be the most efficient way of using the limited (logistical and political) resources of peasant groups and their allies. At times, such mistargeted actions have unnecessarily drained pro-reform allies within the DAR of their energy and tolerance for mobilizations from below. It has also enabled other state agencies, and the anti-reform forces therein, to go about their business free from the pressure of intense rural social movement claim-making initiatives. And it is hardly the case that a cluster of state reformists will emerge in any state agency on their own, without being provoked by sustained engagement with autonomous societal actors. Latent allies and adversaries of redistributive land reform remain latent unless directly provoked by mass mobilizations "from below" — at least this has largely been the experience with most Philippine local state agencies, especially the DAR.

In short, the repertoire of peasant collective actions beyond their localities has jumped from one extreme to another: from the purely agit-prop, "expose and oppose" type of action spearheaded by the ND rural social movement in the 1980s (and the ND continues to promote this approach up to the time of this writing) to the specific estate-by-estate case resolution type. This historical development of peasant movements and their patterns of mass mobilizations has largely accounted for the types of CARP outcomes over time. However, the weaknesses of these types of collective actions have been spotted by some groups both within the ranks of the rural social movements and by state reformists within the DAR. Certain adjustments have been introduced in response, although still with relatively limited impact. These adjustments, discussed below, have aimed to compensate for the gaps in the approach discussed above.

Reformist initiatives "from below"

This second type of pro-reform state–society interface is an extension of the first type, but is an attempt to systematize the scope and extend its impact to a broader terrain. While it pertains to initiatives originally conceived and proposed by rural social movement organizations, in this type of interaction, state reformists have been drawn in. While this second type involves local and national peasant organizations, the NGOs take a more active role in the actual agenda setting, policy analysis, and actions, as compared to the first type, which comprises mainly peasant-based actions. In this second type, resolution of specific cases remains a major agenda item, but due attention is given to three other issues: improving and systematizing implementation mechanisms to speed up and broaden the scope of land redistribution, pushing for policy reforms, and, to some extent, actually mapping possible additional target landholdings. Thus, this second type of approach is more programmatic than the first, although its form is "less dramatic" and so the national media and other analysts do not notice or give much value to it; others make the crude conclusion that such state–society interface means co-optation and uncritical collaboration.

In March 1997, 190 DAR officials and NGO peasant social group community organizers and leaders participated in the second national DAR-NGO-peasant organization workshop (the first was in 1996) on how to "fast-track" CARP implementation. The workshop was convened by "National Task Force 24," an initiative of the PEACE Foundation to hasten CARP implementation in twenty-four provinces identified as areas where there were significant and highly contested large landholdings. The political initiative also aspired to "defend CARPed lands threatened by land use conversions and other anti-agrarian reform moves." The conference vowed to "promote productivity and income improvement in tenancy-free communities" and to push for a positive policy environment for a more just and meaningful agrarian reform and rural development."[82] This workshop, which drew in the DAR, is a good example of the second type of state–society interface. It is necessary to elaborate:

In 1994, the PEACE Foundation and its network of local, autonomous peasant organizations and NGOs initiated a dialogue with the DAR regarding specific landholdings scheduled for expropriation in the twenty-four provinces, where its network had direct operations. Instead of dealing separately and on individual basis to resolve each case, PEACE proposed that a more systematic joint PEACE-DAR team be formed to resolve the cases and work out operational mechanisms for implementation. The workshop formed a working committee called "Task Force 24," whose main objective was to fast-track land acquisition and distribution in the said provinces.

Thereafter, TF-24 focused on the twenty-four provinces where the positive interaction between state reformists within the DAR and peasants organizations and NGOs were most needed, given the potentially and actually strong landlord resistance to reform. This committee facilitated collective efforts among the state and societal pro-reform forces to identify major landholdings or ongoing local land disputes, and joint strategizing on how to defeat the landlords' resistance in order to expedite expropriation and distribution of the land. Distinct roles for each of the involved parties were agreed upon mutually. The NGOs and peasant organizations' main responsibilities were organizing the potential peasant beneficiaries, especially on the contentious issue of beneficiary inclusion-exclusion; carrying out mass mobilizations locally, regionally, and nationally and even mobilizing support internationally; and identifying the local DAR officials they wanted removed from office or a particular position. Meanwhile, the DAR's responsibilities were preparing legal documents and drafting legal decisions that were then brought back to the NGOs and peasant organizations for feedback before finalization; coordinating with other state agencies; checking and preventing possible violence from landlords; and removing from office or position local DAR officials about whom the NGOs and peasant organizations had filed complaints. These joint plans usually had set deadlines.

The dynamic and oftentimes conflict-ridden interaction between local DAR officials and local NGOs and peasant organizations was mediated by national-level DAR officials and NGOs. Many pro-reform societal organizations found that in this type of arrangement even those local DAR officials who had a strong tendency to be "fence-sitters," rent-seekers, or outright opponents to land reform were partly neutralized or even converted to reformism, since they knew that the top DAR leadership valued the joint state–society effort. As one veteran activist said, "When the local officials know that your organization has connections with their higher officials, they respect you and pay attention to your demands. But when they know that you have no contacts at the top, most won't even give you the minimum attention, let alone respect."[83]

The joint initiative proved relatively effective in hastening the process of land reform implementation. Later, the coverage of this joint committee expanded to thirty-two provinces (and the committee was renamed Task Force 32) and a major national rural social movement coalition, PARRDS, joined. Still later, the number of NGO and peasant organization participants expanded to include the social-democratic network AR Now! The Task Force's area of operation also expanded, to forty provinces. The campaign was renamed "Project 40 Now!" It became the main mechanism under the Garilao DAR through which peasant groups and NGOs interfaced with the reformist officials of the DAR in a systematic and programmatic way (although the first type of pro-reform state–society interface discussed above continued in parallel). This interface mechanism was also replicated at the lower levels of the provinces, where it became known as ProCARRD (Provincial Consultation/Campaign for Agrarian Reform and Rural Development) and at the municipal level (MuCARRD or Municipal Consultation/Campaign for Agrarian Reform and Rural Development).[84]

The regions that witnessed widespread and sustained state–society interface around specific land redistribution–focused initiatives and within the tradition of TF-24, TF-32, and Project 40 Now! were regions 3, 4, 6, 7, 8, 10, and 11. Other regions had experienced this type of state–society interaction, but to a far lesser extent and with less frequency than the regions cited here. But again, these pro-reform state–society interactions were highly uneven and varied between and within these regions.

While Task Force 24 and, later, Project 40 Now!, focused on land redistribution, another initiative was ongoing: TriPARRD, the Tripartite

Partnership for Agrarian Reform and Rural Development. TriPARRD was a generously funded project relying on the tripartite partnership between government, NGOs, and peasant organizations. It focused on "softer" landholdings and on making these farms productive through development projects. It started early in the Garilao administration and was conceptualized and implemented by the DAR, PhilDHRRA, and PAKISAMA (see Liamzon, 1996). TriPARRD was virtually stopped, however, toward the end of the Garilao administration, due to its less than successful outcomes. TriPARRD had been carried out in a few pilot municipalities in a few regions, notably, regions 5, 6, and 10.

Project 40 Now! was not maintained during this period, due to divisions within the rural social movement groups with regard to terms of engagement with the Morales DAR. During the Morales period, the relatively broad and systematic interface mechanism was "Task Force Fast-Track," which involved most of the ex-ND and PopDem groups in pushing for land redistribution nationwide. Other NGOs and peasant organizations, however, opted to boycott this initiative. Despite the boycott, the short-lived TF Fast-Track carried out relatively comprehensive work, especially in terms of locating "operational bottlenecks" in the land acquisition and redistribution process. It made sensible recommendations on how to improve the operational mechanisms for quick and decisive expropriation actions. Unfortunately, however, TF Fast-Track's recommendations, which were finalized in December 2000, would not be transformed into actual practice, since Morales would be ousted from office the following month.[85]

The formal and systematic state–society interface tradition of Project 40 Now! and even TF Fast-Track were completely dismantled during the Braganza DAR and after. Instead, Secretary Braganza insisted that what the DAR needed were lawyers to resolve pending cases and the promotion of voluntary land transfers (VLT) to avoid more legal cases. In general, President Macapagal-Arroyo supported Braganza in his thoughts about how to move ahead with CARP, although the sustained peasant protest against him eventually forced the president to remove him from his position in the DAR. Braganza's successor, Roberto Pagdanganan, delivered similar performance and met a similar fate: being ousted from office by the force of peasant protest and mobilization.

In short, the reformist initiatives "from below" just described were an attempt to complement the more peasant-led and less programmatic collective actions, by incorporating policy-oriented and operational issues in the interface with the DAR. Value-added gains were made in this complementary effort.

However, many of the gaps left by the peasant-led collective actions were not fully covered by the complementary initiative operated mainly by NGOs. For example, while the agenda included issues like systematic operational mechanisms and other policy reforms, the bulk of efforts exerted remained limited to the pending cases put forward by autonomous peasant organizations and NGOs. The initiative failed to broaden its scope to cover, for instance, agendas that the state refused to table, such as a systematic accounting of the "missing lands" from the CARP scope. This interface mechanism also failed to realize the importance of public lands under the DAR and DENR jurisdictions. Moreover, the same interface mechanism has also at times resulted in a tendency among some NGO leaders to self-appoint themselves as "negotiators" or "brokers" between the government and local peasant associations, which is not helpful in the development of the organizational autonomy and capacity of peasant groups. Overall, however, like the first approach of peasant-led collective actions, the second type, with both its strengths and its weaknesses, contributed to shaping the nature, character, and extent of CARP land redistribution outcomes over time. The third and last type of interface mechanism between pro-reform state and societal forces complements the first two, but, in practice, will prove unable to substantially fill the still-existing gaps.

Reformist initiatives "from above"

State actors do not simply react to pressures from societal actors. State reformists, on their own, conceive and instigate initiatives that later pull in societal actors. The first major and mainstay initiative of the DAR that slowly drew in the active participation of NGOs and peasant organizations was the Agrarian Reform Community (ARC) development program launched in 1993. An ARC was defined as a *barangay* or a cluster of contiguous *barangays* where a critical mass of farmers and farm workers were awaiting the full implementation of agrarian reform. "These farmers and farm workers will anchor the integrated development of the areas" (DAR-BARBD, 2000: 18). By 2000, the DAR was able to launch some 1,000 ARCs nationwide, involving about a million hectares of (supposedly) "land reformed" landholdings.

Earlier, most NGOs and peasant organizations had been critical of and inactive in the ARC development program, but over time they slowly began to be drawn into it. This interface between pro-reform forces within the state and in society has been relatively different from the land dispute–centred political dynamics of land reform. In an ARC project, the conflict is primarily about the control over the nature, pace, extent, and direction of development projects, such as training and education programs for micro-credit and "social preparation" programs for infrastructure projects like road construction. In an ARC development project, the main challenge for state and non-state reform actors revolves around the issue of making the reform sector socioeconomically productive and viable, an undertaking that requires capacity and skills different from those at the land reform stage.

The ARC strategy, which was the "brainchild" of Garilao, contributed to some extent to the cause of agrarian reform in the country. This is seen in at least three ways: First, the ARC concept was partly responsible for reinvigorating the interest of foreign donors in CARP. Within four years, through the ARC projects, the Garilao DAR had mobilized close to a billion dollars in foreign development assistance.[86] Second, the ARC concept partly shielded CARP from the attacks of the anti-land reform forces that contended that lands awarded to peasants became unproductive. Whatever the limitations and drawbacks of the ARC concept, strategy, and actual implementation, the Garilao DAR was able to produce empirical evidence that agrarian reform actually works, especially when systematic support services are delivered to the reform sector. The Garilao DAR used the ARC program in its perennial arguments with members of congress during annual budget deliberations. In addition, with the serious and renewed interest of the foreign donor community, other anti-CARP state actors hesitated to attack the program, careful not to antagonize the international donors. Finally, overall the ARC strategy can be seen as a "training ground" for pro-reform forces within the state and in society for capacity-building and skills development related to rural development (see Lourie, 2001). For these reasons, subsequent administrations at the DAR decided to continue the ARC strategy and programs.

Nevertheless, in general, autonomous rural social movement groups have remained critical of the ARC concept, strategy, and outcomes. Among the issues they raise is the exclusionary character of the ARC strategy, since only a fraction of land reform beneficiaries are actually covered by the program. Many have realized, however, that defaulting on post-land reform development undertakings may only give ammunition to those looking for ways to edge land reform off of the state policy agenda. Hence, despite actual differences of opinion on rural development strategies, increasingly, societal actors have begun interfacing with the DAR officials in ARC developments.

Eventually, although uneven, integration of autonomous rural social movement groups in the ARC program has resulted in at least two unexpected outcomes: On the one hand, and on a positive note, NGOs have discovered that many of the communities that were declared as ARCs in fact have pending land redistribution-related issues. Thus, while these communities were on record as having no pending issues about land tenure, NGO activists have discovered otherwise. Some of these NGOs have therefore ended up not only doing development projects but also assisting peasants to consummate their land reform struggles. Such situations cut across ARC development levels, from those that are top rated to those with lacklustre performance in development. The three sub-national comparative studies done by Franco and her colleagues (namely, the "35 weakest ARC organizations," 1999c; "top ARCs," 1998a; and "ARC and rural democratization," 2000)[87] are revealing: Most formally declared ARCs in fact have substantial unresolved land disputes, so that many of those who benefit from the state development support are not the peasant beneficiaries but the local elite, and many of the existing ARCs do not necessarily reflect the interests of the previously landless and land-poor segments of the communities.

On the other hand, many NGOs were attracted to the ARC programs primarily because these projects offered generous funds. One of the most significant effects of many NGOs jumping onto the ARC bandwagon was, arguably, a relative drain of activist NGOs and individuals working on the land redistribution struggle. The latter has become increasingly unattractive to local and foreign NGOs, because it is politically contentious, victorious outcomes are uncertain and unpredictable, and it involves project components that are not easily funded (e.g., political mobilizations and organizing expenses). By the late 1990s, few international NGOs and development agencies were providing substantial support for land redistribution campaigns. Rather, "good governance, local governance" and micro-finance within and outside ARCs became favourites, despite the largely unresolved land question in the country. The DAR, many NGOs (national and international), and bilateral and multilateral agencies justify these choices, contending that after "widespread" land transfers, the focus of development work now must be on farm development. While in theory such contentions do not negate the need to continue working on land redistribution, actual funding and projects have largely ceased flowing to the politically contentious land redistribution component of CARP. Interestingly, and unfortunately, this kind of argument is the same as that used by anti–land reform elites within and outside government. The agriculture secretary under the Macapagal-Arroyo administration, the banana magnate Luis Lorenzo Jr. for example, declared,

> Additional land acquisition under the land reform program should be put on hold until the original owners have been properly and fairly paid, and until the land reform beneficiaries have been provided with all the tools (including training and market access). This is to ensure the farmers can properly nurture the land to produce goods that will help them secure a better life.[88]

5.5 CONFRONTATION WITH ANTI-REFORM COALITIONS

While the existence of pro-reform state–society alliances increases the possibility of successful implementation of land reform policy, such alliances do not guarantee automatic positive outcomes. This is because most anti-reform manoeuvres are also marked by a coalition between state and societal actors. The earlier theoretical discussion in this study explained this point in detail. This section demonstrates how and why confrontation with anti-reform coalitions does not always result in positive outcomes. The actual balance of power between the contending sets of actors largely determines the outcomes of struggles, whether the contestations relate to a specific case or are policy-related. A few empirical examples, both case-related and policy-related, are discussed below.

Case-related examples

A good example of a pro-reform state–society coalition that pushed for the expropriation of a specific landholding but was overpowered by an anti-reform alliance was the NDC land in Langkaan, Dasmariñas, Cavite, in 1990. The case did not even involve a private landlord; rather, the 230 hectares of farmland was owned by the governmental NDC. Elites within the Aquino Cabinet wanted the land converted to industrial-commercial uses tied in with a Japanese company, but it was officially up for redistribution under CARP. DAR Secretary Abad sided with the Langkaan peasants, and was backed by a broad national coalition of peasant organizations, the Peasants' Forum (CPAR + FFF + Sanduguan). The "pro–private capital accumulation" elite within the Aquino Cabinet was led by Jose Concepcion and supported by the provincial elite led by Cavite Governor Juanito Remulla and the Japanese giant company Marubeni. Together, they actively blocked the redistribution of the NDC land. Pro-reform forces lost the case in the sense that this conflict was largely used by anti-reform activists within the Congress to refuse to confirm Abad's appointment as DAR secretary. Abad resigned in April, after four months in office; the peasants failed to secure ownership and control of the land.

Similarly, toward the late 1990s, the case of Mapalad involving the landholding of the politically well-connected Quisumbing family in Bukidnon (Region 10, Mindanao) witnessed a top-level pro-reform state–society coalition push for the redistribution of the land. It was among the agrarian reform disputes in CARP's history that received the widest media coverage nationally and internationally, especially because of the dramatic hunger strike launched by the protesting peasants. But the Quisumbings proved too influential, and the regional elite and government bureaucrats stood solidly behind the landlord. The pro-reform forces eventually lost the case (see Gatmaytan, 2000; Villarin, 1999; Quitoriano, 2000).

Other cases that suffered similar fates were some of those described in chapter 3. However, there are also cases where successful expropriation was carried out, despite a strong anti-reform coalition, as shown by the cases in chapter 4. An example in this latter category was the Reyes estate case in Catulin, Buenavista, Quezon. The 174-hectare coconut farm was owned by the largest landlord in Bondoc Peninsula, Quezon (Domingo Reyes). The DAR placed it under compulsory acquisition. The landlord opposed the expropriation and expelled the peasants from the farm. A series of attempts to put the peasants in possession of the land failed due to the escalating and increasingly violent opposition of the landlord. The landlord was extremely powerful and well connected nationally and controlled the local police. The Morales DAR, in coordination with NGOs, peasant organizations, and the national media, organized a national-level inter-agency team (including the DENR, the Department of Justice, the national police, the Armed Forces of the Philippines, and the Office of the President). It brought in a company-sized military and police contingent, which rolled through the town in military tanks, helicopters, and armed personnel carriers, forcibly putting the land in the peasants' actual possession. This was a widely publicized triumph for land reform against a powerful landlord (Franco, forthcoming).

Policy-related examples

The pro-reform state–society coalitions, despite their joint mobilizations, have lost a number of policy-related cases. One example was the eventual exclusion of fishponds from CARP coverage through a congressional initiative toward the mid-1990s. The pro-reform coalition (MORE-AR, Movement to Oppose More Exemptions from Agrarian Reform) mounted a series of mobilizations to block the initiative to exclude farms that are less dependent on land, such as fishponds, salt beds, and poultry farms. Yet, despite sustained mobilizations, the anti-reform coalition proved too strong. The law further diluting CARP was passed and enacted — although, partly in response to the opposition to it, some labour-oriented reforms were included such as mandatory production and profit sharing schemes on such farms.

The pro-reform coalition also lost in courts a number of important legal cases that may have policy-related implications for CARP, such as the Mapalad case regarding the power of local government units to reclassify land use (see, e.g., Gatmaytan, 2000). Moreover, the perennial problem of CARP budget slashing by Congress constitutes an important defeat for pro-reform forces.

However, there are also cases where the pro-reform alliance was able to secure important victories, such as the CARP extension law in early 1998 and the campaign against the World Bank's market-led agrarian reform. These two cases deserve further elaboration.

The original CARP law (RA 6657) explicitly directed the government to finish the land redistribution component of CARP within ten years, or by June 1998. Toward the end of 1997, there was much legal and political uncertainty: CARP was only halfway through its land redistribution implementation, but the legal timetable was to expire the following year. Anti-reform members of Congress were already preparing to use the expiration date to move toward the decisive demise of the CARP law. This was the opportunity that most landlords had been awaiting to have their landholdings excluded from expropriation due to the legal technicality of CARP's expired timetable. A new law, which would have to be approved by the landlord-dominated Congress, was required if CARP's legal existence was to be extended and fresh funds were to be allocated, because the original PhP 50 billion budget for 1988–1998 was already fully spent. The Garilao DAR and the broad rural social movement organizations held a series of consultations and strategy sessions on how to pass a new law. There was a major problem: The congressional session was due to end by February 1998, national elections (congressional and presidential) would be held in May, and the next congressional session would resume only in July and with a new (and as yet unknown) representation composition. The political dynamics were uncertain, but the pro-reform forces turned the seemingly negative constellation of factors into a positive one.

The DAR leadership worked on House Speaker Jose de Venecia, to convince him of the importance of passing a law on CARP extension and additional funding. De Venecia, a close ally of President Ramos, was running for president (against, among others, Joseph Estrada). DAR Secretary Garilao convinced him that the passage of a CARP extension law would boost his chances of election victory, with millions of votes coming from the peasantry. At the time, De Venecia was trailing behind Estrada in the polls. Meanwhile, autonomous rural social movement organizations were working closely with progressive members of congress (specifically with Wigberto Tañada and Edcel Lagman) to help pass the law.

Convinced of the electoral value of a CARP extension law, De Venecia prepared the congressional stage to do an almost impossible thing: sponsor a bill, rush it through different levels of formal committee and plenary deliberations, ensure that it passed through the bicameral committee (Upper and Lower Houses of Congress), and have it signed into law by President Ramos, all within a span of a few days.

The actual political process on the congressional floor and lobby was almost comic, but the outcome carried a profound and far-reaching policy implication: the continuity of CARP beyond June 1998. Congress approved the final bill on a day when there was not even a quorum, as most congress members were absent from the sessions, including the most anti-land reform representatives such as John Osmeña, busy as they were preparing for electoral campaigns in their districts. President Ramos signed into law RA 8532 on 23 February 1998, granting a ten-year extension to land redistribution and appropriating another PhP 50 billion budget (the same amount as for the 1988–1998 period).

Meanwhile, the World Bank made its first attempt to recruit government officials to embrace its market-led agrarian reform (MLAR) program in 1996, insinuating that the Philippine government must halt CARP's land distribution implementation, especially in the 5–24 hectare land size category, because of its distorting the land market. Instead, the World Bank counselled, the country should adopt the MLAR's "willing seller–willing buyer" approach.[89] The DAR under Ernesto Garilao flatly rejected the World Bank's proposal and gave the NGO community a copy of the World Bank's confidential document regarding MLAR in the Philippines. Subsequent noisy public protest from agrarian reform activist circles led by PARRDS drove World Bank officials hastily away from the Philippine CARP. They returned, however, three years later, with renewed vigour and persistence.

In early 1999, the World Bank officials came to the Philippines to convince the then new DAR leadership to at least support a small pilot MLAR project (see Franco, 1999d, 1999e; Reyes, 1999). For different reasons, including the hope for new loans amidst a creeping lack of public funds, the DAR leadership expressed interest in exploring the possibilities of MLAR as a complementary approach to existing CARP schemes. The World Bank, however, later informed the DAR that no fresh funds would be allocated for the MLAR project; instead the existing World Bank–supported infrastructure project for CARP's ARC program would be diverted to finance the MLAR project.[90] Tensions between the DAR and World Bank officials ensued. Finally, they agreed that a much smaller project — a feasibility study — would be carried out instead.[91] Again, throughout 1999 and after, NGOs and peasant movements from the broad political spectrum rejected the MLAR program and any pilot program for it (see, e.g., UNORKA, 2000b). By 2003, the DAR and the World Bank moved on to upgrade the feasibility study into a small pilot program in ten provinces, as explained in chapter 3 — amidst protests from the rural social movement organizations.

Summarizing the examples

In short, pro-reform actions by state actors and societal organizations have been launched as joint actions and as separate but parallel initiatives. While the pro-reform state–societal coalition seems the most promising strategy to secure real redistributive reform gains, it does not guarantee automatic, full, and permanent victory, whether in a specific land dispute or in a policy-oriented struggle. As the discussion above illustrates, the political dynamics that determine the actual balance of power between various competing actors are constantly shifting. The pre-existing structural and institutional settings are an important context and object of these state–society contestations. These, in turn, shape and reshape the degree, extent, and forms of their interactions, pro-reform or otherwise. The reflections of Ernesto Garilao (1999: xix–xxi), former DAR secretary, about his experience in the pro-reform coalition more or less capture the essential points put forward so far in this chapter:

> The civil society partners of the DAR were given all the opportunities to penetrate the state agrarian reform apparatus, get into alliances with national and local DAR bureaucrats, and use legal and extralegal political action to assert and seek favourable resolution of issues, concerns and interests .... Not all the agrarian reform partners fully utilized this opening. But PARRDS and the PEACE Foundation saw this democratic opening and maximized [their] gains .... When reforms do not move as fast, it is easy to accuse government of lacking political will and sincerity, and other pejorative terms in the civil society cookbook. In many cases, reforms do not move fast because social pressure from the constituency is weak. Many have the mistaken notion that press releases and letters to the editor constitute sufficient social pressure .... [P]easant social mobilizations complemented by friendly media support is a more effective combination. State reforms are rarely won by state reformists alone. They are won ... when the alliance between autonomous peasant organizations and state reformists is much stronger than whatever coalition of the anti-reformists within and outside government can mount.

5.6 STATE–SOCIETY INTERACTIONS AND SPATIAL VARIATIONS IN POLICY OUTCOMES

The outcomes of land redistribution in the country have been varied and uneven temporally and spatially. The main cause of such variations is not the mere presence or absence of social movement groups, nor is it the mere presence or absence of pro-reform state actors, in a given place and time.

Rather, it is the nature and character of state–society interactions that largely shape the variegated outcomes through time and across geographic spaces. It is relevant to briefly explain:

Table 5.2 offers a comparative tabulation of regional land reform outcomes, viewing it against the degree of presence and influence of rural social movements and pro-reform state–society interactions. The last column in the table shows the extent of anti-reform outcomes as well, for instance, VLT practices, questionable land distribution scope deductions, and so on. The data and information used in this table have been, to varying extents, discussed and explained in chapters 2–4. Some further clarification about the data and information is, however, necessary. The basis for the land redistribution output estimate used here is not simply the official data; rather it is the official land reform data scrutinized through the analytic lens presented in this study, that is, what is and what is not truly redistributive reform. Hence, a region might have very high land redistribution accomplishment, except for the fact that VLT practices and questionable land distribution scope deduction were equally high; and so, the real picture is not as rosy as the official claims would have us believe. Moreover, the data and information for rural social movements and state–society interactions also build on the author's more than two decades of direct participant-observation of these political processes, although this has been reinforced by the interviews with key actors carried out for this study. Finally, the classifications of "low," "medium," and "high" (and sometimes some combination of these) are approximations; certainly regions that are both classified as "low" (e.g., Ilocos and Cagayan) may still have significant variations between them.

Some relevant insights can be deduced from table 5.2. First, at the lowest end of the table in terms of land reform outcome and reformist actors and political process is ARMM. In this region, there are no significant autonomous rural social movements pushing for land reform, nor are there pro-reform state actors working for this reform. The result is the low level of land reform output, amidst a high degree of questionable transactions and outcomes, such as fake land titles sold to the DAR. Second, in contrast, the best (in relative terms of course) region so far is Central Luzon — on "average" performance, that is. It is to be recalled that this region has been the site of cycles of land claim–making protest actions by peasants during much of the past century. The first and second observations offer a range of interesting insights: On the one hand, the ARMM is not host to any significant modern plantations for exports. In fact for the most part, its agriculture is marked by (sub)subsistence farming; and yet, land reform there was extremely difficult due to the absence

State–Society Interactions for Redistributive Land Reform | 277

Table 5.2 State–society interactions and spatial variations in policy outcomes

Region	Land redistribution output	Degree of presence and influence of rural social movements engaged in CARP implementation	Degree of presence and influence of pro-reform state–society interaction	Extent of anti-reform outcomes (VLT, questionable public lands, land distribution scope deduction, and so on)
National	Medium	Medium-High	Medium	Medium-High
Cordillera (CAR)	Low	Low	Low	Medium
1 – Ilocos	Low	Low	Low	High
2 – Cagayan	Low	Low	Low	Medium-High
3 – Central Luzon	Medium-High	Medium-High	Medium	Medium
4-A – CALABARZON	Low-Medium	Medium	Low-Medium	High
4-B – MIMAROPA	Low	Low	Low	Medium-High
5 – Bicol	Low-Medium	Low-Medium	Low-Medium	Medium-High
6 – Western Visayas	Low-Medium	High	Low-Medium	Medium-High
7 – Central Visayas	Low-Medium	Medium	Low-Medium	Medium
8 – Eastern Visayas	Low-Medium	Medium	Low-Medium	Medium
9 – Western Mindanao	Low	Low	Low	Medium-High
10 – Northern Mindanao	Low	Low-Medium	Low	Medium-High
11 – Southern Mindanao	Low-Medium	High	Low-Medium	High
12 – Central Mindanao	Low	Low-Medium	Low	High
13 – Northeastern Mindanao	Low	Low	Low	High
ARMM – Muslim Mindanao	Low-Low	Low-Low	Low-Low	High-High

of social movements and reform-oriented bureaucrats. Central Luzon, on the other hand, is dominated by rice farms where landlords have been politically and economically weakened over time, partly due to cycles of tenancy and land reforms. The main opposition in this region comes from the real estate interest. Its proximity to the national capital facilitated the faster elevation of legal and political agrarian cases from the local to the national levels of the bureaucracy for quicker case resolution. Peasants in this region usually bypass the local bureaucracy and tend to go straight to the national DAR offices, threatening national media exposure if their demands are not immediately met.

Third, the right-hand column in table 5.2 shows that all regions have a fairly high level of anti-reform outcomes — such as VLT and land reform scope deductions, among others — regardless of pre-existing agrarian structures and institutions and the degree of presence or absence of social movements and reform-oriented bureaucrats. However, it is quite apparent that in those regions where social movements and reform-oriented officials were absent, such anti-reform practices were carried out to the maximum, such as in the cases of Ilocos and Central Mindanao regions where anti-reform VLT practices were most rampant.

Fourth, table 5.2 shows that a high level of social movements does not guarantee a high level of land reform outcomes. The cases of the Western Visayas (sugar cane) and Southern Mindanao (modern plantation belt) regions demonstrate situations where despite very high and sustained social movement mobilizations over time, the best outcome that could be achieved is "medium." On the other hand, however, there are no regions with a high-level presence of social movements where the land reform process resulted in insignificant outcomes. Conversely, there are no regions where social movements were insignificant but where land redistribution outcomes were significant.

Fifth, meanwhile, the presence of strong social movements does not guarantee equally strong pro-reform state–society interaction. Again the cases of Western Visayas and Southern Mindanao regions demonstrate this. But there does seem to be a pattern where the level of pro-reform state–society interactions corresponds to the level of land reform outcome in a region — that is, if the interaction is low, the land reform outcome is low, and vice versa. It is important to note at this point, however, that regional state–society interactions cannot be separated empirically and analytically from the conditions of state–society interaction at the national level. The national level actors intervene quite closely in the regional dynamics, shaping the latter in significant ways. It is not only the physical proximity of a region to the national capital that provokes national intervention; equally relevant is the national significance of regional issues, such as when the issue involves major transnational companies (as in the case of Southern Mindanao) or entrenched rent-seeking landowning families (as in the case of Western Visayas).

In short, structural and institutional factors do indeed matter in establishing regional patterns of land redistribution. However, more generally, it is the nature, character, and extent of state–society interactions that largely influence the sub-national variation and unevenness in land reform processes and outcomes. This conclusion reinforces our view of the issue, which goes beyond both society-centred and state-centred explanations of policy outcomes.

5.7 CONCLUDING REMARKS

This chapter presented evidence showing that the nature and extent of CARP land redistribution outcomes are largely influenced by the nature and extent of the pro-reform state–society coalition pushing for land reform. It showed the importance of autonomous rural social movements in the struggle for redistributive land reform. But the chapter also demonstrated that by themselves rural social movements are not sufficient to achieve a greater degree of success in land redistribution campaigns. Reformist initiatives by state actors autonomously emerged over time and proved important in the subsequent swing in CARP implementation towards greater reformism. However, evidence presented showed the inherent limitations of state reformists. The chapter demonstrated that in the case of CARP, the symbiotic interaction between state reformists "from above" and autonomous rural social movements "from below" is the most promising strategy for achieving a greater degree of successful implementation of redistributive land reform. This is demonstrated during the 1992–2000 period.

This strategy has been popularly referred to in the Philippines as the "*bibingka* strategy" (Borras, 1999, 2001; Franco, forthcoming). Jonathan Fox (1993) refers to it as the "sandwich strategy" in the context of rural Mexico.[92] However, forging such a coalition does not automatically guarantee successful land redistribution, because anti-reform forces attempt to block the reform process through their own state–society alliances. It is when the anti-reform forces are fragmented while the pro-reform alliance remains strong that the chances of successful land redistribution are highest. The extent of pro-reform state–society alliances has been highly uneven and varied across different geographic regions of the country and over time. This unevenness has largely accounted for the variations in land redistribution outcomes between regions and over time. The most important weakness of this strategy is the fact that it relies on two broad sets of actors, state and civil society, and any unfavourable changes — usually the waning of reformist interest and currents within the state — can paralyze the land reform initiative despite persistent actions from below by peasant organizations and their allies (Franco and Borras, 2005). This is demonstrated by the periods before 1992 and after 2000 in the Philippines.

THE CHALLENGE OF REDISTRIBUTIVE LAND REFORM: CONCLUSIONS AND IMPLICATIONS

C.1 INTRODUCTION

This study has demonstrated that to be truly redistributive, a land reform must effect on a pre-existing agrarian structure a change in ownership of and/or control over land resources, wherein such a change flows strictly from the landed to the landless and land-poor classes or from rich landlords to poor peasants and rural workers. Here "ownership and/or control over land resources" means the *effective control* over the nature, pace, extent, and direction of surplus production and distribution. Moreover, pre-existing socioeconomic structures and socio-political institutions influence the struggles for and outcomes of redistributive land reform by the extent to which they shape and condition prior distribution of land-based wealth and political power among different contending social classes and groups in a given state and society. They do not, however, pre-determine outcomes. Structural and institutional settings are important contexts and objects of state–society political contestations that, in turn, shape and reshape the degree and forms of pro- and anti-reform interactions. These political processes dynamically alter the pre-existing limits to and opportunities for redistributive land reform, facilitating or obstructing the land redistribution process. The political actions and strategies of pro-reform state and societal actors can influence land reform policy processes and outcomes by defeating anti-reform resistance and surmounting obstacles erected by structural and institutional factors, usually resulting in highly varied and uneven outcomes both spatially and temporally.

This chapter elaborates on the conclusions of this study, which revolve around three themes: the meaning of redistributive land reform (section C.2), structural and institutional influences on the limits to and opportunities for redistributive land reform (section C.3), and the role of the political actions and strategies of various state and societal actors (section C.4). The final section further explores the possible implications of this study for land reform theories, policies, politics, and research methods in the Philippines and elsewhere.

C.2 RETHINKING REDISTRIBUTIVE LAND REFORM

The conventional definition of land reform is founded on the concept of the formal, statist private-public land property rights dichotomy. This has influenced the subsequent literature's bias on the transfer of (private) ownership rights, the defining feature of which is the redistribution of the right to alienate. This fixation on the redistribution of formal proprietary ownership has led to only partially correct explanations of land reform processes and outcomes. These explanations cannot fully account for the types of outcomes shown in the tales of the five agrarian cases recounted at the beginning of the introduction.

This study has shown that the problem with conventional wisdom on land reform manifests in three ways: (i) in the *a priori* exclusion of redistribution accomplishment in public lands, (ii) in the *a priori* inclusion of all officially reported "redistribution" in private lands, and (iii) in the inconsistent exclusion-inclusion of share tenancy/leasehold reform in considering what is and what is not redistributive land reform.

On the *a priori* exclusion of redistribution in public lands

Contrary to the popular assumption in the literature that land reform in public lands does not constitute redistributive reform, a number of empirical cases studied here showed that redistributive reform can be, and has been, achieved in public lands. The case of the (multinational corporation) Dole-controlled pineapple plantation (DARBCI, chapter 3) shows that redistributive land reform had been achieved when the plantation was redistributed to farm workers in 1989, although the subsequent post–land transfer "leaseback arrangement," whose terms are so onerous, effectively cancelled out the earlier redistributive gains made by farm workers. Meanwhile, the case of the Aquino estate (chapter 4) demonstrates that redistributive reform can, and did, occur in the public forestland category (under the CBFM program) of the Philippine land reform law (CARP). The formal rights and the effective control of the landlord over the (public) lands were transferred to the peasants. Hundreds of thousands, perhaps a few million hectares of this type of lands (which in official documents are classified as forestlands without tenants, when in fact they are croplands tilled by tenants and are controlled by landlords) are host to a great number of poor peasants in the Philippines today.

Clarification of the notion of redistributive land reform in the context of public lands can facilitate a better understanding of successful land reform experiences, as in the cases of South Korea and Taiwan, where public lands were in fact an important component of land reform, and of less successful past attempts at land reform, such as in Colombia in the 1960s, where elite-controlled public lands escaped the analytic lens of many land reform scholars. The reconceptualization put forward in this regard will also facilitate better understanding of the challenges facing redistributive land reform and land policies in many developing countries today, such as in Thailand, Indonesia. and Bolivia, as well as in African countries where significant quantities of public lands have ended up under the control of private elites.

On the *a priori* inclusion of all officially reported "redistribution" in private lands

While the conventional land reform literature has been quite "strict" about its definition of redistributive land reform to exclude redistribution in public lands (and share tenancy/leasehold reform), it has been conceptually unsystematic with regard to its attitude toward private lands. Conventional land reform literature has been biased towards private property, and while many studies have raised criticisms with regard to acceptance of all official data about land redistribution, most of these studies have been framed to include *a priori* all officially reported "redistribution" in private lands. The current study has demonstrated that this perspective has partly allowed the entry of the notion of "market-based land reform" into the redistributive land reform theoretical, policy, and political debate, leading to confusing and even muddled terms and direction of the debate.

This study has shown that some of the officially reported and popularly accepted land redistribution accomplishments in private lands are in fact devoid of the essential elements of redistributive reform. In this study, outcomes are considered non-redistributive when there is no transfer of power from the landed elite to landless and land-poor peasants to effectively control the nature, pace, extent, and direction of surplus production and extraction and the disposition of such surplus from the land — even when official records claim otherwise. Real change in who holds power over the land does occur on occasion when it does *not* constitute redistributive reform, because the direction of change is within and among elites (landed or not), or from the landless and land-poor peasants to the landed elite. Taking off from this assumption, this study has shown that the Philippine CARP's non-redistributive outcomes have been significant and have also occurred in the private land category.

The non-redistributive CARP outcomes can be seen in the different variants of the voluntary land transfer (VLT) scheme (chapter 3). These VLT cases were usually faked redistribution via "paper sales" and/or the use of "on-paper beneficiaries" who are either family members, poor and non-poor peasant dummies, coerced tenants and farm workers, or people completely unaware of the transaction. Many landlords use VLT to perpetuate their control over land resources, although they make it appear as though they have complied with the spirit of land redistribution. This explains, for example, why banana landlord Antonio Floirendo is selling his land at a price sixteen times lower than what the local courts say is the "just price" for his land, and why Danding Cojuangco and the banana company Marsman are "giving" away their lands "for free." These schemes are non-redistributive because they do not involve essential transfer of wealth and power to the landless and land-poor peasants and farm workers. The terms of land use in post–land transfer contracts in these cases ensure the perpetual control of these landlords over the plantations.

Meanwhile, the minuscule MLAR pilot test in the country shows how local elites almost always manipulate market friendly and decentralized processes in land transactions to their sole benefit. A combination of corruption, anti-poor outcomes, and a general anti-reform impact has characterized MLAR in the Philippines (chapter 3). The stock distribution option (SDO) has been another scheme devoid of any dimension of redistributive reform. Under CARP, corporate farms are spared from expropriation if they opt to redistribute corporate stocks equivalent to the value of the land asset of the corporation. Theoretically, this scheme is non-redistributive when there is no essential pro-poor transfer of significant wealth and power within the corporate farm. And as predicted, corporations depressed the value of their land, jacked up the value of the non-land assets of the company, and manipulated financial accounting to show perennially low income, and therefore low dividends, resulting in the beneficiaries ending up with a negligible share of in the company's assets and power. This was the case, for example, in Hacienda Luisita, the sugar cane plantation owned by the family of former president Corazon Cojuangco-Aquino.

Overpriced land transfers via the voluntary offer-to-sell (VOS) scheme are another variant of apparent-but-not-real CARP land redistribution outcomes. In this study, especially as explained in Chapter 1, land is considered to have multiple dimensions, that is, political, economic, social, and cultural. Thus, its value cannot be reduced to solely monetary terms, and so the notion of "overpricing" in the context of land reform is in itself a contested concept. Yet, in the context of land reform policies, it still is possible to detect some practices of straightforward monetary overpricing. Here, an overpriced land transfer transaction occurs when the discrepancy between what is a generally acceptable price level (the one pegged by the LBP) is overruled in favour of a much higher land value based on the decision of a regular court or the DARAB. The case of the "Garchitorena land scam" in Bicol is a good example of overpricing through VOS resulting in the non-redistributive nature of the transaction.

In some cases, beneficiaries are unable to take actual possession of formally awarded lands due to strong, violent opposition from a landlord, who oftentimes has a pending legal appeal about the process. It is indeed non-redistributive when the peasants who the official records claim are the beneficiaries of land reform have in fact failed to take effective control of the awarded lands due to ongoing landlord opposition. Thus, this is another case of official records claiming achievement in redistributive land reform, while in reality there was none — or at the very least none yet. This is illustrated, for example, in the Benedicto estate in Negros Occidental (chapter 3) and on the Mitra farm in Bicol (chapter 4). In addition, one of the most commonly cited cases of unrealized reform, showing a discrepancy between official records and reality, is the problem of deliberate, fraudulent padding of accomplishment reports. This study showed a few examples of such fraud (chapter 3), as in the case of redistribution reports about government-owned lands during the Braganza DAR (2001–2002). Finally, the sale of fictitious land titles to government via VOS is another fraud: a straightforward non-redistributive CARP outcome that has made it to the official land redistribution accomplishment report. This phenomenon has occurred to a significant extent in the ARMM.

Clarification of the notion of redistributive land reform has provided this study with an analytic tool to examine and segregate land reform outcomes in private lands that are devoid of any elements of redistributive reform. This reconceptualization can contribute toward a better understanding of the land reform experiences in many other countries in the past where non-redistributive outcomes might have occurred even in private lands, such as some of the possibly overpriced land sales during the Frei administration in Chile in the mid-1960s. This conceptual clarification can also contribute toward a better understanding of the current debate on land reform where the market-led agrarian reform policy model has been aggressively promoted by the World Bank in several countries, including Brazil, Colombia, and South Africa.

On the *a priori* and inconsistent inclusion, or exclusion, of share tenancy/leasehold reform

The conventional land reform literature rejects redistribution accomplishment in public lands, and it is inconsistent in including or excluding those reforms achieved or attempted through share tenancy/leasehold reform. This study argues for another approach by using the reconceptualized notion of redistributive reform explained earlier. In fact, this study shows that redistribution of wealth and power can, and in many cases did, occur through leasehold reform. This is demonstrated in the case of the Zoleta property (chapter 4), where the tenants' share of the regular harvest doubled after conversion to leasehold arrangements (and the landlord's share was reduced by half) and their long-term tenure security ensured.

This study's conceptual reconsideration of the particular case of share tenancy in the context of redistributive reform can contribute toward a fuller understanding of the political economy of tenancy relations (and reforms) that have persisted in many parts of the world since ancient times. It is also useful for placing in a proper context within the debate on redistributive land reform the experiences of Taiwan and of *Operation Barga* in West Bengal (India) on the one hand and the less than desirable outcomes of leasehold reform in post-Apartheid South Africa on the other hand.

Thus, as shown in the discussion above, the conventional land reform literature has generally failed to account for the two broad types of land redistribution outcomes: that is, (Herring's, 1983) "real" and "apparent-but-not-real" outcomes. In fact, this study has shown that redistributive reform can occur in both private and public lands, through redistribution of full formal property rights, including the right to alienate and via leasehold reforms, and through a variety of formal land redistribution and tenure reform policy instruments. By problematizing the concept of redistributive land reform where the issue of power relations between different actors competing for effective control over land resources is the central issue, the weaknesses of conventional thinking are brought under a brighter analytic spotlight, and redistributive land reform is defined more precisely.

This study also concludes that while it is extremely difficult to ascertain the exact extent of redistributive reform in light of our findings in this study, it is possible to get a general sense of it. The extent of CARP's redistributive land reform outcome is far below the official claims in government statistics, but it also surpasses the pessimistic predictions and current claims of CARP critics (see chapter 2). The existence of actual redistributive reform side by side with apparent-but-not-real outcomes has rendered it extremely difficult to render a statistically exact account of land redistribution output.

Overall, the reconceptualization of the notion of redistributive reform provides a useful analytic tool for examining the tales of the five agrarian cases outlined at the start of the introduction and for putting the recent proposition of the market-led agrarian reform (MLAR) policy model in its proper perspective (i.e., in understanding that MLAR does not constitute and promote redistributive land reform). Our conceptual reconsideration is also useful in the discussion of the next set of theoretical themes: the limits-centred and opportunities-centred views in the study of land reform.

C.3 STRUCTURAL AND INSTITUTIONAL INFLUENCES ON THE LIMITS TO AND OPPORTUNITIES FOR REDISTRIBUTIVE LAND REFORM

The nature and extent of land reform outcomes are, to varying degrees, influenced by pre-existing structural and institutional conditions, specifically by the ways the latter have shaped prior distribution of wealth and political power among different contending groups and classes in a given state and society. Historically, countries with an important agrarian sector usually have a state that is heavily influenced by the land-owning classes and their allies. Thus, the actual distribution of wealth (including land) and political power is heavily concentrated in the hands of the landed elite. The land reform literature has recognized this and offered systematic analyses of the interlinked issues of land monopoly and political power. However, this study also pointed out that while in many settings the pre-existing macroeconomic structures and socio-political institutions are actually operative to the point of obstructing redistributive land reforms, there are also institutions that, while they do not automatically undermine the power of the landowning classes, can be mobilized to counter anti-reform manoeuvres. Thus, pre-existing structures and institutions do not pre-determine policy outcomes. The structural and institutional settings are important as the context and object of these political contestations that shape and reshape the degree and forms of the interactions.

The problems in the conventional land reform literature with regard to the actual role of structures and institutions are largely reflected in the persistence of two contending views, namely, the limits-centred and opportunities-centred perspectives.

On the one hand, the problem with the limits-centred approach is its overemphasis on the obstacles to redistributive land reforms to the extent that it overlooks the actual and potential opportunities. For example, the central state, an important actor in redistributive land reform, has been reconfigured during the neoliberal era amidst a simultaneous triple squeeze: "from above" through globalization, "from below" through (partial) decentralization, and "from the sides" through privatization of some of its regulatory powers (chapters 2–5). But this era also witnessed the emergence of new types of autonomous, polycentric (rural) social movements (chapter 5) that can potentially and actually contribute to keeping and/or reviving land reform on the policy agendas where it is absent — or kept dormant, such as in the case of Indonesia from the 1960s to the 1990s — and push for its fuller implementation where it actually exists, such as in Brazil in the 1990s.

On the other hand, the problem with the opportunities-centred perspective is its overemphasis on the favourable factors for land reform to the extent that it fails to understand the actual and potential limits to reforms. For example, while some landlords would go (and some have actually gone) bankrupt amidst agricultural trade reforms and so more farms would be expected to enter the land market, redistributive land reform is not automatically — or easily — implemented on these estates. The case of sugar cane plantations and cattle ranches in the Philippines (chapter 2) and the experience of Brazil show that despite the sharp fall in land prices due to agricultural trade reforms in the 1990s, landlords have remained vehemently opposed to land reform.

More fundamentally, the lack of systematic conceptual understanding in both camps about redistributive land reform has resulted in the conflation of and confusion over basic concepts in land reform scholarship, which in turn has resulted in even more confusion in the discussion about the limits to and possibilities for redistributive land reform. One camp may be discussing limits to a redistributive land reform, the other camp may be discussing opportunities for a non-redistributive "land reform," and so on. By problematizing the concept of redistributive reform, and locating the discussion about the limits to and opportunities for land reform within this core concept, the terms of the debate on contemporary land reform can be better clarified, as has been attempted in this study (chapters 2–5). The two dominant perspectives have certainly raised important and relevant issues, which must not be dismissed altogether. Building on these issues, however, this study has attempted a more balanced but critical view, acknowledging the necessity to look into the roles played by state and societal actors.

C.4 THE PRO-REFORM STATE–SOCIETY INTERACTION FOR REDISTRIBUTIVE LAND REFORM

In the context of determining the role of state and societal actors in redistributive land reform, the conventional literature is broadly divided into two dominant camps: the state-centred and the society-centred perspective. Both have explanatory power, but both have weaknesses as well. The state-centred approach puts too much emphasis on the role of state actors in carrying out redistributive land reform and thus overlooks the influence of social structures and institutions. Meanwhile, the society-centred approach puts too much weight on the role of social structures and institutions in redistributive land reform and thus overlooks the significance of the autonomous initiatives by pro-reform state actors. This study employed Jonathan Fox's "interactive approach" to the study of state–society relations to build on the strengths of the two dominant perspectives, while trying to fill the remaining gaps. This approach posits that a symbiotic interaction between autonomous social movements "from below" and initiatives by state reformists "from above" constitutes the most promising strategy for carrying out redistributive land reform. Using the interactive approach, this study found that the political actions and strategies of pro-reform state and societal actors have, to a significant extent, determined the nature, pace, extent, and direction of land redistribution processes and outcomes by defeating the anti-reform opposition and overcoming the constraints and surmounting the obstacles posed by pre-existing structural and institutional factors.

Many land reform studies emphasize the role of local peasant organizations and movements in achieving redistributive land reform. However, while highly autonomous and capable local peasant organizations are a necessary ingredient for achieving a greater degree of successful land redistribution, they are not sufficient because landlords evade reform by working in arenas far beyond (and beyond the reach of) the local community. Most of the local agrarian reform cases discussed in chapter 3 show that despite mobilization of local peasant groups for land reform, successful redistribution was far from being realized because anti-reform adversaries mounted their opposition to reform at levels beyond the reach of local peasant associations.

Moreover, the pre-existing distribution of political power is uneven in favour of the landowning classes and their allies. But, as said earlier, there are socio-political institutions that, while they do not automatically undermine anti-reform power, can be mobilized to counter anti-reform forces. Thus, societal allies are crucial in terms of augmenting the power of peasant organizations and extending the reach of their collective actions beyond their locality. Traditionally, peasants' allies for redistributive reform have been progressive (electoral) political parties (more commonly communist and socialist parties), progressive elements in churches and their organizations, and other middle-class intellectuals. In the Philippines, electoral political parties have not played a crucial role in the struggle for land, mainly because programmatic party politics have largely failed to take root in the country's predominantly personality-oriented electoral politics. However, other political parties and movements have played important roles in the struggle for land and power, for instance, communist parties and other leftist social movements, as well as progressive elements in churches and their associations. But the most significant ally of the landless and land-poor peasants that has emerged since the 1980s has been the progressive rural-oriented NGOs that consider themselves part of broader rural social movements.

These societal allies (political parties, social movements, churches, and NGOs) have at various times played an important role in maintaining the issue of land reform on the national policy agenda: during the 1986–1988 policymaking process for CARP (chapter 2) and in the continuing revisions of the CARP law; in the lobby in the mid-1990s against further exclusions of land redistribution coverage; during the 1997–1998 campaign for the ten-year extension of the CARP law; and in the lobby against the exclusion of retrenched farm workers from land reform on commercial plantations (chapters 3 and 4). These societal allies have also provided material and non-material resources to local peasant groups, for example, in the form of transportation support for mass mobilizations in key urban centres, legal assistance, and facilitated media coverage, as exemplified in the struggle of the banana farm workers in the case of DAPCO (chapter 4). As shown in chapters 2–4, most of the local struggles for land would have remained localized and could have easily been defeated by landlords had it not been for the societal allies who assisted in elevating the level of struggle beyond the village or municipal boundaries. These allies also facilitated both horizontal and vertical integration among local peasant associations, which would otherwise have remained scattered. This was the case, for example, in the PEACE Foundation's assistance in the formation of KMP in the mid-1980s, in the formation of DKMP in the early 1990s, and in the founding of UNORKA in the late 1990s (chapter 5).

The ability of local peasant groups to link with and mobilize societal allies can bring them closer to their goals. However, even when they are strong, pro-reform societal coalitions are far from achieving their goal because landlords usually evade reform in alliance with state actors. Hence, further alliances with reformists within the state is crucial to further increase the power of pro-reform forces, especially because state reformists, by themselves, even when capable of launching autonomous reformist initiatives, cannot easily defeat the state–societal anti-reform alliance. The uneven emergence of pro-reform state actors can be understood from the perspective of the state being "comprised of a range of actors" that must maintain a minimum level of political legitimacy while pursuing the process of capital accumulation for both private and state interests at all times.

The conflict-ridden political processes that led to either the real or apparent-but-not-real land redistribution outcomes examined in this study show the crucial influence of the pro-reform state–society alliance. The unexpected positive outcomes in land redistribution during the Garilao DAR (1992–1998) and to some extent during the Morales DAR (1998–2000) can only be attributed to the nature and scale of the pro-reform state–society alliance. From the perspective of specific agrarian cases, this study has shown that the pro-reform state–society alliance played the most crucial role in securing victories for redistributive land reform. These victories occurred in both private lands and public lands, as well as through leasehold reform, as discussed earlier. The state–society reformist alliance has been necessary in agrarian cases that went through expropriation (compulsory acquisition and operation land transfer), as demonstrated in the cases of the De los Reyes estate, Hacienda Roxas, the Salomon estate, DAPCO, the Mitra farm, and the Candaba–San Luis ricelands (chapter 4). This alliance was also crucial to the successful resolution of agrarian cases through various land transfer modalities that are traditionally (but erroneously) believed to be "non-conflictive," such as VOS, as in the case of Superior Agro and the Benedicto estate, lands controlled by government financial institutions such as the CIIF estate, and public lands such as the Aquino farm and DARBCI (chapter 4).

However, pro-reform state–society alliances do not guarantee automatic and easy achievement of their goals in land reform because they have to surmount the obstacles erected by the anti-reform state–society coalition. This study has shown that despite the joint and/or parallel actions by the pro-reform state and societal actors and coalition, some major defeats in the cause of redistributive land reform occurred both in specific cases and at the policy level. The case of the Langkaan estate in Cavite that led to the resignation of reformist DAR secretary Florencio Abad in 1990 is an example. The gaining ground of non-redistributive VLT in several cases, such as the Danding Cojuangco orchard and the banana plantations of Floirendo and Marsman (chapter 3), attests to the fact that the pro-reform state–society alliance is not invincible.

The anti-reform forces can be defeated when their ranks are divided horizontally (e.g., with cleavages between different local elite groups) and vertically (e.g., with the losses of allies "at the top" or within the state), while the ranks of pro-reform forces remain solid, united, and persistent. The cases of the banana farm workers in DAPCO, the Salomon estate, the Candaba-San Luis ricelands, and Superior Agro (chapter 4) exemplify this. In addition, the pro-reform state–society alliance can facilitate redistributive reform outcomes in the contested boundaries of inclusion in the land reform policy of some landholdings and peasants and the exclusion of others. The "inclusion-exclusion" issues in CARP coverage are not absolute, automatic, and permanent as claimed in official records, as proclaimed by laws, or as assumed by analysts. There are farm types marked for exemption, and thus assumed to be automatically excluded from land reform, that have been expropriated, either partially or fully. This is demonstrated in the cases of Fort Magsaysay in Nueva Ecija (a military reservation), the University of the Philippines Land Grant in Basilan (an educational landholding), and the Aquafil estate in Mindoro Occidental (a fishpond), as discussed in chapter 4. Though critics have simply assumed that such exclusion is automatic, the cases studied here demonstrate that it is not. But again, the political processes examined here have shown that sustained political mobilizations by pro-reform state and societal actors were responsible for the expropriation of these estates. However, not all collective actions resulted in successful expropriation, as we see in the pending case of the Davao Penal Colony. In addition, this study looked into the contentious issue of beneficiary "inclusion-exclusion." The poorer, more vulnerable strata of the peasantry, on many occasions predominantly women, were usually de-prioritized with regard to — or even completely excluded from — land reform. However, through sustained collective action within the pro-reform state and societal alliance, some peasants who were inherently disadvantaged in the land reform process have successfully resisted exclusionary currents. This was the case, for example, of farm workers who struggled against the exclusionary DAR administrative order no. 6 series of 1998 (chapter 4).

Moreover, the nature and extent of state–society interactions largely determine the nature, pace, extent, and direction of redistributive land reform, nationally and sub-nationally, over time. These interactions put into operational mode the limits and opportunities facilitated or imposed by pre-existing structural and institutional conditions in a given society. The highly uneven nature and spread of these pro-reform state–society alliances have resulted in varied and uneven outcomes of land reform policy, spatially and temporally.

In short, through the pro-reform state–society alliance, successful implementation of redistributive land reform has become possible but not automatic, difficult but not impossible. The lesson from the Philippines with regard to the role of political actions and strategies of societal and state actors is also useful for understanding past experiences in land reform policies and politics. While contending explanations of land reform processes have gravitated around either the state-centred perspective or society-centred explanations, the preliminary review of these experiences hints at the likelihood that the symbiotic interactions between pro-reform state and societal actors have accounted for the push toward redistributive land reforms, such as in Kerala (India), in Mexico during the administration of Lazaro Cardenas in the 1930s, in Chile during the Allende era, and even in China during the first wave of the communist land redistribution campaign. And like the lessons from these historical cases, this strategy has significant limitations as recently shown in the Philippine case as well: that it is dependent on two broad sets of state and societal actors — and usually, when reformism starts to wane within the state, the overall land reform initiative suffers important setbacks. The reconceptualization of state–society relations in the context of redistributive land reform is useful to obtain a fuller understanding of the limits to and opportunities for redistributive land reform in a contemporary context, especially amidst complex debates about the possible roles of societal actors and the state.

C.5 IMPLICATIONS: RECASTING SOME CONCEPTS, REVISING SOME PRACTICES

A number of possible implications of this study may be advanced. Theoretically, the argument put forward with regard to the more precise definition of redistributive land reform to mean redistribution of wealth and power entails a recasting of some conventional assumptions and conclusions about past and current land reform experiences. Whether popularly perceived as successful or otherwise, the nature and extent of these outcomes and their distribution across public and private lands may be reassessed in this new light. The definition of redistributive land reform offered in this study may at first appear too strict and exclusionary. However, in a deeper sense, this reconceptualized definition is in fact more inclusionary because, unlike the traditional definition, it includes redistributive reforms not only in private lands but also in public lands, and it includes not only land transfers that involve the right to alienate but also leasehold reforms stewardship. Indeed, the conventional *a priori* rejection of land reforms in public lands, *a priori* acceptance of all officially reported land redistribution accomplishment in private lands, and *a priori* inconsistent exclusion-inclusion of leasehold reforms must be cast away in any rigorous theorizing on redistributive land reform.

A related implication is that the two broad types of land redistribution outcomes (i.e., real and apparent-but-not-real) explained in this study may alter traditional conclusions regarding many past land reform experiences. Meanwhile, the rejection of market-led agrarian reform on the basis that, theoretically and in reality, it does not constitute and will not promote redistributive land reform must be relentlessly pursued.

The debate surrounding the limits to and opportunities for redistributive land reform, as well as the political strategies necessary to attain redistributive land reform, must also be re-examined from the basic starting point of what does and what does not constitute redistributive reform. Dichotomous views must be set aside in favour of a more balanced, critical, and dynamic assessment that does not assume that structures and institutions predetermine policy outcomes. The dichotomous state- and society-centred perspectives on redistributive land reform must also be revised in favour of a more interactive approach to state–society relations that is founded on the symbiotic interactions between social movements "from below" and initiatives by state reformists "from above" — but at the same time remains aware of the limits of such a strategy in the real world, as demonstrated in the Philippine case.

Finally, an implication of this study in theorizing about redistributive land reform is that a move toward a multidisciplinary development studies perspective is warranted. The land reform literature can be greatly enriched by other disciplines, specifically those specialized in community-based natural resource management, environmental studies, forest studies, and law and development. A more systematic integration of studies on state–society relations and social movements into the land reform scholarship has become an imperative.

In terms of research methodology, the reconceptualized notion of redistributive land reform requires that research methods be revised accordingly. Future studies require the critical use of official state statistics, but also non-official data and information gathered within and outside the state apparatus. Studies further require critical use of data aggregated at the national level and below. This study showed that nationally aggregated data can impart important information, and so it must always be used. However, below the national level, data and information are fantastically varied and so offer opportunities for richer analysis and interpretation. Below the national level are multiple levels, from regional to provincial, municipal, village, and farm. Thus, sub-national and cross-country sub-national comparative research methods can extend the explanatory reach of an inquiry. The varied and diverse outcomes within and between these levels and the processes that occur within and between them involving different, often competing, state and societal actors can more fully explain policy outcomes and processes.

In terms of policy, some implications of this study are noteworthy: For one, there is a need to develop better instruments to actually measure the degree of redistributive land reform, given that formal quantitative statistics offer an important but insufficient means of assessment. The task of actually measuring outcomes in redistributive reform policies based on the framework put forward in this study may bring the issue closer to other concepts such as democratization and empowerment, which are themselves difficult to measure. Furthermore, this study implies that future policies on redistributive land reform will have to cast away the conventional bias against public lands and leasehold reform. In fact, this study suggests that there is a necessary and urgent policy task: to re-examine and possibly reformulate existing land reform policies to address concerns related to these types of lands and reforms in a more integrated manner. Moreover, based on the findings of this study, it is imperative to move policy analyses away from the "official policy scope-centred" approach in order to address the urgent concerns that are usually left outside the parameters of the official scope of policy. Specifically, policy analyses and policy formulation in the future must systematically deal with the landholdings and peasant households that have been formally excluded from the official policy scope, for example, the "missing" CARP land distribution scope. Finally, based on the starting point of this study — that is, putting forward a sharper definition of redistributive land reform — these findings imply that the market-led agrarian reform policy model and its variants, such as CARP's VLT, must be rejected as a policy option because they neither constitute nor promote redistributive reform.

The findings in this study also have political implications: It is important for rural social movement organizations, such as NGOs and peasant organizations, to maintain perspective on their strategic role and task in resolving the land question in their respective countries in favour of the landless and land-poor peasants. It may thus be necessary for many of them to go beyond the narrow project-based view of the land reform struggle. It is also necessary for some NGOs and peasant organizations to review the notion of "conflict-free" state–society partnership currently being promoted by donor and governmental agencies. It is necessary for peasant movements and NGOs to seriously address the need for widespread militant but pragmatic forms of struggle for land and power. In addition, international development agencies, government and nongovernmental alike, may too need to rethink their general bias in favour of "conflict-free" development projects and reconsider embarking on renewed assistance to the political struggles for land redistribution in most developing countries.

Moreover, peasant organizations and NGOs may have to move away from "official policy scope–centred" political advocacy and mobilizations in order to broaden their agendas to include issues and concerns that the state usually refuses to include in its official policy discourse. One example is the landholdings that are kept outside the scope of official land reform policy. Closely related to this issue, it is necessary and urgent for peasant movements and their allies to organize and mobilize around the issue of land redistribution in public lands and reforms in share tenancy arrangements in a more systematic and integrated manner vis-à-vis the private land category of their country's land reform policy. This is especially because the World Bank has been aggressively promoting policies to privatize public lands, a move that, if implemented as conceived by the World Bank, may lead to further inegalitarian land ownership distribution.

This study also suggests that peasant movements and their NGO allies must escalate and further systematize their opposition to the neoliberal land policies. Local, national, and international initiatives by peasant movements and their NGO allies against the World Bank's attempt to implement its pro-market land policies are under way, notably those carried out by *La Via Campesina* and IPC for Food Sovereignty, but these need further consolidation and strengthening (Rosset, Patel and Courville, 2006).[1]

Moreover, the findings of this study imply that while it is the main duty of peasant movements to develop and maintain their autonomy and capacity at a high level at all times in the context of their struggle for land and power, their need to build capacity while preserving autonomy poses difficult challenges for would-be allies, especially national and international NGOs and state reformists. These allies must respect and assist in consolidating these twin dimensions of peasant organizational power.

Peasant struggles for land and power in the Philippines, and in many parts of the world, have persisted into the 21st century. As long as significant degrees of land-based exploitation, poverty, social exclusion, and rural political conflicts remain, these struggles will likely continue, and these will be marked by ebbs and flows. The dynamic ups and downs in the push for redistributive land reform will be determined, to a lesser degree, by the capacity of peasant movements and their societal allies to, themselves, launch political initiatives or by the technocratic state actors' ability to carry out autonomous reform actions. To a greater degree, however, successful outcomes will be determined by the ability of pro-reform societal and state actors to forge alliances and launch joint and/or parallel collective actions for redistributive land reform.

Finally, this study has shown that the 6 million hectares of lands officially reported to have been redistributed to 3 million peasant households in the Philippines is unrealistically high. However, this study also does not support the pessimistic predictions and sweeping dismissal by some critics of the land reform accomplishment. However, the partial-but-significant land redistribution outcome that has been achieved, and whatever potential it has got in terms of poverty reduction and national development may easily, and could likely, be cancelled out by a convergence of interlinked factors: First, the rapid population growth rates easily overtake the rate of land redistribution; as some lands are redistributed to land claim makers, more new people are in need of land to be tilled. Second, while there is an ever increasing number of potential land claim–makers amidst shrinking political possibilities for further redistribution, the land frontier has clearly been fully exhausted — meaning, there are no more significant possibilities for opening up new farms out of forested lands. This makes the government promise of giving a piece of land to every one who needs it an empty promise and the rural social movements' advocacy for the same increasingly problematic. Third, while some lands were redistributed to peasants, no significant support packages were extended to land reform communities. In fact the highly uneven process of social differentiation in land reform communities is now easily observable with many land reform beneficiaries starting to sell or rent out their awarded farmlands. Fourth, in the midst of insignificant public support to the reform sector, the macro-socioeconomic policies affecting the agricultural sector and the national economy are becoming increasingly hostile to family farms (see Borras, 2007). These issues are complex and should be the subject of a separate, comprehensive scientific study. It is, however, not totally without basis to say at this point that if these creeping problems are not addressed more fundamentally, any significant achievement gained through the partial land reform in the Philippines during the past two decades may one day soon be cancelled out.

NOTES

INTRODUCTION

1. For the most recent policy-oriented studies on land reform in the current context, refer to Cotula, Toulmin and Quan (2006) with special reference to the African debate; Leite with Avila (2006) for a general discussion with special reference to Latin America; Merlet, Thirion and Garces (2006) with special emphasis on state, market, and civil society roles in agrarian reform; and Rosset (2006) with special reference to food sovereignty, human rights, and social movements. The first three papers were presented at the International Conference on Agrarian Reform and Rural Development (ICARRD) in Brazil in March 2006, while Rosset's was presented at an international conference at the Institute of Social Studies in The Hague in January 2006, although it later formed an important part of a collective paper presented by civil society organizations at ICARRD.
2. The terms "peasant" and "peasantry" are highly contested terms and concepts in the literature. The clarification as to what "peasants" mean in this book is sufficient for the purposes of this study. For further insights about this debate, refer to Wolf (1966) and Landsberger (1974).
3. See, for example, the varying explanations by El-Ghonemy (1990, 2001), Griffin (1976), Bell (1974), and Brockett (1991).
4. Refer to Barraclough (2001), although how exactly the two sets of actors (state and societal) relate to each other is not systematically explored and explained in this particular work.
5. For a discussion on Asian experiences within this context, see Griffin, Khan and Ickowitz (2002). Although as Paige (1996: 127) argued, "The causes and consequences of land reform are revolutionary. Land reform is not really reform at all. In an agrarian society, land reform is a revolutionary act because it redistributes the major source of wealth, social standing, and political power."

6 Refer to de Janvry (1981), Dorner (1992), Thiesenhusen (1989, 1995), and Kay (1998) for Latin America; Herring (1983) for South Asia; Tai (1974) for Southeast and East Asia; El-Ghonemy (1990, 2001) for northern Africa and the Middle East; King (1977), Kay (2002b), Ghose (1983), and Prosterman, Temple and Hanstad (1990) for transcontinental comparative surveys; Tuma (1965) for historical (beginning in ancient times) and global comparative studies. For the emerging literature on gender and land rights, refer to the following excellent works: Deere (1985), Deere and Leon (2001), Razavi (2003), Agarwal (2003, 1994), and Whitehead and Tsikata (2003).

7 For various discussions, refer to Kay (1998), Herring (2003), Bernstein (2002), and Akram-Lodhi, Borras and Kay (2007).

8 For recent re-articulation of this issue, see, for example, Dorner (2001), Barraclough (2001), Thiesenhusen (1989, 1995), Griffin, Khan and Ickowitz (2002), and Herring (2003).

9 Refer for example to Meszaros (2000a, 2000b), Wolford (2003a, 2003b, 2004, 2005), Wright and Wolford (2003), Petras (1997, 1998), Brass (2003a, 2003b, 2000), Petras and Veltmeyer (2001), Veltmeyer (2005a, 2005b, 1997), Harvey (1998), Moyo (2007), and Moyo and Yeros (2005), among others.

10 The phrase "pro-market academic and policy circles" here is taken in a broad sense to mean theoretical and policy tendencies that reject the past practice of state-led development policy approaches while they actively propose the more market-led alternative approaches in development. Adherents to more formal neoclassical and neo-institutional economics are included in this definition of the phrase. See, for example, World Bank (2003), Deininger (1999), and Deininger and Binswanger (1999).

11 See the arguments by Hernando de Soto (2000); compare these with the World Bank's (2003).

12 For critical insights, refer to Manji (2006), Cousins and Claassens (2006), and Nyamu-Musembi (2006) in the context of Africa.

13 In the context of sub-Saharan Africa, refer to the critical works of Cousins and Claassens (2006), Manji (2006), Toulmin and Quan (2000), Platteau (1996), and Ellis (2000: 131–35); in Latin America see Kay and Urioste (2007) and Nuijten (2003); in Asia see Borras (2006b); in the context of economies in transition, refer to Spoor (1997, 2003, 2007), Akram-Lodhi (2005, 2007), Ho and Spoor (2006), and Sikor (2006).

14 See, for example, Dorner (2001) and Barraclough (2001).

15 Refer to the example of El Salvadorian debate in this regard by following the different views of Prosterman (1976) and Paige (1996). See also Herring (2003) and Ross (1998: Ch. 5) for broader perspectives.

16 Refer to Deininger and Binswanger (1999) and Deininger (1999) for the basic discussion of the pro-market critique of state-led land reform; see also Atkins (1988).

17 Furthermore, most of the quantitative data from the DAR and other CARP implementing agencies are collected and formatted according to the needs of the government, which are not always consistent with the questions and objectives of this study. This study therefore embarked on the time-consuming, almost Herculean, task of recomputing and reformatting vast amounts of quantitative data. Moreover, to facilitate easier access to, or verification of, the data used here by other researchers, the specific government offices within larger government departments are cited in the references section. For example, instead of simply using "DAR" as the data source, the specific office is mentioned, e.g., "DAR-MIS" or "DAR-PSRS."

CHAPTER 1

1 The degree of "eroded value" due to inflation over time is an important factor to consider in understanding net redistribution of land-based wealth as well.
2 See also related discussion in Leach, Mearns and Scoones (1999) about the "extended entitlement" approach in the context of environmental studies.
3 While between them there are significant differences and contradictions, the following studies do provide insights that are relevant for land reform scholarship: Peluso (1992), Ribot and Peluso (2003), Vandergeest and Peluso (1995), Ribot and Larson (2005), Lynch (1998), Lynch and Talbott (1995), Leach, Mearns and Scoones (1999), Agarwal (2005), Sato (2000), and Johnson and Forsyth (2002), among others.
4 Refer also to the relevant discussion in Whitehead and Tsikata (2003). For relevant broader discussions about rights and how to make them real in terms of actual benefits for poor people (and therefore involving power and power relations between actors), refer to Cousins (1997), Fox (2005) and Newell and Wheeler (2006).
5 At the more local level, the organization of production at the settlements level also provides critical insights regarding the relationship between land redistribution and development. Wendy Wolford's (2003b) insights from the experience of MST in Brazil offer important, relevant insights.
6 Hence, the liberalization of land markets is one of the main pillars of the neoliberal land policies. The Egyptian case is a good example of these ideas, how they have been carried out, and what their impact has been. See the critical examination by Ray Bush (2002).
7 For interesting and relevant debates and discussions about these issues in the context of Latin America, refer to the edited volume by Tom Brass (2003a).
8 See, e.g., Petras (1997, 1998), Veltmeyer (1997), Desmarais (2003, 2001), Rosset (2006, 2001), Robles (2001), Wright and Wolford (2003), Harvey (1998), Ghimire (2005), Brass (1994, 2000), Borras (2004), and McMichael (2006a, 2006b).
9 However, as Carmen Diana Deere and Magdalena León (2001: 350) explain, "Agriculture is no longer the main source of wealth in most countries, as evidenced

by the dramatic fall in the share of agriculture in GDP. One would think that under these conditions land would be much easier to redistribute. However, in Latin American countries agricultural exports are still key, and indeed, are the focus of the neoliberal model, providing one explanation for why the political will continues to be missing to carry out a fundamental redistribution of landed property."

10 Refer also to O'Brien (1996) and O'Brien and Lianjiang (2006) in the context of contemporary rural China, which, while not exactly within the same framework as "everyday forms of peasant resistance," has significant overlaps with the latter in terms of context and conditions for the rural poor people's actions.

CHAPTER 2

1 For scholarly analyses of the Marcos land reform and related tenancy conditions, refer to Putzel (1992), Riedinger (1995), van den Muijzenberg (1991), Wurfel (1989, 1988, 1983), Kerkvliet (1979), Ledesma, Makil and Miralao, (1983), and Carroll (1983); for the performance of agricultural and national economic development, refer, among others, to the works of Boyce (1993) and Hawes (1987); see also Bello, Kinley and Elinson (1982) for an analysis of the World Bank support to the Marcos dictatorship.

2 Refer to Banzon-Bautista (1989) for a study of the impact of foreign currency remittances and inhabitants' quest to go abroad on the agrarian structure of a rural village.

3 President Gloria Macapagal-Arroyo was one of the staunchest promoters of neoliberal policies during her stint in the Senate in the 1990s. See Bello (1996; 2001) for a powerful critique of the neoliberal paradigm in the context of southeast and northeast Asian countries; see also the related analyses of De Dios (1998), Lim (1996, 1998), and Sta. Ana (1998); see Republic of the Philippines (n.d.) for a general overview. For a recent and comprehensive Asian regional development context, refer to the IDS Bulletin special issue on Asia edited by Robinson and Farrington (2006).

4 For incisive analyses of the development of capitalism in Philippine agriculture, see Ofreneo (1980), Hawes (1987), Tadem, Reyes and Magno (1984), Rivera (1994), Tiglao (1982, 1983), David et al. (1983), Billig (1993, 2003), Aguilar (1998, 1994), and Koppel (1990).

5 Refer to the concise historical analyses in Constantino (1975), McCoy and de Jesus (1982), and Corpuz (1997).

6 The economic history of the country by Corpuz (1997) offers fresh materials on the topic.

7 Refer to Constantino (1975) and Corpuz (1997).

8 Refer to Constantino (1975), Corpuz (1997), Aguilar (1998), Lopez-Gonzaga (1994), McCoy and de Jesus (1982), McCoy (1983, 1982), Billig (2003, 1993), and Owen (1982, 1999).

9   See Kerkvliet (1977), Corpuz (1997), Monk (1996: 7), and Starner (1961).
10 For analyses of the impact of settlements on the pre-existing agrarian structure, refer to Rodil (1994), Abinales (2000), Gaspar (2000), Fianza (1999), Turner, May and Turner (1992), Vidal (2004), and Gutierrez and Borras (2004).
11 See Wurfel (1983), Monk (1996), Constantino and Constantino (1978), Gleeck (1993), and Putzel (1992).
12 See Bello, Kinley and Elinson (1982), Feder, (1983), Boyce (1993), Fegan (1989), Rocamora and Panganiban (1975), and Parreño (2003).
13 In a more general and recent critical reflection related to this issue, Henry Bernstein (2006: 403–404) appropriately raises the questions of the near impossibility of producing precise data about "peasant population," "small farmers' population," or the difference between those who are full-time and those who are part-time farmers and so on, largely because of the extreme diversity and fluidity of (rural-urban) livelihoods that have emerged partly as a result of recent neoliberal global agrarian restructuring. The discussion about official census data on the Philippine agricultural population should be viewed in the light of Bernstein's caution/warning.
14 This is more or less the same as the estimate by Putzel (1992: 26), though he used the entire rural population as a base figure.
15 The Malthusian argument of too many people and too rapid population growth as the key reason for poverty cannot be easily dismissed, because indeed there is empirical evidence showing a relationship between population, poverty, and poverty eradication. In the context of the Philippines, the population-poverty argument is very much part of the land reform debate. But Robin Broad and John Cavanagh (1993: 143) put it quite correctly in the Philippine context; they said, "Current Philippine population growth rates are unsustainable. But rapid population growth is motivated primarily by widespread poverty; the root problem is inequity. A sustainable and equitable development path, in attacking the root causes of poverty, is likely to be the best population policy — and the best environmental policy as well."
16 For explanations of various measurements and sub-national variations of poverty incidence, see Balisacan (1999); for sub-national variations in poverty incidence, see Monsod and Monsod (1999).
17 The sugar cane sector itself has been an anomaly within the Philippine agricultural sector because of the political and economic clout of the sugar planters and because of the history of special trade arrangements with the United States. But it is important to note that even during the peak period of sugar cane exportation, the mass of destitute landless farmworkers existed in a state of abject poverty and social exclusion. For critical historical analysis, see Aguilar (1998, 1994), Lopez-Gonzaga (1994), Regalado (1992), and McCoy and de Jesus (1982). The persistence of the inefficient sugar cane sector in the Philippines reminds one of Marc Edelman's (1992) explanation of the persistence of large, inefficient *latifundia* in Costa Rica.

18 The American economist James K. Boyce (1993: 241), in his excellent analysis of the political economy of development and poverty in the Philippines during the Marcos era explained, "The actions of the state, whether in creating the preconditions for markets or in redressing market failures, are invariably shaped by the prevailing distribution of power. In a setting of marked political and economic inequalities, one can expect state policies with respect to the natural environment to favor the interests of the rich and powerful over those of the poor and the powerless. If environmental degradation benefits the former at the expense of the latter, it will continue until such time as it is blocked by the mobilization of countervailing power. Herein lies the vital link between environmentalism and democracy." This extended quote from Boyce is an important analytic guide in the overall discussion in this book — but should be most interesting and should be recalled when one reaches the discussion about "contested public forest lands" and land redistribution in chapters 3 and 4.

19 The various works of Kerkvliet (1977, 1990, 1993, 1995) explore and explain the complexities of politics in the rural Philippines. This body of work constitutes perhaps the most authoritative study on the subject in the country. Also important are Wurfel (1988), Rutten (2000a, 2000b, and 1996), Wolters (1984), Fegan (1989), McCoy (1993a), Sidel (1999), Lacaba (1995), Franco (2005, 2001a, 1994), and Doronila (1992, 1985).

20 *Huk* commander Luis Taruc, Pedro Abad Santos in the 1930s, Juan Feleo of *Pambansang Katipunan ng Magbubukid* (PKM) in the 1930s–1940s, Jeremias Montemayor of the Federation of Free Farmers from the 1950s through the 1990s, and KMP's Felicisimo "Ka Memong" Patayan, Basilio Propongo, Simon Sagnip, Nilo Oracion, Jaime Tadeo, and Rafael Mariano in the 1980s are some examples.

21 The same dynamic process of state-building affecting pre-existing notions of indigenous and community land rights has been profoundly affecting and dynamically transforming much of the public/community forested uplands (Wiber, 1990; Lynch, 1998; Lynch and Talbott, 1995; Cabarle and Lynch, 1996; Sajor, 1999). This would later prove to have impact on land reform processes more generally (Borras, 2006b).

22 See also Franco (1998b), Manapat (1991), Gutierrez (1994), Gutierrez, Torrente and Narca, (1992), Sidel (1999), Hutchcroft (1991), Parreño (2003), and Salonga (2000).

23 For general analysis of the policymaking process and the nature of Congress, see Gutierrez (1994), Gutierrez, Torrente and Narca, (1992), Putzel (1992), Riedinger (1995), Lara (1986), and Lara and Morales (1990).

24 It is important at this point to clarify some issues with regard to CBFM. In 1996, the DENR formally adopted the community-based approach to its forestry program. The CBFM integrates existing related government programs: the Integrated Social Forestry Program (ISFP), the Community Forestry Program (CFP), the Forest Land Management Program (FLMP), the Regional Resources Management Program (RRMP), the Low Income Upland Development Program (LIUCP), the

Coastal Environment Program (CREP), and the Ancestral Domains/Land Claims Program (ADMP) (La Viña, 1999: 18). Not all of these programs are within the CARP scope. The ISFP remains the major CARP component. In reality, however, there are several overlaps between these programs, especially between CARP's CBFM and the ancestral domain claims, which are now handled by another government agency, the National Commission for the Indigenous Peoples (NCIP), under another law, the Indigenous Peoples' Rights Act (IPRA). The confusion remains, e.g., it is unclear how much of the reported CBFM accomplishment data are in fact ancestral domain claims (and vice versa). The available DENR data are not disaggregated according to CBFM sub-programs (see also Gauld, 2000). For a useful background on the CBFM program, see Garilao, Soliman and Cristobal (1999), and especially La Viña (1999), Bulatao (1999), and Cristobal (1999). See also Bello et al. (1998), Utting (2000), Broad (1994), and Borras (2006b).

25 In early 2004, the government was able to recover more than US$ 600 million from the Marcos loot, and the bulk of this money was supposed to go to the agrarian reform fund (after deducting the court-mandated compensation for 10,000 human rights violation victims during the Marcos dictatorship). The money was exhausted at the eve of the presidential election of 2004, and it is widely believed that the Macapagal-Arroyo administration used this money to finance their campaign. This issue is still being investigated by the Senate up to the time of writing. See Rimban (2005).

26 For background on implementation procedures, see Bacuñgan, Froilan and Associates and DAR (2000); DAR (1995). The implementing guidelines and administrative orders are as follows: DAR (n.d.a, n.d.b, n.d.c., n.d.d., n.d.e. and n.d.f.).

27 For varying analyses, see Putzel (1992), Riedinger (1995), Lara (1986), Lara and Morales (1990), IBON (1996, 1988), Adriano (1992), Otsuka (1996), Cornista (1990), Goodno (1991), Hawes (1989), and Thiesenhusen (1990).

28 The most important scholar on agrarian reform in the Philippines, and the sharpest critic of CARP, James Putzel, later revised his perspective on CARP and admitted that the program, despite a number of problems, has redistributed far more lands than earlier predicted (Putzel, 2002).

29 Refer also to Bello, with Marissa de Guzman, (2001: 192–199); CPAR (1990, 1989, 1988), KMP (2000), and Reyes (2000).

CHAPTER 3

1 Refer to PARC-AMIC (2001, 1997, 1996, 1995 and 1994).
2 PARC-AMIC (1997), 1996–1997, section on DAR, p. 10. The preponderance of this type of VLT was confirmed by several top DAR officials interviewed for this study. Interview with Gerry Bulatao, 21 January 2002, Quezon City. In separate interviews with the author, two former DAR secretaries (Ernesto Garilao and

Horacio Morales) and two undersecretaries for operations (Ding Navarro and Hector Soliman) also shared Bulatao's thoughts about VLT, while almost all of the interviewed DAR national bureau and regional directors shared this view of VLT. Similar manipulation has been committed under the DENR CARP program. The PARC-AMIC audit team, for example, has been able to uncover several anomalies such as the one in the province of Leyte: "In *Barangay* Guinciaman, San Miguel, Leyte, 59 hectares of public land was covered with Free Patent titles and given to unqualified awardees ... [who] are all residing in Tacloban City, some 40 kilometers away... Other awardees... are residents of Quezon City. No profession or occupation is recorded except for [one] awardee ... who is a doctor of medicine." (PARC-AMIC, 2001: 3–4, under the section on DENR).

3 Interview with Soltero Coronel (pseudonym), brother of four "paper beneficiaries" in the said case.
4 This is from the AMIC-PARC report for 1996–1997 (PARC-AMIC, 1999), section IV, p. 7.
5 This is from the AMIC-PARC report for 1995 (PARC-AMIC, 1996), section on DAR, p. 17.
6 PARO Jose Grageda (Camarines Sur); Interview, 14 January 2002, Mandaluyong City; see also AMIC-PARC report for 1998, section on DAR.
7 Data for this case study was gathered largely during field work conducted in early 2002. This included interviews with several actors: VLT-CARP beneficiaries contracted by Dole in *barangays* Berada and Meohao, Kidapawan, and North Cotabato; several local DAR officials (in the DAR municipal office of Kidapawan); the municipal agrarian reform officer of Makilala; the provincial agrarian reform officer of North Cotabato; the chairman of the BARC of Meohao; as well as a number of NGO community organizers, including Nestor Tapia of the PEACE Foundation and Joey Gloria of the Philippine Rural Reconstruction Movement (PRRM).
8 Interview with DAR Secretary Ernesto Garilao, Makati, 2001.
9 Interview with peasant leader and PARC member Basilio Propongo, San Enrique, Negros Occidental, 2001; interview Fr. Rod Anoran of the NGO NCPERD, Pulupandan, Negros Occidental, 2001.
10 Parreño (2003: 200–202) offers some revealing details of parts of the process in this deal.
11 Interview with DAR Secretary Horacio Morales Jr., 2001, Quezon City; DAR Undersecretary Conrado Navarro, Quezon City, 2001.
12 The data and information for this case are based on informal and formal discussions with key DARBCI leaders and the voluminous documents related to the case. An interview with one of the key leaders of the pro-Dole farmworkers' faction was also an important source of insights. Interviews with key regional and national DAR officials provided crucial data and information. For a study on lease rentals on commercial plantations, see DAR-PSRS (1997).

13 This amount was roughly equivalent to a worker's minimum monthly wage during the late 1980s. By the second half the 1990s the real value was substantially eroded — it was insufficient to meet even the month-long food needs of an average sized family. But each beneficiary did not get the full lease rent amount because the annual land payment amortization was automatically deducted.

14 Primary data for the Floirendo and Marsman case studies are drawn from a variety of sources: contracts and interviews with key actors, namely, Roberto Sebastian; Rodolfo del Rosario (brother-in-law of Don Antonio Floirendo, Sr., and incumbent governor of Davao del Norte in 2002); top leaders of the pro-Floirendo cooperative (who requested to remain anonymous in this paper); top leaders of autonomous cooperatives (Enrico Cabanit of Floirendo's Worldwide Agricultural Development Corporation [WADECOR; see Franco, 2005] — Cabanit was later assassinated by masked armed men in Panabo in April 2006); Ben Isidro of Floirendo's Tagum Agricultural Development Corporation or TADECO-Central; Komersendo Canias of Marsman; several NGO organizers and activists; an NGO representative to the Provincial Agrarian Reform Committee, Davao del Norte, Ernest Reyes; banana private sector entrepreneurs George Mercado and Antonio Javellana; as well as numerous DAR officials. Interviews were carried out between June 2001 and March 2002, except for the much earlier series of discussions with the late Antonio Javellana. Numerous interviews and discussions with ordinary farmworkers — beneficiaries or otherwise — on the Floirendo- and Sebastian-controlled plantations took place between 1998 and early 2002. Useful background was provided by Lara (2001), a study on the cooperative bias in land redistribution on commercial plantations. Franco (2005) provides critical insights about the politico-legal complexities, while de la Rosa (2005), Ofreneo (1980), Tadem, Reyes and Magno (1984), and Hawes (1987), among others, offer excellent political-economic background.

15 The banana industry is the most lucrative sub-sector in Philippine agriculture with an annual production value per hectare ten times greater than that of irrigated ricelands. The number of affected farmworkers is almost the same as the number of hectares, with the banana plantation having a 1:1 hectare:worker ratio (so the average size of the awards on banana plantations is one hectare per beneficiary). For historical background, refer to Tadem, Reyes and Magno (1984), Hawes (1987), Alano and Hipolito (1999), Feranil (2001), de León and Escobido (2004), and Ang (2001). Interviews with Davao del Norte governor and TADECO vice-president Rodolfo del Rosario, Tagum City, 2001; Antonio Javella, 2001; George Mercado, 2001; and Roberto Sebastian, president of Marsman, 2001 provided banana sector insiders' points of view and opinions.

16 Interview with Romeo Fernando Cabanial, Land Valuation Officer, LBP-XI, 5 February 2002, Davao City.

17 LBP XI's Cabanial said that based on the study of the Land Bank of the Philippines, if the land price was PhP 350,000, the lease rent per hectare per year would be PhP 45,000 based on the prevailing industry standards.

18 These points have been underscored by Enrico Cabanit, Ben Isidro, and Komersiando Canias of the various autonomous farmworkers' groups who opposed the schemes of Floirendo and Marsman. Interviews with the three peasant leaders were conducted 18 February, 16 February, 9 February, respectively, in Davao in 2002 (except for the interview with Cabanit, which was held in Quezon City). Even the top leaders of the pro-Floirendo groups have started to complain about the onerous character of the contracts, but they refused to confront Floirendo openly for fear of violent reprisal. Such was confided to the author by leaders of pro-management cooperatives in the WADECOR and TADECO-Central Floirendo plantations in interviews in February 2002 in Davao.

19 In 1999, Klaus Deininger of the World Bank talked with the owner of Marsman about how the latter viewed the possibility of having his land subjected to the MLAR model. Marsman's owner reportedly readily endorsed the MLAR concept and volunteered his plantation for the pilot project, but with a sky-high PhP 1.2 million per hectare (spot-cash) price tag. No follow-up negotiation with Marsman regarding MLAR occurred after that. This study also benefited from an interview with Marsman president and former Department of Agriculture Secretary Roberto Sebastian in Davao City in 2001.

20 Interview with PARC members Basilio Propongo and Romulo Tapayan, Quezon City, 2003 and 2004.

21 Interview with Danny Carranza, veteran community organizer who also lives within the perimeter of the hacienda (Quezon City, 4 February 2002), and interview with DAR Secretary Morales (Quezon City, 18 January 2002).

22 Interview with DAR Secretary Morales.

23 For a background analysis of the controversial Hijo case, refer to Franco (1999b), Franco and Acosta (1999), and Feranil (2001).

24 Teves was not the only one who was harassed by the court on the same issue. George Mercado, an activist-entrepreneur in the banana sector in Davao del Norte was also slapped with contempt of court charges in February 2002 when he criticized the SAC of Tagum, Davao del Norte, with regard to the Hijo case. The author was interviewing Davao del Norte Governor Rodolfo del Rosario when George Mercado was brought in to the governor's mansion in Tagum City by his arresting police officer. Before and after his arrest, Mercado gave interviews for this research. Mercado would later in 2004 be assassinated by masked men, and, like the case of Cabanit, Mercado's assassination remains unsolved up to this time of writing.

25 The strong lobby was actually facilitated by former Quezon member of Congress and pro–land reform activist Oscar Santos who is personally close to the new executive secretary, Alberto Romulo.

26 The Nagasi peasants were able to take possession of the land some time in August 2003 with the intervention of DAR national leadership (under Secretary Roberto Pagdanganan). The point that this study is making, however, is that between

1999 and mid-2003, no redistributive reform occurred on the estate despite formal claims in official records. And there is an actual threat in this case that the peasants might be driven away from the land again by the landlord.

27 For details, refer to Mission (1999).
28 For elaboration, refer to Borras (2002b: 13–14). Among the documents used for this information are DAR-SSO (1997) and DAR-XII (1995, 2002).
29 Interviews with several DAR officials at the national and Region 4 offices who requested anonymity on this issue.
30 This is arrived at by assuming the real average annual output between 1990 and 1994 was 20,000 hectares, then subtracting the excess quantity of land; see DAR-PS (2001b).
31 Interview with various regional officials, including DAR Director Narciso Nieto, September 2003, Quezon City.
32 Fieldwork for this case was carried out in 2003. Refer also to the overview offered in Feranil and Taipa (2003).
33 Based on interviews with Fr. Peter Geremia, PIME, other regional and provincial DAR officials, Hernani Abella of Sultan Kudarat–based peasant group DEMASKU, Rey Magbanua of PhilNET-RDI in Sultan Kudarat, and DAR Region 12 Director Shio Mambuay. Refer also to the analytic insights of Aida Vidal (2004).
34 Refer to the annual audit reports of PARC-AMIC (1994, 1995, 1996, 1997, 1999, 2001).
35 According to various interviews with banana sector elite players, e.g., George Mercado and Antonio Javellana, top national and regional DAR officials, and leaders of farmworker organizations. The eventual exclusion, under certain conditions, of fishponds, poultry farms, and salt beds from land redistribution also carried a provision for mandatory production and profit sharing. There is no discussion within or data from the DAR about this; and NGOs seem to have ignored this reform altogether.
36 The author has been able to directly observe numerous dialogues between civil society organizations and the DAR. Moreover, the author also led in 2004–2005 a large research study launched by more than a dozen rural-oriented development NGOs to try to understand this problem, the first ever systematic undertaking in this regard.
37 Based on various discussions between the author and DAR Secretary Horacio Morales in 1999, and in 2001 and 2002.
38 The feasibility study started in October 2000 (World Bank, 2000a: 3) with funding of US$ 398,000 [letter from Assistant Secretary Toinette Raquiza to DAR Secretary Horacio Morales Jr. dated 27 February 2001]. This is different from, although broadly related to, the DENR project on land management and administration with US$ 5.4 million funding from the World Bank and AusAid (World Bank, 2000b); information was also taken from various internal documents: Baniqued (2001a, 2001b), Ponce (2001a, 2001b, 2000), and Wilson (2001a, 2001b). Throughout

1999 and after, NGOs and peasant movements from the broad political spectrum rejected MLAR or any pilot program for it (see Franco, 1999a, 1999b; Reyes, 1999; UNORKA, 2000b), forcing the World Bank to relabel MLAR the "Philippines Community-Managed Agrarian Reform Program" or CMARP. See also Borras (2005) and de Asis (forthcoming).
39 From a letter dated 30 October 2001 from DAR's Assistant Secretary Jose Mari Ponce to World Bank Country Director Robert Vance Pulley. The money would come from a grant by the Japan Social Development Fund (JSDF).
40 All field visits at the CMARPRP project sites were carried out in 2005. I thank Leslie Inso, Danny Gatche, Wendy Ludovico, Bong Gonzal, Santiago Corpuz and Roni Buenaventura for their very helpful research assistance.
41 For a study on CMARPRP in the context of state-community partnership, refer to the article by Karlo de Asis (forthcoming).
42 Interview, 16 January 2002, Quezon City.
43 Interview, 21 January 2002, Quezon City.
44 Interview, 18 January 2002, Quezon City.
45 Interview, 1 March 2002, Quezon City.
46 Interview, 29 January 2002, Quezon City.
47 Interview with DAR Secretary Horacio Morales Jr., Quezon City, 2002. See Gutierrez and Borras (2004).

CHAPTER 4

1 Refer, for example, in the discussion-debate on the El Salvadorian experience to the analysis on the non-coverage of the export-oriented crops, such as coffee (Paige, 1996). For a broadly similar Costa Rican historical case, refer to Edelman (1992).
2 Data and information for this case study are drawn from interviews with various community organizers and peasant leaders, including *Ka** Vangie Mendoza, Malu Perpetua, and Danny Mendoza. The author was also present at several confrontation-dialogues with national DAR officials that addressed several land cases, including the De los Reyes estate. Franco (2001b) is also useful.

   * *Ka* is short for *kasama*, which means comrade. Leaders of progressive, militant peasant groups like Mendoza's are always popularly addressed with *Ka* before their first names.
3 Interviews with veteran community organizers at the PEACE Foundation.
4 Interview with Evangeline "*Ka* Vangie" Mendoza, Quezon City, February 2002.
5 The LDC was also affected by the split. It would have to regroup later within the reformist network of the PEACE Foundation and rename itself AGAPE, still working largely in Laguna (see Franco, 2001b).
6 Intercropping means planting secondary crops in between principal crops. The most common practice in the Philippines is to plant shorter crops such as corn and rice in between coconut trees. *Lanzones* is a tropical fruit found in the Philippines and some parts of Indonesia.

7 Data and information for this case study are drawn from various interviews with peasant leaders and community organizers, including Joel Calla, Rustom Suruiz, Vangie Mendoza, Danny Carranza, Albay PARO Olayre, and DAR Region 5 Director Dominador Andres. For a general background on land reform in coconut land, see DAR-PSRS (1998a).

8 This case study is reproduced from Borras (1999) with minor revisions and updates. The data and information are drawn from numerous formal and informal discussions and interviews, including those with top DAR officials at the national, regional, and provincial levels; NGO activists, especially those working at the Mindanao Farmworkers Development Center (MFDC) and the Alternate Forum for Research in Mindanao (AFRIM); numerous farmworker leaders and ordinary farmworkers; and some banana elite players, especially the late Antonio Javellana (one of the former owners of DAPCO). Refer also to de la Rosa (2005) for a similar analysis on DAPCO; refer to Franco (2005) for a broader and deeper analysis of the legal-political institutional terrain within which the DAPCO case has been embedded.

9 For a nuanced study of the power relations of contract farming in Mindanao, refer to Vellema (2002); see also Borras and Franco (2005).

10 See also Alano and Hipolito (1999).

11 The CARP law states that land redistribution will commence in the deferred commercial farms either after the tenth year or upon the expiration of the existing lease contracts, whichever comes first.

12 The particular group was the FoodFirst Information and Action Network (FIAN).

13 This is reproduced from Borras (1999) with minor revisions. Data and information for this case study are drawn from interviews with various key actors, including Argee Esquejo, Alan Bernardino, and the various peasant leaders and community organizers directly involved in the case.

14 NEPAD, later became EMPOWERMENT.

15 The data and information for this case study are drawn primarily from a series of focus group discussions with three groups of actors directly involved in the case, prior to and after the actual land redistribution: the executive board of KAMAHARI, the team of development workers-activists of the Western Batangas Project of the PBSP (Philippine Business for Social Progress), and representatives of various government agencies at the municipal and provincial levels. Interviews with veteran PEACE activists and DAR officials are also useful sources of insights, as well as informal discussions with Atty Mabel Arias, the lawyer assisting the peasants. For a nuanced legal study of this agrarian case, refer to Arias (2004).

16 Interview with one KAMAHARI leader, hacienda site, 2001.

17 This case study is from Borras (1999, 2001) with minor revisions and updates. Data and information for this case are drawn from various informal and formal interviews and discussions with the peasants and peasant leaders in Candaba–San Luis between 1998 and 2002. Interviews with PEACE community organizers

who directly worked on this case are equally important sources of information. Moreover, interviews with local and national DAR officials provided useful insights.

18 Kerkvliet's (1977) excellent book about the *Huk* rebellion offers a good background on this case. The author also participated in numerous dialogue-confrontations between the peasants and government officials about this case. For excellent critical analyses on the Marcos era land reform in rice and corn, especially in Central Luzon, see Ledesma, Makil and Miralao (1983), Wurfel (1983, 1988), van den Muijzenberg (1991), Wolters (1984), and Kerkvliet (1979).

19 Data and information for this case study are drawn from informal discussions with peasant leaders from Superior Agro and the KMBP (Bondoc-wide peasant movement) and community organizers of the PEACE Foundation, especially Danny Carranza, Edwin Pancho, Bong Gonzal, and Danny Gatche. Franco (2005, 2000) and Carranza (2000) are important sources of background data and information. The author also participated in numerous picket-confrontation dialogues between the peasants and DAR officials about this case.

20 GTZ is the German aid agency for international development. For a background discussion on the German-funded project, refer to Franco (2005) and Santoalla, Parreño and Quitoriano (2001). See also the documentary film *Paglaya ng Lupa* (2006) by Janina Dannenberg and Johannes Richter.

21 The film was made by Howie Severino of *The Probe Team*.

22 The data and information for this case study are drawn from various formal and informal discussions with peasant leaders, PEACE's community organizations, Oscar Santos, and Manuel Quiambao. Carranza (2000), a well-written case profile and excellent analysis of the CIIF case, is also an excellent source of data, information, and insights. Franco (2005) is an equally important source of insights.

23 Interview with COIR's Joey Faustino, Quezon City, 2002. For a general background on the CIIF, see Parreño (2003).

24 See Putzel (1992: 53–54).

25 See Putzel's discussion (1992: 56).

26 The data and information for this case study are drawn primarily from a focus group discussion with more than a dozen peasants and peasant leaders on the estate, plus several one-on-one formal and informal discussions with them. Many requested anonymity in this study. Data and information from interviews with the PEACE Foundation community organizers and leaders of KMBP and UNORKA, as well as provincial-regional-national DAR officials also offered insights. Carranza (2000), Corpuz (2000), and Franco (2000, 2005) are other important sources of information and insight.

27 This is a kind of "forced taxation" imposed by the revolutionary groups on landlords. In exchange for the payment of this "tax," the rebels refrain from harming the landlords and from encouraging people to agitate for land reform in the landlord's landholdings.

28 For relevant policy studies on the legal difficulty of implementing leasehold, refer to Arias (1998) and Ocampo (2000).
29 Data and information for this case study are drawn from various informal and formal interviews with PEACE Foundation community organizers, especially Ruben Esquejo, and other regional and national DAR officials.
30 For obvious reasons, details about this specific case cannot be divulged here.
31 Data and information for this case study are drawn from focus group discussions with the NGO (KFI, or Kasangyaham Foundation, Inc.) working with farmworkers on this landholding, as well as a separate focus group with the executive board of the farmworkers-beneficiaries' cooperative in Basilan in 2001. A one-on-one interview with veteran trade union leader and KFI President Bong Malonzo is also an important source of information and insights. (These interviews were conducted by the author for the purpose of another research project, not this book).
32 Data and information for this case study are drawn from a series of formal and informal discussions with peasants and peasant leaders directly involved in the dispute, especially *Ka* Simon Sagnip during the period between 1986 and 2006. Discussions with top DAR officials with regard the issue and as well as the video production of the Philippine Peasant Institute (PPI) on this case in the late 1980s, are important sources of information and insights. Fuentes and Paring (1992) is also useful.
33 Data and information for this case study are drawn from numerous formal and informal discussions with various groups directly involved in the dispute: leaders and members of the three different groups of settlers who accused the Floirendos of having forcibly ejected them from the land in the 1960s and 1970s; leaders and members of various farmworkers' groups in the Floirendo plantation, especially those under the umbrella of UFEARBAI-UNORKA, including Eric Cabanit and Ben Isidro, Governor Rodolfo del Rosario, the late Antonio Javellana, and provincial, regional, and national DAR officials. The author also participated in numerous collective actions launched by the various groups of claim-makers in this case, both in Davao and Manila. Manapat (1991) is also a useful source of information. See also Borras and Franco (2005).
34 Second generation "problems" and political conflicts have occurred in many post–land redistribution settings, such as the conflicts, for instance, between the land reform beneficiaries and the farmworkers in Kerala (see Narayanan, 2003).
35 Refer to Rimban (1997) for details of this case.
36 Data and information for this case study are drawn from various formal and informal discussions with farmworkers and workers' organizations in Davao, and with several NGOs and top regional and national DAR officials between 1998 and 2006. The author also participated in numerous direct actions by farmworkers and in internal discussions within the DAR bureaucracy concerning the debate about the fate of retrenched farmworkers, and in several dialogue-confrontations

between farmworkers' groups, NGOs and DAR officials. This case study also draws on Borras and Franco (2005) and Franco (2005).

37 But some banana plantations were redistributed much earlier, even before the 1998 expiration of the deferment period for the banana commercial farms. The retrenched farmworkers were categorically excluded in these early redistribution efforts. Thus, there are cases when only a fraction of farmworkers benefited from the reformed plantation. Some peasants boasted of becoming rich under the new circumstances, but clearly at the expense of expelling a sizeable number of their fellow farmworkers. This was the case for example of Checkered Farm in Davao del Norte. See Cuarteros (2001), but also Borras and Franco (2005) and contrast the latter with Rodriguez (2000).

38 This is assuming that the average awarded land is nearly 2 hectares; there is no disaggregated data on this. The average size of awarded land is usually smaller for private lands compared to public lands.

39 Region 8 with 77 percent, Region 12 with 75 percent, CAR with 71 percent, and Region 13 with 67 percent.

40 This information is based on various discussions with DAR top officials, including several discussions with DAR Undersecretary Benny Madronio.

CHAPTER 5

1 Refer to Constantino (1975), Agoncillo (1965), Ileto (1979), and Kerkvliet (1977).

2 As, for example, in the case of the PKM, *Pambansang Katipunan ng Magbubukid*, or National Council of Peasants. Refer to the autobiographical book *Tatang* (1988) for enlightening experiences in this regard from the 1920s through the 1970s. Kerkvliet (1977) offers excellent empirical and theoretical analyses relevant to the point made here.

3 The FFF was founded by Jeremias Montemayor, a lawyer. For more general discussion on this theme, refer to Contantino and Constantino (1978), Ileto (1979), Franco (1994), and Huizer (1972).

4 For theoretical background, see Tilly (1984). For scholarly studies on the historical process of state building in the Philippines, refer to Abinales (2000) and Hutchcroft (2000). For the most comprehensive studies on "everyday forms of peasant resistance" in the Philippines, refer to the various works of Kerkvliet (1977, 1990, 1993) and Scott and Kerkvliet (1986).

5 For a first-hand account, refer to the autobiographical book of Felicisimo "*Ka Memong*" Patayan (Patayan, 1998), a veteran FFF leader who was recruited to radical left-wing politics and eventually joined the ND movement. He later co-founded KMP, and later, DKMP.

6 Franco (1994, 2001b) traces the early initiatives in this regard and offers excellent analyses.

7 For general background on the NGO phenomenon in the Philippines, refer to the scholarly works of Clarke (1998), Silliman and Noble (1998), and Hilhorst (2003).

8 Other rural-oriented legal ND movements are the peasant women's group AMIHAN (see Lindio-McGovern, 1997), the National Federation of Sugar Workers (NFSW, see the various works of Rosanne Rutten: 2000a, 2000b, 1996) and the fisherfolk organization PAMALAKAYA (*Pambansang Pederasyon ng Maliliit na Mamamalakaya ng Pilipinas* or National Federation of Subsistence Fisherfolk of the Philippines; see Putzel, 1995).
9 See KMP (1986a, 1986b, 1988).
10 For excellent analyses of this political process, refer to Lara (1986), Lara and Morales (1990), Riedinger (1995), Kasuya (1995), and Putzel (1992).
11 For the various criticisms against CARP coming from the rural social movement groups, refer to Lara (1986), Lara and Morales (1990), and CPAR (1988), and compare these to the earlier proposals by some of these groups: KMP (1986a, 1986b, 1988) and CPAR (1988, 1989, 1990).
12 Basilio Propongo, co-founder of the Small Farmers' Association of Negros (SFAN), KMP's Vice-Chairman for the Visayas (1985-1990), and KMP's Secretary-General (1990-1993). He is a small rice farmer from *Barangay* Guintorilan, San Enrique, Negros Occidental. Data are also taken from the minutes of the KMP "Expanded" National Council meeting in early 1992 (KMP, 1992a, see also 1992b, 1993, 1991).
13 Scholarly studies that inquire into the series of land occupation initiatives during the second half of the 1980s and also address the role of the ND movement are Kerkvliet (1993), Putzel (1995), and Canlas (1992, 1994). Refer also to Padilla (1990), Rutten (2000a, 2000b), Hawes (1990), and Borras (1999: 52-59). The author also directly participated in most of the major assessment conferences conducted by KMP and its NGO allies with regard the land occupation experience.
14 Refer to a local case study in Bicol in Padilla (1990).
15 Various interviews with *Ka* Taning (pseudonym), Head of the National Peasant Secretariat (NPS) of the CPP from 1988 to 1993. The question of land and tenancy reform in the context of communist insurgents' revolution is not new and distinct to the Philippine experience. It is a question confronted by most communist movements in developing countries, as in the case of the Vietnamese communist movement before its victory in 1953. As White (1983) explained "Always, in the end, the land policy is subordinated to the [insurgents'] military agenda," where such a campaign must only be launched in liberated areas and must be selective: "sparing landlords and rich peasants who cooperate." Furthermore, White explained that "part of the success of the 1953 land rent reduction campaign was the fact there was no significant land and tenancy reform policy that the Bao Dai government could offer to the peasants." White's conclusion throws light on the Philippine experience, where in fact the government has something relatively significant to offer to the peasants.
16 For example, refer to Putzel (1992), Riedinger (1995), and Lara and Morales (1990) for analyses of the role played by KMP during the policy debates in the 1986 Constitutional Commission and the CARP policymaking in 1987-1988.

17 The NPS's strategy was outlined in an essay and was popularly referred to as the "September Thesis"; for a summary, see Franco (2001b).
18 KMP (1992a, 1992b). Some data for this study are also based on various interviews with *Ka* Taning and other veteran NPS cadres.
19 Refer to Franco's (2001b) revealing account and analysis of the ND movement's influence within the PEACE network from 1977 onward, with fresh historical and empirical data not published previously in any form. Franco's insights are not only related and relevant to PEACE and its network members but also extremely important for a fuller understanding of the history and evolution of the ND social movements, rural and urban, in the Philippines.
20 Interviews with *Ka* Taning, and other veteran community organizers directly involved in the trailblazing work of the NPS, for example, Ernest Reyes, Danny Mendoza, Ruben Esquejo, and Arnel Caravana. KMP (1992a) also provides insights in terms of actual quantitative data on membership and number of *barangays* and municipalities covered by the KMP and the NPS work during the reorientation campaign.
21 Interview with *Ka* Taning; CPP (1993a, 1993b, 1989, 1988).
22 See also CPP (1993a, 1993b).
23 Data and information about the 1992–1993 split are drawn from a variety of internal documents, including KMP (1991, 1992a, 1992b, 1993).
24 Refer also to Rocamora (1994), Weekley (2001), Reid (2000), and Abinales (2001).
25 Data and information for the DKMP are drawn from a variety of sources, including DKMP (1993, 1995a) and KMP (1993). The author actively participated in the earlier consolidation of DKMP from 1993 to 1996.
26 Refer to the various internal documents of DKMP (1993, 1995a, 1995b).
27 Refer also to CPAR (1992), Putzel (1995, 1998), and Franco (1999a).
28 The political movement co-founded by Horacio Morales Jr. and colleagues, such as Edicio de la Torre, Gerry Bulatao, Oscar Francisco, Isagani Serrano, and Joel Rocamora. It started as a "special political project" within the ND movement but later became an independent political force. It has been influential in setting up a number of other NGOs, including the Philippine Rural Reconstruction Movement or PRRM (which was originally founded in the early 1950s but was re-invigorated and reconstituted in 1986), the Education for Life Foundation, and the Institute for Popular Democracy. Refer to Clarke (1998) for a background on PRRM.
29 For a background on this group, refer to Boudreau (2001).
30 See PAKISAMA (1996), PhilDHRRA (1997), and Riedinger (1995).
31 Information on these are drawn from various informal discussions within the NGO community. Specific validation during the interview with Egad Ligon, formerly of the PAKISAMA secretariat, is also important. Other key PAKISAMA leaders were interviewed, including *Ka* Aning Loza, president.
32 Interview with Armando Jarilla, Task Force Mapalad Land Reform Campaign consultant. Influential on this group is former DAR undersecretary (from the Garilao time) Jose Olano (see, e.g., Olano, 2001).

33 Interviews with several key cadres from the ex-ND peasant community. Other key data and information were directly observed by the author.
34 UNORKA (2001a, 2000a). Interview with DAR Secretaries Garilao and Morales and DAR Undersecretaries Bulatao, Navarro, and Nieto.
35 Interview with *Ka* Cenon, Secretary-General, PKSK.
36 Their most important NGO ally is CARET (Center for Agrarian Reform, Empowerment and Transformation).
37 Interview with Vic Ojano, chairperson of KASAMA-KA.
38 Interview with Romulo Tapayan, Secretary-General of KAMMPIL.
39 Interview with BUKLOD leader *Ka* Memo Palomera.
40 Especially after Tadeo was ousted from the LBP board of directors a year after Macapagal-Arroyo came to power; DKMP would, a few years later, rename itself Paragos.
41 Another NGO involved in this type of work is SENTRA (*Sentro para sa Tunay na Repormang Agraryo* or Center for Genuine Agrarian Reform), which works closely only with KMP. In 2001, another NGO of this orientation, the Agrarian Justice Fund (AJF) was established by people like Conrado Navarro and Wigberto Tañada.
42 One example is local chapters of KMP in Eastern Visayas. This assertion is based on interviews with some of their leaders in 2001.
43 For example, a well-educated, highly skilled senior official at the operations office earns a gross monthly salary of some PhP 18,000 (US$ 350).
44 Interview with DAR Secretaries Garilao and Morales.
45 Interview with DAR Regional Director Dominador Andres, Legaspi, 2001.
46 Interview with former PARO Joe Grageda, himself having more than a dozen administrative cases filed against him by landlords.
47 See Po and Montiel (1980). Refer to Wurfel (1983, 1988, 1989), Kerkvliet (1979), Ledesma, Makil and Miralao (1983), Monk (1996), Putzel (1992), Boyce (1993), Bello, Kinley and Elinson (1982), and Riedinger (1995) for varying emphases in analyzing the Marcos land reform.
48 Refer to Putzel's (1992: 310–312) excellent and detailed analysis of this period.
49 Refer to Putzel (1992: 319–323). For an interesting self-reflection on her stint at the DAR, refer to Santiago (1994: 147–193).
50 She would later run for president in 1992, placing second to Fidel Ramos.
51 Abad teamed with Bonifacio Gillego and Edcel Lagman in fighting for more progressive land reform bills, which were defeated in Congress.
52 Refer to Putzel (1992: 326).
53 One example of these groups is Sanduguan, headed by Benjamin Cruz.
54 For a general background on municipal-level DAR employees' dynamics, refer to DAR-PSRS (n.d.).
55 Refer to Borras (1999: 47, 147).
56 Interview, Gerry Bulatao, 21 January 2002, Quezon City.
57 Interview with Ernesto Garilao, 11 January 2002, Makati City.

58 Interview with Ernesto Garilao, 11 January 2002, Makati City.
59 Soliman, Burkeley, and Bulatao were all associated with the NGO KAISAHAN at the time of their recruitment to the bureaucracy. They all played critical role in the formation of KAISAHAN in 1990, and they turned it into an important NGO that specializes on agrarian reform policy analysis and legal assistance (together with ex-DAR Secretary Florencio Abad). KAISAHAN would play an important role in assisting the Garilao administration in terms of policy direction and bias in legal interpretation of the CARP law. Butch Olano was the former director of another NGO closely associated with the Jesuits, the PhilDHRRA. Meanwhile Joe Grageda and Gerry Bulatao both had past associations with the revolutionary Communist left, although both had earlier left the mainstream movement in the 1980s and joined NGOs that are associated with other "popular-democrats" (those who officially left the mainstream revolutionary movement and started to experiment with new approaches to organizing and mobilization work among the poor).
60 Interviews with Ernesto Garilao, 11 January 2002 and 14 July 2005, both in Makati City.
61 Ernesto Garilao (1999: xix).
62 Interviews with Ernesto Garilao, Hector Soliman, and Gerry Bulatao.
63 Interviews with Garilao in 2001 and 2005.
64 In fact, it appeared that "special deals" with the Aquino and Ramos administrations were made in order to lift the sequestration orders on the properties of these cronies, especially their landholdings. It seemed that only one crony was partially affected by land reform process during the Aquino and Ramos administrations, namely, the Campos family. Refer to Manapat (1991), Parreño (2003), Salonga (2000), and Hutchcroft (1991). The vast landholdings controlled by Danding Cojuangco in Davao del Sur, Agusan del Sur, Bukidnon, Negros Occidental, Palawan, and Tarlac remained largely unaffected by expropriation at the time of this writing. It was only recently that the landholdings of the Benedictos and Floirendos were being placed under expropriation, but under the "regular" process — i.e., these were not treated as Marcos crony–owned landholdings which could have been quickly expropriated without compensation.
65 For a scholarly analysis of the post-1986 work of PRRM, refer to Clarke (1998).
66 Interview with Morales, Quezon City, 2002. Additional information and insights were gathered by the author as a "participant-observer," having been one of Morales's policy advisers in the period 1988–2000.
67 The groups that called for the ouster of Morales primarily came from the ranks of the broad social-democratic and other independent political groups, such as BISIG. The reasons for their strained relationship with the Morales leadership are contested: Some perceived the groups as believing that Estrada and Morales were not serious about implementing land reform, while others thought their attitude toward the Morales DAR was in fact subsumed by their broader and deeper anti-Estrada stance. In an interview with the author, Morales said that he felt that he

was being regarded and treated unfairly by some of these groups, lamenting that these same groups blamed him for lost cases that he had nothing to do with, such as the Mapalad and Hacienda Looc cases, since these were decided during the tenure of the past administration. In the same interview with the author, he also lamented that he was accused of carrying out the special land reform deal in the Danding Cojuangco orchard in Negros Occidental, when in fact the VLT-based distribution was also made during the past administration. For an analysis of how the complex political turmoil that started to unfold in 2000 affected rural social movements and their struggle for land reform, refer to Franco (2004) and Franco and Borras (2005); refer also to Pacuribot and Gatmaytan (2000) and KMP (2000). For helpful comparisons of the reformist tendencies between the different DAR leaderships (from 1988 to 2002), interviews with several key actors in the autonomous rural social movement groups are useful: Ranier Almazan of PAKISAMA, Soc Banzuela of PARFUND (Philippine Agrarian Reform Fund), *Ka* Vic Fabe and *Ka* Aning Loza of PAKISAMA, Joey Faustino of COIR, Salvador Feranil of PhilNET-RDI, Egad Ligon and Reggie Guillen, formerly of PAKISAMA, who have been with the PBSP Batangas land reform project since 2002, Armando Jarilla of Task Force Mapalad, Eddie Lopez of KMBP, Dodo Macasaet of PASCRES (People's Alternative Center for Research and Education in Social Development), *Ka* Vangie Mendoza of UNORKA, Atty Magis Mendoza of KAISAHAN, focus group discussions with the Mindanao Farmworkers' Development Center or MFDC, Abelardo Nayal of KABAKAS, *Ka* Vic Ojano of KASAMA-KA, Edwin Pancho of the German-funded Bondoc Development Program (BDP), Basilio Propongo of NOFFA (Negros Occidental Federation of Farmers' and Farmworkers' Associations), Fr. Rodrigo Anoran of NCPERD (Negros Center for People's Empowerment and Rural Development), and Manuel Quiambao of PEACE, among others.

68 For an analysis of the controversial issue of Estrada and "Cojuangco as godfather of land reform," refer to Borras (2000). Interviews with UNORKA leaders informed this study about the particular land cases for which Estrada lobbied the DAR to approve land use conversions; most of these landholdings were in Cavite and Tagaytay City in Southern Tagalog.

69 For empirical analyses of the nature and character of the remaining lands slated for reform after Morales came to office, refer to Borras (2000) and Morales (1999).

70 When Danilo Lara died, another Caviteño, former Kawit mayor Poblete, a close ally of Juanito Remulla, took over the position. For an excellent analysis of the Cavite politics relevant to land reform and within the context of "local bossism," refer to Sidel (1999) and Lacaba (1995); see also Bankoff (1996).

71 See, e.g., Franco (2004) and Franco and Borras (2005).

72 For empirical analysis in this regard, refer to Borras (2000).

73 For an excellent analysis of this "people's power" with reference to land reform, see Franco (2004). Reyes (2001) provides a good background.

74 Luis Lorenzo Jr. is from the Lorenzo conglomerate in Davao, one of the biggest banana plantation owners (see Gutierrez and Borras, 2004, for a general

historical background). Their family was extremely well connected politically and economically; most of their plantations were eventually exempted from expropriation for dubious reasons. He himself has called for a stop to CARP implementation (see *Philippine Daily Inquirer*, 26–27 March 2001).
75 Perhaps an exception would be Undersecretary for PPLAO Gil de los Reyes, who demonstrated himself as the only Braganza top official to have some affinity with militant rural social mobilizations and understanding of the political dimension of the land reform process. He was even among those endorsed by some NGOs and peasant organizations to replace Braganza.
76 Refer to UNORKA (2001a, 2001b, 2002, 2000a) and to the detailed analysis in Franco and Borras (2005). At one point in August 2001, some 500 UNORKA peasants were frustrated to have travelled to Manila to discover that Braganza would not honour his promise of an audience with the peasants, who had come from a number of different provinces. The peasants padlocked the Office of the Secretary in protest against the absentee secretary, and refused to leave the fourth-floor lobby of the central DAR office for two nights and three days. In another case, in Davao, UNORKA peasants padlocked the main gate of the regional DAR office in protest against the slow decision process in their land cases. DAR security guards shot at the padlock, indirectly hitting a number of peasant protestors. These kinds of scenes were never witnessed during the Garilao period.
77 *Philippine Daily Inquirer*-GMA online interview with President Macapagal-Arroyo, 6 March 2002, posted at: www.inq7.net/exclusive/2002/mar/06/Macapagal-Arroyo_03-6-2.htm, accessed 5 May 2002.
78 See also Manasan and Mercado (2001).
79 Philippine state–society interaction in far broader contexts, that is, beyond the question of redistributive land reform, is an important context for the discussion in this book. For this purpose, Abinales and Amoroso (2005) offer highly accessible scholarly presentation and examination of this interaction from an historical perspective.
80 One must take into consideration the financial hardships that land claim–makers tend to suffer during the course of their struggle for land. As explained by Anne Lanfer (2006) in her study of the impact of land reform on peasant households in Bondoc peninsula, usually the livelihoods of land claim–makers are dislocated when landlords resist land redistribution, thereby prolonging the process of reform and throwing peasants livelihoods into a state of great uncertainty and precariousness.
81 Discussions and interview with Ernesto Garilao.
82 Refer to PARRDS (1997).
83 Interview with Manuel Quiambao.
84 Interviews with Ernesto Garilao, Gerry Bulatao, Hector Soliman, and other DAR regional directors.
85 DAR-TFFT (2000) is the terminal report of the Task Force Fast-Track. The document includes the most detailed profile of the cases confronted by the task force.

86 For critical empirical studies of ARCs, refer to the three important works by Franco (1999c for an analysis of the so-called top ARCs; 1998a for an analysis of weak ARCs using thirty-five case studies nationwide; and 2000 for an analysis of the relationship between ARCs and rural democratization). Other relevant studies are Quitoriano (2001, 1998) and Santoalla, Parreño and Quitoriano (2001).
87 The first two studies were commissioned by the FAO, the third by UNDP; see also Meliczek (1999).
88 *Philippine Daily Inquirer*, 26–27 March 2001.
89 Refer to World Bank (1997b, 1997a, and 1996); see also Borras (2005).
90 For a background on the World Bank–supported infrastructure project referred to here, see Fox and Gershman (2000).
91 The feasibility study started in October 2000 (World Bank, 2000a: 3) with funding of US$ 398,000 (from a letter from Assistant Secretary Toinette Raquiza to DAR Secretary Horacio Morales Jr. dated 27 February 2001). This is different from — although broadly related to — the DENR project on land management and administration with its US$ 5.4 million funding from the World Bank and the Australian Agency for International Development (World Bank, 2000b).
92 The argument in this book has greatly benefited, albeit in varying degrees and contexts, from Tendler's "good government" argument (1997); Evans's "state–society synergy" (1995, 1997); Migdal's and Migdal and his colleagues' "state-in-society" concept (Migdal, 1988, 2001; Migdal, Kohli and Shue, 1994); Wang's (1999) "mutual empowerment of state and society," Wang's (1997) "mutual empowerment of state and peasantry"; Heller's (2000) notion of mutually reinforcing "redistributive conflict," Ackerman's (2004) "co-governance for accountability," "the politics of inclusion" by Houtzager and Moore (2003), Hohn Harriss's related discussion on "social capital" (2002), as well as Ron Herring's (1983) state–society discussion in the context of land reforms in South Asia.

CONCLUSION

1 See also FIAN-Via Campesina (2003), Monsalve (2003), Paasch (2003), Desmarais (2003, 2001), Baranyi, Deere and Morales (2004), McMichael (2006a, 2006b), and Borras (2004).

LIST OF ABBREVIATIONS

A&D	alienable and disposable (lands)
ADB	Asian Development Bank
ADMP	Ancestral Domains/Land Claims Program
AFRIM	Alternate Forum for Research in Mindanao
AGAPE	Advocates for Genuine Alternative for People's Empowerment
AJF	Agrarian Justice Fund
ALDA	Active Leadership for the Development of AgriWorkers
AMA	*Aniban ng Manggagawa sa Agrikultura* (Unity of Agricultural Workers)
AMGL	*Alyansa ng Magsasaka sa Gitnang Luson* (Alliance of Central Luzon Farmers)
AMIC	Audit Management and Investigation Committee
AMIHAN*	National Federation of Rural Women's Organizations
AO	administrative order
ARC	Agrarian Reform Community
ARMM	Autonomous Region of Muslim Mindanao
AR Now!	Agrarian Reform Now!
ARPT	Agrarian Reform Program Technician
ASEAN	Association of Southeast Asian Nations
BARC	*Barangay* Agrarian Reform Committee
BDP	Bondoc Development Program
BISIG	*Bukluran sa Ikauunlad ng Sosyalismo sa Isip at Gawa* (Unity for the Advancement of Socialism in Theory and Practice)
BUKLOD	*Bukluran ng Malayang Magbubukid* (Council of Free Farmers)

---

* This is not, strictly speaking, an acronym, but the name is always given in all capital letters.

BUTIL	*Bukluran ng mga Tagapaglikha ng Butil* (Federation of Grain Producers)
CA	compulsory acquisition
CADC	Certificate of Ancestral Domain Claim
CAFGU	Citizens Armed Force Geographic Units
CALABARZON	Cavite, Laguna, Batangas, Rizal, Quezon
CAR	Cordillera Autonomous Region
CARET	Center for Agrarian Reform, Empowerment, and Transformation
CARL	Comprehensive Agrarian Reform Law
CARP	Comprehensive Agrarian Reform Program
CBFM	Community-Based Forest Management
CFP	Community Forestry Program
CIIF	Coconut Industry Investment Fund
CLOA	Certificate of Land Ownership Award
CLT	certificate of land transfer
CMARP	Philippines Community-Managed Agrarian Reform Program
CMARPRP	Community-Managed Agrarian Reform and Poverty Reduction Program
COIR	Coconut Industry Reform Movement
CPAR	Congress for a People's Agrarian Reform
CPP	Communist Party of the Philippines
CREP	Coastal Environment Program
CSC	Certificate of Stewardship Contract
DA	Department of Agriculture
DAPCO	Davao Abaca Plantation Corporation
DAPECOL	Davao Penal Colony
DAR	Department of Agrarian Reform
DARAB	Department of Agrarian Reform Adjudication Board
DARBCI	Dole Agrarian Reform Beneficiaries Cooperative Incorporated
DAREA	Department of Agrarian Reform Employees' Association
DENR	Department of Environment and Natural Resources
DKMP	*Demokratikong Kilusang Magbubukid ng Pilipinas* (Democratic Peasant Movement of the Philippines)
DOJ	Department of Justice
EP	emancipation patent
FFF	Federation of Free Farmers
FGD	focus group discussion
FIAN	FoodFirst Information and Action Network
FLMP	Forest Land Management Program
GAA	General Appropriations Act
GFI	government financial institution
GOL	government-owned lands

HLI	Hacienda Luisita, Inc.
HMB	*Hukbong Mapagpalaya ng Bayan* (People's Liberation Army)
HPI	Hijo Plantation, Inc.
ICARRD	International Conference on Agrarian Reform and Rural Development
ICCO	Inter-Church Organization for Development and Cooperation
IPRA	Indigenous Peoples' Rights Act
ISFP	Integrated Social Forestry Program
ISI	Import-Substitution Industrialization
KAISAHAN*	*Kaisahan Tungo sa Kaunlaran ng Kanayunan at Repormang Pansakahan* (Unity towards the Development of the Countryside and Agrarian Reform)
KAMAHARI	*Katipunan ng mga Magbubukid sa Hacienda Roxas, Inc.* (Council of Peasants in Hacienda Roxas)
KAMMPIL	*Kalipunan ng Maliliit na Magniniyog sa Pilipinas* (Federation of Small Coconut Farmers and Farmworkers' Organizations)
KASAMA-KA	*Kalipunan ng mga Samahaang Magsasaka sa Kanayunan* (Federation of People's Organizations in the Countryside)
KASAMA-TK	*Katipunan ng mga Samahang Magbubukid sa Timog Katagalugan* (Council of Peasant Organizations in Southern Tagalog)
KFI	The Kasangyahan Foundation, Inc.
KKK	*Kilusang Kabuhayan at Kaunlaran*
KMBP	*Kilusang Magbubukid ng Bondoc Peninsula* (Peasant Movement of Bondoc Peninsula)
KMP	*Kilusang Magbubukid ng Pilipinas* (Peasant Movement of the Philippines)
KPD	*Kilusan para sa Pambansang Demokrasya* (Movement for National Democracy)
LAMP	Land Administration and Management Program
LBP	Land Bank of the Philippines
LIUCP	Low Income Upland Development Program
LnM	*Laban ng Masa* (Struggle of the Masses).
LRAN	Land Research and Action Network
LUCF	land use conversion filed
MAKISAKA	*Malayang Kaisahan ng mga Samahang Magbubukid sa Nueva Ecija* (Movement of Free Peasant Associations)
MARO	Municipal Agrarian Reform Officer
MFDC	Mindanao Farmworkers' Development Center
MFDF	Mindanao Farmworkers Development Foundation
MLAR	market-led agrarian reform
MMCSL	*Malayang Magbubukid sa Candaba at San Luis* (Free Farmers of Candaba and San Luis)

MNC	multinational corporation
MODE	Management and Organizational Development for Empowerment
MORE-AR	Movement to Oppose More Exemptions from Agrarian Reform
MOU	memorandum of understanding
MPD	Movement for Popular Democracy (PopDem)
MuCARRD	Municipal Consultation/Campaign for Agrarian Reform and Rural Development
NAMASTAN	*Nagkakaisang Manggagawa ng Stanfilco* (United Workers of Stanfilco)
NARBMCI	Nagasi Agrarian Reform Beneficiaries Multi-Purpose Cooperative, Inc.
NAPC	National Anti-Poverty Commission
NCIP	National Commission for the Indigenous Peoples
NCPERD	Negros Center for People's Empowerment and Rural Development
ND	National-Democrat, "Nat-Dem"
NDC	National Development Corporation
NDF	National Democratic Front
NEPAD	Nueva Ecija People's Assistance for Development
NFA	National Food Authority
NFSW	National Federation of Sugar Workers
NGO	nongovernmental organization
NMGL	*Nagkakaisang Magsasaka sa Gitnang Luson* (United Farmers in Central Luzon)
NOFFA	Negros Occidental Federation of Farmers' and Farmworkers' Associations
NPA	New People's Army
NPS-CPP	National Peasant Secretariat of the Communist Party of the Philippines
OLH	Operation Leasehold
OLT	Operation Land Transfer
OP	Office of the President
OSG	Office of the Solicitor General
PACOFA	Paulog Coconut Farmers' Association
PAGC	Presidential Anti-Graft Commission
PAKISAMA	*Pambansang Katipunan ng mga Samahang Magsasaka* (National Movement of Farmers' Associations)
PAMALAKAYA	*Pambansang Pederasyon ng Maliliit na Mamamalakaya ng Pilipinas* (National Federation of Subsistence Fisherfolk of the Philippines)
PARAD	Provincial Agrarian Reform Adjudicator

PARC	Presidential Agrarian Reform Council
PARCode	People's Agrarian Reform Code
PARCCOM	Provincial Agrarian Reform Consultative Committee
PARFUND	Philippine Agrarian Reform Fund
PARO	Provincial Agrarian Reform Officer
PARRDS	Partnership for Agrarian Reform and Rural Development Services
PASCRES	People's Alternative Center for Research and Education in Social Development
PBSP	Philippine Business for Social Progress
PCA	Philippine Coconut Authority
PCGG	Presidential Commission on Good Government
PD 27	Presidential Decree No. 27
PDI	Project Development Institute
PEACE	Philippine Ecumenical Action for Community Empowerment
PhilDDHRA	Philippine Partnership for the Development of Human Resources in Rural Areas
PhilNET-RDI	Philippine Network of Rural Development Institutes
PKM	*Pambansang Katipunan ng Magbubukid* (National Council of Peasants)
PKMM	*Pambansang Katipunan ng Makabayang Magbubukid* (National Federation of Nationalist Peasants)
PKP	*Partido Komunista ng Pilipinas*
PKSK	*Pambansang Kilusan ng mga Samahan sa Kanayunan* (National Federation of Organizations in the Countryside)
PPI	Philippine Peasant Institute
PPLAO	Policy Planning and Legal Affairs Office
PPS	production and profit sharing
ProCARRD	Provincial Consultation/Campaign for Agrarian Reform and Rural Development
PRRM	Philippine Rural Reconstruction Movement
RARAD	Regional Agrarian Reform Adjudicator
Region 1	Ilocos
Region 2	Cagayan Valley
Region 3	Central Luzon
Region 4	Southern Tagalog
Region 5	Bicol
Region 6	Western Visayas
Region 7	Central Visayas
Region 8	Eastern Visayas
Region 9	Southwestern Mindanao
Region 10	Northern Mindanao

Region 11	Southern Mindanao
Region 12	Central Mindanao
Region 13	Northeastern Mindanao
ROD	Registry of Deeds
RRMP	Regional Resources Management Program
SAC	Special Agrarian Court
SAMALA	*Samahan ng Malayang Magsasaka sa Lupaing Aquino* (Association of Free Peasants of the Aquino Estate)
SCS	Special Concerns Staff
SDO	stock distribution option
SEARBAI	Stanfilco Employees and Agrarian Reform Beneficiaries Association, Inc.
SEC	Securities and Exchange Commission
SENTRA	*Sentro para sa Tunay na Repormang Agraryo* (Center for Genuine Agrarian Reform)
SFAN	Small Farmers' Association of Negros
SMBSAI	*Samahan ng mga Magsasakang Benepisyaryo ng Superior Agro Inc.* (Association of Peasant Beneficiaries in Superior Agro, Inc.)
TADECO	Tagum Agricultural Development Corporation
TF-24	Task Force 24
TFM	Task Force Mapalad
TMI	*Tinig ng Magsasaka sa Imok*
TriPARRD	Tripartite Partnership for Agrarian Reform and Rural Development
UFEARBAI	United Floirendo Employees Agrarian Reform Beneficiaries Association, Inc.
UNORKA	*Pambansang Ugnayan ng Nagsasariling Lokal na mga Samahang Mamamayan sa Kanayunan* (National Coordination of Autonomous Local Rural People's Organizations)
USAID	US Agency for International Development
VLT	voluntary land transfer
VOS	voluntary offer-to-sell

REFERENCES

A. BOOKS, JOURNAL ARTICLES, CONFERENCE PAPERS AND OTHER DOCUMENTS

Abinales, Patricio (2001) *Fellow Traveler: Essays on Filipino Communism.* Quezon City: University of the Philippines Press.

———— (2000) *Making Mindanao: Cotabato and Davao in the Formation of the Philippine Nation-State.* Quezon City: Ateneo de Manila University Press.

Abinales, Patricio and Donna Amoroso (2005) *State and Society in the Philippines.* Manila: Anvil.

Adams, Martin and John Howell (2001) "Redistributive Land Reform in Southern Africa," *National Resource Perspectives,* (64): 1–6. London: ODI.

ADB (2005) *Poverty in the Philippines: Income, Assets and Access.* Manila: Asian Development Bank.

Adnan, Shapan (2007) "Departures from Everyday Resistance and Flexible Strategies of Domination: The Making and Unmaking of a Poor Peasant Mobilization in Bangladesh," *Journal of Agrarian Change,* 7(2): 183–224.

Adriano, Lourdes (1992) "A Critique of Agrarian Reform under the Aquino Administration." Quezon City: KAISAHAN. Unpublished mimeo.

Agarwal, Arun (2005) *Environmentality: Technologies of Government and the Making of Subjects.* Durham, NC: Duke University Press.

Agarwal, Bina (2003) "Gender and Land Rights Revisited: Exploring New Prospects via the State, Family and Market," *Journal of Agrarian Change,* 3(1/2): 184–224.

———— (1994) *A Field of One's Own: Gender and Land Rights in South Asia.* Cambridge, UK: Cambridge University Press.

Agoncillo, Teodoro (1965) *The Revolt of the Masses* (2002 ed.). Quezon City: University of the Philippines.

Aguilar, Filomeno, Jr. (1998) *Clash of Spirits: The History of Power and Sugar Planter Hegemony on a Visayan Island.* Honolulu: University of Hawaii Press.

—— (1994) "Sugar Planter-State Relations and Labour Processes in Colonial Philippine *Haciendas*," *Journal of Peasant Studies*, 22(1): 50–80.

Akram-Lodhi, Haroon (2007) "Land Markets and Rural Livelihoods in Vietnam," in H. Akram-Lodhi, S. Borras and C. Kay (eds.) *Land, Poverty and Livelihoods in an Era of Neoliberal Globalization: Perspectives from Developing and Transition Countries*. London: Routledge.

—— (2005) "Vietnam's Agriculture: Processes of Rich Peasant Accumulation and Mechanisms of Social Differentiation," *Journal of Agrarian Change*, 5(1): 73–116.

—— (2004) "Are Landlords Taking Back the Land: An Essay on the Agrarian Transition of Vietnam," *European Journal of Development Research*, 16(2): 757–789.

Akram-Lodhi, Haroon, Saturnino M. Borras Jr. and Cristóbal Kay (eds.) (2007) *Land, Poverty and Livelihoods in an Era of Neoliberal Globalization: Perspectives from Developing and Transition Countries*. London: Routledge.

Alano, Lisa and Rommel Hipolito (1999) "The Situation of Small Banana Growers of Stanfilco in Davao and Compostela Valley Provinces," *Mindanao Focus Journal* 1999(4): 3–38. Davao: Alternate Forum for Research in Mindanao.

Alavi, Hamza (1973) "Peasant Classes and Primordial Loyalties," *Journal of Peasant Studies*, 1(1): 43–59.

Anderson, Benedict (1988) "Cacique Democracy in the Philippines: Origins and Dreams," *New Left Review*, (169): 3–29.

Andrews, Mercia (2006) "Struggling for a Life in Dignity," in L. Ntsebeza and R. Hall (eds.) *The Land Question in South Africa: The Challenge of Transformation and Redistribution*. Cape Town: HSRC Press.

Ang, Suzanne (2001) "Agrarian Reform Implementation in the Banana Industry," *Bantaaw*, 14(2/3): 1–12. Davao: Alternate Forum for Research in Mindanao.

Angeles, Leonora (1999) "The Political Dimension in the Agrarian Question: Strategies of Resilience and Political Entrepreneurship of Agrarian Elite Families in a Philippine Province," *Rural Sociology*, 64(4): 667–692.

Apthorpe, Raymond (1979) "The Burden of Land Reform in Taiwan: An Asian Model Land Reform Re-Analysed," *World Development*, 7(4–5): 513–530.

Arias, Mabel (2004) "Scope and Status Validation of the Philippine Comprehensive Agrarian Reform Program: Case Study for Batangas Province." Unpublished draft research paper, Davao: Alternative Forum for Research in Mindanao (AFRIM).

—— (1998) "The Legal Rationale for an Agricultural Tenant's Non-Culpability for Estafa in Instances of Default in the Payment of Lease Rental or Delivery of the Landlord's Share." *KAISAHAN Occasional Papers* (July 1998). Quezon City: KAISAHAN.

ASEAN (2004) *Statistical Yearbook, 2004*. Jakarta: ASEAN.

Assies, Willen, Gemma van der Haar and A.J. Hoekma (1998) *The Challenge of Diversity: Indigenous Peoples and Reform of the State in Latin America*. Amsterdam: CEDLA.

Atkins, Fiona (1988) "Land Reform: A Failure of Neoclassical Theorization?," *World Development*, 16(8): 935–946.

Bachriadi, Dianto and Noer Fauzi (2006) "The Resurgence of Agrarian Movements in Indonesia: Scholar-Activists, Popular Education and Peasant Mobilization." Paper presented at the International Conference on Land, Poverty and Development at the Institute of Social Studies (ISS), The Hague, Netherlands, 9-14 January 2006.

Bacuñgan, Froilan and Associates and DAR (2000) *Agrarian Law and Jurisprudence.* Quezon City: Department of Agrarian Reform (DAR)/United Nations Development Programme (UNDP).

Bak, Janos (ed.) (1975) "The German Peasant War of 1525," *Journal of Peasant Studies,* 3(1): 1-135.

Balisacan, Arsenio (1999) "What Do We Really Know — or Don't Know — about Economic Inequality and Poverty in the Philippines?," in A. Balisacan and S. Fujisaki (eds.) *Causes of Poverty: Myths, Facts and Policies: A Philippine Study,* pp. 1-50. Quezon City: University of the Philippines Press.

Balisacan, Arsenio and Hall Hill (2003) "An Introduction to the Key Issues," in A. Balisacan and H. Hill (eds.) *The Philippine Economy: Development, Policies, and Challenges,* pp. 3-44. Quezon City: Ateneo de Manila University Press.

Banerjee, Abhijit (1999) "Land Reforms: Prospects and Strategies." A Paper prepared for the Annual Bank Conference on Development Economics, Washington, DC.

Banerjee, Abhijit, Paul Gertler and Maitreesh Ghatak (2002) "Empowerment and Efficiency: Tenancy Reform in West Bengal," *Journal of Political Economy,* 110(2): 239-280.

Bankoff, Gregg (1996) "Legacy of the Past, Promise of the Future: Land Reform, Land Grabbing, and Land Conversion in Calabarzon," *Bulletin of Concerned Asian Scholars,* 28(1): 39-51.

Banzon-Bautista, Cynthia (1989) "The Saudi Connection: Agrarian Change in a Pampanga Village, 1977-1984," in G. Hart, A. Turton and B. White (eds.) *Agrarian Transformations: Local Processes and the State in Southeast Asia,* pp. 144-158. Berkeley: University of California Press.

―――― (1984) "Marxism and the Peasantry: The Philippine Case," in *Marxism in the Philippines: Marx Centennial Lectures,* pp. 155-188. Quezon City: Third World Studies Center, University of the Philippines.

Baranyi, Stephen, Carmen Diana Deere and Manuel Morales (2004) *Scoping Study on Land Policy Research in Latin America.* Ottawa: The North-South Institute/ International Development Research Centre (IDRC).

Barraclough, Solon (2001) "The Role of the State and Other Actors in Land Reform," in K. Ghimire (ed.) *Land Reform and Peasant Livelihoods: The Social Dynamics of Rural Poverty and Agrarian Reform in Developing Countries,* pp. 26-64. Geneva: URISD/ London: ITDG.

Barraclough, Solon (ed.) (1973) *Agrarian Structure in Latin America: A Resume of the CIDA Land Tenure Studies of Argentina, Brazil, Chile, Colombia, Ecuador, Guatemala, Peru.* Lexington, MA: Lexington Books.

Barros, Flavia, Sergio Sauer and Stephan Schwartzman (eds.) (2003) *The Negative Impacts of World Bank Market-Based Land Reform.* Brazil: Comissao Pastoral da Terra,

Movimento dos Trabalhadores Rurais Sem Terra (MST), FoodFirst Information and Action Network (FIAN).

Baruah, Sanjib (1990) "The End of the Road in Land Reform? Limits to Redistribution in West Bengal," *Development and Change*, 21(1): 119-146.

Baumeister, Eduardo (2000) "Institutional Change and Responses at the Grassroots Level: Examples from Nicaragua, Honduras and El Salvador," in A. Zoomers and G.v.d. Haar (eds.) *Current Land Policy in Latin America: Regulating Land Tenure Under Neo-Liberalism*, pp. 249-268. Amsterdam: Royal Tropical Institute (KIT).

Bell, Clive (1974) "Ideology and Economic Interests in Indian Land Reform," in D. Lehmann (ed.) *Peasants, Landlords and Governments: Agrarian Reform in the Third World*, pp. 190-220. New York: Holmes and Meier Publishers.

Bellisario, Antonio (2007a) "The Chilean Agrarian Transformation: Agrarian Reform and Capitalist 'Partial' Counter-Agrarian Reform, 1964-1980. Part 2: CORA, Post-1980 Outcomes and the Emerging Agrarian Class Structure," *Journal of Agrarian Change*, 7(2): 145-182.

―――― (2007b) "The Chilean Agrarian Transformation: Agrarian Reform and Capitalist 'Partial' Counter-Agrarian Reform, 1964-1980. Part 1: Reformism, Socialism, and Free-Market Neo-liberalism," *Journal of Agrarian Change*, 7(1): 1-34.

―――― (2006) "The Chilean Agrarian Transformation: The Pre-Agrarian Reform Period (1955-1965)," *Journal of Agrarian Change*, 6(2): 167-204.

Bello, Rolando, Ma. Angeles Catelo, Corazon Rapera, Sining Cuevas and Alvin Paul Dirain (1998) *Study on the Impact of CARP on the Preservation of Ancestral Lands and Welfare of Indigenous Communities – Final Report*. Los Baños: College of Economics and Management, University of the Philippines at Los Baños, and UNDP-DAR SARDIC Programme. Unpublished document.

Bello, Walden (2001) *The Future in the Balance: Essays on Globalization and Resistance*. Quezon City: University of the Philippines Press.

―――― (1996) "Neither Market Nor State: The Development Debate in Southeast Asia," *The Ecologist*, 26(4): 167-175.

Bello, Walden, Herbert Docena, Marissa de Guzman and Marylou Malig (2004) *The Anti-Development State: The Political Economy of Permanent Crisis in the Philippines*. Quezon City: University of the Philippines Press.

Bello, Walden with Marissa de Guzman (2001) "Why Land Reform Is No Longer Possible without Revolution," in W. Bello, *The Future in the Balance: Essays on Globalization and Resistance*, pp. 192-199. Quezon City: University of the Philippines Press.

Bello, Walden and John Gershman (1992) "Democratization and Stabilization in the Philippines," *Critical Sociology*, 17(1): 34-56.

Bello, Walden, David Kinley and Elaine Elinson (1982) *Development Debacle: The World Bank in the Philippines*. San Francisco: Institute for Food and Development Policy.

Bernstein, Henry (2006) "Once Were/Still Are Peasants? Farming in a Globalising 'South,' " *New Political Economy*, 11(3): 399-406.

—— (2004) "Changing before Our Very Eyes: Agrarian Questions and the Politics of Land in Capitalism Today," *Journal of Agrarian Change*, 4(1/2): 190–225.

—— (2003) "Land Reform in Southern Africa in World-Historical Perspective," *Review of African Political Economy*, 96: 21–46

—— (2002) "Land Reform: Taking a Long(er) View," *Journal of Agrarian Change*, 2(4): 433–463.

—— (1998) "Social Change in the South African Countryside? Land and Production, Poverty and Power," *Journal of Peasant Studies*, 25(4): 1–32.

Berry, Sara (2002) "Debating the Land Question in Africa," *Comparative Study in Society and History*, 44(4): 638–668.

Bhandari, Ravi (2006) "Searching for a Weapon of Mass Production in Nepal: Can Market-Assisted Land Reforms Live Up to Their Promise?," *Journal of Developing Societies*, 22(2): 111–143.

Billig, Michael (2003) *Barons, Brokers, and Buyers: The Institutions and Cultures of Philippine Sugar*. Quezon City: Ateneo de Manila University Press.

—— (1993) "Syrup in the Wheels of Progress?: The Inefficient Organization of the Philippine Sugar Industry," *Journal of Southeast Asian Studies*, 24(1): 122–147.

Binswanger, Hans (1996a) "The Political Implications of Alternative Models of Land Reform and Compensation," in J.v. Zyl, J. Kirsten and H.P. Binswanger (eds.) *Agricultural Land Reform in South Africa: Policies, Markets and Mechanisms*, pp. 139–146. Oxford, UK: Oxford University Press.

—— (1996b) "Rural Development and Poverty Reduction," in J.v. Zyl, J. Kirsten and H.P. Binswanger (eds.) *Agricultural Land Reform in South Africa: Policies, Markets and Mechanisms*, pp. 147–160. Oxford, UK: Oxford University Press.

Binswanger, Hans and Klaus Deininger (1997) "Explaining Agricultural and Agrarian Policies in Developing Countries." A paper presented at the FAO Technical Consultation of Decentralization and Rural Development, Rome, 16–18 Dec. 1997.

—— (1996) "South African Land Policy: The Legacy of History and Current Options," in J. v. Zyl, J. Kirsten and H.P. Binswanger (eds.) *Agricultural Land Reform in South Africa: Policies, Markets and Mechanisms*, pp. 64–104. Oxford, UK: Oxford University Press.

Blair, Harry (2000) "Participation and Accountability at the Periphery: Democratic Local Governance in Six Countries," *World Development*, 28(1): 21–39.

Bobrow-Strain, Aaron (2004) "(Dis)Accords: The Politics of Market-Assisted Land Reforms in Chiapas, Mexico," *World Development*, 32(6): 887–903.

Boone, Catherine (1998) "State-Building in the African Countryside: Structure and Politics at the Grassroots," *Journal of Development Studies*, 34(4): 1–31.

Borras, Saturnino, Jr. (2007) " 'Free Market,' Export-Led Development Strategy and Its Impact on Rural Livelihoods, Poverty and Inequality: The Philippine Experience Seen from a Southeast Asian Perspective," *Review of International Political Economy*, 14(1): 143–175.

―― (2006a) "The Philippine Land Reform in Comparative Perspective: Conceptual and Methodological Implications," *Journal of Agrarian Change*, 6(1): 69–101.

―― (2006b) "Redistributive Land Reform in Public (Forest) Lands? Rethinking Theory and Practice with Evidence from the Philippines," *Progress in Development Studies*, 6(2): 123–145.

―― (2005) "Can Redistributive Reform Be Achieved via Market-Based Land Transfer Schemes? Lessons and Evidence from the Philippines," *Journal of Development Studies*, 41(1): 90–134.

―― (2004) "*La Via Campesina*: An Evolving Transnational Social Movement." *TNI Briefing Paper Series* 2004/6, 30pp. Amsterdam: Transnational Institute; PDF available online at: www.tni.org.

―― (2003a) "Questioning Market-Led Agrarian Reform: Experiences from Brazil, Colombia and South Africa," *Journal of Agrarian Change*, 3(3): 367–394.

―― (2003b) "Inclusion-Exclusion in Public Policies and Policy Analyses: The Case of Philippine Land Reform, 1972-2002," *Journal of International Development*, 15(8): 1049–1065.

―― (2003c) "Questioning the Pro-Market Critique of State-Led Agrarian Reform," *European Journal of Development Research*, 15(2): 105–128.

―― (2002a) "Problems and Prospects of Redistributive Land Reform in Mindanao, 1972–2002," *Mindanao Focus Journal*, 2002(1): 1–45. Davao: Alternate Forum for Research in Mindanao (AFRIM).

―― (2002b) "Towards a Better Understanding of the Market-Led Agrarian Reform in Theory and Practice: Focusing on the Brazilian Case," *Land Reform, Land Settlement and Cooperatives*, 1: 32–51.

―― (2001) "State-Society Relations in Land Reform Implementation in the Philippines," *Development and Change*, 32(3): 545–575.

―― (2000) "CARP in Its 12th Year: A Closer Examination of the Agrarian Reform Performance," *IPD Political Brief*, 8(6): 1–35. Quezon City: Institute for Popular Democracy.

―― (1999) *The Bibingka Strategy in Land Reform Implementation: Autonomous Peasant Movements and State Reformists in the Philippines*. Quezon City: Institute for Popular Democracy.

Borras, Saturnino, Jr., Danilo Carranza and Ricardo Reyes (2007) "Land Reform, Poverty Reduction and State-Society Interaction in the Philippines," in H. Akram-Lodhi, S. Borras and C. Kay (eds.) *Land, Poverty and Livelihoods in an Era of Neoliberal Globalization: Perspectives from Developing and Transition Countries*. London: Routledge.

Borras, Saturnino and Jennifer Franco (2006) "The National Land Reform Campaign in the Philippines." Paper prepared for the Citizens' Participation in National Policy Processes Project of the Institute of Development Studies (IDS), Sussex, and the Ford Foundation.

―― (2005) "Struggles for Land and Livelihood: Redistributive Reform in Philippine Agribusiness Plantations," *Critical Asian Studies*, 37(3): 331–361.

Borras, Saturnino, Jr., Cristóbal Kay and Haroon Akram Lodhi (2007) "Agrarian Reform and Rural Development: Historical Overview and Current Issues," in. H. Akram-Lodhi, S. Borras and C. Kay (eds.), *Land, Poverty and Livelihoods: Perspectives from Developing and Transition Countries.* London: Routledge.

Borras, Saturnino Jr., Cristobal Kay and Edward Lahiff, eds. (forthcoming) "Market-Led Agrarian Reform: Critical Reflections," *Third World Quarterly,* special issue (December 2007).

Borras, Saturnino and Terry McKinley (2006) "The Unresolved Land Reform Debate: Beyond the State-Led and Market-Led Models." *IPC Policy Brief* No. 2. Brasilia: UNDP International Poverty Centre; available online at: www.undp-poverty centre.org.

Borras, Saturnino, Jr. and Eric Ross (2007) "Land Rights, Conflict and Violence amid Neo-liberal Globalization," *Peace Review,* 19(1): 1–5.

Boudreau, Vincent (2001) *Grass Roots and Cadre in the Protest Movement.* Quezon City: Ateneo de Manila University Press.

Boyce, James (1993) *The Political Economy of Growth and Impoverishment in the Marcos Era.* Quezon City: Ateneo de Manila University Press.

——— (1992) "Of Coconuts and Kings: The Political Economy of an Export Crop," *Development and Change,* 23(4): 1–25.

Bramall, Chris (2004) "Chinese Land Reform in Long-Run Perspective and in the Wider East Asian Context," *Journal of Agrarian Change,* 4(1/2): 107–141.

Branford, Sue and Jan Rocha (2002) *Cutting the Wire: The Story of the Landless Movement in Brazil.* London: Latin American Bureau.

Brass, Tom (2003a) "Latin American Peasants — New Paradigms for Old?," in T. Brass (ed.) *Latin American Peasants,* pp. 1–40. London: Frank Cass.

——— (2000) *Peasants, Populism and Postmodernism: The Return of the Agrarian Myth.* London: Frank Cass.

Brass, Tom (ed.) (2003b) *Latin American Peasants.* London: Frank Cass.

——— (1994) *The New Farmers' Movements in India.* London: Frank Cass.

Bratton, Michael (1990) "Ten Years after Land Redistribution in Zimbabwe, 1980–1990," in R. Prosterman, M. Temple and T. Hanstad (eds.) *Agrarian Reform and Grassroots Development: Ten Case Studies,* pp. 265–291. Boulder, CO: Lynne Rienner.

Bright, Charles and Susan Harding (1984) "An Introduction," in Bright and Harding (eds.) *Processes of Statemaking and Popular Protest: Essays in History and Theory.* Ann Arbor, MI: University of Michigan Press.

Broad, Robin (1994) "The Poor and the Environment: Friends or Foe?," *World Development,* 22(6): 811–822.

Broad, Robin and John Cavanagh (1993) *Plundering Paradise: The Struggle for the Environment in the Philippines.* Berkeley: University of California Press.

Brockett, Charles (1991) "The Structure of Political Opportunities and Peasant Mobilization in Central America," *Comparative Politics,* 23(3): 253–274.

Broegaard, Rikke (2005) "Land Tenure Insecurity and Inequality in Nicaragua," *Development and Change,* 36(5): 845–864.

Bromley, Daniel (1991) *Environment and Economy: Property Rights and Public Policy*. Oxford: Blackwell.
Bryant, Coralie (1996) "Strategic Change through Sensible Projects," *World Development*, 24(9): 1539–1550.
Bryceson, Deborah, Cristóbal Kay and Jos Mooij (eds.) (2000) *Disappearing Peasantries? Rural Labour in Africa, Asia and Latin America*. London: Intermediate Technology Publications.
Buainain, Márcio Antonio, José Maria da Silveira, Hildo Meireles Souza and Marcelo Magalhães (1999) "Community-Based Land Reform Implementation in Brazil: A New Way of Reaching Out to the Marginalized?" A paper presented at the First Annual Development Conference, Global Development Network, Bonn, Germany, 5–8 December 1999; accessed 21 June 2001 at: www.gdnet.org/bonn99/confpapers.f1ml.
Buainain, Márcio Antonio, José Maria da Silveira and Edson Teófilo (1998) "Agrarian Reform, Development and Participation: A Discussion of Necessary and Possible Transformations." Unpublished document.
Bulatao, Gerardo (1999) "Community-Based Forest Management in Cotabato: More Attention to Socio-economic Aspects, Please," in E. Garilao, H. Soliman and A. Cristobal Jr. (eds.) *Saving the Plains from the Floods: Strengthening National Government–Local Government Partnership in Community-Based Forest Management*, pp. 57–72. Makati City, Philippines: Asian Institute of Management.
Bush, Ray (ed.) (2002) *Counter Revolution in the Egyptian Countryside*. London: Zed Books.
Byres, Terence (2004a) "Introduction: Contextualizing and Interrogating the GKI Case for Redistributive Land Reform," *Journal of Agrarian Change*, 4(1/2): 1–16.
—— (2004b) "Neo-Classical Neo-Populism 25 Years On: Déjà Vu and Deja Passe: Towards a Critique," *Journal of Agrarian Change*, 4(1/2): 17–44.
—— (1995) "Political Economy, the Agrarian Question and the Comparative Method," *Journal of Peasant Studies*, 22(4): 561–580.
—— (1983) "Historical Perspectives on Sharecropping," in T.J. Byres (ed.) Sharecropping and Sharecroppers special issue, *Journal of Peasant Studies*, 10(2/3): 7–40.
—— (1974) "Land Reform, Industrialization and the Marketed Surplus in India: An Essay on the Power of Rural Bias," in D. Lehmann (ed.) *Peasants, Landlords and Governments: Agrarian Reform in the Third World*, pp. 221–261. New York: Holmes and Meier Publishers.
Cabarle, Bruce and Owen Lynch (1996) "Conflict and Community Forestry: Legal Issues and Responses." Rome: FAO. Commissioned paper in PDF format.
Canlas, Corinne (1994) "In Search of Land: Three Cases of Land Occupation in San Antonio, Mandayao and Hacienda Tison in Negros Occidental," in Reyes-Cantos (ed.) *Waging the Battle for Land Ownership (Part II): Case Studies of Peasant-Initiated Land Occupations*, pp. 35–84. Quezon City: Philippine Peasant Institute.

―――― (1992) "BUGKOS and BUFFALO: Two Stories of Peasant-Initiated Land Occupations in Bukidnon," in F. Lim (ed.) *Waging the Battle for Land Ownership: Case Studies of Peasant Initiated Land Occupations*, pp. 69–87. Quezon City: Philippine Peasant Institute.

Caouette, Dominique (2004) "Persevering Revolutionaries: Armed Struggle in the 21st Century, Exploring the Revolution of the Communist Party of the Philippines." Ph.D. dissertation, Cornell University.

Carranza, Danilo (2006) "Dilemmas, Difficulties and Challenges in Carrying out Pro-poor Property Rights Reforms in Public Lands in the Philippines," *Agrarian Notes*, PEACE Foundation; available online at: www.peace.net.ph; accessed 23 October 2006.

―――― (2005) "Hacienda Luisita Massacre: A Tragedy Waiting to Happen," *Agrarian Notes*, PEACE Foundation; available online at: www.peace.net.ph; accessed 18 May 2006.

―――― (2000) "Case Study No. 1: Barangay Cambuga, Bondoc Peninsula." Quezon City: UNDP/Institute for Popular Democracy. Unpublished document.

―――― (1994) "Failing a Reform: The Hacienda Luisita Formula." *SENTRA Monograph* 1, Series of 1992, pp. 1–35. Quezon City: SENTRA.

Carranza, Danilo and Pepito Mato (2006) "Subverting Peasants' Land Rights: The Supreme Court Decision Exempting Livestock Areas from the Coverage of Agrarian Reform," *Agrarian Notes*, (May), PEACE Foundation; available online at: www.peace.net.ph; accessed on 12 April 2007.

Carroll, John, S.J. (1983) "Agrarian Reform, Productivity and Equity: Two Studies," in A. Ledesma, S.J., P. Makil and V. Miralao (eds.) *Second View from the Paddy*, pp. 15–23. Quezon City: Institute of Philippine Culture, Ateneo de Manila University.

Carter, Michael (2000) "Old Questions and New Realities: Land in Post-liberal Economies," in A. Zoomers and G.v.d. Haar (eds.) *Current Land Policy in Latin America: Regulating Land Tenure Under Neo-liberalism*, pp. 29–44. Amsterdam: Royal Tropical Institute (KIT).

Carter, Michael and Dina Mesbah (1993) "Can Land Market Reform Mitigate the Exclusionary Aspects of Rapid Agro-Export Growth?," *World Development*, 21(7): 1085–1100.

Carter, Michael and Ramón Salgado (2001) "Land Market Liberalization and the Agrarian Question in Latin America," in A. de Janvry, G. Gordillo, J.P. Platteau and E. Sadoulet (eds.) *Access to Land, Rural Poverty, and Public Action*, pp. 246–278. Oxford: Oxford University Press.

Christodoulou, D. (1990) *The Unpromised Land: Agrarian Reform and Conflict Worldwide*. London: Zed Books.

Ciamarra, Ugo Pica (2003) "State-Led and Market-Assisted Land Reforms: History, Theory, and Insight from the Philippines." Paper prepared for the VII Spring Meeting of Young Economists, Leuven, Belgium, 3–5 April 2003.

Clarke, Gerard (1998) *The Politics of NGOs in South-East Asia: Participation and Protest in the Philippines*. London/New York: Routledge.

Collins, Joseph with Frances Moore Lappé and N. Allen (1982) *What Difference Could a Revolution Make? Food and Farming in the New Nicaragua*. San Francisco: Institute for Food and Development Policy.

Connolly, Michael, S.J. (1992) *Church Lands and Peasant Unrest in the Philippines: Agrarian Conflict in 20th Century Luzon*. Quezon City: Ateneo de Manila University Press.

Constantino, Renato (1975) *The Philippines: A Past Revisited*. Quezon City: Renato Constantino.

Constantino, Renato and Letizia R. Constantino (1978) *The Philippines: The Continuing Past*. Quezon City: The Foundation for Nationalist Studies.

Cornista, Luzviminda (1990) "The Philippine Agrarian Reform Program: Issues, Problems and Prospects." *IAST Occasional Papers Series* (30): 1–11. Los Baños: Institute of Agrarian Studies, College of Economics and Management, University of the Philippines at Los Baños.

Corpuz, O.D. (1997) *An Economic History of the Philippines*. Quezon City: University of the Philippines Press.

Corpuz, Santiago (2000) "Barangay Bagong Silang and Villa Batabat, Buenavista, Bondoc Peninsula." Quezon City: Institute for Popular Democracy (IPD)/United Nations Development Programme (UNDP) – SARDIC Programme. Unpublished document.

Cotula, Lorenzo, Camilla Toulmin and Julian Quan (2006) "Policies and Practices for Securing and Improving Access to Land." Paper presented at the International Conference on Agrarian Reform and Rural Development (ICARRD), Porto Alegre, Brazil, 6–10 March 2006; available online at: www.icarrd.org/en/icarrd_docs_issues.html; accessed 18 May 2006.

Cousins, Ben (1997) "How Do Rights Become Real? Formal and Informal Institutions in South Africa's Land Reform," *IDS Bulletin*, 28(4): 59–67.

Cousins, Ben and Aninka Claassens (2006) "More Than Simply 'Socially Embedded': Recognizing the Distinctiveness of African Land Rights." Keynote address at the international symposium At the Frontier of Land Issues: Social Embeddedness of Rights and Public Policy, Montpellier, France, 17–19 May 2006.

CPAR (1992) "Proceedings of the Congress for a People's Agrarian Reform — Inter-Federation Conference held on 5–9 October 1992 in Antipolo, Rizal." Quezon City: Congress for a People's Agrarian Reform (CPAR). Unpublished document.

——— (1990) "Assessment of the Second Year of CARP." Quezon City: CPAR. NGO pamphlet.

——— (1989) *Popular Grassroots Initiatives towards Genuine Agrarian Reform: A Descriptive Report (with Assessment of the First-Year Implementation of CARP)*. Quezon City: CPAR.

——— (1988) *A Primer on Agrarian Reform*. Quezon City: CPAR.

CPP (1993a) "Executive Committee of the Central Committee's Clarification Regarding the September Thesis of the National Peasant Secretariat (NPS), dated April 1993." Internal document, Communist Party of the Philippines.

—— (1993b) "Memorandum from the Executive Committee of the Central Committee of the CPP to the National Peasant Secretariat (NPS) Regarding the Reformist Activities of the NPS's Leadership, 18 April 1993." Internal document.

—— (1989) "Tasks of the Revolutionary Peasant Movement for Advancing in the 1990s." Political Bureau, internal document.

—— (1988) "September Thesis of the National Peasant Secretariat." NPS-CPP internal document.

CPRC (2005) *The Chronic Poverty Report 2004–05*. Manchester, UK: Chronic Poverty Research Centre, University of Manchester.

Cramer, Christopher (2003) "Does Inequality Cause Conflict?," *Journal of International Development*, 15(4): 397–412.

Cristobal, Adrian, Jr. (1999) "Community-Based Forest Management: A Case Study on the Municipality of Mauban, Province of Quezon," in E. Garilao, H. Soliman and A. Cristobal Jr. (eds.) *Saving the Plains from the Floods: Strengthening National Government–Local Government Partnership in Community-Based Forest Management*, pp. 37–66. Makati City, Philippines: Asian Institute of Management.

Cuarteros, Gladstone (2001) "Upgrading Possibilities for Philippine Banana Co-operatives." Unpublished M.A. thesis, The Hague: Institute of Social Studies.

David, C. (2003) "Agriculture," in A. Balisacan and H. Hill (eds.) *The Philippine Economy: Development, Policies, and Challenges*, pp. 175–218. Quezon City: Ateneo de Manila University Press.

David, Randolf, Temario Rivera, Patricio Abinales and Oliver Teves (1983) "Transnational Corporations and the Philippine Banana Export Industry," in S.D. Randolf, Teresita Gimenez-Maceda and Sheila Coronel (eds.) *Political Economy of Philippine Commodities*, pp. 1–134. Quezon City: Third World Studies Center, University of the Philippines.

de Asis, Karlo (forthcoming) "State-Community Partnership in Agrarian Reform in the Philippines," *Asian Studies* journal, University of the Philippines.

de Bremond, Ariane (2006) "The *Programa de Transferencia de Tierras* (PTT) and Livelihoods in the Making of a Future: State-Market Hybrids and the Post-war Resettlement of Agrarian Landscapes in El Salvador." Paper presented at the International Conference on Land, Poverty and Development at the Institute of Social Studies (ISS) in The Hague, Netherlands, 9–14 January 2006.

de Dios, Emmanuel (1998) "Between Nationalism and Globalization," in Filomeno Sta. Ana III (ed.) *The State and the Market: Essays on a Socially Oriented Philippine Economy*, pp. 17–32. Quezon City: Action for Economic Reforms/Ateneo de Manila University Press.

Deere, Carmen Diana (2003) "Women's Land Rights and Social Movements in the Brazilian Agrarian Reform," *Journal of Agrarian Change*, 3(1/2): 257–288.

―――― (2000) "Towards a Reconstruction of Cuba's Agrarian Transformation: Peasantization, De-peasantization and Re-peasantization," in D. Bryceson, C. Kay and J. Mooij (eds.) *Disappearing Peasantries? – Rural Labour in Africa, Asia and Latin America*, pp. 139–158. London: ITDG.

―――― (1985) "Rural Women and State Policy: The Latin American Agrarian Reform Experience," *World Development*, 13(9): 1037–1053.

Deere, Carmen Diana and Leonilde de Medeiros (2007) "Agrarian Reform and Poverty Reduction: Lessons from Brazil," in H. Akram-Lodhi, S. Borras and C. Kay (eds.) *Land, Poverty and Livelihoods in an Era of Neoliberal Globalization: Perspectives from Developing and Transition Countries*. London: Routledge.

Deere, Carmen Diana and Magdalena León (2001) "Who Owns the Land: Gender and Land-Titling Programmes in Latin America," *Journal of Agrarian Change*, 1(3): 440–467.

Deininger, Klaus (2002) "Agrarian Reforms in Eastern European Countries: Lessons from International Experience," *Journal of International Development*, 14(7): 987–1003.

―――― (1999) "Making Negotiated Land Reform Work: Initial Experience from Colombia, Brazil and South Africa," *World Development*, 27(4): 651–672.

―――― (1995) "Collective Agricultural Production: A Solution for Transition Economies?," *World Development*, 23(8): 1317–1334.

Deininger, Klaus and Hans Binswanger (1999) "The Evolution of the World Bank's Land Policy: Principles, Experience and Future Challenges," *The World Bank Research Observer*, 14(2): 247–276.

Deininger, Klaus, Francisco Lara Jr., Miet Maertens and Agnes Quisumbing (2000) "Agrarian Reform in the Philippines: Past Impact and Future Challenges." World Bank document, unpublished.

Deininger, Klaus and Julian May (2000) "Is There Scope for Growth with Equity? The Case of Land Reform in South Africa." World Bank document, unpublished.

de Janvry, Alain (1981) *The Agrarian Question and Reformism in Latin America*. Baltimore, MD: The Johns Hopkins University Press.

de Janvry, Alain, Gustavo Gordillo, Jean-Philippe Platteau and Elisabeth Sadoulet (2001a) "Access to Land and Land Policy Reforms," in A. de Janvry, G. Gordillo, J.P. Platteau and E. Sadoulet (eds.) *Access to Land, Rural Poverty, and Public Action*, pp. 1–26. Oxford: Oxford University Press.

―――― (eds.) (2001b) *Access to Land, Rural Poverty, and Public Action*. Oxford: Oxford University Press.

de Janvry, Alain and Elisabeth Sadoulet (1989) "A Study in Resistance to Institutional Change: The Lost Game of Latin American Land Reform," *World Development*, 17(9): 1397–1407.

de Janvry, Alain, Elisabeth Sadoulet and Rinku Murgai (1999) "Access to Land via Land Markets." www.worldbank.org/landpolicy; accessed 18 January 2001.

de Janvry, Alain, Elisabeth Sadoulet, and Wendy Wolford (2001) "The Changing Role of the State in Latin American Land Reform," in de Janvry, G. Gordillo, J.P. Platteau and E. Sadoulet (eds.) *Access to Land, Rural Poverty, and Public Action*, pp. 279–303. Oxford: Oxford University Press.

de la Rosa, Romulo (2005) "Agrarian Reform Movement in Commercial Plantations: The Experience of the Banana Sector in Davao del Norte," in J. Franco and S. Borras (eds.) *On Just Grounds: Struggling for Agrarian Justice and Exercising Citizenship Rights in the Rural Philippines*. Quezon City: Institute for Popular Democracy/ Amsterdam: Transnational Institute.

de la Rosa, Romulo, Jr. (1994) *CAP and the European Market for Coconut Oil and Copra Meal*. Davao: AFRIM.

de León, Teresita and Gema Escobido (2004) *The Banana Export Industry and Agrarian Reform*. Davao: AFRIM.

Delville, Philippine Lavigne (2000) "Harmonising Formal Law and Customary Land Rights in French-Speaking West Africa," in C. Toulmin and J. Quan (eds.) *Evolving Land Rights, Policy and Tenure in Africa*. London: DFID/IIED/NRI.

Desmarais, Annette (2003) "The Via Campesina: Peasants Resisting Globalization." Ph.D. dissertation, University of Calgary.

——— (2001) "The Via Campesina: Consolidating an International Peasant and Farm Movement," *Journal of Peasant Studies*, 29(2): 91–124.

de Soto, Hernando (2000) *The Mystery of Capital: Why Capitalism Triumphs in the West and Fails Everywhere Else*. New York: Basic Books.

Diskin, Martin (1989) "El Salvador: Reform Prevents Change," in W. Thiesenhusen (ed.) *Searching for Agrarian Reform in Latin America*, pp. 429–450. Boston: Unwin Hyman.

DKMP (1995a) "Five-Year Rural Development Program," 1995–2000. Unpublished internal document.

——— (1995b) "Three Stories of Land Reform Struggles," (illustrated). Quezon City: DKMP.

——— (1993) "Proceedings of the National Congress of DKMP held on November 26-29, 1993 in Quezon City." Unpublished internal document.

Dorner, Peter (2001) "Technology and Globalization: Modern-Era Constraints on Local Initiatives for Land Reform," in K. Ghimire (ed.) *Land Reform and Peasant Livelihoods: The Social Dynamics of Rural Poverty and Agrarian Reform in Developing Countries*, pp. 86–104. Geneva: UNRISD/London: ITDG.

——— (1992) *Latin American Land Reforms in Theory and Practice*. Madison, WI: University of Wisconsin Press.

Doronila, Amando (1992) *The State, Economic Transformation, and Political Change in the Philippines, 1946–1972*. Singapore: Oxford University Press.

——— (1985) "The Transformation of Patron-Client Relationship and Its Political Consequences in Postwar Philippines," *Journal of Southeast Asian Studies*, 16(1): 99–116.

Edelman, Marc (1999) *Peasants against Globalization: Rural Social Movements in Costa Rica*. Stanford: Stanford University Press.

—— (1992) *The Logic of the Latifundio: The Large Estates of the Northwestern Costa Rica since the Late Nineteenth Century*. Stanford, CA: Stanford University Press.

Edillion, Rosemarie (2001) *Economic Analysis of the Community-Managed Agrarian Reform Pilot (CMARP)*. Unpublished study commissioned by the ARCDP-DAR. Quezon City: ARCDP-DAR.

El-Ghonemy, Riad (2001) "The Political Economy of Market-Based Land Reform," in K. Ghimire (ed.) *Land Reform and Peasant Livelihoods: The Social Dynamics of Rural Poverty and Agrarian Reform in Developing Countries*, pp. 105–133. Geneva: UNRISD/London: ITDG.

—— (1990) *The Political Economy of Rural Poverty: The Case for Land Reform*. New York/London: Routledge.

Ellis, Frank (2000) *Rural Livelihoods and Diversity in Developing Countries*. Oxford: Oxford University Press.

Engels, Frederick (1956) *The Peasant War in Germany*. Moscow: Progress Publishers.

Esguerra, Manny (2001) *The Community-Managed Agrarian Reform Project (CMARP): A Feasibility Study*. Unpublished study commissioned by ARCDP-DAR. Quezon City: DAR-ARCDP, February 2001.

Estrella, Conrado (1978) *Tenant Emancipation in the Philippines*. Quezon City: Ministry of Agrarian Reform.

Evans, Peter (1995) *Embedded Autonomy: States and Industrial Transformation*. Princeton, NJ: Princeton University Press.

Evans, Peter (ed.) (1997) *State–Society Synergy: Government and Social Capital in Development*. Berkeley: University of California.

Fairhead, J. and M. Leach (2000) "Fashioned Forest Pasts, Occluded Histories? International Environmental Analysis in West African Locales," in M. Doornbos, A. Saith and B. White (eds.) Forests: Nature, People, People special issue, *Development and Change*, 31(1): 35–59.

Feder, Ernest (1983) *Perverse Development*. Manila: Foundation for Nationalist Studies.

—— (1970) "Counterreform," in R. Stavenhagen (ed.) *Agrarian Problems and Peasant Movements in Latin America*, pp. 173–224. New York: Anchor Books.

Fegan, Brian (1989) "The Philippines: Agrarian Stagnation under a Decaying Regime," in G. Hart, A. Turton and B. White (eds.) *Agrarian Transformations: Local Processes and the State in Southeast Asia*, pp. 125–143. Berkeley: University of California Press.

Felstehausen, Herman (1971) "Agrarian Reform: Colombia," in P. Dorner (ed.) *Land Reform in Latin America*, pp. 165–184. Madison, WI: Land Economics, University of Wisconsin-Madison.

Feranil, Salvador (2005) "Evolving Peasant Movements in the Negros Occidental," in J. Franco and S. Borras (eds.) *On Just Grounds: Struggling for Agrarian Justice and Citizenship Rights in the Rural Philippines*. Quezon City: Institute for Popular Democracy/Amsterdam: Transnational Institute.

—— (2001) "The Politics of Agrarian Reform in Philippine Commercial Banana Plantations: The Case of Hijo Plantation in Davao." Unpublished M.A. thesis, Institute of Social Studies, The Hague.

Feranil, Salvador and Nestor Tapia (2003) "Insights from the Margins: Exploring Land Reform Implementation in Settlement Lands," *Bantaaw Economic and Social Indicators of Mindanao*, 16(1–2): 1–11.

FIAN-Via Campesina (2003) "Commentary on Land and Rural Development Policies of the World Bank." Heidelberg/Honduras: FoodFirst Information and Action Network/Via Campesina; see also www.fian.org, www.ciacampesina.org.

Fianza, Myrthena (1999) "Conflicting Land Use and Ownership Patterns and the 'Moro Problem' in Southern Philippines," in M.C. Ferrer (ed.) *Sama-Sama: Facets of Ethnic Relations in South East Asia*, pp. 21–70. Quezon City: Third World Studies Center, University of the Philippines.

FitzGerald, E.V.K. (1985) "Agrarian Reform as a Model of Accumulation: The Case of Nicaragua since 1979," *Journal of Development Studies*, 22(1): 208–220.

Flores, Edmundo (1970) "The Economics of Land Reform," in R. Stavenhagen (ed.) *Agrarian Problems and Peasant Movements in Latin America*, pp. 139–158. New York: Anchor Books.

Foley, Michael (1997) "Land and Peace in Postwar El Salvador: Structural Adjustment, Land Reform and Social Peace in the Salvadoran Countryside." Research for the Washington Office on Latin America (WOLA) on the World Bank and agrarian policy in post-war El Salvador. Unpublished document.

—— (1991) "Agenda for Mobilization: The Agrarian Question and Popular Mobilization in Contemporary Mexico," *Latin American Research Review*, 26(2): 39–74.

Foley, Michael and Karl Yambert (1989) "Anthropology and Theories of the State," in B. Orlove, M. Foley and T. Love (eds.) *State, Capital, and Rural Society*, pp. 39–67. Boulder, CO: Westview Press.

Forero, Roberto (1999) "Evaluacion de Proyectos Piloto de Reforma Agraria en Colombia: Informe Preliminar, Junio 15 de 1999." World Bank document, unpublished.

Fortin, Elizabeth (2005) "Reforming Land Rights: The World Bank and the Globalisation of Agriculture," *Social and Legal Studies*, 14(2): 147–177.

Fortmann, Louise (1995) "Taking Claims: Discursive Strategies in Contesting Property," *World Development*, 23(6): 1053–1063.

Foweraker, Joe (1990) "Popular Movements and Political Change in Mexico," in J. Foweraker and A.L. Craig (eds.) *Popular Movements and Political Change*, pp. 3–20. Boulder, CO: Lynne Rienner.

Fox, Jonathan (2005) "Empowerment and Institutional Change: Mapping 'Virtuous Circles' of State-Society Interaction," in R. Alsop (ed.) *Power, Rights, and Poverty: Concepts and Connections*, pp. 68–82. Washington DC: World Bank.

—— (1996) "Does Civil Society Thicken? The Political Construction of Social Capital in Rural Mexico," *World Development*, 24(6): 1089–1103.

―― (1995) "Governance and Rural Development in Mexico: State Intervention and Public Accountability," *Journal of Development Studies*, 32(1): 1–30.

―― (1994a) "Latin America's Emerging Local Politics," *Journal of Democracy*, 5(2): 105–116.

―― (1994b) "The Difficult Transition from Clientilism to Citizenship: Lessons from Mexico," *World Politics*, 46(2): 151–184.

―― (1994c) "Political Change in Mexico's New Peasant Economy," in M.L. Cook, K. Middlebrook, and J.M. Horcasitas (eds.) *The Politics of Economic Restructuring: State–Society Relations and Regime Change in Mexico*, pp. 243–276. San Diego: The Center for U.S.-Mexican Studies, University of California, San Diego.

―― (1993) *The Politics of Food in Mexico: State Power and Social Mobilization*. Ithaca, NY: Cornell University Press.

―― (1992) "Democratic Rural Development: Leadership Accountability in Regional Peasant Organizations," *Development and Change*, 23(2): 1–36.

Fox, Jonathan, and John Gershman (2000) "The World Bank and Social Capital: Lessons from Ten Rural Development Projects in the Philippines and Mexico," *Policy Sciences*, 33(3/4): 399–419.

Fox, Jonathan (ed.) (1990) *The Challenges of Rural Democratisation: Perspectives from Latin America and the Philippines*. London: Frank Cass.

Franco, Jennifer (forthcoming) "Making Land Rights Accessible: Social Movement Innovation and Political-Legal Strategies in the Philippines," *Journal of Development Studies*.

―― (2007) "Again, They Are Killing Peasants in the Philippines: Lawlessness, Murder and Impunity," *Critical Asian Studies*, 39(2).

―― (2006) "Making Land Rights Accessible: Potentials and Challenges of a Human Rights Approach to Land Issues." Paper presented at the March 2006 international workshop of the High-Level Commission for the Legal Empowerment of the Rural Poor. Available online at: www.tni.org; accessed 21 October 2006.

―― (2005) "Making Property Rights Accessible: Movement Innovation in the Political-Legal Struggle to Claim Land Rights in the Philippines." IDS Working Paper Series, no. 244 (June 2005) Institute of Development Studies (IDS), Brighton.

―― (2004) "Philippines: Fractious Civil Society, Competing Visions of Democracy," in M. Alagappa (ed.) *Political Change in Asia: The Role of Civil Society*, Stanford, CA: Stanford University Press.

―― (2001a) *Elections and Democratization in the Philippines*. New York: Routledge/ Quezon City: Institute for Popular Democracy.

―― (2001b) "Building Alternatives, Harvesting Change: PEACE Network and the Institutionalization of *Bibingka* Strategy." Quezon City: PEACE Foundation. Internal document (unpublished).

―― (2000) "Agrarian Reform Communities and Rural Democratization in Quezon Province." Quezon City: Institute for Popular Democracy (IPD)/United Nations Development Programme (UNDP) – SARDIC Programme. Unpublished paper.

―――― (1999a) "Between Uncritical Collaboration and Outright Opposition: An Evaluative Report on the Partnership for Agrarian Reform and Rural Development Services, PARRDS." *IPD Occasional Papers* No 12. Quezon City: Institute for Popular Democracy; available online at: http://ipd.org.ph.
―――― (1999b) "Post-CARP Banana Split Turns Deadly: What Went Wrong at Hijo Plantation," *Conjuncture*, 11(3): 1–2, 7. Quezon City: Institute for Popular Democracy.
―――― (1999c) *Organizational Strength Appraisal of Organizations in Top Agrarian Reform Communities (ARCs)*. Unpublished study commission by the Food and Agriculture Organization (FAO), SARC-TSARRD Programme: Quezon City.
―――― (1999d) "Is Agrarian Reform on the Way Out?," *Philippine Daily Inquirer*, 7 March, 1999, p. 9.
―――― (1999e) "Market-Assisted Land Reform in the Philippines: Round Two – Where Have All the Critics Gone," *Conjuncture*, 11(2): 1–6. Quezon City: Institute for Popular Democracy; available online at: http://ipd.org.ph.
―――― (1998a) "Problems-Needs Assessment of Agrarian Reform Communities (ARC) Organizations in the Least Developed ARCs." Quezon City: Food and Agriculture Organization, SARC-TSARRD Programme.
―――― (1998b) "Between Honesty and Hope on the Agrarian Front: Wrestling with Warlords in the Bondoc Peninsula," *Conjuncture*, 10(4): 1–4, 5, 8. Quezon City: Institute for Popular Democracy.
―――― (1994) "Philippine Electoral Politics and the Peasant-Based Civic Movement in the 1980s," *Rural Development Studies*, 10(2): 1–107. Quezon City: Philippine Peasant Institute.
Franco, Jennifer and Norman Acosta (1999) "The Banana War: Part Two, Conclusion," *Conjuncture*, 11(10): 12–15, Quezon City: Institute for Popular Democracy.
Franco, Jennifer and Saturnino M. Borras Jr. (2007) "Struggles over Land Resources in the Philippines," *Peace Review*, 19(1): 67–75.
Franco, Jennifer and Saturnino M. Borras Jr. (eds.) (2005) *On Just Grounds: Struggling for Agrarian Justice and Citizenship Rights in the Rural Philippines*. Amsterdam: Transnational Institute/Manila: Institute for Popular Democracy.
Friedmann, Harriet (2005) "Feeding the Empire: The Pathologies of Globalized Agriculture," in L. Panitch and C. Leys (eds.) *The Empire Reloaded*. Toronto: Socialist Register.
Fuentes, Anna Luisa and Emma Paring (1992) "Learning Lessons from Struggle: The Land Occupation of the Aquafil Estate in Occidental Mindoro," in F. Lim (ed.) *Waging the Battle for Land Ownership: Case Studies of Peasant Initiated Land Occupations*, pp. 27–77. Quezon City: Philippine Peasant Institute.
Garilao, Ernesto (1999) "Foreword," in S. Borras, *The Bibingka Strategy in Land Reform Implementation*, pp. xix–xxi. Quezon City: Institute for Popular Democracy.
―――― (1998) *The Ramos Legacy in Agrarian Reform: A Transition Report*. Quezon City: DAR.

Garilao, Ernesto, Hector Soliman and Adrian Cristobal Jr. (eds.) (1999) *Saving the Plains from the Floods: Strengthening National Government–Local Government Partnership in Community-Based Forest Management*. Makati City, Philippines: Asian Institute of Management.

Gaspar, Karl, C.Ss.R. (2000) *The Lumad's Struggle in the Face of Globalization*. Davao: Alternate Forum for Research in Mindanao (AFRIM).

Gasper, Des (1990) "What Happened to the Land Question in Zimbabwe?: Rural Reform in the 1980s." *ISS Working Paper Series* 91. The Hague: Institute of Social Studies.

Gatmaytan, Dan (2000) "Discretionary Justice: The Story and Folly of Fortich v. Corona." *KAISAHAN Occasional Paper* (June 2000). Quezon City: KAISAHAN.

Gauld, Richard (2000) "Maintaining Centralized Control in Community-Based Forestry: Policy Construction in the Philippines," *Development and Change*, 31(1): 229–254.

Gauster, Susana (2006) "The Impacts of World Bank's Land Policy Implementation in Guatemala." Paper presented at the International Conference on Land, Poverty and Development at the Institute of Social Studies (ISS), The Hague, Netherlands, 9–14 January 2006.

Gaventa, John (2002) "Exploring Citzenship, Participation and Accountability," *IDS Bulletin*, 33(2): 1–11.

Geremia, Peter, PIME (1986) *Dreams and Bloodstains: The Diary of a Missioner in the Philippines*. Quezon City: Claretian Publications.

German, Milagros (1995) *Share and Leasehold Tenancy in RA No. 1199 and RA No. 3844 as Amended, Annotated with Commentaries and the Comprehensive Agrarian Reform Law RA No. 6657*. Mandaluyong City, Philippines: National Bookstore.

Gershman, John (1999) "Coda: Market-Assisted Agrarian Reform," *Conjuncture*, 11(2): 5. Quezon City: Institute for Popular Democracy; available online at http://ipd.org.ph.

Ghimire, Krishna (2005) "Markets and Civil Society in Rural Transformation: An Overview of Principal Issues, Trends and Outcomes," in K. Ghimire (ed.) *Civil Society and the Market Question: Dynamics of Rural Development and Popular Mobilization*. Geneva: UNRISD/London: Palgrave Macmillan.

——— (2001a) "Land Reform at the End of the Twentieth Century: An Overview of Issues, Actors and Processes," in K. Ghimire (ed.) *Land Reform and Peasant Livelihoods: The Social Dynamics of Rural Poverty and Agrarian Reform in Developing Countries*, pp. 1–26. Geneva: UNRISD/London: ITDG.

——— (2001b) "Peasants' Pursuit of Outside Alliances and Legal Support in the Process of Land Reform," in K. Ghimire (ed.) *Land Reform and Peasant Livelihoods: The Social Dynamics of Rural Poverty and Agrarian Reform in Developing Countries*, pp. 134–163. Geneva: UNRISD/London: ITDG.

Ghimire, Krishna (ed.) (2001c) *Land Reform and Peasant Livelihoods: The Social Dynamics of Rural Poverty and Agrarian Reform in Developing Countries*. Geneva: UNRISD/London: ITDG.

Ghimire, Krishna and Bruce Moore (eds.) (2001) *Whose Land? Civil Society Perspectives on Land Reform and Rural Poverty Reduction: Regional Experiences from Africa, Asia and Latin America*. Rome/Geneva: International Fund for Agricultural Development (IFAD) and the Popular Coalition to Eradicate Hunger and Poverty/UNRISD.

Ghose, Ajit Kumar (ed.) (1983) *Agrarian Reform in Contemporary Countries*. London: Croom Helm/New York: St. Martin's Press.

Gleeck, Lewis, Jr. (1993) *The Third Philippine Republic, 1946–1972*. Quezon City: New Day Publishers.

Goodno, James (1991) *The Philippines: Land of Broken Promises*. London: Zed Books.

Gordillo, Gustavo de Anda (1997) "The Reconstruction of Rural Institutions." A paper presented at the FAO Technical Consultation on Decentralisation and Rural Development, Rome, December 1997, available online at: www.fao.org/sd/ltdirect/lr96/gordillo.htm.

Gordillo, Gustavo de Anda and Frank Boening (1999) "Latin American Land Reforms in the 1990s." A paper presented at the Workshop on Land: New Context, New Claims, New Concepts, organized by CEDLA, Amsterdam, May 1999.

Griffin, Keith (1980) "Economic Development in a Changing World," *World Development*, 9(3): 221–226.

—— (1976) *Land Concentration and Rural Poverty*. London: Macmillan Press.

Griffin, Keith, Azizur Rahman Khan and Amy Ickowitz (2002) "Poverty and Distribution of Land," *Journal of Agrarian Change*, 2(3): 279–330.

Grindle, Merilee (1986) *State and Countryside: Development Policy and Agrarian Politics in Latin America*. Baltimore, MD: The Johns Hopkins University Press.

Grindle, Merilee and John Thomas (1989) "Policy Makers, Policy Choices, and Policy Outcomes: The Political Economy of Reform in Developing Countries," *Policy Sciences*, 22(2): 213–248.

Groppo, Paolo, Hernan Mora Corrales, Adolfo Hurtado, Celso Luis Vegro, José Kleber Costa Pereira, Luis Carlos de Aquino Pereira, Maria Leuda Candido and Armando Gomes Marques (1998) "Avaliacão Sintètica do Projeto Cédula da Terra." Unpublished study commissioned by Convêvio FAO/INCRA, Fortaleza-CE, Maio de 1998.

Guerrero, Amado (pseudonym) (1970) *Philippine Society and Revolution*. Oakland, CA: International Association of Filipino Patriots.

Gutierrez, Eric (1994) *The Ties That Bind: A Guide to Family, Business and Other Interests in the Ninth House of Representatives*. Manila: Philippine Center for Investigative Journalism.

Gutierrez, Eric and Saturnino Borras Jr. (2004) "The Moro Conflict: Landlessness and Misdirected State Policies." East-West Center, Washington *Policy Studies Series 8*, pp. 1–89; for PDF version, see http://washington.eastwestcenter.org/Publications/psseriespublications2.htm.

Gutierrez, Eric, Ildefonso Torrente and Noli Narca (1992) *All in the Family: A Study of Elites and Power Relations in the Philippines*. Quezon City: Institute for Popular Democracy.

Gwynne, Robert and Cristóbal Kay (2004) *Latin America Transformed: Globalization and Modernity* (2nd ed.). London: Arnold.
Hall, Anthony (1990) "Land Tenure and Land Reform in Brazil," in R. Prosterman, M. Temple and T. Hanstad (eds.) *Agrarian Reform and Grassroots Development: Ten Case Studies*, pp. 205–232. Boulder, CO: Lynne Rienner Publishers.
Hall, Ruth (2004) "A Political Economy of Land Reform in South Africa," *Review of African Political Economy*, 31(100): 213–227.
Hammersley, Martyn (1992) *What's Wrong with Ethnography?* London/New York: Routledge.
Handy, Jim (1994) *Revolution in the Countryside: Rural Conflict and Agrarian Reform in Guatemala, 1944–1954*. Chapel Hill, NC: University of North Carolina Press.
Harriss, John (2002) *Depoliticizing Development: The World Bank and Social Capital*. London: Anthem Press.
—— (1993) "What Is Happening in Rural West Bengal? Agrarian Reform, Growth and Distribution," *Economic and Political Weekly*, 28: 1237–1247.
Harriss, John (ed.) (1982) *Rural Development: Theories of Peasant Economy and Agrarian Change*. London: Routledge.
Hart, Gillian (1995) "Clothes for Next to Nothing: Rethinking Global Competition," *South African Labour Bulletin*, 9(6): 41–47.
—— (1989) "Agrarian Change in the Context of State Patronage," in G. Hart, A. Turton and B. White (eds.) *Agrarian Transformations: Local Processes and the State in Southeast Asia*, pp. 31–49. Berkeley: University of California Press.
Harvey, Neil (1998) *The Chiapas Rebellion: The Struggle for Land and Democracy*. Durham, NC: Duke University Press.
Hawes, Gary (1990) "Theories of Peasant Revolution: A Critique and Contribution from the Philippines," *World Politics*, 42(2): 261–298.
—— (1989) "Aquino and Her Administration: A View from the Countryside," *Pacific Affairs*, 62(1): 9–28.
—— (1987) *The Philippine State and the Marcos Regime: The Politics of Export*. Ithaca, NY: Cornell University Press.
Hayami, Yuhiro, Agnes Quisumbing and Lourdes Adriano (1990) *Toward an Alternative Land Reform Paradigm: A Philippine Perspective*. Quezon City: Ateneo de Manila University Press.
Heller, Patrick (2000) "Degrees of Democracy: Some Comparative Lessons from India," *World Politics*, 52(2): 484–519.
Hellman, Judith Adler (1992) "The Study of New Social Movements in Latin America and the Question of Autonomy," in S. Alvarez and A. Escobar (eds.) *The Making of Social Movements in Latin America: Identity, Strategy, and Democracy*, pp. 52–61. Boulder, CO: Westview Press.
Heredia, Beatriz, Leonilde Medeiros, Moacir Palmeira, Rosangla Cintrao and Sergio Pereira Leite (2006) "Regional Impacts of Land Reform in Brazil," in P. Rosset, R. Patel and M. Courville (eds.) *Promised Land: Competing Visions of Agrarian Reform*, pp. 277–300. Oakland, CA: FoodFirst Books.

Herring, Ronald (2003) "Beyond the Political Impossibility Theorem of Agrarian Reform," in P. Houtzager and M. Moore (eds.) *Changing Paths: International Development and the New Politics of Inclusion*, pp. 58-87. Ann Arbor, MI: University of Michigan Press.

—— (2002) "State Property Rights in Nature (with Special Reference to India)," in F. Richards (ed.) *Land, Property, and the Environment*, pp. 263-297. Oakland, CA: Institute for Contemporary Studies.

—— (1990) "Explaining Anomalies in Agrarian Reform: Lessons from South India," in R. Prosterman, M. Temple, and T. Hanstad (eds.) *Agrarian Reform and Grassroots Development: Ten Case Studies*, pp. 49-76. Boulder, CO: Lynne Rienner Publishers.

—— (1983) *Land to the Tiller: The Political Economy of Agrarian Reform in South Asia*. New Haven, CT: Yale University Press.

Hilhorst, Dorothea (2003) *The Real World of NGOs: Discourses, Diversity and Development*. London: Zed/Quezon City: Ateneo de Manila University Press.

Hirschman, Alberto (1967) *Journeys toward Progress*. New York: Twentieth Century Fund.

Hirtz, Frank (2003) "It Takes Modern Means to Be Traditional: On Recognizing Indigenous Cultural Communities in the Philippines," *Development and Change*, 34(5): 887-917.

—— (1998) "The Discourse That Produces Silence: Farmers' Ambivalence towards Land Reform in the Philippines," *Development and Change*, 29(2): 247-275.

Ho, Peter and Max Spoor (guest eds.) (2006) "Whose Land? The Political Economy of Land Titling in Transition Economies," special issue, *Land Use Policy*, 23(4): 580-587.

Hobsbawm, Eric (1974) "Peasant Land Occupations," *Past and Present*, (62): 120-152.

—— (1965) *Primitive Rebels*. New York: Norton [original, 1959].

Holt-Gimenez, Eric (2006) *Campesino a Campesino: Voices from Latin America's Farmer to Farmer Movement for Sustainable Agriculture*. Oakland, CA: FoodFirst Books.

Houtzager, Peter (2001) "Collective Action and Political Authority: Rural Workers, Church, and State in Brazil," *Theory and Society*, 30(1): 1-45.

—— (2000) "Social Movements amidst Democratic Transitions: Lessons from the Brazilian Countryside," *Journal of Development Studies*, 36(5): 59-88.

Houtzager, Peter and Jennifer Franco (2003) "When the Poor Make Law: Comparisons Across Brazil and the Philippines." Research note, Law, Democracy, and Development Program. Sussex: Institute of Development Studies.

Houtzager, Peter and Mick Moore (eds.) (2003) *Changing Paths: International Development and the New Politics of Inclusion*. Ann Arbor, MI: University of Michigan Press.

Huizer, Gerrit (2001) "Peasant Mobilization for Land Reform: Historical Case Studies and Theoretical Considerations," in K. Ghimire (ed.) *Land Reform and Peasant Livelihoods: The Social Dynamics of Rural Poverty and Agrarian Reform in Developing Countries*, pp. 164-198. Geneva: UNRISD/London: ITDG.

―――― (1975) "How Peasants Become Revolutionaries: Some Cases from Latin America and Southeast Asia," *Development and Change*, 6(3): 27–56.

―――― (1972) "Agrarian Unrest and Peasant Organizations in the Philippines." *ISS Occasional Papers*, No. 1. The Hague: Institute of Social Studies.

Hutchcroft, Paul (2000) "Colonial Masters, National Politicos, and Provincial Lords: Central Authority and Local Autonomy in the American Philippines," *Journal of Asian Studies*, 59(2): 277–306.

―――― (1991) "Oligarchs and Cronies in the Philippine State: The Politics of Patrimonial Plunder," *World Politics*, 43(3): 414–450.

IBON (1996) *The Comprehensive Agrarian Reform Program: More Misery for the Philippine Peasantry*. Manila: IBON.

―――― (1988) *Land Reform in the Philippines*. Manila: IBON Databank.

Ileto, Reynaldo Clemeña (1979) *Pasyon and Revolution: Popular Movements in the Philippines, 1840–1910*. Quezon City: Ateneo de Manila University Press.

Jacoby, Erich (with Charlotte Jacoby) (1971) *Man and Land: The Fundamental Issue in Development*. London: André Deutsch.

Johnson, Craig and Tim Forsyth (2002) "In the Eyes of the State: Negotiating a 'Rights-Based Approach' to Forest Conservation in Thailand," *World Development*, 30(9): 1591–1605.

Jones, P.M. (1991) "The 'Agrarian Law': Schemes for Land Redistribution during the French Revolution," *Past and Present*, (133): 96–133.

Jorgensen, Hans (2006) "The Inter-War Land Reforms in Estonia, Finland and Bulgaria: A Comparative Study," *Scandinavian Economic History Review*, 54(1): 64–97.

Juul, Kristine and Christian Lund (2002) "Negotiating Property in Africa: Introduction," in K. Juul and C. Lund (eds.) *Negotiating Property in Africa*, pp. 1–10. Portsmouth, NH: Heinemann.

Kabeer, Naila (1999) "Resources, Agency, Achievement: Reflections on the Measurement of Women's Empowerment," *Development and Change*, 30(3): 435–464.

Karshenas, Massoub (2004) "Urban Bias, Intersectoral Resource Flows and the Macroeconomic Implications of Agrarian Relations: The Historical Experience of Japan and Taiwan," *Journal of Agrarian Change*, 4(1/2): 170–189.

Kasuya, Yuko (1995) "The 'Failure' of Agrarian Reform in Transitional Democracy, Philippines 1986–1992." *ISS Working Paper* No. 194. The Hague: Institute of Social Studies.

Kay, Cristóbal (2004) "Rural Livelihoods and Peasant Futures," in R. Gwynne and C. Kay (eds.) *Latin America Transformed: Globalization and Modernity* (2nd ed.), pp. 232–250. London: Arnold.

―――― (2002a) "Chile's Neoliberal Agrarian Transformation and the Peasantry," *Journal of Agrarian Change*, 2(4): 464–501.

―――― (2002b) "Why East Asia Overtook Latin America: Agrarian Reform, Industrialization and Development," *Third World Quarterly*, 23(6): 1073–1102.

—— (2001) "Reflections on Rural Violence in Latin America," *Third World Quarterly*, 22(5): 741–775.
—— (1998) "Latin America's Agrarian Reform: Lights and Shadows," *Land Reform, Land Settlements and Cooperatives*, 1998(2): 9–31.
—— (1992a) "Agrarian Reform and the Class Struggle," in C. Kay and P. Silva (eds.) *Development and Social Change in the Chilean Countryside: From the Pre–Land Reform Period to the Democratic Consolidation*, pp. 129–151. Amsterdam: CEDLA.
—— (1992b) "Political Economy, Class Alliances and Agrarian Change," in C. Kay and P. Silva (eds.) *Development and Social Change in the Chilean Countryside: From the Pre–Land Reform Period to the Democratic Consolidation*, pp. 33–54. Amsterdam: CEDLA.
—— (1983) "The Agrarian Reform in Peru: An Assessment," in A.K. Ghose (ed.) *Agrarian Reform in Contemporary Developing Countries*, pp. 185–239. London/New York: Croom Helm Ltd/St. Martin's Press.
Kay, Cristóbal and Miguel Urioste (2007) "Bolivia's Unfinished Reform: Rural Poverty and Development Policies," in H. Akram-Lodhi, S. Borras and C. Kay (eds.) *Land, Poverty and Livelihoods in an Era of Neoliberal Globalization: Perspectives from Developing and Transition Countries*. London: Routledge.
Kay, Cristóbal and Patricio Silva (eds.) (1992) *Development and Social Change in the Chilean Countryside: From the Pre–Land Reform Period to the Democratic Consolidation*. Amsterdam: CEDLA.
Kerkvliet, Benedict (2006) "Agricultural Land in Vietnam: Markets Tempered by Family, Community and Socialist Practices," *Journal of Agrarian Change*, 6(3): 285–305.
—— (2005) *The Power of Everyday Politics: How Vietnamese Peasants Transformed National Policy*. Ithaca, NY: Cornell University Press.
—— (1995) "Toward a More Comprehensive Analysis of Philippine Politics: Beyond the Patron-Client, Factional Framework," *Journal of Southeast Asian Studies*, 26(2): 401–419.
—— (1993) "Claiming the Land: Take-Overs by Villagers in the Philippines with Comparisons to Indonesia, Peru, Portugal, and Russia," *Journal of Peasant Studies*, 20(3): 459–493.
—— (1990) *Everyday Politics in the Philippines: Class and Status Relations in a Central Luzon Village*. Berkeley: University of California Press.
—— (1979) "Land Reform: Emancipation or Counterinsurgency?," in D.A. Rosenberg (ed.) *Marcos and Martial Law in the Philippines*, pp. 113–144. Berkeley: University of California Press.
—— (1977) *The Huk Rebellion: A Study of Peasant Revolt in the Philippines*. Berkeley: University of California Press.
King, Russell (1977) *Land Reform: A World Survey*. London: B. Bell and Sons Ltd.
KMP (2000) "Ang Kalagayan ng Masang Magbubukid sa Ilalim ng Rehimeng US-Estrada." Quezon City: Kilusang Magbubukid ng Pilipinas. Pamphlet.
—— (1993) "Minutes of the National Council Meeting held on January 23–26, 1993 in Quezon City." Internal document.

—— (1992a) "Proceedings of the KMP's Strategic Assessment and Planning Conducted by the National Council on January 27–31, 1992, Tagaytay City." Internal document.

—— (1992b) "KMP's Three-Year Development Program." Quezon City: KMP. Computer print-out.

—— (1991) "Proceedings of the National Peasant Consultation on Socio-economic Work held on 28–31 May 1991 at the University of the Philippines at Los Baños." Internal document.

—— (1988) "Sowing the Seed: Proceedings of the International Solidarity Conference for the Filipino Peasants held in Metro Manila on October 11–21, 1986." Quezon City: KMP.

—— (1986a) "Program for Genuine Land Reform." Quezon City: KMP. Pamphlet.

—— (1986b) "Policy Proposals for Agricultural and Countryside Development." Quezon City: KMP. Pamphlet.

Koppel, Bruce (1990) "Mercantile Transformations: Understanding the State, Global Debt and Philippine Agriculture," *Development and Change*, 21(4): 579–619.

Korovkin, Tanya (2000) "Weak Weapons, Strong Weapons: Hidden Resistance and Political Protest in Rural Ecuador," *Journal of Peasant Studies*, 27(3): 1–29.

Kurtz, Marcus (2000) "Understanding Peasant Revolution: From Concept to Theory and Case," *Theory and Society*, 29(10): 93–124.

Lacaba, Jose (1995) *Boss: Five Cases of Local Politics on the Philippines*. Quezon City: Philippine Center for Investigative Journalism.

Lahiff, Edward (2006) "State, Market or the Worst of Both? Experimenting with Market-Based Land Reform in Southern Africa." Paper presented at the International Conference on Land, Poverty and Development at the Institute of Social Studies (ISS), The Hague, Netherlands, 9–14 January 2006.

—— (2003) "Land Reform and Sustainable Livelihood in South Africa's Eastern Cape Province." *IDS Research Paper* No. 9 (March 2003). Brighton: Institute of Development Studies.

—— (2001) "Land Reform in South Africa: Is It Meeting the Challenge?" *PLAAS Policy Brief – Debating Land Reform and Rural Development* (1): 1–6. Cape Town: PLAAS, University of Western Cape.

Lahiff, Edward and Ian Scoones (2000) "Sustainable Livelihoods in Southern Africa: Institutions, Governance and Policy Processes." *Sustainable Livelihood Southern Africa (SLSA) Research Paper* 2. Brighton, Sussex: Institute of Development Studies.

Landsberger, Henry and Cynthia Hewitt (1970) "Ten Sources of Weaknesses and Cleavage in Latin American Peasant Movements," in R. Stavenhagen (ed.) *Agrarian Problems and Peasant Movements in Latin America*, pp. 559–583. New York: Anchor Books.

Landsberger, Henry (ed.) (1974) *Rural Protest: Peasant Movements and Social Change*. London: Macmillan.

Lanfer, Anne (2006) "The Philippine Land Reform and Their Impact on Rural Households." Bachelorarbeit (thesis), University of Kiel, Germany.

Lara, Francisco (2001) "Cooperative Bias in the Redistribution of Commercial Farms and Agribusiness Plantations: The 'Illogic' of Collective Action." Unpublished paper.

——— (1986) "Land Reform in the Proposed Constitution: Landmarks and Loopholes," *Agricultural Policy Studies*, 1, Quezon City: Philippine Peasant Institute.

Lara, Francisco, Jr. and Horacio Morales Jr. (1990) "The Peasant Movement and the Challenge of Democratisation in the Philippines," in J. Fox (ed.) The Challenge of Rural Democratisation: Perspectives from Latin America and the Philippines special issue, *Journal of Development Studies*, 26(4): 143–162.

La Viña, Antonio (1999) "The State of Community-Based Forest Management in the Philippines and the Role of Local Governments," in E. Garilao, H. Soliman and A. Cristobal Jr. (eds.) *Saving the Plains from the Floods: Strengthening National Government–Local Government Partnership in Community-Based Forest Management*, pp. 11–36. Makati City, Philippines: Asian Institute of Management.

Layder, Derek (1994) *Understanding Social Theory*. London/Thousand Oaks/New Delhi: Sage Publications.

Leach, Melissa, Robin Mearns and Ian Scoones (1999) "Environmental Entitlement: Dynamics and Institutions in Community-Based Natural Resource Management," *World Development*, 27(2): 225–247.

Lebert, Tom (2001) "Tinkering at the Edges: Land Reform in South Africa – 1994 to 2001." A Paper prepared for the International Conference on Access to Land: Innovative Agrarian Reforms for Sustainability and Poverty Reduction, Bonn, Germany, 19–23 March 2001.

Ledesma, Antonio, S.J., Perla Makil and Virginia Miralao (eds.) (1983) *Second View from the Paddy*. Quezon City: Institute of Philippine Culture, Ateneo de Manila University.

Lehmann, David (1974a) "Introduction," in D. Lehmann (ed.) *Peasants, Landlords and Governments: Agrarian Reform in the Third World*, pp. 13–24. New York: Holmes and Meier Publishers.

Lehmann, David (ed.) (1974b) *Peasants, Landlords and Governments: Agrarian Reform in the Third World*. New York: Holmes and Meier Publishers.

Leite, Sergio with Rodrigo Avila (2006) "Agrarian Reform, Social Justice and Sustainable Development." Paper presented at the International Conference on Agrarian Reform and Rural Development (ICARRD), Porto Alegre, Brazil, 6–10 March 2006; available online at: www.icarrd.org/en/icarrd_docs_issues.html; accessed 18 May 2006.

Leonen, Marvic (1993) "The Philippines: Dwindling Frontiers and Agrarian Reform," in M. Colchester and L. Lohnmann (eds.) *The Struggle for Land and the Fate of the Forests*, pp. 264–290. London: Zed.

Levin, Richard and Daniel Weiner (eds.) (1997) *Struggles for Land in Mpumalanga, South Africa*. NJ/Eritrea: Africa World Press.

Levin, Richard and Daniel Weiner (1996) "The Politics of Land Reform in South Africa after Apartheid: Perspectives, Problems and Prospects," *Journal of Peasant Studies*, 23(2/3): 93–119.
Li, Tania Murray (1996) "Images of Community: Discourse and Strategy in Property Relations," *Development and Change*, 27(3): 501–527.
Liamzon, Cristina (1996) "Agrarian Reform: A Continuing Imperative or an Anachronism?," *Development in Practice*, 6(4): 315–323.
Lichauco, Luis (1956) "Land Settlement in the Philippines," in K. Parsons, R. Penn and P. Raup (eds.) "Land Tenure: Proceedings of the International Conference on Land Tenure and Related Problems in World Agriculture," held at Madison, WI, 1951, pp. 188–197. Madison: The University of Wisconsin Press.
Lichbach, Mark (1994) "What Makes Rational Peasants Revolutionary? Dilemma, Paradox, and Irony in Peasant Collective Action," *World Politics*, 46(3): 383–418.
Lieten, G.K. (1996) "Land Reforms at Centre Stage: The Evidence on West Bengal," *Development and Change*, 26(1): 111–130.
Lim, Joseph (1998) "The Economy in a Globalized Setting," in F. Sta. Ana III (ed.) *The State and the Market: Essays on a Socially Oriented Philippine Economy*, pp. 33–87. Quezon City: Action for Economic Reforms/Ateneo de Manila University Press.
——— (1996) "Issues Concerning the Three Major Agricultural Crops and GATT," in Judith Reyes (ed.) *The General Agreement on Tariffs and Trade: Philippine Issues and Perspectives*, pp. 28–86. Quezon City: Philippine Peasant Institute.
Lindio-McGovern, Ligaya (1997) *Filipino Peasant Women: Exploitation and Resistance*. Philadelphia: University of Pennsylvania Press.
Lipton, Michael (1993) "Land Reform as Commenced Business: The Evidence against Stopping," *World Development*, 21(4): 641–657.
——— (1974) "Towards a Theory on Land Reform," in D. Lehmann (ed.) *Peasants, Landlords and Governments: Agrarian Reform in the Third World*, pp. 269–315. New York: Holmes and Meier Publishers.
Lo, Frances Theresa (2004) "Cancellation of Land Titles: Pulling the Rug from under Agrarian Reform." *KAISAHAN Occasional Papers*. Quezon City: KAISAHAN.
Long, Norman (1988) "Sociological Perspectives on Agrarian Development and State Intervention," in A. Hall and J. Midgley (eds.) *Development Policies: Sociological Perspectives*, pp. 108–133. Manchester: Manchester University Press.
Lopez-Gonzaga, Violeta (1994) *Land of Hope, Land of Want: A Socio-economic History of Negros, 1571–1985*. Quezon City: Philippine National Historical Society.
Lourie, Menachem (2001) "Participation of Stakeholders in Developing Agrarian Reform Communities in the Philippines," *Land Reform, Land Settlement and Cooperatives*, 2000(1): 9–20.
Loveman, Brian (1976) *Struggle in the Countryside: Politics and Rural Labor in Chile, 1919–1973*. Bloomington: Indiana University Press.
Lund, Christian (1998) *Law, Power and Politics in Niger: Land Struggles and the Rural Code*. Hamburg: LIT.

Lynch, Owen (1998) "Law, Pluralism and the Promotion of Sustainable Community-Based Forest Management," *Unasylva*, 194: 1–7. Rome: FAO.

Lynch, Owen and Kirk Talbott (1995) *Balancing Acts: Community Based Forest Management and National Law in Asia and the Pacific*. Washington DC: World Resources Institute.

Magadia, Jose (2003) *State–Society Dynamics: Policy Making in a Restored Democracy*. Quezon City: Ateneo de Manila University Press.

Mamon, Roque (2001) *Community-Managed Agrarian Reform Project (CMARP) Pilot – Individual [Technical Adviser] Report*. Unpublished document, Quezon City: DAR-ARCDP.

Manapat, Ricardo (1991) *Some Are Smarter Than Others*. New York: Alethia Publishing.

Manasan, Rosario and Ruben Mercado (2001) *An Evaluation of the Fiscal Aspect of the Comprehensive Agrarian Reform Program (CARP) – Final Report*. Unpublished study prepared for the Department of Agrarian Reform. Quezon City: Department of Agrarian Reform (PSRS Office).

Manji, Ambreena (2006) *The Politics of Land Reform in Africa: From Communal Tenure to Free Markets*. London: Zed.

Marsman (2002) "Briefing Kit and Collated Documents with Regard to the Proposed Land Donation and Land Use in Marsman Banana Plantation as submitted to the Presidential Agrarian Reform Council dated August 2002." Unpublished document, available at the PARC Secretariat, Quezon City.

Marx, Karl (1968) "The Eighteenth Brumaire of Louis Bonaparte," in *Marx/Engels: Selected Works in One Volume*. London: Lawrence and Wishart.

Mathieu, Paul, Mahamadou Zongo and Lacinan Pare (2002) "Monetary Land Transactions in Western Burkina Faso: Commoditisation, Papers and Ambiguities," *European Journal of Development Research*, 14(2): 109–128.

Matondi, Prosper and Sam Moyo (2003) "Experiences with Market Based Land Reform in Zimbabwe," in F. Barros et al. (eds.) *The Negative Impacts of World Bank Market Based Land Reform*, pp. 323–402. Brazil: CPT and MST.

McAdam, Doug, J. McCarthy and M. Zald (eds.) (1996) *Comparative Perspectives on Social Movements: Political Opportunity, Mobilizing Structures, and Cultural Framings*. Cambridge, UK: Cambridge University Press.

McAndrew, John (1994) *Urban Usurpation: From Friar Lands to Industrial Estates in a Philippine Hinterland*. Quezon City: Ateneo de Manila University Press.

McAuslan, Patrick (2000) "Only the Name of the Country Changes: The Diaspora of 'European' Land Law in Commonwealth Africa," in C. Toulmin and J. Quan (eds.) *Evolving Land Rights, Policy and Tenure in Africa*. London: DFID/IIED/NRI.

McClintock, Cynthia (1984) "Why Peasants Rebel: The Case of Peru's Sendero Luminoso," *World Politics*, 37(1): 48–84.

McCoy, Alfred (1993a) "An Anarchy of Families: The Historiography of State and Family in the Philippines," in A. McCoy (ed.) *An Anarchy of Families: State and Family in the Philippines*, pp. 1–32. Madison, WI: Center for Southeast Asian Studies, University of Wisconsin Press.

——— (1983) "The Extreme Unction: The Philippine Sugar Industry," in S.D. Randolf, Teresita Gimenez-Maceda and Sheila Coronel (eds.) *Political Economy of Philippine Commodities*. Quezon City: Third World Studies Center, University of the Philippines.

——— (1982) "Introduction," in A. McCoy and E. de Jesus (eds.) *Philippine Social History: Global Trade and Local Transformations*, pp. 1–18. Quezon City: Ateneo de Manila University Press.

McCoy, Alfred (ed.) (1993b) *An Anarchy of Families: State and Family in the Philippines*. Madison, WI: Center for Southeast Asian Studies, University of Wisconsin Press.

McCoy, Alfred and Ed de Jesus (eds.) (1982) *Philippine Social History: Global Trade and Local Transformations*. Quezon City: Ateneo de Manila University Press.

McMichael, Philip (2006a) "Peasant Prospects in the Neoliberal Age," *New Political Economy*, 11(3): 407–418.

——— (2006b) "Reframing Development: Global Peasant Movements and the New Agrarian Question," *Canadian Journal of Development Studies*.

Meinzen-Dick, Ruth and Anna Knox (1999) "Collective Action, Property Rights, and Devolution of Natural Resource Management: A Conceptual Framework." Washington DC: IFPRI.

Meliczek, Hans (1999) "Issues and Problems Related to Impact Assessment of Agrarian Reform Programmes: The Philippines Case," *Land Reform, Land Settlements, and Cooperatives*, 1999(1/2): 63–74.

Melucci, Alberto (1992) "Liberation or Meaning? Social Movements, Culture and Democracy," *Development and Change*, 23(3): 43–77.

——— (1985) "The Symbolic Challenge of Contemporary Movements," *Social Research*, 52(4): 787–816.

Merlet, Michel, Samuel Thirion and Vicent Garces (2006) "States and Civil Society: Access to Land and Rural Development and Capacity Building for New Forms of Governance." Paper presented at the International Conference on Agrarian Reform and Rural Development (ICARRD), Porto Alegre, Brazil, 6–10 March 2006; available online at: www.icarrd.org/en/icarrd_docs_issues.html; accessed 18 May 2006.

Meszaros, George (2000a) "No Ordinary Revolution: Brazil's Landless Workers' Movement," *Race and Class*, 42(2): 1–18

——— (2000b) "Taking the Land into Their Hands: The Landless Workers Movement and the Brazilian State," *Journal of Law and Society*, 27(4): 517–541.

Meyer, David and Suzanne Staggenborg (1996) "Movements, Countermovements, and Structure of Political Opportunity," *American Journal of Sociology*, 101(6): 1628–1660.

Migdal, Joel (2001) *State in Society: Studying How States and Societies Transform and Constitute One Another*. Cambridge, UK: Cambridge University Press.

——— (1988) *Strong Societies and Weak States: State–Society Relations and State Capabilities in the Third World*. Princeton, NJ: Princeton University Press.

—— (1974) *Peasants, Politics, and Revolution: Pressures toward Political and Social Changes in the Third World*. Princeton, NJ: Princeton University Press.
Migdal, Joel, Atul Kohli and Vivienne Shue (eds.) (1994) *State Power and Social Forces: Domination and Transformation in the Third World*. Cambridge, UK: Cambridge University Press.
Mission, Gina (1999) "Big Swindle in Hacienda Looc?," originally published online on CyberDyaryo, archived on the Gina Mission home page at: http://gina.ph/CyberDyaryo/features/cd1999_0826-002.htm.
Molyneux, Maxine and Shahra Razavi (2002) *Gender Justice, Development and Rights*. Oxford: Oxford University Press.
Mondragon, Hector (2003) "Colombia: Either Land Markets or Agrarian Reform," in F. Barros et al. (eds.) *The Negative Impacts of World Bank Market Based Land Reform*, pp. 103–168. Brazil: CPT and MST.
Monk, Paul (1996) *Truth and Power: Robert S. Hardie and Land Reform Debates in the Philippines, 1950–1987* (rev. ed.). Quezon City: New Day Publishers.
Monsalve, Sofia (2003) "Access to Land and Justiciability," *Right to Food Journal*, 2 (December 2003) Heidelberg: FoodFirst Information and Action Network (FIAN). Pamphlet.
Monsod, Solita and Toby Monsod (1999) "International and Intranational Comparisons of Philippine Poverty," in A. Balisacan and S. Fujisaki (eds.) *Causes of Poverty: Myths, Facts and Policies – A Philippine Study*, pp. 51–93. Quezon City: University of the Philippines Press.
Montinola, Gabriella (1999) "Politicians, Parties, and the Persistence of Weak States: Lessons from the Philippines," *Development Change*, 30(4): 739–774.
Moore, Barrington, Jr. (1967) *Social Origins of Dictatorship and Democracy: Lord and Peasant in the Modern World*. Harmondsworth: Penguin.
Morales, Horacio, Jr. (1999) "Afterword," in S. Borras, *The Bibingka Strategy in Land Reform Implementation*, pp. 191–199. Quezon City: Institute for Popular Democracy.
Mosley, Paul (1985) "Achievements and Contradictions of the Peruvian Agrarian Reform: A Regional Perspective," *Journal of Development Studies*, 21(3): 440–448.
Moyo, Sam (2007) "Land Policy, Poverty Reduction and Public Action in Zimbabwe," in H. Akram-Lodhi, S. Borras and C. Kay (eds.) *Land, Poverty and Livelihoods in an Era of Neoliberal Globalization: Perspectives from Developing and Transition Countries*. London: Routledge.
—— (2000) "The Political Economy of Land Acquisition and Redistribution in Zimbabwe, 1990–1999," *Journal of Southern African Studies*, 26(1): 5–28.
Moyo, Sam and Paris Yeros (2005) "The Resurgence of Rural Movements under Neoliberalism," in S. Moyo and P. Yeros (eds.) *Reclaiming the Land: The Resurgence of Rural Movements in Africa, Asia and Latin America*, pp. 8–66. London: Zed.
MUCEP (2001) "Proposal for the Preparation of Area Development Plan and Household Level Farm Business Plans for World Bank-DAR-CMARP Project in Sibula, Lopez Jaena, Misamis Occidental." A Project Proposal by the Misamis

University Community Extension Program (MUCEP) submitted to the ARCDP-DAR. Misamis Occidental: MUCEP/Quezon City: DAR-ARCDP.
Mukherjee, Chandan and Marc Wuyts (1998) "Thinking with Quantitative Data," in A. Thomas, J. Chataway and M. Wuyts (eds.) *Finding Out Fast: Investigative Skills for Policy and Development*, pp. 237-260. London/Thousand Oaks/New Delhi: Sage Publications in association with the Open University.
Murray, Colin (1996) "Land Reform in the Eastern Free State: Policy Dilemmas and Political Conflicts," *Journal of Peasant Studies*, 23(2/3): 209-244.
Narayanan, N.C. (2003) "Against the Grain: The Political Ecology of Land Use in a Kerala Region, India." Ph.D. dissertation, The Hague: Institute of Social Studies/Maastricht: Shaker Publishing.
Navarro, Zander (1998) "The 'Cédula da Terra' Guiding Project — Comments on the Social and Political-Institutional Conditions of Its Recent Development." www.dataetrra.org.br. Unpublished document, World Bank.
Newell, Peter and Joanna Wheeler (2006) "Rights, Resources and the Politics of Accountability: An Introduction," in P. Newell and J. Wheeler (eds.) Rights, Resources and the Politics of Accountability, pp. 1-36. London: Zed.
Nordlinger, Eric (1987) "Taking the State Seriously," in M. Weiner and S.P. Huntington (eds.) *Understanding Political Development*, pp. 353-390. Boston: Little Brown.
Ntsebeza, Lungisile (2006) *Democracy Compromised: Chiefs and the Politics of the Land in South Africa*. Leiden: Brill.
Ntsebeza, Lungisile and Ruth Hall (eds.) (2006) *The Land Question in South Africa: The Challenge of Transformation and Redistribution*. Cape Town: HSRC Press.
Nuijten, M. (2003) "Family Property and the Limits of Intervention: The Article 27 Reforms and the PROCEDE Programme in Mexico," *Development and Change*, 34(3): 475-497.
Nyamu-Musembi, Celestine (2006) Breathing Life into Dead Theories about Property Rights: de Soto and Land Relations in Rural Africa. *IDS Working Paper* No. 272. Brighton: IDS.
O'Brien, Kevin (1996) "Rightful Resistance," *World Politics* 49(October): 31-55.
O'Brien, Kevin and Li Lianjiang (2006) *Rightful Resistance in China*. Cambridge, UK: Cambridge University Press.
Ocampo, David Isidoro (2000) "The Plight of Farmers Charged with Theft or Qualified Theft." *KAISAHAN Occasional Papers* (August 2000). Quezon City: KAISAHAN.
O'Donnell, Guillermo (1993) "On the State, Democratization and Some Conceptual Problems: A Latin American View with Glances at Some Postcommunist Countries," *World Development*, 21(8): 1355-1369.
Ofreneo, Rene (1980) *Capitalism in Philippine Agriculture* (updated ed.). Quezon City: Foundation for Nationalist Studies.
Olano, Jose Noel (2001) "The Role of Peasants' Organizations in Managing Agrarian Conflict," in K. Ghimire (ed.) *Land Reform and Peasant Livelihoods: The Social Dynamics of Rural Poverty and Agrarian Reform in Developing Countries*, pp. 199-229. Geneva: UNRISD/London: ITDG.

O'Laughlin, Bridget (1996) "Through a Divided Glass: Dualism, Class and the Agrarian Questions in Mozambique," *Journal of Peasant Studies*, 23(4): 1–39.

——— (1995) "Past and Present Options: Land Reform in Mozambique," *Review of African Political Economy*, (63): 99–106.

Oorthuizen, Joost (2003) *Water, Works and Wages: The Everyday Politics of Irrigation Management Reform in the Philippines*. Wageningen, The Netherlands: Wageningen University Water Resources Series/Hyderabad: Orient Longman.

Ostrom, Elinor (2001) "The Puzzle of Counterproductive Property Rights Reforms: A Conceptual Analysis," in A. de Janvry, G. Gordillo, J.P. Platteau and E. Sadoulet (eds.) *Access to Land, Rural Poverty, and Public Action*, pp. 129–150. Oxford: Oxford University Press.

Otsuka, Keijiro (1996) "Land Reform in the Philippines: Lessons from the Past and Direction for the Future," in E. de Dios and R. Fabella (eds.) *Choice, Growth and Development: Emerging and Enduring Issues (Essays in Honor of José Encarnacion)*, pp. 171–192. Quezon City: University of the Philippines Press.

Owen, Norman (1999) *The Bikol Blend: Bikolanos and Their History*. Quezon City: New Day Publishers.

——— (1982) "Abaca in Kabikolan: Prosperity without Progress," in A. McCoy and E. de Jesus (eds.) *Philippine Social History: Global Trade and Local Transformations*, pp. 191–216. Quezon City: Ateneo de Manila University Press.

Paasch, Armin (2003) "The Failure of Market-Assisted Land Reforms and Some Necessary Consequences: Comments on the World Bank's Policy Research Report." www.worldbank.org/landpolicy/; accessed 2 May 2004.

Pacuribot, Ma. Lourdes Zenaida and Dante Gatmaytan (2000) "Agrarian Reform in Retreat: A Critique of Joint Economic Enterprises." *KAISAHAN Occasional Paper* (June 2000). Quezon City: KAISAHAN.

Padilla, Sabino, Jr. (1990) *Agrarian Revolution: Peasant Radicalization and Social Change in Bicol*. Manila: Kalikasan Press.

Paige, Jeffrey (1996) "Land Reform and Agrarian Revolution in El Salvador," *Latin American Research Review*, 31(2): 1127–1139.

——— (1975) *Agrarian Revolution: Social Movements and Export Agriculture in the Underdeveloped World*. New York: Free Press.

PAKISAMA (1996) *Peasant Initiatives*. Quezon City: PAKISAMA.

Palmer, Robin (2000a) "Land Policy in Africa: Lessons from Recent Policy and Implementation Processes," in C. Toulmin and J. Quan (eds.) *Evolving Land Rights, Policy and Tenure in Africa*, pp. 267–288. London: DFID/IIED/NRI.

——— (2000b) "Mugabe's 'Land Grab' in Regional Perspective," in T.A.S. Bowyer-Bower and C. Stoneman (eds.) *Land Reform in Zimbabwe: Constraints and Prospects*, pp. 15–23. Aldershot, Hampshire, UK: Ashgate.

PARRDS (2002) "Absence of Transparency and Statistical Scams Go Together in DAR." Press statement, dated 29 May 2002. Quezon City: PARRDS.

—— (1997) "Executive Summary, Second DAR-NGO-PO Workshop: Fast-Tracking CARP Implementation." Quezon City: PARRDS. Unpublished document.
Parreño, Earl (2003) *Boss Danding*. Quezon City: Earl Parreño/First Quarter Storm Foundation.
Parsons, Kenneth (1956) "Part 1: Introduction — Land Reform and Agricultural Development," in K. Parsons, R. Penn and P. Raup (eds.) "Land Tenure — Proceedings of the International Conference on Land Tenure and Related Problems in World Agriculture," pp. 3–22, held at Madison, WI, 1951. Madison: The University of Wisconsin Press.
Patayan, Felicisimo (1998) *Struggle: An Autobiography* (ed. by E. Quitoriano and L. Mercado-Carreon). Quezon City: Felicisimo Patayan.
Patel, Rajeev (2006) "International Agrarian Restructuring and the Practical Ethics of Peasant Movement Solidarity," *Journal of Asian and African Studies*, 41(1&2): 71–93.
Patel, Rajeev, Radhika Balakrishna and Uma Narayan (2007) "Explorations on Human Rights," *Feminist Economics*, 13(1): 87–116.
Pearce, Jenny (1998) "From Civil War to Civil Society: Has the End of the Cold War Brought Peace in Central America?," *International Affairs*, 74(3): 587–615.
Peluso, Nancy (2007) "Violence, Decentralization and Resource Access in Indonesia," *Peace Review*, 19(1): 23–32.
—— (1992) *Rich Forests, Poor People: Resource Control and Resistance in Java*. Berkeley: University of California Press.
Peña, Teodorico (1996) "Agrarian Reform in Negros Occidental," *KAISAHAN Occasional Paper* 96-01. Quezon City: KAISAHAN.
Pereira, João Marcio (forthcoming) "The World Bank's 'Market-Assisted' Land Reform as a Political Issue: Evidence from Brazil (1997–2006)," *European Review of Latin American and Caribbean Studies*.
Peters, Pauline (2004) "Inequality and Social Conflict over Land in Africa," *Journal of Agrarian Change*, 4(3): 269–314.
Petras, James (1998) "The Political and Social Basis of Regional Variation in Land Occupations in Brazil," *Journal of Peasant Studies*, 25(4): 124–133.
—— (1997) "Latin America: The Resurgence of the Left," *New Left Review*, (223): 17–47.
Petras, James and Henry Veltmeyer (2003) "The Peasantry and the State in Latin America: A Troubled Past, an Uncertain Future," in T. Brass (ed.) *Latin American Peasants*, pp. 41–82. London: Frank Cass.
—— (2001) "Are Latin American Peasant Movements Still a Force for Change?," *Journal of Peasant Studies*, 28(2): 83–118.
PhilDHRRA (1997) *Making Agrarian Reform Work: Securing the Gains of Land Tenure Improvement*. Quezon City: Philippine Partnership for the Development of Human Resources in Rural Areas (PhilDHRRA).
Philippine Daily Inquirer, 26–27 March 2001, p. 8.

Philippine Daily Inquirer, GMA online interview with President Macapagal-Arroyo, 6 March 2002; posted at: www.inq7.net/exclusive/2002/mar/06/Macapagal-Arroyo_03-6-2.htm; accessed 5 May 2002.
Pimentel, Benjamin (1991) *Rebolusyon: A Generation of Struggle in the Philippines*. New York: Monthly Review Press.
Platteau, Jean-Philippe (1996) "The Evolutionary Theory of Land Rights as Applied to Sub-Saharan Africa: A Critical Assessment," *Development and Change*, 27(1): 29–86.
——— (1995) "A Framework for the Analysis of Evolving Patron-Client Ties in Agrarian Economies," *World Development*, 23(5): 767–786.
Po, Blondie and Cristina Montiel (1980) *Rural Organizations in the Philippines*. Quezon City: Institute of Philippine Culture. Ateneo de Manila University.
Pons-Vignon, Nicolas and Henri-Bernard Solignac Lecomte (2004) "Land, Violent Conflict and Development." Working Paper No. 233. OECD Development Centre.
Prosterman, Roy (1976) "IRI: A Simplified Predictive Index of Rural Instability," *Comparative Politics*, 8(3): 339–354.
Prosterman, Roy and Jeffrey Riedinger (1987) *Land Reform and Democratic Development*. Baltimore, MD: Johns Hopkins University Press.
Prosterman, Roy, Mary Temple and Timothy Hanstad (eds.) (1990) *Agrarian Reform and Grassroots Development: Ten Cases*. Boulder, CO: Lynne Rienner.
Putzel, James (2002) "The Politics of Partial Reform in the Philippines," in V.K. Ramachandran and M. Swaminathan (eds.) *Agrarian Studies: Essays on Agrarian Relations in Less-Developed Countries*, pp. 213–229. New Delhi: Tulika Books [2003, London: Zed].
——— (2000) "Land Reforms in Asia: Lessons from the Past for the 21st Century." *LSE Working Paper Series*, No. 00-04. London: London School of Economics.
——— (1999) "The Survival of an Imperfect Democracy in the Philippines," *Democratization*, 6(1): 198–223.
——— (1998) "Non-governmental Organizations and Rural Poverty," in G.S. Silliman and L.G. Noble (eds.) *Organizing for Democracy: NGOs, Civil Society, and the Philippine State*, pp. 77–112. Quezon City: Ateneo de Manila University Press.
——— (1995) "Managing the 'Main Force': The Communist Party and the Peasantry in the Philippines," *Journal of Peasant Studies*, 22(4): 645–671.
——— (1992) *A Captive Land: The Politics of Agrarian Reform in the Philippines*. London: Catholic Institute for International Relations/New York: Monthly Review Press/Quezon City: Ateneo de Manila University Press.
Quan, Julian (2000) "Land Tenure, Economic Growth and Poverty in Sub-Saharan Africa," in C. Toulmin and J. Quan (eds.) *Evolving Land Rights, Policy and Tenure in Africa*, pp. 31–49. London: DFID/IIED/NRI.
Quimpo, Nathan (2005) Review Article: "Oligarchic Patrimonialism, Bossism, Electoral Clientilism and Contested Democracy in the Philippines," *Comparative Politics*, 37(2).

Quitoriano, Eddie (2001) "Agrarian Reform: Who Calls the Shots at the Local Level?," *Bantaaw*, 14(4/5): 1–12. Davao: Alternate Forum for Research in Mindanao (AFRIM).

────── (2000) *Agrarian Struggles and Institutional Change: The MAPALAD Struggle for Land*. Quezon City: Management and Organization for Development and Empowerment (MODE).

────── (1998) "Agrarian Reform Communities in the Philippines." Quezon City: NCOS-Pilipinas [n.b., this organization is now known as 11.11.11]. Unpublished document.

Ragin, Charles (1992) " 'Casing' and the Process of Social Inquiry," in C. Ragin and H. Becker (eds.) *What Is a Case?: Exploring the Foundations of Social Inquiry*, pp. 217–326. Cambridge, UK: Cambridge University Press.

Ramos, Charmaine (2000) *State Intervention and Private Sector Participation in Philippine Rice Marketing*. Quezon City: Management and Organizational Development for Empowerment (MODE) and Southeast Asian Council for Food Security and Fair Trade.

Razavi, Shahra (2003) "Introduction: Agrarian Change, Gender and Land Rights," special issue, *Journal of Agrarian Change*, 3(1/2): 2–32.

Redclift, Michael (1978) *Agrarian Reform and Peasant Organization on the Ecuadorian Coast*. London: University of London/The Athlone Press.

Regalado, Aurora (1992) "Barriers in the Development of the Sugar Industry," *Rural Development Studies*, 8(4) (August): 1–42. Quezon City: Philippine Peasant Institute.

Reid, Ben (2005) "Poverty Alleviation and Participatory Development in the Philippines," *Journal of Contemporary Asia*, 35(1): 29–53.

────── (2000) *Philippine Left: Political Crisis and Social Change*. Manila/Sydney: Journal of Contemporary Asia Publishers.

Resurreccion, Bernadette (2006) "Gender, Identity and Agency in the Philippine Upland Development," *Development and Change*, 37(2): 375–400.

Reyes, Cecilia (2002) "Impact of Agrarian Reform on Poverty." *PIDS Discussion Paper Series* No. 2002-02. Manila: Philippine Institute for Development Studies.

Reyes, Ricardo (2001) "People Power Comes into the New Millennium," *IPD Political Brief*, 9(2): 1–30. Quezon City: Institute for Popular Democracy.

────── (2000) "CARP Past the Deadline: Where's the Beef?," in "The Impact of Agrarian Reform and Changing Market on Rural Households." *MODE Research Papers*, 1(4): 7–56. Quezon City: MODE.

────── (1999) "Market-Assisted Land Reform: An Indecent Proposal." Available on the website of the Philippine European Solidarity Centre (PESC-KSP) at: www.philsol.nl/A99a/RicReyes-WB-mar99.htm.

Ribot, Jesse and Anne Larson (2005) *Democratic Decentralisation through a Natural Resource Lens*. London: Routledge.

Ribot, Jesse and Nancy Peluso (2003) "A Theory of Access," *Rural Sociology*, 68(2): 153–181.

Riedinger, Jeffrey (1995) *Agrarian Reform in the Philippines: Democratic Transitions and Redistributive Reform*. Stanford, CT: Stanford University Press.

Riedinger, Jeffrey, Wan-Ying Yang and Karen Brook (2001) "Market-Based Land Reform: An Imperfect Solution," in H. Morales and J. Putzel (eds.) *Power in the Village: Agrarian Reform, Rural Politics, Institutional Change and Globalization*, pp. 363–378. Quezon City: University of the Philippines Press.

Rigg, Jonathan (2006) "Land, Farming, Livelihoods, and Poverty: Rethinking the Links in the Rural South," *World Development*, 34(1): 180–202.

Rimban, Luz (2005) "Did Marcos Wealth and Taxpayers Bankroll GMA Campaign?"; posted 28 August 2005 on the website of the Philippine Center for Investigative Journalism at: http://pcij.org/stories/print/2005/farmfunds2.html; accessed 21 October 2006.

—— (1997) "Women Being Winnowed out of Agrarian Reform," *The Manila Times*, 3–4 March 1997.

Rivera, Temario (1994) *Landlords and Capitalists: Class, Family, and State in Philippine Manufacturing*. Quezon City: University of the Philippines Press.

Robinson, Mark and John Farrington (eds.) (2006) Sustaining Growth and Ending Poverty in Asia special issue, *IDS Bulletin*, 37(3).

Robles, Wilder (2001) "The Landless Rural Workers Movement (MST) in Brazil," *Journal of Peasant Studies*, 28(2): 146–161.

Rocamora, Joel (1994) *Breaking Through: The Struggle within the Communist Party of the Philippines*. Manila: Anvil.

Rocamora, J. Eliseo and Corazon Panganiban (1975) *Rural Development Strategies: The Philippine Case*. Quezon City: Institute of Philippine Culture, Ateneo de Manila University.

Rodil, B.R. (1994) *The Minoritization of the Indigenous Communities of Mindanao and the Sulu Archipelago*. Davao: Alternate Forum for Research in Mindanao.

Rodriguez, Joel (2000) "Agrarian Reform in Commercial Farms: Designing an Appropriate Institutional Response." *MODE Research Papers*, 1(3): 1–40. Quezon City: MODE.

—— (1987) *Genuine Agrarian Reform*. Quezon City: Urban-Rural Mission, National Council of Churches in the Philippines.

Roquas, Esther (2002) *Stacked Law: Land, Property and Conflict in Honduras*. Amsterdam: Thela Latin America Series.

—— (2000) "*Muerte a los Jueces Vendidos*: Land Conflicts and the Paradox of Class Justice in Rural Honduras," in A. Zoomers and G.v.d. Haar (eds.) *Current Land Policy in Latin America: Regulating Land Tenure Under Neo-liberalism*, pp. 177–200. Amsterdam: Royal Tropical Institute (KIT).

Ross, Eric (2007) "Clearance as Development Strategy in Colombia," *Peace Review*, 19(1): 59–65.

—— (2003) "Modernisation, Clearance and the Continuum of Violence in Colombia." *ISS Working Paper Series* no. 383. The Hague: Institute of Social Studies.

—— (1998) *The Malthus Factor: Poverty, Politics and Population in Capitalist Development*. London: Zed.
Rosset, Peter (2006) "Agrarian Reform and Food Sovereignty: Inseparable Parts of an Alternative Framework." Paper presented at the International Conference on Land, Poverty and Development at the Institute of Social Studies (ISS), The Hague, Netherlands, 9–14 January 2006.
—— (2001) "Tides Shift on Agrarian Reform: New Movements Show the Way," *Backgrounder*, 7(1): 1–8. Berkeley: FoodFirst Institute.
Rosset, Peter, Raj Patel and Michael Courville (eds.) (2006) *Promised Land: Competing Visions of Agrarian Reform*. Berkeley, CA: FoodFirst Books.
Rutten, Rosanne (2000a) "High-Cost Activism and the Worker Household: Interests, Commitment, and the Costs of Revolutionary Activism in a Philippine Plantation Region," *Theory and Society*, 29(2): 215–252.
—— (2000b) "Changing Sides in Revolutionary Times: The Career of a Lower-Class CPP-NPA Leader in Negros Occidental," in A. McCoy (ed.) *Lives at the Margin: Biography of Filipinos Obscure, Ordinary, and Heroic*, pp. 423–467. Quezon City: Ateneo de Manila University Press.
—— (1996) "Popular Support for the Revolutionary Movement CPP-NPA: Experiences in a Hacienda in Negros Occidental, 1978–1995," in P. Abinales (ed.) *The Revolution Falters: The Left in Philippine Politics after 1986*. Ithaca, NY: Southeast Asia Program Publications, Cornell University.
—— (1993) *Artisans and Entrepreneurs in the Rural Philippines: Making a Living and Gaining Wealth in Two Commercialized Crafts*. Quezon City: New Day Publishers.
Sadoulet, Elisabeth, Rinku Murgai, and Alain de Janvry (2001) "Access to Land via Land Rental Markets," in A. de Janvry, G. Gordillo, J.P. Platteau and E. Sadoulet (eds.) *Access to Land, Rural Poverty, and Public Action*, pp. 196–229. Oxford: Oxford University Press.
—— (1998) "Access to Land via Land Rental Markets." A paper prepared for the WIDER Land Reform Project Conference, Santiago, Chile, 27–29 April 1998.
Saith, Ashwani (1990) "Development Strategies and the Rural Poor," *Journal of Peasant Studies*, 17(2): 171–244.
—— (1985) "Primitive Accumulation, Agrarian Reform and Socialist Transitions: An Argument," *Journal of Development Studies*, 22(1): 1–48.
Sajor, Edsel (1999) "Upland Livelihood Transformations: State and Market Processes and Social Autonomy in the Northern Philippines." Ph.D. dissertation, The Hague: Institute of Social Studies/Maastricht: Shaker Publishing.
Salamini, Heather Fowler (1971) *Agrarian Radicalism in Veracruz, 1920–38*. Lincoln: University of Nebraska Press.
Salonga, Jovito (2000) *Presidential Plunder: The Quest for the Marcos Ill-Gotten Wealth*. Quezon City: University of the Philippines' Center for Leadership, Citizenship and Democracy, College of Public Administration, and Regina Publishing Co.
Sanderson, Susan Walsh (1984) *Land Reform in Mexico: 1920–1980*. London/New York: Academic Press.

Santiago, Miriam (1994) *Cutting Edge: The Politics of Reform in the Philippines*. Metro Manila: Woman Today Publications.

Santoalla, Ed, Earl Parreño and Eddie Quitoriano (eds.) (2001) *Lessons in ODA Theory and Practice*. Quezon City: MODE.

Sato, Jin (2000) "People in Between: Conversion and Conservation of Forest Lands in Thailand," in M. Doornbos, A. Saith and B. White (eds.) Forests: Nature, People, People special issue, *Development and Change*, 31(1): 155–177.

Sauer, Sergio (2003) "A Ticket to Land: The World Bank's Market-Based Land Reform in Brazil," in F. Barros et al. (eds.) *The Negative Impacts of World Bank Market-Based Land Reform*, pp. 45–102. Brazil: Comissao Pastoral da Terra, Movimento dos Trabalhadores Rurais Sem Terra (MST), FoodFirst Information and Action Network (FIAN).

Scott, James (1998) *Seeing Like a State: How Certain Schemes to Improve the Human Condition Have Failed*. New Haven: Yale University Press.

——— (1990) *Domination and the Arts of Resistance: Hidden Transcripts*. New Haven: Yale University Press.

——— (1985) *Weapons of the Weak*. New Haven: Yale University Press.

——— (1976) *The Moral Economy of the Peasant: Rebellion and Subsistence in Southeast Asia*. New Haven: Yale University Press.

Scott, James and Benedict Kerkvliet (1986) "Everyday Forms of Peasant Resistance in Southeast Asia," special issue, *Journal of Peasant Studies*, 13(2).

Shanin, Teodor (ed.) (1987) *Peasant and Peasant Societies* (new ed.). London: Penguin, in association with Basil Blackwell.

Shillinglaw, Geoffrey (1974) "Land Reform and Peasant Mobilization in Southern China, 1947–1950," in D. Lehmann (ed.) *Peasants, Landlords and Governments: Agrarian Reform in the Third World*, pp. 118–155. New York: Holmes and Meier Publishers

Sidel, John (1999) *Capital, Coersion and Crime: Bossism in the Philippines*. Stanford, CA: Stanford University Press.

Sikor, Thomas (2006) "Politics of Rural Land Registration in Post-socialist Societies: Contested Titling in Villages of Northwest Vietnam," *Land Use Policy*, 23(2006): 617–628.

Silliman, Sidney and Lela Noble (eds.) (1998) *Organizing for Democracy: NGOs, Civil Society, and the Philippine State*. Quezon City: Ateneo de Manila University Press.

Skocpol, Theda (1988) "Social Revolutions and Mass Military Mobilizations," *World Politics*, 40(2): 147–168.

——— (1979) *States and Revolution: A Comparative Analysis of France, Russia, and China*. Cambridge, UK: Cambridge University Press.

Slater, David (1990) "Debating Decentralisation — A Reply to Rondinelli [Discussion]," *Development and Change*, 21(3): 501–512.

——— (1989) "Territorial Power and the Peripheral State: The Issue of Decentralisation," *Development and Change*, 20(3): 501–531.

Sobhan, Rehman (1993) *Agrarian Reform and Social Transformation*. London: Zed.
Spoor, Max (2002) "Policy Regimes and Performance of the Agricultural Sector in Latin America and the Caribbean during the Last Three Decades," *Journal of Agrarian Change*, 2(3): 381–400.
Spoor, Max and Oane Visser (2004) "Restructuring Postponed: Large Russian Farm Enterprises 'Coping with the Market,' " *Journal of Peasant Studies*, 31(3/4): 515–551.
Spoor, Max (ed.) (forthcoming) *Contested Land in the "East": Land and Rural Markets in Transition Economies*. London: Routledge.
―――― (2003) *Transition, Institutions, and the Rural Sector*. New York: Lexington.
―――― (1997) *The "Market Panacea": Agrarian Transformation in Developing Countries and Former Socialist Economies*. London: Intermediate Technology Publications.
Sta. Ana, Filomeno, III (ed.) (1998) *The State and the Market: Essays on a Socially Oriented Philippine Economy*. Quezon City: Action for Economic Reforms; Ateneo de Manila University Press.
Starner, Frances (1961) *Magsaysay and the Philippine Peasantry: The Agrarian Impact on Philippine Politics, 1953–1956*. Berkeley: University of California Press.
Stiglitz, Joseph (2002) *Globalization and its Discontents*. London: The Penguin Press.
Striffler, Steve (2002) *In the Shadows of State and Capital: The United Fruit Company, Popular Struggle, and Agrarian Reform Restructuring in Ecuador, 1900–1995*. Durham, NC: Duke University Press.
Sturtevant, David (1976) *Popular Uprisings in the Philippines, 1840–1940*. Ithaca, NY: Cornell University Press.
Tadem, Eduardo, Johnny Reyes and Linda Susan Magno (1984) *Showcases of Underdevelopment in Mindanao: Fishes, Forests, and Fruits*. Davao: Alternate Forum for Research in Mindanao (AFRIM).
Tai, Hung-Chao (1974) *Land Reform and Politics: A Comparative Analysis*. Berkeley: University of California Press.
Tannenbaum, Frank (1929) *The Mexican Agrarian Revolution*. New York: Archon Books [republished in 1968].
Tarrow, Sidney (1998) *Power in Movement: Social Movements and Contentious Politics* (2nd ed.). Cambridge, UK: Cambridge University Press.
―――― (1996) "States and Opportunities: The Political Structure of Social Movements," in McAdam et al. (eds.) *Comparative Perspectives on Social Movements: Political Opportunity, Mobilizing Structures and Cultural Framings*, pp. 41–61. Cambridge, UK: Cambridge University Press.
―――― (1994) *Power in Movement: Social Movements, Collective Action and Politics*. Cambridge, UK: Cambridge University Press.
"Tatang" (pseudonym) (1988) *Ang Talambuhay ni Tatang: Sa Tungki ng Ilong ng Kaaway*. Quezon City: LINANG.
Tendler, Judith (1997) *Good Government in the Tropics*. Baltimore, MD: The Johns Hopkins University Press.

Thelen, Kathleen and Sven Steinmo (1992) "Historical Institutionalism in Comparative Politics," in S. Steinmo, K. Thelen and F. Longstreth (eds.) *Structuring Politics: Historical Institutionalism in Comparative Analysis*, pp. 1–32. Cambridge: Cambridge University Press.

Thiesenhusen, William (1995) *Broken Promises: Agrarian Reform and the Latin American Campesino*. Boulder, CO: Westview.

—— (1990) "Recent Progress toward Agrarian Reform in the Philippines," *Land Reform, Land Settlements and Cooperatives*, 1989(1/2): 57–77.

—— (1971) "Colonization: Alternative or Supplement to Agrarian Reform," in P. Dorner (ed.) *Land Reform in Latin America*, pp. 209–226. Madison, WI: Land Economics, University of Wisconsin-Madison.

Thiesenhusen, William (ed.) (1989) *Searching for Agrarian Reform in Latin America*. Boston: Unwin Hyman.

Thomas, John and Merilee Grindle (1990) "After the Decision: Implementing Policy Reforms in Developing Countries," *World Development*, 18(8): 1163–1181.

Thome, Joseph (1997) "Land Rights and Agrarian Reform: Latin American and South African Perspectives," in J. Fuandez (ed.) *Good Government and Law: Legal and Institutional Reform in Developing Countries*, pp. 201–224. London: Macmillan.

—— (1989) "Law, Conflict, and Change: Frei's Law and Allende's Agrarian Reform," in W. Thiesenhusen (ed.) *Searching for Agrarian Reform in Latin America*, 188–215. Boston: Unwin Hyman.

—— (1971) "Agrarian Reform Legislation: Chile," in P. Dorner (ed.) *Land Reform in Latin America*. Madison, WI: Land Economics, University of Wisconsin-Madison.

Thompson, Mark (1996) *The Anti-Marcos Struggle: Personalistic Rule and Democratic Transition in the Philippines*. New Haven, CT: Yale University Press.

Tiglao, Rigoberto (1983) "The Political Economy of the Philippine Coconut Industry," in S.D. Randolf, Teresita Gimenez-Maceda and Sheila Coronel (eds.) *Political Economy of Philippine Commodities*, pp. 181–272. Quezon City: Third World Studies Center, University of the Philippines.

—— (1982) "Tenancy in Underdeveloped Capitalism," in T. Rivera et al. (eds.) *Feudalism and Capitalism in the Philippines: Trends and Implications*, pp. 45–59. Quezon City: Foundation for Nationalist Studies.

Tilly, Charles (1988) "Social Movements, Old and New," *Research in Social Movements, Conflicts and Change*, (10): 1–18.

—— (1984) "Social Movements and National Politics," in C. Bright and S. Harding (eds.) *Statemaking and Social Movements: Essays in History and Theory*. Ann Arbor: University of Michigan Press.

Toulmin, Camilla and Julian Quan (eds.) (2000) *Evolving Land Rights, Policy and Tenure in Africa*. London: DFID/IIED/NRI.

Tsing, Anna (2002) "Land as Law: Negotiating the Meaning of Property in Indonesia," in F. Richards (ed.) *Land, Property, and the Environment*, 94–137. Oakland, CA: Institute for Contemporary Studies.

Tuma, Elias (1965) *Twenty-Six Centuries of Agrarian Reform: A Comparative Analysis*. Berkeley: University of California Press.

Turner, Mark, R.J. May and Lulu Respall Turner (eds.) (1992) *Mindanao: Land of Unfulfilled Promise*. Quezon City: New Day.

UNORKA (2002) "Ang Kampanyang 7/11 ng UNORKA. October 2002." Discussion paper on its campaign for the ouster of DAR Secretary Braganza. Internal document.

───── (2001a) "Status Report of 519 Agrarian Cases Directly Handled by UNORKA." Internal document.

───── (2001b) "Beyond the Peasant Barricades: Who We Are, Why We Went to Manila on 13 August 2001, and Why We Were Forced to Invade the DAR's Office of the Secretary for Three Days and Two Nights." Statement by the UNORKA Consultative Council on 20 August 2001. Quezon City: UNORKA.

───── (2000a) "Minutes of the First Executive Committee Meeting held on 23 June 2000." Internal document.

───── (2000b) "No to the World Bank's Market-Assisted Land Reform." Statement circulated during the International Conference on Agrarian Reform and Rural Development, Tagaytay City, Philippines, December 2000. Mimeo.

UPSARDFI (2001) *Families and Households in the ARC: Focusing ARCDP II for Greater and Lasting Impact in the Rural Countryside – A Final Report on the Social Assessment for the Second Phase of the Agrarian Reform Communities Development Project*, prepared by the University of the Philippines Action and Research for Development Foundation, Inc. (UPSARDFI) for the ARCDP-DAR. Quezon City: UPSARDFI, College of Social Work and Community Development, U.P.-Diliman; DAR.

Utting, Peter (ed.) (2000) *Forest Policy and Politics in the Philippines: The Dynamics of Participatory Conservation*. Quezon City: Ateneo de Manila University Press.

van Acker, Frank (2005) "'Where Did All the Land Go?' Enclosure and Social Struggle in Kivu (D.R. Congo)," *Review of African Political Economy*, 32(103): 79–98.

van den Brink, Rogier, Mike de Klerk and Hans Binswanger (1996) "Rural Livelihoods, Fiscal Costs and Financing Options: A First Attempt at Quantifying the Implications of Redistributive Land Reform," in J.v. Zyl, J. Kirsten and H.P. Binswanger (eds.) *Agricultural Land Reform in South Africa: Policies, Markets and Mechanisms*, pp. 423–460. Oxford: Oxford University Press.

van den Muijzenberg, Otto (1991) "Tenant Emancipation, Diversification and Social Differentiation in Central Luzon," in J. Breman and S. Mundle (eds.) *Rural Transformation in Asia*, pp. 313–337. Oxford: Oxford University Press.

Vandergeest, Peter and Nancy Peluso (1995) "Territorialization and State Power in Thailand," *Theory and Society*, 24(3): 385–426.

van Donge, Jan Kees with George Eiseb and Alfons Mosimane (2007) "Land Reform in Namibia: Issues of Equity and Poverty," in H. Akram-Lodhi, S. Borras and C. Kay (eds.) *Land, Poverty and Livelihoods in an Era of Neoliberal Globalization: Perspectives from Developing and Transition Countries*. London: Routledge.

van Schalkwyk and Johan van Zyl (1996) "The Land Market," in J.v. Zyl, J. Kirsten and H.P. Binswanger (eds.) *Agricultural Land Reform in South Africa: Policies, Markets and Mechanisms*, pp. 310–335. Oxford: Oxford University Press.

van Zyl, Johan and Hans Binswanger (1996) "Market-Assisted Land Reform: How Will It Work?," in J.v. Zyl, J. Kirsten and H.P. Binswanger (eds.) *Agricultural Land Reform in South Africa: Policies, Markets and Mechanisms*, pp. 413–422. Oxford: Oxford University Press.

van Zyl, Johan, Johann Kirsten and Hans Binswanger (1996) "Introduction," in J.v. Zyl, J. Kirsten and H.P. Binswanger (eds.) *Agricultural Land Reform in South Africa: Policies, Markets and Mechanisms*, pp. 3–17. Oxford: Oxford University Press.

Vellema, Sietze (2002) "Making Contract Farming Work?: Society and Technology in Philippine Transnational Agribusiness." Ph.D. dissertation, Wageningen, The Netherlands: Wageningen University/Maastricht: Shaker Publishing.

Velmonte, Jose (1956) "Farm Ownership and Tenancy in the Philippines," in K. Parsons, R. Penn and P. Raup (eds.) "Land Tenure: Proceedings of the International Conference on Land Tenure and Related Problems in World Agriculture," held at Madison, WI, 1951, pp. 180–188. Madison: University of Wisconsin Press.

Veltmeyer, Henry (2005a) "The Dynamics of Land Occupation in Latin America," in S. Moyo and P. Yeros (eds.) *Reclaiming the Land*, pp. 285–316. London: Zed.

——— (2005b) "The Dynamics of Market-Led Rural Development in Latin America: The Experience of Mexico, Ecuador, Bolivia and Peru," in K. Ghimire (ed.) *Civil Society and the Market Question*, pp. 100–131. New York: Palgrave Macmillan/Geneva: UNRISD.

——— (1997) "New Social Movements in Latin America: The Dynamics of Class and Identity," *Journal of Peasant Studies*, 25(1): 139–169.

Vidal, Aida (2004) *The Politics and Formation of Indigenous Peoples' Right to Land: The Case of Mindanao with Special Reference to the Subanen*. Davao: AFRIM.

Villarin, Tom (1999) "The Mapalad Farmers' Case: Advocacy through the Courts." *KAISAHAN Occasional Papers* (June 1999). Quezon City: KAISAHAN.

von Benda-Beckmann, Franz (2001) "Legal Pluralism and Social Justice in Economic and Political Development," *IDS Bulletin*, 32(1): 46–56.

——— (1993) "Scapegoat and Magic Charm: Law in Development Theory and Practice," in M. Hobart (ed.) *An Anthropological Critique of Development: The Growth of Ignorance*, pp. 116–134. London: Routledge.

Waeterloos, Evert and Blair Rutherford (2004) "Land Reform in Zimbabwe: Challenges and Opportunities for Poverty Reduction among Commercial Farm Workers," *World Development*, 32(3): 537–553.

Walinsky, Louis (ed.) (1977) *Agrarian Reform as Unfinished Business: The Selected Papers of Wolf Ladejinsky*. Oxford: Oxford University Press.

Walker, Cherryl (2003) "Piety in the Sky? Gender Policy and Land Reform in South Africa," *Journal of Agrarian Change*, 3(1/2): 113–148.

Walt, Stephen (1992) "Revolution and War," *World Politics*, 44(3): 321–368.

Wang, Xu (1999) "Mutual Empowerment of State and Society: Its Nature, Conditions, Mechanisms, and Limits," *Comparative Politics*, 31(2): 231–249.

——— (1997) "Mutual Empowerment of State and Peasantry: Grassroots Democracy in Rural China," *World Development*, 25(9): 1431–1442.

Warriner, Doreen (1969) *Land Reform in Principle and Practice*. Oxford: Clarendon Press.

Watkins, Kevin (1996) "Agricultural Trade and Food Security." Paper presented at the South East Asian NGO Conference on Food Security and Fair Trade, University of the Philippines, Quezon City, 13–16 February, 1996. Proceedings published, Quezon City: Management and Organization for Development and Empowerment (MODE).

Watts, Michael (1994) "Life under Contract: Contract Farming, Agrarian Restructuring, and Flexible Accumulation," in P.D. Little and M. Watts (eds.) *Living under Contract: Contract Farming and Agrarian Transformation in Sub-Saharan Africa*, pp. 21–77. Madison: University of Wisconsin Press.

Weekley, Kathleen (2001) *The Communist Party of the Philippines, 1968–1993: A Story of Its Theory and Practice*. Quezon City: University of the Philippines Press.

White, Ben (1997) "Agroindustry and Contract Farmers in Upland West Java," *Journal of Peasant Studies*, 24(3): 100–136.

——— (1989) "Problems in the Empirical Analysis of Agrarian Differentiation," in G. Hart, A. Turton and B. White (eds.) *Agrarian Transformations: Local Processes and the State in Southeast Asia*, pp. 15–30. Berkeley: University of California Press.

White, Christine (1983) "Peasant Mobilization and Anti-colonial Struggle in Vietnam: The Rent Reduction Campaign of 1953," *Journal of Peasant Studies*, 10(4): 187–213.

Whitehead, Anne and Dzodzi Tsikata (2003) "Policy Discourse on Women's Land Rights in Sub-Saharan Africa: The Implications of the Re-turn to the Customary," *Journal of Agrarian Change*, 3(1/2): 67–112.

Wiber, Melanie (1990) "Who Profits from Custom? Jural Constraints on Land Accumulation and Social Stratification in Benguet Province, Northern Philippines," *Journal of Southeast Asian Studies*, 21(2): 329–339.

Wiradi, Gunawan (2005) "Agrarian Reform Movement in Indonesia: Past and Present." Paper presented at the workshop on "Food Sovereignty and Agrarian Reform Movement in Indonesia," organized by the CCFD, Paris, 3 February 2005.

Wolf, Eric (1969) *Peasant Wars of the Twentieth Century*. New York/London: Harper and Row.

——— (1966) *Peasants*. Englewood Cliffs, NJ: Prentice-Hall.

Wolford, Wendy (2005) "Agrarian Moral Economies and Neoliberalism in Brazil: Competing Worldviews and the State in the Struggle for Land," *Environment and Planning*, 37(2): 241–261.

——— (2004) "The Land Is Ours Now: Spatial Imaginaries and the Struggle for Land in Brazil," *Annals of the Association of American Geographers*, 94(2): 409–424.

——— (2003a) "Families, Fields, and Fighting for Land: The Spatial Dynamics of Contention in Rural Brazil," *Mobilization*, 8(2): 157–172.

——— (2003b) "Producing Community: The MST and Land Reform Settlements in Brazil," *Journal of Agrarian Change*, 3(4): 500–520.

Wolters, Willem (1984) *Politics, Patronage and Class Conflict in Central Luzon*. Quezon City: New Day.

Worby, Eric (2001) "A Redivided Land? New Agrarian Conflicts and Questions in Zimbabwe," *Journal of Agrarian Change*, 1(4): 475–509.

World Bank (2003) *Land Policies for Growth and Poverty Reduction*. A World Bank Policy Research Report prepared by Klaus Deininger. Washington, DC: World Bank/Oxford: Oxford University Press.

——— (2000a) "Philippines – Second Agrarian Reform Communities Development Project, or ARCDP-2, Project Concept Document," Manila: World Bank, East Asia and Pacific Region Office, Philippine Country Department.

——— (2000b) *World Bank Report No. 20755-PH – Land Administration and Management Project*. Washington, DC: World Bank.

——— (1997a) "Philippines: Promoting Equitable Rural Growth," confidential/draft, January 1997. Washington, DC: Agriculture and Environment Operations Division, Country Department 1, East Asia Pacific Region. Unpublished.

——— (1997b) "Philippines: Promoting Equitable Rural Growth," confidential/draft, May 1997. Washington, DC: Agriculture and Environment Operations Division, Country Department 1, East Asia Pacific Region. Unpublished.

——— (1996) *A Strategy to Fight Poverty: Philippines*. Washington, DC: Agriculture and Environment Operations Division, Country Department 1, East Asia Pacific Region.

——— (n.d.) "The Theory Behind Market-Assisted Land Reform." www.worldbank.org/landpolicy/; accessed 18 January 2001.

Wright, Angus and Wendy Wolford (2003) *To Inherit the Earth: The Landless Movement and the Struggle for a New Brazil*. Oakland, CA: FoodFirst Books.

Wurfel, David (1989) "Land Reform: Contexts, Accomplishments and Prospects under Marcos and Aquino," *Pilipinas* 12(Spring): 35–54.

——— (1988) *Filipino Politics: Development and Decay*. Ithaca, NY: Cornell University Press.

——— (1983) "The Development of Post-war Philippine Land Reform: Political and Sociological Explanations," in A. Ledesma, S.J., P. Makil and V. Miralao (eds.) *Second View from the Paddy*, pp. 1–14. Quezon City: Institute of Philippine Culture, Ateneo de Manila University.

Yashar, Deborah (1999) "Democracy, Indigenous Movements, and the Postliberal Challenge in Latin America," *World Politics*, 52(1): 76–104.

Zoomers, Annelies and Gemma van der Haar (eds.) (2000) *Current Land Policy in Latin America: Regulating Land Tenure Under Neo-liberalism*. Amsterdam: Royal Tropical Institute (KIT).

B. LIST OF KEY INFORMANTS INTERVIEWED

B.1 Under pseudonyms

"Ababago, Marianne" (pseudonym), former activist supporting peasant struggle in Central Mindanao Region (Region 12) both underground and aboveground and currently leader of an NGO working with and for the peasants in the same region. Quezon City, February 2002.

"Abadiba, Clarito" (pseudonym), top official of a cooperative that is working very closely with the plantation owners, Don Antonio Floirendo Sr. Davao, early 2002.

"Abante, Julio" and others (pseudonym), land reform beneficiaries of a VLT-scheme under the special arrangement (lease-to-own). Focus group discussion at plantation site in North Cotabato, early 2002.

"Abatago, Edmundo" (pseudonym), top official of a cooperative that is working very closely with the plantation owner, Don Antonio Floirendo Sr. Davao, early 2002.

"Alyansa Group" (pseudonym), group of peasant leaders in a landholding in Bondoc peninsula who successfully got the land from the landlord but through the DENR's CBFM; the peasants also used to be the core group of support unit for the New People's Army (NPA) in the area. Focus group discussion in Mulanay, Quezon, third quarter of 2001.

"Anino, Janis" (pseudonym), local DAR official in a municipality of the North Cotabato, explaining and criticizing the lease-to-own scheme being promoted by her superiors. Plantation site in North Cotabato, early 2002.

"*Ka* Julian" (pseudonym), former member of the Mindanao Commission of the Communist Party of the Philippines. Handwritten notes [interview was not tape recorded], The Netherlands, June 1997.

"*Ka* Taning" (pseudonym), former head of the National Peasant Secretariat (NPS) under the Central Committee of the Communist Party of the Philippines (CPP). Quezon City, early 2002.

"Kapitan" (pseudonym), a long-time barangay captain in one of the villages of Mulanay, Quezon. Mulanay, third quarter of 2001.

"Ka-tropa" (pseudonym), group of peasants who were displaced by a decision of the DENR to award a public land in Laguna to a big private company to be developed for tourism. Focus group discussion in Quezon City, last quarter of 2001.

"Negosyanteng Puti" (pseudonym), a foreign national conducting export business in banana based in Davao. Davao City, early 2002.

"Soltero Coronel" (pseudonym), sibling of VLT "paper beneficiaries" in Central Luzon. Quezon City, 22 February 2001.

B.2 In their legal identity

Abela, Hernani, vice chairperson, *Demokratikong Kilusang Magbubukid ng Pilipinas* (DKMP), Sultan Kudarat. Takorong City, 15 March 2002.

Abella, Mr., provincial agrarian reform officer (PARO) for North Cotabato (formerly PARO of Sultan Kudarat), DAR Provincial Office. Kidapawan City, North Cotabato, 13 February 2002.

AFRIM, Alternate Forum for Research in Mindanao, program staff focus group discussion. AFRIM Office, Davao City, 5 July 2001.

Alano, Lisa, head, Policy Advocacy Department of AFRIM. Davao City, 8 February 2002.

Alim, Guiamel, executive director, Kadtuntaya Foundation, Inc. (KFI), an NGO working with Muslim rural and urban communities; also a veteran activist in the Muslim communities especially of Region 12 and ARMM areas. Cotabato City, 12 February 2002.

Almazan, Ranier, national coordinator, PAKISAMA. TESDA Training Center, Marikina City, 25 February 2002.

Andres, Dominador, DAR regional director for Region 5 (at the time of the interview); former director, Region 6. DAR Regional Office, Legaspi City, 30 January 2002.

Baniqued, Bert, program management officer (PMO), Agrarian Reform Community Development Program (ARCDP) with funding from the World Bank. (The ARCDP program implemented the pilot-test of MLAR in the Philippines.) ARCDP Office, DAR Central Office, Quezon City, 16 January 2002.

Banzuela, Soc, executive director, Philippine Agrarian Reform Fund (PARFUND); also formerly with PhilDHRRA; a veteran agrarian reform activist. Quezon City, 19 March 2002.

Barbon, Wilson, program manager of Agri-Aqua Development Coalition. Davao City, 11 February 2002.

Bernal, Danny, community organizer, QUARRDDS-Quezon; veteran community organizer for agrarian reform, especially in the central part of Quezon; member of PARCCOM-Quezon I. Quezon City, 20 February 2002.

Bulatao, Gerry, former undersecretary, Field Operations and Support Services Office (FOSSO) of the DAR (during Secretary Garilao's administration), also held various positions within the DAR, and a veteran agrarian reform activists beginning in the FFF radicalism in the late 1960s–early 1970s; former underground (NDF) leader. Quezon City, 21 January 2002.

Cabanial, Romeo Fernando, head, Land Valuation Office, Land Bank of the Philippine Region 11. LBP Region 11 office, Davao City, 5 February 2002.

Cabanit, Enrico, aspiring land reform beneficiary in a Floirendo-owned banana plantation (WADECOR); secretary-general, UNORKA-Mindanao; vice president, UFEARBAI. Quezon City, 18 February 2002.

Calla, Joel, veteran agrarian reform activist, coordinator of PEACE Foundation in Region 5. Quezon City, 22 February 2002.

Canias, Komersendo, chairperson, Marsman Employees Agrarian Reform Beneficiaries Association, Inc. (MEARBAI). Barangay Tibalog, Municipality of Sto. Tomas, Davao del Norte, 9 February 2002.

Carranza, Danny, executive director QUARRDDS-Quezon; also currently the coordinator of Agrarian Reform Program of the PEACE Foundation; veteran agrarian reform activist, worked in Hacienda Luisita in Tarlac, Bulacan, and Quezon. Quezon City, 4 February 2002.

"*Ka* Cenon," chairperson, PKSK. CARET Office, Quezon City, 5 February 2002.

Cudilla, Canuto, Sr., senior agrarian reform program officer (SARPO), North Cotabato Provincial DAR office. Kidapawan City, North Cotabato, 13 March 2002.

Cueto, Malu, program staff, PhilNET-Commercial Farms Project in Davao; also a veteran agrarian reform activist, and did community organizing work in southern Tagalog and Lanao del Norte. Tagum, Davao del Norte, 6 February 2002.

DARBCI, focus group discussion with board members. Davao City, 25 June 2001.

de la Rosa, Billy, executive director, Alternate Forum for Research in Mindanao (AFRIM); also veteran activist specializing in peasant-related work in Mindanao. AFRIM Office, Davao City, 15 February 2002.

de Leon, Tess, media-liaison officer, AFRIM. Davao City, 8 February 2002.

de Los Reyes, Gil, DAR Undersecretary for Policy Planning and Legal Affairs Office (PPLAO), PPLAO Office, DAR Central Office. Quezon City, 1 February 2002.

Del Rosario, Rodolfo, governor of Davao del Norte; president of the Governor's League of the Philippines; president of the Union of Local Authorities of the Philippines (ULAP); many times member of Congress; brother in-law of Antonio Floirendo Sr. Governor's Mansion House, Tagum City, Davao del Norte, 6 February 2002.

Esquejo, Ruben, executive director of (the now defunct) NEPAD (later of EMPOWERMENT) in Nueva Ecija; taped interview/transcript conducted by Jennifer Franco for the *Komite ng Sambayanng Pilipino* (KSP). Utrecht, The Netherlands, 10 November 1996.

Fabe, Vic, secretary-general, PAKISAMA. Marikina City, 25 February 2002.

Faustino, Joey, coordinator, Coconut Industry Reform Movement (COIR), Quezon City, 26 February 2002.

Feranil, Malut, researcher, AFRIM. Davao City, 10 February 2002.

Feranil, Salvador, former PhilNET Commercial Plantations Program Coordinator in Davao. Davao City, 16 February 2002.

Garilao, Ernesto, former secretary, Department of Agrarian Reform (July 1992 to June 1998), Asian Institute of Management (AIM). Makati City, 11 January 2002.

Gatche, Danny, executive director of ACCORD-Central Luzon and member of PARCCOM-Bulacan; also veteran agrarian reform activist (former program staff of CPAR, community organizer in Davao, Bulacan, Nueva Ecija, and Quezon); has current work in Hacienda Luisita and other estates in Tarlac. Quezon City, 6 February 2002.

Geremia, Peter (Fr.), diocesan coordinator of Tribal Filipino Program, Diocese of Kidapawan, North Cotabato; veteran activist for the rights and welfare of the rural poor. Kidapawan City, March 2002.

Gloria, Joey, branch manager, Philippine Rural Reconstruction Movement (PRRM), North Cotabato Branch. Davao City, 9 February 2002.

Gonzal, Bong, community organizing program officer, Quezon Agrarian Reform, Rural Development and Democratization Services (QUARRDDS); veteran community organizer for agrarian reform especially in Bulacan, Cavite, and Quezon. Quezon City, 6 February 2002.
Grageda, Joe, former provincial agrarian reform officer, Camarines Sur. Mandaluyong City, 14 January 2002.
Guillen, Reggie, Land Tenure Improvement (LTI) Program head, PBSP-Western Batanagas Project; also veteran agrarian reform activist, formerly with PAKISAMA and CPAR. Quezon City, 2 March 2002.
Gumbao, Pete, DAR's provincial agrarian reform officer (PARO) for Davao del Norte (formerly of South Cotabato). DAR Region Office, Davao City, 11 February 2002.
Hamada, director, regional director of DENR Region 5. DENR Region 5 office, Legaspi City, 31 January 2002.
Hermocilla, Alejandro, Jr., land reform beneficiary in a banana plantation, board member of CFEARBAI (Checkered Farm Employees Agrarian Reform Beneficiaries Association, Inc.), Municipality of Carmen, Davao del Norte (Region 11). Barangay Sto. Niño, Carmen, Davao del Norte, 8 February 2002.
Herrera, Rene, DAR regional director for Region 4 (also formerly, and again, currently, Region 3). DAR Region 4 office, Pasig City, 24 January 2002.
Inson, Rudy, former DAR regional director for Region 11 (and, currently, DAR Regional Director for Region 7), also veteran agrarian reform activist beginning during the FFF radicalism in the early 1970s in Davao. DAR Region 11 office, Davao City, 11 February 2002.
Isidro, Ben, aspiring land reform beneficiary in a banana plantation, board member, LINDEARBAI (Linda District Employees Agrarian Reform Beneficiaries Association, Inc.) in the Linda District of Floirendo's TADECO; Chairperson, UFEARBAI. Davao City, 16 February 2002.
Jarilla, Armando, coordinator, Land Tenure Improvement (LTI) Program of the Philippine Development Assistance Program (PDAP), a Canadian CIDA-supported NGO in the Philippines; also a veteran agrarian reform activist. Quezon City, 28 February 2002.
KAMAHARI, *Katipunan ng Magbubukid sa Hacienda Roxas* (Association of Peasants in Hacienda Roxas), focus group discussion with the board members. Nasugbo, Batangas, 25 July 2001.
Kidapawan Municipal Agrarian Reform Office, focus group discussion with four DAR municipal officers. Kidapawan City, North Cobato, 13 February 2002.
Layan, Alejandro, vice chairperson of PAKISAMA-Davao del Norte (*Kapunungan sa mga Bundok Mag-uuma sa Davao*, KBMD). Sitio Pagiusa, Barangay Talumo, Municipality of Sto. Tomas, Davao del Norte, 9 February 2002.
Ligon, Egad, veteran agrarian reform activist, formerly with PAKISAMA (1991–1997), and currently with the Philippine Business for Social Progress (PBSP) Agrarian Reform project in Western Batangas. He was also deeply involved in the national campaign of and for the Mapalad case. Quezon City, 1 February 2002.

Lopez, Eddie, coconut peasant-farmer and land reform beneficiary in the Domingo Reyes estate in Catulin, Buenavista, Quezon (Bondoc peninsula); chairperson, KMBP (*Kilusang Magbubukid ng Bondoc Peninsula*, Peasant Movement of Bondoc Peninsula); National Chairperson of UNORKA for one quarter in 2001. UNORKA Office, Quezon City, 12 July 2002.

Loza, Ananias, national chairperson, PAKISAMA; also, long-time leader of a local peasant organization in Sorsogon, Region 5. TESDA Training Center, Marikina City, 25 February 2002.

Macasaet, Dodo, veteran agrarian reform activist, also with PASCRES, a research NGO specializing in rural issues. Quezon City, 20 March 2002.

Magbanua, Rey, executive director, PhilNET-RDI in Sultan Kudarat (Region 12). Takorong, Sultan Kudarat, 14 March 2002.

Makilala, municipal agrarian reform officer (MARO), North Cotabato. Kidapawan City, 13 February 2002.

Mambuay, Faisal, DAR regional director for Region 12. Cotabato City, 12 February 2002.

Mendoza, Danny, community organizing program officer, AGAPE-Laguna; veteran agrarian reform activist. Quezon City, 7 February 2002.

Mendoza, Evangeline, secretary-general, UNORKA; also a land reform beneficiary in the de Los Reyes Estate, Imok, Calauan, Laguna (Region 4). UNORKA Office, Quezon City, 5 February 2002.

Mendoza, Magis, agrarian lawyer, and executive director of KAISAHAN. Quezon City, 22 February 2002.

Mercado, George, private entrepreneur in the banana industry in Davao. Davao City, 1 February 2002.

MFDC, Mindanao Farmworkers' Development Center, focus group discussion with program staff. Davao City, 25 June 2001.

Mora, Ed, Chairperson, PKMP; also long-time leader of KASAMA-TK, the regional chapter of KMP in Southern Tagalog (Region 4). PKMP Office, Quezon City, 7 March 2002.

Morales, Horacio, Jr., former DAR secretary (July 1998 – December 2000). Quezon City, 18 January 2002.

Morales, Tiburcio, Jr., DAR Regional Director (Region 8). Leyte, June 2004.

Navarro, Conrado, former DAR undersecretary for Field Operations and Support Services Office (FOSSO) during Secretary Morales's administration; currently board member of the Agrarian Justice Fund (AJF), a newly formed NGO supporting the legal needs of peasants. Quezon City, 16 January 2002.

Nayal, Abelardo, Executive Director of KABAKAS, an NGO specializing in agrarian reform and sustainable agriculture work in Davao provinces, especially in Davao Oriental (Region 11); also a veteran activist working with the peasants. Davao City, 6 February 2002.

Nieto, Narciso, Director of the Bureau of Land Development (BLD) of the DAR; also, formerly: assistant regional director for central Luzon, and regional director for

Region 8; Head, National Task Force to Fast-Track Land Redistribution, 1999–2000. BLD Office, DAR Central Office, Quezon City, 26 January 2002.

Ojano, Vic, chairman, KASAMA-KA. Quezon City, 5 February 2002.

Olayres, provincial agrarian reform officer (PARO) for Albay. Regional DAR Office, Legaspi City, 30 January 2002.

Palomera, Memo, veteran peasant leader since the early 1970s with the FFF; currently president of BUKLOD. Quezon City, 5 February 2002.

Pancho, Edwin, agrarian reform specialist, Bondoc Development Program, supported and operated by the German GTZ in Bondoc Peninsula, Quezon (Region 4). Quezon City, 22 February 2002.

Panes, Marino, chairman of the Barangay Agrarian Reform Committee of Meohao, Kidapawan, North Cotabato, 12 February 2002.

PBSP, Philippine Business for Social Progress, focus group discussion with the program staff of the Agrarian Reform Program in Western Batangas. Nasugbo, Batangas, 26 July 2002.

Perpetua, Malu, community organizer, PEACE Foundation in Southern Tagalog since the late 1980s until the mid-1990s, handwritten notes [interview was not tape recorded]. Amsterdam, 30 June 1997.

Propongo, Basilio, member of the Presidential Agrarian Reform Council (PARC), 1998–onward; veteran peasant leader; former secretary-general of KMP-national and DKMP-National; PD 27 land reform beneficiary and a rice farmer in San Enrique, Negros Occidental, coming from a sakada family. He has assisted in the formation of Negros Federation of Farmers' Associations (NOFFA). Quezon City, 24 January 2002.

Quiambao, Manuel, president of the PEACE Foundation Network, veteran agrarian reform activist. Quezon City, 4 February 2002.

Quibod, Atty, lawyer for land reform claimants especially in the plantation areas of Region 11. Davao City, 15 February 2002.

Rebaja, Chato, banana plantation farmworker, chairperson of DAFCO (DAFCO Association of Farmworkers Cooperative). Barangay DAPCO, Panabo, Davao del Norte, 8 February 2002.

Reyes, Ernest, community organizing program head, Mindanao Farmworkers Development Center (MFDC), and veteran community organizer among farmworkers in plantations in Mindanao. MFDC office, Davao City, 7 February 2002.

Reyes, Lorenz, assistant secretary, DAR Adjudication Board (DARAB), also one of the most senior permanent members of the DARAB. DARAB office, Quezon City, 29 January 2002.

Reyes, Mirasol, executive director, Mindanao Farmworkers Development Center (MFDC); also veteran agrarian reform activist and cooperative-building expert; formerly of FARMCoop. MFDC Office, Davao City, 8 February 2002.

Rivera, Ian, national coordinator, MAKABAYAN national peasant organization. Quezon City, 16 February 2002.
Robles, Marlene, division chief, Landowner Assistance and Administrative Division, Land Bank of the Philippines Region 5. Legaspi City, 31 January 2002.
Ruiz, Rustom, aspiring land reform beneficiary, Mitra estate in Albay (Region 5); also regional coordinator of UNORKA for Region 5. Quezon City, 22 February 2002.
San Andres, Ding, director of the Internal Audit Service (IAS) of DAR and head, PARC's AMIC. IAS Office, DAR Central Office, Quezon City, 1 March 2002.
Sebastian, Roberto, president, Marsman company, also former secretary of the Department of Agriculture under the Ramos presidency. Marsman Office, Davao City, 9 February 2002.
Soliman, Hector (Atty), agrarian reform lawyer and former DAR undersecretary (Legal Affairs and also Operations). Quezon City, 18 January 2002.
Suaybagiou, Ed, acting regional director for Region 11. Davao City, 10 February 2002.
Sytia, Ms., supervising agrarian reform program officer (SUARPO), also former acting PARO for Masbate, DAR Region 5. DAR Region 5 office, Legaspi City, 22 January 2002.
Tabadora, Edna, executive director, CARP Secretariat, DENR. Quezon City, June 2004.
Tanguihan, Gil, land reform beneficiary in a banana plantation, vice chairperson of SEARBEMCO. Barangay DAPCO, Panabo, Davao del Norte, 8 February 2002.
Tapayan, Romulo, secretary-general, KAMMPIL; also veteran peasant leader in Mindanao with KMP until 1992; member of the Presidential Agrarian Reform Council (PARC), 1988–onward. KAMMPIL Office, Quezon City, 6 February 2002.
Tapia, Nestor, community organizer, PEACE Foundation in North Cotabato (before, also in Davao del Norte); also, formerly connected with the indigenous peoples program of PhilNET in Davao. Tagum, Davao del Norte, 6 February 2002.

C. Government Documents Consulted

ARMM-DAR (2002) "CARP Accomplishment Status Report for the Autonomous Region of Muslim Mindanao." Internal document prepared for the National Assessment and Strategic Planning, 5–8 February 2002, DAP-Tagaytay. Cotabato: ARMM-DAR (document also available at DAR-Region XII).

DAR (1995) *Handbook for CARP Implementors*. Quezon City: DAR.

——— (n.d.a) *DAR Compilation of Administrative Issues and Pertinent Vital Documents, Book 5, 1998–1999*. Quezon City: Department of Agrarian Reform.

——— (n.d.b) *DAR Compilation of Administrative Issues and Pertinent Memorandum Circulars, Book 4, January 1997–March 1998*. Quezon City: Department of Agrarian Reform.

——— (n.d.c) *DAR Compilation of Administrative Issues and Pertinent Memorandum Circulars, Book 3, 1994–1996*. Quezon City: Department of Agrarian Reform.

——— (n.d.d) *DAR Compilation of Administrative Issues and Pertinent Memorandum Circulars, Book 2, 1991–1993*. Quezon City: Department of Agrarian Reform.

(n.d.e) *DAR Compilation of Administrative Issues and Pertinent Memorandum Circulars, Book 1, 1987–1990.* Quezon City: Department of Agrarian Reform.

(n.d.f) Comprehensive Agrarian Reform Program (CARP): A Compilation of R.A. 6657, Presidential Issuances, Implementing Rules and Procedures, Book I, Book II, Book III, Book IV, Book V, Ra 1199, RA 3844, RA 6389, DARAB Revised Rules and Procedures. Quezon City: Department of Agrarian Reform.

DAR-IV (2002) "List of Approved and Disapproved Land Use Conversion Applications as of June 1998." Computer print-out. Pasig City: DAR.

DAR-V (2002) "Special Operations for DAR-V, Bicol." Internal Document clarifying the internal plans to speed up land redistribution. Legaspi: DAR Region V, Office of the Regional Director.

(1999) "Accomplishment Report on Agrarian Legal Assistance, 1988–1998." Legaspi: DAR Office of the Regional Director.

DAR-VI (2000) "Field Operations Group (FOG) Queries, Regional Target Setting for Region VI prepared for the Regional Directors' Conference, Quezon City, 31 July to 4 August 2000." Computer print-out.

DAR-XI (2001) "Status of Deferred Commercial Farms as of March 31, 2001 for Region XI." Davao: DAR.

(1998) "Production and Profit Sharing Compliance, 1988–98 of Selected Companies in Region 11." Computer print-out. Davao: DAR.

(n.d.) "List of Land Use Conversion Applications." Computer print-out. Davao City: DAR.

DAR-XII (2002) *Accomplishment Report CY-2001*, prepared for the National Assessment and Planning Conference, 5–8 February 2002, DAP, Tagaytay City. Cotabato City: DAR Office of the Regional Director (ORD).

(1995) "Status of Homelots and Farmlots, as of June 1995 Inventory, Sultan Kudarat Resettlement Project No. 1, Phase 2, Banayal, Tulunan, North Cotabato." North Cotabato: DAR.

DAR-ARCDP (2001) *Community-Managed Agrarian Reform Program (CMARP) Project Operations Manual.* Quezon City: DAR-ARCDP.

DAR-BARBD (2000) *Agrarian Reform Communities (ARCs): Situationer Report, as of December 2000.* Quezon City: DAR, Bureau of Agrarian Reform Beneficiaries Development (BARBD).

DAR-MIS (2006) "Land Acquisition and Distribution Status (Table 4) as of March 31, 2006." Photocopy. Quezon City: Management of Information System (MIS), DAR.

(2005) "Land Acquisition and Distribution Status (Table 4) as of December 31, 2005." Photocopy. Quezon City: Management of Information System (MIS), DAR.

(2001a) "Land Acquisition and Distribution Status (Table 4) as of December 31, 2001." Photocopy. Quezon City: Management of Information System (MIS), DAR.

——— (2001b) "Land Distribution Accomplishment, 1972–2000, Area in Hectares by Land Type, Region, Province, Year and Administration." Photocopy. Quezon City: Management of Information System (MIS), DAR.

——— (1998a) "Deductibles [Deducted] from Scope, by Land Type, Region, Province, and by Deduction Reasons." Quezon City: MIS.

——— (1998b) "Cancelled Emancipation Patents and Certificate of Land Ownership Awards (EPs/CLOAs) as of July 31, 1998." Quezon City: MIS.

DAR-PS (2003) *National Leasehold Accomplishment Report, 1972–2003.* Quezon City: DAR, Planning Service.

——— (2001a) *National Leasehold Accomplishment Report, 1972–2000.* Quezon City: DAR, Planning Service.

——— (2001b) "Department of Agrarian Reform, President's Budget (F-101 & F-158), 1988 – 2000 [F-101 = Annual General Appropriations Act and F-158 = PARC Report]." Computer print-out. Quezon City: DAR's Planning Service (PS).

DAR-PSRS (1998a) *The Agrarian Situation in Coconut Lands.* Unpublished study prepared by the Economic and Socio-Cultural Research Division, Policy and Strategic Research Service (PSRS). Quezon City: DAR (PSRS Office).

——— (1998b) *An Assessment of Payment of Land Amortization by Agrarian Reform Beneficiaries (ARBs).* Unpublished study by the Economic and Socio-Cultural Research Division, Policy and Strategic Research Division, DAR. Quezon City: DAR (PSRS Office).

——— (1997) *Determination of Lease Rental for Major Commercial Crops.* Unpublished, internal policy study conducted by the Economic and Socio-Cultural Research Division of the Policy and Strategic Research Service (PSRS) of the DAR. Photocopy. Quezon City: DAR.

——— (n.d.) "MAROs Perception Survey on their Roles in CARP Implementation." Unpublished document. Quezon City: DAR, Policy and Strategic Research Service (PSRS).

DAR-SSO (1997) Memorandum dated 15 September 1997 by DAR Assistant Secretary Aristotle Alip addressed to DAR Region XII Director Antonietta Borra with Subject: Settlement Development Program. Quezon City: Office of the Assistant Secretary for Support Service Office (SSO); Cotabato City: Office of the Regional Director. [Note: This is a package of documents including the status reports of some settlement projects.]

DAR-TFFT (2000) Memorandum, Subject: Terminal Report of Task Force Fast Track. Internal document from the Task Force, created in 1999 to expedite land redistribution and headed by Director Narciso Nieto. [The memorandum, dated 8 December 2000, was addressed to DAR Secretary Morales, among others.] Quezon City: DAR (OSEC).

DENR (2004) "Land Distribution Accomplishment for A&D Lands and CBFM Program, as of June 2004." Photocopy. Quezon City: DENR CARP-Secretariat.

––––––– (n.d.a) "Targets and Accomplishments as of December 2001, Forest Management Service." Computer print-out. Quezon City: Forest Management Service, Department of Environment and Natural Resources.

––––––– (n.d.b) "Summary of DENR's Land Distribution Accomplishments by Land Type, by Region, July 1987–December 2000." Computer print-out. Quezon City: DENR, CARP Secretariat.

––––––– (n.d.c) *CARP Secretariat Report on A&D and CBFM Distribution as of 2001.* Quezon City: DENR CARP-Secretariat.

DENR-V (2001) "DENR Region V Briefing Kit." Legaspi: DENR Region V.

LBP (2002) "Selected CARP Cases: LBP Valuation versus Court Valuation." Makati City: Land Bank of the Philippines.

––––––– (2001) "Comparative Average Land of PD 27 Lands and RA 6657 Lands, per Year, 1988–2000." Makati City: Land Bank of the Philippines.

PAGC (2002) "Compilation of Documents Regarding the Formal Complaint of the DAR Employees Association against DAR Secretary Hernani Braganza for Graft and Corruption (PAGC-ADM 0105-02), 5 September 2002." Manila: Presidential Anti-Graft Commission (PAGC).

PARC (2002a) PARC Secretariat memorandum addressed to the PARC Executive Committee on the subject of highlights of the CARP CY 2001 Accomplishment Report. Photocopy. Quezon City: Presidential Agrarian Reform Council.

––––––– (2002b) "Minutes of the 88th Presidential Agrarian Reform Council Executive Committee Meeting, 20 March 2002, DAR-OSEC Boardroom, DAR Central Office." Photocopy. Quezon City: PARC. [Note: This document is a package of documents that includes assorted types of memoranda and other vital documents.]

––––––– (2002c) "PARC Resolution No. 2002-31-01: Approval of the Agreements Regarding the Alternative Venture Agreement (AVA) Between Marsman Estate Plantation Inc. (MEPI) and Davao Marsman Agrarian Reform Beneficiaries Development Cooperative (DAMARBDEVCO)." Quezon City: PARC Secretariat.

––––––– (2001a) PARC Secretariat memorandum addressed to the PARC Executive Committee on the subject of pending SDO applications, dated 5 November 2001. Photocopy. Quezon City: Presidential Agrarian Reform Council.

––––––– (2001b) "Minutes of the 87th Presidential Agrarian Reform Council Executive Committee Meeting, 7 November 2001, DAR-OSEC Boardroom, DAR Central Office." Photocopy. Quezon City: PARC.

––––––– (2001c) *CARP Annual Report for CY 2000.* Quezon City: DAR-PARC Secretariat. [Note: This is a package of documents that includes assorted types of memoranda and other vital documents.]

––––––– (2000) "Accomplishment on Processing of Stock Distribution Proposals, as of December 2000." Internal document prepared for PARC by the Task Force on Production and Profit Sharing (PPS), Stoch Distribution Option (SDO), and Commercial Farms Deferment (CFD) under the Field Operations and Support Services Offices (FOSSO). Quezon City: DAR (PARC Secretariat).

―――― (1997) Memorandum from the PARC Secretariat addressed to the PARC Executive Committee regarding DENR's New Revised Scope on Public Alienable and Disposable (A&D) Lands, dated 27 January 1997. Photocopy. Quezon City: PARC.

―――― (n.d.) "Complete List of Community-Based Forest Management (CBFM) CARP Sites." Quezon City: PARC Secretariat.

PARC-AMIC (2001) *Comprehensive Agrarian Reform Program Final Audit Report Covering the Year 1998*. Unpublished report by the Presidential Agrarian Reform Council (PARC) and the Audit Management and Investigation Committee (AMIC). Quezon City: PARC.

―――― (1999) *Comprehensive Agrarian Reform Program Final Audit Report Covering the Year 1996-1997*. Unpublished report by the Presidential Agrarian Reform Council (PARC) and the Audit Management and Investigation Committee (AMIC). Quezon City: PARC.

―――― (1997) *Comprehensive Agrarian Reform Program Final Audit Report Covering the Year 1996-1997*. Unpublished report by the Presidential Agrarian Reform Council (PARC) and the Audit Management and Investigation Committee (AMIC). Quezon City: PARC.

―――― (1996) *Comprehensive Agrarian Reform Program Final Audit Report Covering the Year 1995*. Unpublished report by the Presidential Agrarian Reform Council (PARC) and the Audit Management and Investigation Committee (AMIC). Quezon City: PARC.

―――― (1995) *Comprehensive Agrarian Reform Program Final Audit Report Covering the Year 1994*. Unpublished report by the Presidential Agrarian Reform Council (PARC) and the Audit Management and Investigation Committee (AMIC). Quezon City: PARC.

―――― (1994) *Comprehensive Agrarian Reform Program Final Audit Report Covering the Years 1992-1993*. Unpublished report by the Presidential Agrarian Reform Council (PARC) and the Audit Management and Investigation Committee (AMIC). Quezon City: PARC.

PARC-EC (2002) Memorandum from the PARC Executive Committee addressed to the PARC Council with the subject: Disapproval of Nice Stock Distribution Option (SDO) Applications. Quezon City: PARC Secretariat.

―――― (1997) Memorandum from the PARC Secretariat addressed to the PARC Executive Committee with the subject: DENR's New Revised Scope on Public Alienable and Disposable (A&D) Lands. Quezon City: PARC Secretariat. [Note: This is a package of various vital documents related to the subject.]

Regional Development Council, RDC (1997) *The Southern Tagalog Regional Development Plan, 1999-2004: Directions for the 21st Century*. Southern Tagalog: Regional Development Council (RDC) Region IV coordinated by the National Economic and Development Authority (NEDA), December 1997.

Regional Development Council (1992) *Southern Tagalog Regional Development Plan, 1993–1998*. Southern Tagalog: Regional Development Council (RDC) Region IV coordinated by the National Economic and Development Authority (NEDA), December 1992.

Republic of the Philippines, R.P. (n.d.) *Medium-Term Philippine Development Plan, 1999–2004* (Angat Pinoy 2004). Pasig: National Economic and Development Authority (NEDA).

D. Other Selected Written Materials

Baniqued, Adelberto (2001a), ARCDP project director, Memorandum for Jose Mari Ponce, assistant secretary for Support Services and Foreign-Assisted Projects Office, dated 15 August 2001, with regard to Credit Fund for the MLAR projects.

——— (2001b) Memorandum to the provincial agrarian reform officers (PAROs) of Quezon II and Misamis Occidental, dated 9 November 2001, with regard the MLAR pilot projects.

DAPCO (1985) Lease Agreement between Dole-Philippines/Stanfilco and the DAPCO company, dated November 1985 (notarized 31 December 1985).

Ponce, Jose Mari (2001a), assistant secretary for Support Services and Foreign-Assisted Projects Office, letter to Robert Vance Pulley, country director of the World Bank Office Manila, dated 30 October 2001, regarding the MLAR project in the Philippines.

——— (2001b), assistant secretary for Support Services and Foreign-Assisted Projects Office, letter to NEDA Director General Dante Canlas, dated 11 December 2001, with regard to the MLAR pilot project and the entry of the Japan Social Development Fund "to scale up the [MLAR] piloting."

——— (2000), assistant secretary for Support Services and Foreign-Assisted Projects Office, letter to Director Felizardo Virtucio of NEDA, dated 20 September 2000, with regard to the MLAR pilot project.

Sibula CMARP Pilot Project Committee, Minutes of the meeting held on 19 March 2001.

Virtucio, Felizardo (of NEDA), letter to ARCDP's Adelberto Baniqued, dated 18 September 2000, with regard the MLAR project.

WEARBEMPCO (2000) Memoranda of Agreement between WEARBEMPCO and WADECOR on the terms of the Voluntary Land Transfer Scheme and the Subsequent Leaseback Arrangement, signed 3 January 2000.

Wilson, Mark (2001a) (World Bank, East Asia and Pacific Region), letter to DAR Secretary Hernani Braganza, dated 23 July 2001, with regard the ARCDP Assessment and MLAR Pilot Project.

——— (2001b) (World Bank), letter to DAR Secretary Hernani Braganza, dated 30 October 2001, with regard the MLAR Pilot Project.

E. Other Materials

(i) *Paglaya ng Lupa*: Peasant Land Struggle in Bondoc Peninsula (2006) A documentary film by Janina Dannenberg and Johannes Richter. See: www.bondoc-solidarity.de.

(ii) "Hunger for Land" (1989) Video. Philippine Peasant Institute and North-South Films.

(iii) "The Philippine Statistics, 2001 Edition." CD-ROM. Makati City: National Statistical Coordination Board.

(iv) A compilation of various (position) papers from different groups before, during, and right after the split/s within the Communist Party of the Philippines (CPP) in 1991–1993. [This is referred to by some Philippine leftist activists as the "red book" (it has a red cover); there is no official publisher of this compilation.]

(v) Various statements and pamphlets during the KMP split in 1993.

(vi) Various contracts on land redistribution and post–land redistribution schemes including those on leaseback and SDO.

(vii) Compilation of voluminous CMARPRP project reports from ten provinces, as of 2005.

INDEX

"t" refers to table and "n" refers to notes.

A

Abad, Florencio, 243, 271, 292
Active Leadership for the Development of AgriWorkers (ALDA), 176-78, 260
A&D. *See* alienable and disposable land (A&D)
ADB. *See* Asian Development Bank (ADB)
administrative order (AO), 203-4
ADMP. *See* Ancestral Domains/Land Claims Program (ADMP)
Advocates for Genuine Alternative for People's Empowerment (AGAPE), 310n5
Africa, 42, 64
AFRIM. *See* Alternate Forum for Research in Mindanao (AFRIM)
AGAPE. *See* Advocates for Genuine Alternative for People's Empowerment (AGAPE)
Agrarian Justice Fund (AJF), 317n41
Agrarian Law 160, 57
Agrarian Reform Community (ARC), 268-70, 274
Agrarian Reform Community Development Program, 144-45
Agrarian Reform Now! (AR Now!), 231, 260, 266
Agrarian Reform Program Technician (ARPT), 112
AJF. *See* Agrarian Justice Fund (AJF)
Akbayan, 233, 236
ALDA. *See* Active Leadership for the Development of AgriWorkers (ALDA)
alienable and disposable land (A&D)
  Aquino Estate, Quezon, 192-93
  DENR's accomplishment (1987-2001), 211, 212t4.2, 214
  public lands under different classifications, 108-9
  reclassifications, 138
Alliance for Progress 41
Alliance of Central Luzon Farmers. *See Alyansa ng Magsasaka sa Gitnang Luson* (AMGL)
Alternate Forum for Research in Mindanao (AFRIM), 235
Alyansa ng Magsasaka sa Gitnang Luson (Alliance of Central Luzon Farmers) (AMGL), 222
AMA. *See Aniban ng Manggagawa sa Agrikultura* (Unity of Agricultural Workers) (AMA)

385

AMGL. *See Alyansa ng Magsasaka sa Gitnang Luson* (Alliance of Central Luzon Farmers) (AMGL)
AMIC. *See* Audit Management and Investigation Committee (AMIC)
AMIHAN. *See* National Federation of Rural Women's Organizations (AMIHAN)
Ancestral Domains/Land Claims Program (ADMP), 305n24
Angara, Edgardo, 249
Aniban ng Manggagawa sa Agrikultura (Unity of Agricultural Workers) (AMA), 234
Añonuevo, Carlito, 250
AO. *See* administrative order (AO)
Aquafil estate, 200–201, 292
Aquino Estate, Quezon, 192–97, 282, 291
AR Now!. *See* Agrarian Reform Now! (AR Now!)
ARC. *See* Agrarian Reform Community (ARC)
ARMM. *See* Autonomous Region of Muslim Mindanao (ARMM)
ARPT. *See* Agrarian Reform Program Technician (ARPT)
Arroyo, President Miguel, 130, 236, 251–54, 267, 302n3
Arsenio A. Acuña Corporation, 158
ASEAN. *See* Association of Southeast Asian Nations (ASEAN)
Asia, 6, 8, 28, 30–31, 45, 47t1.2
Asian Development Bank (ADB), 12–13, 91, 323, 329
Association of Free Peasants of the Aquino Estate. *See Samahan ng Malayang Magsasaka sa Lupaing Aquino* (SAMALA)
Association of Peasant Beneficiaries in Superior Agro, Inc. *See Samahan ng mga Magsasakang Benepisyaryo ng Superior Agro Inc.* (SMBSAI)

Association of Southeast Asian Nations (ASEAN), 94
Ateneo de Manila University, 247
Audit Management and Investigation Committee (AMIC), 112, 121
autonomous farmworkers' group (FARM), 133
autonomous peasant associations, 98, 165–66, 216, 237, 242–43, 248, 252, 259–63, 265, 268, 275
Autonomous Region of Muslim Mindanao (ARMM)
  CA distribution, 209–11
  DAR land distribution in private hands, 206t4.1, 207–8
  DAR's land distribution (1972-2005), 148t3.2
  deductions from CARP scores (2005), 150, 151t3.3
  deductions on legal grounds, 153t3.4b
  DENR's accomplishment in A&D lands and CBFM, 211, 212t4.2, 214
  overpriced land valuation, 160
  state-society interactions and policy outcomes, 275–79, 277t5.2

B

Barangay Agrarian Reform Committee (BARC), 112
Barangay Hagonghong, 144
Barangay Imok, Calauan, Laguna, 167
Barangay Sibula, 143–44
BARC. *See Barangay* Agrarian Reform Committee (BARC)
BARC-MARO decision, 179–80
Batanes province, 210
BDP. *See* Bondoc Development Program (BDP)
Becca, Ate, 189
Benedicto sugar cane plantation, 134, 141, 149, 248, 285, 291
beneficiaries
  CARP, 109, 114, 114t2.11

farmworker, 130
labourer/worker, 130
land reform, 16
non-indigenous, 138
paper, 123
peasant, DAR (1972-2000), 114, 114t2.11
preferred, 122
selecting, 50–51
uninstalled, voluntary land transfer (VLT), 120, 134–35, 156
bibingka strategy, 279
Bicol provinces, 233
Bicol (Region 5)
    CA distribution, 209–11
    DAR land distribution in private hands, 206t4.1, 207–8
    DAR's land distribution (1972-2005), 148t3.2
    deductions from CARP scores (2005), 150, 151t3.3
    deductions on legal grounds, 153t3.4b
    DENR's accomplishment in A&D lands and CBFM, 211, 212t4.2, 213
    Mitra Farm, Albay, 170–71
    state-society interactions and policy outcomes, 275–79, 277t5.2
    VOS distribution, 208–9
BISIG. *See Bukluran sa Ikauunlad ng Sosyalismo sa Isip at Gawa* (Unity for the Advancement of Socialism in Theory and Practice) (BISIG)
Bolivia, 28, 283
Bondoc Development Program (BDP), 188, 195
Braganza, Hernani, 154, 251–53, 256, 267
Brazil
    compulsory acquisition (CA), 165
    land occupation by MST, 68
    land prices, drop in, 288
    land redistribution, 13
    land reform, liberal, 43
    land reform, socio-political bases for, 47 t1.2
    land reform laws, 107
    market-led agrarian reform policy, 286
    MLAR model, 57, 59–60
    neo-liberalism and impact on power, 61–62
    opportunities-centred approach, 63
    political conflicts, land-based, 48
    redistributive reform, 23
BUKLOD. *See Bukluran ng Malayang Magbubukid* (Council of Free Farmers) (BUKLOD)
Bukluran ng Malayang Magbubukid (Council of Free Farmers) (BUKLOD), 234
Bukluran ng mga Tagapaglikha ng Butil (Federation of Grain Producers) (BUTIL), 180, 225
Bukluran sa Ikauunlad ng Sosyalismo sa Isip at Gawa (Unity for the Advancement of Socialism in Theory and Practice) (BISIG), 228, 230, 233
Bulatao, Gerry, 243–46, 253, 255
Burkeley, Clifford, 246, 318n59
BUTIL. *See Bukluran ng mga Tagapaglikha ng Butil* (Federation of Grain Producers) (BUTIL)

C
CA. *See* compulsory acquisition (CA)
Cabanit, Eric, 130, 237, 254, 313n33
CADC. *See* Certificate of Ancestral Domain Claim (CADC)
CAFGU. *See* Citizens Armed Force Geographic Units (CAFGU)
Cagayan province, 210, 276, 277t5.2
Cagayan Valley (Region 2), 136
    CA distribution, 209–11
    DAR land distribution in private hands, 206t4.1, 207–8
    DAR's land distribution (1972-2005), 148t3.2

deductions from CARP scores (2005), 150, 151t3.3
deductions on legal grounds, 153t3.4b
DENR's accomplishment in A&D lands and CBFM, 211, 212t4.2, 213
OLT distribution, 209
state-society interactions and policy outcomes, 275-79, 277t5.2
CALABARZON. *See* Cavite, Laguna, Batangas, Rizal, Quezon (CALABARZON)
Candaba-San Luis community, 186
Candaba-San Luis farms, 185, 291-92
CAR. *See* Cordillera Autonomous Region (CAR)
CARET. *See* Center for Agrarian Reform, Empowerment, and Transformation (CARET)
CARL. *See* Comprehensive Agrarian Reform Law (CARL)
CARP (Comprehensive Agrarian Reform Program)
  acquisition fund, 109
  Aquino administration, 106-7
  Aquino Estate, Quezon, 192-97, 282, 291
  ARC program, 274
  beneficiaries, 109, 114, 114t2.11
  compulsory acquisition (CA), 108, 166
  criticisms, key, 112
  DAR redistribution of government-owned lands, 107
  exclusions, 110
  implementation, 67
  key features of, 107-12, 111t2.8
  landless peasants (1985), 87-88
  leasehold accomplishments (1986-2003), 114, 115t2.12
  leasehold reform benefits, 107
  «on-paper» land transfers, 32-33, 168
  outcomes, 112-16, 113t2.9-113t2.10, 114t2.11, 115t2.12, 116-17
  over priced land transfers, 32-33
  passage into law, 13
  policy making, negotiations on, 100
  private land acquisition, 108-9
  redistributed land, 32-33
  rejection by peasants, 106-7
  scope, revisions to, 110
  share tenancy declared illegal, 197
  VLT and landlord cooperation, 32-33, 108
  VOS and reduced landlord resistance, 108
CARP's non-redistributive policies and outcomes
  Barangay Hagonghong, 144
  Barangay Sibula, 143-44
  Benedicto landholdings, Negros Occidental, 141, 149, 285
  beneficiaries, farmworker, 130
  beneficiaries, non-indigenous, 138
  beneficiaries, paper, 123
  beneficiaries, preferred, 122
  CARP scope, shrinking, 120, 139-41, 140t3.1
  Central Mindanao settlements, 137-38
  cheating in production and profit sharing, 120
  commercial farms and land redistribution deferment, 100, 139
  compulsory production, pre-exemption of, 138-39
  DAR's land distribution (1972-2005), 146-47
  deductions, extent and geographic distribution, 150, 151t3.3
  deductions based on "problematic lands," 152, 154
  deductions by land type and legal grounds, 140t3.1, 154, 155t3.5, 156
  deductions from CARP score, 151t3.3
  deductions on legal grounds, 150, 151t3.4a, 151t3.4b, 152, 153t3.4b

Index | 389

extent and geographic distribution, 146–61
fictitious titles sold to DAR, 120, 142, 161, 285
Floirendo banana plantations, 141, 203–4
Garchitorena land scam (Bicol), 285
land redistribution, failed attempts at, 120, 141, 161
land reform evasion, 120, 122–23
land reform reversals, 120, 135–36, 156
land use conversion, extent and geographical distribution, 157
leaseback, extent and geographical distribution, 125, 127–29, 157–58
leasehold accomplishments (1986-2003), 114, 115t2.12
"*Listasaka*" land registration programme, 149–50
Mapalad in Bukidnon, 141
Masbate, anti-reform landlord, 149
Mindoro Occidental site, 145
non-installation, voluntary, 137
non-redistributive, defined, 119
non-redistributive practices, 120
outcomes, apparent-but-not-real, 137–38, 285, 294
overpriced land acquisitions, 120, 133–34, 285
overpriced land evaluations, 159–60, 286
padding of reports, deliberate, 120, 136–37, 160–61
profit sharing, pre-exemption of, 138–39
public lands, problems in, 137–38
Puyat estates in Bulacan, 141
Quezon Province, 145–46
Samal Island (Davao Province), 146
scope reduction, extent and geographic distribution, 149–56
settlement areas, problems in, 137–38
stock distribution option (SDO), 120, 158–59, 284
Sultan Kudarat settlement, 138
ten-year land rental/sales prohibition, 122

CARP's redistributive policies and outcomes
Aquafil estate, Mindoro Occidental, 200–201
boundaries, contested, 198–204
CA mode, distribution of, 209–11
cattle ranches, 199–200
CBFM, distribution of, 211–13, 212t4.2
"coerced volunteerism" and voluntary offer-to-sell (VOS), 164, 187–89
compulsory acquisition (CA), 164–204
DAPCO, Davao del Norte, 171–78, 291
DAR land distribution in private hands, 205, 206t4.1
DAR's government-owned land, 206t4.1, 211
De los Reyes estate, Laguna, 166–70
DENR's A&D, distribution of, 211–13, 212t4.2
farmland "inclusion-exclusion" issues, 199–202
farms controlled by educational institutions, 200
fishponds, 200, 272
Fort Magsaysay, Nueva Ecija, 199
Garchitorena land scam (Bicol), 244
government financial institution-owned lands (GFI), 190–91
Hacienda Gonzales, 179
Hacienda Roxas, Batangas, 182–84, 291
leasehold, 197–98
leasehold reform, distribution of, 213
Ligao Farm Systems, Inc., 170–71
Mitra Farm, Albay, 170–71, 285, 291
NDC land, South Cotabato, 191–92
OLT, distribution of, 209
operation land transfer (OLT) in rice and corn lands, 164–65, 184–87

peasant claimant "inclusion-exclusion" issues, 202–4
private land accomplishments, 205–8, 206t4.1
private lands except VLT, 208
public lands, redistributive reform on, 191–97
redistribution of landholdings and GFIs, 164
redistribution of public lands, 164
redistributive outcomes, possible extent of, 205–13
Salomon Estate, Nueva Ecija, 178–82, 291
Superior Agro corporation, 187–88, 291
University of the Philippines (UP), 200
VOS, distribution of, 208–9
VOS as apparent-but-not-real outcome, 285
Zoleta property, 197, 286
Catanduanes, 210
Catholic Bishops Conference of the Philippines (CBCP), 236
Catholic Church, 83–84, 120, 218, 226, 229, 243, 249
Cavendish banana sector, 166, 178, 201–2
Cavite, Laguna, Batangas, Rizal, Quezon (CALABARZON), 148t3.2, 151t3.3, 206t4.1, 277t5.2
CBCP. *See* Catholic Bishops Conference of the Philippines (CBCP)
CBFM. *See* Community-Based Forest Management (CBFM)
Center for Agrarian Reform, Empowerment, and Transformation (CARET), 317n35
central Asia, 47 t1.2
Central Luzon
beneficiaries, paper, 123
DKMP influence, 229
land reform, low levels, 276, 278

NPS strategy, reoriented, 226
reform battles, 233, 256
Central Luzon (Region 3)
CA distribution, 209–11
DAR land distribution in private hands, 206t4.1, 207–8
DAR's land distribution (1972-2005), 148t3.2
deductions from CARP scores (2005), 150, 151t3.3
deductions on legal grounds, 153t3.4b
DENR's accomplishment in A&D lands and CBFM, 211, 212t4.2, 213
OLT distribution, 209
Salomon Estate, Nueva, 178–82
state-society interactions and policy outcomes, 275–79, 277t5.2
Central Mindanao (Region 12), 138
CA distribution, 209–11
DAR land distribution in private hands, 206t4.1, 207–8
DAR's land distribution (1972-2005), 148t3.2
deductions from CARP scores (2005), 150, 151t3.3
deductions on legal grounds, 153t3.4b
DENR's accomplishment in A&D lands and CBFM, 211, 212t4.2, 213
private lands except VLT, 208
state-society interactions and policy outcomes, 275–79, 277t5.2
Central Philippines, 226, 229, 233–34
Central Visayas (Region 7)
CA distribution, 209–11
DAR land distribution in private hands, 206t4.1, 207–8
DAR's land distribution (1972-2005), 148t3.2
deductions from CARP scores (2005), 150, 151t3.3
deductions on legal grounds, 153t3.4b
DENR's accomplishment in A&D lands and CBFM, 211, 212t4.2, 213

state-society interactions and policy outcomes, 275–79, 277t5.2
Centro Saka, Inc. (CSI), 234
Certificate of Ancestral Domain Claim (CADC), 138
Certificate of Land Ownership Award (CLOA), 109, 127, 170
certificate of land transfer (CLT), 86–87
Certificate of Stewardship Contract (CSC), 193, 324
CFP. *See* Community Forestry Program (CFP)
Chile
　agribusiness redistribution, 45
　land reform, liberal, 43, 293
　land reform as geopolitical instrument, 42
　overpriced land sales, 286
　political parties and land reform, 102
　redistributive reform, 23
　rice and corn yield, 96t2.6
　voluntary offer-to-sell (VOS), 34
China
　land reform, economic bases of, 47 t1.2
　land reform, liberal, 44, 293
　land reform as geopolitical instrument, 42
　pro-reform forces, 78
　pro-reform forces and state/society alliance, 77–78
　redistributive reform, 23
　state-society interactions, 64
Chiquita, 129, 201
CIDA, 231
CIIF. *See* Coconut Industry Investment Fund (CIIF)
Citizens' Action Party, 233, 236
Citizens Armed Force Geographic Units (CAFGU), 181
CLOA. *See* Certificate of Land Ownership Award (CLOA)
CLT. *See* certificate of land transfer (CLT)

CMARPRP. *See* Community-Managed Agrarian Reform and Poverty Reduction Program (CMARPRP)
Coastal Environment Program (CREP), 305n24, 324
Coconut Industry Investment Fund (CIIF), 190
Coconut Industry Reform Movement (COIR), 312n23, 319n67, 324
coconut levy fund, 190
COIR. *See* Coconut Industry Reform Movement (COIR)
Cojuangco, Danding, 125–26, 190, 248, 254, 284, 292
Cojuangco, Jose "Peping," 166, 225
Cojuangco, Margarita "Tingting," 166
Cojuangco-Aquino, President Corazon
　anti-land reform president, 246
　anti-reform lobby and, 106
　Aquino Estate, Quezon, 192–97, 282, 291
　bombings and arrests, military's indiscriminate, 224
　CARP as conservative legislation, 106
　CARP implementation and public scandals, 242
　Catholic Church and industrial complex, 243
　Comprehensive Agrarian Reform Law, 227
　DAR and "50 hectare and above" landholding, 168
　DAR and de los Reyes estate, 168
　DAR secretaries, turnover of, 243–44
　Defensor-Santiago, Mirian, 242–43
　Hacienda Luisita, 131–33, 158–59, 166, 244, 284
　Hacienda Luisita and murdered workers, 133
　KMP exposure of, 220
　Malacañang Palace, killing of protestors, 106, 219

Mendiola Bridge massacre, 106
militarization of countryside, 191, 224
Mitra Farm, Albay, 170–71
NDC land in Langkaan, 271
political institutions, restored, 82
"pro–private capital accumulation" elite, 271
SAMALA association, 195–97
"special deals," 318n64
state co-opted peasant associations, 67
stock distribution option (SDO), 131–33
"total war" policy against communist insurgents, 224, 258
Colombia, 30–31, 57–60, 62–63, 283, 286
Communist Party of the Philippines. *See Partido Komunista ng Pilipinas* (PKP) (Communist Party of the Philippines)
Community-Based Forest Management (CBFM), 107–9, 193, 196, 211–13, 212t4.2, 282
Community Forestry Program (CFP), 304n24, 324
Community-Managed Agrarian Reform and Poverty Reduction Program (CMARPRP), 144–46
Comprehensive Agrarian Reform Law (CARL), 227
Comprehensive Agrarian Reform Program. *See* CARP (Comprehensive Agrarian Reform Program)
compulsory acquisition (CA)
  Brazil, 165
  CARP pro-poor redistributive reforms, 108, 164–83
  CARP's redistributive policies and outcomes, 32–32, 108, 164–204
  DAR land distribution, total, 113t2.9, 148t3.2
  DAR land distribution in private hands, 206t4.1

  DAR reduction in land distribution, 150
  De los Reyes estate (Catulin), 160–70, 272, 291
  private agricultural land (PAL), 154, 156
  private lands non-redistributed, 242
  private lands redistributed, 156, 164
  redistributive reform, real, 164, 213
  Zimbabwe, 165
Concepcion, Jose, 243, 271
Congress for a People's Agrarian Reform (CPAR), 101–2, 219, 230, 258, 271
Constantino-David, Karina, 251
Cordaid, 229, 231
Cordillera Autonomous Region (CAR)
  DAR land distribution in private hands, 206t4.1, 207–8
  DAR's land distribution (1972-2005), 148t3.2
  deductions from CARP scores (2005), 150, 151t3.3
  deductions on legal grounds, 153t3.4b
  state-society interactions and policy outcomes, 275–79, 277t5.2
Costa Rica, 78
Council of Free Farmers. *See Bukluran ng Malayang Magbubukid* (BUKLOD)
Council of Peasant Organizations in Southern Tagalog. *See Katipunan ng mga Samahang Magbubukid sa Timog Katagalugan* (KASAMA-TK)
Council of Peasants in Hacienda Roxas. *See Katipunan ng mga Magbubukid sa Hacienda Roxas, Inc.* (KAMAHARI)
CPAR. *See* Congress for a People's Agrarian Reform (CPAR)
CREP. *See* Coastal Environment Program (CREP)
CSC. *See* Certificate of Stewardship Contract (CSC)

D

DAPCO. *See* Davao Abaca Plantation Corporation (DAPCO)
DAPCO, Davao del Norte, 171–78, 291
DAPECOL. *See* Davao Penal Colony (DAPECOL)
DAR. *See* Department of Agrarian Reform (DAR)
DAR Internal Audit Service, 121
DARAB. *See* Department of Agrarian Reform Adjudication Board (DARAB)
DARBCI. *See* Dole Agrarian Reform Beneficiaries Cooperative Incorporated (DARBCI)
DAREA. *See* Department of Agrarian Reform Employees' Association (DAREA)
Davao Abaca Plantation Corporation (DAPCO), 171, 291
Davao-Cotabato plantation, 202–3, 226, 229, 233, 263
Davao del Norte plantation, 203–9
Davao Penal Colony (DAPECOL), 201–2, 292
De los Reyes estate, Laguna, 166–70
Defensor-Santiago, Miriam, 242–43
Del Monte, 158, 192
Deles, Ging, 251
Demokratikong Kilusang Magbubukid ng Pilipinas (Democratic Peasant Movement of the Philippines) (DKMP), 17, 169, 200, 228–30, 232
DENR. *See* Department of Environment and Natural Resources (DENR)
Department of Agrarian Reform Adjudication Board (DARAB), 110, 174
Department of Agrarian Reform (DAR), 16
  "50 hectare and above" landholding, 168
  bureaucracy, "clean-up" operation of, 246–47
  bureaucracy, erosion of, 252
  bureaucracy, huge, 239–41
  data-bank, improving quality of, 248
  De los Reyes estate, 168
  established, 87
  fictitious titles sold to, 120, 142, 161, 285
  Field Operations Office, 141
  government-owned lands, 107, 206t4.1, 211
  government-owned lands, redistribution of, 107, 114
  land distribution, reduction in, 150
  land distribution (1972-2005), 111t2.5, 146–47, 148t3.2, 149
  land distribution by CA, 113t2.9, 148t3.2
  land distribution by VLT, 146–47, 148t3.2, 149
  land distribution in private hands, 205, 206t4.1
  land redistribution (1972-2005), 113t2.9
  peasant beneficiaries (1972-2000), 114, 114t2.11
  Philippine, 19–17
  scope of, 110
  secretaries, turnover of, 243–44
  Secretary Braganza, 267
  Secretary Ernesto Garilao, 121, 160, 231, 241, 246–49, 273
  Secretary Florencio Abad, 243, 271, 292
  Secretary Horacio Morales Jr., 135, 159, 204, 249
  Secretary Hernani Braganza, 251
  Secretary Roberto Pagdanganan, 253, 267
Department of Agrarian Reform Employees' Association (DAREA), 252
Department of Agriculture (DA), 241

Department of Environment and Natural Resources (DENR)
  A&D, land distribution, 211–13, 212t4.2
  A&D and CBFM, 211–13, 212t4.2
  CARP program, 136
  government-owned lands redistributed, 107–8, 114
  inter-agency team, 272
  jurisdiction, 110
  land evaluation and amortization payments, 263
  land redistribution by land type, 113t2.10
  peasant beneficiaries (1972-2000), 114t2.11
Department of Justice (DOJ), 201, 272
Department of National Defense, 243
Department of Trade and Industry (DTI), 243
DKMP. *See Demokratikong Kilusang Magbubukid ng Pilipinas* (Democratic Peasant Movement of the Philippines) (DKMP)
DOJ. *See* Department of Justice (DOJ)
Dole, 124–25, 158, 171–78, 192
Dole Agrarian Reform Beneficiaries Cooperative Incorporated (DARBCI), 127–28, 282
Dole-DARBCI, 124–25, 127–29, 282
DTI. *See* Department of Trade and Industry (DTI)
Dutch Cebemo, 229
Dutch ICCO, 230–31, 235

E

Eastern Europe, 47 t1.2
Eastern Visayas (Region 8)
  CA distribution, 209–11
  DAR land distribution in private hands, 206t4.1, 207–8
  DAR's land distribution (1972-2005), 148t3.2
  deductions from CARP scores (2005), 150, 151t3.3
  deductions on legal grounds, 153t3.4b
  DENR's accomplishment in A&D lands and CBFM, 211, 212t4.2, 213
  state-society interactions and policy outcomes, 275–79, 277t5.2
Ecija, Nueva, 134
Ecuador, 39, 68
Egypt, 42, 57–58, 60
El Salvador, 41, 47 t1.2
emancipation patent (EP), 156, 324
EP. *See* emancipation patent (EP)
Estrada, President Joseph
  budget for land redistribution, 254
  Catholic Church, support of, 249
  Cojuangco, Jr., Eduardo "Danding," 126–27, 132
  Danding Cojuangco, "godfather of land reform," 250, 254, 319n68
  DKMP's leader, Jaime Tadeo, 232
  Horacio Morales Jr., 249–53, 318n67
  Office of the President (OP), peasant appeal, 135
  presidency, short-lived, 82
Estrella, Conrado, 154, 242
European Catholic development agencies, 231

F

Federation of Free Farmers (FFF) activists, 101, 217, 234
Federation of Grain Producers. *See Bukluran ng mga Tagapaglikha ng Butil* (BUTIL)
Federation of People's Organizations in the Countryside. *See Kalipunan ng mga Samahaang Magsasaka sa Kanayunan* (KASAMA-KA)
FFF. *See* Federation of Free Farmers (FFF)

FIAN. *See* FoodFirst Information and Action Network (FIAN)
fictitious titles sold to DAR, 120, 142, 161, 285
fishponds, 200, 272
FLMP. *See* Forest Land Management Program (FLMP)
Floirendo, Don Antonio, 125, 129–30, 201, 248, 284
Floirendo banana plantations, 141, 203–9, 292
FoodFirst Information and Action Network (FIAN), 57
Ford Foundation, 229, 231
Forest Land Management Program (FLMP), 304n24, 324
Fort Magsaysay (Nueva Ecija), 199, 292
France, 42
Free Farmers of Candaba and San Luis. *See Malayang Magbubukid sa Candaba at San Luis* (MMCSL)

G

GAA. *See* General Appropriations Act (GAA)
Galbraith, John K., 63
Garchitorena land scam (Bicol), 244, 285
Garilao, Ernesto
    DAR leadership, 17, 231, 241, 246–49, 273
    parole of Jaime Tadeo, 245
    peasant mobilization, anger against, 260–61
    record padding, 160
    reflections of, 275
    voluntary land transfer (VLT), 121
    World Bank, rejected proposal, 274
General Appropriations Act (GAA), 109
German Bread for the World, 229
German Misereor, 229
GFI. *See* government financial institution (GFI)

GOL. *See* government-owned lands (GOL)
government financial institution (GFI), 108, 114, 190–91
government-owned lands (GOL), 140t3.1, 155t3.5, 324
Grageda, Joe, 246
Green Revolution, 81–82, 87, 92
Guatemala, 42, 46

H

Hacienda Gonzales, 179
Hacienda Looc (Batangas), 238, 248
Hacienda Luisita, Inc. (HLI), 132
Hacienda Luisita SDO, 132–33, 158–59, 166, 242, 244, 284
Hacienda Roxas, Batangas, 182–84, 291
Hijo Plantation, Inc. (HPI), 133–34
HLI. *See* Hacienda Luisita, Inc. (HLI)
HMB. *See Hukbong Mapagpalaya ng Bayan* (People's Liberation Army) (HMB)
HPI. *See* Hijo Plantation, Inc. (HPI)
Hukbong Mapagpalaya ng Bayan (People's Liberation Army) (HMB), 185

I

ICARRD. *See* International Conference on Agrarian Reform and Rural Development (ICARRD)
ICCO. *See* Inter-Church Organization for Development and Cooperation (ICCO)
Ilocos (Region 1)
    CA distribution, 209–11
    DAR land distribution in private hands, 206t4.1, 207–8
    DAR's land distribution (1972-2005), 148t3.2
    deductions from CARP scores (2005), 150, 151t3.3
    deductions on legal grounds, 153t3.4b
    DENR's accomplishment in A&D lands and CBFM, 211, 212t4.2, 213

OLT distribution, 209
private lands except VLT, 208
state-society interactions and policy outcomes, 275–79, 277t5.2
VOS distribution, 208–9
Import-Substitution Industrialization (ISI), 62
India, 45, 71, 102, 107, 293
Indigenous Peoples' Rights Act (IPRA), 138, 305n24, 325
Indonesia, 13, 28, 30–31, 60, 93t2.4, 94, 96t2.6, 283
Integrated Social Forestry Program (ISFP), 193, 212, 304–5n24, 325
Inter-Church Organization for Development and Cooperation (ICCO), 229–30, 232
International Conference on Agrarian Reform and Rural Development (ICARRD), 299n1, 325
International Rice Research Institute, 87
IPRA. *See* Indigenous Peoples' Rights Act (IPRA)
ISFP. *See* Integrated Social Forestry Program (ISFP)
ISI. *See* Import-Substitution Industrialization (ISI)

J
Japan, 42–43, 205
Javellana, Antonio, 175
Juico, Philip, 242

K
Kaisahan Tungo sa Kaunlaran ng Kanayunan at Repormang Pansakahan (Unity towards the Development of the Countryside and Agrarian Reform) (KAISAHAN), 233
Kalinga, 210
Kalipunan ng Maliliit na Magniniyog sa Pilipinas, (Federation of Small Coconut Farmers and Farmworkers' Organizations) (KAMMPIL), 225
Kalipunan ng mga Samahaang Magsasaka sa Kanayunan (Federation of People's Organizations in the Countryside) (KASAMA-KA), 233–34
KAMAHARI. *See Katipunan ng mga Magbubukid sa Hacienda Roxas, Inc.* (Council of Peasants in Hacienda Roxas) (KAMAHARI)
KAMMPIL. *See Kalipunan ng Maliliit na Magniniyog sa Pilipinas,* (Federation of Small Coconut Farmers and Farmworkers' Organizations) (KAMMPIL)
KASAMA-KA. *See Kalipunan ng mga Samahaang Magsasaka sa Kanayunan* (Federation of People's Organizations in the Countryside) (KASAMA-KA)
kasamá (share tenancy) system, 183, 197, 286
KASAMA-TK. *See Katipunan ng mga Samahang Magbubukid sa Timog Katagalugan* (Council of Peasant Organizations in Southern Tagalog) (KASAMA-TK)
The Kasangyahan Foundation, Inc.(KFI), 235
Katipunan ng mga Magbubukid sa Hacienda Roxas, Inc. (Council of Peasants in Hacienda Roxas) (KAMAHARI), 184–85
Katipunan ng mga Samahang Magbubukid sa Timog Katagalugan (Council of Peasant Organizations in Southern Tagalog) (KASAMA-TK), 222
KFI. *See* The Kasangyahan Foundation, Inc.(KFI)
Kilos AR, 235–36
Kilusan para sa Pambansang Demokrasya (Movement for National Democracy) (KPD), 233

Kilusang Kabuhayan at Kaunlaran (KKK) land category, 136
Kilusang Magbubukid ng Bondoc Peninsula (Peasant Movement of Bondoc Peninsula) (KMBP), 189, 196
Kilusang Magbubukid ng Pilipinas (Peasant Movement of the Philippines) (KMP), 17, 101, 168–69
  land occupation campaign, 219–24
  mass mobilization (1985-1991), 223t5.1
  media-related activities, 224
  militant peasant movement, 223, 237, 260
  political networking activities, 224
  Visayas, 222–23, 223t5.1
KKK. *See Kilusang Kabuhayan at Kaunlaran* (KKK)
KMBP. *See Kilusang Magbubukid ng Bondoc Peninsula* (Peasant Movement of Bondoc Peninsula) (KMBP)
KMP. *See Kilusang Magbubukid ng Pilipinas* (Peasant Movement of the Philippines) (KMP)
KPD. *See Kilusan para sa Pambansang Demokrasya* (Movement for National Democracy) (KPD)

L

La Via Campesina, 57, 296
Laban ng Masa (Struggle of the Masses) (LnM), 228, 236
Lagman, Edcel, 273, 317n51
Lagman, Popoy, 228
Laguna Development Center (LDC), 167
LAMP. *See* Land Administration and Management Program (LAMP)
Lanao del Sur province, 210
Land Administration and Management Program (LAMP), 89
Land Bank of the Philippines (LBP), 110, 133, 232, 263

land reform studies
  actors, state and societal, 11–12
  agency, definition, 14
  agrarian reform, market-driven, 6
  agrarian sector, Philippines, 12–13
  CARP, passage into law, 13
  communist insurgencies, peasant-based, 7
  data and data collection, 15–18
  development, post-land transfer, 4, 58–59 t1.3
  focus group discussions (FGDs), 16
  historical institutionalism, 14
  land, defined, 4
  land redistribution, questionable outcomes, 1
  land reform, apparent *vs.* real, 8–9
  land reform, expropriationary, 4
  land reform, non-redistributive, 7–8
  land reform, relevance of Philippine, 12–14
  land reform beneficiaries, 16
  land rentals, 6
  land rights, community, 6
  limits-centred approach, 10
  methodological issues, 14–18
  militant political action by peasants, 5
  opportunities-centred perspective, 11
  peasants, defined, 4
  political-economic structural factors, 14
  power to control, 10
  private sector actors, 16
  problems, five types of agrarian, 1–2
  redistributive land reforms, state-led, 5–6
  research questions and arguments, 9–12
  revolts and mobilization, peasant, 13
  rural livelihoods, insecurity, 5
  rural poor, lacking control over land, 5
  rural social movement actors, 16
  societal actors, defined, 15
  socioeconomic structures, 14

state actors, 16
state reformists, defined, 15
structural-actor-oriented approach, 14
World Bank, 7, 13–14
Land Research and Action Network (LRAN), 57
land use conversion filed (LUCF), 157
Langkaan estate (Cavite), 291–92
Lara, Pancho, 250
Latin America, 28, 30, 34, 76
LBP. *See* Land Bank of the Philippines (LBP)
leaseback
  Del Monte and VLT, 158, 192
  Dole and VLT, 158
  Dole-DARBC and VLT, 124–25, 127–29
  extent and geographical distribution, 125, 127–29, 157–58
  Floirendo and VLT, 125, 129–30
  Negros Occidental haciendas and VLT, 158
  plantations in Mindanao and VLT, 158
  voluntary land transfer (VLT), 124–25
leasehold
  accomplishments (1986-2003), 114, 115t2.12
  CARP's redistributive policies, 197–98
  reform, 35–37
  reform, distribution of, 213
  reform and landlord opposition, 35–36
  reform benefits, 107
Leong, Benjamin, 244
Ligao Farm Systems, Inc., 170–71
"*Listasaka*" land registration programme, 149–50
LIUCP. *See* Low Income Upland Development Program (LIUCP)
Liwanag, Armando, 228
LnM. *See Laban ng Masa* (Struggle of the Masses) (LnM)
Local Government Code, 157
Lorenzo Jr., Luis, 251–52, 270

Low Income Upland Development Program (LIUCP), 304n24, 325
LRAN. *See* Land Research and Action Network (LRAN)
LUCF. *See* land use conversion filed (LUCF)
Lumad group, 138

M

Macapagal, Diosdado, 251
Macapagal-Arroyo, President Gloria
  anti-land reform elites within government, 270
  Cojuangco, Jr., Eduardo "Danding," 126
  corruption, massive, 82–83, 133, 236
  Danding Cojuangco land deal, perpetuated, 254
  DAR bureaucracy, erosion of, 252
  DAR secretary Hernani Braganza, 251, 267
  DAR secretary Roberto Pagdanganan, 253, 267
  Hacienda Luisita, refused to investigate, 133, 159
  Marcos loot, used to finance campaign, 305n25
  Marsman profit-sharing scheme, 130–31
  neo-liberal policies, 251, 302n3
  peasants' lobby against, 135
  pro-land reform personalities, 251
  violence, era of, 254
  VLT adopted as main strategy, 120
Makabayan, 234
MAKISAKA. *See Malayang Kaisahan ng mga Samahang Magbubukid sa Nueva Ecija* (Movement of Free Peasant Associations) (MAKISAKA)
Malacañang Palace killings, 106, 219
Malayang Kaisahan ng mga Samahang Magbubukid sa Nueva Ecija (Movement of Free Peasant

Associations) (MAKISAKA), 180, 182
Malayang Magbubukid sa Candaba at San Luis (Free Farmers of Candaba and San Luis) (MMCSL), 186
Malaysia, 93t.4
Management and Organizational Development for Empowerment (MODE), 235
Mapalad agrarian case (Bukidnon), 141, 231, 248, 272–73
Marcos, President Ferdinand
 Benedicto sugar cane plantation, 134
 coconut levy fund, 225
 elite allies and power brokers, 106
 Green Revolution, 81–82, 87, 92
 land redistribution outcome, 86, 103
 land reform in rice and corn lands, 13, 86–87, 108
 Malibu Agro Corporation, 134
 martial law regime, 86
 ND peasant mobilization strategy, 257–58
 Operation Leasehold (OLH) program, 86
 public lands, segregated, 108
 wealth, ill-gotten, 109, 305n25
market-led agrarian reform (MLAR)
 Brazil, 57, 59–60
 land reform, politics of, 53–60
market-led agrarian reform, 53–60, 287
 Mexico, 62
 non-redistributive land reform, 287
 operational manual, 143
 Philippines, 57
 pilot test, 284
 post-land purchase farm and beneficiary development, 56
 program financing, 56–60, 59 t1.3
 South Africa, 57, 59–60
 state-led *vs.*, 57
 World Bank opposed, 145
 World Bank supported, 274

MARO. *See* Municipal Agrarian Reform Officer (MARO)
Marsman banana plantation, 284, 292
Masbate provinces, 98, 122, 149, 233
memorandum of understanding (MOU), 174–77
Mendoza, Evangeline, 168–70
Mexico
 Chiapas and land reform, 47 t1.2
 Chiapas political condition, 70
 effective control of land, 39
 land reform, economic bases of, 47 t1.2
 land reform, liberal, 44, 293
 MLAR model, 62
 neo-liberalism and military action, 61
 opportunities-centred approach, 62
 peasant organizations, Veracruz, 77
 political conflicts, land-based, 48
 redistributive reform, 23
 voluntary offer-to-sell (VOS), 34
MFDC. *See* Mindanao Farmworkers' Development Center (MFDC)
MFDF. *See* Mindanao Farmworkers' Development Foundation (MFDF)
Mindanao Farmworkers' Development Center (MFDC), 311n8, 319n67, 325, 376
Mindanao Farmworkers' Development Foundation (MFDF), 175
Mindanao plantations, 178
Mindanao Rice Company (Minrico), 172
Mindoro Occidental fishpond, 292
Mindoro Occidental site, 145
Misereor, 231
Mitra Farm, Albay, 170–71, 285, 291
MLAR. *See* market-led agrarian reform (MLAR)
MMCSL. *See Malayang Magbubukid sa Candaba at San Luis* (Free Farmers of Candaba and San Luis) (MMCSL)
MNC. *See* multinational corporation (MNC)

MODE. *See* Management and Organizational Development for Empowerment (MODE)
Montemayor, Leonardo, 154, 241, 251
Morales Jr., Horacio
  DAR Secretary, 135, 159, 204, 249
  Estrada, President Joseph, 249–53, 318n67
  influence of Ernesto Garilao, 250
  record padding, 160
MORE-AR. *See* Movement to Oppose More Exemptions from Agrarian Reform (MORE-AR)
MOU. *See* memorandum of understanding (MOU)
Movement for National Democracy. *See Kilusan para sa Pambansang Demokrasya* (KPD)
Movement for Popular Democracy (PopDem) (MPD), 249, 326
Movement of Free Peasant Associations. *See Malayang Kaisahan ng mga Samahang Magbubukid sa Nueva Ecija* (MAKISAKA)
Movement to Oppose More Exemptions from Agrarian Reform (MORE-AR), 272
Mozambique, 42
MPD. *See* Movement for Popular Democracy (PopDem) (MPD)
MuCARRD. *See* Municipal Consultation/Campaign for Agrarian Reform and Rural Development (MuCARRD)
multinational corporation (MNC), 171–73, 326
Municipal Agrarian Reform Officer (MARO), 112
Municipal Consultation/Campaign for Agrarian Reform and Rural Development (MuCARRD), 266, 326

N

Nagasi Agrarian Reform Beneficiaries Multi-Purpose Cooperative, Inc. (NARBMCI), 134–35
Nagkakaisang Magsasaka sa Gitnang Luson (United Farmers in Central Luzon) (NMGL), 235
Nagkakaisang Manggagawa ng Stanfi lco (United Workers of Stanfilco) (NAMASTAN), 173
NAMASTAN. *See Nagkakaisang Manggagawa ng Stanfi lco* (United Workers of Stanfilco) (NAMASTAN)
Namibia, 46, 60
NAPC. *See* National Anti-Poverty Commission (NAPC)
NARBMCI. *See* Nagasi Agrarian Reform Beneficiaries Multi-Purpose Cooperative, Inc. (NARBMCI)
Nat-Dem. *See* National-Democrat (Nat-Dem) (ND)
National Anti-Poverty Commission (NAPC), 241
National Commission for the Indigenous Peoples (NCIP), 305n24, 326
National Council of Peasants. *See Pambansang Katipunan ng Magbubukid* (PKM)
National-Democrat (Nat-Dem) (ND), 17
  agrarian revolution program, 220
  communist-led, 218
  peasant mass mobilization, 257–58, 264
  statist attitude, 222
National Democratic Front (NDF), 249, 326
National Development Corporation (NDC), 192
National Federation of Organizations in the Countryside. *See Pambansang Kilusan ng mga Samahan sa Kanayunan* (PKSK)

Index | 401

National Federation of Rural Women's Organizations (AMIHAN), 315n8, 323
National Federation of Sugar Workers (NFSW), 183, 315n8, 326
National Food Authority (NFA), 225
National Housing Regulatory Board, 263
National Irrigation Authority, 263
National Movement of Farmers' Associations. *See Pambansang Katipunan ng mga Samahang Magsasaka* (PAKISAMA)
National Peasant Secretariat of the Communist Party of the Philippines (NPS-CPP), 225, 258
National Rural Congress (NRC), 237
National Task Force 24 (TF-24), 265–66
Navarro, Conrado, 250
NCIP. *See* National Commission for the Indigenous Peoples (NCIP)
NCPERD. *See* Negros Center for People's Empowerment and Rural Development (NCPERD)
ND. *See* National-Democrat (Nat-Dem) (ND)
NDC. *See* National Development Corporation (NDC)
NDC land, South Cotabato, 191–92
NDC land in Langkaan, 271
NDF. *See* National Democratic Front (NDF)
Negros Center for People's Empowerment and Rural Development (NCPERD), 306n9, 319n67, 326
Negros Occidental Federation of Farmers' and Farmworkers' Associations (NOFFA), 319n67, 326
Negros Occidental province, 231, 262
Negros Occidental sugar cane sector, 263
Nemenzo, President Francisco, 236
neo-liberalism, 61–62

NEPAD. *See* Nueva Ecija People's Assistance for Development (NEPAD)
Nepal, 60
New People's Army (NPA), 104, 196, 218–19
NFA. *See* National Food Authority (NFA)
NFSW. *See* National Federation of Sugar Workers (NFSW)
NGO. *See* nongovernmental organization (NGO)
Nicaragua, 42
NMGL. *See Nagkakaisang Magsasaka sa Gitnang Luson* (United Farmers in Central Luzon) (NMGL)
NOFFA. *See* Negros Occidental Federation of Farmers' and Farmworkers' Associations (NOFFA)
nongovernmental organization (NGO), 15, 101, 168, 218, 262, 265–66, 290, 296
Norte, Davao del, 130
North Korea, 42
Northeastern Mindanao (Region 13)
  CA distribution, 209–11
  DAR land distribution in private hands, 206t4.1, 207–8
  DAR's land distribution (1972-2005), 148t3.2
  deductions from CARP scores (2005), 150, 151t3.3
  deductions on legal grounds, 153t3.4b
  DENR's accomplishment in A&D lands and CBFM, 211, 212t4.2, 213
  state-society interactions and policy outcomes, 275–79, 277t5.2
Northern Mindanao (Region 10)
  CA distribution, 209–11
  DAR land distribution in private hands, 206t4.1, 207–8

DAR's land distribution (1972-2005), 148t3.2
deductions from CARP scores (2005), 150, 151t3.3
deductions on legal grounds, 153t3.4b
DENR's accomplishment in A&D lands and CBFM, 211, 212t4.2, 213
private lands except VLT, 208
state-society interactions and policy outcomes, 275–79, 277t5.2
NPA. *See* New People's Army (NPA)
NPS-CPP. *See* National Peasant Secretariat of the Communist Party of the Philippines (NPS-CPP)
NRC. *See* National Rural Congress (NRC)
NSFW. *See* National Federation of Sugar Workers (NFSW)
Nueva Ecija People's Assistance for Development (NEPAD), 180, 182

O

Office of the President (OP), 135, 171
Office of the Solicitor General (OSG), 196
Olano, Jose, 246
OLH. *See* Operation Leasehold (OLH)
OLT. *See* Operation Land Transfer (OLT)
"on-paper" land transfers, 32–33, 168
OP. *See* Office of the President (OP)
Operation Land Transfer (OLT), 86, 114, 184–87
Operation Leasehold (OLH), 86
OSG. *See* Office of the Solicitor General (OSG)
Osmeña, John, 274
Ostrom schema, 25–26

P

PACOFA. *See* Paulog Coconut Farmers' Association (PACOFA)
PAGC. *See* Presidential Anti-Graft Commission (PAGC)

Pagdanganan, Roberto, 253–54, 256, 267
PAKISAMA. *See Pambansang Katipunan ng mga Samahang Magsasaka* (National Movement of Farmers' Associations) (PAKISAMA)
Pambansang Katipunan ng Magbubukid (National Council of Peasants) (PKM), 304n20, 314n1, 327
Pambansang Katipunan ng Makabayang Magbubukid (National Federation of Nationalist Peasants) (PKMM), 233
Pambansang Katipunan ng mga Samahang Magsasaka (National Movement of Farmers' Associations) (PAKISAMA), 231, 235, 260
Pambansang Kilusan ng mga Samahan sa Kanayunan (National Federation of Organizations in the Countryside) (PKSK), 233, 235
Pambansang Pederasyon ng Maliliit na Mamamalakaya ng Pilipinas (National Federation of Subsistence Fisherfolk of the Philippines) (PAMALAKAYA), 315n8, 326
Pambansang Ugnayan ng Nagsasariling Lokal na mga Samahang Mamamayan sa Kanayunan (National Coordination of Autonomous Local Rural People's Organizations) (UNORKA), 17, 232, 235–36, 252
Pampanga, Central Luzon, 185–87
PARAD. *See* Provincial Agrarian Reform Adjudicator (PARAD)
PARC. *See* Presidential Agrarian Reform Council (PARC)
PARC Secretariat, 121
PARCCOM. *See* Provincial Agrarian Reform Consultative Committee (PARCCOM)
PARCode. *See* People's Agrarian Reform Code (PARCode)
PARO. *See* Provincial Agrarian Reform Officer (PARO)

Partido Komunista ng Pilipinas (PKP) (Communist Party of the Philippines), 104, 185, 218–19, 224, 227–28, 234
Partnership for Agrarian Reform and Rural Development Services (PARRDS), 102, 230, 236, 252
Paulog Coconut Farmers' Association (PACOFA), 170
PBSP. *See* Philippine Business for Social Progress (PBSP)
PCGG. *See* Presidential Commission on Good Government (PCGG)
PCT. *See Projeto Cédula da Terra* (PCT)
PD 27. *See* Presidential Decree No. 27 (PD 27)
PD27 (rice and corn reform), 242
PDI. *See* Project Development Institute (PDI)
PEACE. *See* Philippine Ecumenical Action for Community Empowerment (PEACE)
PEACE Foundation, 167–68, 180, 188, 191, 226, 229–30, 232, 263, 265
Peasant Movement of Bondoc Peninsula. *See Kilusang Magbubukid ng Bondoc Peninsula* (KMBP)
Peasant Movement of the Philippines. *See Kilusang Magbubukid ng Pilipinas* (KMP)
People's Agrarian Reform Code (PARCode), 220
People's Alternative Center for Research and Education in Social Development (PASCRES), 319n67, 327
People's Liberation Army. *See Hukbong Mapagpalaya ng Bayan* (HMB)
Peru, 42, 47 t1.2
Philippine Agrarian Reform Fund (PARFUND), 319n67, 327
Philippine Business for Social Progress (PBSP), 184

Philippine Coconut Authority (PCA), 241
Philippine Ecumenical Action for Community Empowerment (PEACE), 17, 101, 170
Philippine land and tenancy reforms
agricultural exports, loss of comparative advantage, 96–97, 97t2.7
agricultural exports/imports, total value, 93–94, 93t2.4
agricultural sector within national economy, 91–98, 93t2.4, 95t2.5, 96t2.6, 97t2.7
agriculture, gross value added (GVA), 92
CARP, key features of, 107–12, 111t2.8
CARP policy making, negotiations on, 100
churches and, 101, 192
class domination and land ownership, 105–6
collective action against state, 104
collective action of rural poor, 101
commercial farms and land redistribution deferment, 100, 139
Communist Party of the Philippines (CPP), 104
Congress, landlord-dominated, 106
context, structural and institutional, 81–98
elite response to peasant unrest, 104–5
export plantation crops, exempted, 100
farms, size distribution, 89–-90, 89t2.2
GDP, agricultural sector, 91
grievances and, 102
income distribution, Gini coefficient, 92
Land Administration and Management Program (LAMP), 89
land ownership, concentration of agricultural, 90–91, 90t2.3
land ownership, Gini coeffecint in, 90

land reforms, neo-liberal, 97–98
livestock areas, agrarian reform exemption, 98
New People's Army (NPA), 104
non-traditional crops, export value, 94–95, 95t2.5
outcomes, initial, 112–16, 113t2.9–113t2.10, 114t2.11, 115t2.12
overt actions by peasants, 104
peasant mobilization for, 103
political opportunities for peasants, 102–3, 288
political parties and, 101–2, 290
poverty incidence, rural, 91–92
rice and corn, comparative yield, 94, 96, 96t2.6
ruling elite and landowning, 99–100
rural politics, 98–107
share tenancy, 88–89, 100, 183, 197, 286
state agenda, imperative of, 98–99
state police and military repression, 98
structure, agrarian, 83–91, 88t2.1, 89t2.2, 90t2.3
violent upheavals and injustice, 100–101
Philippine Network of Rural Development Institutes (PhilNET-RDI), 234
Philippine Partnership for the Development of Human Resources in Rural Areas (PhilDHRRA), 231
Philippine Peasant Institute (PPI), 101, 234–35
Philippine Rural Reconstruction Movement (PRRM), 306n6, 316n28, 327, 374
Philippines
  CARP implementation, 67
  conflict, peasants *vs.* landlord, 79
  Green Revolution, 81–82, 87, 92
  indigenous communities, 85
  land reform as geopolitical instrument, 42
  MLAR model, 57
  peasant rebellions, armed, 85
  political opportunity structure, 79
  population, agricultural, 89
  population (1961-1999), 88t2.1
  property rights, Western, 84
  resettlement programs, 84–85
  Revolution (1896), 83–84
  Rural Progress Administration, 86
  state-society conflictive interaction, 71–72
  Torrens land titling system, 84
  US Central Intelligence Agency, 85–86
  US invasion, 84
Philippines Community-Managed Agrarian Reform Program (CMARP), 144–46, 310n38, 310n40–41, 324, 384
PhilNET-RDI. *See* Philippine Network of Rural Development Institutes (PhilNET-RDI)
PKM. *See Pambansang Katipunan ng Magbubukid* (National Council of Peasants) (PKM)
PKMM. *See Pambansang Katipunan ng Makabayang Magbubukid* (National Federation of Nationalist Peasants) (PKMM)
PKP. *See Partido Komunista ng Pilipinas* (PKP) (Communist Party of the Philippines)
PKSK, *Pambansang Kilusan ng mga Samahan sa Kanayunan* (National Federation of Organizations in the Countryside) (PKSK)
Policy Planning and Legal Affairs Office (PPLAO), 250, 320n74, 327
Ponce, Cheli, 254
PopDem. *See* Movement for Popular Democracy (PopDem) (MPD)
post-land transfer, 4, 58–59 t1.3
PPI. *See* Philippine Peasant Institute (PPI)

PPLAO. *See* Policy Planning and Legal Affairs Office (PPLAO)
PPS. *See* production and profit sharing (PPS)
Presidential Agrarian Reform Council (PARC), 110, 112, 136
Presidential Anti-Graft Commission (PAGC), 252, 326, 381
Presidential Commission on Good Government (PCGG), 190
Presidential Decree No. 27 (PD 27), 156, 159, 242, 327
ProCARRD. *See* Provincial Consultation/Campaign for Agrarian Reform and Rural Development (ProCARRD)
production and profit sharing (PPS), 139
Project 40 Now!, 266–67
Project Development Institute (PDI), 235
Projeto Cédula da Terra (PCT), 57
Provincial Agrarian Reform Adjudicator (PARAD), 110, 134, 198
Provincial Agrarian Reform Consultative Committee (PARCCOM), 112
Provincial Agrarian Reform Officer (PARO), 112
Provincial Consultation/Campaign for Agrarian Reform and Rural Development (ProCARRD), 266
Puyat estates in Bulacan, 141

Q
Quezon, President, 120
Quisumbing family (Bukidnon), 271–72

R
Ramos, Fidel, 82, 135, 154, 245–46, 249
Raquiza, Toinette, 250, 309n38, 321n91
RARAD. *See* Regional Agrarian Reform Adjudicator (RARAD)
redistributive land reform, politics of
  agrarian reform, market-led, 46, 48

"apparent" land redistribution, 35, 285, 294
associational autonomy, 77
beneficiaries, selecting, 50–51
bundle of powers *vs.* property rights, 39–40
CARP redistributed land, 32–33
caudillo phenomena, 74–75
census data, reliance on official, 37–38
citizen right and resource access, 40
conflict and transformed state/societal actors, 71
corruption-ridden implementation, 51–52
decentralization and self government, 25
dominant views, problems with, 26–40
effective control as defining factor, 38–40
effective control of land, 39
environmental concerns, 48 t1.2
fixed rent tenancy, 36
formal property rights, 38
gender and land rights, 40, 48 t1.2
human rights-based approaches, 48 t1.2
Import-Substitution Industrialization (ISI), 62
independence *vs.* autonomy, 76–77
indigenous peoples, rights of, 48 t1.2
informal land market transactions, 38–39
informal tenure, 27
institutions and land reform, 69–70
"land-banking" by landlords, 51–52
land reform, conservative, 43
land reform, economic and sociopolitical bases, 47–48 t1.2
land reform, imperatives for, 47 t1.2
land reform, liberal, 43
land reform, rethinking, 21–26
land reform, revolutionary, 43

land reform, state-led, 49
land reform and poverty reduction, 43
land reform and social structure, 43
land reform as geopolitical instrument, 42
land reform outcomes, 44–45
land rental market, liberalization of, 54
land size ceiling, 50
land tenure as power problem, 63
landlord compensation mechanism, 24
landlords' resistance to land reform, overcoming, 78–79
landlords subverting policy, 50
landowning classes and central state, 70
leasehold reform, 35–37
leasehold reform and landlord opposition, 35–36
limits-centred perspective, beyond, 60–63
market-led agrarian reform (MLAR) model, 53–60, 287
market price *vs.* actual compensation, 23
multinational agribusinesses, 39
neo-liberal land reform, 34–35
NGOs as actors, 48 t1.2
Olstrom schema, 25–26
opportunities-centred perspective, beyond, 60–63
organizations, co-opted *vs.* autonomous, 77
ownership/ control, defined, 22
peasant allies, 74–75
peasant mobilization, horizontal/ vertical, 73–75
peasant movement activists, 34
peasant organizations, government sponsored, 65
peasant organizations, independent of state, 66
"peasant wars," 72–73
political conflicts, land-based, 46, 48

"political will," 65
power, state *vs.* state institutions, 64
private lands, 32–35
private property concept, 25
pro-market land policy model, 53–56
pro-market thinking, contemporary, 49–60
pro-reform forces and state/society actors, 76–78
pro-reform forces and state/society alliance, 77–78
pro-reform initiatives by state actors, 75–76
pro-reform social groups, 77–78
property rights, lacking clear private, 50
property rights, types of, 25–26
public lands, possible outcomes, 26–32, 33t1.1
public settlement program (colonization), 27–28
public/state lands, 53
redistributive reform, defined, 21–22
redistributive reform by matter of degree, 22–23
"rule of law" reforms, 48 t1.2
rural social mobilizations "from below," 72–75
share tenancy reform, 36–37, 286
sharecropping arrangement, 36
shared rent tenancy, 36
shared tenancy, 35–37
social function of land, 24
social justice, 24, 75
society actors, transformation of, 67
society-centred approach, 66
sovereign guarantee concept, 52
state-led land reforms, 41–49
state-society approach, 64–66
state-society interactive approach, 68–72
state *vs.* society-centred approach, 67–68

theory of access, 39
value of land, 24
violence, drugs and ethnic concerns, 48 t1.2
voluntary land transfer (VLT), 32–33
voluntary offer-to-sell (VOS), 32–33
redistributive land reform challenges
 concepts, recasting, 293–97
 effective control of land, 281
 practices, revising, 293–97
 private land redistribution, *a priori* conclusion, 283–86
 pro-reform state-society interaction, 289–93
 public land redistribution, *a priori* conclusion, 282–83
 share tenancy/leasehold, inconsistency, 286–87
 structural and institutional influences, 287–89
Region 1. *See* Ilocos (Region 1)
Region 2. *See* Cagayan Valley (Region 2)
Region 3. *See* Central Luzon (Region 3)
Region 4. *See* Southern Tagalog (Region 4)
Region 5. *See* Bicol (Region 5)
Region 6. *See* Western Visayas (Region 6)
Region 7. *See* Central Visayas (Region 7)
Region 8. *See* Eastern Visayas (Region 8)
Region 9. *See* Southwestern Mindanao (Region 9)
Region 10. *See* Northern Mindanao (Region 10)
Region 11. *See* Southern Mindanao (Region 11)
Region 12. *See* Central Mindanao (Region 12)
Region 13. *See* Northeastern Mindanao (Region 13)
Regional Agrarian Reform Adjudicator (RARAD), 110
Regional Resources Management Program (RRMP), 304n24, 328

Registry of Deeds (ROD), 263
Remulla, Governor Juanito, 250, 271, 319n70
revolutionary tax, 194
Reyes, Domingo, 272
Reyes, Geronimo de los, 166
Reyes, Lorenz, 147
Reyes estate (Catulin), 166–70, 272, 291, 310n2
ROD. *See* Registry of Deeds (ROD)
Rosa, Billy de la, 127, 307n14
Roxas, President, 120
RRMP. *See* Regional Resources Management Program (RRMP)
Russia, 41

S

SAC. *See* Special Agrarian Court (SAC)
Sagnip, Simon, 200, 304n20, 313n32
Salomon, Pablo, 179
Salomon Estate, Nueva Ecija, 178–82, 291–92
Samahan ng Malayang Magsasaka sa Lupaing Aquino (Association of Free Peasants of the Aquino Estate) (SAMALA), 195–96
Samahan ng mga Magsasakang Benepisyaryo ng Superior Agro Inc. (Association of Peasant Beneficiaries in Superior Agro, Inc.) (SMBSAI), 189
SAMALA. *See Samahan ng Malayang Magsasaka sa Lupaing Aquino* (Association of Free Peasants of the Aquino Estate) (SAMALA)
"sandwich strategy," 279
Santos, Oscar, 191, 308n25, 312n22
SCS. *See* Special Concerns Staff (SCS)
SDO. *See* stock distribution option (SDO)
SEARBAI. *See* Stanfilco Employees and Agrarian Reform Beneficiaries Association, Inc. (SEARBAI)

Sebastian, Roberto, 130–31, 154, 248, 307n14–307n15, 308n19, 378
SEC. *See* Securities and Exchange Commission (SEC)
Securities and Exchange Commission (SEC), 328
SENTRA. *See Sentro para sa Tunay na Repormang Agraryo* (Center for Genuine Agrarian Reform) (SENTRA)
Sentro para sa Tunay na Repormang Agraryo (Center for Genuine Agrarian Reform) (SENTRA), 317n41, 328
SFAN. *See* Small Farmers' Association of Negros (SFAN)
Sitio Poultry peasants, 181–82
Small Farmers' Association of Negros (SFAN), 315n11, 328
SMBSAI. *See Samahan ng mga Magsasakang Benepisyaryo ng Superior Agro Inc.* (Association of Peasant Beneficiaries in Superior Agro, Inc.) (SMBSAI)
Soliman, Dinky, 251
Soliman, Hector, 147, 246, 251, 305n24, 306n2, 318n59, 378
South Africa
 agrarian reform, market-led, 46
 land redistribution, 13
 land reform, socio-political bases for, 47 t1.2
 land reform as geopolitical instrument, 42, 286
 market-led agrarian reform policy, 286
 MLAR model, 57, 59–60
 neo-liberalism and impact on power, 61–62
 opportunities-centred approach, 63
 property rights, ambiguous, 28
South Korea
 land reform, liberal, 43

 land reform, successful, 205, 283
 land reform as geopolitical instrument, 42
 public land, 30
South Vietnam, 41
Southeast Asia, 45
Southern Mindanao (Region 11)
 CA distribution, 209–11
 DAPCO, Davao del Norte, 171–78
 DAR land distribution in private hands, 206t4.1, 207–8
 DAR's land distribution (1972-2005), 148t3.2
 deductions from CARP scores (2005), 150, 151t3.3
 deductions on legal grounds, 153t3.4b
 DENR's accomplishment in A&D lands and CBFM, 211, 212t4.2, 213
 state-society interactions and policy outcomes, 275–79, 277t5.2
 VOS distribution, 208–9
Southern Tagalog, 226, 229, 256
Southern Tagalog (Region 4)
 Barangay Imok, Calauan, Laguna, 167
 CA distribution, 209–11
 DAR land distribution in private hands, 206t4.1, 207–8
 DAR's land distribution (1972-2005), 148t3.2
 De los Reyes estate, Laguna, 166–70
 deductions from CARP scores (2005), 150, 151t3.3
 deductions on legal grounds, 153t3.4b
 DENR's accomplishment in A&D lands and CBFM, 211, 212t4.2, 213
 Roxas Hacienda, Batangas, 182–84
 state-society interactions and policy outcomes, 275–79, 277t5.2
Southwestern Mindanao (Region 9)
 CA distribution, 209–11
 DAR land distribution in private hands, 206t4.1, 207–8

Index | 409

DAR's land distribution (1972-2005), 148t3.2
deductions from CARP scores (2005), 150, 151t3.3
deductions on legal grounds, 153t3.4b
DENR's accomplishment in A&D lands and CBFM, 211, 212t4.2, 213
private lands except VLT, 208
state-society interactions and policy outcomes, 275-79, 277t5.2
Special Agrarian Court (SAC), 110
Special Concerns Staff (SCS), 261
Standard Philippine Fruit Company, 171-78
Stanfilco, 171-78
Stanfilco Employees and Agrarian Reform Beneficiaries Association, Inc. (SEARBAI), 172-76
state-society interactions for redistributive land reform
activists, political *vs.* developmental, 221
anti-reform coalitions, confrontations with, 271-80, 291
case-related examples, 271-72
collective action with specific demands, 255-64
guerrilla zone preparation (GZPrep), 226-27
Malacañang Palace, 106, 219
peasant organizational power, 217
policy outcomes, spatial variations in, 275-79, 277t5.2
policy related examples, 272-75
political agitation, mass, 217-18
private armies and military, 220
pro-reform state-society alliances, 254-70
reformist initiatives by peasants, 264-68
reformist initiatives from «above,» 268-70

reformist inititiates by pro-reform state actors, 238-54
rural social movements, autonomous peasant, 216-38, 223t5.4
summarizing examples, 275
stock distribution option (SDO)
extent and geographical distribution, 158-59
peasant beneficiaries (1972-2000), 114, 114t2.11
redistributive reform, lacking, 284
voluntary land transfer(VLT), 120, 131-33
Struggle of the Masses. *See Laban ng Masa* (LnM)
sub-Saharan Africa, 28
Superior Agro corporation, 187-88, 196-97, 291-92, 312n19

T

TADECO. *See* Tagum Agricultural Development Corporation (TADECO)
Tadeo, Jaime, 232, 244-45, 257, 304n20, 317n40
Tagum Agricultural Development Corporation (TADECO), 139, 307n14-307n15, 308n18, 328
Taiwan
effective control of land, 39
land reform, liberal, 43
land reform, successful, 205, 283, 286
land reform as geopolitical instrument, 42
public land, 30
redistributive reform, 23
Tañada, Wigberto, 253, 273
Task Force 24 (TF-24), 265-66
Task Force 32 (TF-32), 266
Task Force Fast-Track, 267
Task Force Mapalad (TFM), 231, 262
tersyung baliktad (inverted sharing arrangement), 194-95, 197

Teves, President Margarito, 134
TF-24. *See* Task Force 24 (TF-24)
TFM. *See* Task Force Mapalad (TFM)
Thailand, 30–31, 93t2.4, 94, 96t2.6, 283
Tiglao, Rigoberto, 251
Tinig ng Magsasaka sa Imok (TMI), 167–68
TMI. *See Tinig ng Magsasaka sa Imok* (TMI)
TriPARRD. *See* Tripartite Partnership for Agrarian Reform and Rural Development (TriPARRD)
Tripartite Partnership for Agrarian Reform and Rural Development (TriPARRD), 266–67
Tulunan settlement, 138

U

"uninstalled" beneficiaries, 120, 134–35, 156
United Floirendo Employees Agrarian Reform Beneficiaries Association, Inc. (UFEARBAI), 139, 204, 260
United States, 41, 84, 96t2.6
United Workers of Stanfilco. *See Nagkakaisang Manggagawa ng Stanfilco* (NAMASTAN)
Unity for the Advancement of Socialism in Theory and Practice. *See Bukluran sa Ikauunlad ng Sosyalismo sa Isip at Gawa* (BISIG)
Unity of Agricultural Workers. *See Aniban ng Manggagawa sa Agrikultura* (AMA)
Unity towards the Development of the Countryside and Agrarian Reform. *See Kaisahan Tungo sa Kaunlaran ng Kanayunan at Repormang Pansakahan* (KAISAHAN)
University of the Philippines (UP), 200, 292
UNORKA. *See Pambansang Ugnayan ng Nagsasariling Lokal na mga Samahang Mamamayan sa Kanayunan* (National Coordination of Autonomous Local Rural People's Organizations) (UNORKA)
UP. *See* University of the Philippines (UP)
US Agency for International Development (USAID), 142
US Central Intelligence Agency, 85–86
USAID. *See* US Agency for International Development (USAID)

V

Venecia, Jose de, 154, 273
Vietnam, 47 t1.2, 53, 93t2.4, 96t2.6
VLT. *See* voluntary land transfer (VLT)
voluntary land transfer (VLT), 120–31, 284
  anti-reform outcomes, 276, 277t5.2
  Benedicto sugar cane plantation, 134, 285, 291
  CARP program, 32–33, 108
  Catholic Church, confiscating lands of, 120
  Danding Cojuangco joint venture, 125–27
  DAR's land distribution (1972-2005), 146–47, 148t3.2, 149
  Ecija, Nueva, 134
  Garilao, DAR Secretary Ernesto, 121, 160
  Hacienda Looc case, 135–36
  Hacienda Luisita, Inc. (HLI), 132–33, 158–59, 284
  Hijo Plantation, Inc (HPI), 133–34
  land reform evasion, 122–23
  land reform reversals, 120, 135–36, 156
  landlords and anti-reform formula, 130
  lease to own schemes, 124–25
  leaseback, Del Monte, 158, 192
  leaseback, Dole, 158
  leaseback, Dole-DARBCI, 124–25, 127–29

Index | 411

leaseback, extent and geographical distribution, 157–58
leaseback, Floirendo, 125, 129–30
leaseback, Negros Occidental haciendas, 158
leaseback, plantations in Mindanao, 158
Macapagal-Arroyo administration, 120
Marsman profit-sharing scheme, 125, 130–31
multinational companies, 124
non-redistributive outcomes, 120–31
padding of reports, deliberate, 120, 136–37, 160–61
pending cases and lawyers, 267
Quezon's administration, 120
rent-seeking, widespread, 123–24
Roxas administration, 120
stock distribution option (SDO), 120, 131–33, 284
uninstalled beneficiaries, 120, 134–35, 156
VLT-based integrated schemes, 125–31
voluntary offer-to-sell (VOS), 32–34, 108
VOS. *See* voluntary offer-to-sell (VOS)

W

West Africa, 38
West Bengal, 42, 47 t1.2, 286
Western Visayas (Region 6)
  CA distribution, 209–11
  DAR land distribution in private hands, 206t4.1, 207–8
  DAR's land distribution (1972-2005), 148t3.2
  deductions from CARP scores (2005), 150, 151t3.3

deductions on legal grounds, 153t3.4b
DENR's accomplishment in A&D lands and CBFM, 211, 212t4.2, 213
state-society interactions and policy outcomes, 275–79, 277t5.2
VOS distribution, 208–9
World Bank
  Agrarian Reform Community Development Program, 144–45
  CARP, pessimism towards, 116
  distributive model, failure of, 161
  land ownership distribution, non-egalitarian, 296
  land reform model, 7, 13–14
  market-driven agrarian reform, 142–46, 273, 286
  MLAR concept, opposed, 145
  MLAR concept, supported, 274

Y

Yap, Tarlac Provincial Governor Apeng, 132

Z

Zambales province, 145
Zamora, Secretary, 135
Zimbabwe
  compulsory acquisition (CA), 165
  informal land market transactions, 38–39
  land redistribution, 13
  land reform, 34, 47 t1.2
  land reform laws, 107
  neo-liberalism and impact on power, 61–62
  opportunities-centred approach, 63
Zoleta property, 197, 286

STUDIES IN INTERNATIONAL DEVELOPMENT AND GLOBALIZATION

Development has often been understood as economic growth and industrialization. Yet it also refers to the social, cultural, and political changes that accompany changes in economic and industrial structure. It can thus entail new forms of exploitation as well as opportunities for individuals, communities, and states. In the era of globalization, transnational corporations, often more powerful than states, have emerged as new agents of development. New social movements have also arisen with the goal of facilitating social justice rather than simply economic growth and industrialization that may benefit only a few. These social movements also make wide use of transnational linkages. The field of development and globalization is an interdisciplinary study of these changes, as well as a critique of current practices, with the goal of creating a more just human future.

The objective of the University of Ottawa Studies in Development and Globalization is to promote new perspectives in the interdisciplinary studies of development and globalization. The collection publishes French and English books in this field. Edited volumes are sought on a range of research topics, including indigenous peoples and development, women and development, social movements and development, and international labour issues. Single-author books are sought in the different disciplines that contribute to the academic debates on development and globalization. Preference will be given to critical works that reveal the tensions and conflicts of development, as well as the quest for social justice in global contexts.

Editorial Committee

Caroline Andrew
Stephen Brown
Dominique Caouette
Abdoulaye Gueye
Cristina Rojas
Scott Simon
Nancy Thede

Printed and bound in August 2007
by TRI-GRAPHIC PRINTING, Ottawa, Ontario,
for THE UNIVERSITY OF OTTAWA PRESS

Typeset in 10 on 13 Book Antiqua by Brad Horning
by Brad Horning

Edited by Trish O'Reilly
Proofread by David Bernardi
Indexed by Clive Pyne
Cover designed by Cathy Maclean

Printed on Rolland Opaque Text Natural Smooth 50 lb